Electronic Nanodevices

Electronic Nanodevices

Editor

Antonio Di Bartolomeo

MDPI • Basel • Beijing • Wuhan • Barcelona • Belgrade • Manchester • Tokyo • Cluj • Tianjin

Editor
Antonio Di Bartolomeo
University of Salerno
Italy

Editorial Office
MDPI
St. Alban-Anlage 66
4052 Basel, Switzerland

This is a reprint of articles from the Special Issue published online in the open access journal *Nanomaterials* (ISSN 2079-4991) (available at: https://www.mdpi.com/journal/nanomaterials/special_issues/nano-electronic_devices).

For citation purposes, cite each article independently as indicated on the article page online and as indicated below:

LastName, A.A.; LastName, B.B.; LastName, C.C. Article Title. *Journal Name* **Year**, *Volume Number*, Page Range.

ISBN 978-3-0365-5021-3 (Hbk)
ISBN 978-3-0365-5022-0 (PDF)

© 2022 by the authors. Articles in this book are Open Access and distributed under the Creative Commons Attribution (CC BY) license, which allows users to download, copy and build upon published articles, as long as the author and publisher are properly credited, which ensures maximum dissemination and a wider impact of our publications.

The book as a whole is distributed by MDPI under the terms and conditions of the Creative Commons license CC BY-NC-ND.

Contents

About the Editor vii

Antonio Di Bartolomeo
Electronic Nanodevices
Reprinted from: *Nanomaterials* **2022**, *12*, 2125, doi:10.3390/nano12132125 1

Peng Cui and Yuping Zeng
Effect of Device Scaling on Electron Mobility in Nanoscale GaN HEMTs with Polarization Charge Modulation
Reprinted from: *Nanomaterials* **2022**, *12*, 1718, doi:10.3390/nano12101718 5

Monica La Mura, Patrizia Lamberti and Vincenzo Tucci
Numerical Evaluation of the Effect of Geometric Tolerances on the High-Frequency Performance of Graphene Field-Effect Transistors
Reprinted from: *Nanomaterials* **2021**, *11*, 3121, doi:10.3390/nano11113121 17

Mirko Poljak, Mislav Matić, Tin Župančić and Ante Zeljko
Lower Limits of Contact Resistance in Phosphorene Nanodevices with Edge Contacts
Reprinted from: *Nanomaterials* **2022**, *12*, 656, doi:10.3390/nano12040656 31

Enver Faella, Kimberly Intonti, Loredana Viscardi, Filippo Giubileo, Arun Kumar, Hoi Tung Lam, Konstantinos Anastasiou, Monica F. Craciun, Saverio Russo and Antonio Di Bartolomeo
Electric Transport in Few-Layer ReSe$_2$ Transistors Modulated by Air Pressure and Light
Reprinted from: *Nanomaterials* **2022**, *12*, 1886, doi:10.3390/nano12111886 43

Khalil Tamersit, Jaya Madan, Abdellah Kouzou, Rahul Pandey, Ralph Kennel and Mohamed Abdelrahem
Role of Junctionless Mode in Improving the Photosensitivity of Sub-10 nm Carbon Nanotube/Nanoribbon Field-Effect Phototransistors: Quantum Simulation, Performance Assessment, and Comparison
Reprinted from: *Nanomaterials* **2022**, *12*, 1639, doi:10.3390/nano12101639 55

Khalil Tamersit, Abdellah Kouzou, Hocine Bourouba, Ralph Kennel and Mohamed Abdelrahem
Synergy of Electrostatic and Chemical Doping to Improve the Performance of Junctionless Carbon Nanotube Tunneling Field-Effect Transistors: Ultrascaling, Energy-Efficiency, and High Switching Performance
Reprinted from: *Nanomaterials* **2022**, *12*, 462, doi:10.3390/nano12030462 71

Mitsue Takahashi and Shigeki Sakai
Area-Scalable 10^9-Cycle-High- Endurance FeFET of Strontium Bismuth Tantalate Using a Dummy-Gate Process
Reprinted from: *Nanomaterials* **2021**, *11*, 101, doi:10.3390/nano11010101 89

Juan B. Roldán, Gerardo González-Cordero, Rodrigo Picos, Enrique Miranda, Félix Palumbo, Francisco Jiménez-Molinos, Enrique Moreno, David Maldonado, Santiago B. Baldomá, Mohamad Moner Al Chawa, Carol de Benito, Stavros G. Stavrinides, Jordi Suñé and Leon O. Chua
On the Thermal Models for Resistive Random Access Memory Circuit Simulation
Reprinted from: *Nanomaterials* **2021**, *11*, 1261, doi:10.3390/nano11051261 103

**Sara Bernardes, Ricardo A. Marques Lameirinhas, João Paulo N. Torres
and Carlos A. F. Fernandes**
Characterization and Design of Photovoltaic Solar Cells That Absorb Ultraviolet, Visible and Infrared Light
Reprinted from: *Nanomaterials* **2021**, *11*, 78, doi:10.3390/nano11010078 . . . . **149**

**Francisco Duarte, João Paulo N. Torres, António Baptista
and Ricardo A. Marques Lameirinhas**
Optical Nanoantennas for Photovoltaic Applications
Reprinted from: *Nanomaterials* **2021**, *11*, 422, doi:10.3390/nano11020422 . . . . **165**

T. F. Alhamada, M. A. Azmah Hanim, D. W. Jung, A. A. Nuraini and W. Z. Wan Hasan
A Brief Review of the Role of 2D Mxene Nanosheets toward Solar Cells Efficiency Improvement
Reprinted from: *Nanomaterials* **2021**, *11*, 2732, doi:10.3390/nano11102732 . . . . **191**

**Hua Wang, Tianyi Li, Ahmed M. Hashem, Ashraf E. Abdel-Ghany, Rasha S. El-Tawil,
Hanaa M. Abuzeid, Amanda Coughlin, Kai Chang, Shixiong Zhang, Hazim El-Mounayri,
Andres Tovar, Likun Zhu and Christian M. Julien**
Nanostructured Molybdenum-Oxide Anodes for Lithium-Ion Batteries: An Outstanding Increase in Capacity
Reprinted from: *Nanomaterials* **2022**, *12*, 13, doi:10.3390/nano12010013 . . . . **209**

About the Editor

Antonio Di Bartolomeo

Antonio Di Bartolomeo is a professor of Experimental Condensed Matter Physics and the president of the Physics Education Committee at the University of Salerno, Italy, where he teaches semiconductor device physics and nanoelectronics.

His present research interests include optical and electrical properties of nanostructured materials such as carbon nanotubes, graphene, and 2D materials; van der Waals heterostructures; Schottky junctions; field-effect transistors; non-volatile memories; solar cells; photodetectors; field emission devices; supercapacitors; and fuel cells.

Dr. Di Bartolomeo received his PhD in Physics in 1997 from the University of Salerno, where he held the position of researcher in Experimental Physics before his appointment as a professor. His scientific career started at CERN (CH) with collaboration in experiments on neutrino oscillations and heavy-ion collisions. He spent several years in the industry as a semiconductor device engineer (ST Microelectronics, Infineon Technologies, and Intel Corporation) and was a guest scientist at IHP-Microelectronics (Germany) and Georgetown University (Washington, DC).

He has delivered over 100 presentations in international conferences and has authored over 150 publications in peer-reviewed journals, two physics textbooks, and two patents. He is serving as a Section Editor-in-Chief of MDPI *Nanomaterials* and is an Editorial Board Member of several MDPI journals, such as *Materials*, *Electronic Materials*, *Electronics*, and *Sensors*.

Editorial

Electronic Nanodevices

Antonio Di Bartolomeo

Department of Physics "E.R. Caianiello", University of Salerno, 84084 Fisciano, SA, Italy; adibartolomeo@unisa.it; Tel.: +39-089-969189

Citation: Di Bartolomeo, A. Electronic Nanodevices. *Nanomaterials* **2022**, *12*, 2125. https://doi.org/10.3390/nano12132125

Received: 9 June 2022
Accepted: 13 June 2022
Published: 21 June 2022

Publisher's Note: MDPI stays neutral with regard to jurisdictional claims in published maps and institutional affiliations.

Copyright: © 2022 by the author. Licensee MDPI, Basel, Switzerland. This article is an open access article distributed under the terms and conditions of the Creative Commons Attribution (CC BY) license (https://creativecommons.org/licenses/by/4.0/).

The new phenomena observed in nanodevices and the related technological challenges of fabrication and manipulation at the nanoscale have spurred intense theoretical, simulation and experimental research activity. New device structures, materials, simulation and characterization techniques have emerged.

The Special Issue entitled "Electronic Nanodevices" focuses on the design, simulation, fabrication, and modeling of new nanodevices for electronic, optoelectronic and energy applications; it includes articles dealing with nanoscale transistors, phototransistors, memories, and solar cells.

The effects of down-scaling and the introduction of new materials, architectures and fabrication processes in transistors and phototransistors are widely investigated.

High-electron-mobility transistors (HEMTs) are devices designed for high-frequency and high-power applications. An experimental study by P. Cui and Y. Zheng checked the impact of vertical and lateral scaling on low-field electron mobility in GaN HEMTs [1]. Although low-field mobility is expected to stay constant when devices scale down, in GaN HEMTs, the distribution of polarization charges that scatter with the channel electrons, localized in the barrier layer, can change with the device dimensions, thus leading to mobility variations. Indeed, P. Cui and Y. Zheng demonstrate that in InAlN/GaN HEMTs, the mobility decreases as the InAlN barrier and the gate length scale down but increases with the down-scaled source–drain distance. Their study highlights that the polarization charges are an important ingredient to consider in the nanoscale device design.

Owing to their great mechanical, electronic, and carrier transport properties, two-dimensional (2D) materials such as graphene, black phosphorus and transition metal dichalcogenides [2–6], as well as one-dimensional (1D) carbon nanotubes [7,8], are considered promising candidates for future post-silicon electronic and optoelectronic devices. Their use as channel of field effect transistors (FET) has been an important part of the down-scaling process.

M. La Mura and coworkers numerically investigated the effects of device geometry and graphene quality variations on the performance of graphene-field effect transistors (GFETs) [9]. The poor repeatability of GFETs hampers their diffusion in GFET-based commercial RF circuits. Specifically, the impact of geometrical parameters on the RF performance of a GFET-based common-source amplifier is studied in terms of the amplifier transit frequency and maximum oscillation frequency. M. La Mura and coworkers concluded that the most influential factor variation on the transition frequency and the maximum oscillation frequency is the channel length, as expected, because the transistor high-frequency limit is inversely proportional to the time the carriers need to cross the channel. They show that reducing the channel length increases the transition and the maximum frequency and point out that the accurate control the channel length is essential to reducing unwanted fluctuations of the transistors' cut-off frequency. They also highlight that the improvement provided by increasing the accuracy of the other geometrical parameters, such as channel width or top oxide thickness, is very limited.

M. Poljak and coworkers dealt with the contact resistance in black phosphorus nanoribbons (PNRs) with edge contacts using atomistic quantum transport simulations [10]. The acceptable bandgap and the high carrier mobility of monolayer black phosphorus (or phosphorene) make it more advantageous than other 2D materials for nanoscale FETs. The impact of PNR size down-scaling on the contact resistance is analyzed for technologically relevant PNR widths and lengths. It is shown that the contact resistance decreases with the width down-scaling but increases considerably when the length decreases. Significant metallization effects become visible in the deterioration of electronic and transport properties for nanoribbon lengths below ~8 nm. It is pointed out that for optimized metal edge contacts, a weakly interacting metal is best suited to ultra-short nanoribbons. The numerical results indicate that in ultra-narrow PNR devices, the quantum intrinsic limits of the contact resistance, i.e., minimum achievable contact resistance, could be as low as ~14 Ω μm, a level acceptable to the CMOS industry.

E. Faella et al. fabricated back-gated FETs based on few-layer $ReSe_2$ with Cr contacts and presented their optoelectronic characterization [11]. The devices show n-type conduction due to the to the alignment of the Cr Fermi level with the $ReSe_2$ conduction band. It is demonstrated that the $ReSe_2$ FETs are strongly affected by air pressure and undergo a dramatic increase in conductivity when the air pressure is lowered below the atmospheric pressure. The exposure to air suppresses the channel conductivity as an effect of electron capture by oxygen and water molecules adsorbed on the material surface. The reversible pressure behavior allows the devices to be used as air pressure gauges. Finally, a negative photoconductivity in the $ReSe_2$ channel is found and explained as back-gate-dependent trapping of the photo-excited charges.

K. Tamersit and coworkers performed numerical simulations by self-consistently solving the Poisson equation with the mode space non-equilibrium Green's function formalism in the ballistic limit to investigate carbon nanotube/nanoribbon junctionless phototransistors, endowed with sub-10 nm photogate lengths [12]. The light-induced modulation of electrostatics through the photogate is employed as a photosensing principle and the impact of the light illumination on the transport of carbon-based junctionless phototransistors is analyzed via the energy-position-resolved electron density. They find that the junctionless approach is efficient in boosting the photosensitivity of phototransistors by dilating the potential barrier while mitigating the tunneling currents and improving the subthreshold characteristics. They also compare graphene nanoribbon and carbon nanotube junctionless phototransistors, concluding that the former exhibit higher photosensitivity.

The same group in another computational work proposed an efficient approach based on the synergy of electrostatic and chemical-doping engineering to boost the subthreshold and switching performance of sub–10 nm junctionless-carbon-nanotube-tunnel field-effect transistors [13]. Their doping approach, also favored by ferroelectric-based gating, is exploited to shrink the band-to-band tunneling window and dilate the direct source-to-drain tunneling window.

Ferroelectric gates are also considered by M. Takahashi and S. Sakai who fabricated a new strontium bismuth tantalate (SBT) ferroelectric-gate FET with channel lengths of 85 nm by a replacement-gate process [14]. Their device is demonstrated to be suitable for non-volatile memories with long stable data retention of 10^5 s and high erase-and-program endurance up to 10^9 cycles. In the fabrication process, they prepared dummy-gate transistor patterns and then replaced the dummy substances with an SBT precursor which is subsequently annealed for SBT crystallization. The proposed process has good channel-area scalability in geometry depending on the lithography ability.

Memory devices are also treated in a review paper by Juan B. Roldán and coworkers, dedicated to resistive random access memories (RRAMs) [15]. RRAMs are based on resistive switching mechanisms to modulate their conductance in a non-volatile manner and exhibit a set of technological features that make them ideal candidates for applications related to non-volatile memories, hardware cryptography, and neuromorphic computing. The review is focused on RRAM models dealing with temperature effects, which are very important considering that the physical mechanisms behind resistive switching are thermally activated. The authors describe models of different complexity to integrate thermal effects in complete compact models that account for the kinetics of the chemical reactions behind resistive switching and the current calculation. Specifically, among other issues, they treat different geometries, operation regimes, lateral heat losses, etc. to characterize each conductive filament.

Driven by the ever-increasing need for sustainable energy sources, the design, fabrication, and characterization of solar cells have also attracted a great deal of research endeavor.

S. Bernardes and coworkers numerically studied the lattice-matched GaInP/GaInAs/Ge triple-junction solar cell, which is currently being used in most satellites and concentrator photovoltaic systems [16]. They first analyzed the three subcells individually and then they simulated the whole cell by extracting the typical figures-of-merit. They compared the simulated results with the actual experimental results, confirming that the cell is emulated successfully. After that, they investigated the effect of temperature, which is relevant for space applications, and proceeded with the optimization of the cell, in terms of thickness and doping, so that the maximum efficiency can be reached. As an important guideline for fabrication, they also highlighted how the doping can significantly boost the cell efficiency.

F. Duarte and coworkers used COMSOL Multiphysics® software to study nanometric optical antennas, with dimensions smaller than the wavelength of the incident electromagnetic wave, for solar energy harvesting on photovoltaic cells [17]. The use of optical antennas has received significant interest as they represent a viable alternative to the traditional energy harvesting technologies. To increase the efficiency of solar cells, the behavior of optical aperture nanoantennas, which consist of a metal sheet with apertures of dimensions smaller than the wavelength, is studied for materials such as aluminum, gold, and platinum. With several simulations in different conditions, F. Duarte and coworkers showed that all three metals exhibit the optical transmission phenomenon, i.e., they transmit a greater amount of light than might naively be expected. The enhanced transmission is due to the coupling of light with surface plasmon polaritons on the surface of the metallic nanoantennas. Furthermore, it is shown that aluminum is superior to the other materials because of its transmission and reflection coefficients.

Efficient solar cells can also be achieved through the development of innovative materials. Among them, two-dimensional metal MXenes, consisting of transition-metal nitrides or carbides, have emerged for their outstanding transparency, metallic electrical conductivity, and mechanical characteristics. Recent applications of MXene materials in solar cells and new perspectives to achieve higher power conversion efficiency with an excellent quality–cost ratio are offered in a review paper by T. F. Alhamada and coworkers [18]. The review details the basic principles for the creation of each 2D transition-metal MXene structure, the tunable characteristics depending on the transition-metal composition and summarizes all previously reported work on incorporating MXene into solar cells. The roles that MXenes play to improve solar power generation, operational stability and power conversion efficiency are reviewed.

Efficient energy storage is another important aspect of the sustainable development. Currently, lithium-ion batteries (LIBs) have become one of the most important energy storage technologies and their progress requires the development of high-capacity electrode materials [19]. Molybdenum oxides such as MoO_2 and MoO_3 are considered as promising anode materials for LIBs due to the broad spectrum of electrical properties ranging from metallic (MoO_2) to wide band gap semiconducting (MoO_3) character. In this direction, H. Wang and coworkers used orange peel extract as an effective chelating agent to synthesize molybdenum oxides [20]. MoO_2 and MoO_3 are prepared in vacuum and in air, respectively, at a temperature of 450 °C. Extensive morphological and structural characterization along with electrical and electrochemical analysis are performed to show their outstanding properties in terms of capacity upgrading upon cycling and as an anode in material for Li-ion batteries.

In summary this Special Issue offers a good overview of the recent research in nanoscale transistors, based on 1D and 2D materials, solar cells, memory devices, and electrochemical devices.

Funding: This research received no external funding.

Institutional Review Board Statement: Not applicable.

Informed Consent Statement: Not applicable.

Data Availability Statement: Data might be available from the Authors of the cited papers.

Conflicts of Interest: The author declares no conflict of interest.

References

1. Cui, P.; Zeng, Y. Effect of Device Scaling on Electron Mobility in Nanoscale GaN HEMTs with Polarization Charge Modulation. *Nanomaterials* **2022**, *12*, 1718. [CrossRef] [PubMed]
2. Urban, F.; Martucciello, N.; Peters, L.; McEvoy, N.; Di Bartolomeo, A. Environmental Effects on the Electrical Characteristics of Back-Gated WSe2 Field-Effect Transistors. *Nanomaterials* **2018**, *8*, 901. [CrossRef] [PubMed]
3. Di Bartolomeo, A. Emerging 2D Materials and Their Van Der Waals Heterostructures. *Nanomaterials* **2020**, *10*, 579. [CrossRef] [PubMed]
4. Urban, F.; Lupina, G.; Grillo, A.; Martucciello, N.; Di Bartolomeo, A. Contact Resistance and Mobility in Back-Gate Graphene Transistors. *Nano Ex.* **2020**, *1*, 010001. [CrossRef]
5. Di Bartolomeo, A.; Pelella, A.; Urban, F.; Grillo, A.; Iemmo, L.; Passacantando, M.; Liu, X.; Giubileo, F. Field Emission in Ultrathin PdSe 2 Back-Gated Transistors. *Adv. Electron. Mater.* **2020**, *6*, 2000094. [CrossRef]
6. Grillo, A.; Pelella, A.; Faella, E.; Giubileo, F.; Sleziona, S.; Kharsah, O.; Schleberger, M.; Di Bartolomeo, A. Memory Effects in Black Phosphorus Field Effect Transistors. *2D Mater.* **2022**, *9*, 015028. [CrossRef]
7. Capista, D.; Passacantando, M.; Lozzi, L.; Faella, E.; Giubileo, F.; Di Bartolomeo, A. Easy Fabrication of Performant SWCNT-Si Photodetector. *Electronics* **2022**, *11*, 271. [CrossRef]
8. Di Bartolomeo, A.; Giubileo, F.; Grillo, A.; Luongo, G.; Iemmo, L.; Urban, F.; Lozzi, L.; Capista, D.; Nardone, M.; Passacantando, M. Bias Tunable Photocurrent in Metal-Insulator-Semiconductor Heterostructures with Photoresponse Enhanced by Carbon Nanotubes. *Nanomaterials* **2019**, *9*, 1598. [CrossRef] [PubMed]
9. La Mura, M.; Lamberti, P.; Tucci, V. Numerical Evaluation of the Effect of Geometric Tolerances on the High-Frequency Performance of Graphene Field-Effect Transistors. *Nanomaterials* **2021**, *11*, 3121. [CrossRef] [PubMed]
10. Poljak, M.; Matić, M.; Župančić, T.; Zeljko, A. Lower Limits of Contact Resistance in Phosphorene Nanodevices with Edge Contacts. *Nanomaterials* **2022**, *12*, 656. [CrossRef] [PubMed]
11. Faella, E.; Intonti, K.; Viscardi, L.; Giubileo, F.; Kumar, A.; Lam, H.T.; Anastasiou, K.; Craciun, M.F.; Russo, S.; Di Bartolomeo, A. Electric Transport in Few-Layer ReSe2 Transistors Modulated by Air Pressure and Light. *Nanomaterials* **2022**, *12*, 1886. [CrossRef] [PubMed]
12. Tamersit, K.; Madan, J.; Kouzou, A.; Pandey, R.; Kennel, R.; Abdelrahem, M. Role of Junctionless Mode in Improving the Photosensitivity of Sub-10 Nm Carbon Nanotube/Nanoribbon Field-Effect Phototransistors: Quantum Simulation, Performance Assessment, and Comparison. *Nanomaterials* **2022**, *12*, 1639. [CrossRef] [PubMed]
13. Tamersit, K.; Kouzou, A.; Bourouba, H.; Kennel, R.; Abdelrahem, M. Synergy of Electrostatic and Chemical Doping to Improve the Performance of Junctionless Carbon Nanotube Tunneling Field-Effect Transistors: Ultrascaling, Energy-Efficiency, and High Switching Performance. *Nanomaterials* **2022**, *12*, 462. [CrossRef] [PubMed]
14. Takahashi, M.; Sakai, S. Area-Scalable 109-Cycle-High-Endurance FeFET of Strontium Bismuth Tantalate Using a Dummy-Gate Process. *Nanomaterials* **2021**, *11*, 101. [CrossRef] [PubMed]
15. Roldán, J.B.; González-Cordero, G.; Picos, R.; Miranda, E.; Palumbo, F.; Jiménez-Molinos, F.; Moreno, E.; Maldonado, D.; Baldomá, S.B.; Moner Al Chawa, M.; et al. On the Thermal Models for Resistive Random Access Memory Circuit Simulation. *Nanomaterials* **2021**, *11*, 1261. [CrossRef] [PubMed]
16. Bernardes, S.; Lameirinhas, R.A.M.; Torres, J.P.N.; Fernandes, C.A.F. Characterization and Design of Photovoltaic Solar Cells That Absorb Ultraviolet, Visible and Infrared Light. *Nanomaterials* **2021**, *11*, 78. [CrossRef] [PubMed]
17. Duarte, F.; Torres, J.P.N.; Baptista, A.; Marques Lameirinhas, R.A. Optical Nanoantennas for Photovoltaic Applications. *Nanomaterials* **2021**, *11*, 422. [CrossRef] [PubMed]
18. Alhamada, T.F.; Azmah Hanim, M.A.; Jung, D.W.; Nuraini, A.A.; Hasan, W.Z.W. A Brief Review of the Role of 2D Mxene Nanosheets toward Solar Cells Efficiency Improvement. *Nanomaterials* **2021**, *11*, 2732. [CrossRef] [PubMed]
19. Askari, M.B.; Salarizadeh, P.; Beheshti-Marnani, A.; Di Bartolomeo, A. NiO-Co3O4-rGO as an Efficient Electrode Material for Supercapacitors and Direct Alcoholic Fuel Cells. *Adv. Mater. Interfaces* **2021**, *8*, 2100149. [CrossRef]
20. Wang, H.; Li, T.; Hashem, A.M.; Abdel-Ghany, A.E.; El-Tawil, R.S.; Abuzeid, H.M.; Coughlin, A.; Chang, K.; Zhang, S.; El-Mounayri, H.; et al. Nanostructured Molybdenum-Oxide Anodes for Lithium-Ion Batteries: An Outstanding Increase in Capacity. *Nanomaterials* **2021**, *12*, 13. [CrossRef] [PubMed]

Article

Effect of Device Scaling on Electron Mobility in Nanoscale GaN HEMTs with Polarization Charge Modulation

Peng Cui [1,*] and Yuping Zeng [2,*]

[1] Institute of Novel Semiconductors, Shandong University, Jinan 250100, China
[2] Department of Electrical and Computer Engineering, University of Delaware, Newark, DE 19716, USA
* Correspondence: pcui@sdu.edu.cn (P.C.); yzeng@udel.edu (Y.Z.)

Abstract: We have experimentally investigated the impact of vertical and lateral scaling on low-field electron mobility (μ) in InAlN/GaN high-electron-mobility transistors (HEMTs). It is found that μ reduces as InAlN barrier (T_B) and gate length (L_G) scale down but increases with the scaled source–drain distance (L_{SD}). Polarization Coulomb Field (PCF) scattering is believed to account for the scaling-dependent electron mobility characteristic. The polarization charge distribution is modulated with the vertical and lateral scaling, resulting in the changes in μ limited by PCF scattering. The mobility characteristic shows that PCF scattering should be considered when devices scale down, which is significant for the device design and performance improvement for RF applications.

Keywords: GaN HEMTs; scaling; electron mobility; scattering; polarization charge

1. Introduction

Due to the high breakdown voltage, high two-dimensional electron gas densities, and high electron saturation velocity, gallium nitride (GaN) high-electron-mobility transistors (HEMTs) have been ideal for high-frequency and high-power applications, such as radar communications, electronic countermeasures, 5G applications, small base stations, new communication microsatellites, power transmission and automotive electronics [1–5]. Yan Tang et al. fabricated the AlN/GaN/AlGaN double heterojunction HEMTs with fully passivation and n$^+$-GaN ohmic contact regrowth technology, demonstrating a record high current/power gain cutoff frequency f_T/f_{max} of 454/444 GHz on a 20 nm-gate-length HEMT with gate–source and gate–drain spacings of 50 nm [6]. Jeong-Gil Kim et al. reported an AlGaN/GaN HEMT structure on the high-quality undoped thick AlN buffer layer with a high breakdown voltage of 2154 V and a very high figure of merit (FOM) of ~1.8 GV$^2 \cdot \Omega^{-1} \cdot$cm^{-2} [7]. Xiaoyu Xia et al. reported a new type of AlGaN/GaN HEMTs with a microfield plate (FP) with a breakdown voltage increase from 870 V to 1278 V by adjusting the distribution of the potential and channel electric field [8]. Maddaka Reddeppa et al. demonstrated high photoresponse and the electrical transport properties of a pristine GaN nanorod-based Schottky diode with an optimized Schottky barrier height [9]. Kedhareswara Sairam Pasupuleti et al. developed the integration of conductive polypyrrole (Ppy) and GaN nanorods for high-performance self-powered UV-A photodetectors, exhibiting superior photoresponse properties such as detectivity, responsivity, external quantum efficiency, good stability and reproducibility [10].

To further improve device performance, device scaling in GaN HEMTs is necessary [6,11,12]. The effects of scaling on short-channel effects (SECs), leakage current, electron velocity, frequency characteristics have been studied [13–18], providing insightful guidance for device design and performance improvement. However, few studies about the impact of scaling on electron mobility have been reported. In general, low-field mobility should not change when devices scale down. However, due to the spontaneous and piezoelectric polarization in GaN HEMTs, there are polarization charges in the barrier layer [19,20], which is different from conventional transistors (Si, GaAs, et al.). The change in the polarization charge distribution is related to the device dimension and can result in scattering on the channel electrons [21,22], which leads to a possible change in mobility with device scaling. In this article, to demonstrate this influence, the InAlN/GaN HEMTs with various barrier thicknesses, source–drain distances, and gate lengths are fabricated and the effect of scaling on electron mobility is studied.

2. Experiment

The lattice-matched In$_{0.17}$Al$_{0.83}$N/GaN HEMT structure is grown by metal–organic chemical vapor deposition on a Si substrate, as shown in Figure 1, consisting of a 2 nm GaN cap, an InAlN barrier, a 1 nm AlN interlayer, a 15 nm GaN channel layer, a 4 nm In$_{0.12}$Ga$_{0.88}$N back-barrier and a 2 µm undoped GaN buffer. Here, two different InAlN layers with the thicknesses of 8 nm and 5 nm are grown. The device process started with mesa isolation with Cl$_2$-based inductively coupled plasma (ICP) etching. Then, Ohmic contact was formed with Ti/Al/Ni/Au metal deposition and annealed at 850 °C for 40 s. Ni/Au gate Schottky contact was deposited in the center of the source–drain region to complete the process. For the large devices, the gate length (L_G), gate–source distance (L_{GS}), and gate–drain distance (L_{GD}) of the devices are all 2 µm. For the RF devices, two types of devices are fabricated. For type I, L_G of the devices is fixed at 50 nm and L_{SD} is 2, 1, and 0.6 µm, respectively. For type II, L_{SD} of the devices is fixed at 1 µm and L_G is 50, 100, and 150 nm, respectively. Here, the gate of all the devices is located between the source and drain regions, and the gate width is 2 × 20 µm. The current–voltage (I–V) and capacitance–voltage (C–V) measurements were carried out by using an Agilent B1500A semiconductor parameter analyzer (Agilent Technologies, Santa Clara, CA, USA).

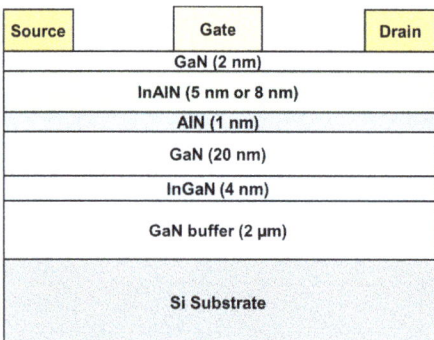

Figure 1. Schematic cross-section of the fabricated InAlN/GaN HEMT with two different InAlN barrier thickness (8 nm and 5 nm, respectively).

3. Results and Discussion

Figure 2a,b show the measured capacitances (C) of the InAlN/GaN circle diodes with both InAlN barrier thicknesses (T_B). Here, six devices are measured and a good consistency is presented. An improved C and a subthreshold voltage (V_T) shift are observed due to the reduced InAlN barrier thickness ($C = \varepsilon/T_B$, ε is the dielectric constant of InAlN barrier). Through integrating C-V curves, electron density (n_{2D}) is extracted as shown in Figure 2c,d. It shows that the InAlN/GaN heterostructure with 8 nm InAlN barrier presents higher electron density. Figure 3 shows the simulated band structure and 2DEG electron density as a function of the distance from the material surface of the InAlN/GaN heterostructure, which is calculated by self-consistently solving Schrodinger's and Poisson's equations [23,24]. Compared with the 5 nm InAlN barrier, the InAlN/GaN heterostructure with an 8 nm InAlN barrier also shows a higher electron density peak. In GaN HEMTs, the surface states are identified as the source of channel electrons. Due to the spontaneous polarization filed, the increase in InAlN barrier thickness can increase the energy of the surface states, resulting in higher electron density [25,26].

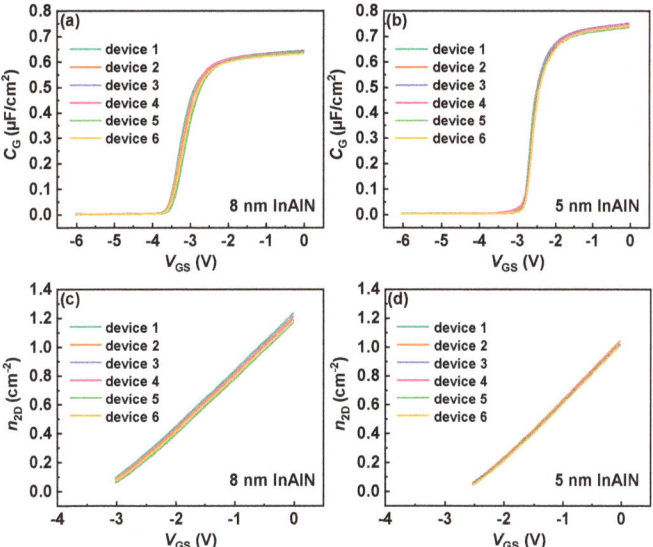

Figure 2. Gate capacitance (C_G) of the InAlN/GaN diode with (**a**) 8 nm InAlN and (**b**) 5 nm InAlN, respectively. Two-dimensional electron gas electron density (n_{2D}) of the InAlN/GaN diode with (**c**) 8 nm InAlN and (**d**) 5 nm InAlN, respectively.

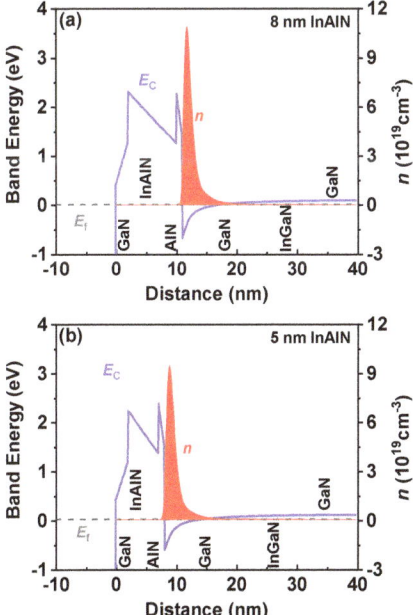

Figure 3. Simulated band structure and 2DEG electron density as a function of the distance from the material surface of the InAlN/GaN heterostructure with (**a**) 8 nm InAlN and (**b**) 5 nm InAlN, respectively.

Figure 4 shows the output characteristics of the InAlN/GaN HEMTs with different InAlN thickness. The L_G, L_{GS}, and L_{GD} of the devices are all 2 μm. To extract low-field mobility, the drain current (I_D) at V_{DS} = 0.1 V in the output characteristics are used. At V_{GS} = 0 V, the total source–drain resistance (R_{SD}) can be written as

$$R_{SD} = \frac{V_{DS}}{I_{DS}} = 2R_C + \frac{L_G + L_{GS} + L_{GD}}{n_{2D0}q\mu_0} \quad (1)$$

where R_C is the ohmic contact resistance, q is the electron charge, and μ_0 and n_{2D0} are the electron mobility and electron density under the gate region with V_{GS} = 0 V. Here, only μ_0 and R_C are unknown. Electron mobility in GaN HEMTs is limited by polar optical phonon (μ_{POP}), polarization Coulomb field (μ_{PCF}), acoustic phonon (μ_{AP}), interface roughness (μ_{IFR}), and dislocation (μ_{DIS}) scatterings [22,27,28]. PCF scattering is related to the nonuniformity of polarization charge distribution [21,22]. At V_{GS} = 0 V, the polarization charge distribution is uniform, and the PCF can be neglected. Based on the two-dimensional (2D) scattering theory and the obtained n_{2D0} [27], μ_0 can be calculated with $1/\mu_0 = 1/\mu_{POP} + 1/\mu_{AP} + 1/\mu_{IFR} + 1/\mu_{DIS}$, and then R_C can be determined with (1). Based on the obtained n_{2D0} and μ_0, the electron mobility μ under the gate region under different V_{GS} can be extracted from

$$\frac{V_{DS}}{I_{DS}} = 2R_C + \frac{L_G}{n_{2D}q\mu} + \frac{L_{GS} + L_{GD}}{n_{2D0}q\mu_0} \quad (2)$$

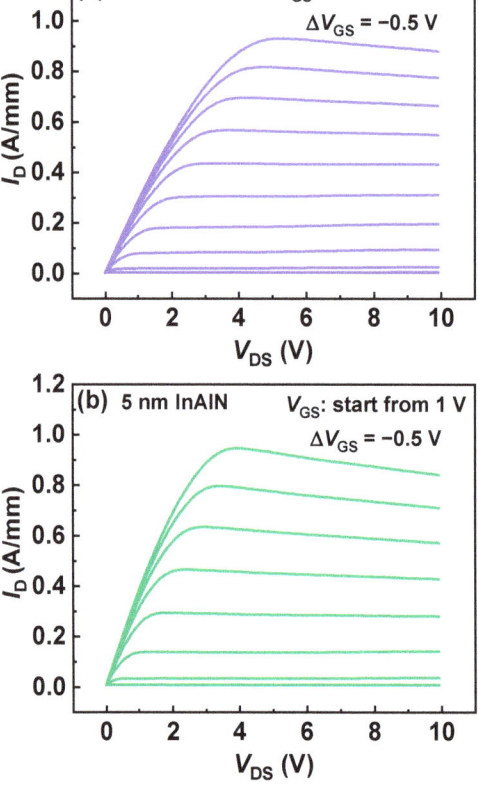

Figure 4. Output characteristics of the InAlN/GaN HEMTs with (a) 8 nm InAlN and (b) 5 nm InAlN, respectively.

Figure 5 depicts the extracted μ versus V_{GS} for both samples. At V_{GS} = 0 V, μ of the devices with 8 nm InAlN and 5 nm InAlN is 1221 and 1651 cm^2/V·s, respectively. The improved electron mobility with a thinner barrier is also confirmed with the Hall measurement (1242 cm^2/V·s for 8 nm InAlN and 1663 cm^2/V·s for 5 nm InAlN) and the electron mobility of Fat-FETs (with L_G of 96 μm and L_{SD} of 100 μm, 1101 cm^2/V·s for 8 nm InAlN and 1670 cm^2/V·s for 5 nm InAlN) [29].

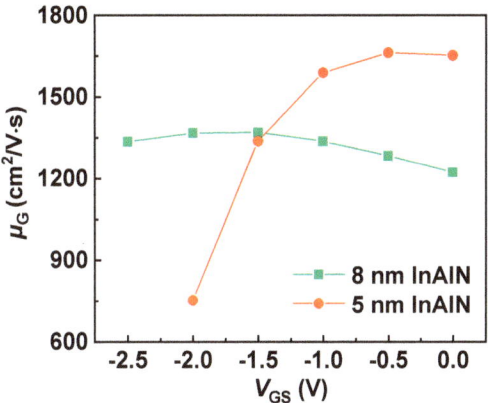

Figure 5. Extracted μ versus V_{GS} of the devices with 8 nm and 5 nm InAlN.

As shown in Figure 5, μ presents a different trend versus V_{GS} for the devices with different InAlN thickness. As V_{GS} increases, μ of the device with 8 nm InAlN deceases, but that of the device with 5 nm InAlN increases. Figure 6a,b show the calculated μ limited by different scatterings for both devices [21,30,31]. The calculated μ (μ_{CAL}, lines in the figures) by using 2D scattering theory shows good agreement with the extracted μ (scatters in the figures), which proves the accuracy of the calculation. As V_{GS} increases, μ_{POP} and μ_{IFR} decrease, μ_{DIS} and μ_{PCF} increase, and μ_{AP} presents a slight change. μ_{POP} and μ_{PCF} play more significant roles among all the scatterings. Figure 7 compares μ_{POP} and μ_{PCF} for both devices. When the InAlN barrier decreases from 8 nm to 5 nm, μ_{POP} increases while μ_{PCF} decreases. The reduced n_{2D} with a 5 nm InAlN barrier decreases the collision probability between channel electrons and polar optical phonons (POPs), resulting in the improved μ_{POP} [27,28]. Due to the spontaneous polarization, there are polarization charges (ρ_0) in the InAlN barrier near the InAlN/GaN interface. When V_{GS} is applied on the gate terminal, the polarization charges (ρ_G) under the gate region are changed due to the inverse piezoelectric effect [32], as shown in Figure 8. The polarization charge distribution is not uniform, and the potential periodicity is broken, resulting in polarization Coulomb field (PCF) scattering. The PCF scattering potential is from the additional polarization charges ($\sigma = \rho_0 - \rho_G$) and is written as [21,22]

$$V(x,y,z) = -\frac{q}{4\pi\varepsilon}\int_{-L_{GS}-\frac{L_G}{2}}^{\frac{L_G}{2}} dx' \int_0^{W_G} \frac{\sigma}{\sqrt{(x-x')^2+(y-y')^2+z^2}} dy' \\ -\frac{q}{4\pi\varepsilon}\int_{\frac{L_G}{2}}^{L_{GD}+\frac{L_G}{2}} dx' \int_0^{W_G} \frac{\sigma}{\sqrt{(x-x')^2+(y-y')^2+z^2}} dy' \quad (3)$$

where ε is the dielectric constant of GaN and W_G is the gate width. Based on inverse piezoelectric effect, σ can be calculated by using $\sigma = \rho_0 - \rho_G = -ne_{33}{}^2V_{GS}/(C_{33}d)$ [32]. n is the fitting parameter, and e_{33} and C_{33} are the piezoelectric coefficient and the elastic stiffness tensor of InAlN, respectively. d is the gate-to-channel distance, which is the sum of the thicknesses of the GaN cap layer (2 nm), InAlN barrier (8 or 5 nm), and AlN interlayer (1 nm). Figure 9 depicts the calculated σ versus V_{GS} with an 8 and 5 nm InAlN barrier. σ increases with the decreased T_B and V_{GS}, resulting in the enhanced PCF scattering as the

InAlN barrier thickness and V_{GS} decrease. Therefore, μ_{PCF} increases with V_{GS}. Because the device with a 5 nm InAlN barrier shows an enhanced PCF scattering, μ increases with V_{GS}. This fact is more pronounced, especially in the more negative V_{GS} region. For the device with an 8 nm InAlN barrier, the PCF scattering became weaker and the POP scattering dominates μ, leading to a slight decrease in μ when V_{GS} increases.

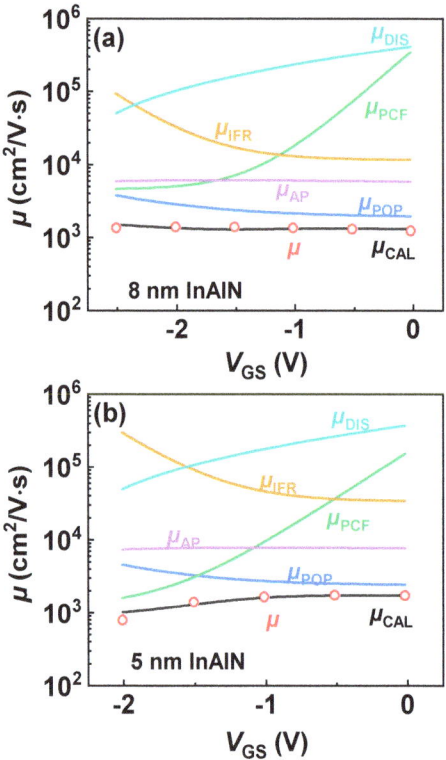

Figure 6. (**a**,**b**) Calculated μ limited by different scattering mechanisms, extracted μ (μ, scatters), and calculated μ (μ_{CAL}, lines) versus V_{GS} of both samples.

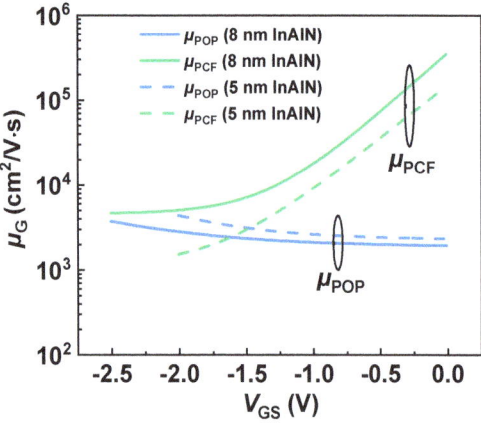

Figure 7. Comparison of μ_{POP} and μ_{PCF} versus V_{GS} of both samples.

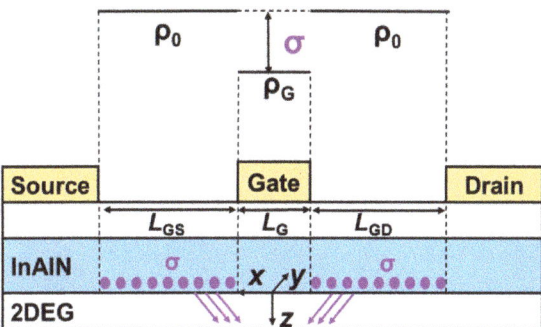

Figure 8. Schematic of the additional polarization charge (σ) distribution in InAlN barrier.

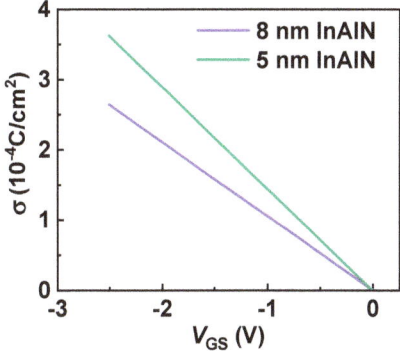

Figure 9. Additional polarization charge (σ) versus V_{GS} with 8 nm and 5 nm InAlN barrier.

From the above discussions, the vertical scale will increase σ and thus enhance PCF scattering, leading to a reduced μ. The lateral scaling is also experimentally investigated on the devices by varying L_{SD} and L_G using the same electron mobility extraction methodology. As the device laterally scales, n_{2D} is not changed, so POP, AP, IFR, and DIS scatterings are not affected. Only PCF scattering can be changed due to the modulation of the polarization change distribution. Figure 10a,b present μ versus V_{GS} at V_{DS} = 0.1 V for the devices with L_G of 50 nm and L_{SD} of 2, 1, 0.6 μm with 8 nm and 5 nm InAlN. μ presents an increase with the decrease in L_{SD}. The corresponding μ_{PCF} is also calculated and plotted in Figure 10c,d. As shown in Figure 11a,b, as L_{SD} scales down, the number of σ is reduced and the effect of σ on the electron under the gate region is weakened, resulting in the increased μ_{PCF} and μ. Because PCF scattering in the device with 8 nm InAlN is weaker, the increase in μ due to the downscaling of L_{SD} is more significant. Here, μ of the devices with L_G of 2 μm is also plotted for comparison, and a significant decrease in μ in the device with an L_G of 50 nm is observed. Although the number of σ is the same under the same V_{GS}, the effect of σ on the 50 nm gate is stronger and thus PCF scattering is enhanced, leading to a decreased μ.

Figure 12a,b present the μ versus V_{GS} for the devices with L_{SD} of 1 μm and L_G of 50, 100, 150 nm with 8 nm and 5 nm InAlN. The electron mobility of all devices presents an increase with V_{GS}. This means PCF scattering plays a dominant role in the electron mobility. As V_{GS} increases from a negative value to 0 V, the electric field under the gate region decreases, resulting in the increase in μ_{PCF} and μ. For the devices with different gate lengths, μ presents an increase as L_G increases. This means the increase in gate length can increase the electron mobility. To explain this phenomenon, the corresponding μ_{PCF} is calculated and plotted in Figure 12c,d. It shows that the increase in L_G can weaken PCF scattering and increase μ_{PCF}. Because L_{SD} is fixed, as shown in Figure 13, the decreased L_G means the increased L_{GS} and L_{GD}, resulting in the enhanced effect of σ on the electrons under the gate region. Thus, PCF scattering becomes stronger and μ reduces with the downscaled L_G.

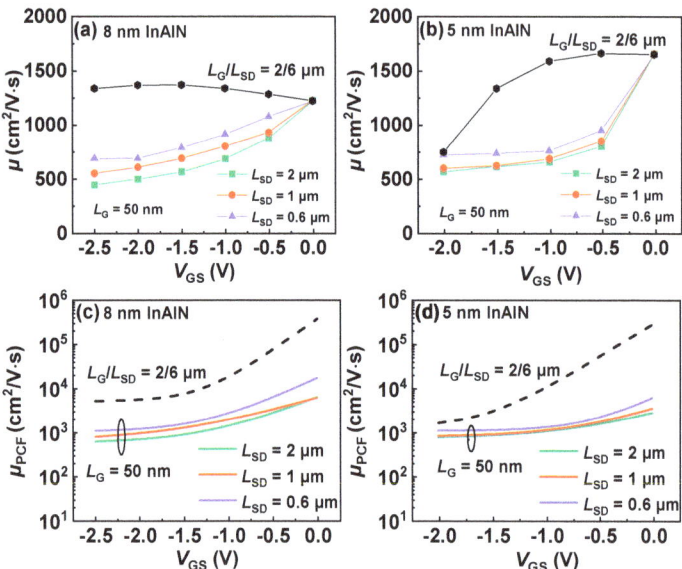

Figure 10. μ versus V_{GS} for the devices with L_G of 50 nm and L_{SD} of 2, 1, 0.6 µm with (**a**) 8 nm and (**b**) 5 nm InAlN. The device with L_G/L_{SD} of 2/6 µm is also plotted for comparison. Calculated μ_{PCF} versus V_{GS} of the same devices with (**c**) 8 nm and (**d**) 5 nm InAlN. The device with L_G/L_{SD} of 2/6 µm is also plotted for comparison.

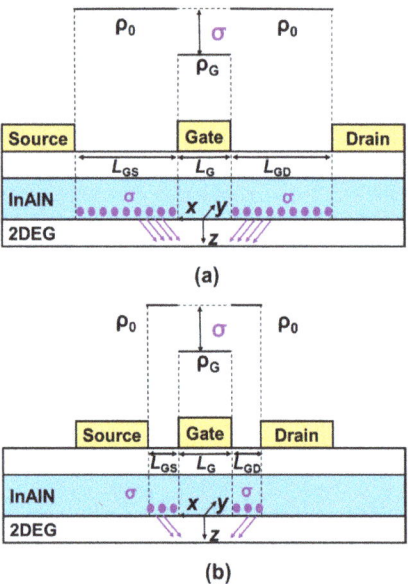

Figure 11. Schematic of the additional polarization charge (σ) distribution in InAlN barrier with (**a**) large and (**b**) small source–drain spacing L_{SD}. The gate length is fixed.

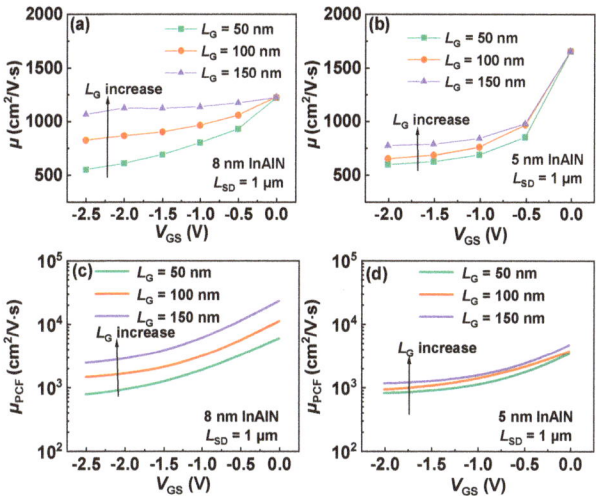

Figure 12. (**a**,**b**) μ versus V_{GS} for the devices with L_{SD} of 1 µm and L_G of 50, 100, 150 nm with 8 nm and 5 nm InAlN. (**c**,**d**) Calculated μ_{PCF} versus V_{GS} of the same devices with 8 nm and 5 nm InAlN.

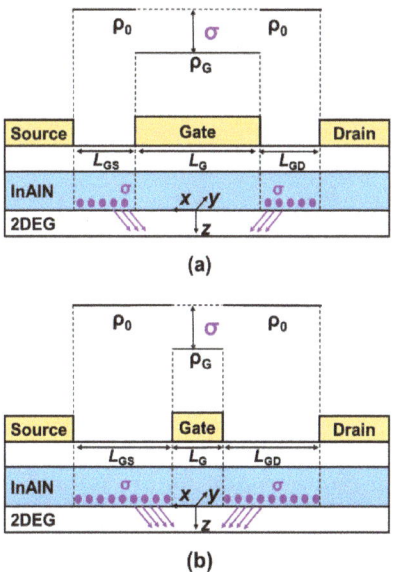

Figure 13. Schematic of the additional polarization charge (σ) distribution in InAlN barrier with (**a**) large and (**b**) small gate length L_G. The source–drain spacing L_{SD} is fixed.

4. Conclusions

In summary, the effect of down-scaling on electron mobility is experimentally demonstrated. It shows that the downscaling of barrier thickness and L_G results in a decrease in μ, but downscaled L_{SD} leads to an increase in μ. This is because the polarization charge distribution is modulated with the vertical and lateral scale, resulting in a change in PCF scattering. When GaN HEMTs scale down, the effect of PCF scattering should be considered, providing an insightful guidance for the device geometry design and performance improvement for RF application.

Author Contributions: P.C. and Y.Z. contributed to the research design, experiment measurements, data analysis, and manuscript preparation. All authors have read and agreed to the published version of the manuscript.

Funding: This research was funded in part by the NASA International Space Station under Grant 80NSSC20M0142, and in part by Air Force Office of Scientific Research under Grant FA9550-19-1-0297, Grant FA9550-21-1-0076 and Grant FA9550-22-1-0126.

Institutional Review Board Statement: Not applicable.

Informed Consent Statement: Not applicable.

Data Availability Statement: The data presented in this study are available upon request from the corresponding author.

Conflicts of Interest: The authors declare no conflict of interest.

References

1. Hamza, K.H.; Nirmal, D. A review of GaN HEMT broadband power amplifiers. *AEU—Int. J. Electron. Commun.* **2020**, *116*, 153040. [CrossRef]
2. Ma, C.-T.; Gu, Z.-H. Review of GaN HEMT applications in power converters over 500 W. *Electronics* **2019**, *8*, 1401. [CrossRef]
3. Keshmiri, N.; Wang, D.; Agrawal, B.; Hou, R.; Emadi, A. Current status and future trends of GaN HEMTs in electrified transportation. *IEEE Access* **2020**, *8*, 70553–70571. [CrossRef]
4. Li, L.; Nomoto, K.; Pan, M.; Li, W.; Hickman, A.; Miller, J.; Lee, K.; Hu, Z.; Bader, S.J.; Lee, S.M. GaN HEMTs on Si with regrown contacts and cutoff/maximum oscillation frequencies of 250/204 GHz. *IEEE Electron Device Lett.* **2020**, *41*, 689–692. [CrossRef]
5. Cui, P.; Mercante, A.; Lin, G.; Zhang, J.; Yao, P.; Prather, D.W.; Zeng, Y. High-performance InAlN/GaN HEMTs on silicon substrate with high $fT \times Lg$. *Appl. Phys. Express* **2019**, *12*, 104001. [CrossRef]
6. Tang, Y.; Shinohara, K.; Regan, D.; Corrion, A.; Brown, D.; Wong, J.; Schmitz, A.; Fung, H.; Kim, S.; Micovic, M. Ultrahigh-Speed GaN High-Electron-Mobility Transistors With f_T/f_{max} of 454/444 GHz. *IEEE Electron Device Lett.* **2015**, *36*, 549–551. [CrossRef]
7. Kim, J.-G.; Cho, C.; Kim, E.; Hwang, J.S.; Park, K.-H.; Lee, J.-H. High breakdown voltage and low-current dispersion in AlGaN/GaN HEMTs with high-quality AlN buffer layer. *IEEE Trans. Electron Devices* **2021**, *68*, 1513–1517. [CrossRef]
8. Xia, X.; Guo, Z.; Sun, H. Study of Normally-Off AlGaN/GaN HEMT with Microfield Plate for Improvement of Breakdown Voltage. *Micromachines* **2021**, *12*, 1318. [CrossRef]
9. Reddeppa, M.; Park, B.-G.; Pasupuleti, K.S.; Nam, D.-J.; Kim, S.-G.; Oh, J.-E.; Kim, M.-D. Current–voltage characteristics and deep-level study of GaN nanorod Schottky-diode-based photodetector. *Semicond. Sci. Technol.* **2021**, *36*, 035010. [CrossRef]
10. Pasupuleti, K.S.; Reddeppa, M.; Park, B.-G.; Oh, J.-E.; Kim, S.-G.; Kim, M.-D. Efficient Charge Separation in Polypyrrole/GaN-Nanorod-Based Hybrid Heterojunctions for High-Performance Self-Powered UV Photodetection. *Phys. Status Solidi (RRL)—Rapid Res. Lett.* **2021**, *15*, 2000518. [CrossRef]
11. Schuette, M.L.; Ketterson, A.; Song, B.; Beam, E.; Chou, T.-M.; Pilla, M.; Tserng, H.-Q.; Gao, X.; Guo, S.; Fay, P.J. Gate-recessed integrated E/D GaN HEMT technology with f_T/f_{max} > 300 GHz. *IEEE Electron Device Lett.* **2013**, *34*, 741–743. [CrossRef]
12. Downey, B.P.; Meyer, D.J.; Katzer, D.S.; Roussos, J.A.; Pan, M.; Gao, X. SiN$_x$/InAlN/AlN/GaN MIS-HEMTs With 10.8 THz·V Johnson Figure of Merit. *IEEE Electron Device Lett.* **2014**, *35*, 527–529. [CrossRef]
13. Jessen, G.H.; Fitch, R.C.; Gillespie, J.K.; Via, G.; Crespo, A.; Langley, D.; Denninghoff, D.J.; Trejo, M.; Heller, E.R. Short-channel effect limitations on high-frequency operation of AlGaN/GaN HEMTs for T-Gate devices. *IEEE Trans. Electron Devices* **2007**, *54*, 2589–2597. [CrossRef]
14. Shinohara, K.; Regan, D.C.; Tang, Y.; Corrion, A.L.; Brown, D.F.; Wong, J.C.; Robinson, J.F.; Fung, H.H.; Schmitz, A.; Oh, T.C. Scaling of GaN HEMTs and Schottky diodes for submillimeter-wave MMIC applications. *IEEE Trans. Electron Devices* **2013**, *60*, 2982–2996. [CrossRef]
15. Shinohara, K.; Regan, D.; Milosavljevic, I.; Corrion, A.; Brown, D.; Willadsen, P.; Butler, C.; Schmitz, A.; Kim, S.; Lee, V. Electron velocity enhancement in laterally scaled GaN DH-HEMTs with f_T of 260 GHz. *IEEE Electron Device Lett.* **2011**, *32*, 1074–1076. [CrossRef]
16. Shinohara, K.; Regan, D.; Corrion, A.; Brown, D.; Burnham, S.; Willadsen, P.; Alvarado-Rodriguez, I.; Cunningham, M.; Butler, C.; Schmitz, A. Deeply-scaled self-aligned-gate GaN DH-HEMTs with ultrahigh cutoff frequency. In Proceedings of the 2011 International Electron Devices Meeting, Washington, DC, USA, 5–7 December 2011; pp. 11–14.
17. Medjdoub, F.; Alomari, M.; Carlin, J.-F.; Gonschorek, M.; Feltin, E.; Py, M.; Grandjean, N.; Kohn, E. Barrier-layer scaling of InAlN/GaN HEMTs. *IEEE Electron Device Lett.* **2008**, *29*, 422–425. [CrossRef]
18. Lee, D.S.; Lu, B.; Azize, M.; Gao, X.; Guo, S.; Kopp, D.; Fay, P.; Palacios, T. Impact of GaN channel scaling in InAlN/GaN HEMTs. In Proceedings of the 2011 International Electron Devices Meeting, Washington, DC, USA, 5–7 December 2011; pp. 11–14.
19. Ambacher, O.; Foutz, B.; Smart, J.; Shealy, J.; Weimann, N.; Chu, K.; Murphy, M.; Sierakowski, A.; Schaff, W.; Eastman, L. Two dimensional electron gases induced by spontaneous and piezoelectric polarization in undoped and doped AlGaN/GaN heterostructures. *J. Appl. Phys.* **2000**, *87*, 334–344. [CrossRef]

20. Yu, E.; Sullivan, G.; Asbeck, P.; Wang, C.; Qiao, D.; Lau, S. Measurement of piezoelectrically induced charge in GaN/AlGaN heterostructure field-effect transistors. *Appl. Phys. Lett.* **1997**, *71*, 2794–2796. [CrossRef]
21. Luan, C.; Lin, Z.; Lv, Y.; Zhao, J.; Wang, Y.; Chen, H.; Wang, Z. Theoretical model of the polarization Coulomb field scattering in strained AlGaN/AlN/GaN heterostructure field-effect transistors. *J. Appl. Phys.* **2014**, *116*, 044507. [CrossRef]
22. Cui, P.; Mo, J.; Fu, C.; Lv, Y.; Liu, H.; Cheng, A.; Luan, C.; Zhou, Y.; Dai, G.; Lin, Z. Effect of Different Gate Lengths on Polarization Coulomb Field Scattering Potential in AlGaN/GaN Heterostructure Field-Effect Transistors. *Sci. Rep.* **2018**, *8*, 9036. [CrossRef]
23. Lin, Z.; Zhao, J.; Corrigan, T.D.; Wang, Z.; You, Z.; Wang, Z.; Lu, W. The influence of Schottky contact metals on the strain of AlGaN barrier layers. *J. Appl. Phys.* **2008**, *103*, 044503. [CrossRef]
24. Guo, L.; Wang, X.; Wang, C.; Xiao, H.; Ran, J.; Luo, W.; Wang, X.; Wang, B.; Fang, C.; Hu, G. The influence of 1 nm AlN interlayer on properties of the $Al_{0.3}Ga_{0.7}N$/AlN/GaN HEMT structure. *Microelectron. J.* **2008**, *39*, 777–781. [CrossRef]
25. Ibbetson, J.P.; Fini, P.; Ness, K.; DenBaars, S.; Speck, J.; Mishra, U. Polarization effects, surface states, and the source of electrons in AlGaN/GaN heterostructure field effect transistors. *Appl. Phys. Lett.* **2000**, *77*, 250–252. [CrossRef]
26. Goyal, N.; Fjeldly, T.A. Analytical modeling of AlGaN/AlN/GaN heterostructures including effects of distributed surface donor states. *Appl. Phys. Lett.* **2014**, *105*, 023508. [CrossRef]
27. Gurusinghe, M.; Davidsson, S.; Andersson, T. Two-dimensional electron mobility limitation mechanisms in $Al_xGa_{1-x}N$/GaN heterostructures. *Phys. Rev. B* **2005**, *72*, 045316. [CrossRef]
28. Fang, T.; Wang, R.; Xing, H.; Rajan, S.; Jena, D. Effect of optical phonon scattering on the performance of GaN transistors. *IEEE Electron Device Lett.* **2012**, *33*, 709–711. [CrossRef]
29. Kordoš, P.; Gregušová, D.; Stoklas, R.; Čičo, K.; Novák, J. Improved transport properties of Al_2O_3/AlGaN/GaN metal-oxide-semiconductor heterostructure field-effect transistor. *Appl. Phys. Lett.* **2007**, *90*, 123513. [CrossRef]
30. Cui, P.; Lv, Y.; Fu, C.; Liu, H.; Cheng, A.; Luan, C.; Zhou, Y.; Lin, Z. Effect of Polarization Coulomb Field Scattering on Electrical Properties of the 70-nm Gate-Length AlGaN/GaN HEMTs. *Sci. Rep.* **2018**, *8*, 12850. [CrossRef]
31. Cui, P.; Liu, H.; Lin, W.; Lin, Z.; Cheng, A.; Yang, M.; Liu, Y.; Fu, C.; Lv, Y.; Luan, C. Influence of different gate biases and gate lengths on parasitic source access resistance in AlGaN/GaN heterostructure FETs. *IEEE Trans. Electron Devices* **2017**, *64*, 1038–1044. [CrossRef]
32. Anwar, A.; Webster, R.T.; Smith, K.V. Bias induced strain in AlGaN/GaN heterojunction field effect transistors and its implications. *Appl. Phys. Lett.* **2006**, *88*, 203510. [CrossRef]

Article

Numerical Evaluation of the Effect of Geometric Tolerances on the High-Frequency Performance of Graphene Field-Effect Transistors

Monica La Mura *, Patrizia Lamberti and Vincenzo Tucci

Department of Information and Electrical Engineering and Applied Mathematics, University of Salerno, Via Giovanni Paolo II, 132, 84084 Fisciano, SA, Italy; plamberti@unisa.it (P.L.); vtucci@unisa.it (V.T.)
* Correspondence: mlamura@unisa.it

Abstract: The interest in graphene-based electronics is due to graphene's great carrier mobility, atomic thickness, resistance to radiation, and tolerance to extreme temperatures. These characteristics enable the development of extremely miniaturized high-performing electronic devices for next-generation radiofrequency (RF) communication systems. The main building block of graphene-based electronics is the graphene-field effect transistor (GFET). An important issue hindering the diffusion of GFET-based circuits on a commercial level is the repeatability of the fabrication process, which affects the uncertainty of both the device geometry and the graphene quality. Concerning the GFET geometrical parameters, it is well known that the channel length is the main factor that determines the high-frequency limitations of a field-effect transistor, and is therefore the parameter that should be better controlled during the fabrication. Nevertheless, other parameters are affected by a fabrication-related tolerance; to understand to which extent an increase of the accuracy of the GFET layout patterning process steps can improve the performance uniformity, their impact on the GFET performance variability should be considered and compared to that of the channel length. In this work, we assess the impact of the fabrication-related tolerances of GFET-base amplifier geometrical parameters on the RF performance, in terms of the amplifier transit frequency and maximum oscillation frequency, by using a design-of-experiments approach.

Keywords: design of experiments; GFET; graphene; high-frequency; RF devices; tolerance analysis

1. Introduction

The research in high-frequency electronics has been historically driven by the development of advanced radiofrequency (RF) wireless telecommunication systems.

Despite the advances in CMOS-based RF devices, unsolved issues related to losses and noise have determined the rise of III-V compound semiconductors technology, which made great achievements in high-frequency applications thanks to high electron mobility [1–4]. Meanwhile, graphene has already proven to have remarkable electron mobility and thermal conductivity, and the issues related to its zero-bandgap (that prevents graphene-based devices from turning off completely) are of secondary importance in analogue RF electronics [5–9]. Hence, a great number of graphene field effect transistors (GFETs) [6,10] has been proposed, pursuing a clear current saturation [11–13] and improved voltage gain [8,14] targeting RF applications [15–21], and demonstrating the capabilities of graphene-based RF electronics. As of now, cut-off frequencies in the range of f_T = 100–300 GHz [16,22], and above [23] have been experimentally demonstrated for GFETs, in line with the best silicon-based FETs. The GFET maximum oscillation frequency, though, is strongly limited below 70 GHz [20,24] by the poor current saturation, the high graphene/metal contact resistance at the Gate terminal [25–27], and the unclean graphene transfer process. Exceptionally, values as high as f_{MAX} = 200 GHz [28] were measured, which continue to be lower than the values theoretically achievable with graphene-based devices.

Even though these results are not comparable to the best-performing III–V HEMTs, graphene RF devices are still considered appealing due to the possibility of taking advantage of the GFET current ambipolarity, which enables a strong reduction in the transistor count and favours additional miniaturization capabilities [29]. This feature is extremely interesting, for example, for the aerospace field, particularly because it is accompanied by graphene's inherent tolerance to radiation [30–32]. For these reasons, several examples of graphene-based RF devices have been proposed in recent years, including antennas [33,34], transmitters and receivers [35–37], modulators and demodulators [38–43], shields [44], power and signal amplifiers [45–48], mixers [49–51], and oscillators [52–54]. Important milestones were recently reached towards the large-scale fabrication of graphene electronic devices [55] and their integration into traditional semiconductor fabrication lines [56]. On this basis, graphene can be considered very promising for the development of breakthrough RF electronics.

In this scenario, one important challenge to address is the reliability of fabricated devices. The uncontrollable variations related to the manufacturing process tolerances determine an unavoidable non-uniformity across the devices, both fabricated on different wafers and on the same wafer. This inter-wafer and intra-wafer variability of the characteristics of the fabricated devices affects the uniformity of the performance of the fabricated devices. The process-related variations of nanomaterial-based electronic devices can be gathered in two categories of factors: factors related to the layout definition, and factors related to the material properties, as stated in [57]. The first category includes the geometrical parameters defined by the lithography (for the lateral dimensions) or by the growth/deposition process (for the vertical dimensions). The second category includes the parameters expressing the graphene quality (i.e., mobility, doping caused by traps and impurities, defects), which are determined by the capability of the growth or transfer process to not degrade the material electrical properties. These two categories of factors are independent and can be treated separately. In this paper, we focus on the first category of parameters.

Extracting a mathematical relationship between the GFET parameters variability and the performance variability, e.g., in the form of a regression model, is useful to predict the uncertainty resulting from the wafer processing. To optimize the number of runs necessary to get accurate modelling of the performance variation, design of experiments (DoE) techniques can be used [58–60].

In this work, we perform a tolerance analysis of a GFET common-source amplifier, originally proposed in [45] as the first high-frequency voltage amplifier obtained by using large-area CVD-grown graphene. The device performance is assessed by means of circuit simulations, designed according to a full factorial design of experiments, and performed using a large-signal charge-based compact model of a GFET described and validated in [61]. The Advanced Design System® (Keysight Technologies, Inc., Santa Rosa, CA, USA) simulation environment is used by varying channel width, W, the channel length, L, and the top oxide thickness, t_{OX}, in order to investigate the impact of geometry variations caused by the fabrication of process-related tolerances. Following the study presented in [62], where we discussed the impact of tolerances on the amplifier's transconductance, g_m, and output conductance, g_{ds}, the influence of the same variations is reported here on the high-frequency performance described in terms of f_T and f_{MAX}.

2. GFET Simulation Design

2.1. Input Parameter Space

The geometrical parameters determine the device input capacitance, output capacitance, and trans-capacitance, which limit the high-frequency performance of a field-effect transistor. In particular, the capacitances depend on the channel width, W, the channel length, L, and the top gate oxide thickness, t_{OX}. The unevenness of these parameters, thus, impairs the uniformity of the fabricated devices' high-frequency capabilities. In [57], it was observed that FETs based on nanowires and nanotubes are more robust to process-related geometry variations as compared to bulk silicon-based MOS devices and FinFETs, from the point of view of the direct current and of the input capacitance; the impact of the same parameters on the drain-source current of a GFET was assessed in [63]. Concerning graphene-based devices, the range of variation that should be considered for the geometrical factors is very process-dependent. The channel area is affected by an uncertainty generated either by the graphene sheet irregular shape (in the case of mechanical exfoliation and transfer of graphene flakes) [64], or by the lithography and/or etching steps (in the case of large-area CVD-grown graphene transfer) [65]. The accuracy of the thickness of the top-gate oxide depends on the thickness control capabilities of the growth or deposition technique and on the resulting roughness, and is also affected by inherent process variations [66].

In this work, the factors chosen for the tolerance analysis are W, L, and t_{OX}, and in the absence of an initial estimate of the process tolerances, a variation $\pm \Delta$ within the 10% of the nominal value is considered for each factor, in analogy with the approach proposed in [62,63,67–69].

The response variables of interest were computed in correspondence of all the combinations of the minimum value, centre value, and maximum value of each input factor, following a 3-factors, 3-levels full-factorial design of simulations. Hence, $3^3 = 27$ combinations of the input settings were considered. This approach allows accounting for simultaneous variations of all the considered input factors, enabling the investigation of possible interaction effects between the factors. In the proposed analysis, the factors are represented in the form of coded variables $x_{i,c}$, where the minimum, nominal, and maximum values are represented by the values -1, 0, and 1, to provide an immediate matching with the regression model coefficients [60]. Including the centre point allows assessing the linearity of the response variable, with the scope of selecting the most suitable order for the regression model.

Table 1 reports the minimum, nominal, and maximum values of the simulation input parameters. The centre values for the three factors W, L, t_{OX} refer to the nominal design of the device described in [45] and investigated in [62,70].

Table 1. Input factors levels in the performed simulations.

Factor		Minimum	Nominal [45]	Maximum
x_1	W (µm)	27	30	33
x_2	t_{OX} (nm)	3.6	4	4.4
x_3	L (µm)	0.45	0.5	0.55
	Coded	-1	0	-1

2.2. Output Regression Model

The chosen performance indicators, computed in correspondence of the n_c combinations of the input factors, are processed in accordance with the design of experiments techniques to evaluate the regression model coefficients. Depending on the linearity of the response variation with respect to the $m = 3$ factors $x_{i,c}$, the regression model for the performance y obtainable from the 3-by-3 full factorial plan of simulation can be [60]:

- A first-order model, including only the linear dependence on the factors (main effects model):

$$y \approx y_0 + \beta_1 \, x_1 + \beta_2 \, x_2 + \beta_3 \, x_3 \tag{1}$$

- A first-order model with interactions, including a small curvature in the response by means of the mixed product terms:

$$y \approx y_0 + \beta_1 \, x_1 + \beta_2 \, x_2 + \beta_3 \, x_3 + \beta_{12} \, x_1 \, x_2 + \beta_{23} \, x_2 \, x_3 + \beta_{31} \, x_3 \, x_1 \tag{2}$$

- A second order model, including quadratic terms (response surface model):

$$y \approx y_0 + \beta_1 \, x_1 + \beta_2 \, x_2 + \beta_3 \, x_3 + \beta_{11} \, x_1^2 + \beta_{22} \, x_2^2 + \beta_{33} \, x_3^2 + \beta_{12} \, x_1 \, x_2 + \beta_{23} \, x_2 \, x_3 + \beta_{31} \, x_3 \, x_1 \tag{3}$$

2.3. Response Variables

To assess the high-frequency operation capabilities of RF devices, the most common figures of merit are the transition frequency, f_T, and the maximum oscillation frequency, f_{MAX}.

In particular, f_T is defined as the frequency at which the current gain with the output in the short circuit condition reaches unity. By representing the common-source amplifier with a two-port network in which the input port is the gate-source terminal pair and the output port is the drain-source pair, the short-circuit current gain is the h_{21} parameter, which can be computed from the scattering parameters (S-parameters) matrix according to [71]:

$$h_{21} = -2S_{21} \left[(1 - S_{11})(1 + S_{22}) + S_{12} S_{21} \right]^{-1} \quad (4)$$

The computation of the S-parameters is preferred because their evaluation does not require short-circuiting or open circuiting the input and output ports. These conditions are never satisfied perfectly at very high frequencies.

Despite its common use, f_T is not the most important figure of merit [72] in RF electronics. Amplifiers are useful as long as they are able to deliver power to the load, rather than current, and for this reason, it is important to also evaluate the transistor's f_{MAX}. This parameter is the frequency at which the maximum available gain (MAG), the frequency-dependent maximum power that can be transferred to the load in the impedance matching condition, reaches unity. f_{MAX} is, thus, the frequency over which the transistor is not able to amplify the input power in any case. This frequency is also called the maximum oscillation frequency because it is the frequency at which the transistor can trigger and sustain stable oscillations in oscillator circuit design. f_{MAX} is usually lower than f_T, and the most interesting frequency between the two depends on the application.

2.4. Simulation Environment Setup

To assess the impact of the fabrication-related tolerance affecting the geometrical parameters on a GFET-based amplifier RF performance, a GFET small-signal model [73,74] can be used to compute the quantities of interest according to [6,29,73]

$$f_T = \frac{g_m}{2\pi \left\{ \left(C_{gs} + C_{gd} \right) [1 + g_{ds}(R_S + R_D)] + C_{gd} g_m (R_S + R_D) \right\}} \quad (5)$$

$$f_{MAX} = \frac{g_m}{4\pi \left(C_{gs} + C_{gd} \right) \left[g_{ds}(r_i + R_S + R_G) + g_m R_G \frac{C_{gd}}{C_{gs} + C_{gd}} \right]^{1/2}} \quad (6)$$

where C_{gs} is the gate-source capacitances and C_{gd} is the drain-source capacitance, R_S, R_D, R_G, are the source, drain, and gate resistances, and $r_i = 1/(2 g_m)$ is the intrinsic resistance [75].

Nevertheless, compact models for the simulation of the GFET electrical behaviour in large-signal operations have been developed and made compatible with most circuit simulators [61,76–78]. In this work, we use the charge-based large-signal GFET compact model presented in [61] and written in the hardware description language Verilog-A. This model preserves charge conservation and considers non-reciprocal self-capacitances and transcapacitances, contrarily to the Meyer's and Meyer-like models commonly used [61]. The simulated device is the GFET common-source amplifier, made of high-quality single-layer CVD-grown graphene transferred onto a silicon oxide substrate, with an ultrathin high-k dielectric gate oxide [79] and a 6-finger embedded gate, presented in [45] as the first high-frequency voltage amplifier obtained by using large-area graphene and already simulated in [62,70]. The compact model used for the circuit simulations requires setting the input parameters related to the geometry, to the oxide material properties, and to the graphene characteristics. The nominal settings were obtained by Pasadas et al. in [70] by fitting the experimental I–V curve reported in [45], and are listed here in Table 2.

Table 2. Input parameters of the circuit model at the nominal design point.

Parameter	Value [70]	Description
L	0.5 µm	Channel length
W	30 µm	Channel width
t_{ox}	4 nm	Top oxide thickness
ε_{top}	12	Top oxide relative permittivity
V_{GS0}	0.613 V	Top gate voltage offset
Δ	0.095 eV	Electrostatic potential inhomogeneity due to electron-hole puddles
$\hbar\omega$	0.12 eV	Effective energy of substrate optical phonon emission
μ	4500 cm^2/Vs	Effective carrier mobility

Concerning the resistance at the transistor's terminals, they are taken into account by adding external lumped resistors. In [70], the values indicated for the drain and source contact resistances R_D and R_S for the nominal design of the considered device are dependent on the channel width and equal to $R_D = R_S = 435\ \Omega\ \mu m$, whereas the gate resistance R_G is a fixed resistance $R_G = 14\ \Omega$. Nevertheless, the contact resistance is known to impact strongly on the high-frequency limits of the GFET [80]. Therefore, in the performed simulations, the drain and source resistances and the gate resistance are increased proportionally to the channel width and to the channel length, respectively, in order to include the effect of the geometry variation. On the contrary, the dependence of the contact resistance upon other parameters related to the channel transport properties at different field intensities are not addressed here, since these properties are not related to the geometrical parameters that are the focus of this paper.

The circuit schematic can be seen in Figure 1.

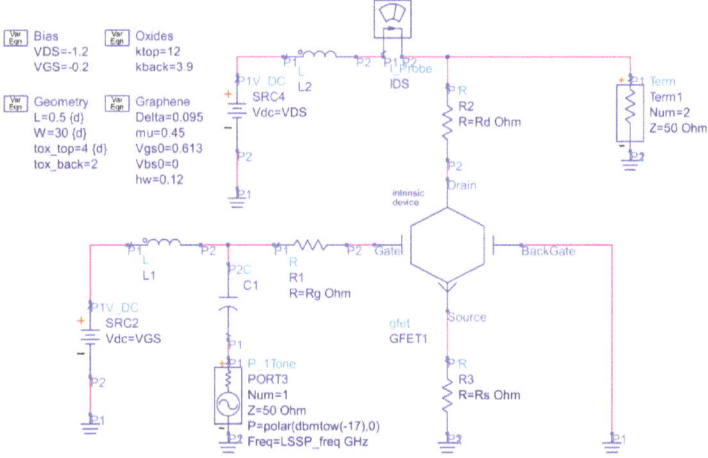

Figure 1. Schematic for the GFET amplifier large-signal S-parameters (LSSP) analysis.

Simulations are run in the Advanced Design System—ADS (®Keysight, Inc., Santa Rosa, CA, USA) software environment, which performs a DC analysis to choose the bias point and large-signal S-parameters (LSSP) analysis to take into account the device nonlinearity in the computation of the S-parameters. Figure 2 shows the drain current I_D computed by varying the drain-source and gate-source bias voltage. As can be observed by viewing the surface curvature, the saturation of the drain current can be obtained in a certain bias region. Since the choice of the bias point is of great importance to achieve optimum performance [81], it was carefully chosen to achieve the maximum intrinsic voltage gain $A_V = g_m\ g_{ds}^{-1}$. Searching for the optimal bias point, the applied V_{DS} was intentionally limited to prevent the effects of the carrier velocity saturation and the possible self-heating that intervene in high-field conditions, as these phenomena are not addressed by the model. On this basis, the bias point was set to $V_{GS} = -0.2$ V, $V_{DS} = -1.2$ V, as found in [62]. The output conductance g_{ds} on top of the drain current I_D output characteristic is shown in Figure 3a, and the transconductance g_m on top of the I_D transfer curve is shown in Figure 3b.

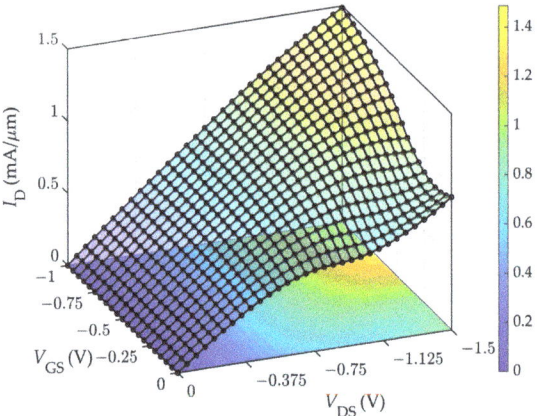

Figure 2. Surface plot of the drain current I_D computed by varying the V_{GS} and V_{DS}.

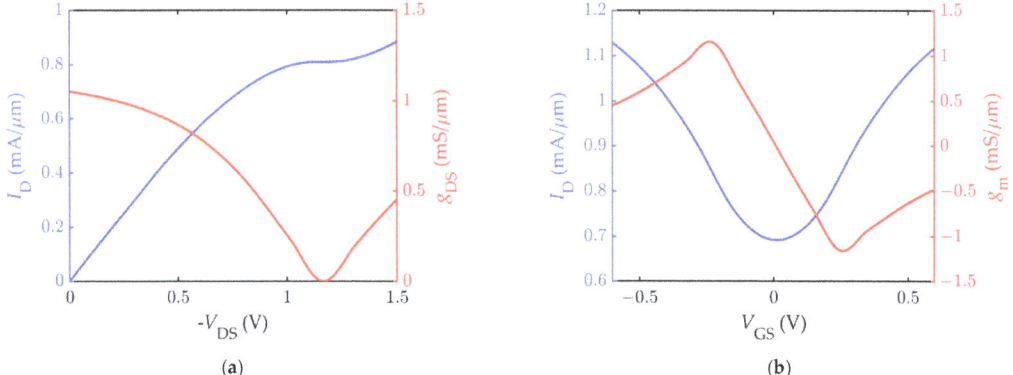

Figure 3. The DC characteristic of the simulated GFET: (**a**) the drain current I_D (in blue) against the drain-source voltage at $V_{GS} = -0.2$ V, with superimposed output conductance g_{ds} (in red); (**b**) the drain current I_D (in blue) against the gate-source voltage at $V_{DS} = -1.2$ V, with superimposed transconductance g_m (in red).

2.5. Validation of the Simulated GFET Behaviour

In order to validate the simulation results, the f_T and f_{MAX} obtained by the circuit simulator for the nominal design of the GFET were compared with the measured values reported in [45]. For this purpose, the analysis was performed by biasing the transistor at $V_{GS} = -0.1$ V, $V_{DS} = -1.2$ V, as reported in the paper. In addition, the values computed by means of the small-signal relations reported in Equations (5) and (6) are also reported. As can be observed, the results obtained by using Equations (5) and (6) agree neither with the experiment nor with the simulation, probably due to the nonlinear behaviour of the device and to the model being based on nonreciprocal capacitances. The simulation results replicate the measurements quite well, especially concerning the f_{MAX}, as can be seen in Table 3. Differences between the simulation and the measurement can be caused by the imperfect value attributed to some of the graphene-related input parameters reported in Table 2, and can be reduced by applying optimization techniques to find the parameters' values that improve the fitting of the measured current curves.

Table 3. Simulated and measured f_T, f_{MAX} at V_{GS} = −0.1 V, V_{DS} = −1.2 V.

	Simulated	Measured [45]	Computed
f_T (GHz)	9.3	8.2	7.2
f_{MAX} (GHz)	6.1	6.2	4.0

The simulated h_{21} and MAG at the optimal bias point V_{GS} = −0.2 V, V_{DS} = −1.2 V, instead, return a nominal value for the f_T and f_{MAX} of $f_{T,n}$ = 29.40 GHz and $f_{MAX,n}$ = 14.84 GHz and are shown in Figure 4.

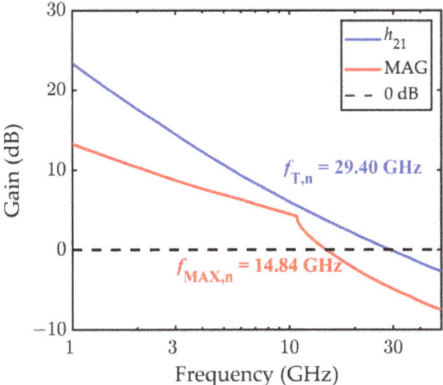

Figure 4. Short-circuit current gain h_{21} and maximum available gain MAG computed in correspondence of the nominal set of input parameters, at the bias point V_{GS} = −0.2 V, V_{DS} = −1.2 V. The nominal cut-off frequency is $f_{T,n}$ = 29.40 GHz, and the nominal maximum oscillation frequency is $f_{MAX,n}$ = 14.84 GHz.

3. Tolerance Analysis Results

3.1. f_T Sensitivity

To extract the f_T from the simulation results, the short-circuit current gain h_{21} was computed for the 27 combinations of the input factors, and the scattered data is plotted against the factors in Figure 5a, showing the main effects plot, and against the factor-mixed products in Figure 5b, showing the interaction effects plot. By looking at Figure 5 it can be concluded that the transition frequency f_T is by far more sensitive to the channel length L rather than to the other parameters, as the L factor variation causes the highest location shift of the mean performance, indicated by the blue dots for each level taken by the input factors. This result confirms expectations, since the peak cut-off frequency is reported to have a $1/L$ dependence in FETs with short gate lengths, and a $1/L^2$ dependence in FETs with long gate lengths [16]. The two other factors have the same influence on the f_T, and both are much less effective than L. As can be observed from the f_T main effects and interaction effects values reported in Table 4, the main effect of the channel length L, ME_3 = −7.11, is by far the highest contribution to the f_T variability. The interactions between the channel length L and the other two factors (i.e., IE_{13} and IE_{23}) are very similar, and comparable to the main effects of t_{OX} and W, ME_1, and ME_2. They are less than 10% of the main effect of the L, meaning that W and t_{OX} and their interactions with L impact the response variability by less than 10% of the impact of L.

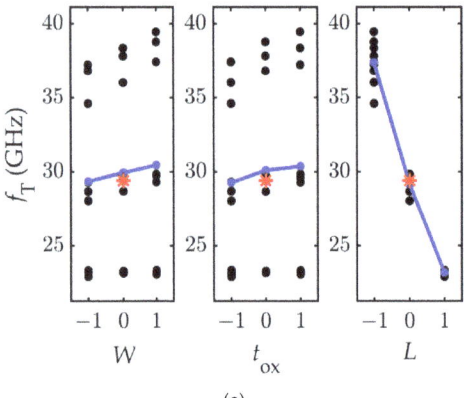
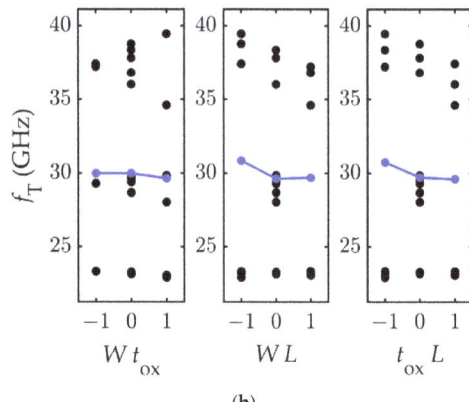

Figure 5. Computed values of f_T against (**a**) the input factors and (**b**) the factor-mixed products. The blue lines connect the f_T average values, and the red star marks the response computed at the nominal set of the input parameters.

Table 4. f_T main effects and interaction effects.

	x_1 (W)	x_2 (t_{OX})	x_3 (L)
x_1 (W)	$ME_1 = 0.557$	$IE_{12} = -0.166$	$IE_{13} = -0.575$
x_2 (t_{OX})		$ME_2 = 0.549$	$IE_{23} = -0.570$
x_3 (L)			$ME_3 = -7.11$

Concerning the linearity of the response, the f_T variation induced by the variation of the factors of 10% is approximately linear; in fact, the blue line connecting the average f_T computed at the different levels of the input factors is pretty straight, and closely passes the nominal response $f_{T,n}$.

To account for the slight nonlinearity of the response variable in the regression model, the interaction effects shown in Figure 5b can be considered. The interaction effects are computed by calculating the slope of the line connecting the average values of f_T computed when the product of the coded factors equals -1 and $+1$. The introduction of such effects can model the small curvatures in the response.

On this basis, the f_T variability can be modelled by:

$$f_T = 29.4 + 0.557\,W + 0.549\,t_{OX} - 7.11\,L - 0.166\,W\,t_{OX} - 0.575\,W\,L - 0.57\,t_{OX}\,L \quad (7)$$

where W, t_{OX}, and L are varying between -1 and $+1$, following the coding reported in Table 1.

3.2. f_{MAX} Sensitivity

The f_{MAX} variation in response to the variation of the input factors is shown in Figure 6a,b, which report the main effects plot and the interaction effect plot, respectively. As in the previous case, the blue lines connect the f_{MAX} average values computed in correspondence of each level of the factors, and the red star indicates the nominal response $f_{MAX,n}$.

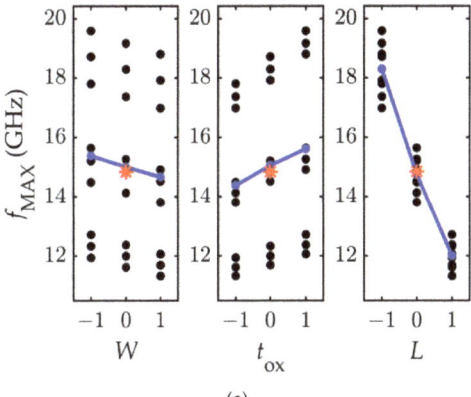
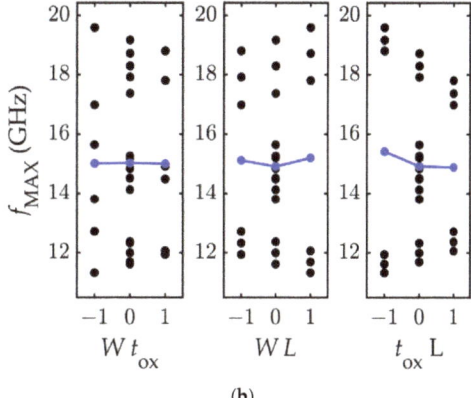

Figure 6. Computed values of f_{MAX} against (**a**) the input factors and (**b**) the factor-mixed products. The blue lines connect the f_{MAX} average values, and the red star marks the response computed at the nominal set of the input parameters.

By looking at Figure 6, it can be observed that the factor most influential on the f_{MAX} is, as for the f_T, the channel length L. However, contrarily to what was observed for f_T, the increase of the channel width W causes a decrease of the f_{MAX}. Another noticeable result is that, in this case, the response dependence on the three factors is very linear. In fact, the plots in Figure 6b show that there is no interaction between W and t_{OX}, and that the interaction between W and L is one order of magnitude smaller than the lowest main effect. Moreover, while for the f_T the factors W and t_{OX} had a similar impact on the response, for the f_{MAX} it is observed that the t_{OX} is the second most influential parameter, as its main effect doubles the main effect of W, and is ≈20% the main effect of L. This is clearer by observing the computed values of the main effects and interaction effects reported in Table 5.

Table 5. f_{MAX} main effects and interaction effects.

	x_1 (W)	x_2 (t_{OX})	x_3 (L)
$x_1(W)$	$ME_1 = 0.356$	$IE_{12} \approx 0$	$IE_{13} = 0.042$
$x_2(t_{OX})$		$ME_2 = 0.615$	$IE_{23} = -0.263$
$x_3(L)$			$ME_3 = -3.14$

These values allow extracting the linear regression model representing the variability of the PF f_{MAX}, which is:

$$f_{MAX} = 14.84 - 0.356\,W + 0.615\,t_{OX} - 3.14\,L + 0.042\,W\,L - 0.263\,t_{OX}\,L \qquad (8)$$

4. Conclusions

An analysis of the impact on the fabrication-related tolerances of the GFET geometrical parameters was performed by means of designed circuit simulations.

The factor variation most influential on the transition frequency and the maximum oscillation frequency uniformity for a GFET-based common-source amplifier is the channel length L, coherently with the concept that the transistor high-frequency limit is inversely proportional to the time the carriers need to cross the channel. Reducing the channel length has great benefits on the transition frequency improvement and helps to improve the maximum frequency, too. Hence, being able to control the channel length reliably and applying all the possible measures to limit the occurrence of any uncontrollable phenomenon interfering with the channel length accuracy is the best way to reduce unwanted fluctuations of the fabricated transistors' cut-off frequency, and therefore improve the intra-wafer and inter-wafer performance uniformity. The improvement provided by increasing the accuracy of the other geometrical parameters, instead, is very limited. In fact, this analysis has shown that the impact of the channel width W and the top oxide thickness t_{OX} on the f_T is the same, and it is less than 10% of the impact of the channel length L. The interaction between L and the other two factors has an impact comparable to the W and t_{OX} main effect, and must therefore be included in the regression model for the f_T. Concerning the f_{MAX}, the t_{OX} is the second most influential factor, with the main effect that is about 20% of the L main effect. The W impacts on the f_{MAX} by less than 10% the impact of the L. A first-order regression model accounting for interaction between the factors is provided for both the considered performance indicators, allowing both the prediction of the expected variability when the tolerance of process parameters is known, and the definition of a region of acceptability for the factors' tolerances when the variability of the observed performance is constrained.

In conclusion, the reduction of the variability of W and t_{OX} would improve the uniformity of the f_T and f_{MAX} far less than a reduction of the variability of L by an equal percentage amount. The quantitative evaluation of this improvement can be done by using the provided mathematical relations between the quantities of interest. These considerations can support the cost/benefit analysis for the planning of investments to improve the ability of the manufacturing process to control the geometric parameters.

Further work includes the tolerance analysis of different GFET devices found in the literature, in order to compare the robustness of different device layouts and different processes to the fabrication-related tolerances. Moreover, the impact of graphene quality on the RF performance could be assessed quantitatively, providing the model with different inputs depending on the graphene quality indicators.

Author Contributions: Conceptualization, M.L.M.; methodology, M.L.M. and P.L.; software, M.L.M.; investigation, M.L.M. and P.L.; visualization, M.L.M.; writing—original draft preparation, M.L.M.; writing—review and editing, P.L. and V.T.; supervision, P.L. and V.T.; project administration, P.L.; funding acquisition, P.L. All authors have read and agreed to the published version of the manuscript.

Funding: This project has received funding from the European Union's Horizon 2020 research and innovation programme under the grant agreement GrapheneCore3 881603.

Acknowledgments: The authors acknowledge Francisco Pasadas for providing the GFET compact model used for the circuit simulations.

Conflicts of Interest: The authors declare no conflict of interest.

References

1. Passlack, M.; Zurcher, P.; Rajagopalan, K.; Droopad, R.; Abrokwah, J.; Tutt, M.; Park, Y.B.; Johnson, E.; Hartin, O.; Zlotnicka, A.; et al. High mobility III-V MOSFETs for RF and digital applications. In Proceedings of the 2007 IEEE International Electron Devices Meeting, Washington, DC, USA, 10–12 December 2007; pp. 621–624.
2. Barratt, C.A. III-V Semiconductors, a History in RF Applications. *ECS Trans.* **2009**, *19*, 79. [CrossRef]
3. Saravanan, M.; Parthasarathy, E. A review of III-V Tunnel Field Effect Transistors for future ultra low power digital/analog applications. *Microelectron. J.* **2021**, *114*, 105102. [CrossRef]
4. Ajayan, J.; Nirmal, D. A review of InP/InAlAs/InGaAs based transistors for high frequency applications. *Superlattices Microstruct.* **2015**, *86*, 1–19. [CrossRef]
5. Ferrari, A.C.; Bonaccorso, F.; Fal'ko, V.; Novoselov, K.S.; Roche, S.; Bøggild, P.; Borini, S.; Koppens, F.H.L.; Palermo, V.; Pugno, N.; et al. Science and technology roadmap for graphene, related two-dimensional crystals, and hybrid systems. *Nanoscale* **2015**, *7*, 4598–4810. [CrossRef]
6. Schwierz, F. Graphene transistors. *Nat. Nanotechnol.* **2010**, *5*, 487–496. [CrossRef]
7. Fiori, G.; Bonaccorso, F.; Iannaccone, G.; Palacios, T.; Neumaier, D.; Seabaugh, A.; Banerjee, S.K.; Colombo, L. Electronics based on two-dimensional materials. *Nat. Nanotechnol.* **2014**, *9*, 768–779. [CrossRef] [PubMed]
8. Fiori, G.; Neumaier, D.; Szafranek, B.N.; Iannaccone, G. Bilayer graphene transistors for analog electronics. *IEEE Trans. Electron Devices* **2014**, *61*, 729–733. [CrossRef]
9. Neumaier, D.; Zirath, H. High frequency graphene transistors: Can a beauty become a cash cow? *2D Mater.* **2015**, *2*, 030203. [CrossRef]

10. Lemme, M.C.; Echtermeyer, T.J.; Baus, M.; Kurz, H. A graphene field-effect device. *IEEE Electron Device Lett.* **2007**, *28*, 282–284. [CrossRef]
11. Meric, I.; Han, M.Y.; Young, A.F.; Ozyilmaz, B.; Kim, P.; Shepard, K.L. Current saturation in zero-bandgap, top-gated graphene field-effect transistors. *Nat. Nanotechnol.* **2008**, *3*, 654–659. [CrossRef]
12. Meric, I.; Dean, C.; Young, A.; Hone, J.; Kim, P.; Shepard, K.L. Graphene field-effect transistors based on boron nitride gate dielectrics. In Proceedings of the Technical Digest-International Electron Devices Meeting, IEDM, San Francisco, CA, USA, 6–8 December 2010.
13. Peng, S.; Jin, Z.; Ma, P.; Yu, G.; Shi, J.; Zhang, D.; Chen, J.; Liu, X.; Ye, T. Heavily p-type doped chemical vapor deposition graphene field-effect transistor with current saturation. *Appl. Phys. Lett.* **2013**, *103*, 223505. [CrossRef]
14. Szafranek, B.N.; Fiori, G.; Schall, D.; Neumaier, D.; Kurz, H. Current saturation and voltage gain in bilayer graphene field effect transistors. *Nano Lett.* **2012**, *12*, 1324–1328. [CrossRef]
15. Lin, Y.-M.; Jenkins, K.A.; Valdes-Garcia, A.; Small, J.P.; Farmer, D.B.; Avouris, P. Operation of graphene transistors at gigahertz frequencies. *Nano Lett.* **2008**, *9*, 422–426. [CrossRef] [PubMed]
16. Wu, Y.; Lin, Y.M.; Bol, A.A.; Jenkins, K.A.; Xia, F.; Farmer, D.B.; Zhu, Y.; Avouris, P. High-frequency, scaled graphene transistors on diamond-like carbon. *Nature* **2011**, *472*, 74–78. [CrossRef] [PubMed]
17. Meric, I.; Dean, C.R.; Han, S.J.; Wang, L.; Jenkins, K.A.; Hone, J.; Shepard, K.L. High-frequency performance of graphene field effect transistors with saturating IV-characteristics. In Proceedings of the Technical Digest-International Electron Devices Meeting, IEDM, Washington, DC, USA, 5–7 December 2011.
18. Rawat, B.; Paily, R. Analysis of graphene tunnel field-effect transistors for analog/RF applications. *IEEE Trans. Electron Devices* **2015**, *62*, 2663–2669. [CrossRef]
19. Lyu, H.; Lu, Q.; Liu, J.; Wu, X.; Zhang, J.; Li, J.; Niu, J.; Yu, Z.; Wu, H.; Qian, H. Deep-submicron graphene field-effect transistors with state-of-art f_{max}. *Sci. Rep.* **2016**, *6*, 35717. [CrossRef]
20. Bonmann, M.; Asad, M.; Yang, X.; Generalov, A.; Vorobiev, A.; Banszerus, L.; Stampfer, C.; Otto, M.; Neumaier, D.; Stake, J. Graphene field-effect transistors with high extrinsic f_T and f_{max}. *IEEE Electron Device Lett.* **2019**, *40*, 131–134. [CrossRef]
21. Vorobiev, A.; Bonmann, M.; Asad, M.; Yang, X.; Stake, J.; Banszerus, L.; Stampfer, C.; Otto, M.; Neumaier, D. Graphene field-effect transistors for millimeter wave amplifiers. In Proceedings of the 2019 44th International Conference on Infrared, Millimeter, and Terahertz Waves (IRMMW-THz), Paris, France, 1–6 September 2019. [CrossRef]
22. Liao, L.; Lin, Y.-C.; Bao, M.; Cheng, R.; Bai, J.; Liu, Y.; Qu, Y.; Wang, K.L.; Huang, Y.; Duan, X. High-speed graphene transistors with a self-aligned nanowire gate. *Nature* **2010**, *467*, 305–308. [CrossRef] [PubMed]
23. Wu, Y.; Jenkins, K.A.; Valdes-Garcia, A.; Farmer, D.B.; Zhu, Y.; Bol, A.A.; Dimitrakopoulos, C.; Zhu, W.; Xia, F.; Avouris, P.; et al. State-of-the-art graphene high-frequency electronics. *Nano Lett.* **2012**, *12*, 3062–3067. [CrossRef]
24. Guo, Z.; Dong, R.; Chakraborty, P.S.; Lourenco, N.; Palmer, J.; Hu, Y.; Ruan, M.; Hankinson, J.; Kunc, J.; Cressler, J.D.; et al. Record maximum oscillation frequency in C-face epitaxial graphene transistors. *Nano Lett.* **2013**, *13*, 942–947. [CrossRef]
25. Giubileo, F.; Di Bartolomeo, A. The role of contact resistance in graphene field-effect devices. *Prog. Surf. Sci.* **2017**, *92*, 143–175. [CrossRef]
26. Giubileo, F.; Di Bartolomeo, A.; Martucciello, N.; Romeo, F.; Iemmo, L.; Romano, P.; Passacantando, M. Contact resistance and channel conductance of graphene field-effect transistors under low-energy electron irradiation. *Nanomaterials* **2016**, *6*, 206. [CrossRef] [PubMed]
27. Farmer, D.B.; Valdes-Garcia, A.; Dimitrakopoulos, C.; Avouris, P. Impact of gate resistance in graphene radio frequency transistors. *Appl. Phys. Lett.* **2012**, *101*, 143503. [CrossRef]
28. Wu, Y.; Zou, X.; Sun, M.; Cao, Z.; Wang, X.; Huo, S.; Zhou, J.; Yang, Y.; Yu, X.; Kong, Y.; et al. 200 GHz maximum oscillation frequency in CVD graphene radio frequency transistors. *ACS Appl. Mater. Interfaces* **2016**, *8*, 25645–25649. [CrossRef]
29. Wang, H.; Hsu, A.L.; Palacios, T. Graphene electronics for RF applications. *IEEE Microw. Mag.* **2012**, *13*, 114–125. [CrossRef]
30. Zhang, C.X.; Wang, B.; Duan, G.X.; Zhang, E.X.; Fleetwood, D.M.; Alles, M.L.; Schrimpf, R.D.; Rooney, A.P.; Khestanova, E.; Auton, G.; et al. Total ionizing dose effects on hBN encapsulated graphene devices. *IEEE Trans. Nucl. Sci.* **2014**, *61*, 2868–2873. [CrossRef]
31. Paddubskaya, A.; Batrakov, K.; Khrushchinsky, A.; Kuten, S.; Plyushch, A.; Stepanov, A.; Remnev, G.; Shvetsov, V.; Baah, M.; Svirko, Y.; et al. Outstanding radiation tolerance of supported graphene: Towards 2D Sensors for the space millimeter radioastronomy. *Nanomaterials* **2021**, *11*, 170. [CrossRef]
32. Childres, I.; Jauregui, L.A.; Foxe, M.; Tian, J.; Jalilian, R.; Jovanovic, I.; Chen, Y.P. Effect of electron-beam irradiation on graphene field effect devices. *Appl. Phys. Lett.* **2010**, *97*, 173109. [CrossRef]
33. Perruisseau-Carrier, J. Graphene for antenna applications: Opportunities and challenges from microwaves to THz. In Proceedings of the 2012 Loughborough Antennas & Propagation Conference (LAPC), Loughborough, UK, 12–13 November 2012. [CrossRef]
34. Yang, X.; Vorobiev, A.; Yang, J.; Jeppson, K.; Stake, J. A Linear-Array of 300-GHz Antenna Integrated GFET Detectors on a Flexible Substrate. *IEEE Trans. Terahertz Sci. Technol.* **2020**, *10*, 554–557. [CrossRef]
35. Han, S.-J.J.; Garcia, A.V.; Oida, S.; Jenkins, K.A.; Haensch, W. Graphene radio frequency receiver integrated circuit. *Nat. Commun.* **2014**, *5*, 1–6. [CrossRef]

36. Bonmann, M.; Andersson, M.A.; Zhang, Y.; Yang, X.; Vorobiev, A.; Stake, J. An Integrated 200-GHz Graphene FET Based Receiver. In Proceedings of the International Conference on Infrared, Millimeter, and Terahertz Waves, IRMMW-THz, Nagoya, Japan, 9–14 September 2018; Volume 2018.
37. Saeed, M.; Hamed, A.; Wang, Z.; Shaygan, M.; Neumaier, D.; Negra, R. Graphene integrated circuits: New prospects towards receiver realisation. *Nanoscale* **2018**, *10*, 93–99. [CrossRef]
38. Sensale-Rodriguez, B.; Fang, T.; Yan, R.; Kelly, M.M.; Jena, D.; Liu, L.; Xing, H. Unique prospects for graphene-based terahertz modulators. *Appl. Phys. Lett.* **2011**, *99*, 113104. [CrossRef]
39. Sensale-Rodriguez, B.; Yan, R.; Kelly, M.M.; Fang, T.; Tahy, K.; Hwang, W.S.; Jena, D.; Liu, L.; Xing, H.G. Broadband graphene terahertz modulators enabled by intraband transitions. *Nat. Commun.* **2012**, *3*, 1–7. [CrossRef] [PubMed]
40. Phare, C.T.; Daniel Lee, Y.-H.; Cardenas, J.; Lipson, M. Graphene electro-optic modulator with 30 GHz bandwidth. *Nat. Photonics* **2015**, *9*, 511–514. [CrossRef]
41. Habibpour, O.; He, Z.S.; Strupinski, W.; Rorsman, N.; Ciuk, T.; Ciepielewski, P.; Zirath, H. Graphene FET gigabit ON-OFF keying demodulator at 96 GHz. *IEEE Electron Device Lett.* **2016**, *37*, 333–336. [CrossRef]
42. Dalir, H.; Xia, Y.; Wang, Y.; Zhang, X. Athermal broadband graphene optical modulator with 35 GHz Speed. *ACS Photonics* **2016**, *3*, 1564–1568. [CrossRef]
43. Ahmadivand, A.; Gerislioglu, B.; Ramezani, Z. Gated graphene island-enabled tunable charge transfer plasmon terahertz metamodulator. *Nanoscale* **2019**, *11*, 8091–8095. [CrossRef]
44. Hong, S.K.; Kim, K.Y.; Kim, T.Y.; Kim, J.H.; Park, S.W.; Kim, J.H.; Cho, B.J. Electromagnetic interference shielding effectiveness of monolayer graphene. *Nanotechnology* **2012**, *23*, 455704. [CrossRef]
45. Han, S.J.; Jenkins, K.A.; Valdes Garcia, A.; Franklin, A.D.; Bol, A.A.; Haensch, W. High-frequency graphene voltage amplifier. *Nano Lett.* **2011**, *11*, 3690–3693. [CrossRef]
46. Hanna, T.; Deltimple, N.; Khenissa, M.S.; Pallecchi, E.; Happy, H.; Frégonèse, S. 2.5 GHz integrated graphene RF power amplifier on SiC substrate. *Solid. State. Electron.* **2017**, *127*, 26–31. [CrossRef]
47. Hamed, A.; Asad, M.; Wei, M.-D.; Vorobiev, A.; Stake, J.; Negra, R. Integrated 10-GHz Graphene FET Amplifier. *IEEE J. Microw.* **2021**, *1*, 821–826. [CrossRef]
48. Yu, C.; He, Z.; Song, X.; Gao, X.; Liu, Q.; Zhang, Y.; Yu, G.; Han, T.; Liu, C.; Feng, Z.; et al. Field effect transistors and low noise amplifier MMICs of monolayer graphene. *IEEE Electron Device Lett.* **2021**, *42*, 268–271. [CrossRef]
49. Wang, H.; Hsu, A.; Wu, J.; Kong, J.; Palacios, T. Graphene-based ambipolar RF mixers. *IEEE Electron Device Lett.* **2010**, *31*, 906–908. [CrossRef]
50. Habibpour, O.; Cherednichenko, S.; Vukusic, J.; Yhland, K.; Stake, J. A subharmonic graphene FET mixer. *IEEE Electron Device Lett.* **2012**, *33*, 71–73. [CrossRef]
51. Andersson, M.A.; Zhang, Y.; Stake, J. A 185-215-GHz subharmonic resistive graphene FET integrated mixer on silicon. *IEEE Trans. Microw. Theory Tech.* **2017**, *65*, 165–172. [CrossRef]
52. Schall, D.; Otto, M.; Neumaier, D.; Kurz, H. Integrated ring oscillators based on high-performance graphene inverters. *Sci. Rep.* **2013**, *3*, 1–5. [CrossRef]
53. Guerriero, E.; Polloni, L.; Bianchi, M.; Behnam, A.; Carrion, E.; Rizzi, L.G.; Pop, E.; Sordan, R. Gigahertz integrated graphene ring oscillators. *ACS Nano* **2013**, *7*, 5588–5594. [CrossRef]
54. Safari, A.; Dousti, M. Ring oscillators based on monolayer graphene FET. *Analog Integr. Circuits Signal Process.* **2020**, *102*, 637–644. [CrossRef]
55. Coletti, C.; Romagnoli, M.; Giambra, M.A.; Mišeikis, V.; Pezzini, S.; Marconi, S.; Montanaro, A.; Fabbri, F.; Sorianello, V.; Ferrari, A.C. Wafer-scale integration of graphene-based photonic devices. *ACS Nano* **2021**, *15*, 3171–3187. [CrossRef]
56. Neumaier, D.; Pindl, S.; Lemme, M.C. Integrating graphene into semiconductor fabrication lines. *Nat. Mater.* **2019**, *18*, 525–529. [CrossRef]
57. Paul, B.C.; Fujita, S.; Okajima, M.; Lee, T.H.; Wong, H.S.P.; Nishi, Y. Impact of a process variation on nanowire and nanotube device performance. *IEEE Trans. Electron Devices* **2007**, *54*, 2369–2376. [CrossRef]
58. Taguchi, G. *System of Experimental Design: Engineering Methods to Optimize Quality and Minimize Costs*; UNIPUB/Kraus International Publications: New York, NY, USA, 1987; ISBN 978-0527916213.
59. Hinkelmann, K. *Design and Analysis of Experiments*; American Psychological Association: Washington, DC, USA, 2012; Volume 3.
60. Montgomery, D.C. *Design and Analysis of Experiments*, 9th ed.; John Wiley & Sons: Hoboken, NJ, USA, 2017; ISBN 9781119113478.
61. Pasadas, F.; Jiménez, D. Large-signal model of graphene field-effect transistors-part I: Compact modeling of GFET intrinsic capacitances. *IEEE Trans. Electron Devices* **2016**, *63*, 2936–2941. [CrossRef]
62. Lamberti, P.; La Mura, M.; Pasadas, F.; Jiménez, D.; Tucci, V. Tolerance analysis of a GFET transistor for aerospace and aeronautical application. In Proceedings of the IOP Conference Series: Materials Science and Engineering, Salerno, Italy, 2–4 September 2020; Volume 1024.
63. Spinelli, G.; Lamberti, P.; Tucci, V.; Pasadas, F.; Jiménez, D. Sensitivity analysis of a graphene field-effect transistors by means of design of experiments. *Math. Comput. Simul.* **2020**, *183*, 187–197. [CrossRef]
64. Jmai, B.; Silva, V.; Mendes, P.M. 2D electronics based on graphene field effect transistors: Tutorial for modelling and simulation. *Micromachines* **2021**, *12*, 979. [CrossRef] [PubMed]

65. Cabral, P.D.; Domingues, T.; Machado, G.; Chicharo, A.; Cerqueira, F.; Fernandes, E.; Athayde, E.; Alpuim, P.; Borme, J. Clean-room lithographical processes for the fabrication of graphene biosensors. *Materials* **2020**, *13*, 5728. [CrossRef]
66. Gupta, A.; Fang, P.; Song, M.; Lin, M.R.; Wollesen, D.; Chen, K.; Hu, C. Accurate determination of ultrathin gate oxide thickness and effective polysilicon doping of CMOS devices. *IEEE Electron Device Lett.* **1997**, *18*, 580–582. [CrossRef]
67. La Mura, M.; Bagolini, A.; Lamberti, P.; Savoia, A.S. Impact of the variability of microfabrication process parameters on CMUTs performance. In Proceedings of the IEEE International Ultrasonics Symposium, IUS, Las Vegas, NV, USA, 7–11 September 2020.
68. Lamberti, P.; Sarto, M.S.; Tucci, V.; Tamburrano, A. Robust design of high-speed interconnects based on an MWCNT. *IEEE Trans. Nanotechnol.* **2012**, *11*, 799–807. [CrossRef]
69. Lamberti, P.; Tucci, V. Impact of the variability of the process parameters on CNT-based nanointerconnects performances: A comparison between SWCNTs bundles and MWCNT. *IEEE Trans. Nanotechnol.* **2012**, *11*, 924–933. [CrossRef]
70. Pasadas, F.; Jiménez, D. Large-signal model of graphene field-effect transistors-part II: Circuit performance benchmarking. *IEEE Trans. Electron Devices* **2016**, *63*, 2942–2947. [CrossRef]
71. Pozar, D.M. *Microwave Engineering*, 4th ed.; John Wiley & Sons Inc.: Hoboken, NJ, USA, 2012; pp. 1–756.
72. Fiori, G.; Iannaccone, G. Multiscale modeling for graphene-based nanoscale transistors. *Proc. IEEE* **2013**, *101*, 1653–1669. [CrossRef]
73. Thiele, S.A.; Schaefer, J.A.; Schwierz, F. Modeling of graphene metal-oxide-semiconductor field-effect transistors with gapless large-area graphene channels. *J. Appl. Phys.* **2010**, *107*. [CrossRef]
74. Rodriguez, S.; Vaziri, S.; Smith, A.; Fregonese, S.; Ostling, M.; Lemme, M.C.; Rusu, A. A comprehensive graphene FET model for circuit design. *IEEE Trans. Electron Devices* **2014**, *61*, 1199–1206. [CrossRef]
75. Asad, M.; Bonmann, M.; Yang, X.; Vorobiev, A.; Jeppson, K.; Banszerus, L.; Otto, M.; Stampfer, C.; Neumaier, D.; Stake, J. The dependence of the high-frequency performance of graphene field-effect transistors on channel transport properties. *IEEE J. Electron Devices Soc.* **2020**, *8*, 457–464. [CrossRef]
76. Fregonese, S.; Magallo, M.; Maneux, C.; Happy, H.; Zimmer, T. Scalable electrical compact modeling for graphene FET transistors. *IEEE Trans. Nanotechnol.* **2013**, *12*, 539–546. [CrossRef]
77. Landauer, G.M.; Jimenez, D.; Gonzalez, J.L. An accurate and verilog-a compatible compact model for graphene field-effect transistors. *IEEE Trans. Nanotechnol.* **2014**, *13*, 895–904. [CrossRef]
78. Aguirre-Morales, J.D.; Fregonese, S.; Mukherjee, C.; Wei, W.; Happy, H.; Maneux, C.; Zimmer, T. A Large-signal monolayer graphene field-effect transistor compact model for RF-circuit applications. *IEEE Trans. Electron Devices* **2017**, *64*, 4302–4309. [CrossRef]
79. Han, S.J.; Reddy, D.; Carpenter, G.D.; Franklin, A.D.; Jenkins, K.A. Current saturation in submicrometer graphene transistors with thin gate dielectric: Experiment, simulation, and theory. *ACS Nano* **2012**, *6*, 5220–5226. [CrossRef]
80. Parrish, K.N.; Akinwande, D. Impact of contact resistance on the transconductance and linearity of graphene transistors. *Appl. Phys. Lett.* **2011**, *98*, 183505. [CrossRef]
81. Chauhan, J.; Liu, L.; Lu, Y.; Guo, J. A computational study of high-frequency behavior of graphene field-effect transistors. *J. Appl. Phys.* **2012**, *111*. [CrossRef]

Article

Lower Limits of Contact Resistance in Phosphorene Nanodevices with Edge Contacts

Mirko Poljak *, Mislav Matić, Tin Župančić and Ante Zeljko

Computational Nanoelectronics Group, Faculty of Electrical Engineering and Computing, University of Zagreb, HR 10000 Zagreb, Croatia; mislav.matic@fer.hr (M.M.); tin.zupancic@fer.hr (T.Ž.); ante.zeljko@fer.hr (A.Z.)
* Correspondence: mirko.poljak@fer.hr

Abstract: Edge contacts are promising for improving carrier injection and contact resistance in devices based on two-dimensional (2D) materials, among which monolayer black phosphorus (BP), or phosphorene, is especially attractive for device applications. Cutting BP into phosphorene nanoribbons (PNRs) widens the design space for BP devices and enables high-density device integration. However, little is known about contact resistance (R_C) in PNRs with edge contacts, although R_C is the main performance limiter for 2D material devices. Atomistic quantum transport simulations are employed to explore the impact of attaching metal edge contacts (MECs) on the electronic and transport properties and contact resistance of PNRs. We demonstrate that PNR length downscaling increases R_C to 192 Ω μm in 5.2 nm-long PNRs due to strong metallization effects, while width downscaling decreases the R_C to 19 Ω μm in 0.5 nm-wide PNRs. These findings illustrate the limitations on PNR downscaling and reveal opportunities in the minimization of R_C by device sizing. Moreover, we prove the existence of optimum metals for edge contacts in terms of minimum metallization effects that further decrease R_C by ~30%, resulting in lower intrinsic quantum limits to R_C of ~90 Ω μm in phosphorene and ~14 Ω μm in ultra-narrow PNRs.

Keywords: phosphorene; black phosphorus; nanoribbon; edge contact; contact resistance; quantum transport; NEGF; metallization; broadening

1. Introduction

Two-dimensional (2D) materials are considered to be feasible candidates for future post-silicon electron devices due to their atomic thickness and exceptional mechanical, electronic, and carrier transport properties [1–5]. Among monoelemental 2D materials, monolayer black phosphorus (BP) or phosphorene is frequently identified as promising for future nanoscale field-effect transistors (FETs) due to its acceptable bandgap and carrier mobility that should enable appropriate switching and current-driving performance of phosphorene-based electron devices [6,7]. Recently, experimental demonstration and characterization results have been reported for micro-scale BP FETs [7–9], while theoretical and numerical simulation reports have been published for short-channel and wide-gate phosphorene FETs [4,10,11]. However, phosphorene nanoribbons (PNRs) that are quasi-one-dimensional phosphorene nanostructures are less explored, despite the opportunity provided by quantum confinement to adjust the material and device properties [12–16]. An additional motivation for further research on PNRs is provided by recent reports on fabricated and characterized ultra-narrow PNRs with the widths down to ~0.5 nm [17,18].

While 2D materials and their nanostructures seem promising for nanodevices, they suffer from high contact resistance (R_C), which limits their performance and conceals their exceptional transport properties. For micro-scale BP FETs, R_C was measured in the range from ≈1750 Ω μm [19] and ≈1100 Ω μm [9], over ≈700 Ω μm [20], down to ≈400 Ω μm [21] and 310 Ω μm [22]. Even the best reported R_C values are unacceptably high for transistors in future high-density integrated circuits and, additionally, very little is known about R_C levels and its behavior in PNR-based devices [23]. The most promising avenue toward low R_C in 2D material-based devices seems to be the concept of edge contacts, i.e., one-dimensional contacts connected only at the edges of the nanostructure. Edge contacts are scalable, not limited by current transfer length as top contacts, and they allow the encapsulation of the 2D material that preserves its exceptional properties and enables long-term stability [24,25]. Almost all theoretical research on 2D material or nanoribbon-based FETs assumes ideal contacts, which only provides upper limits to device performance since the parasitic contact resistance is completely ignored [4,10,11].

In this work, we explore the contact resistance in PNRs with edge contacts using atomistic quantum transport simulations. We describe the metal electrodes by the wide-band limit model that is capable of reproducing metal-induced broadening and metallization effects. The impact of PNR size downscaling on R_C is analyzed for technologically relevant PNR widths (<5.5 nm) and lengths (<16 nm). We reveal significant metallization effects visible in the deterioration of electronic and transport properties of PNRs, which are especially detrimental for nanoribbon lengths under ~8 nm. Contact resistance decreases with the width downscaling but increases considerably when the length decreases. Surprisingly, we show that even in the two-probe simulation setup there exists the optimum metal-nanoribbon interaction parameter that results in the minimum R_C for a given PNR size. With metal edge contacts, optimum electrode material for PNRs is a more strongly-interacting metal in the case of longer devices, whereas ultra-short nanoribbons with lengths under ~6 nm demand contacts with a weaker interaction strength. Our results indicate that the quantum intrinsic limits of R_C, i.e., minimum achievable R_C, in large-area phosphorene devices could be as low as ~90 Ω μm. Moreover, an even lower R_C of ~14 Ω μm can be obtained in 0.5 nm-wide PNRs with a careful choice of the electrode material. Our results give an encouraging perspective on the suitability of phosphorene and PNR FETs for future nanoscale electron devices and contribute towards theoretical understanding and practical minimization of contact resistance in nanodevices with edge contacts.

2. Methods

A multi-band tight-binding (TB) model from [26] is used for the construction of armchair PNR Hamiltonians that enter the retarded Green's function within the non-equilibrium Green's function (NEGF) formalism for quantum transport. This TB model agrees well with more advanced GW simulations for electron energies up to ~2 eV away from the Fermi level. While a more advanced Hamiltonian, e.g., one resulting from *ab initio* simulations, would improve the bandstructure accuracy in ultra-narrow PNRs [16], we choose a simpler model to reduce the computational burden since we investigate numerous devices of different sizes and contact-device interaction strengths. Regarding device size, we focus on technologically relevant extremely-scaled PNRs with the widths (W) under ~5.5 nm and lengths (L) below ~16 nm. The largest PNR under study consists of 2312 phosphorus atoms, and as many orbitals in the Hamiltonian matrix.

Atomistic NEGF calculations are employed to investigate the electronic and transport properties of ultra-scaled PNRs, and to calculate contact resistance that emerges in PNRs after attaching metal edge contacts (MECs). Ballistic transport simulations are carried out by assuming a two-probe configuration, i.e., two MECs attached on the left and right edge of the nanoribbon, as illustrated in Figure 1. The NEGF formalism solves the Schrödinger's equation for a given system with open boundary conditions (OBCs) [27,28]. The retarded Green's function of the device is given by:

$$G^R(E) = \left[(E + i0^+)I - H - \Sigma_1^R(E) - \Sigma_2^R(E)\right]^{-1} \quad (1)$$

where E is the energy, I is the identity matrix, H is the device Hamiltonian, and Σ matrices are the retarded contact self-energies that account for OBCs in the nanoribbon imposed by the two attached MECs (left contact or contact 1, and right contact or contact 2). Our existing NEGF code, written in C/C++ and Compute Unified Device Architecture (CUDA) for heterogenous CPU-GPU execution, and previously demonstrated on graphene, silicene, germanene and phosphorene nanostructures [29,30], is used for calculations in this work.

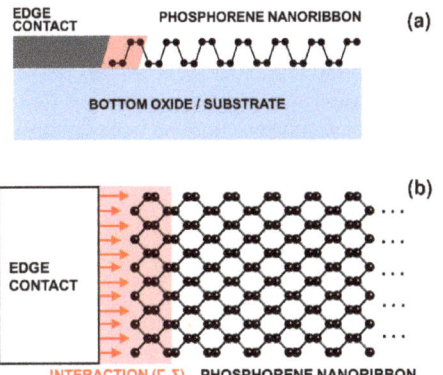

Figure 1. (**a**) Side-view and (**b**) top-view of the left metal edge contact attached to the PNR. Light red shaded area indicates the extent of metal-nanoribbon interaction across the closest super-cell, described by the broadening parameter (Γ) or contact-self energy (Σ).

Regarding the OBCs, we study the impact of attaching ideal and metal edge contacts on the electronic and transport properties of PNRs. The ideal edge contacts (IECs) are semi-infinite regions with the same geometry and bandstructure as the central region. Setting IECs in NEGF simulations is common throughout the literature, and this approach eliminates destructive interference at contact-device interfaces and results in perfect step-like transmission functions. In this work, MECs are treated with the wide-band limit (WBL) model in which only the constant imaginary part of contact self-energy matrices is retained [28]. As shown previously in the case of GNRs [31], we set the initial value of the nanoribbon-MEC interaction strength to $-\mathrm{Im}\Sigma^R = 0.9$ eV, in accordance with the average hopping parameter in the TB model for phosphorene, and with the expected density of states (DOS) in the model metal near the Fermi level [28,31]. We analyze the effects of changing $-\mathrm{Im}\Sigma^R$ from the initial to lower and higher values, thus exploring the consequences of attaching weakly and strongly-interacting metals to the PNR, respectively. The MECs are assumed to be Ohmic so tunnel or Schottky barriers are disregarded to solely study the impact of metal-induced broadening or metallization effects. We note that our approach could be applied to large top contacts as well, but contact and device sizes are limited by the available computational facilities since atomistic NEGF simulations are very computationally intensive.

After transmission is calculated from the retarded Green's function [32], we find the PNR conductance at 300 K from the expression:

$$G = \frac{2e^2}{h}\int_0^\infty T(E)(-\partial f(E-E_F)/\partial E)dE, \tag{2}$$

where $T(E)$ is the transmission function, $f(E-E_F)$ is the Fermi–Dirac distribution function, E_F is the Fermi level set to 50 meV away from the conduction band minimum, e is the electronic charge, and h is the Planck's constant. Attaching WBL contacts induces broadening and decreases the transmission and conductance in the conduction and valence bands [31,33]. Therefore, by comparing the conductance values between the IEC and MEC cases, we can calculate the added contact resistance introduced by edge metal contacts using

$$R_C = \frac{1}{G_{MEC}} - \frac{1}{G_{IEC}}, \tag{3}$$

where G_{MEC} and G_{IEC} are PNR conductances with either metal or ideal edge contacts, respectively.

3. Results and Discussion

First, we focus on investigating the impact of PNR width downscaling from 5.4 nm to 0.5 nm on the electronic and transport properties of PNRs with IECs and MECs. Figure 2a shows the DOS in 2.5 nm-wide PNRs and we observe oscillations in DOS in the case of MECs, in contrast to van Hove singularities obtained for ideal contacts. These oscillations are known to occur in graphene and other nanodevices with metallic contacts [34], and can be easily understood from an analytical solution for a one-dimensional atomic chain. For the atomic chain, electron dispersion can be found to be $E(k) = E_0 + 2t\cos(ka)$, where k is the wave-vector or crystal momentum, E_0 is the local orbital energy, t is the hopping parameter, and a is the distance between atoms in the chain. Setting $\Sigma_1 = \Sigma_2 = -i\Gamma/2$ for the MEC case, where Γ is the broadening parameter, and using Equation (1) for the Green's function, we analytically obtain the following spectral function:

$$A(E) = G^R(\Gamma_1 + \Gamma_2)G^A = \frac{2\Gamma}{(E - E_0)^2 + \Gamma^2} \quad (4)$$

where G^A is the advanced Green's function. Therefore, $A(E)$ and density of states defined as $DOS(E) = A(E)/\pi$ are clearly Lorentzian curves centered at E_0, i.e., at band center, that decrease towards ban edges. This characteristic is in stark contrast to the case of ideal contacts that exhibits singularities at band edges and minimum DOS at the band center in 1D structures [27].

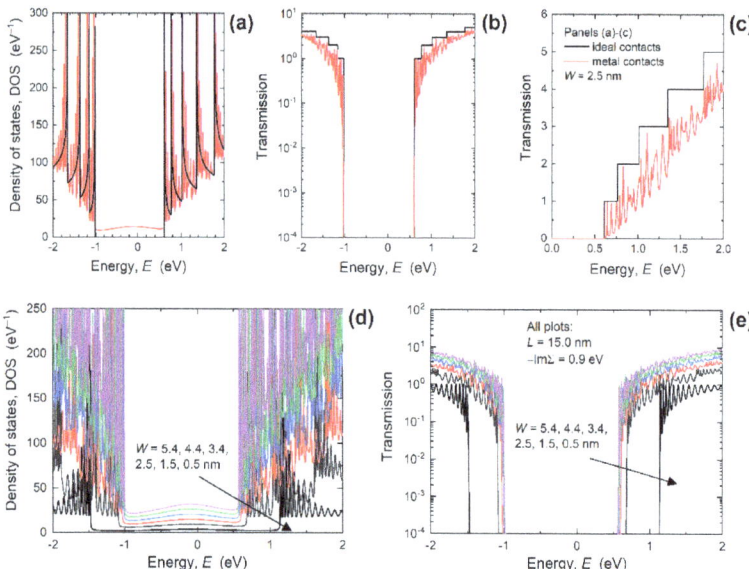

Figure 2. (a) DOS in linear, and transmission in (b) logarithmic and (c) linear scale for 15 nm-long and 2.5 nm-wide PNRs with ideal and metal edge contacts. Impact of width scaling on (d) DOS and (e) transmission in 15 nm-long PNRs with MECs. For all MEC-PNRs, $-Im\Sigma^R = 0.9$ eV.

The impact of attaching MECs is also visible in the appearance of metal-induced gap states (MIGS) between the valence band maximum (VBM) and conduction band minimum (CBM). However, these states are clearly strongly localized as can be seen in Figure 2b that reports the transmission through the 2.5 nm-wide PNR with IECs and MECs.

The transmission is extremely low inside the bandgap so the transport gap (E_{TG}) exists. Therefore, MIGS do not contribute to transport, which is beneficial for FETs that need a transport gap to achieve efficient switching between the ON and OFF states. These findings demonstrate that PNRs are a more plausible solution of ultra-scaled FETs than GNRs given the considerable metallization-induced E_{TG} decrease reported for GNRs with MECs [31]. While the energy gap of PNRs is immune to MEC-induced metallization effects, the characteristic shown in linear scale in Figure 2c demonstrates a significant transmission suppression by MECs. Lorentzian oscillations are also reported in the transmission as in the DOS curves, and the reasons are given in the Supplementary Materials—Supplementary Note S1. In contrast to ideal contacts that result in unitary transmission probability for each conducting mode and a step-like transmission function, attaching MECs described within the WBL model allows destructive interference for electron waves injected from the contact into the nanoribbon [31,33,34].

Figure 2d,e plots the DOS and transmission, respectively, for MEC PNRs with L = 15 nm and for various widths. When W decreases from 5.4 nm to 0.5 nm, the MIGS decrease in intensity due to shorter edge contacts in narrower nanoribbons. At the same time, reducing W increases the transport gap of PNRs, with Lorentzian oscillations existing in the transmission functions for all PNRs irrespective of the width. Therefore, in PNR nanodevices with MECs we expect a considerable deterioration of the current driving capabilities, even in the ballistic transport case that presents an upper intrinsic limit to device performance. Assessing device performance is beyond the scope of this work, but the presented data allows the calculation of relevant conductance values and enables the extraction of R_C introduced by MECs, as described in Section 2.

The influence of decreasing nanoribbon width on the conductance calculated for E_F = CBM + 50 meV at 300 K is reported in Figure 3a for 15 nm-long PNRs. The conductance deteriorates in narrower devices due to lower transmission (see Figure 2e), which itself is a consequence of a lower number of modes or bands in narrower PNRs. In the case of IECs, the conductance decreases from 1.64 (constant $2e^2/h$ is omitted for clarity) to 0.87 in the examined W range, whereas the conductance drops from 0.43 to 0.24 when MECs are connected to the PNRs. Comparing the two edge contact cases, we find that the conductance deterioration with MECs equals 74% for W = 5.4 nm and 72% in 0.5 nm-wide PNRs. Using Equation (3), we extract the contact resistance introduced by MECs and plot R_C versus PNR width in Figure 3b. As the width decreases, R_C increases from 22 kΩ (W = 5.4 nm) to 38.3 kΩ (W = 0.5 nm), which demonstrates that the narrower PNRs are more susceptible to MEC-induced metallization effects through the transmission deterioration. Figure 3c depicts the width-dependence of the width-normalized R_C, i.e., $R_C W$, which is a common contact resistance figure of merit for electron devices. In contrast to R_C behavior in Figure 3b, $R_C W$ monotonically decreases with the downscaling of nanoribbon width, from 119 Ω μm for W = 5.4 nm down to 19 Ω μm for W = 0.5 nm.

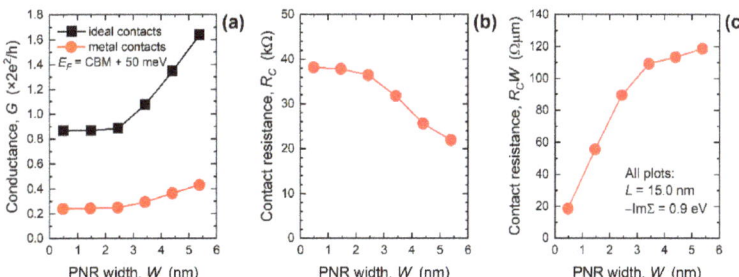

Figure 3. Width-dependence of (**a**) conductance, (**b**) contact resistance, and (**c**) width-normalized contact resistance in 15 nm-long PNRs. For all MEC-PNRs, $-\text{Im}\Sigma^R$ = 0.9 eV.

In comparison to GNRs [31], phosphorene nanodevices exhibit a 62% higher R_C for the widest nanoribbons, whereas the narrowest PNRs offer a 10% lower R_C (at $W \sim 0.5$ nm). By extrapolating the results for wide nanoribbons to large-area 2D material devices, our results indicate that micro-scale phosphorene devices should have a significantly higher R_C than graphene devices. This finding agrees with the literature that reports the best R_C of 400 Ω μm [21] to 310 Ω μm [22] for phosphorene FETs, whereas the best reported R_C for graphene FETs is ~80 Ω μm [35]. On the other hand, R_C is very low in narrowest PNRs which means that patterning phosphorene into nanoribbons offers a promising avenue for R_C minimization in ultra-scaled devices that enable high-density integration. The best reported experimental R_C for phosphorene devices is ~300 Ω μm, so the space for improvement of the contact resistance exists and is quite extensive since the quantum limit of $R_C W$ reported above (~20 Ω μm) is more than 15× lower than the best-reported measured $R_C W$ value.

Width scaling provides an opportunity to expand the design space through confinement effects, however, length scaling is also important because in modern CMOS industry the channel length decrease is the main driving force behind FET performance improvement. Hence, in the following paragraphs we set a common $W = 3.4$ nm and analyze the electronic and transport properties, and R_C for PNRs with the lengths from ~16 nm down to ~5 nm. Figure 4a shows the DOS of MEC-PNRs for various lengths with a zoomed-in energy range around the CBM reported in Figure 4b. The DOS again exhibits Lorentzians instead of van Hove singularities due to metallization effects. In the case of L scaling, MIGS are present but the magnitude of localized states inside the bandgap does not change with PNR length. In contrast, Figure 4b shows that DOS inside the conduction band changes considerably when L decreases, with the first DOS peak closest to CBM being shifted away from the CBM when the PNR length is scaled down. The CBM is positioned at $E = 583$ meV in the case of IECs, whereas the closest Lorentzian peak is situated at $E = 595$ meV for $L = 15.9$ nm in PNRs with MECs. Decreasing the length to 7.9 nm moves the first peak to $E = 623$ meV, while for $L = 5.2$ nm the first peak is positioned at $E = 677$ meV, i.e., shifted by 94 meV from the CBM. In addition to significant qualitative changes, we observe that DOS values decrease when L is scaled down, which is expected to decrease the ability of ultra-short PNRs to generate enough charge carriers for acceptable performance of PNR-based FETs.

As reported in Figure 4c, the transmission curves exhibit variations similar to those seen in the DOS. Decreasing L reduces the number of Lorentzians and shifts the first peak away from the CBM. The transmission is greatly reduced in PNRs with MECs, which is especially evident for $L = 5.2$ nm for which the transmission is almost completely suppressed in the entire energy range corresponding to the first transmission step of the PNR with IECs. Results presented in Figure 4c seem to indicate that the downscaling of the length of PNRs with MECs leads to the increase of the transmission gap, but Figure 4d that reports the transmission in logarithmic scale reveals a more complicated picture. Namely, while the transmission decreases with L downscaling in the energy range above the CBM, the opposite is true inside the bandgap. As the PNR length decreases, transmission probability below the CBM increases considerably, which leads to the contraction of the transport gap. If we define the transport gap as the energy range where the transmission is lower than 0.001, we find that E_{TG} decreases by 56 meV when $L = 7.9$ nm and by 252 meV in the 5.2 nm-long PNR. Since the existence and value of E_{TG} is very important for the practical realization of FETs, this finding clearly shows that broadening or metallization effects must be included into the physical framework used for the simulation of nanoscale electron devices. We have previously reported that in ultra-short GNRs the transport gap closes completely due to these metallization effects [31], but PNRs are evidently more resilient to the influence of metal edge contacts than GNRs since E_{TG} still exists, albeit being somewhat smaller.

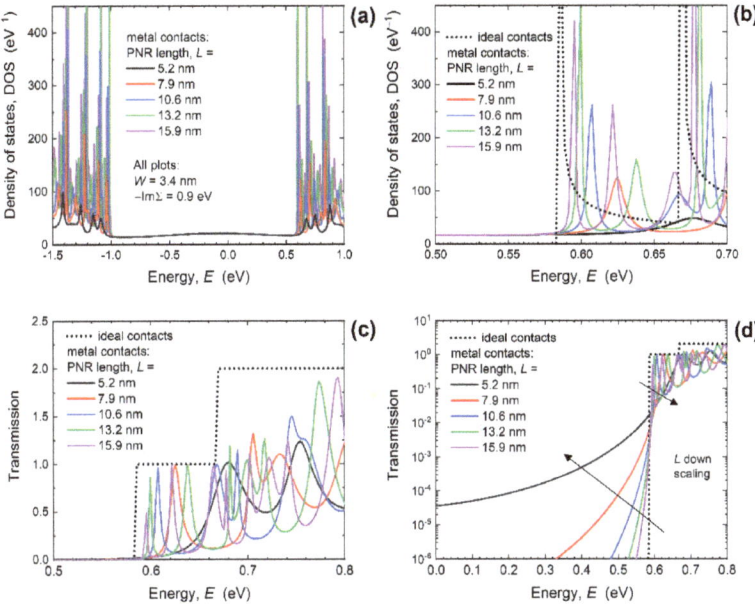

Figure 4. DOS in (**a**) entire energy range, and (**b**) in the conduction band for 3.4 nm-wide PNRs of various lengths with ideal and metal edge contacts. Influence of length downscaling on transmission in the (**c**) linear and (**d**) logarithmic scale. For all MEC-PNRs, $-\mathrm{Im}\Sigma^R = 0.9$ eV.

The observed strong suppression of transmission near the CBM consequently decreases the conductance and induces contact resistance at the two MEC-nanoribbon interfaces. Figure 5a reports the conductance calculated for E_F = CBM + 50 meV and 300 K versus PNR length for 3.4 nm-wide PNRs with IECs and MECs. While the conductance is length-independent in the case of ideal contacts, it noticeably decreases for $L < 8$ nm when MECs are attached to PNRs. Hence, conductance difference between the two contact configurations is largest in the shortest devices, which is also seen in the extracted R_C shown in Figure 5b. As the length is downscaled, R_C increases from 31.9 kΩ (L = 15.9 nm) to 56.6 kΩ (L = 5.2 nm), which is a consequence of the greatly decreased transmission near the CBM in 5.2 nm-long PNRs (see Figure 4c). After width-normalization the contact resistance curve in Figure 5c stays qualitatively the same as in Figure 5b. The R_CW equals 109 Ω μm for L = 15.9 nm, stays almost constant down to L = 7.9 nm, and then increases to 192 Ω μm in MEC-PNRs that are only 5.2 nm long. In addition to transport gap decrease, the observed boost of R_CW is yet another negative consequence of attaching metal contacts if we consider ultra-scaled PNRs as channel material for future FETs.

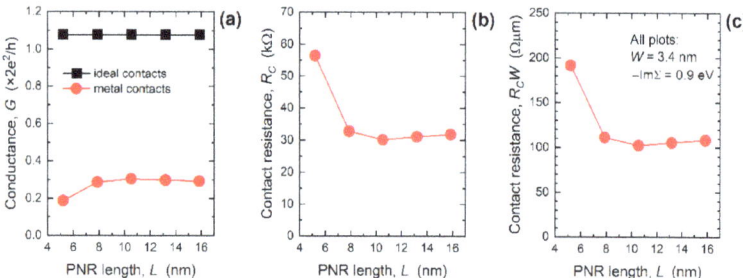

Figure 5. Length-dependence of (**a**) conductance, (**b**) contact resistance, and (**c**) width-normalized contact resistance in 3.4 nm-wide PNRs. For all MEC-PNRs, $-\text{Im}\Sigma^R = 0.9$ eV.

All the results considered so far are based on using $-\text{Im}\Sigma^R = 0.9$ eV in MEC self-energy matrices, which presents a model metal material with moderately-strong interactions with the nanoribbon. However, we have recently shown for FETs based on various monoelemental 2D materials that there exists the optimum interaction parameter value leading to the lowest transmission decrease, which enables the minimization of R_C in such nanodevices [23]. An example concerning optimum $-\text{Im}\Sigma^R$ for transmission is given for a 2.45 nm-wide and 15 nm-long PNR in the Supplementary Materials—Supplementary Note S2, Figure S1. This finding is in accordance with the study dealing with reflections and transmissions in atomic chains and carbon nanotubes connected to wide-band leads reported in [36]. An illustrative example based on 1D atomic chains about the evolution of eigenstates and transmission functions, and the existence of the optimum interaction parameter is provided in Supplementary Materials—Supplementary Note S3, Figures S2–S4. For phosphorene FETs with 15 nm-long channels, the optimum $-\text{Im}\Sigma^R$ of ~2 eV was reported in [23]. Therefore, it seems reasonable to assume that such optimum interaction parameters will exist also in the case of a two-probe setup assessed in this work with the aim of finding quantum limits of R_C in PNRs with metal edge contacts. In the following discussions, we calculate R_CW for MEC-PNRs of various dimensions, and for $-\text{Im}\Sigma^R$ that ranges from 0.01 eV to 20 eV. The $-\text{Im}\Sigma^R$ value range is chosen according to studies on graphene-metal and carbon nanotube-metal contacts in [37,38]. While we do not perform *ab initio* interface studies for phosphorene-metal systems as in [39–41] due to heavy computational burden of doing so for a large variety of nanoribbon sizes and metal choice, the WBL approach allows us to explore the impact of weakly, moderately and strongly-interacting metal electrodes on the contact resistance in PNR nanodevices. Generally, the low $-\text{Im}\Sigma^R$ values in our approach correspond to weakly interacting metals such as Al, Ag, Au, Cu, and higher $-\text{Im}\Sigma^R$ values describe strongly interacting metals such as Cr, Ni, Pd, Ti, where the interaction strength is assessed in detail by *ab initio* calculations in [39].

Figure 6a reports the dependence of R_CW on the interaction strength in 2.45 nm-wide and 15 nm-long phosphorene nanoribbons. Starting from very weakly interacting metals ($-\text{Im}\Sigma^R = 0.01$ eV) where $R_CW = 11.2$ kΩ μm, the resistance first decreases and reaches a minimum of 61 Ω μm for the optimum $-\text{Im}\Sigma^R$ of 2 eV, and then increases to 247 Ω μm when strongly-interacting ($-\text{Im}\Sigma^R = 20$ eV) MECs are attached to the PNR. In comparison to the initial resistance value of 90 Ω μm for $W = 2.45$ nm in Figure 3c, a careful choice of contact material can reduce R_CW by 32%. Assuming the optimum interaction parameter of 2 eV for all 15 nm-long devices, in Figure 6b, we report R_CW values for the entire examined PNR width range. In this case the resistance decreases from 84 Ω μm for $W = 5.4$ nm down to 14 Ω μm in the 0.5 nm-wide MEC-PNR. The improvement is almost constant and equals ~30% for nanoribbon widths down to ~1.5 nm, whereas R_CW drops by 23% for 0.5 nm-wide PNRs with MECs and $-\text{Im}\Sigma^R = 2$ eV. The characteristics reported in Figure 6b indicate that a minimum R_CW of ~90 Ω μm is achievable in large-area phosphorene devices with edge contacts, which puts these lower quantum limits of R_C in phosphorene close to the best reported contact resistance in graphene devices [24,35]. In addition, our results show that the contact resistance can be further minimized to ~14 Ω·µm by using ultra-narrow PNRs as channel material in ultra-scaled FETs.

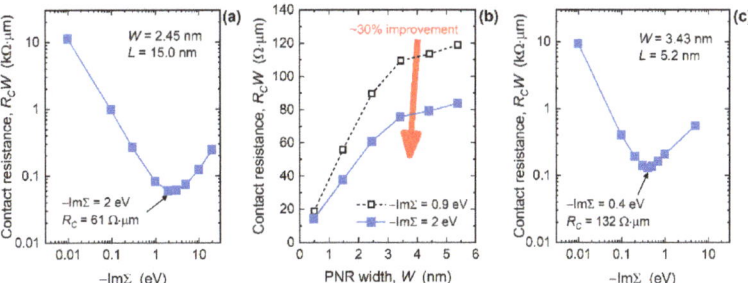

Figure 6. (**a**) Dependence of width-normalized contact resistance on interaction strength in 2.45 nm-wide and 15 nm-long PNRs with MECs. (**b**) Impact of PNR width downscaling on R_CW for the two $-\text{Im}\Sigma^R$ values, initial and the optimum one. (**c**) R_CW versus interaction strength in 3.43 nm-wide and 5.2 nm-long PNRs with MECs.

Concerning the PNR length scaling, optimum $-\text{Im}\Sigma^R$ stays the same down to about $L = 10$ nm (not shown), and then decreases. Figure 6c plots R_CW versus the interaction parameter $-\text{Im}\Sigma^R$ for 3.4 nm-wide PNRs with a length of 5.2 nm. For this device, R_CW starts at 5.5 kΩ·µm in the case of weakly-interacting WBL edge contacts, then decreases and reaches the optimum value of 132 Ω·µm for $-\text{Im}\Sigma^R = 0.4$ eV, after which R_CW increases to 559 Ω·µm for the strongest-interacting MECs considered. The improvement of R_CW in 5.2 nm-long PNRs with $-\text{Im}\Sigma^R = 0.4$ eV, over the initial case where $-\text{Im}\Sigma^R$ was 0.9 eV, amounts to 31%. Hence, even in the shortest devices, the contact resistance can be significantly reduced despite the very strong metallization-induced effects. Nevertheless, the choice of optimum electrode material changes in shorter devices that clearly benefit from less-interacting MECs (optimum $-\text{Im}\Sigma^R = 0.4$ eV) than longer PNRs (optimum $-\text{Im}\Sigma^R = 2$ eV) and, by extrapolation, large-area phosphorene devices with edge contacts.

4. Conclusions

Using atomistic quantum transport simulations, we studied the consequences of attaching metal electrodes in the edge-contact configuration on the electronic and transport properties of ultra-scaled PNRs. Since we ignore tunnel and Schottky barriers, our approach allows us to explore upper performance limits and lower limits on contact resistance in these devices. Attaching MECs leads to Lorentzian peaks in the DOS and transmission characteristics, appearance of localized MIGS inside the bandgap, noticeable narrowing of the transport gap, and overall suppression of the transmission in the conduction and valence bands. This suppression decreases the device conductance and introduces additional contact resistance at electrode-nanoribbon interfaces. We have shown that PNR width downscaling in the 5.4–0.5 nm range decreases R_CW from 119 Ω·µm down to 19 Ω·µm. Therefore, patterning phosphorene into PNRs provides a compelling way to minimize contact resistance to levels acceptable to the CMOS industry for nanoscale FETs. In contrast to width scaling, R_CW increases with decreasing PNR length from 109 Ω·µm when $L = 15.9$ nm to 192 Ω·µm in 5.2 nm-long PNRs with MECs. In addition to E_{TG} decrease, the boosted R_CW in ultra-short PNRs also limits their feasibility as channel material in ultra-scaled FETs, and emphasizes the importance of including metallization effects in device simulation at this scale. Finally, we have demonstrated the existence of optimum interaction parameters or optimum electrode materials that can significantly improve R_CW (30% in comparison to the initial case of $-\text{Im}\Sigma^R = 0.9$ eV). Surprisingly, shorter PNRs favor less-interacting metals (optimum $-\text{Im}\Sigma^R = 0.4$ eV), whereas longer PNRs profit from more strongly interacting electrodes (optimum $-\text{Im}\Sigma^R = 2$ eV) that reduce R_CW to very low levels, i.e., ~14 Ω·µm in the narrowest PNRs. Our work proves that there is enough room for $R_C W$ improvement in BP and PNR devices since quantum limits of $R_C W$ reported in this work are an order of magnitude lower than the best reported measured contact resistance. Regarding large-area phosphorene devices with edge contacts, we show that $R_C W$ of ~90 Ω μm is achievable, which is close to the best reported contact resistance in graphene devices.

Supplementary Materials: The following supporting information can be downloaded at: https://www.mdpi.com/article/10.3390/nano12040656/s1, pdf document containing additional simulation results, mainly on 1D atomic chains to illustrate the emergence of contact resistance and existence of optimum electrode material in nanodevices with edge contacts: Figure S1: Transmission of 15 nm-long and 2.45 nm-wide PNRs with MECs for various contact self-energy or interaction parameter values ranging from 0.09 eV to 20 eV, Figure S2: Transmission function of a 5-atom chain with ideal and metal contacts for different ratios of the contact self-energy and inter-atomic hopping parameter $-\text{Im}\{\Sigma\}/t$ that ranges from 0.1 to 10, Figure S3: The same as in Figure S2 but for $-\text{Im}\{\Sigma\}/t$ values that range from 0.9 to 1.5, Figure S4: Transmission in a 5-atom chain for weakly and very strongly interacting MECs, and dependence of eigenvalues on the interaction strength.

Author Contributions: Conceptualization, M.P.; methodology, M.P., M.M. and T.Ž.; data curation, M.M., A.Z., T.Ž. and M.P.; writing—original draft preparation, M.P., M.M. and A.Z.; writing—review and editing, M.P.; project administration, M.P.; funding acquisition, M.P. All authors have read and agreed to the published version of the manuscript.

Funding: This work was supported by the Croatian Science Foundation (CSF) under the project CONAN2D (Grant No. UIP-2019-04-3493). The work of doctoral student A. Zeljko was also supported by CSF through the Program "Young researchers' career development project—training of doctoral students" (Grant No. DOK-2020-01-7349).

Institutional Review Board Statement: Not applicable.

Informed Consent Statement: Not applicable.

Data Availability Statement: The data presented in this study are contained within the article and are available on request from the corresponding author.

Conflicts of Interest: The authors declare no conflict of interest.

References

1. Fiori, G.; Bonaccorso, F.; Iannaccone, G.; Palacios, T.; Neumaier, D.; Seabaugh, A.; Banerjee, S.K.; Colombo, L. Electronics Based on Two-Dimensional Materials. *Nat. Nanotechnol.* **2014**, *9*, 768–779. [CrossRef] [PubMed]
2. Briggs, N.; Subramanian, S.; Lin, Z.; Li, X.; Zhang, X.; Zhang, K.; Xiao, K.; Geohegan, D.; Wallace, R.; Chen, L.-Q.; et al. A Roadmap for Electronic Grade 2D Materials. *2D Mater.* **2019**, *6*, 022001. [CrossRef]
3. Pizzi, G.; Gibertini, M.; Dib, E.; Marzari, N.; Iannaccone, G.; Fiori, G. Performance of Arsenene and Antimonene Double-Gate MOSFETs from First Principles. *Nat. Commun.* **2016**, *7*, 12585. [CrossRef] [PubMed]
4. Klinkert, C.; Szabó, Á.; Stieger, C.; Campi, D.; Marzari, N.; Luisier, M. 2-D Materials for Ultrascaled Field-Effect Transistors: One Hundred Candidates under the Ab Initio Microscope. *ACS Nano* **2020**, *14*, 8605–8615. [CrossRef] [PubMed]
5. Afzalian, A. Ab Initio Perspective of Ultra-Scaled CMOS from 2D-Material Fundamentals to Dynamically Doped Transistors. *NPJ 2D Mater. Appl.* **2021**, *5*, 5. [CrossRef]
6. Liu, H.; Neal, A.T.; Zhu, Z.; Luo, Z.; Xu, X.; Tománek, D.; Ye, P.D. Phosphorene: An Unexplored 2D Semiconductor with a High Hole Mobility. *ACS Nano* **2014**, *8*, 4033–4041. [CrossRef]
7. Das, S.; Demarteau, M.; Roelofs, A. Ambipolar Phosphorene Field Effect Transistor. *ACS Nano* **2014**, *8*, 11730–11738. [CrossRef]
8. Li, L.; Yu, Y.; Ye, G.J.; Ge, Q.; Ou, X.; Wu, H.; Feng, D.; Chen, X.H.; Zhang, Y. Black Phosphorus Field-Effect Transistors. *Nat. Nanotechnol.* **2014**, *9*, 372–377. [CrossRef]
9. Haratipour, N.; Robbins, M.C.; Koester, S.J. Black Phosphorus P-MOSFETs with 7-nm HfO_2 Gate Dielectric and Low Contact Resistance. *IEEE Electron Device Lett.* **2015**, *36*, 411–413. [CrossRef]
10. Cao, X.; Guo, J. Simulation of Phosphorene Field-Effect Transistor at the Scaling Limit. *IEEE Trans. Electron Devices* **2015**, *62*, 659–665. [CrossRef]
11. Afzalian, A.; Pourtois, G. ATOMOS: An ATomistic MOdelling Solver for Dissipative DFT Transport in Ultra-Scaled HfS_2 and Black Phosphorus MOSFETs. In Proceedings of the 2019 International Conference on Simulation of Semiconductor Processes and Devices (SISPAD), Udine, Italy, 4–6 September 2019; pp. 1–4.
12. Guo, H.; Lu, N.; Dai, J.; Wu, X.; Zeng, X.C. Phosphorene Nanoribbons, Phosphorus Nanotubes, and van Der Waals Multilayers. *J. Phys. Chem. C* **2014**, *118*, 14051–14059. [CrossRef]

13. Taghizadeh Sisakht, E.; Zare, M.H.; Fazileh, F. Scaling Laws of Band Gaps of Phosphorene Nanoribbons: A Tight-Binding Calculation. *Phys. Rev. B* **2015**, *91*, 085409. [CrossRef]
14. Poljak, M.; Suligoj, T. Immunity of Electronic and Transport Properties of Phosphorene Nanoribbons to Edge Defects. *Nano Res.* **2016**, *9*, 1723–1734. [CrossRef]
15. Poljak, M.; Matić, M. Quantum Transport Simulations of Phosphorene Nanoribbon MOSFETs: Effects of Metal Contacts, Ballisticity and Series Resistance. In Proceedings of the 2020 International Conference on Simulation of Semiconductor Processes and Devices (SISPAD), Kobe, Japan, 23 September–6 October 2020; pp. 371–374.
16. Poljak, M.; Matić, M. Bandstructure and Size-Scaling Effects in the Performance of Monolayer Black Phosphorus Nanodevices. *Materials* **2022**, *15*, 243. [CrossRef] [PubMed]
17. Watts, M.C.; Picco, L.; Russell-Pavier, F.S.; Cullen, P.L.; Miller, T.S.; Bartuś, S.P.; Payton, O.D.; Skipper, N.T.; Tileli, V.; Howard, C.A. Production of Phosphorene Nanoribbons. *Nature* **2019**, *568*, 216–220. [CrossRef]
18. Zhang, W.; Enriquez, H.; Tong, Y.; Mayne, A.J.; Bendounan, A.; Smogunov, A.; Dappe, Y.J.; Kara, A.; Dujardin, G.; Oughaddou, H. Flat Epitaxial Quasi-1D Phosphorene Chains. *Nat. Commun.* **2021**, *12*, 5160. [CrossRef]
19. Du, Y.; Liu, H.; Deng, Y.; Ye, P.D. Device Perspective for Black Phosphorus Field-Effect Transistors: Contact Resistance, Ambipolar Behavior, and Scaling. *ACS Nano* **2014**, *8*, 10035–10042. [CrossRef] [PubMed]
20. Li, X.; Yu, Z.; Xiong, X.; Li, T.; Gao, T.; Wang, R.; Huang, R.; Wu, Y. High-Speed Black Phosphorus Field-Effect Transistors Approaching Ballistic Limit. *Sci. Adv.* **2019**, *5*, eaau3194. [CrossRef]
21. Telesio, F.; le Gal, G.; Serrano-Ruiz, M.; Prescimone, F.; Toffanin, S.; Peruzzini, M.; Heun, S. Ohmic Contact Engineering in Few–Layer Black Phosphorus: Approaching the Quantum Limit. *Nanotechnology* **2020**, *31*, 334002. [CrossRef]
22. Haratipour, N.; Namgung, S.; Grassi, R.; Low, T.; Oh, S.; Koester, S.J. High-Performance Black Phosphorus MOSFETs Using Crystal Orientation Control and Contact Engineering. *IEEE Electron Device Lett.* **2017**, *38*, 685–688. [CrossRef]
23. Poljak, M.; Matić, M.; Zeljko, A. Minimum Contact Resistance in Monoelemental 2D Material Nanodevices with Edge-Contacts. *IEEE Electron Device Lett.* **2021**, *42*, 1240–1243. [CrossRef]
24. Wang, L.; Meric, I.; Huang, P.Y.; Gao, Q.; Gao, Y.; Tran, H.; Taniguchi, T.; Watanabe, K.; Campos, L.M.; Muller, D.A.; et al. One-Dimensional Electrical Contact to a Two-Dimensional Material. *Science* **2013**, *342*, 614–617. [CrossRef] [PubMed]
25. Jain, A.; Szabó, Á.; Parzefall, M.; Bonvin, E.; Taniguchi, T.; Watanabe, K.; Bharadwaj, P.; Luisier, M.; Novotny, L. One-Dimensional Edge Contacts to a Monolayer Semiconductor. *Nano Lett.* **2019**, *19*, 6914–6923. [CrossRef] [PubMed]
26. Rudenko, A.N.; Katsnelson, M.I. Quasiparticle Band Structure and Tight-Binding Model for Single- and Bilayer Black Phosphorus. *Phys. Rev. B* **2014**, *89*, 201408. [CrossRef]
27. Datta, S. *Quantum Transport: Atom to Transistor*, 2nd ed.; Cambridge University Press: New York, NY, USA, 2005; ISBN 0-521-63145-9.
28. Pourfath, M. *The Non-Equilibrium Green's Function Method for Nanoscale Device Simulation*; Computational Microelectronics; Springer: Wien, Austria, 2014; ISBN 978-3-7091-1799-6.
29. Poljak, M.; Glavan, M.; Kuzmić, S. Accelerating Simulation of Nanodevices Based on 2D Materials by Hybrid CPU-GPU Parallel Computing. In Proceedings of the 2019 42nd International Convention on Information and Communication Technology, Electronics and Microelectronics (MIPRO), Opatija, Croatia, 20–24 May 2019; pp. 51–56.
30. Poljak, M. Electron Mobility in Defective Nanoribbons of Monoelemental 2D Materials. *IEEE Electron Device Lett.* **2020**, *41*, 151–154. [CrossRef]
31. Poljak, M.; Matić, M. Metallization-Induced Quantum Limits of Contact Resistance in Graphene Nanoribbons with One-Dimensional Contacts. *Materials* **2021**, *14*, 3670. [CrossRef]
32. Datta, S. Nanoscale Device Modeling: The Green's Function Method. *Superlattices Microstruct.* **2000**, *28*, 253–278. [CrossRef]
33. Liang, G.; Neophytou, N.; Lundstrom, M.S.; Nikonov, D.E. Contact Effects in Graphene Nanoribbon Transistors. *Nano Lett.* **2008**, *8*, 1819–1824. [CrossRef]
34. Liang, G.; Neophytou, N.; Lundstrom, M.S.; Nikonov, D.E. Ballistic Graphene Nanoribbon Metal-Oxide-Semiconductor Field-Effect Transistors: A Full Real-Space Quantum Transport Simulation. *J. Appl. Phys.* **2007**, *102*, 054307. [CrossRef]
35. Meersha, A.; Variar, H.B.; Bhardwaj, K.; Mishra, A.; Raghavan, S.; Bhat, N.; Shrivastava, M. Record Low Metal—(CVD) Graphene Contact Resistance Using Atomic Orbital Overlap Engineering. In Proceedings of the 2016 IEEE International Electron Devices Meeting (IEDM), San Francisco, CA, USA, 3–7 December 2016; pp. 119–122.
36. Nemec, N.; Tománek, D.; Cuniberti, G. Modeling Extended Contacts for Nanotube and Graphene Devices. *Phys. Rev. B* **2008**, *77*, 125420. [CrossRef]
37. Fediai, A.; Ryndyk, D.A.; Cuniberti, G. The Modular Approach Enables a Fully Ab Initio Simulation of the Contacts between 3D and 2D Materials. *J. Phys. Condens. Matter* **2016**, *28*, 395303. [CrossRef] [PubMed]
38. Fediai, A.; Ryndyk, D.A.; Seifert, G.; Mothes, S.; Claus, M.; Schröter, M.; Cuniberti, G. Towards an Optimal Contact Metal for CNTFETs. *Nanoscale* **2016**, *8*, 10240–10251. [CrossRef] [PubMed]
39. Pan, Y.; Wang, Y.; Ye, M.; Quhe, R.; Zhong, H.; Song, Z.; Peng, X.; Yu, D.; Yang, J.; Shi, J.; et al. Monolayer Phosphorene–Metal Contacts. *Chem. Mater.* **2016**, *28*, 2100–2109. [CrossRef]

40. Li, J.; Sun, X.; Xu, C.; Zhang, X.; Pan, Y.; Ye, M.; Song, Z.; Quhe, R.; Wang, Y.; Zhang, H.; et al. Electrical Contacts in Monolayer Blue Phosphorene Devices. *Nano Res.* **2018**, *11*, 1834–1849. [CrossRef]
41. Zhang, X.; Pan, Y.; Ye, M.; Quhe, R.; Wang, Y.; Guo, Y.; Zhang, H.; Dan, Y.; Song, Z.; Li, J.; et al. Three-Layer Phosphorene-Metal Interfaces. *Nano Res.* **2018**, *11*, 707–721. [CrossRef]

Article

Electric Transport in Few-Layer ReSe$_2$ Transistors Modulated by Air Pressure and Light

Enver Faella [1,2], Kimberly Intonti [1], Loredana Viscardi [1], Filippo Giubileo [2], Arun Kumar [1], Hoi Tung Lam [3], Konstantinos Anastasiou [3], Monica F. Craciun [3], Saverio Russo [3] and Antonio Di Bartolomeo [1,2,*]

[1] Department of Physics "E.R. Caianiello", University of Salerno, 84084 Fisciano, SA, Italy; efaella@unisa.it (E.F.); k.intonti@studenti.unisa.it (K.I.); l.viscardi7@studenti.unisa.it (L.V.); akumar@unisa.it (A.K.)
[2] CNR-SPIN, 84084 Fisciano, SA, Italy; filippo.giubileo@spin.cnr.it
[3] University of Exeter, Stocker Road 6, Exeter EX4 4QL, Devon, UK; o.lam@exeter.ac.uk (H.T.L.); ka391@exeter.ac.uk (K.A.); m.f.craciun@exeter.ac.uk (M.F.C.); s.russo@exeter.ac.uk (S.R.)
* Correspondence: adibartolomeo@unisa.it; Tel.: +39-089-96-9189

Abstract: We report the fabrication and optoelectronic characterization of field-effect transistors (FETs) based on few-layer ReSe$_2$. The devices show n-type conduction due to the Cr contacts that form low Schottky barriers with the ReSe$_2$ nanosheet. We show that the optoelectronic performance of these FETs is strongly affected by air pressure, and it undergoes a dramatic increase in conductivity when the pressure is lowered below the atmospheric one. Surface-adsorbed oxygen and water molecules are very effective in doping ReSe$_2$; hence, FETs based on this two-dimensional (2D) semiconductor can be used as an effective air pressure gauge. Finally, we report negative photoconductivity in the ReSe$_2$ channel that we attribute to a back-gate-dependent trapping of the photo-excited charges.

Keywords: 2D materials; rhenium; selenides; ReSe$_2$; field-effect transistor; pressure; negative photoconductivity

1. Introduction

Rhenium diselenide (ReSe$_2$) is a member of the layered transition metal dichalcogenides (TMDs), which has attracted a lot of attention due to the extremely anisotropic electrical, optical and mechanical properties stemming from the strong in-plane anisotropy consequence of its reduced crystal symmetry [1–4]. Contrary to other hexagonal TMDs, the room temperature thermodynamically stable 1T phase for ReSe$_2$ has a distorted triclinic symmetry, which endows the material with anisotropic responses in many properties [5–7].

Monolayer ReSe$_2$ has an indirect bandgap of 1.34 eV [8–10], reducing to 0.98 eV [6] for bulk ReSe$_2$, with a weak layer dependency. In general, an increase in the layer thickness causes a reduction in band-gap energy and the loss of electric properties of thick ReSe$_2$ [11].

ReSe$_2$ has been employed in various electronic and optoelectronic functional devices in order to study its electrical and optical properties. Yang et al. reported that the mobility of ReSe$_2$ nanosheets increases when the number of layers decreases and highlighted that the properties of ReSe$_2$ can be tuned by the number of layers and gas molecule gating, making ReSe$_2$ a promising material for future functional device applications [11]. Optically biaxial and highly anisotropic Mo-doped ReSe$_2$ (Mo:ReSe$_2$) was used to investigate the effects of physisorption of gas molecules on few-layer nanosheet-based photodetectors, reporting different sensitivity to the surrounding environment, prompt photoswitching, and high photoresponsivity [12].

The anisotropic nature of ReSe$_2$ was revealed by Raman spectroscopy under linearly polarized excitations in a study by Zhang et al., who fabricated top-gate ReSe$_2$ field-effect transistors (FETs), with a high on/off current ratio and a well-developed current saturation in the current–voltage characteristics at room temperature [7]. They synthesized

ReSe$_2$ directly onto hexagonal boron nitride (h-BN) substrates to improve the electron and hole mobility and demonstrated that the ReSe$_2$-based photodetectors exhibit polarization-sensitive photoresponsivity due to the intrinsic linear dichroism, originating from high in-plane optical anisotropy, thus, identifying ReSe$_2$ as a highly anisotropic two-dimensional (2D) material for novel electronic and optoelectronic applications.

Similarly, a near-infrared ReSe$_2$ photodetector featuring high photoresponsivity and a short photoresponse time, in the order of 10 ms, was demonstrated by Kim and coworkers, achieving high photo and temporal responses simultaneously by applying a p-doping technique based on hydrochloric acid to a selected ReSe$_2$ region [13].

Ambipolar FETs were obtained from multi-layer ReSe$_2$, mechanically exfoliated onto a SiO$_2$ layer by Pradhan et al., who demonstrated that it is possible to utilize the ambipolarity to fabricate logical elements or digital synthesizers [10]. Similarly, ambipolar all-2D ReSe$_2$ FET with a h-BN gate dielectric and graphene contacts were investigated by Lee and coworkers, who used the ambipolar transfer characteristics, attributed to the tunable Fermi level of the graphene contact, to demonstrate an inverter in a logic circuit [14].

Corbet et al. proposed a method to improve the contact resistance in few-layer ReSe$_2$ FETs, by up to three orders of magnitude, using ultra-high-vacuum annealing [15]. A low contact resistance was also obtained in single-layer ReSe$_2$, encapsulated in h-BN using scandium/gold contacts, and this enabled Khan and coworkers [16] to measure a large field-effect charge carrier mobility and responsivity.

Xing et al. addressed the challenge of the controlled synthesis of high-quality ultrathin ReSe$_2$, developing an approach for synthesizing 2D ReSe$_2$ flakes with a thickness down to monolayer by chemical vapor transport, through carefully tuning the growth kinetics [17]. The FETs fabricated with such flakes showed n-type semiconducting behavior with mobility of a few cm^2 V^{-1} s^{-1}, comparable to the values measured using mechanically exfoliated flakes.

Polarization-resolved ReSe$_2$ photodetectors were recently studied by Tian and Liu, who reported a van der Waals heterojunction ReSe$_2$/WSe$_2$-based photodetector, with high responsivity and detectivity at room temperature. Remarkably, they demonstrated that the photoresponse of their devices is a function of the polarized angle of the incident light, indicating the effective polarized light detection [18].

Pressure is commonly used to understand the interlayer interaction in layered materials. High-hydrostatic pressures of several kbar were applied to ReSe$_2$ (and ReS$_2$) exfoliated flakes and the effect on their optical properties was investigated, finding that the energies of the two main excitonic transitions decrease in energy with increasing pressure [19]. The negative pressure coefficients were attributed to the destabilization of the p$_z$ orbital with increasing pressure, demonstrating that ReSe$_2$ does not exhibit a strong electronic decoupling and, hence, the optoelectronic properties of few-layered ReSe$_2$ could be drastically different from the bulk form.

Conversely, the effect of low pressure on ReSe$_2$ has been rarely investigated in the literature.

In the present study, we fabricate back-gate FETs with a few-layer ReSe$_2$ channel and study the electric transport from room pressure down to 10^{-5} mbar. We find that air pressure has a dramatic effect on the channel conductivity, which increases by more than two orders of magnitude when the pressure decreases. We explain such behavior in terms of the desorption of oxygen and water molecules from the ReSe$_2$ surface in high vacuum. Importantly, we observe that the effect of air pressure is reversible, highlighting that back-gate ReSe$_2$ FETs can be exploited as effective pressure gauges. Moreover, we report a reduction of the channel conductivity when the device is illuminated, i.e., a negative photoconducticity, that has not been reported before for ReSe$_2$. The dependence of the negative photoconductivity on the gate voltage suggests that photo-excited free charge carriers are attracted towards the gate and captured at the interface, with the dielectric layer contributing to the observed loss of conductivity.

2. Materials and Methods

Ultrathin ReSe$_2$ flakes were exfoliated from bulk ReSe$_2$ single crystals using a standard mechanical exfoliation method by adhesive tape. The flakes were transferred onto highly doped n-type (resistivity 0.005 Ω cm) silicon substrates, covered by 290 nm thick SiO$_2$, which serves as a global back gate. Photolithography and standard lift-off process of evaporated Cr/Au (5 nm/100 nm) were applied to define metal contacts. Figure 1a reports the crystal structure and Figure 1b shows the schematic of a ReSe$_2$ FET with the circuit used to control the Si/SiO$_2$ back-gate and the source-drain bias on the 2D semiconducting channel. We adopted an interdigitated layout with 4 parallel channels corresponding to a total channel width W = 26.0 μm and length L = 0.78 μm. An optical top view of a typical device is shown in Figure 1c. The thickness of the flake was measured by an atomic force microscope (Nanosurf AG, Liestal, Switzerland), obtaining the height profile displayed in Figure 1d that confirms a thickness of 1.84 nm, corresponding to 3 layers [20].

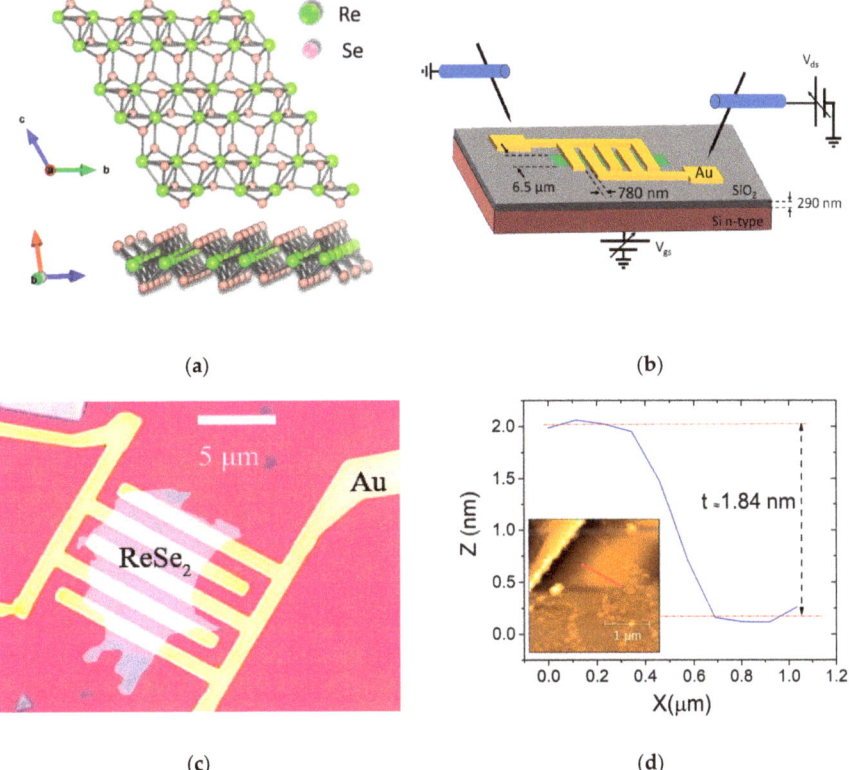

Figure 1. (a) Top view and side view of ReSe$_2$ atomic structure (the green and pink dots represent the Re and Se atoms, respectively); (b) schematic of the ReSe$_2$ back-gated FET with interdigitated source/drain leads. (c) Optical image of the ReSe$_2$ device with interdigitated Cr/Au leads. The flake is highlighted. (d) AFM vertical profile showing the flake thickness of 1.84 nm.

Electric measurements were carried out in two-probe configuration in a Janis ST-500 Probe Station (Lake Shore Cryotronics, Inc., Westerville, OH, USA) equipped with nanoprobes connected to the source/drain leads (Figure 1b). The back-gate voltage was applied through the sample holder of the probe station which was in direct electrical contact to the Ag-pasted n-Si substrate. The measurements were performed by the source-measurement units of a semiconductor characterization system Keithley 4200 SCS (Tektronix, Inc., Beaverton, OR, USA), with current and voltage sensitivity better than 1 pA and 2 µV, respectively. For the transistor characterization, the source was grounded while the drain (V_{ds}) and gate (V_{gs}) voltages were either swept or stepped while the drain (I_d) and gate (I_g) currents were monitored. The measured gate leakage current was always < 10 pA, confirming the integrity of the SiO_2 gate dielectric.

The electric measurements were performed at controlled air pressure, from room pressure to 10^{-5} mbar. Under the combined action of a rotatory and a turbomolecular pump connected in series to a probe station and a valve system, it was possible to control the pressure stepwise. The pressure was monitored through the pressure gauge TPG261 (Pfeiffer, Asslar, Deutschland). The photoresponse of the device was investigated using an array of 144 white LEDs with a spectrum ranging from 400 to 750 nm and peaks at 450 nm and 540 nm, a color temperature of 6000 K, and with 1 mW/cm^2 intensity.

3. Results and Discussion

Initially, the ReSe$_2$ transistor was characterized in dark and at room temperature and pressure, followed by investigating the effect of the lowering pressure in the same conditions of temperature and darkness. Finally, we explored the photoresponse of the fabricated device.

3.1. Transistor Characterization

Figure 2a,b report the output ($I_d - V_{ds}$ at fixed V_{gs}) and transfer ($I_d - V_{gs}$ at fixed V_{ds}) characteristics of the fabricated ReSe$_2$ FET, respectively. We limited the drain bias to 3 V and gate voltage range to ± 30 V to prevent damage to the device and, in particular, to the SiO_2 gate dielectric. The $I_d - V_{ds}$ curves (Figure 2a) show that the drain current is modulated by the gate voltage V_{gs} and stays below 10 pA for negative V_{gs} but increases abruptly for positive V_{gs}. This behavior is typical of a n-type transistor [21,22]. Furthermore, for all gate voltages, the $I_d - V_{ds}$ curves are asymmetric, with slightly higher current at positive V_{ds}, pointing to the formation of low Schottky barriers at the ReSe$_2$/Cr/Au contacts [23–26]. The presence of a Schottky barrier is confirmed also by the limited current that reaches the maximum of 20 nA at $V_{ds} = 3$ V.

The $I_d - V_{gs}$ transfer curves of Figure 2b, shown on both the linear and logarithmic scale, confirm the n-type behavior of the transistor, with off-state at $V_{gs} < 20$ V and on-state for $V_{gs} > 20$ V. The curve on the logarithmic scale shows an on/off current ratio higher than two orders of magnitude and a modest subthreshold swing SS $\simeq$ 2.8 V/decade, typical of back-gate 2D transistors with limited gate efficiency and high interface defect density [27–30]. The smooth rise of I_d at negative V_{gs} indicates the appearance of a hole-type conduction. The carrier type can be controlled via the metal contacts. Dominant n-type behavior is obtained in ReSe$_2$ transistors with low-work-function metal contacts, such as Al or Ti, whose Fermi level aligns above the conduction band minimum of ReSe$_2$ [7,14,31]. As the conduction band minimum of ReSe$_2$ is around of 4.5 eV and the valence band maximum is around 5.6 eV [31], the Fermi levels of Cr and Au that have work functions of 4.5 and 5.1 eV, respectively, align within the ReSe$_2$ bandgap and can favor ambipolar conduction.

The transfer curve on the linear scale is used to estimate the field-effect mobility, μ_{FE}, in the on-state of the transistor for $V_{gs} > 20$ V. The mobility, evaluated as $\mu_{FE} = \frac{L}{W} \frac{1}{C_{ox}V_{ds}} \frac{dI_{ds}}{dV_{gs}}$ (here $C_{ox} = 1.15 \times 10^{-8}$ F cm^{-2} is the gate dielectric capacitance per unit area), results $\mu_{FE} \simeq 0.03$ cm^2 V^{-1} s^{-1} slightly lower than the $\mu_{FE} \sim 0.1 - 10$ cm^2 V^{-1} s^{-1}, typically measured in few-layer ReSe$_2$ FETs [5,7,10,11]. We also note that an increase in layer thickness causes a loss of electric properties in ReSe$_2$ and, in particular, that few-layer ReSe$_2$ exhibits lower mobility of two orders of magnitude or more than single-layer ReSe$_2$ [11]. Furthermore, the presence of a Schottky barrier at the contacts [32,33], as well as intrinsic defects in the material and impurities located at the interface with the SiO_2 layer or adsorbates on top of the channel from air exposure during the fabrication and the measurement process [10,34,35], acting as scattering or trapping centers, can contribute to decrease the mobility.

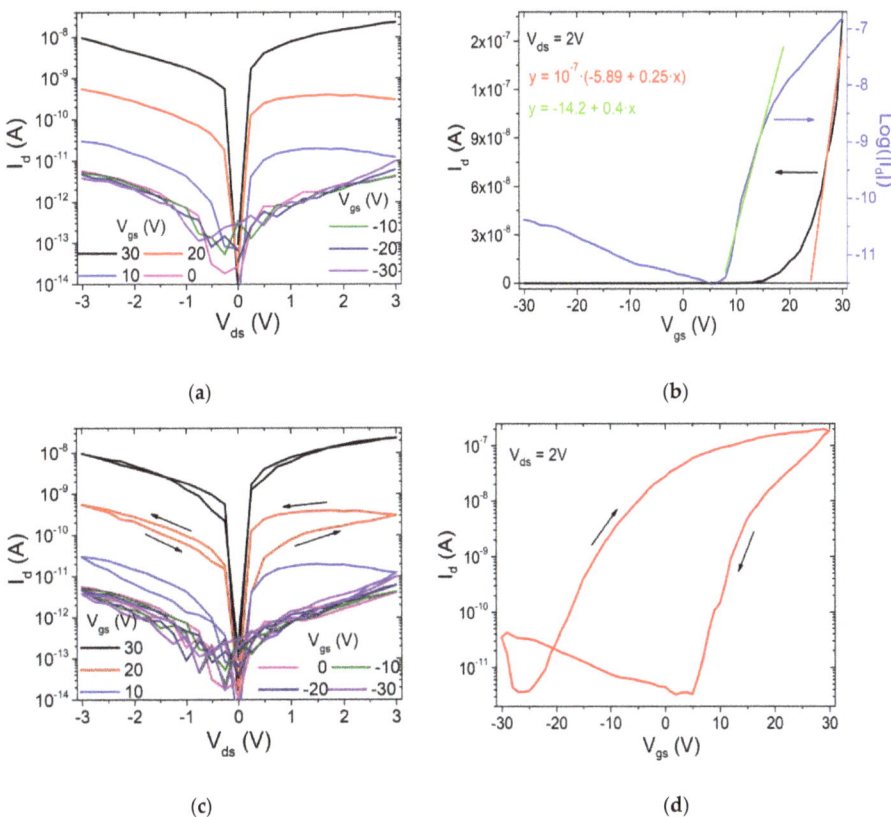

Figure 2. Electrical measurements at normal atmospheric pressure: (**a**) Output curves for reverse V_{ds} sweep (single). (**b**) Transfer curve on linear (black) and logarithmic (blue) scale. (**c**) Output curves for forward and reverse V_{ds} sweeps. (**d**) Transfer curves for forward and reverse V_{gs} sweeps, showing a wide hysteresis.

The x-axis intercept of the straight line that fits the transfer curve on the linear scale in Figure 2b is assumed as the threshold voltage V_{th} of the transistor and is about 20 V, indicating a n-type enhancement mode device.

More insights in the electric transport through the $ReSe_2$ channel can be gained from Figure 2c,d, which display a hysteresis on both the output and transfer curves when V_{ds} or V_{gs} are swept in a loop (the forward and reverse sweeps yield different curves). The presence of large hysteresis in the $I_d - V_{ds}$ characteristics has been reported before in monolayer MoS_2 devices, where it was attributed to the multigrain structure of the material and exploited to enable resistive switching devices. The presence of grain boundaries provides the opportunity to fabricate memristors, owing to the phenomenon of migration of defects, such as sulphur vacancies at grain boundaries, by applying a high electric field [36]. The hysteretic behavior in Figure 2c points to a defective $ReSe_2$ channel, possibly with Se vacancies, consistent with the n-type intrinsic doping and the low mobility. The presence of intrinsic and interfacial defects is confirmed by the huge hysteresis observed in the transfer curve in Figure 2d. Hysteresis in the transfer characteristic is very common in 2D-material-based transistors and has been widely studied and attributed to charge trapping inside the channel material, interface trap states or surface adsorbates [37,38]. The interaction with the SiO_2 dielectric, i.e., the $ReSe_2/SiO_2$ interface, is of paramount importance. Indeed, the substitution of the SiO_2 layer by a high-quality h-BN-insulating substrate, which is atomically flat and free of charge trapping sites, has been shown to result in a strong mitigation of the hysteresis [39].

3.2. Pressure Behavior

To investigate the effect of air pressure on the ReSe$_2$ channel conductivity, we performed an electric transport measurement, lowering the atmospheric pressure down to 10^{-5} mbar. The measurements were performed after keeping the device at the given pressure for several hours to achieve a steady state. Figure 3a shows the output characteristics at three different pressures (room pressure, 3 mbar and 8×10^{-5} mbar) for increasing gate voltages, ranging from 0 V to 30 V, with steps of 10 V. It can be observed that the channel current increases at lower pressure while the hysteresis decreases, and the asymmetric behavior is unchanged. The reduced hysteresis indicates that surface adsorbates play an important role.

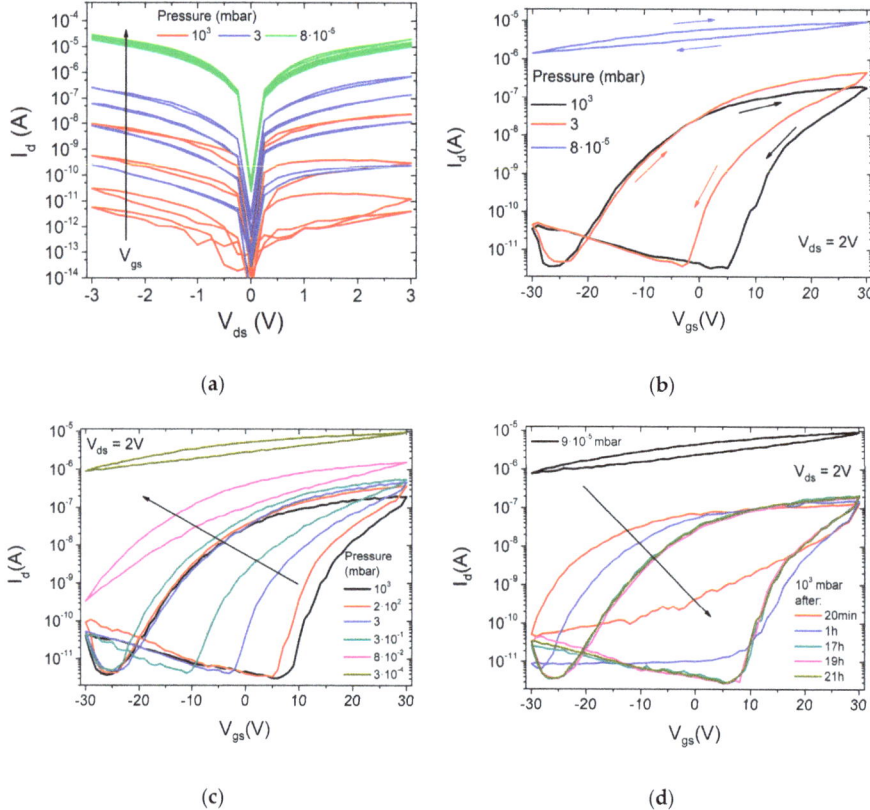

Figure 3. (a) Output curves at different gate voltages (V_{gs} = 0, 10, 20, 30 V) for three different air pressures (atmospheric, 3 mbar, 8×10^{-5} mbar). (b) Transfer curves for three different air pressures (atmospheric, 3 mbar, 8×10^{-5} mbar). The arrows show the direction of voltage gate sweeping starting from 30 V. Transfer characteristics (c) for lowering pressure, and (d) at different times after reaching the room pressure.

The same trend with increased current and reduced hysteresis at low pressure is displayed also by the transfer characteristics in Figure 3b. The low pressure, in particular, causes a dramatic change in the transfer characteristics with the transistor that does not turn off over the applied V_{gs} range. The lowering pressure causes a left shift in the transfer characteristics, corresponding to a reduction in the threshold voltage V_{th}, pointing to an increased n-type doping density. Such behavior can be explained as desorption of adsorbates from the ReSe$_2$ surface. Adsorbed oxygen and water molecules, being electronegative, subtract electrons to the channel, thus, decreasing the conductivity (otherwise stated, oxygen and water counter-dope the n-type channel with holes). Their desorption has the two-fold beneficial effect of increasing the n-type doping and the mobility (see following), resulting in increased conductivity.

Figure 3c,d, which display the transfer characteristics for lowering and raising pressures, respectively, demonstrate that the transformation of the transfer curves is gradual and reversible. While the plot in Figure 3c shows the dynamic evolution of the transfer curves during the pressure change, the plot in Figure 3d monitors the time evolution of the transfer curves after a sudden change from 8×10^{-5} mbar to room pressure, showing that the recovery of the pristine state is a slow process, requiring a few hours. The reversible change of current with pressure demonstrates that the device can be used as an air pressure gauge.

Figure 4a,b detail the behavior of the mobility μ_{FE} and of the current in the on state (I_{on}) as a function of pressure. The mobility was evaluated using both the forward (V_{gs} sweep from -30 V to 30 V) and reverse (V_{gs} sweep from 30 V to -30 V) branches of transfer characteristics. Both forward μ_{FE} and I_{on} decrease for increasing pressure, following a power law, as demonstrated by the linear log–log plots in the respective insets. Conversely, the threshold voltage V_{th} increases up to 10^{-1} mbar, above which it reaches a plateau (Figure 4c), demonstrating that the desorption of the adsorbates becomes effective at a pressure below 10^{-1} mbar. Finally, Figure 4d shows that the hysteresis width (here defined as the difference between the V_{gs} corresponding to the current $I_d = 1$ nA in the reverse and forward sweep) is also increased by the rising pressure. The contribution of adsorbates to hysteresis in 2D-material-based transistors has been widely studied and demonstrated [34,40,41]. The easier the charge transfer between the channel and the adsorbates, the wider the hysteresis [38].

3.3. Photoresponse

As ReSe$_2$ nanosheets have been widely used in efficient photodetectors [7,13,42], we checked the photoresponse of the ReSe$_2$ FET by exposing it to the light of an array of white LEDs at a pressure of 8×10^{-5} mbar.

Figure 5a shows that the current I_d decreases when the device is illuminated, a phenomenon referred to as negative photoconductivity. The decrease in the current under light is enhanced at $V_{gs} = 30$ V. Illumination normally generates additional carriers in a semiconductor material, which increase its conductivity. Conversely, negative photoconductivity has been reported in a few 1D and 2D materials, and explained as a photogating effect due to trap centers, light-induced desorption of surface gas molecules or surface plasmons [43–47]. The origin and role of the negative photoconductivity in low-dimensional materials is still poorly understood. Moreover, negative photoconductivity has not been observed before in ReSe$_2$ and requires deep investigation that will be the subject of a forthcoming study. Here, we note that the photocurrent ($I_{ph} = I_{light} - I_{dark}$) increases with the drain bias and has the absolute value tunable by the gate voltage, as shown in Figure 5b. The increase in the photocurrent with V_{ds} is easily understood because a higher horizontal field favors charge collection to the drain. The increasing $|I_{ph}|$ with the higher gate bias instead suggests a mechanism for the negative photoconductivity, as gate-induced photo-excited charges separation and trapping. The photogenerated electron-hole pairs are separated by the vertical gate field, which attracts electrons at the ReSe$_2$/SiO$_2$ interface, where they become trapped. The excess holes in the channels combine with electrons of the n-type ReSe$_2$, causing a counter-doping effect, i.e., a reduction in the channel conductivity.

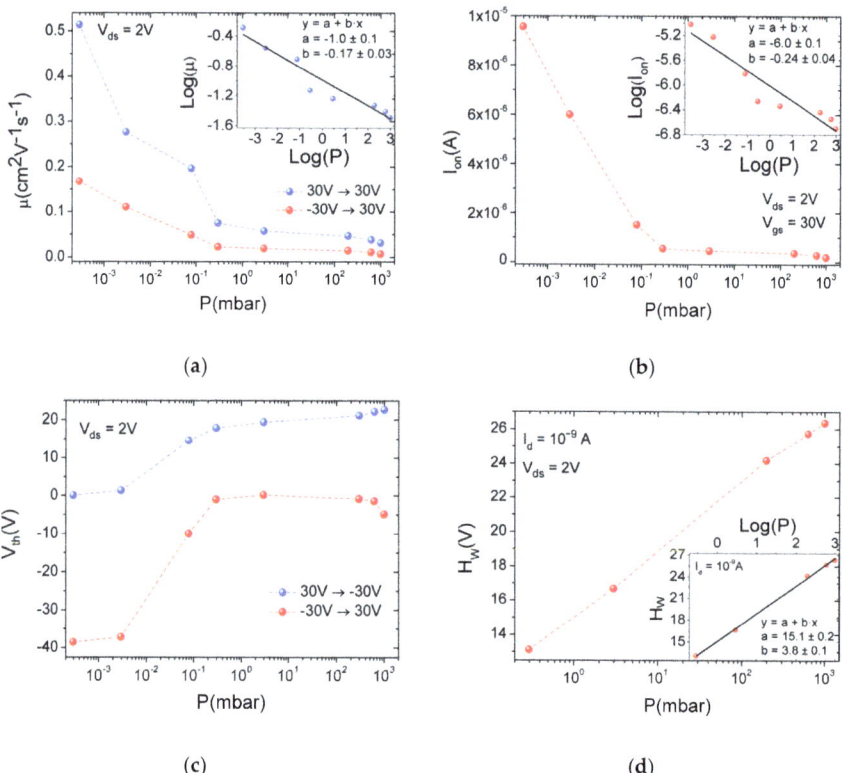

Figure 4. (**a**) Forward and reverse mobility as function of pressure. Linear fit of the data on log–log scale in the inset, (**b**) current in the on state as function of pressure. Linear fit of the data on log–log scale in inset, (**c**) forward and reverse threshold voltage as function of pressure, and (**d**) hysteresis width at $I_d = 1$ nA versus air pressure. Linear fit of data on semi-log scale in the inset.

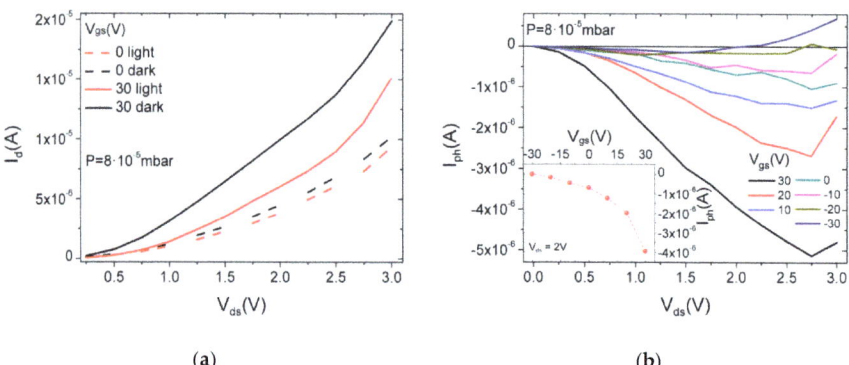

Figure 5. (**a**) $I_{ds} - V_{ds}$ curves in dark and light at $V_{gs} = 0$ and $+30$ V (dashed and solid lines); (**b**) $I_{ph} - V_{ds}$ curves at different V_{gs}. I_{ph} vs. V_{gs} at $V_{ds} = 2$ V in the inset.

4. Conclusions

We fabricated a back-gate field-effect transistor with ReSe$_2$ nanosheets and Cr/Au contacts and studied its electric transport. We showed that the transistor has a dominant n-type character due to the alignment of the Cr Fermi level with the ReSe$_2$ conduction band minimum. We investigated the effect of low pressure on the material conductivity and found that the device is strongly affected by air pressure. The exposure to air suppresses the channel conductivity as an effect of electron capture by oxygen and water molecules adsorbed on the material surface. The desorption of adsorbates in high vacuum increases the channel conductivity. We pointed out that the reversible pressure behavior allows the device to be used as an air pressure gauge. Furthermore, we showed that the n-type channel and the gate-driven separation and trapping of photogenerated electrons can lower the channel conductivity under illumination, the origin of the observed negative photoconductivity.

Author Contributions: Conceptualization, S.R. and A.D.B.; methodology, H.T.L., M.F.C., E.F., F.G. and K.A.; software, E.F., K.I., A.K. and L.V.; validation, A.D.B., M.F.C., F.G. and S.R.; formal analysis, E.F., K.I. and L.V.; investigation, E.F., K.I., L.V, H.T.L., K.A. and A.K.; resources, S.R. and A.D.B.; data curation, E.F., K.I., L.V. and A.K.; writing—original draft preparation, A.D.B. and E.F.; writing—review and editing, A.D.B., F.G., M.F.C. and S.R.; visualization, E.F., K.I., H.T.L. and K.A.; supervision, A.D.B. and S.R.; project administration, A.D.B., M.F.C. and S.R.; funding acquisition, F.G. and M.F.C. All authors have read and agreed to the published version of the manuscript.

Funding: This research was funded by the University of Salerno, Italy, grant number ORSA218189 and ORSA200207. The APC was funded by A.D.B.

Institutional Review Board Statement: Not applicable.

Informed Consent Statement: Not applicable.

Data Availability Statement: The data presented in this study are available on request from the corresponding author.

Conflicts of Interest: The authors declare no conflict of interest.

References

1. Friemelt, K.; Lux-Steiner, M.C.; Bucher, E. Optical Properties of the Layered Transition-Metal-Dichalcogenide ReS$_2$: Anisotropy in the van Der Waals Plane. *J. Appl. Phys.* **1993**, *74*, 5266–5268. [CrossRef]
2. Ho, C.H.; Huang, C.E. Optical Property of the Near Band-Edge Transitions in Rhenium Disulfide and Diselenide. *J. Alloys Compd.* **2004**, *383*, 74–79. [CrossRef]
3. Dumcenco, D.O.; Huang, W.Y.; Huang, Y.S.; Tiong, K.K. Anisotropic Optical Characteristics of Au-Doped Rhenium Diselenide Single Crystals. *J. Alloys Compd.* **2009**, *480*, 104–106. [CrossRef]
4. Di Bartolomeo, A. Emerging 2D Materials and Their Van Der Waals Heterostructures. *Nanomaterials* **2020**, *10*, 579. [CrossRef] [PubMed]
5. Cui, F.; Li, X.; Feng, Q.; Yin, J.; Zhou, L.; Liu, D.; Liu, K.; He, X.; Liang, X.; Liu, S.; et al. Epitaxial Growth of Large-Area and Highly Crystalline Anisotropic ReSe$_2$ Atomic Layer. *Nano Res.* **2017**, *10*, 2732–2742. [CrossRef]
6. Ho, C.H.; Huang, Y.S.; Tiong, K.K. In-Plane Anisotropy of the Optical and Electrical Properties of ReS$_2$ and ReSe$_2$ Layered Crystals. *J. Alloy. Compd.* **2001**, *317*, 222–226. [CrossRef]
7. Zhang, E.; Wang, P.; Li, Z.; Wang, H.; Song, C.; Huang, C.; Chen, Z.-G.; Yang, L.; Zhang, K.; Lu, S.; et al. Tunable Ambipolar Polarization-Sensitive Photodetectors Based on High-Anisotropy ReSe$_2$ Nanosheets. *ACS Nano* **2016**, *10*, 8067–8077. [CrossRef]
8. Wolverson, D.; Crampin, S.; Kazemi, A.S.; Ilie, A.; Bending, S.J. Raman Spectra of Monolayer, Few-Layer, and Bulk ReSe$_2$: An Anisotropic Layered Semiconductor. *ACS Nano* **2014**, *8*, 11154–11164. [CrossRef]
9. Hart, L.S.; Webb, J.L.; Dale, S.; Bending, S.J.; Mucha-Kruczynski, M.; Wolverson, D.; Chen, C.; Avila, J.; Asensio, M.C. Electronic Bandstructure and van Der Waals Coupling of ReSe$_2$ Revealed by High-Resolution Angle-Resolved Photoemission Spectroscopy. *Sci. Rep.* **2017**, *7*, 5145. [CrossRef]
10. Pradhan, N.R.; Garcia, C.; Isenberg, B.; Rhodes, D.; Feng, S.; Memaran, S.; Xin, Y.; McCreary, A.; Walker, A.R.H.; Raeliarijaona, A.; et al. Phase Modulators Based on High Mobility Ambipolar ReSe$_2$ Field-Effect Transistors. *Sci. Rep.* **2018**, *8*, 12745. [CrossRef]
11. Yang, S.; Tongay, S.; Li, Y.; Yue, Q.; Xia, J.-B.; Li, S.-S.; Li, J.; Wei, S.-H. Layer-Dependent Electrical and Optoelectronic Responses of ReSe$_2$ Nanosheet Transistors. *Nanoscale* **2014**, *6*, 7226. [CrossRef] [PubMed]

12. Yang, S.; Tongay, S.; Yue, Q.; Li, Y.; Li, B.; Lu, F. High-Performance Few-Layer Mo-Doped ReSe$_2$ Nanosheet Photodetectors. *Sci. Rep.* **2015**, *4*, 5442. [CrossRef] [PubMed]
13. Kim, J.; Heo, K.; Kang, D.; Shin, C.; Lee, S.; Yu, H.; Park, J. Rhenium Diselenide (ReSe$_2$) Near-Infrared Photodetector: Performance Enhancement by Selective P-Doping Technique. *Adv. Sci.* **2019**, *6*, 1901255. [CrossRef] [PubMed]
14. Lee, K.; Yang, S.; Sung, Y.; Chang, Y.; Lin, C.; Yang, F.; Li, M.; Watanabe, K.; Taniguchi, T.; Ho, C.; et al. Analog Circuit Applications Based on All-2D Ambipolar ReSe$_2$ Field-Effect Transistors. *Adv. Funct. Mater.* **2019**, *29*, 1809011. [CrossRef]
15. Corbet, C.M.; Sonde, S.S.; Tutuc, E.; Banerjee, S.K. Improved Contact Resistance in ReSe$_2$ Thin Film Field-Effect Transistors. *Appl. Phys. Lett.* **2016**, *108*, 162104. [CrossRef]
16. Khan, M.F.; Rehman, S.; Akhtar, I.; Aftab, S.; Ajmal, H.M.S.; Khan, W.; Kim, D.; Eom, J. High Mobility ReSe$_2$ Field Effect Transistors: Schottky-Barrier-Height-Dependent Photoresponsivity and Broadband Light Detection with Co Decoration. *2D Mater.* **2019**, *7*, 015010. [CrossRef]
17. Xing, L.; Yan, X.; Zheng, J.; Xu, G.; Lu, Z.; Liu, L.; Wang, J.; Wang, P.; Pan, X.; Jiao, L. Highly Crystalline ReSe$_2$ Atomic Layers Synthesized by Chemical Vapor Transport. *InfoMat* **2019**, *1*, 552–558. [CrossRef]
18. Tian, X.; Liu, Y. Van Der Waals Heterojunction ReSe$_2$/WSe$_2$ Polarization-Resolved Photodetector. *J. Semicond.* **2021**, *42*, 032001. [CrossRef]
19. Oliva, R.; Laurien, M.; Dybala, F.; Kopaczek, J.; Qin, Y.; Tongay, S.; Rubel, O.; Kudrawiec, R. Pressure Dependence of Direct Optical Transitions in ReS$_2$ and ReSe$_2$. *Npj 2D Mater. Appl.* **2019**, *3*, 20. [CrossRef]
20. Tongay, S.; Sahin, H.; Ko, C.; Luce, A.; Fan, W.; Liu, K.; Zhou, J.; Huang, Y.-S.; Ho, C.-H.; Yan, J.; et al. Monolayer Behavior in Bulk ReS$_2$ Due to Electronic and Vibrational Decoupling. *Nat. Commun.* **2014**, *5*, 3252. [CrossRef]
21. Di Bartolomeo, A.; Urban, F.; Passacantando, M.; McEvoy, N.; Peters, L.; Iemmo, L.; Luongo, G.; Romeo, F.; Giubileo, F. A WSe$_2$ Vertical Field Emission Transistor. *Nanoscale* **2019**, *11*, 1538–1548. [CrossRef] [PubMed]
22. Urban, F.; Martucciello, N.; Peters, L.; McEvoy, N.; Di Bartolomeo, A. Environmental Effects on the Electrical Characteristics of Back-Gated WSe$_2$ Field-Effect Transistors. *Nanomaterials* **2018**, *8*, 901. [CrossRef] [PubMed]
23. Grillo, A.; Di Bartolomeo, A. A Current–Voltage Model for Double Schottky Barrier Devices. *Adv. Electron. Mater.* **2021**, *7*, 2000979. [CrossRef]
24. Di Bartolomeo, A.; Grillo, A.; Urban, F.; Iemmo, L.; Giubileo, F.; Luongo, G.; Amato, G.; Croin, L.; Sun, L.; Liang, S.-J.; et al. Asymmetric Schottky Contacts in Bilayer MoS$_2$ Field Effect Transistors. *Adv. Funct. Mater.* **2018**, *28*, 1800657. [CrossRef]
25. Ezhilmaran, B.; Patra, A.; Benny, S.; Sreelakshmi, M.R.; Akshay, V.V.; Bhat, S.V.; Rout, C.S. Recent Developments in the Photodetector Applications of Schottky Diodes Based on 2D Materials. *J. Mater. Chem. C* **2021**, *9*, 6122–6150. [CrossRef]
26. Giubileo, F.; Di Bartolomeo, A. The Role of Contact Resistance in Graphene Field-Effect Devices. *Prog. Surf. Sci.* **2017**, *92*, 143–175. [CrossRef]
27. Pelella, A.; Grillo, A.; Urban, F.; Giubileo, F.; Passacantando, M.; Pollmann, E.; Sleziona, S.; Schleberger, M.; Di Bartolomeo, A. Gate-Controlled Field Emission Current from MoS$_2$ Nanosheets. *Adv. Electron. Mater.* **2021**, *7*, 2000838. [CrossRef]
28. Di Bartolomeo, A.; Pelella, A.; Urban, F.; Grillo, A.; Iemmo, L.; Passacantando, M.; Liu, X.; Giubileo, F. Field Emission in Ultrathin PdSe$_2$ Back-Gated Transistors. *Adv. Electron. Mater.* **2020**, *6*, 2000094. [CrossRef]
29. Sun, J.; Passacantando, M.; Palummo, M.; Nardone, M.; Kaasbjerg, K.; Grillo, A.; Di Bartolomeo, A.; Caridad, J.M.; Camilli, L. Impact of Impurities on the Electrical Conduction of Anisotropic Two-Dimensional Materials. *Phys. Rev. Appl.* **2020**, *13*, 044063. [CrossRef]
30. Di Bartolomeo, A.; Urban, F.; Pelella, A.; Grillo, A.; Iemmo, L.; Faella, E.; Giubileo, F. Electrical Transport in Two-Dimensional PdSe2 and Mos2 Nanosheets. In Proceedings of the 2020 IEEE 20th International Conference on Nanotechnology (IEEE-NANO), Montreal, QC, Canada, 28–31 July 2020; pp. 276–281.
31. Kang, B.; Kim, Y.; Cho, J.H.; Lee, C. Ambipolar Transport Based on CVD-Synthesized ReSe$_2$. *2D Mater.* **2017**, *4*, 025014. [CrossRef]
32. Urban, F.; Lupina, G.; Grillo, A.; Martucciello, N.; Di Bartolomeo, A. Contact Resistance and Mobility in Back-Gate Graphene Transistors. *Nano Express* **2020**, *1*, 010001. [CrossRef]
33. Pelella, A.; Kharsah, O.; Grillo, A.; Urban, F.; Passacantando, M.; Giubileo, F.; Iemmo, L.; Sleziona, S.; Pollmann, E.; Madauß, L.; et al. Electron Irradiation of Metal Contacts in Monolayer MoS$_2$ Field-Effect Transistors. *ACS Appl. Mater. Interfaces* **2020**, *12*, 40532–40540. [CrossRef] [PubMed]
34. Di Bartolomeo, A.; Genovese, L.; Giubileo, F.; Iemmo, L.; Luongo, G.; Foller, T.; Schleberger, M. Hysteresis in the Transfer Characteristics of MoS$_2$ Transistors. *2D Mater.* **2017**, *5*, 015014. [CrossRef]
35. Giubileo, F.; Iemmo, L.; Passacantando, M.; Urban, F.; Luongo, G.; Sun, L.; Amato, G.; Enrico, E.; Di Bartolomeo, A. Effect of Electron Irradiation on the Transport and Field Emission Properties of Few-Layer MoS$_2$ Field-Effect Transistors. *J. Phys. Chem. C* **2019**, *123*, 1454–1461. [CrossRef]
36. Sangwan, V.K.; Jariwala, D.; Kim, I.S.; Chen, K.-S.; Marks, T.J.; Lauhon, L.J.; Hersam, M.C. Gate-Tunable Memristive Phenomena Mediated by Grain Boundaries in Single-Layer MoS$_2$. *Nat. Nanotechnol.* **2015**, *10*, 403–406. [CrossRef] [PubMed]
37. Di Bartolomeo, A.; Pelella, A.; Liu, X.; Miao, F.; Passacantando, M.; Giubileo, F.; Grillo, A.; Iemmo, L.; Urban, F.; Liang, S. Pressure-Tunable Ambipolar Conduction and Hysteresis in Thin Palladium Diselenide Field Effect Transistors. *Adv. Funct. Mater.* **2019**, *29*, 1902483. [CrossRef]
38. Urban, F.; Giubileo, F.; Grillo, A.; Iemmo, L.; Luongo, G.; Passacantando, M.; Foller, T.; Madauß, L.; Pollmann, E.; Geller, M.P.; et al. Gas Dependent Hysteresis in MoS$_2$ Field Effect Transistors. *2D Mater.* **2019**, *6*, 045049. [CrossRef]

39. Lee, C.; Rathi, S.; Khan, M.A.; Lim, D.; Kim, Y.; Yun, S.J.; Youn, D.-H.; Watanabe, K.; Taniguchi, T.; Kim, G.-H. Comparison of Trapped Charges and Hysteresis Behavior in HBN Encapsulated Single MoS$_2$ Flake Based Field Effect Transistors on SiO$_2$ and HBN Substrates. *Nanotechnology* **2018**, *29*, 335202. [CrossRef]
40. Knobloch, T.; Rzepa, G.; Illarionov, Y.Y.; Waltl, M.; Schanovsky, F.; Stampfer, B.; Furchi, M.M.; Mueller, T.; Grasser, T. A Physical Model for the Hysteresis in MoS$_2$ Transistors. *IEEE J. Electron Devices Soc.* **2018**, *6*, 972–978. [CrossRef]
41. Shu, J.; Wu, G.; Guo, Y.; Liu, B.; Wei, X.; Chen, Q. The Intrinsic Origin of Hysteresis in MoS$_2$ Field Effect Transistors. *Nanoscale* **2016**, *8*, 3049–3056. [CrossRef]
42. Silva, B.; Rodrigues, J.; Sompalle, B.; Liao, C.-D.; Nicoara, N.; Borme, J.; Cerqueira, F.; Claro, M.; Sadewasser, S.; Alpuim, P.; et al. Efficient ReSe$_2$ Photodetectors with CVD Single-Crystal Graphene Contacts. *Nanomaterials* **2021**, *11*, 1650. [CrossRef] [PubMed]
43. Han, Y.; Zheng, X.; Fu, M.; Pan, D.; Li, X.; Guo, Y.; Zhao, J.; Chen, Q. Negative Photoconductivity of InAs Nanowires. *Phys. Chem. Chem. Phys.* **2016**, *18*, 818–826. [CrossRef] [PubMed]
44. Di Bartolomeo, A.; Urban, F.; Faella, E.; Grillo, A.; Pelella, A.; Giubileo, F.; Askari, M.B.; McEvoy, N.; Gity, F.; Hurley, P.K. PtSe$_2$ Phototransistors with Negative Photoconductivity. *J. Phys. Conf. Ser.* **2021**, *1866*, 012001. [CrossRef]
45. Urban, F.; Gity, F.; Hurley, P.K.; McEvoy, N.; Di Bartolomeo, A. Isotropic Conduction and Negative Photoconduction in Ultrathin PtSe$_2$ Films. *Appl. Phys. Lett.* **2020**, *117*, 193102. [CrossRef]
46. Grillo, A.; Faella, E.; Pelella, A.; Giubileo, F.; Ansari, L.; Gity, F.; Hurley, P.K.; McEvoy, N.; Di Bartolomeo, A. Coexistence of Negative and Positive Photoconductivity in Few-Layer PtSe$_2$ Field-Effect Transistors. *Adv. Funct. Mater.* **2021**, *31*, 2105722. [CrossRef]
47. Cui, B.; Xing, Y.; Han, J.; Lv, W.; Lv, W.; Lei, T.; Zhang, Y.; Ma, H.; Zeng, Z.; Zhang, B. Negative Photoconductivity in Low-Dimensional Materials. *Chin. Phys. B* **2021**, *30*, 028507. [CrossRef]

Article

Role of Junctionless Mode in Improving the Photosensitivity of Sub-10 nm Carbon Nanotube/Nanoribbon Field-Effect Phototransistors: Quantum Simulation, Performance Assessment, and Comparison

Khalil Tamersit [1,2,3,*], Jaya Madan [4], Abdellah Kouzou [5,6,7], Rahul Pandey [4], Ralph Kennel [7] and Mohamed Abdelrahem [7,8,*]

1. Department of Electronics and Telecommunications, Université 8 Mai 1945 Guelma, Guelma 24000, Algeria
2. Department of Electrical and Automatic Engineering, Université 8 Mai 1945 Guelma, Guelma 24000, Algeria
3. Laboratory of Inverse Problems, Modeling, Information and Systems (PIMIS), Université 8 Mai 1945 Guelma, Guelma 24000, Algeria
4. VLSI Centre of Excellence, Chitkara University Institute of Engineering and Technology, Chitkara University, Rajpura, Punjab, India; jaya.madan@chitkara.edu.in (J.M.); rahul.pandey@chitkara.edu.in (R.P.)
5. Applied Automation and Industrial Diagnosis Laboratory (LAADI), Faculty of Science and Technology, Djelfa University, Djelfa 17000, Algeria; kouzouabdellah@ieee.org
6. Electrical and Electronics Engineering Department, Nisantasi University, Istanbul 34398, Turkey
7. Institute for Electrical Drive Systems and Power Electronics (EAL), Technical University of Munich (TUM), Munich, Germany; ralph.kennel@tum.de
8. Electrical Engineering Department, Faculty of Engineering, Assiut University, Assiut 71516, Egypt

* Correspondence: tamersit_khalil@hotmail.fr or khalil.tamersit@univ-guelma.dz (K.T.); mohamed.abdelrahem@tum.de (M.A.)

Abstract: In this article, ultrascaled junctionless (JL) field-effect phototransistors based on carbon nanotube/nanoribbons with sub-10 nm photogate lengths were computationally assessed using a rigorous quantum simulation. This latter self-consistently solves the Poisson equation with the mode space (MS) non-equilibrium Green's function (NEGF) formalism in the ballistic limit. The adopted photosensing principle is based on the light-induced photovoltage, which alters the electrostatics of the carbon-based junctionless nano-phototransistors. The investigations included the photovoltage behavior, the I-V characteristics, the potential profile, the energy-position-resolved electron density, and the photosensitivity. In addition, the subthreshold swing–photosensitivity dependence as a function of change in carbon nanotube (graphene nanoribbon) diameter (width) was thoroughly analyzed while considering the electronic propieties and the quantum physics in carbon nanotube/nanoribbon-based channels. As a result, the junctionless paradigm substantially boosted the photosensitivity and improved the scaling capability of both carbon phototransistors. Moreover, from the point of view of comparison, it was found that the junctionless graphene nanoribbon field-effect phototransistors exhibited higher photosensitivity and better scaling capability than the junctionless carbon nanotube field-effect phototransistors. The obtained results are promising for modern nano-optoelectronic devices, which are in dire need of high-performance ultra-miniature phototransistors.

Keywords: junctionless; zigzag carbon nanotube; armchair-edge graphene nanoribbon; quantum simulation; sub-10 nm; phototransistors; photosensitivity; subthreshold swing

1. Introduction

Optoelectronic devices based on carbon nanotubes (CNTs) and graphene nanoribbons (GNRs), namely, GNR/CNT-based cells, carbon-based phototransistors, and carbon-based photodetectors, have attracted significant interest in recent years [1–5]. Indeed, CNT/GNR-based phototransistors have gained keen focus owing to their promising features such as the unique light–CNT/GNR interaction, high photoresponsivity, fast response, high detectivity, high photosensitivity, extensive detection range, and especially, the low noise in comparison to the conventional photodiodes [6–10]. Most of these promising features are attributed to the unique characteristics that the CNTs and GNRs exhibit in terms of the physical, electrical, optical properties and are synergically correlate with their atomistic structures [11,12]. Therefore, the applications of the CNT/GNR-based phototransistors are highly effective in imaging, optical communication, and sophisticated (bio)sensing applications (e.g., the photoplethysmography) [13], which makes them suitable for futuristic nano-optoelectronics.

The photogating paradigm is one of the most efficient and straightforward principles in phototransistors that allows the conversion of the light information into an electrical signal (change in drain current) through light-induced electrostatic and transport modulations [6,14–16]. In fact, the concept of the light-induced gate photovoltage [17] has given the ability to mostly confine the light's electrical effect at the sensitive component (i.e., the photogate), and thus the field-effect devices act as transducers while greatly simplifying the photosensing mechanism, which is somewhat complicated when the light affects all phototransistor components including the sensing and transducing parts [18,19]. Recently, the light-induced photovoltage approach has made it possible to simply combine cutting-edge field-effect transistors, generally based on emerging 2D materials, with particular photosensing gates while forming advanced high-performance phototransistors [20–22]. In this context, some improvement approaches have been proposed to boost the modern carbon-based phototransistors such as, the use of an ultra-sensitive photogate producing improved photovoltage under specific illumination [23,24], exploiting the high-sensitivity of the GNR channel to the light-induced electrostatic modulation [22], and the identification of a photosensing regime, in which the phototransistors can provide better photosensing performance [10]. However, to the best of our knowledge, the role of the junctionless (JL) paradigm in improving the sub-10 nm CNT/GNR phototransistors and the performance comparison between ultrascaled CNT-based phototransistors and ultrascaled GNR-based phototransistors in junctionless mode and inversion mode (IM) are still questionable, which deserves experimental and computational investigation. More importantly, it is obvious that, with the continuous miniaturization of modern electronics and the progress experienced in large-scale integration, optoelectronics needs high-performance, easy-to-make, and miniature (sub-10-nm) phototransistors [10].

Further, doping is an essential process for ensuring the appropriate functioning of nanotransistors. Implant and/or diffusion processes are commonly used to create chemical doping in semiconductors, wherein the process and material parameters such as implantation dose, energy, diffusion time, temperature and solid solubility limit play a crucial role in determining the doping profile of concentration and junction depth. However, for CNT, graphene, and the other 2D-material-based FETs, the chemical route of doping is quite cumbersome as these nanoscale devices demand the formation of very high doping gradient–based junctions [25]. Therefore, electrostatic doping, which potentially replaces the conventional donor/acceptor dopant–based chemical doping with image charge, i.e., free-electron/hole, has been adopted for nanoscale devices [26–28]. The difference in the photosensitive gate and CNT/GNR work function, applied voltage, energy bandgap, trap engineering, and their interactions result in an electrostatic connection that governs the carrier density for the formation of the p-channel in the proposed phototransistor. Electrostatic doping allows the formation of a virtual junction near the source and drain by emulating a p-channel beneath the polarity gate, where it has merit in controlling the concentration by applying a specific voltage to the polarity gate electrode. This technique also results in formation of ultra-sharp junctions with a controlled doping profile with the feature of lower defect density. Therefore, the foundation of utilizing the junctionless technology in designing the proposed phototransistor mitigates the limitations such as high thermal budget, random dopant fluctuations, and costly millisecond annealing techniques, also known as rapid thermal annealing [29].

In this regard, for the first time, this study assesses the role of junctionless mode in improving the photosensing performance of GNR/CNT-based sub-10 nm phototransistors while targeting the facility of fabrication and improving the electrical and photosensing performance. In addition, this computational investigation fairly compares the IM/JL CNT phototransistors performance against the IM/JL GNR phototransistors' performance, while deeply analyzing the relevant quantum transport including the impact of bandgap, effective mass, and tunneling components on the photosensing performance. The numerical investigation proposed in this paper is based on a quantum simulation, which self-consistently solves the Poisson solver and the mode-space non-equilibrium Green's function (NEGF) formalism in the ballistic limit, where the Hamiltonian of GNR and CNT, which have been presented in previous works, have been normally employed in the NEGF computation [30–33]. The double-gate (DG) configuration has been adopted for the JL/IM GNR-based phototransistors, while the coaxial-gate (CG) geometry has been considered for the JL/IM CNT-based phototransistors. The presented study included the transfer characteristics, the photosensitivity, the dependence subthreshold swing-photosensitivity, quantum transport (energy bandgap, effective mass, direct and band-to-band tunneling currents), the photo-electrostatics, and the impact of change in CNT/GNR energy bandgap (through diameter/width variation) on the subthreshold domain, which was adopted as photosensing regime.

The rest of this paper is organized as follows: Section 2 presents the nano-phototransistors structures. Section 3 summarizes the adopted NEGF-based quantum simulation approach. Section 4 shows and analyzes the results. Section 5 is a conclusion outlining the main findings of the investigation presented in this paper.

2. Device Structure

Figure 1a shows a sketch of the two-dimensional armchair-edge GNR (AGNR) with its detailed atomic structure. It is a well-known fact that the bandgap of AGNR depends on its width [11,34]. Therefore, in this investigation, we considered the semiconducting families (i.e., n = 3p and n = 3p + 1). Simultaneously for a fair comparison, the ZCNT bandgap was also accounted for. Figure 1b shows a schematic of the ZCNT. Similar to AGNR, the bandgap of the ZCNT depends on its diameter, thus we considered the appropriate diameters in this comparative study [35]. It can be clearly noted form Figure 1a,b that the ZCNT can be formed by rolling the AGNR. This important aspect tremendously simplifies the quantum simulation in terms of NEGF computations in mode-space (MS) representation [35–37]. However, from the point of view of the electrostatics, the coaxial-gate configuration and double-gate structure were treated differently using the finite difference method (FDM) and finite element method (FEM). Figure 1c shows the 3D perspective of the ultrascaled double-gate junctionless graphene nanoribbon field-effect phototransistor. An AGNR is considered as channel material, which is sandwiched between two hafnium oxide layers. The germanium-based photogates are placed at the medium of the nanodevice over and under the oxide materials. Figure 1d shows the three-dimensional (3D) structure of the ultrascaled coaxially photogated junctionless carbon nanotube field-effect phototransistor. A zigzag-type carbon nanotube is considered as channel material, which is coaxially sandwiched in a hafnium oxide cylinder acting as an insulator. Note that the use of high-k HfO_2 oxide in the two carbon-based phototransistors aims to provide a good electrostatics control over the carrier transport [35–37]. The germanium-based photogate is placed at the nanodevice medium with a gate-all-around (GAA) configuration. The source and drain electrode are clearly shown in the same figure while assuming an ohmic contact. Figure 1e shows the lengthwise cut view of both carbon-based nano-phototransistors. As shown, the cross-sectional view is similar with the same components, materials (excepting the channel material), and parameters. We emphasize that the interior of the zigzag carbon nanotube is considered an air environment [35]. Figure 1f shows the considered junctionless n-type doping in both nano-phototransistors, devoid of metallurgical junctions that complicate the nanofabrication of such ultrascaled transistors [29,38]. It is worth noting that the main benefits of junctionless FETs are the simplification of fabrication on one hand and the improvement in subthreshold behavior on the other hand [38–40]. From the fabrication point of view, the production of an array configuration of such nanodevices is expected to be profitable since the elementary devices can be manufactured identically [41], because no junctions and no doping concentration gradients are needed [29,38]. Table 1 shows the physical, dimensional, and electrical parameters of the nanoscale carbon-based phototransistors under investigation. The doping molar fraction in both FETs is taken to be comparable [30–32]. It is important to note here that a low source-to-drain bias is considered (V_{DS} = 0.3 V), which is beneficial for low-power photosensing applications. It is worth noting that the diameter of the ZCNT and the width of the AGNR, which are tunable parameters to reach a suitable bandgap, were intentionally chosen to provide a comparable energy bandgap for fair comparison.

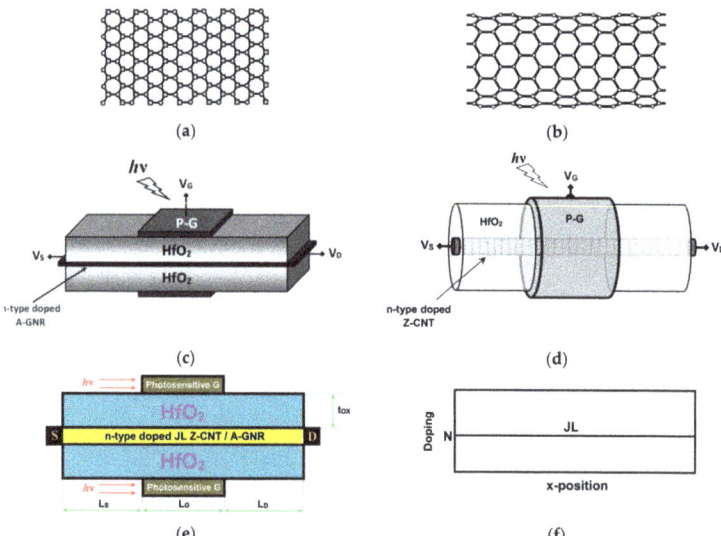

Figure 1. Sketch of (**a**) armchair-edge graphene nanoribbon and (**b**) zigzag carbon nanotube. (**c**) The 3D structure of a double-photogate junctionless graphene nanoribbon field-effect phototransistor. (**d**) The 3D structure of a coaxial-photogate junctionless carbon nanotube field-effect phototransistor. (**e**) Lengthwise cut view of the ultrascaled JL carbon nanotube/nanoribbon field-effect phototransistors under study. (**f**) Uniform n-type doping profile of the junctionless phototransistors under investigation.

Table 1. The physical, dimensional, and electrical parameters of DGJL GNRFET and GAAJL CNTFET.

Parameter	Symbol	DG JL GNRFET	GAA JL CNTFET	Unit
Dimmer number	n	13	13	-
Bandgap	E_G	~0.86	~0.81	eV
Width/diameter	W_{GNR}/d_{CNT}	~1.47	~1	nm
Sensitive gate length	L_G	8	8	nm
S/D length	$L_{S(D)}$	10	10	nm
S/C/D doping	$N_{S/C/D}$	0.56	1.5	nm^{-1}
Oxide thickness	t_{OX}	1.5	1.5	nm
Oxide dielectric constant	ε_{OX}	16	16	-
Temperature	T	300	300	K
Light wavelength	λ	1550	1550	nm
Drain-to-source voltage	V_{DS}	0.3	0.3	V

3. Quantum Simulation Approach

The computational treatment of the armchair-edge graphene nanoribbon and the zigzag carbon nanotube using the mode-space (MS) non-equilibrium Green's function (NEGF) is comparable due to the crystalline similarity between the AGNR and the ZCNT from the mode-space representation point of view [30–33,42,43]. It can be deduced from this comparison that the main difference resides in the Hamiltonian [30–33]. Note that the edge bond relaxation is normally considered in the AGNR's case [30]. As shown in the flowchart of the used quantum simulation method, a potential vector is employed as an initial guess to start the self-consistent procedure between the Poisson equation and the NEGF solver. This latter is initially based on the computation of the retarded Green's function, which is well known and is defined as follows [44,45]:

$$G(E) = [(E + i\eta^+)I - H_{PZ} - \Sigma_S - \Sigma_D]^{-1} \quad (1)$$

where E, η^+, H_{PZ}, I, and $\Sigma_{S(D)}$ are the energy, infinitesimal number, ZCNT/AGNR Hamiltonian matrix based on the atomistic nearest neighbor p_Z-orbital tight-binding (TB) approximation [30–33], identity matrix, and the source (drain) self-energy, respectively. It is worth indicating that the mode-space fashion was adopted in the simulation of both nano-phototransistors in order to save the computational cost [36], which is ordinarily pronounced when using the real-space approach [46]. It is important to note that only the first subband was considered in both cases, which is sufficient from an accuracy point of view [30–32]. The energy level broadening due to the source (drain) contact, $\Gamma_{S(D)}$, and the source (drain) local density of states, $D_{S(D)}$, can now be obtained using the following equations [30–32]:

$$\Gamma_{S(D)} = i(\Sigma_{S(D)} - \Sigma_{S(D)}^\dagger) \quad (2)$$

and

$$D_{S(D)} = G\Gamma_{S(D)}G^\dagger \quad (3)$$

The charge density in AGNR and ZCNT channels can be normally computed using the above NEGF quantities based on the following expression [30–32]:

$$Q_{GNR/CNT}(x) = (-q)\int_{-\infty}^{+\infty} dE \cdot sgn[E - E_N(x)] \times \{D_S(E,x)f(sgn[E - E_N(x)](E - E_{FS})) \\ + D_D(E,x)f(sgn[E - E_N(x)](E - E_{FD}))\} \quad (4)$$

where q, sgn, E_N, f, and $E_{FS(FD)}$ are the electron charge, sign function, charge neutrality level, Fermi function, and source (drain) Fermi level, respectively. As shown in Figure 2, the flowchart of the quantum simulation has a self-consistent procedure, which means that the NEGF solver needs the electrostatic information and the Poisson solver needs a channel charge information. Therefore, the electrostatics should be estimated by solving the Poisson's equation using the finite difference method (FDM) considering the nano-phototransistors' geometry [30–32,47]. It is worth noting that the Neumann boundary conditions were considered for the external interfaces including the source and drain electrodes excepting the applied voltage nodes, which were treated considering the Dirichlet boundary condition, where the photosensing paradigm is embedded by adding to the applied gate voltage, V_{GS}, the so-called light-induced photovoltage, V_{PH}. Hence, the resulting effective gate voltage, V_{GS-EFF}, can be expressed as follows [10,17]:

$$V_{GS-EFF} = V_{GS} + V_{PH} \quad (5)$$

Considering a Ge-based photogate, the photovoltage V_{PH} can be empirically expressed as a function of the incident optical power (P_{INC}) [17]

$$V_{PH} = (nkT/q) \times \ln[1 + (\eta q P_{INC})/(h\nu I_S)] \quad (6)$$

where k, n, T, $h\nu$, I_S, and η are Boltzmann constant, empirical constant (taken to be 0.4), temperature, photon energy, diode leakage current, and quantum efficiency, respectively [10–17].

It is worth noting that the junctionless mode (inversion mode) is computationally treated in the second term of the Poisson equation by considering the same doping concentration (the intrinsic portion) at the channel underneath the gate within the concerned nodes in the FDM.

After obtaining the computational convergence, the current can be calculated by the following integral [30–32]:

$$I = \frac{xq}{\hbar} \int_{-\infty}^{+\infty} dE\, T(E)\, [f(E - E_{FS}) - f(E - E_{FD})] \quad (7)$$

where $\hbar$ is the Planck's constant, x is taken to be 4 for CNT and 2 for GNR, and $T(E)$ is the transmission coefficient given by

$$T(E) = Tr\left[\Gamma_S G \Gamma_D G^\dagger\right] \quad (8)$$

where Tr is the trace operator. Now, the photosensitivity is within reach and can be computed as

$$Ph = \frac{I_{ILLUM} - I_{DARK}}{I_{DARK}} \quad (9)$$

where I_{DARK} denotes the I_{DS} in dark condition and I_{ILLUM} is the drain current under illumination. For more details about the computational methodology, we refer to some relevant works [46–48].

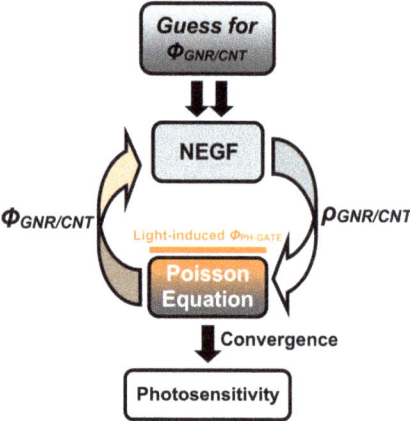

Figure 2. Flowchart of the self-consistent computational approach that considers the Poisson equation solver and the mode-space NEGF solver.

4. Results and Discussion

As known, NEGF-based quantum simulation is a powerful conceptual method and a practical analysis approach to deal with nanoelectronic devices including modern nanotransistors, where the quantum effects, specific electrostatics, and atomistic features play a pivotal role. In fact, the adopted quantum simulation approach contains several computational blocks including the FDM-based Poisson solver, the NEGF-based Schrodinger solver, the non-linear dummy function for convergence efficiency, and an analytical relation describing the light-induced photovoltage. For this reason, the source code of the quantum simulators should be checked while reasonably comparing their outputs with some works in the literature [17,30,32]. For precision's sake, we compared the simulated I_{DS}-V_{DS} output characteristics of the baseline GNRFET and CNTFET with those reported in relevant simulation works considering the same conditions (i.e., ballistic transport), gating configurations, and physical and geometrical parameters and the same simulation approach [30,32]. As shown in Figure 3, an excellent agreement was obtained for both nanotransistors while confirming the soundness and accuracy of the simulator source code. The recorded excellent matching is normally attributed to the use of same simulation parameters, fine spacing mesh in the FDM-based Poisson solver, and efficient non-linear dummy function to speed up and ensure self-consistency.

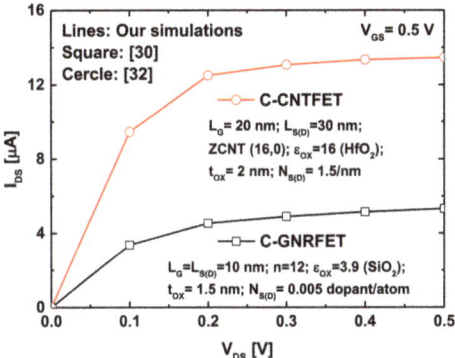

Figure 3. The I_{DS}-V_{DS} output characteristics of the baseline double-gate GNRFET and coaxially gated CNTFET. Lines: results issued from the simulator, symbols: results obtained in [30,32].

Figure 4a shows the experimentally measured photovoltages [17] as a function of the theoretically calculated ones using the above-mentioned empirical relation (Equation (6)) [17]. As shown, a good agreement was noticed for a wide range of incident optical power. Figure 4b shows the Ge photovoltage as a function of the incident optical power considering a monochromatic light wavelength of 1550 nm. It is worth indicating that the curve issued from the empirical relation (Equation (6)) showed excellent agreement with experimental data [17]. Note that the light-induced photovoltage can behave better for a given wavelength and incident optical power by improving the crystal quality and/or applying surface treatments [17]. Other engineered materials [23,24] can also be employed as photosensing gates with some consideration to the band bending. Inspecting the same figure, we can see that the considered range of incident optical power can generate an exploitable amount of photovoltage especially if the nano-phototransistor is operated in the subthreshold regime, where the drain current is more sensitive to the variation of the effective gate voltage [42]. In the literature, it is well known that the FET-based sensors operating with the sensing principles of the measurand-induced modulation in gate voltage are preferably operated in the subthreshold domain targeting optimal sensitivities [42]. In this context, we will show how the junctionless paradigm can not only facilitate the fabrication process by avoiding the integration of sharp junctions but also boost the photosensitivity making the proposed carbon-based nano-phototransistors intriguing candidates for the modern nano-optoelectronics, in which fabrication reliability and high performance are prerequisites.

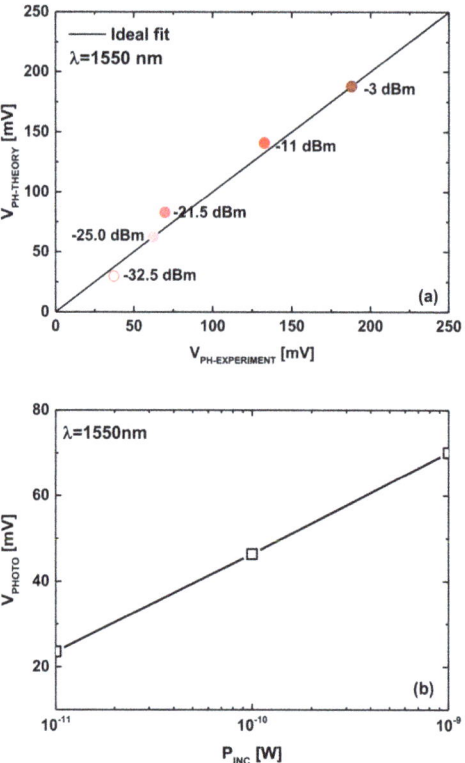

Figure 4. (a) The measured photovoltage [17] versus the modeled photovoltage. (b) The light-induced photovoltage as a function of incident optical power in Ge-based photosensing gate.

In order to clearly show the impact of the infrared light illumination on the quantum transport of the sub-10 nm carbon-based junctionless nano-phototransistors under investigation, we obtained from the NEGF quantities, the electron density spectrum (or equivalently, the energy-position-resolved electron distribution) [31,32] considering a gate bias near the threshold voltage condition. Under the dark condition, we can see in Figure 5a,c that there was no electron flow over the potential barrier, which means that both nanophototransistors were in the optical off-state regime. However, the direct source-to-drain tunneling mechanism (shown in the same figure in the form of some tunneling states through the potential barrier) exists normally due to the considered ultrascaled photogate lengths (sub-10 nm) [35,48,49]. It is worth noting that the junctionless paradigm is found to be very efficient in mitigating the leakage current in both carbon nanotube- and nanoribbon-based nanoFETs, which is very beneficial for low-power optoelectronic systems [39,40]. Under illumination with a monochromatic light with 1550 nm wavelength and 1 nW as incident optical power, we observed a flow of electron from source to drain over the potential barrier, which is attributed to the light-induced photovoltage that lowers the potential barrier while allowing a thermionic emission, which was clearly visible by light spectrum over the barrier from left to right. This behavior explicitly indicates the record of photosensitivity to the considered monochromatic light.

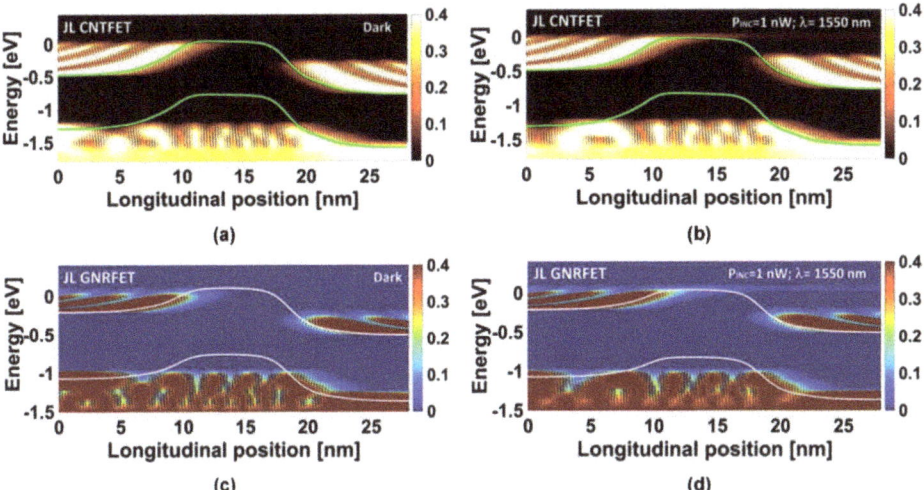

Figure 5. Color-scaled plot for the energy-position-resolved electron distribution along the ZCNT for the JL CNTFET (top figures) and JL GNRFET (bottom figures). The plots (**a**,**c**) are drawn under dark condition, while the plots (**b**,**d**) are drawn under illumination condition (P_{INC} = 1 nW, λ = 1550 nm).

Figure 6 shows the potential distribution of the DG GNRFET-based phototransistor with 8 nm photogate length in dark and illumination conditions, where λ = 1550 nm and P_{INC} = 1 nW were considered. We can see the effect of the photogating (i.e., underneath the Ge photogate) in Figure 6b, where a reduction at the level of potential profile (i.e., 10–18 nm) was recorded in comparison to the dark case in Figure 6a, which is expected according to the gate photovoltage-based photosensing principle. By comparing the two figures, we also observed a shrinking in terms of the potential barrier width in the illumination case. However, no substantial electrostatic modulations were recorded far from the photo-gating region, where the nano-phototransistor was ungated.

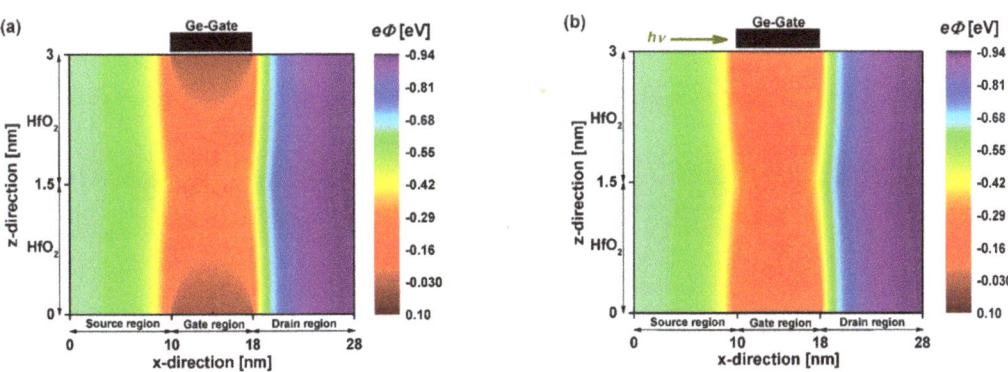

Figure 6. Two-dimensional potential distribution of the sub-10 nm double-gate junctionless carbon nanoribbon field-effect phototransistor before (**a**) and after (**b**) illumination with: V_{DS} = 0.3 V and V_{GS} = 0 V. The infrared light-induced photovoltage is V_{PH} = 0.07 V.

Figure 7 shows the 2D potential distribution of the coaxially photogated CNT field-effect phototransistors extracted after the self-consistency at the longitudinal cross-section (a,b) and the middle cross-section (c,d) of the nanodevice before and after the IR illumination. As recorded in the case of the JL GNR-based phototransistor, the JL CNT-based nano-phototransistor exhibited the same behavior, where the IR illumination-induced reduction in electrostatic gating was clearly pronounced by comparing the dark and light scenarios shown in Figure 7a,c and Figure 7b,d, respectively.

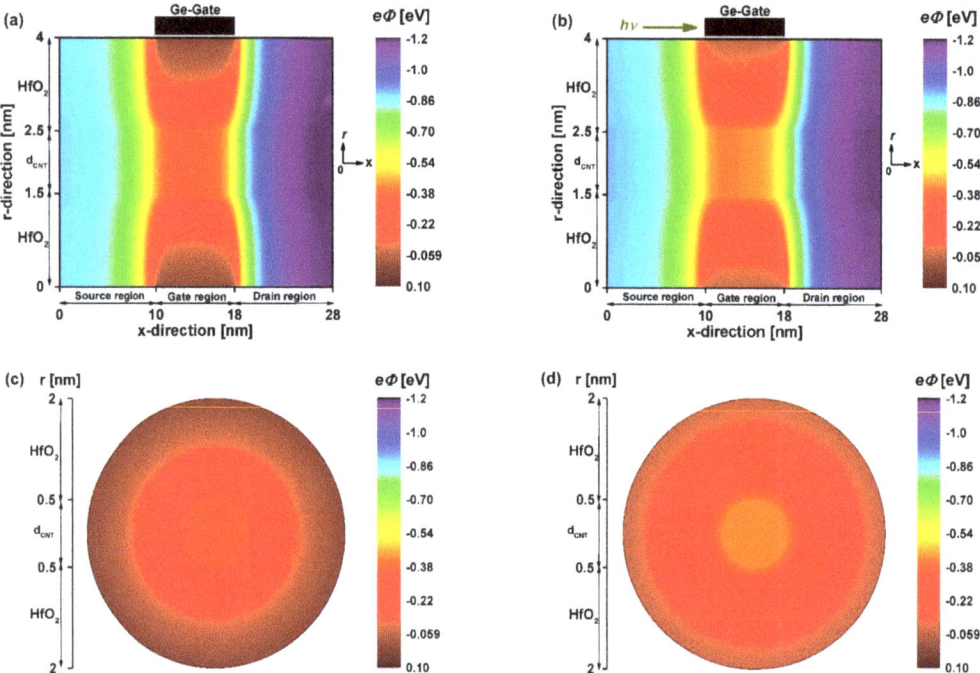

Figure 7. 2D potential distribution of the 8 nm coaxial-gate junctionless carbon nanotube field-effect phototransistor before (**a**,**c**) after (**b**,**d**) illumination at V_{DS} = 0.3 V. The top figures are drawn from the nodes at the lengthwise cut view, while the bottom figures are extracted from the nodes at the middle cross-section of the nano-phototransistor. V_{PH} = 0.07 V is considered as an infrared light-induced photovoltage.

Figure 8 shows the maximum photosensitivities of the nanoscale carbon-based phototransistors under investigation, which were drawn from the subthreshold photosensing regime due to the high sensitivity that it can provide toward the measurand-induced effective V_{GS} modulation [42]. As shown, the junctionless nanoscale carbon-based phototransistors exhibited higher photosensitivities than those provided by inversion-mode nanoscale phototransistors. In addition, on comparing the IM GNR/CNT-based nanoscale phototransistors, the IM-GNRFET exhibited higher photosensitivity than that provided by IM-CNTFET; equivalently, the IM-GNRFET exhibited a steeper optical subthreshold swing. A similar observation was recorded for the junctionless nano-phototransistors, where the JL-GNRFET provides higher photosensitivity than its JL-CNTFET counterpart.

In order to understand the superiority of junctionless nanoscale phototransistors over the inversion-mode nanoscale phototransistors in terms of photosensitivity, we plotted in Figure 9 the transfer characteristics and the potential profile of the ultrascaled carbon-based phototransistors under investigation. Inspecting Figure 9a,b showing the transfer characteristics, we can clearly observe that the junctionless paradigm improved the I_{DS}-V_{GS} propriety of both carbon-based nanoscale photo-FETs, where a decrease in off-current is clearly visible leading to an improvement in terms of subthreshold swing and current while explaining the superiority of JL photo-FETs over IM photo-FETs in terms of photosensitivity, as shown in Figure 8. It is worth noting that the steeper SS is, the higher photosensitivity is, since the photosensing principle is based on the light-induced gate photovoltage and because the subthreshold swing can be viewed as the sensitivity of drain current to the variation in effective gate voltage [49–52]. Figure 9c,d show how the junctionless mode improves the subthreshold characteristics by lowering the leakage current and decreasing the swing factor. As shown, the consideration of the junctionless paradigm or, equivalently, the uniform n-type doping profile, dilated the potential barrier while mitigating the direct source-to-drain tunneling (DSDT), which is more significant in sub-10 carbon nanotube/ribbons-based FETs [39,40]. This junctionless-mode-induced immunity against the DSDT leakage explains the recorded decrease in off-current and subthreshold swing, which were the physical cause of the recorded enhancement in photosensitivity.

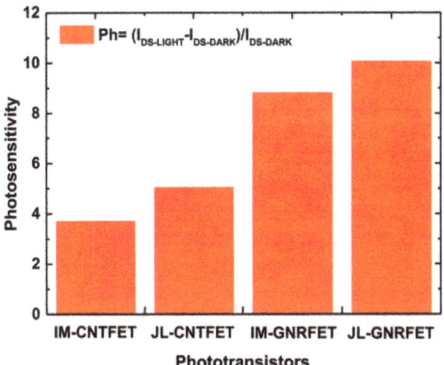

Figure 8. Photosensitivity of IM/JL CNTFET- and IM/JL GNRFET-based nano-phototransistors.

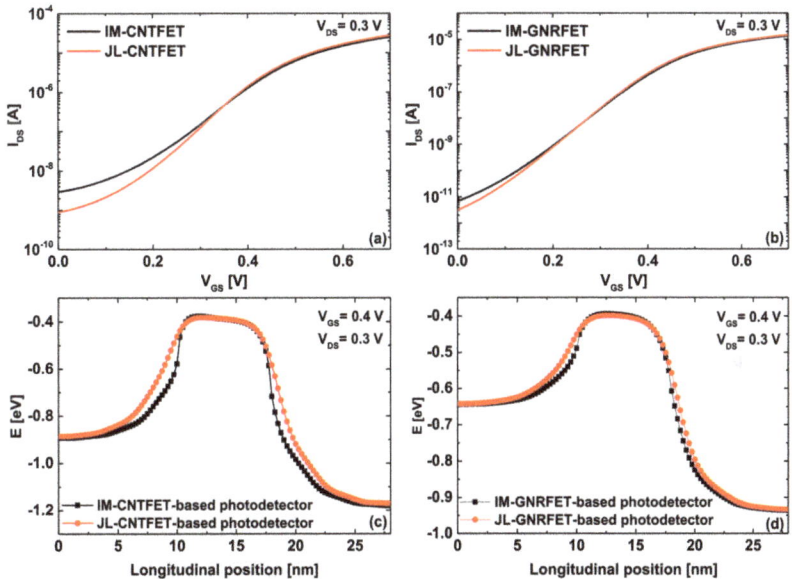

Figure 9. Transfer characteristics of (**a**) IM/JL-CNTFET and (**b**) IM/JL-GNRFET. The potential profile of (**c**) IM/JL-CNTFET and (**d**) IM/JL-GNRFET at V_{GS} = 0.4 V and V_{DS} = 0.3 V.

In the literature, the impact of change in the width (diameter) of the carbon nanoribbon (nanotube) on the GNR(CNT)FET's subthreshold performance has been found significant because of the bandgap/effective mass-width (diameter) dependence [32,42]. For this reason, we plotted in Figure 10 the subthreshold swing and photosensitivity of the nanoscale carbon phototransistors as a function of energy bandgap and diameter/width variation. As described above, the steep nano-FETs (i.e., having low subthreshold swing) are logically expected to have high photosensitivity basing on the principle of the light-induced gate photovoltage. For this reason, we can see in the three plots of Figure 10 that the photosensitivity increased with the subthreshold swing's decrease. Inspecting the figures, one can also see that the diameter/width-decrease-induced energy bandgap energy increase improved the subthreshold swing and photosensitivity of JL CNT/GNR phototransistors. This improvement, caused by the diameter/width-decrease-induced energy bandgap increase, can be explained by the mitigation of tunneling currents including the leakage current known as the band-to-band tunneling [52,53]. Inspecting Figure 10a, one can see that the curvature effects, which can be a concern in the reliability of CNTFET performance, can seriously limit the scalability and the efficiency of the improvement technique based on the CNT diameter variation. On the other hand, in the GNRFET's case (for both families), we can see that ultrascaled widths were required to achieve the ideal FET subthreshold swing (i.e., 60 mV/dec) and the ultimate photosensitivity, which is challenging from the fabrication point of view. More importantly, by comparing the GNRFETs with armchair-edge GNRs of n = 3p with those of n = 3p + 1 dimer, we can clearly observe that the GNRFETs with n = 3p + 1 channels exhibited higher photosensitivity and steeper swing factor than those with n = 3p channels. This is attributed to the larger effective mass of n = 3p + 1 GNRs as well as their higher energy bandgap, which allow better switching with improved SS values due to the resulted mitigation in tunneling subthreshold currents. It is worth noting that the third AGNR family of n = 3p + 2 was not considered because it contains close-to-metallic GNRs with a very small energy bandgap, which are not suitable for FET applications including the phototransistors as in the graphene field-effect transistor (GFET) [53–55].

The swing factor–photosensitivity dependence described above has beneficial technological implications, such that the engineering of dielectric material and its thickness can be normally adopted to improve the electrostatic gating while converging to the ideal SS [39,40] and the optimal photosensitivity. The doping-engineering-based improvement technique (while keeping the junctionless paradigm) [40] can also be employed to improve the subthreshold characteristics via the dilation in the potential barrier. However, the present uniform doping remains less complicated in the manufacturing process, which is beneficial for mass production and advanced optoelectronics based on array configurations. More importantly, since the JL CNT/GNRFET can provide subthermionic subthreshold swing (very high photosensitivity) when they are operated in band-to-band regime [48,52], the assessment and performance projection of nanoscale BTBT GNR/CNT phototransistor can be an exciting matter for further computational investigations. From another perspective, the steep transistors based on tunneling mechanism [56–58] and negative capacitance paradigm [59–65] can be advanced nano-phototransistors while forming a matter for further investigations.

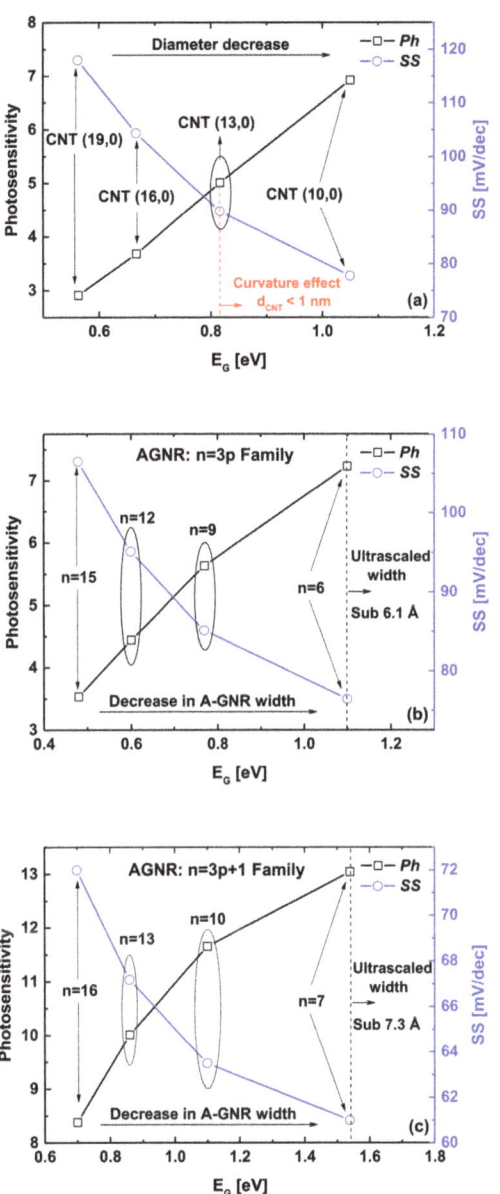

Figure 10. Impact of change in (**a**) ZCNT diameter and (**b**,**c**) AGNR width, on the photosensitivity and SS of the nanoscale phototransistors under investigation. λ = 1550 nm, P_{INC} = 1 nW with V_{PH} = 0.07 V.

5. Conclusions

In this paper, carbon-based junctionless phototransistors endowed with sub-10 nm photogate lengths were computationally assessed using the NEGF simulation. The light-induced modulation of electrostatics through the photogate was employed as a photo-sensing principle. The impact of the light illumination on the transport of carbon-based junctionless phototransistors was thoroughly analyzed via the energy-position-resolved electron density. It was found that the junctionless paradigm is efficient in boosting the photosensitivity of GNR/CNT-based phototransistors by dilating the potential barrier while mitigating the tunneling currents and improving the subthreshold characteristics; however, the thermionic limit imposed a limitation in terms of photosensitivity in both junctionless phototransistors. From the comparison point of view, the GNR-based junctionless phototransistors exhibited higher photosensitivity than the CNT-based junctionless phototransistors. In addition, we also analyzed the role of change in ZCNT (AGNR) diameter (width), in improving the subthreshold and photosensing performance through the modulation in energy bandgap, where the phototransistors based on AGNR with n = 3p + 1 showed intriguing photosensing performance due to the higher effective mass and larger bandgap, which have a direct reflection on the tunneling currents, which are the leading cause of subthreshold swing degradation. Considering the performed comparative analysis on the subthreshold swing–photosensitivity dependence, we believe that the n-n-n JL CNT/GNR field-effect phototransistors operating in the band-to-band regime (i.e., the on-state is controlled by the BTBT current while the off-state is the cause of DSDT current) can open a new way to achieve very high photosensitivity (sub-thermionic subthreshold swing) using an easy-to-make JL-based structure.

Author Contributions: Conceptualization, K.T.; supervision, K.T.; methodology, K.T.; software, K.T.; validation, K.T.; formal analysis, K.T.; resources, K.T.; investigation, K.T. and J.M.; data curation, K.T., J.M., A.K., R.P., M.A., and R.K.; writing—original draft preparation, K.T., J.M., A.K., R.P., M.A., and R.K.; writing—review and editing, K.T., J.M., A.K., R.P., M.A., and R.K.; visualization, K.T., J.M., A.K., R.P., M.A., and R.K. All authors have read and agreed to the published version of the manuscript.

Funding: This research received no external funding.

Institutional Review Board Statement: Not applicable.

Informed Consent Statement: Not applicable.

Data Availability Statement: Not applicable.

Acknowledgments: K.T. would like to thank the DGRSDT, Algeria. The first author would also to thank the Laboratory of Inverse Problems, Modeling, Information, and Systems (PIMIS), Guelma University, Guelma, Algeria, for providing computational support. This work was supported by the German Research Foundation (DFG) and the Technical University of Munich (TUM) in the framework of the Open Access Publishing Program.

Conflicts of Interest: The authors declare no conflict of interest.

References

1. DJariwala, D.; Sangwan, V.K.; Lauhon, L.J.; Marks, T.J.; Hersam, M.C. Carbon nanomaterials for electronics, optoelectronics, photovoltaics, and sensing. *Chem. Soc. Rev.* **2012**, *42*, 2824–2860. [CrossRef] [PubMed]
2. Avouris, P.; Freitag, M.; Perebeinos, V. Carbon-nanotube photonics and optoelectronics. *Nat. Photonics* **2008**, *2*, 341–350. [CrossRef]
3. Garg, R.; Dutta, N.K.; Choudhury, N.R. Work Function Engineering of Graphene. *Nanomaterials* **2014**, *4*, 267–300. [CrossRef] [PubMed]
4. Du, J.; Pei, S.; Ma, L.; Cheng, H.-M. 25th Anniversary Article: Carbon Nanotube- and Graphene-Based Transparent Conductive Films for Optoelectronic Devices. *Adv. Mater.* **2014**, *26*, 1958–1991. [CrossRef]
5. Avouris, P.; Chen, J. Nanotube electronics and optoelectronics. *Mater. Today* **2006**, *9*, 46–54. [CrossRef]
6. Marcus, M.S.; Simmons, J.M.; Castellini, O.M.; Hamers, R.; Eriksson, M.A. Photogating carbon nanotube transistors. *J. Appl. Phys.* **2006**, *100*, 084306. [CrossRef]
7. Chen, H.Z.; Xi, N.; Lai, K.W.C.; Chen, L.L.; Yang, R.; Song, B. Gate dependent photo-responses of carbon nanotube field effect phototransistors. *Nanotechnology* **2012**, *23*, 385203. [CrossRef]
8. Salimian, S.; Araghi, M.E.A. Study of the preparation and spectral response of stacked graphene nanoribbon-carbon nanotube-based phototransistors. *Carbon* **2016**, *107*, 754–764. [CrossRef]
9. Chang, H.; Wu, H. Graphene-Based Nanomaterials: Synthesis, Properties, and Optical and Optoelectronic Applications. *Adv. Funct. Mater.* **2012**, *23*, 1984–1997. [CrossRef]
10. Tamersit, K. Energy-Efficient Carbon Nanotube Field-Effect Phototransistors: Quantum Simulation, Device Physics, and Photosensitivity Analysis. *IEEE Sens. J.* **2021**, *22*, 288–296. [CrossRef]
11. Castro Neto, A.H.; Guinea, F.; Peres, N.M.R.; Novoselov, K.S.; Geim, A.K. The electronic properties of graphene. *Rev. Mod. Phys.* **2009**, *81*, 109–162. [CrossRef]

12. Baughman, R.H.; Zakhidov, A.A.; de Heer, W.A. Carbon Nanotubes—The Route Toward Applications. *Science* **2002**, *297*, 787–792. [CrossRef] [PubMed]
13. Polat, E.O.; Mercier, G.; Nikitskiy, I.; Puma, E.; Galan, T.; Gupta, S.; Montagut, M.; Piqueras, J.J.; Bouwens, M.; Durduran, T.; et al. Flexible graphene photodetectors for wearable fitness monitoring. *Sci. Adv.* **2019**, *5*, eaaw7846. [CrossRef] [PubMed]
14. Voronin, K.V.; Ermolaev, G.A.; Stebunov, Y.V.; Arsenin, A.V.; Bylinkin, A.N.; Jensen, B.B.E.; Jørgensen, B.; Volkov, V.S. Photogating in graphene field-effect phototransistors: Theory and observations. In Proceedings of Inter-National Congress on Graphene, 2d Materials and Applications (2D MATERIALS 2019); AIP Publishing: Woodbury, New York, NY, USA; 2021; Volume 2359, p. 020034. [CrossRef]
15. Vaquero, D.; Clericò, V.; Salvador-Sánchez, J.; Díaz, E.; Domínguez-Adame, F.; Chico, L.; Meziani, Y.M.; Diez, E.; Quereda, J. Fast response photogating in monolayer MoS_2 phototransistors. *Nanoscale* **2021**, *13*, 16156–16163. [CrossRef]
16. Fang, H.; Hu, W. Photogating in Low Dimensional Photodetectors. *Adv. Sci.* **2017**, *4*, 1700323. [CrossRef] [PubMed]
17. Going, R.W.; Loo, J.; Liu, T.-J.K.; Wu, M.C. Germanium Gate PhotoMOSFET Integrated to Silicon Photonics. *IEEE J. Sel. Top. Quantum Electron.* **2013**, *20*, 1–7. [CrossRef]
18. Guo, J.; Alam, M.A.; Yoon, Y. Theoretical investigation on photoconductivity of single intrinsic carbon nanotubes. *Appl. Phys. Lett.* **2006**, *88*, 133111. [CrossRef]
19. Gao, Q.; Guo, J. Quantum mechanical simulation of graphene photodetectors. *J. Appl. Phys.* **2012**, *112*, 084316. [CrossRef]
20. Joshi, S.; Dubey, P.K.; Kaushik, B.K. A Transition Metal Dichalcogenide Tunnel FET-Based Waveguide-Integrated Photodetector Using Ge for Near-Infrared Detection. *IEEE Sens. J.* **2019**, *19*, 9187–9193. [CrossRef]
21. Joshi, S.; Dubey, P.K.; Kaushik, B.K. Photosensor Based on Split Gate TMD TFET Using Photogating Effect for Visible Light Detection. *IEEE Sens. J.* **2020**, *20*, 6346–6353. [CrossRef]
22. Kadri, A.; Djeffal, F.; Ferhati, H.; Menacer, F.; Dibi, Z. Performance analysis of a new graphene based-phototransistor for ultra-sensitive infrared sensing applications. *Optik* **2018**, *176*, 24–31. [CrossRef]
23. Farah, S.; Ferhati, H.; Dibi, Z.; Djeffal, F. Performance analysis of broadband Mid-IR graphene-phototransistor using strained black phosphorus sensing gate: DFT-NEGF investigation. *Superlattices Microstruct.* **2022**, 107187. [CrossRef]
24. Kadri, A.; Ferhati, H.; Djeffal, F. Giant responsivity of a new optically controlled graphene UV-phototransistor using graded band-gap ZnMgO gate. *Sens. Actuators A Phys.* **2021**, *325*, 112701. [CrossRef]
25. Fiori, G.; Bonaccorso, F.; Iannaccone, G.; Palacios, T.; Neumaier, D.; Seabaugh, A.; Banerjee, S.K.; Colombo, L. Electronics based on two-dimensional materials. *Nat. Nanotechnol.* **2014**, *9*, 768–779. [CrossRef] [PubMed]
26. Tamersit, K. A new ultra-scaled graphene nanoribbon junctionless tunneling field-effect transistor: Proposal, quantum simulation, and analysis. *J. Comput. Electron.* **2019**, *19*, 170–176. [CrossRef]
27. Tamersit, K.; Kouzou, A.; Bourouba, H.; Kennel, R.; Abdelrahem, M. Synergy of electrostatic and chemical doping to improve the performance of junctionless carbon nanotube tunneling field-effect transistors: Ultrascaling, energy-efficiency, and high switching performance. *Nanomaterials* **2022**, *12*, 462. [CrossRef]
28. Hammam, A.; Schmidt, M.E.; Muruganathan, M.; Suzuki, S.; Mizuta, H. Sub-10 nm graphene nano-ribbon tunnel field-effect transistor. *Carbon* **2018**, *126*, 588–593. [CrossRef]
29. Colinge, J.P.; Lee, C.W.; Akhavan, N.D.; Yan, R.; Ferain, I.; Razavi, P.; Kranti, A.; Yu, R. Junctionless Transistors: Physics and Properties. In *Semiconductor-On-Insulator Materials for Nanoelec-tronics Applications*; Springer: Berlin/Heidelberg, Germany, 2011; pp. 187–200. [CrossRef]
30. Zhao, P.; Guo, J. Modeling edge effects in graphene nanoribbon field-effect transistors with real and mode space methods. *J. Appl. Phys.* **2009**, *105*, 034503. [CrossRef]
31. Yousefi, R.; Shabani, M.O.; Arjmandi, M.; Ghoreishi, S. A computational study on electrical characteristics of a novel band-to-band tunneling graphene nanoribbon FET. *Superlattices Microstruct.* **2013**, *60*, 169–178. [CrossRef]
32. Koswatta, S.O.; Hasan, S.; Lundstrom, M.S.; Anantram, M.P.; Nikonov, D. Nonequilibrium Green's Function Treatment of Phonon Scattering in Carbon-Nanotube Transistors. *IEEE Trans. Electron Devices* **2007**, *54*, 2339–2351. [CrossRef]
33. Tamersit, K. An ultra-sensitive gas nanosensor based on asymmetric dual-gate graphene nanoribbon field-effect transistor: Proposal and investigation. *J. Comput. Electron.* **2019**, *18*, 846–855. [CrossRef]
34. Son, Y.-W.; Cohen, M.L.; Louie, S.G. Energy Gaps in Graphene Nanoribbons. *Phys. Rev. Lett.* **2006**, *97*, 216803. [CrossRef] [PubMed]
35. Guo, J.; Datta, S.; Lundstrom, M.; Anantam, M.P. Toward Multiscale Modeling of Carbon Nanotube Transistors. *Int. J. Multiscale Comput. Eng.* **2004**, *2*, 257–276. [CrossRef]
36. Ghoreishi, S.S.; Vadizadeh, M.; Yousefi, R.; Afzalian, A. Low-Power Ultradeep-Submicrometer Junctionless Carbon Nanotube Field-Effect Diode. *IEEE Trans. Electron Devices* **2021**, *69*, 400–405. [CrossRef]
37. Tamersit, K. Improving the performance of a junctionless carbon nanotube field-effect transistor using a split-gate. *AEU-Int. J. Electron. Commun.* **2020**, *115*, 153035. [CrossRef]
38. Colinge, J.-P.; Lee, C.-W.; Afzalian, A.; Akhavan, N.D.; Yan, R.; Ferain, I.; Razavi, P.; O'Neill, B.; Blake, A.; White, M.; et al. Nanowire transistors without junctions. *Nat. Nanotechnol.* **2010**, *5*, 225–229. [CrossRef]
39. Tamersit, K. A computational study of short-channel effects in double-gate junctionless graphene nanoribbon field-effect transistors. *J. Comput. Electron.* **2019**, *18*, 1214–1221. [CrossRef]

40. Tamersit, K. Sub-10 nm junctionless carbon nanotube field-effect transistors with improved performance. *AEU-Int. J. Electron. Commun.* **2020**, *124*, 153354. [CrossRef]
41. Liu, M.; Wang, H.; Tang, Q.; Zhao, X.; Tong, Y.; Liu, Y. Ultrathin Air-Stable n-Type Organic Phototransistor Array for Conformal Optoelectronics. *Sci. Rep.* **2018**, *8*, 16612. [CrossRef]
42. Tamersit, K.; Djeffal, F. Double-Gate Graphene Nanoribbon Field-Effect Transistor for DNA and Gas Sensing Applications: Simulation Study and Sensitivity Analysis. *IEEE Sens. J.* **2016**, *16*, 4180–4191. [CrossRef]
43. Tamersit, K. Performance enhancement of an ultra-scaled double-gate graphene nanoribbon tunnel field-effect transistor using channel doping engineering: Quantum simulation study. *AEU-Int. J. Electron. Commun.* **2020**, *122*, 153287. [CrossRef]
44. Datta, S. Nanoscale device modeling: The Green's function method. *Superlattices Microstruct.* **2000**, *28*, 253–278. [CrossRef]
45. Datta, S. *Electronic Transport in Mesoscopic Systems*; Cambridge University Press: Cambridge, UK, 1997.
46. Tamersit, K.; Djeffal, F. A computationally efficient hybrid approach based on artificial neural networks and the wavelet transform for quantum simulations of graphene nanoribbon FETs. *J. Comput. Electron.* **2019**, *18*, 813–825. [CrossRef]
47. Moghaddam, S.; Ghoreishi, S.S.; Yousefi, R.; Aderang, H. Quantum simulation of a junctionless carbon nanotube field-effect transistor under torsional strain. *Superlattices Microstruct.* **2019**, *138*, 106239. [CrossRef]
48. Tamersit, K.; Ramezani, Z.; Amiri, I.S. Improved performance of sub-10-nm band-to-band tunneling n-i-n graphene nanoribbon field-effect transistors using underlap engineering: A quantum simulation study. *J. Phys. Chem. Solids* **2022**, *160*, 110312. [CrossRef]
49. Tamersit, K. A novel band-to-band tunneling junctionless carbon nanotube field-effect transistor with lightly doped pocket: Proposal, assessment, and quantum transport analysis. *Phys. E Low-Dimens. Syst. Nanostruct.* **2021**, *128*, 114609. [CrossRef]
50. Dassi, M.; Madan, J.; Pandey, R.; Sharma, R. Chemical modulation of conducting polymer gate electrode work function based double gate Mg2Si TFET for gas sensing applications. *J. Mater. Sci. Mater. Electron.* **2022**, 1–10. [CrossRef]
51. Mehrad, M.; Zareiee, M. Using Hetro-Structure Window in Nano Scale Junctionless SOI MOSFET for High Electrical Performance. *ECS J. Solid State Sci. Technol.* **2021**, *10*, 111005. [CrossRef]
52. Tamersit, K. New nanoscale band-to-band tunneling junctionless GNRFETs: Potential high-performance devices for the ultrascaled regime. *J. Comput. Electron.* **2021**, *20*, 1147–1156. [CrossRef]
53. Banadaki, Y.M.; Srivastava, A. Investigation of the width-dependent static characteristics of graphene nanoribbon field effect transistors using non-parabolic quantum-based model. *Solid-State Electron.* **2015**, *111*, 80–90. [CrossRef]
54. Banadaki, Y.M.; Srivastava, A. Scaling Effects on Static Metrics and Switching Attributes of Graphene Nanoribbon FET for Emerging Technology. *IEEE Trans. Emerg. Top. Comput.* **2015**, *3*, 458–469. [CrossRef]
55. Tamersit, K.; Kotti, M.; Fakhfakh, M. A new pressure microsensor based on dual-gate graphene field-effect transistor with a vertically movable top-gate: Proposal, analysis, and optimization. *AEU-Int. J. Electron. Commun.* **2020**, *124*, 153346. [CrossRef]
56. Tamersit, K. Improved performance of nanoscale junctionless carbon nanotube tunneling FETs using dual-material source gate design: A quantum simulation study. *AEU-Int. J. Electron. Commun.* **2020**, *127*, 153491. [CrossRef]
57. Anvarifard, M.K.; Ramezani, Z.; Amiri, I.S.; Tamersit, K.; Nejad, A.M. Profound analysis on sensing performance of Nanogap SiGe source DM-TFET biosensor. *J. Mater. Sci. Mater. Electron.* **2020**, *31*, 22699–22712. [CrossRef]
58. Tamersit, K. Boosting the performance of an ultrascaled carbon nanotube junctionless tunnel field-effect transistor using an ungated region: NEGF simulation. *J. Comput. Electron.* **2019**, *18*, 1222–1228. [CrossRef]
59. Jooq, M.K.Q.; Moaiyeri, M.H.; Tamersit, K. Ultra-Compact Ternary Logic Gates Based on Negative Capacitance Carbon Nanotube FETs. *IEEE Trans. Circuits Syst. II Express Briefs* **2020**, *68*, 2162–2166. [CrossRef]
60. Tamersit, K. Improved Switching Performance of Nanoscale p-i-n Carbon Nanotube Tunneling Field-Effect Transistors Using Metal-Ferroelectric-Metal Gating Approach. *ECS J. Solid State Sci. Technol.* **2021**, *10*, 031004. [CrossRef]
61. Tamersit, K.; Jooq, M.K.Q.; Moaiyeri, M.H. Analog/RF performance assessment of ferroelectric junctionless carbon nanotube FETs: A quantum simulation study. *Phys. E Low-Dimens. Syst. Nanostruct.* **2021**, *134*, 114915. [CrossRef]
62. Behbahani, F.; Jooq, M.K.Q.; Moaiyeri, M.H.; Tamersit, K. Leveraging Negative Capacitance CNTFETs for Image Processing: An Ultra-Efficient Ternary Image Edge Detection Hardware. *IEEE Trans. Circuits Syst. I Regul. Pap.* **2021**, *68*, 5108–5119. [CrossRef]
63. Salahuddin, S.; Datta, S. Use of Negative Capacitance to Provide Voltage Amplification for Low Power Nanoscale Devices. *Nano Lett.* **2007**, *8*, 405–410. [CrossRef]
64. Tu, L.; Wang, X.; Wang, J.; Meng, X.; Chu, J. Ferroelectric Negative Capacitance Field Effect Transistor. *Adv. Electron. Mater.* **2018**, *4*, 1800231. [CrossRef]
65. Wong, J.C.; Salahuddin, S. Negative Capacitance Transistors. *Proc. IEEE* **2019**, *107*, 49–62. [CrossRef]

Article

Synergy of Electrostatic and Chemical Doping to Improve the Performance of Junctionless Carbon Nanotube Tunneling Field-Effect Transistors: Ultrascaling, Energy-Efficiency, and High Switching Performance

Khalil Tamersit [1,2,3,*], Abdellah Kouzou [4,5,6], Hocine Bourouba [1,3], Ralph Kennel [6] and Mohamed Abdelrahem [6,7,*]

1. Department of Electronics and Telecommunications, Université 8 Mai 1945 Guelma, Guelma 24000, Algeria; bourouba.hocine@univ-guelma.dz
2. Department of Electrical and Automatic Engineering, Université 8 Mai 1945 Guelma, Guelma 24000, Algeria
3. Laboratory of Inverse Problems, Modeling, Information and Systems (PIMIS), Université 8 Mai 1945 Guelma, Guelma 24000, Algeria
4. Applied Automation and Industrial Diagnosis Laboratory (LAADI), Faculty of Science and Technology, Djelfa University, Djelfa 17000, Algeria; kouzouabdellah@ieee.org
5. Electrical and Electronics Engineering Department, Nisantasi University, Istanbul 34398, Turkey
6. Institute for Electrical Drive Systems and Power Electronics (EAL), Technical University of Munich (TUM), 80333 Munich, Germany; ralph.kennel@tum.de
7. Electrical Engineering Department, Faculty of Engineering, Assiut University, Assiut 71516, Egypt
* Correspondence: tamersit_khalil@hotmail.fr (K.T.); mohamed.abdelrahem@tum.de (M.A.)

Citation: Tamersit, K.; Kouzou, A.; Bourouba, H.; Kennel, R.; Abdelrahem, M. Synergy of Electrostatic and Chemical Doping to Improve the Performance of Junctionless Carbon Nanotube Tunneling Field-Effect Transistors: Ultrascaling, Energy-Efficiency, and High Switching Performance. *Nanomaterials* 2022, 12, 462. https://doi.org/10.3390/nano12030462

Academic Editor: Antonio Di Bartolomeo

Received: 8 December 2021
Accepted: 26 January 2022
Published: 28 January 2022

Publisher's Note: MDPI stays neutral with regard to jurisdictional claims in published maps and institutional affiliations.

Copyright: © 2022 by the authors. Licensee MDPI, Basel, Switzerland. This article is an open access article distributed under the terms and conditions of the Creative Commons Attribution (CC BY) license (https://creativecommons.org/licenses/by/4.0/).

Abstract: The low on-current and direct source-to-drain tunneling (DSDT) issues are the main drawbacks in the ultrascaled tunneling field-effect transistors based on carbon nanotube and ribbons. In this article, the performance of nanoscale junctionless carbon nanotube tunneling field-effect transistors (JL CNTTFETs) is greatly improved by using the synergy of electrostatic and chemical doping engineering. The computational investigation is conducted via a quantum simulation approach, which solves self-consistently the Poisson equation and the non-equilibrium Green's function (NEGF) formalism in the ballistic limit. The proposed high-performance JL CNTTFET is endowed with a particular doping approach in the aim of shrinking the band-to-band tunneling (BTBT) window and dilating the direct source-to-drain tunneling window, while keeping the junctionless paradigm. The obtained improvements include the on-current, off-current, ambipolar behavior, leakage current, I_{60} metric, subthreshold swing, current ratio, intrinsic delay, and power-delay product. The scaling capability of the proposed design was also assessed, where greatly improved switching performance and sub-thermionic subthreshold swing were recorded by using JL CNTTFET with 5 nm gate length. Moreover, a ferroelectric-based gating approach was employed for more enhancements, where further improvements in terms of switching performance were recorded. The obtained results and the conducted quantum transport analyses indicate that the proposed improvement approach can be followed to improve similar cutting-edge ultrascaled junctionless tunnel field-effect transistors based on emerging atomically thin nanomaterials.

Keywords: carbon nanotube; junctionless; tunnel field effect transistors; chemical doping; electrostatic doping; NEGF simulation; band-to-band tunneling; switching performance; nanoscale

1. Introduction

Sub-thermionic subthreshold swing provided by nanoscale-tunnel field-effect transistors (TFETs) enables a decrease in power supply voltage, which is a prerequisite in ultralow power applications, such as the internet of things (IoT) [1,2]. In the last decade, the great progress experienced in nanomaterials science have given an additional asset and new impulses to TFETs technology, which can play a leading role in the extension of Moore's Law that converges to its end [2–5]. In the ultrascaled regime, the accuracy of nanofabrication is crucial for the reliability of elementary nanoelectronic nanodevices, as it can affect the performance of electronic circuits and systems [2–6]. In this context, the junctionless paradigm has shown its efficiency in simplifying the elaboration of ultrascaled FETs on the one hand and in improving their performance on the other hand [6–9]. Combining the benefits of the junctionless paradigm with the amazing features of tunneling transistors has been the subject of promising devices called junctionless-tunnel field-effect transistors (JL TFETs) [9]. In these devices, the channel doping is performed by the electrostatic and chemical doping, while ensuring the operating regime of tunneling FETs with a double benefit in terms of the facility of fabrication and high performance [9,10].

In the literature, the junctionless-carbon-nanotube-tunnel field-effect transistors (JL CNTTFETs) have shown promising subthreshold and switching performance [5,10,11] due to the amazing characteristics of carbon nanotube (CNT) as mature channel material, such as atomic structure, tunable band gap, high electrical conductivity, quasi-ballistic property, high Fermi velocity, and high sensitivity to its surrounded electrostatics (i.e., the electrostatic gating) [12–15]. However, as any electronic nanodevice, the ultrascaled JL CNTTFET suffers from some weaknesses, namely the low on-current and the issue of direct source-to-drain tunneling (DSDT), which is attributed to the low effective mass in the carbon nanotube [16–18]. Note that the DSDT phenomenon is the main cause in degrading the switching and subthreshold performance of CNT tunnel FETs in ultrascaled regime [18]. Recently, an ultrascaled CNTTFET with p-n doping profile has been proposed, showing spectacular improvements in terms of subthreshold and switching performance, including the on-current [18]. However, the p-n junction is still an intractable task even with the experienced progress in nanofabrication, including the doping techniques. A negative-capacitance carbon-nanotube-tunnel field-effect transistor (NC CNTTFET) has also been proposed recently through a quantum simulation study, where improved on-current was recorded by dint of ferroelectric-induced amplified inner-gate voltage [19]. However, the instability in NC-FET is still a concern. Moreover, the heterogeneous structure has been found as an intriguing approach to improve the on-current of CNTTFET with carbon nanotube-GNR heterojunctions [20]. However, the accurate realization of such an atomistic heterojunction is complicated and budget consuming, which is a concern. Therefore, new innovative techniques and simple improvement approaches should be developed while considering the fabrication aspect and TFET performance.

In this computational work, an efficient approach based on the synergy of electrostatic and chemical-doping engineering is proposed to boost the subthreshold and switching performance of sub–10 nm junctionless-carbon-nanotube-tunnel field-effect transistors. The proposed viable approach has been found to be very efficient in shrinking the band-to-band tunneling (BTBT) window and dilating the DSDT barrier, while boosting the subthreshold and switching performance of ultrascaled JL CNTTFET. The improved characteristics include the on-current, off-current, current ratio, subthreshold swing, leakage current, ambipolar behavior, I_{60} factor, power-delay product, and intrinsic delay. The proposed design has also shown high-performance in ultrascaled regime (with 5-nm gate length), where the sub-thermionic SS and high current ratio have been within reach.

The rest of this article is structured as follows. Section 2 details the proposed TFET structure. Section 3 summarizes the quantum simulation approach. Section 4 is devoted to present and discuss the results. Section 5 contains the conclusion.

2. Device Structure

Figure 1a shows the three-dimensional (3D) structure of the junctionless-carbon-nanotube-tunneling field-effect transistor (JL CNTTFET). The shape of the nanodevice follows the cylindricity of the carbon-nanotube channel, and, thus, coaxial gates are considered accordingly. Note that the gate-all-around (GAA) configuration is found to be more efficient in terms of controlling the carrier transport [21,22]. In addition, the GAA structure really supports the assumption of uniform electrostatics in radial direction, thus making the simulation less complex [22]. In this work, a small CNT diameter was used, due to its appropriateness in terms of device electrical performance. Figure 1b shows the lengthwise-cut view of the uniformly doped JL CNTTFET. As shown, the tunneling FET is endowed with an auxiliary gate (P-gate) to electrostatically p-type dope the source side in order to preserve the junctionless aspect on CNT channel while achieving the tunneling FET operating regime [9]. As we can see, the control-gate at the middle of the device governs the FET carrier transport, while the drain side is left undoped. The Hafnium oxide (HfO_2) is considered to be a gate dielectric surrounding the zigzag CNT (Z-CNT). Figure 1c shows the doping profile of the conventional JL CNTTFET, which is uniformly n-type doped from source to drain electrodes. Figure 1d shows the cross-sectional view of the proposed engineered doping (ED)-based design, EDJL CNTTFET. As shown, this latter design is similar to the baseline design shown in Figure 1b, with the exception of three differences. The first is a heavily n-type doped pocket (HDP), which is located between the two coaxial gates with α concentration [23], the second is a lightly n-type doped portion (LDP) near the drain with β concentration, and the third is an electrical p-type doping gate with a tunable applied bias that aims to match the synergy. Figure 1e shows the doping profile of the proposed JL CNTTFET, showing the heavily n-type doped pocket between the P-G and C-G gates and the LDP near the drain electrode. From a fabrication point of view, the proposed non-uniform doping profile can be reached by tuning the exposure time of the concerned CNT portions to the employed chemical dopant and thus varying the doping level as required [13,22].

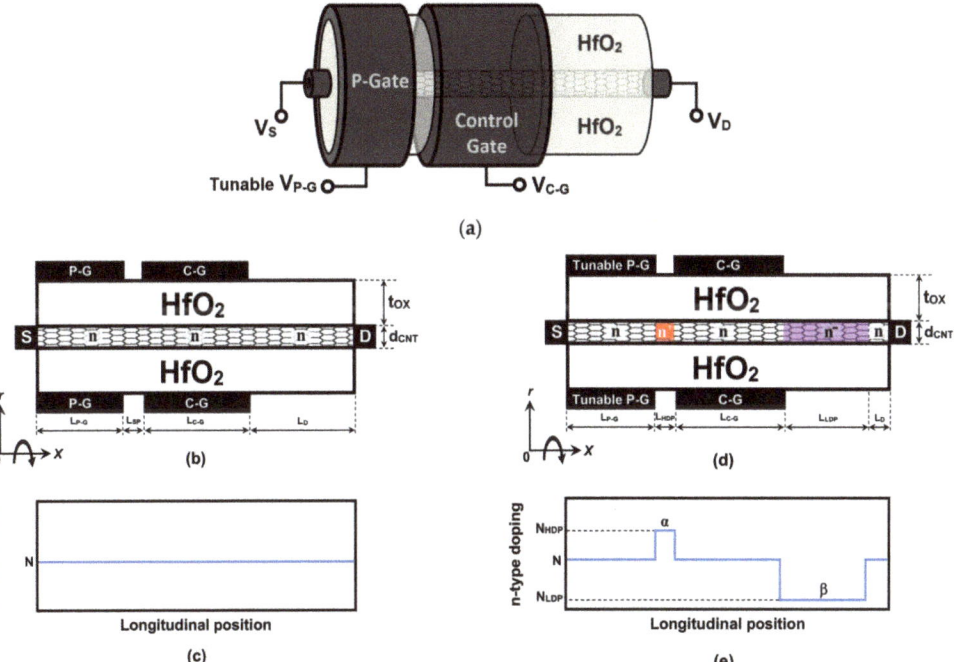

Figure 1. (a) Three-dimensional structure of the JL CNT tunneling FET. (b) Lengthwise-cut view and (c) doping profile of the conventional uniformly n-type doped JL CNT tunnel FET. (d) Lengthwise-cut view and (e) doping profile of the proposed non-uniformly n-type doped JL CNT tunnel FET with tunable P-G voltage.

All physical, electrical, and geometrical design parameters are shown in Table 1. Note that the physical backgrounds and reasons for the adopted chemical and electrical doping and their locations are discussed thoroughly in Section 4.

Table 1. Simulation parameters.

Parameter	Symbol	Value	Unit
Common parameters			
Z-CNT	(n,0)	10	-
Gap energy	E_G	~1.053	eV
CNT diameter	d_{CNT}	~7.82	Å
Gate length	L_{C-G}	10	nm
Drain length	L_D	10	nm
P-gate length	L_{P-G}	8	nm
Space between gates	L_{SP}	2	nm
S/C/D doping (CJL)	N	1	nm^{-1}
Oxide thickness	t_{OX}	1.5	nm
HfO$_2$ dielectric constant	ε_{OX}	16	-
Temperature	T	300	K
Source gate voltage	V_{P-G}	−0.8	V
Drain-to-source voltage	V_{DS}	0.4	V
Additional parameters in the proposed design			
Heavily doped pocket	N_{HDP}	3	nm^{-1}
HDP Length	L_{HDP}	2	nm
Lightly doped pocket	N_{LDP}	N/8	nm^{-1}
LDP Length	L_{LDP}	7.5	nm

3. Simulation Approach

In the literature, the common quantum simulation method used to propose, investigate, and assess advanced nanoscale CNTFETs with full soundness and high accuracy is the self-consistent computation between the non-equilibrium Green's function formalism and the Poisson equation [22–25]. The main assets of this quantum simulation method are its ability to consider most of electrostatic features and the main quantum transport phenomena, including the band-to-band and direct source-to-drain tunneling mechanisms [22–26]. For this reason, we adopted the NEGF simulation in the present computational work. The retarded Green's function is the main equation on which this quantum simulation is based, and it can be expressed in the following matrix form [26]

$$G(E) = [(E + i\eta^+)I - H_{PZ} - \Sigma_S - \Sigma_D]^{-1} \quad (1)$$

where E, η^+, H_{PZ}, I, and $\Sigma_{S(D)}$ are the energy, infinitesimal positive value, Hamiltonian matrix based on the atomistic nearest neighbor p_Z-orbital tight-binding approximation, identity matrix, and the source (drain) self-energy, respectively. In our computation, the mode space (MS) representation is employed to avoid the computational burden while considering only the relevant modes and the ballistic limit conditions [27]. Note that the source (drain) self-energy is analytically computed in accordance with the MS computational fashion [22,27]. The computation of the retarded Green's function and the S/D self-energies allows us to compute the source (drain) local density of states (LDOS), $D_{S(D)}$, using the following expressions [22]

$$D_{S(D)} = G\Gamma_{S(D)}G^\dagger \quad (2)$$

with

$$\Gamma_{S(D)} = i(\Sigma_{S(D)} - \Sigma_{S(D)}^\dagger) \quad (3)$$

where $\Gamma_{S(D)}$ denotes the energy level broadening due to the S/D contact. Now, the channel charge density is within reach, using the following equation [22]:

$$Q(x) = (-q)\int_{-\infty}^{+\infty} dE \cdot \text{sgn}[E - E_N(x)] \times \{D_S(E,x)f(\text{sgn}[E - E_N(x)](E - E_{FS})) \\ + D_D(E,x)f(\text{sgn}[E - E_N(x)](E - E_{FD}))\} \quad (4)$$

where q, sgn, E_N, f, and $E_{FS(FD)}$ are the electron charge, sign function, charge neutrality level, Fermi function, and S/D Fermi level, respectively. In the self-consistent computation, computing the charge-density Equations (1)–(4) needs information on the on-site electrostatic potential, which is approximated by solving the Poisson equation for cylindrical nano-FET structure given by the following equation [22,27]:

$$\nabla^2 U(x,r) = -\frac{\rho(x,r)}{\varepsilon} \quad (5)$$

where U, ε, and ρ are the potential distribution, the dielectric constant, and the Z-CNT charge density, including the chemical doping concentration, respectively. The Poisson equation is solved by using the finite difference method, while assuming that the potential is invariant in the coaxial direction. The Dirichlet boundary conditions are imposed on the gates' nodes, considering the relevant biases, while the Neumann boundary conditions are considered for the remaining external interfaces, including the source and drain electrodes [22,27]. After attaining the self-consistency between the Poisson solver and the MS NEGF solver, the drain current is within reach by using the following equation [22]:

$$I = \frac{4q}{\hbar} \int_{-\infty}^{+\infty} dE\, T(E)[f(E - E_{FS}) - f(E - E_{FD})] \quad (6)$$

where $\hbar$ is the Planck's constant, and $T(E)$ is the transmission coefficient, which can be computed as follows [22]:

$$T(E) = Tr\left[\Gamma_S G \Gamma_D G^\dagger\right] \quad (7)$$

where Tr denotes the trace operator. All NEGF simulations were performed by using MATLAB software. For more information and details regarding the NEGF-based quantum mechanical simulation of nanoscale carbon-nanotube FETs, we refer to our previous relevant works [24,25,28,29], where the validation of the used NEGF simulation against some experimental and theoretical data was reported.

4. Results and Discussion

The nanoscale tunneling FETs are promising nanodevices, due to their assets, namely sub-thermionic subthreshold swing, low-off current, and intriguing scaling capability. However, the low on-current is considered the main disadvantage in these promising nano-FETs. Thereafter, we show interesting improvements in on-current, off-current, and subthreshold swing, using the synergy of both chemical and electrical-doping techniques, while keeping the junctionless paradigm. Figure 2a shows how the increase in doping concentration of the heavily n-type doped pocket boosts the on-current of the JL CNTTFET. When inspecting the same figure, we can observe that the off-current is also slightly improved with the N_{HDP} increase. The recorded off-current (on-current) improvement is principally attributed to the dilation (shrinking) in the DSDT (BTBT) window induced by the heavily doped pocket. Figure 2b shows that the recorded improvement in on-current, using the heavily doped pocket, can be further enhanced by increasing negatively the applied voltage of the auxiliary p-gate that ensures the source p-type doping electrostatically. We can also see that a slight increase in off-current is recorded, while the ambipolar behavior is still the same. The recorded additional improvement in on-current is logically attributed to an additional shrinking in the BTBT window that is induced by the negatively high p-gate voltage. Therefore, in order to increasingly boost the on-current, it is appropriate to combine the HDP technique with that of the negatively high p-gate voltage.

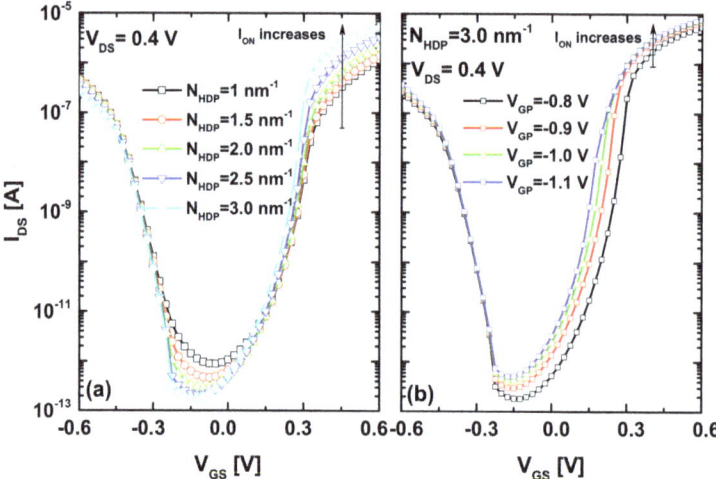

Figure 2. (a) Impact of doping concentration of the heavily n-type doped pocket between gates on the I_{DS}–V_{GS} transfer characteristics of JL CNTTFET. (b) Impact of P-gate voltage on the improved I_{DS}–V_{GS} transfer characteristics of JL CNTTFET endowed with HDP.

In order to decrease the off-current (increased with increasing the negative p-gate voltage as shown in Figure 2b) and improve the subthreshold swing, we adopted, in addition, a lightly doped portion to dilate the direct source-to-drain tunneling window, while keeping the junctionless paradigm. As expected, Figure 3a explicitly shows significant improvements in terms of on-current, off-current, subthreshold swing, and ambipolar behavior, in comparison to the conventional JL CNTTFET. We can clearly see the steep switching of the transfer characteristic, which is a highly desired feature in cutting-edge high-performance digital applications. Figure 3b shows the subthreshold swing in function with the drain current for the conventional and proposed nanoscale TFETs. This indicates that the drawn curves are important and informative, because they reveal the minimum SS on the one hand and the values of SS over the transfer characteristics on the other hand. The same figure also highlights the I_{60} factor, which denotes the highest drain current at which SS = 60 mV/dec is recorded. Note that the ideal region of the I_{60} metric in the plot is on the lower right corner, with a steep SS and high drain currents [30]. As shown, the performance of the proposed design is closest to the aforementioned region of interest, with a higher I_{60} factor in comparison to the baseline TFET. In addition, the proposed JL-CNTTFET exhibits a steeper SS than the conventional TFET over the considered I_{DS} range, and, thus, the average SS of the proposed JL-CNTTFET is smaller than that of the conventional one. It is worth noting that the proposed (conventional) design provides a minimum SS value of ~19 mV/dec (~33 mV/dec), as indicated in Figure 3a.

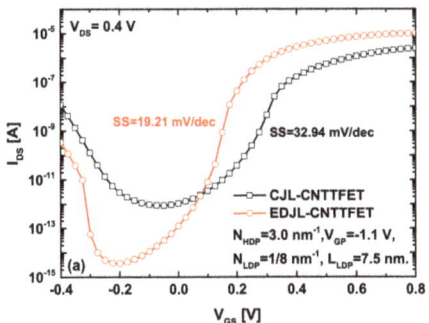 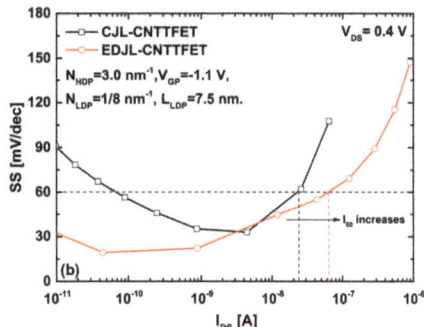

Figure 3. (a) I_{DS}–V_{GS} transfer characteristics of the conventional JL CNTTFET and the proposed JL CNTTFET, which includes the heavily n-type doped pocket, the optimized p-gate voltage, and the LDP near the drain electrode. (b) Subthreshold swing as a function of drain current for the standard and proposed nano-TFET.

Figure 4 shows the potential distribution drawn from the converged Poisson's solutions at the lengthwise-cut region. The electrostatic gating of the p-gate and the main gate is clearly seen. More important, we can see in Figure 4a that the longitudinal potential variation between the two aforementioned electrostatic-gating examples (at the level of the ungated region, framed by a discontinued line) is somewhat wide, while reflecting the long BTBT window responsible for the low on-current. However, by using the V_{PG} adjustment and heavily n-type doped pocket, we can observe a steep longitudinal potential variation at the BTBT region, as shown in Figure 4b. In this latter example, it is also clearly seen the dilation in the DSDT window that is induced by the lightly n-type doped portion near the drain, making the nano-TFET more immune to the DSDT leakage, contrary to the conventional case.

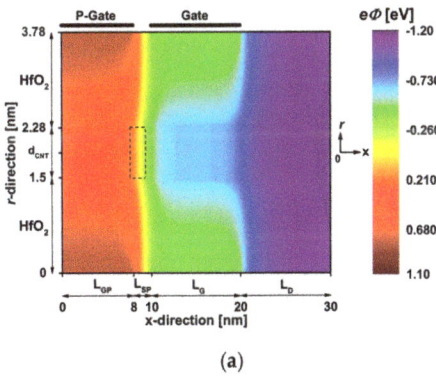 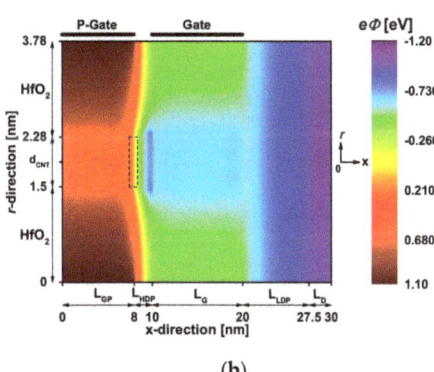

Figure 4. Two-dimensional potential distribution at V_{GS} = 0.4 V and V_{DS} = 0.4 V for (a) the CJL CNTTFET and (b) the proposed JL CNTTFET with chemical- and electrical-doping engineering.

Figure 5 shows how the band diagrams are tuned by using the chemical- and electrical-doping techniques in order to improve the low on-current, which is among the main drawbacks in nanoscale TFETs. In Figure 5, the top (bottom) solid line is the edge of conduction (valence) band edge, E_C (E_V). We can clearly see in all figures that the edge of the conduction band underneath the gate is below the edge of the source valence band, while allowing a band-to-band tunneling mechanism that results in the on-current in tunneling FETs. This indicates that the direct source-to-drain tunneling can also contribute to the BTBT on-current, especially in TFET with ultra-scaled gate lengths, where the DSDT leakage becomes a concern. In Figure 5a, we can clearly see that the BTBT window indicated by two arrows is somewhat long, leading to low TFET on-currents. In Figure 5b, we can see the HDP-induced band lowering, which shrinks the BTBT window while increasing the BTBT components and making the on-current higher, as shown in Figure 2a. It is worth noting that the shorter (longer) BTBT window provides a higher (lower) on-current [18]. The inspection of Figure 5b also reveals a slight dilation in the DSDT window, due to the HDP-induced band lowering, while also explaining the recorded decrease in off-current shown in Figure 2a. Figure 5c shows that the BTBT window becomes somewhat shorter by increasing the p-gate voltage, and, thus, the BTBT on-current is boosted accordingly. Note that the negative increase in p-gate voltage also decreases the DSDT window, leading to the increase in off-current, as recorded in Figure 2b. For more clarification, Figure 5d is plotted to graphically show how the synergy of the HDP-based technique and the P-G voltage adjustment increasingly shrinks the BTBT window responsible for the on-current increase. In fact, the negative increase in P-gate voltage induces a band elevation at the level of source region, as shown in the same figure. Therefore, geometrically, the V_{PG} adjustment-induced band elevation, together with the HDP-induced band lowering, shrinks the BTBT window more and more, making it shorter, while clearly explaining the additional increase in on-current recorded in Figure 2b.

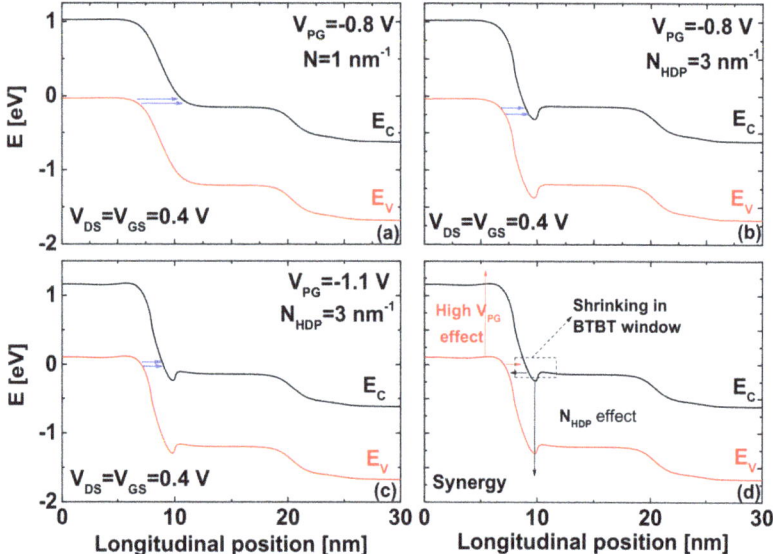

Figure 5. Band diagrams drawn at the on-state condition of (**a**) CJL CNTTFET, (**b**) JL CNTTFET with heavily n-type doped pocket, and (**c**) JL CNTTFET with both highly n-type doped pocket and optimized P-G voltage. (**d**) Doping-induced shrinking in BTBT window.

Figure 6 shows the energy-position-resolved current spectrum drawn from the NEGF quantities for the JL CNTTFETs under investigation. We can see in Figure 6a the band-to-band tunneling from source valence band to the drain conduction band through the BTBT window. In Figure 6b, we can clearly see that the BTBT on-current spectrum becomes higher than that of conventional JL CNTTFET, due to the HDP-induced band lowering that shrinks the BTBT window. Figure 6c obviously shows that the synergy of the p-gate voltage adjustment and heavily doped pocket approaches causes an additional increase in BTBT on-current spectrum (in comparison to other cases), due to the recorded additional shortening in BTBT window, as previously explained and shown in Figure 5.

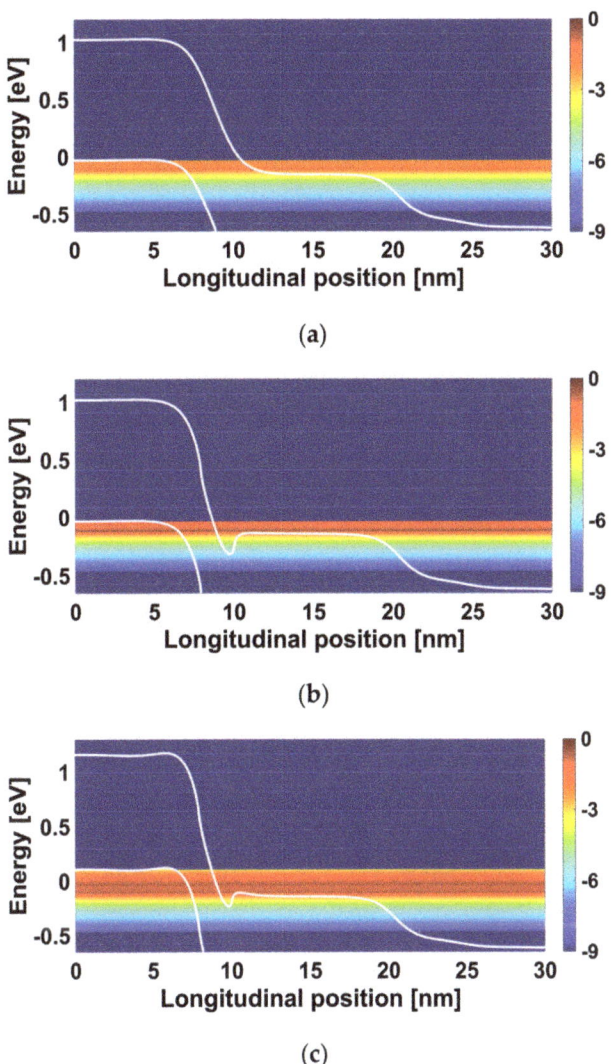

Figure 6. Energy-position-resolved current spectrum at on-state (V_{GS} = 0.4 V and V_{DS} = 0.4 V) of (**a**) the CJL CNTTFET, (**b**) the JL CNTTFET with heavily n-type doped pocket, and (**c**) JL CNTTFET with both HDP (N_{HDP} = 3 nm^{-1}) and optimized p-gate bias (V_{PG} = −1.1 V).

Figure 7 shows the role of the lightly n-type doped ZCNT region near the drain in dilating the direct source-to-drain tunneling window responsible for the tunneling leakage current in ultrascaled TFETs. As shown in Figure 7a, the DSDT window of the JL CNTTFET without the lightly n-type doped pocket is somewhat short (~14 nm), leading to a higher leakage current or, equivalently, a higher DSDT current; thus, a high off-state is recorded, as shown previously in Figure 2. Figure 7b clearly shows the LDP-induced dilation in the DSDT window by elevating the concerned bands via the lightly doped pocket. Please note that this LDP-induced dilation in the DSDT window explains the recorded improvement well in the off-current, I_{60} factor, and sub-thermionic subthreshold swing, as shown above in Figure 3.

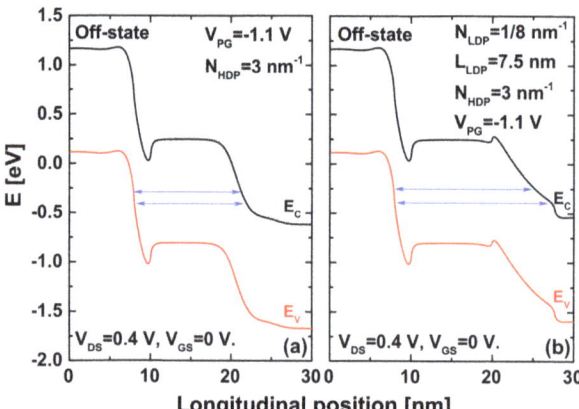

Figure 7. Band diagrams at the off-state for (**a**) JL CNTTFET with HDP and optimized V_{PG}; and (**b**) JL CNTTFET endowed with HDP, optimized V_{PG}, and lightly n-type doped ZCNT portion near the drain electrode.

Figure 8a shows the electron-density distribution throughout the JL CNTTFET, without considering the lightly n-type doped pocket near the drain electrode. We can see that the direct source-to-drain tunneling window is somewhat short; equivalently, the source and drain reservoir are close, thus leading to a significant DSDT mechanism and a high leakage current spectrum, as shown in Figure 8b. Figure 8c shows the electron density per unit energy versus the longitudinal position at off-state for the JL CNTTFET, considering the LDP near the drain electrode. As shown, the source and drain reservoirs diverge, making the DSDT window longer, and, thus, a decrease in DSDT off-current spectrum is recorded, as shown in Figure 8d.

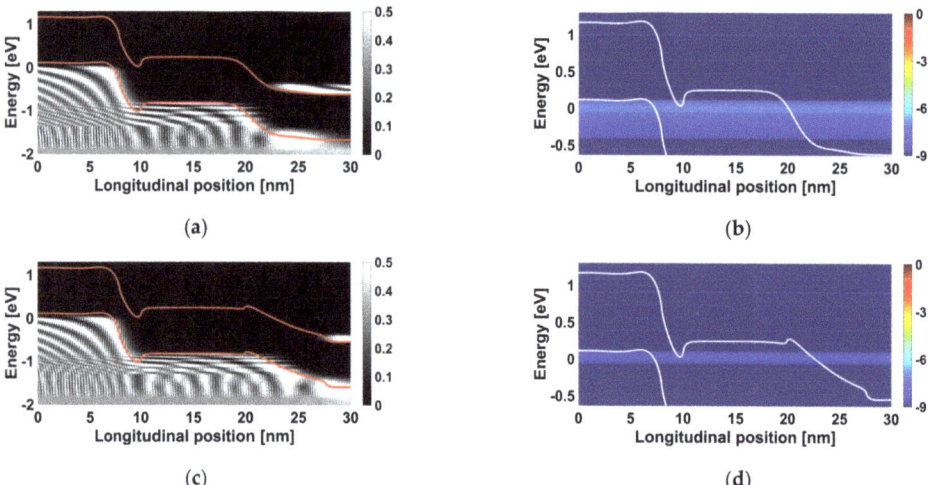

Figure 8. Electron density per unit energy versus the longitudinal position at off-state ($V_{GS} = 0$ V and $V_{DS} = 0.4$ V) for the JL CNTTFET (**a**) without and (**c**) with ($L_{LPD} = 7.5$ nm and $N_{LDP} = 1/8$ nm^{-1}) the lightly n-type doped portion near the drain electrode. Energy-position-resolved current spectrum for the JL CNTTFET (**b**) without and (**d**) with ($L_{LPD} = 7.5$ nm and $N_{LDP} = 1/8$ nm^{-1}) the LDP near the drain electrode.

Figure 9a shows how the decrease in doping concentration of the lightly n-type doped pocket near the drain improves the subthreshold swing and off-current and suppresses the ambipolar behavior. It is worth noting that we have not considered very low doping concentrations in order to keep the junctionless paradigm and avoid the n-type doping-intrinsic abrupt junction. The recorded improvements are attributed to the light doping-induced band elevation that dilates the DSDT window. In Figure 9b, the same improvement behavior is recorded when increasing the length of the LDP, where enhancements in terms of sub-thermionic subthreshold swing, off-current, and ambipolar behavior are recorded, while optimized on-current is within reach by the chemical and electrical-doping techniques near the source, as shown above. Therefore, wide lightly n-type doped ZCNT portions with a low concentration are suitable for improved subthreshold performance; however, there are some considerations regarding the junctionless aspect, the scaling capability, and the ohmic drain contact.

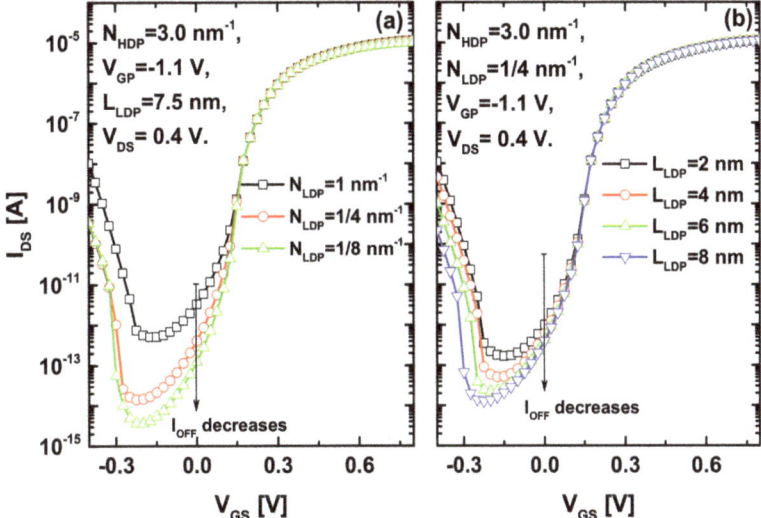

Figure 9. Impact of (**a**) doping concentration of the lightly n-type doped pocket near the drain and (**b**) the length of LDP on the I_{DS}–V_{GS} transfer characteristics of the proposed JL CNTTFET.

Figure 10 shows the switching performance of the conventional and proposed nanoscale TFETs, including the off-current (I_{OFF}); on-current (I_{ON}); current ratio (I_{ON}/I_{OFF}); power-delay product, $PDP = (Q_{ON} - Q_{OFF})V_{DD}$; and the intrinsic delay, $\tau = (Q_{ON} - Q_{OFF})/I_{ON}$. It is to indicate that the intrinsic delay presents how fast the JL CNTTFET can switch, while the power-delay product shows the energy required for a switching event. Note that the curves in Figure 10 are drawn from the concerned transfer characteristics by shifting a switching window with a width of power-supply voltage (V_{DD}) equal to 0.4 V, while extracting the on-state total charge (Q_{ON}) and its current (I_{ON}) at each given $V_{GS\text{-}ON}$, and the corresponding off-state total charge (Q_{OFF}) and its current (I_{OFF}) at $V_{GS\text{-}OFF} = V_{GS\text{-}ON} - V_{DD}$ [31–33].

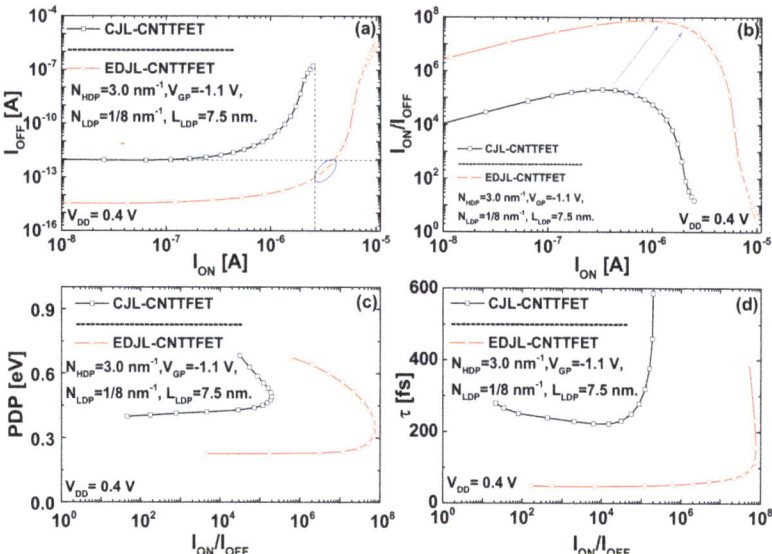

Figure 10. (**a**) Off-current versus on-current, (**b**) I_{ON}/I_{OFF} current ratio in function of the on-current, (**c**) power delay product as a function of current ratio, and (**d**) intrinsic delay versus the I_{ON}/I_{OFF} current ratio for the conventional and proposed JL CNTTFETs.

Figure 10a shows that the proposed JL CNTTFET can provides higher (lower) on-current (off-current) for a shared off-current (on-current) in comparison with the conventional nanodevice. Our inspection of the same figure reveals that the proposed JL CNTTFET, which is endowed with electrical- and chemical-doping engineering, can provide a particular performance (highlighted by a solid circle), where both higher on-current and lower off-current were simultaneously recorded in comparison with the currents of the conventional JL CNTTFET. Figure 10b is drawn from the concerned transfer characteristics, showing that the proposed JL CNTTFET can exhibit a higher maximum reachable current ratio (MRCR) with higher on-current, as indicated by arrows. Note that the MRCR of the proposed device is higher than that of the conventional device by about three orders of magnitude. In addition, we can clearly see that the proposed device exhibits a higher I_{ON}/I_{OFF} current ratio than the conventional device over the shared range of on-currents. Figure 10c shows and compares the power-delay product (PDP) in function of I_{ON}/I_{OFF} current ratio for the proposed and conventional JL CNTTFET. It is clearly seen that the proposed nanodevice exhibits lower PDP (higher I_{ON}/I_{OFF}) than its conventional counterpart over the shared range of current ratio (PDP). In addition, we can observe that the proposed device exhibits a higher MRCR with a lower PDP than that of the CJL CNTTFET. The recorded improvements in terms of PDP empower the proposed design to be an intriguing energy-efficient nano-TFET for high switching applications. Figure 10d shows that the proposed device provides faster (higher) intrinsic delay (current ratio) than its conventional counterpart over the shared range of current ratio (intrinsic delay). In addition, we can also see that the proposed design provides higher MRCR with faster delay than that of the CJL CNTTFET. The substantial decrease in terms of intrinsic delay, together with the recorded current ratios, makes the proposed JL CNTTFET an interesting nanoscale junctionless tunnel FET for high-speed applications.

In order to assess the benefits of the proposed design in the ultrascaled regime, we have performed a quantum-simulation-based comparison between the conventional and the proposed nanodevices, considering the main parameters of switching performance. Table 2 summarizes the main switching figures of merit of the proposed JLCNTTFET with 5 nm gate length. As very interesting results, the current ratio is improved by about 3 orders of magnitude and sub-thermionic SS (43 mV/dec) is well recorded in ultra-scaled regime. In addition, the on-current is boosted, and the off-current, minimum leakage current (I_{MIN}), I_{60} factor, PDP, and intrinsic delay are all decreased, which is very important for high-speed, low-power, and high-performance switching applications.

Table 2. Switching performance of JL CNTTFETs with 5 nm gate length.

Parameter	CJL-CNTTFET	EDJL-CNTTFET
I_{ON} (A)	7×10^{-7}	1.34×10^{-6}
I_{OFF} (A)	3.4×10^{-9}	1.23×10^{-11}
I_{MIN} (µA)	1.41×10^{-3}	2.05×10^{-6}
I_{60} (A)	-	5.6×10^{-8}
I_{ON}/I_{OFF}	205.8	10^5
SS (mV/dec)	128	43
PDP (eV)	0.52	0.31
τ (fs)	300.8	94.3

Basing on the recorded results in terms of the on-current improvement, which is attributed to the doping-induced shrinking in BTBT window, the ferroelectric-based gating can be adopted as additional improvement approach in order to further improve the EDJL-CNTTFET performance via the feature of the FE-induced amplified gate voltage [34], and thus well exploiting the boosted BTBT on-current. In fact, the adoption of ferroelectric (FE) material can take two different designs. The first configuration is based on the metal–ferroelectric–insulator–semiconductor (MFIS) design, while the second arrangement is the metal–ferroelectric–metal–insulator–semiconductor (MFMIS) structure [35]. We adopt in our case the MFMIS configuration due to its benefits in terms of elaboration [35–37], the possibility of separate integration [38], and the simulation simplicity [39–41]. Figure 11a shows an EDJL-CNTTFET design with a MFMIS structure. Note that the MFMIS can be integrated as a coaxial gate [42] or used as separate gating system ideally connected by a wire [25,38,41,43]. From simulation point of view, the ferroelectric field-effect transistors endowed with a MFMIS system can be treated as a baseline field-effect transistor in series with a ferroelectric capacitor [25,40–44]. Therefore, conceptually, the numerical modeling of the negative capacitance (MFMIS) nanodevices is divided into two parts [45]. The first step of simulation deals with the baseline device as mentioned above in the Section 3. After the self-consistency, the gate charge (Q_G) is numerically extracted and used to compute the voltage across the FE material (V_{FE}), using the 1-D steady-state Landau–Khalatnikov equation, which is given as follows [34]:

$$V_{FE} = 2\alpha t_{FE} Q_G + 4\beta t_{FE} Q_G^3 + 6\gamma t_{FE} Q_G^5 \qquad (8)$$

where t_{FE} is the FE thickness; and (α, β, and γ) are the FE Landau coefficients, which are chosen to be as those of the Al-doped HfO_2 FE parameters [25,44–46]. After computing V_{FE}, the external gate voltage (V_{GS}) of the EDJL-CNTTFET is normally computed by using the following equation [25,39–45]:

$$V_{GS} = V_{INT} + V_{FE} \qquad (9)$$

where V_{INT} is the internal metal-gate voltage considered in the baseline self-consistent quantum simulation. For more computational information regarding the quantum simulation of ultrascaled MFMIS FE-FETs, we refer the reader to our previous works [19,25,45].

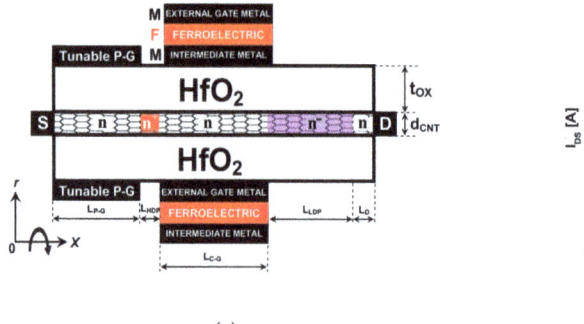 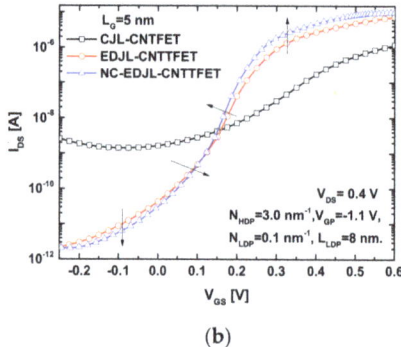

Figure 11. (**a**) Cross-sectional view of the proposed NC-EDJL-CNTTFET with MFMIS structure. (**b**) I_{DS}–V_{GS} transfer characteristics of the conventional JL CNTTFET, the proposed EDJL-CNTTFET, and the proposed NC-EDJL-CNTTFET considering 5 nm gate length.

Figure 11b shows that the proposed electrical- and chemical-doping approach can significantly improve the I_{DS}–V_{GS} transfer characteristics of an ultrascaled JL CNTTFET with 5 nm gate length. We can clearly see the substantial improvements in terms of I_{ON}, I_{OFF}, current ratio, and leakage current. In addition, we can observe that the nanodevice with the MFMIS structure additionally improves the on-current, off-current, and subthreshold swing, due to the FE-induced amplified gate voltage. Note that the recorded sub-thermionic subthreshold swing recorded in EDJL-CNTTFET was decreased from 43 to 35 mV/dec via the FE-based improvement approach. This indicates that the adoption of more appropriate FE nanomaterial with particular coercive field and remnant polarization can increasingly boost the nanodevice performance via enhancing the FE-induced amplified internal gate voltage [45]. In order to find the best device and ferroelectric parameters that can lead to the ultimate best performance, a parametric investigation [47] based on metaheuristic techniques (e.g., ant colony optimization, practical swarm optimization, genetic algorithms [48], etc.) in conjunction with the used NEGF simulation approach can be followed, while solving an advanced optimization problem, which can be a matter for future investigations.

The intriguing results obtained in this computational work can give new impulses to the design, simulation, and optimization of the advanced 2D materials-based nanoscale FETs with ultra-thin dielectrics, which have experienced significant progress [49–57]. In addition, the employment of such intriguing steep-slope nanodevices in advanced sensing applications [48,58–61] can be a matter for future works.

5. Conclusions

In this article, a new approach based on the synergy of the electrostatic and chemical-doping engineering is proposed to boost the performance of nanoscale JL CNTTFETs. The hybrid doping approach was found to be efficient at shrinking the BTBT window and dilating the DSDT spacing, while also boosting the JL CNTTFET performance. The profound quantum transport investigations have included the band diagrams, the potential distributions, and the energy-position-resolved electron density and current spectra. As a result, the subthreshold and switching performance is significantly improved, where sub-thermionic subthreshold swing, mitigated ambipolar behavior, boosted on-current, higher current ratio, reduced off- and leakage-current, faster switching speed, lower switching power, and improved scaling capability were obtained. Moreover, the metal–ferroelectric–metal-based gating approach was employed in order to exploit the recorded improvement in carrier transport, while boosting the JL TFET switching performance. The proposed design based on the synergy of electrostatic and chemical-doping engineering solved the main problems in ultrascaled JL CNTTFETs, and this is promising for the future CNT-based nanoelectronics.

Author Contributions: Conceptualization, K.T.; methodology, K.T.; software, K.T.; validation, K.T., A.K., H.B., M.A. and R.K.; formal analysis, K.T., A.K., H.B., M.A. and R.K.; investigation, K.T., A.K., H.B., M.A. and R.K.; resources, K.T., A.K., H.B., M.A. and R.K.; data curation, K.T., A.K., H.B., M.A. and R.K.; writing—original draft preparation, K.T., A.K., H.B., M.A. and R.K.; writing—review and editing, K.T.; visualization, K.T.; supervision, K.T. All authors have read and agreed to the published version of the manuscript.

Funding: This research received no external funding.

Institutional Review Board Statement: Not applicable.

Informed Consent Statement: Not applicable.

Data Availability Statement: Not applicable.

Acknowledgments: K.T. would like to thank the DGRSDT, Algeria. The first author would also to thank the Laboratory of Inverse Problems, Modeling, Information, and Systems (PIMIS), Guelma University, Guelma, Algeria, for providing computational support. This work was supported by the German Research Foundation (DFG) and the Technical University of Munich (TUM) in the framework of the Open Access Publishing Program.

Conflicts of Interest: The authors declare no conflict of interest.

References

1. Ionescu, A.M.; Riel, H. Tunnel field-effect transistors as energy-efficient electronic switches. *Nature* **2011**, *479*, 329–337. [CrossRef] [PubMed]
2. Sarkar, D.; Xie, X.; Liu, W.; Cao, W.; Kang, J.; Gong, Y.; Kraemer, S.; Ajayan, P.M.; Banerjee, K. A subthermionic tunnel field-effect transistor with an atomically thin channel. *Nature* **2015**, *526*, 91–95. [CrossRef] [PubMed]
3. Avci, U.E.; Morris, D.H.; Young, I. Tunnel Field-Effect Transistors: Prospects and Challenges. *IEEE J. Electron Devices Soc.* **2015**, *3*, 88–95. [CrossRef]
4. Lu, H.; Lu, B.; Zhang, Y.; Zhang, Y.; Lv, Z. Drain Current Model for Double Gate Tunnel-FETs with InAs/Si Heterojunction and Source-Pocket Architecture. *Nanomaterials* **2019**, *9*, 181. [CrossRef]
5. Tamersit, K. A novel band-to-band tunneling junctionless carbon nanotube field-effect transistor with lightly doped pocket: Proposal, assessment, and quantum transport analysis. *Phys. E Low-Dimens. Syst. Nanostruct.* **2021**, *128*, 114609. [CrossRef]
6. Tamersit, K. New nanoscale band-to-band tunneling junctionless GNRFETs: Potential high-performance devices for the ultrascaled regime. *J. Comput. Electron.* **2021**, *20*, 1147–1156. [CrossRef]
7. Lee, C.-W.; Afzalian, A.; Akhavan, N.D.; Yan, R.; Ferain, I.; Colinge, J.-P. Junctionless multigate field-effect transistor. *Appl. Phys. Lett.* **2009**, *94*, 053511. [CrossRef]
8. Tamersit, K. Sub-10 nm junctionless carbon nanotube field-effect transistors with improved performance. *AEU-Int. J. Electron. Commun.* **2020**, *124*, 153354. [CrossRef]
9. Ghosh, B.; Akram, M.W. Junctionless Tunnel Field Effect Transistor. *IEEE Electron Device Lett.* **2013**, *34*, 584–586. [CrossRef]
10. Tamersit, K. Improved performance of nanoscale junctionless carbon nanotube tunneling FETs using dual-material source gate design: A quantum simulation study. *AEU-Int. J. Electron. Commun.* **2020**, *127*, 153491. [CrossRef]
11. Tamersit, K. Boosting the performance of an ultrascaled carbon nanotube junctionless tunnel field-effect transistor using an ungated region: NEGF simulation. *J. Comput. Electron.* **2019**, *18*, 1222–1228. [CrossRef]
12. Nguyen, H.P.T.; Murugathas, T.; Plank, N.O. Comparison of Duplex and Quadruplex Folding Structure AdenosineAptamers for Carbon Nanotube Field Effect Transistor Aptasensors. *Nanomaterials* **2021**, *11*, 2280. [CrossRef] [PubMed]
13. Avouris, P.; Chen, Z.; Perebeinos, V. Carbon-based electronics. *Nat. Nanotechnol.* **2007**, *2*, 605–615. [CrossRef] [PubMed]
14. Browning, L.; Watterson, W.; Happe, E.; Silva, S.; Valenzuela, R.A.; Smith, J.; Dierkes, M.; Taylor, R.; Plank, N.; Marlow, C. Investigation of Fractal Carbon Nanotube Networks for Biophilic Neural Sensing Applications. *Nanomaterials* **2021**, *11*, 636. [CrossRef]
15. La Mura, M.; Lamberti, P.; Tucci, V. Numerical Evaluation of the Effect of Geometric Tolerances on the High-Frequency Performance of Graphene Field-Effect Transistors. *Nanomaterials* **2021**, *11*, 3121. [CrossRef]
16. Shirazi, S.G.; Karimi, G.R.; Mirzakuchaki, S. GAA CNT TFETs structural engineering: A higher on current, lower ambipolarity. *IEEE Trans. Electron Devices* **2019**, *66*, 2822–2830. [CrossRef]
17. Poli, S.; Reggiani, S.; Gnudi, A.; Gnani, E.; Baccarani, G. Computational Study of the Ultimate Scaling Limits of CNT Tunneling Devices. *IEEE Trans. Electron Devices* **2007**, *55*, 313–321. [CrossRef]
18. Tamersit, K. Computational Study of p-n Carbon Nanotube Tunnel Field-Effect Transistor. *IEEE Trans. Electron Devices* **2020**, *67*, 704–710. [CrossRef]
19. Tamersit, K. Improved Switching Performance of Nanoscale p-i-n Carbon Nanotube Tunneling Field-Effect Transistors Using Metal-Ferroelectric-Metal Gating Approach. *ECS J. Solid State Sci. Technol.* **2021**, *10*, 031004. [CrossRef]
20. Yoon, Y.; Salahuddin, S. Barrier-free tunneling in a carbon heterojunction transistor. *Appl. Phys. Lett.* **2010**, *97*, 33102. [CrossRef]

21. Gu, J.; Zhang, Q.; Wu, Z.; Yao, J.; Zhang, Z.; Zhu, X.; Wang, G.; Li, J.; Zhang, Y.; Cai, Y.; et al. Cryogenic Transport Characteristics of P-Type Gate-All-Around Silicon Nanowire MOSFETs. *Nanomaterials* **2021**, *11*, 309. [CrossRef] [PubMed]
22. Guo, J.; Datta, S.; Lundstrom, M.; Anantam, M.P. Toward Multiscale Modeling of Carbon Nanotube Transistors. *Int. J. Multiscale Comput. Eng.* **2004**, *2*, 257–276. [CrossRef]
23. Tamersit, K. Improving the On-Current of Junctionless Carbon Nanotube Tunneling FETs Using a Heavily n-Type Doped Pocket. In Proceedings of the 2021 International Semiconductor Conference (CAS), Sinaia, Romania, 6–8 October 2021; pp. 257–260. [CrossRef]
24. Tamersit, K. Performance Assessment of a New Radiation Dosimeter Based on Carbon Nanotube Field-Effect Transistor: A Quantum Simulation Study. *IEEE Sens. J.* **2019**, *19*, 3314–3321. [CrossRef]
25. Tamersit, K.; Jooq, M.K.Q.; Moaiyeri, M.H. Analog/RF performance assessment of ferroelectric junctionless carbon nanotube FETs: A quantum simulation study. *Phys. E Low-Dimens. Syst. Nanostruct.* **2021**, *134*, 114915. [CrossRef]
26. Datta, S. Nanoscale device modeling: The Green's function method. *Superlattices Microstruct.* **2000**, *28*, 253–278. [CrossRef]
27. Koswatta, S.O.; Hasan, S.; Lundstrom, M.S.; Anantram, M.P.; Nikonov, D. Nonequilibrium Green's Function Treatment of Phonon Scattering in Carbon-Nanotube Transistors. *IEEE Trans. Electron Devices* **2007**, *54*, 2339–2351. [CrossRef]
28. Tamersit, K. Quantum simulation of a junctionless carbon nanotube field-effect transistor with binary metal alloy gate electrode. *Superlattices Microstruct.* **2019**, *128*, 252–259. [CrossRef]
29. Tamersit, K. Improving the performance of a junctionless carbon nanotube field-effect transistor using a split-gate. *AEU-Int. J. Electron. Commun.* **2020**, *115*, 153035. [CrossRef]
30. Lu, H.; Seabaugh, A. Tunnel Field-Effect Transistors: State-of-the-Art. *IEEE J. Electron Devices Soc.* **2014**, *2*, 44–49. [CrossRef]
31. Javey, A.; Tu, R.; Farmer, D.B.; Guo, J.; Gordon, R.G.; Dai, H. High Performance n-Type Carbon Nanotube Field-Effect Transistors with Chemically Doped Contacts. *Nano Lett.* **2005**, *5*, 345–348. [CrossRef]
32. Tamersit, K. Performance enhancement of an ultra-scaled double-gate graphene nanoribbon tunnel field-effect transistor using channel doping engineering: Quantum simulation study. *AEU-Int. J. Electron. Commun.* **2020**, *122*, 153287. [CrossRef]
33. Tamersit, K. A new ultra-scaled graphene nanoribbon junctionless tunneling field-effect transistor: Proposal, quantum simulation, and analysis. *J. Comput. Electron.* **2019**, *19*, 170–176. [CrossRef]
34. Salahuddin, S.; Datta, S. Use of Negative Capacitance to Provide Voltage Amplification for Low Power Nanoscale Devices. *Nano Lett.* **2007**, *8*, 405–410. [CrossRef]
35. Wong, J.C.; Salahuddin, S. Negative Capacitance Transistors. *Proc. IEEE* **2019**, *107*, 49–62. [CrossRef]
36. Tu, L.; Wang, X.; Wang, J.; Meng, X.; Chu, J. Ferroelectric Negative Capacitance Field Effect Transistor. *Adv. Electron. Mater.* **2018**, *4*, 1800231. [CrossRef]
37. Srimani, T.; Hills, G.; Bishop, M.D.; Radhakrishna, U.; Zubair, A.; Park, R.S.; Stein, Y.; Palacios, T.; Antoniadis, D.; Shulaker, M.M. Negative Capacitance Carbon Nanotube FETs. *IEEE Electron Device Lett.* **2017**, *39*, 304–307. [CrossRef]
38. Saeidi, A.; Jazaeri, F.; Stolichnov, I.; Luong, G.V.; Zhao, Q.-T.; Mantl, S.; Ionescu, A.M. Effect of hysteretic and non-hysteretic negative capacitance on tunnel FETs DC performance. *Nanotechnology* **2018**, *29*, 095202. [CrossRef]
39. Sakib, F.I.; Mullick, F.E.; Shahnewaz, S.; Islam, S.; Hossain, M. Influence of device architecture on the performance of negative capacitance MFMIS transistors. *Semicond. Sci. Technol.* **2019**, *35*, 025005. [CrossRef]
40. Jiang, C.; Liang, R.; Xu, J. Investigation of Negative Capacitance Gate-all-around Tunnel FETs Combining Numerical Simulation and Analytical Modeling. *IEEE Trans. Nanotechnol.* **2016**, *16*, 58–67. [CrossRef]
41. Seo, J.; Lee, J.; Shin, M. Analysis of Drain-Induced Barrier Rising in Short-Channel Negative-Capacitance FETs and Its Applications. *IEEE Trans. Electron Devices* **2017**, *64*, 1793–1798. [CrossRef]
42. Sakib, F.I.; Hasan, A.; Hossain, M. Exploration of Negative Capacitance in Gate-All-Around Si Nanosheet Transistors. *IEEE Trans. Electron Devices* **2020**, *67*, 5236–5242. [CrossRef]
43. Behbahani, F.; Jooq, M.K.Q.; Moaiyeri, M.H.; Tamersit, K. Leveraging Negative Capacitance CNTFETs for Image Processing: An Ultra-Efficient Ternary Image Edge Detection Hardware. *IEEE Trans. Circuits Syst. I Regul. Pap.* **2021**, *68*, 5108–5119. [CrossRef]
44. Jooq, M.K.Q.; Moaiyeri, M.H.; Tamersit, K. Ultra-Compact Ternary Logic Gates Based on Negative Capacitance Carbon Nanotube FETs. *IEEE Trans. Circuits Syst. II Express Briefs* **2020**, *68*, 2162–2166. [CrossRef]
45. Tamersit, K.; Jooq, M.K.Q.; Moaiyeri, M.H. Computational Investigation of Negative Capacitance Coaxially Gated Carbon Nanotube Field-Effect Transistors. *IEEE Trans. Electron Devices* **2020**, *68*, 376–384. [CrossRef]
46. Dabhi, C.K.; Parihar, S.S.; Dasgupta, A.; Chauhan, Y.S. Compact Modeling of Negative-Capacitance FDSOI FETs for Circuit Simulations. *IEEE Trans. Electron Devices* **2020**, *67*, 2710–2716. [CrossRef]
47. Dutta, T.; Pahwa, G.; Agarwal, A.; Chauhan, Y.S. Impact of Process Variations on Negative Capacitance FinFET Devices and Circuits. *IEEE Electron Device Lett.* **2017**, *39*, 147–150. [CrossRef]
48. Tamersit, K.; Kotti, M.; Fakhfakh, M. A new pressure microsensor based on dual-gate graphene field-effect transistor with a vertically movable top-gate: Proposal, analysis, and optimization. *AEU-Int. J. Electron. Commun.* **2020**, *124*, 153346. [CrossRef]
49. Bae, G.Y.; Kim, J.; Kim, J.; Lee, S.; Lee, E. MoTe$_2$ Field-Effect Transistors with Low Contact Resistance through Phase Tuning by Laser Irradiation. *Nanomaterials* **2021**, *11*, 2805. [CrossRef]
50. Tamersit, K.; Ramezani, Z.; Amiri, I. Improved performance of sub-10-nm band-to-band tunneling n-i-n graphene nanoribbon field-effect transistors using underlap engineering: A quantum simulation study. *J. Phys. Chem. Solids* **2021**, *160*, 110312. [CrossRef]

51. Zhang, Q.; Iannaccone, G.; Fiori, G. Two-dimensional tunnel transistors based on Bi_2Se_3 thin film. *IEEE Electron Device Lett.* **2014**, *35*, 129–131. [CrossRef]
52. Chen, C.-Y.; Ameen, T.A.; Ilatikhameneh, H.; Rahman, R.; Klimeck, G.; Appenzeller, J. Channel Thickness Optimization for Ultrathin and 2-D Chemically Doped TFETs. *IEEE Trans. Electron Devices* **2018**, *65*, 4614–4621. [CrossRef]
53. Liu, F.; Zhou, Y.; Wang, Y.; Liu, X.; Wang, J.; Guo, H. Negative capacitance transistors with monolayer black phosphorus. *Npj Quantum Mater.* **2016**, *1*, 16004. [CrossRef]
54. Ilatikhameneh, H.; Tan, Y.; Novakovic, B.; Klimeck, G.; Rahman, R.; Appenzeller, J. Tunnel Field-Effect Transistors in 2-D Transition Metal Dichalcogenide Materials. *IEEE J. Explor. Solid-State Comput. Devices Circuits* **2015**, *1*, 12–18. [CrossRef]
55. Fiori, G.; Bonaccorso, F.; Iannaccone, G.; Palacios, T.; Neumaier, D.; Seabaugh, A.; Banerjee, S.K.; Colombo, L. Electronics based on two-dimensional materials. *Nat. Nanotechnol.* **2014**, *9*, 768–779. [CrossRef] [PubMed]
56. Ilatikhameneh, H.; Klimeck, G.; Rahman, R. Can Homojunction Tunnel FETs Scale Below 10 nm? *IEEE Electron Device Lett.* **2015**, *37*, 115–118. [CrossRef]
57. Marin, E.G.; Marian, D.; Iannaccone, G.; Fiori, G. First principles investigation of tunnel FETs based on nanoribbons from topological two-dimensional materials. *Nanoscale* **2017**, *9*, 19390–19397. [CrossRef]
58. Tamersit, K.; Djeffal, F. Double-Gate Graphene Nanoribbon Field-Effect Transistor for DNA and Gas Sensing Applications: Simulation Study and Sensitivity Analysis. *IEEE Sens. J.* **2016**, *16*, 4180–4191. [CrossRef]
59. Tamersit, K.; Djeffal, F. Carbon Nanotube Field-Effect Transistor with Vacuum Gate Dielectric for Label-Free Detection of DNA Molecules: A Computational Investigation. *IEEE Sens. J.* **2019**, *19*, 9263–9270. [CrossRef]
60. Anvarifard, M.K.; Ramezani, Z.; Amiri, I.S.; Tamersit, K.; Nejad, A.M. Profound analysis on sensing performance of Nanogap SiGe source DM-TFET biosensor. *J. Mater. Sci. Mater. Electron.* **2020**, *31*, 22699–22712. [CrossRef]
61. Tamersit, K. An ultra-sensitive gas nanosensor based on asymmetric dual-gate graphene nanoribbon field-effect transistor: Proposal and investigation. *J. Comput. Electron.* **2019**, *18*, 846–855. [CrossRef]

Article

Area-Scalable 10^9-Cycle-High-Endurance FeFET of Strontium Bismuth Tantalate Using a Dummy-Gate Process

Mitsue Takahashi * and Shigeki Sakai

National Institute of Advanced Industrial Science and Technology, 1-1-1 Umezono, Tsukuba, Ibaraki 305-8568, Japan; shigeki.sakai@aist.go.jp
* Correspondence: Mitsue-takahashi@aist.go.jp

Abstract: Strontium bismuth tantalate (SBT) ferroelectric-gate field-effect transistors (FeFETs) with channel lengths of 85 nm were fabricated by a replacement-gate process. They had metal/ferroelectric/insulator/semiconductor stacked-gate structures of Ir/SBT/HfO$_2$/Si. In the fabrication process, we prepared dummy-gate transistor patterns and then replaced the dummy substances with an SBT precursor. After forming Ir gate electrodes on the SBT, the whole gate stacks were annealed for SBT crystallization. Nonvolatility was confirmed by long stable data retention measured for 10^5 s. High erase-and-program endurance of the FeFETs was demonstrated for up to 10^9 cycles. By the new process proposed in this work, SBT-FeFETs acquire good channel-area scalability in geometry along with lithography ability.

Keywords: FeFET; ferroelectric; nonvolatile; semiconductor memory; SBT

Citation: Takahashi, M.; Sakai, S. Area-Scalable 10^9-Cycle-High-Endurance FeFET of Strontium Bismuth Tantalate Using a Dummy-Gate Process. *Nanomaterials* **2021**, *11*, 101. https://doi.org/10.3390/nano11010101

Received: 14 December 2020
Accepted: 29 December 2020
Published: 4 January 2021

Publisher's Note: MDPI stays neutral with regard to jurisdictional claims in published maps and institutional affiliations.

Copyright: © 2021 by the authors. Licensee MDPI, Basel, Switzerland. This article is an open access article distributed under the terms and conditions of the Creative Commons Attribution (CC BY) license (https://creativecommons.org/licenses/by/4.0/).

1. Introduction

Ferroelectric-gate field-effect transistors (FeFETs) comprising SrBi$_2$Ta$_2$O$_9$ (SBT) or Ca$_x$Sr$_{1-x}$Bi$_2$Ta$_2$O$_9$ (CSBT) ferroelectrics have unique characteristics of high endurance against at least 10^8 cycles of program and erase operations [1–12]. CSBT is a kind of SBT family which was derived from original SBT by Sr-site substitution with Ca. The material natures of SBT [13–32] and CSBT [33–36] have been intensively studied previously. FeFETs using CSBT with about x = 0.2 showed larger memory windows than those with SBT [5]. The invention of long-retention FeFET was first reported in 2002 and consisted of a metal/ferroelectric/insulator/semiconductor (MFIS) stacked-gate structure of Pt/SBT/(HfO$_2$)$_{0.75}$(Al$_2$O$_3$)$_{0.25}$(HAO)/Si [37]. Since then, we have investigated characteristics of (C)SBT-FeFETs [1–3,38–44], improved the device performance [4–8,45,46], and developed FeFET-integrated circuits [9–12,47–52]. For improving the single FeFET performance, we succeeded in reducing gate voltage (V_g) from the initial 6~8 [1] to 3.3 V [8]. Another progress was in shrinking gate-metal length (L_m) from the initial 10 μm [1] to 100 nm [7].

The conventional (C)SBT-FeFETs were formed by etching the gate stacks. By decreasing the FeFET gate length, SBT etching-damage problems [29–32] on the gate-stack sidewalls became significant. Since we recognized that L_m = 100 nm was approaching the shortest limit by the conventional method based on etching, we changed the fabrication strategy to shape the gate stacks from etching-down to filling-up. The new (C)SBT-FeFET process is outlined as follows: Dummy-gate transistor patterns with self-aligned source- and drain regions are prepared in advance. The dummy substance is selectively removed to leave grooves which are later filled up with SBT precursor. Gate electrodes are formed. Finally, whole gate stacks of Ir/SBT/HfO$_2$/Si are annealed for SBT crystallization. In the new FeFET process, the (C)SBT sidewall of the gate stack is not exposed to etching plasma. The sidewall is thus free from etching damage problem [6]. Consequently, the ferroelectric becomes more controllable in terms of quality and more scalable in terms of geometry than by the etching. The new FeFET dimensions follow good lithography progress with an adequate height of (C)SBT to show large memory windows increasing with the ferroelectric thickness [3,43]. In this work, SBT-FeFETs with gate channel lengths L_{ch} = 85 nm were first reported by adopting the proposed process. Excellent characteristics were demonstrated such as 10^9 cycle erase-program endurance and long stable retention for 10^5 s. The endurance and retention were as good as those of the conventional (C)SBT-FeFETs formed by the gate-stack etching [1–12].

2. Materials and Methods

2.1. Device Fabrication Process

The fabrication process (schematic drawings shown in Figure 1) in this work is as follows:

- *Step 1: Si substrate preparation.* A *p*-type Si substrate patterned with FET active areas was prepared. Local-oxidation-of-silicon (LOCOS) process was used in the patterning for device isolation. The LOCOS patterns with various channel widths (*W*) were designed in a sample chip. Areas for source-, drain- and substrate-contact holes on the Si were heavily ion-doped. Sacrificial SiO_2 on Si was removed with buffered hydrogen fluoride.
- *Step 2: Insulator deposition.* A 5 nm thick HfO_2 was deposited on the Si substrate by a large-area pulsed-laser deposition system (Vacuum Products Corporation, Kodaira, Tokyo, Japan) [53]. A KrF laser was irradiated on a ceramic HfO_2 target in 15.3 Pa N_2 ambient [54]. The substrate temperature was 220 °C.
- *Step 3: Lithography.* Electron-beam (EB) lithography was performed by spin-coating an organic resist, exposing 130 kV EB, and developing. Resist patterns 550 nm tall were left on the HfO_2/Si. They were later used as ion-implantation mask in *Step 4* and as dummy gates in *Step 7*.
- *Step 4: Ion implantation.* HfO_2 uncovered with resist was etched out by inductively-coupled-plasma reactive-ion etching (ICP-RIE). On the exposed Si, As^+ ions were implanted for source and drain. The energy and dose conditions were 4 keV and $5.0 \times 10^{12}/cm^2$.
- *Step 5: SiO_2 deposition.* An 830 nm thick SiO_2 was deposited to cover the resist patterns on the substrate by 300 W rf sputtering in 0.1 Pa Ar.
- *Step 6: Flattening SiO_2.* The SiO_2 was etched back and flattened by ICP-RIE with 1.0 Pa Ar-CF_4 mixed gas until tops of the resists or dummy gates were exposed.
- *Step 7: Leaving grooves on gates.* The dummy-gate substances were selectively removed by O_2 plasma ashing. There remained grooves in a 410 nm tall SiO_2 isolation. The grooves were located on the HfO_2 with self-aligned source and drain regions prepared in *Step 4*. The whole chip was rapidly annealed at 800 °C in ambient N_2.
- *Step 8: Ferroelectric deposition.* SBT precursor film was deposited to fill up the grooves by a metal-organic-chemical-vapor deposition (MOCVD) system (WACOM R&D, Nihonbashi, Tokyo, Japan). Sources of $Bi(C_5H_{11}O_2)_3$, $Sr[Ta(OC_2H_5)_5(OC_2H_4OCH_3)]_2$ and $Ta(OCH_2CH_3)_5$ (Tri Chemical Laboratories Inc., Uenohara, Yamanashi, Japan) were used [6]. As-deposited precursor-film thickness was estimated as 80 nm on a flat place of the substrate.
- *Step 9: Metal deposition.* Ir was deposited by rf sputtering on the SBT precursor layer. Resist mask was patterned for gate electrodes by EB lithography.
- *Step 10: Forming gate electrodes.* Ir uncovered with resist was etched out by Ar^+ ion milling. Then, the resist mask was removed by O_2 plasma ashing.
- *Step 11: FeFET completed.* SBT precursor was deposited again by MOCVD to cover the substrate [6]. The whole substrate was annealed for crystallization of the SBT to show ferroelectricity. The annealing condition was at 780 °C in an O_2-N_2 mixed gas we investigated before [8]. Finally, contact holes for gate, source, drain and substrate were formed by ultraviolet g-line lithography and Ar^+ ion milling.

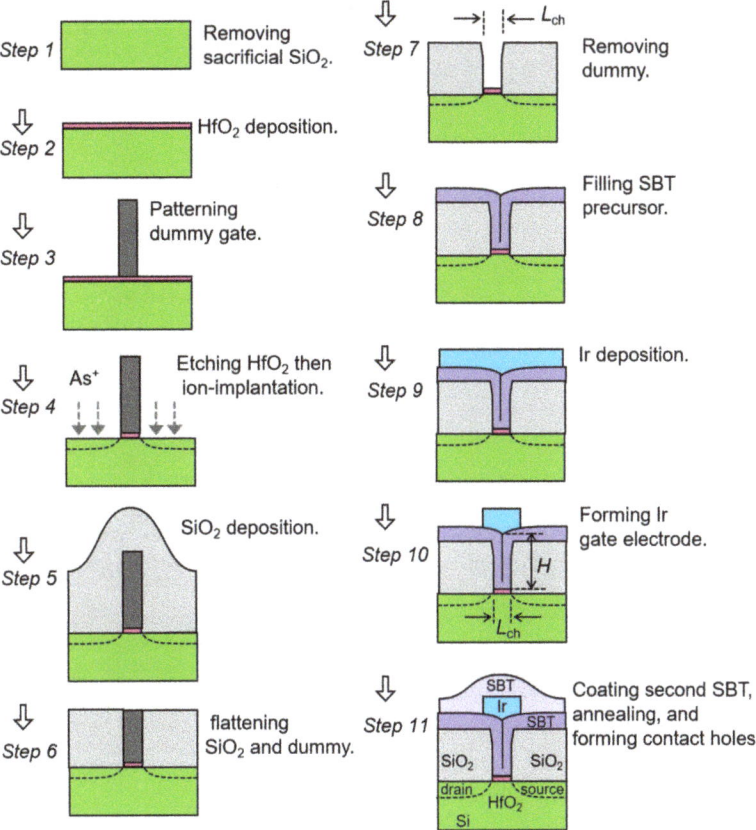

Figure 1. New fabrication process of Strontium bismuth tantalate (SBT)-ferroelectric-gate field-effect transistors (FeFETs) demonstrated in this work.

2.2. Reason for Using SBT in FeFET

The gate stack of MFIS should be regarded as MFI(IL)S, as shown in in Figure 2a, where F, I, IL, S are connected in series. The IL is an interfacial layer between I and S which is formed during the ferroelectric crystallization annealing process of FeFETs [8,39,55–57]. The main component of IL is silicon dioxide with an electric permittivity (ε_{IL}) of ε_{IL} = 3.9. In the MFI(IL)S, $|P_F| \approx \varepsilon_0 \cdot \varepsilon_I \cdot |E_I| = \varepsilon_0 \cdot \varepsilon_{IL} \cdot |E_{IL}| = |Q_S|$ is satisfied in any time. The P_F is ferroelectric polarization. E_I and E_{IL} are electric fields in the I and the IL. The Q_S is charge area density in the semiconductor surface. The ε_I is a relative permittivity of the I. The ε_0 is the vacuum dielectric constant of ε_0 = 8.85 × 10^{-12} F/m. For a simplified explanation, we assumed a virtual equivalent circuit of series capacitance as drawn in Figure 2a which is expressed by $|P_F| \approx |Q_I| = |Q_{IL}| = |Q_S|$ with virtual charges Q_I and Q_{IL} on I and IL, respectively. In MFI(IL)S, the IL suffers from a stress of field $|E_{IL}| \approx |P_F|/(\varepsilon_0 \cdot \varepsilon_{IL})$ = 8.7 MV/cm even at a small $|P_F|$ = 3 µC/cm^2. For example, real IL thickness is 2.6 nm [8] or about 1 nm [55–57]. Electric-field-assisted tunnel current through such a thin SiO$_2$ [58,59] brings charge injection into the gate stack from S across IL. In erase-and-program operations, a large E_{IL} derived from a large P_F swing induces significant trapped-charge accumulation which accelerates endurance degradations [2,52]. According to our experience [43,52,60], $|P_F|$ should normally be less than 2.5 µC/cm^2 all the time and should not exceed 2.0 µC/cm^2 for further high-endurance requirements of the FeFET.

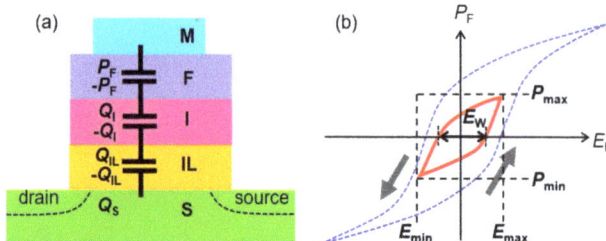

Figure 2. (a) Schematic cross-section of a FeFET with an equivalent circuit of MFI(IL)S gate stack. For convenience of explanation, the circuit is represented using virtual capacitances instead of a strict physical explanation by the electric flux density continuity, D. (b) Schematic drawings of P_F versus E_F. All P_F-E_F loops are drawn in counter-clockwise directions. The inner loop (red solid) is a minor loop corresponding to unsaturated P_F discussed in Section 2.2. Outer loop (blue broken) is a major loop for saturated P_F added as a reference. Every loop has its P_{max} at E_{max} and P_{min} at E_{min}.

Ferroelectric materials show P_F versus E_F hysteresis loops as illustrated in Figure 2b. The E_F is the electric field across the F. We defined E_{max} as the positive maximum E_F and P_{max} as the P_F at $E_F = E_{max}$. Similarly, E_{min} and P_{min} are the negative minimum E_F and the P_F at $E_F = E_{min}$. The loop is called "major" loop when the E_{max} and $|E_{min}|$ are strong enough to force P_F saturated, whereas it is called "minor" loop when P_F is unsaturated by moderate E_F swing. In SBT-FeFETs, restrictions of $P_{max} \leq 2.5 \ \mu C/cm^2$ corresponding to the minor loops are used during all operations as we emphasized in early works [39,43,52,60].

Regarding a ferroelectric hidden in MFI(IL)S, an exact symmetric swing maximum, i.e., $P_{max} = |P_{min}|$ or $E_{max} = |E_{min}|$, is difficult because $|Q_S|$ versus Φ_S is very asymmetric [61,62]. The Q_S is the charge area density of the semiconductor surface and Φ_S is the surface potential. Presence of the flat-band voltage V_{fb} makes the symmetric swing further difficult. However, to simplify the physical explanation, $P_{max} = |P_{min}|$ and $E_{max} = |E_{min}|$ are assumed as shown in Figure 2b with $V_{fb} = 0V$. In every P_F-E_F loop, the E_F width at $P_F = 0$ is defined as E_w being related with a voltage memory window (V_w) by an approximate expression $E_w = 2E_c = V_w/d_F$, where the E_c is a coercive field and d_F is ferroelectric thickness. According to a method we proposed before [43], an important characteristic E_{max} of the ferroelectric can be evaluated which has not been measurable by direct probing on a FeFET. If P_{max} is provided, a gate voltage V_g to achieve a target memory window $V_w = E_w \cdot d_F$ can be estimated as a sum of $E_{max} \cdot d_F$, $E_I \cdot d_I$, $E_{IL} \cdot d_{IL}$ and Φ_S at $Q_S = P_{max}$. An exact discussion can be found in the paper [43].

For instance, Pt/SBT/HAO/Si FeFETs showed $E_w = 18$ kV/cm at $P_{max} = 2.0 \ \mu C/cm^2$ and $E_{max} = 25$ kV/cm [43]. By adopting an advanced process [8], Ir/CSBT/HfO$_2$/Si FeFETs had the best improved values of $E_w = 65$ kV/cm at $P_{max} = 2.0 \ \mu C/cm^2$ and $E_{max} = 140$ kV/cm [3,43]. A good reason for using (C)SBT in Si-based FeFETs is the (C)SBT ferroelectric nature of a convenient minor P_F-E_F loop [14,17,20] which has E_w available and is controllable in a restricted P_F range of $P_{max} \leq 2 \ \mu C/cm^2$ with $E_{max} \leq 140$ kV/cm.

There are some other ferroelectric materials also intensively studied for applications in Si-based MFIS FeFETs. Regarding Pb$_5$Ge$_3$O$_{11}$ (PGO), attempts to develop replacement-gate-type Pt/PGO/ZrO$_2$/Si FeFETs were reported [63] but the erase-program-test results of the FeFETs were not found although the ferroelectric itself showed a good potential P_{max}-E_{max} and $E_w - E_{max}$ judging from hysteresis loops of the PGO metal/ferroelectric/metal capacitors [64]. Regarding another candidate, the ferroelectric HfO$_2$ family [55–57,65–70], the intrinsic material nature may not be suitable for applying to Si-based FeFETs. Informative minor hysteresis loops were reported on Y-doped HfO$_2$ in which E_w seemed nearly equal to 0 V/cm at $P_{max} = 2.0 \ \mu C/cm^2$, although it was as large as about 1 MV/cm at $P_{max} = 10 \ \mu C/cm^2$ [66]. Operation of the FeFETs under the restriction of $P_{max} \leq 2 \ \mu C/cm^2$ may be difficult. Some reports suggested that HfO$_2$-FeFETs cannot help using a large P_{max} ($>>2 \ \mu C/cm^2$) [52,55]. The large P_{max} may induce significant charge injection into the gate stack. As far as we know, fair works on HfO$_2$-FeFETs have not cleared 10^8 cycles endurance in spite of using sophisticated production facilities [56,67–70].

3. Results and Discussion

3.1. Device Dimensions

A cross-sectional scanning-electron-microscope photograph of an Ir/SBT/HfO$_2$/Si FeFET fabricated by the new proposed process is shown in Figure 3a. Figure 3b shows the same picture added with support lines to clarify the material boundaries. The schematic drawing of the FeFET was assigned with four terminals of gate, drain, source and substrate (Figure 3c). The gate-channel length (L_{ch}) was L_{ch} = 85 nm. The gate-channel width was W = 100 μm depending on the initial LOCOS pattern designed in *Step 1* in Section 2.1. The metal-gate length L_m was 150 nm which could be shorter but was not the focus in this work. The SBT precursor film thickness was about 80 nm measured on a flat place. By filling gate grooves with SBT precursor (*Step 8* in Section 2.1.), the effective SBT height (H) was finally about 450 nm which was a distance between Ir and HfO$_2$. Area scalability of the new FeFET was equivalent to that of the dummy gates which are organic resist patterns made by lithography. From the viewpoint of Si transistor technology, L_{ch} = 10 nm is expected to be the critical limit [71]. A significant Curie-temperature decrease in SBT started when particle were sizes of around 20 nm [25]. Thus, the prospective shortest limit of L_{ch} by our proposed FeFET process may be around 20 nm.

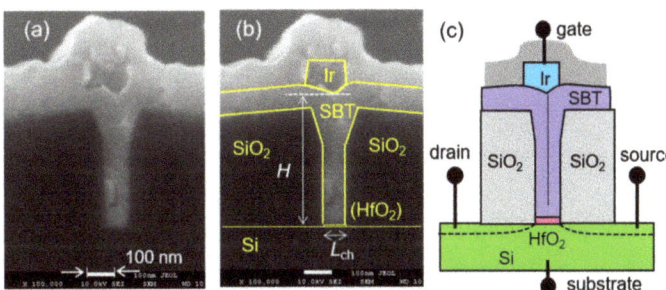

Figure 3. Cross-section of a FeFET with L_{ch} = 85 nm fabricated in this work. (a) Original photo by SEM observation and (b) the photo with supporting lines added to clarify material boundaries. (c) Schematic drawing assigned with gate, drain, source and substrate terminals for electrical characterizations.

3.2. Electrical Characterizations

In this study, memory windows, endurance and retention of FeFETs were investigated at room temperature. A semiconductor parameter analyzer (4156C, Keysight Technologies, Santa Rosa, CA, USA) was used for measuring static drain current versus gate voltage (I_d–V_g) curves of the FeFETs. A pulse generator (81110A, Keysight Technologies, Santa Rosa, CA, USA) was used to apply V_g pulses. The instruments were computer-controlled using programs written by the language of LabVIEW (ver. 10, National Instruments, Austin, TX, USA).

3.2.1. Memory Windows

As an elementary test of the FeFETs, I_d–V_g hysteresis loops were investigated (Figure 4). The I_d was measured by V_g increments and decrements with 0.1 V steps. The V_g sweeping ranges were V_g = 1 ± 4 V, 1 ± 5 V and 1 ± 6 V. Drain voltage (V_d), source voltage (V_s) and substrate voltage (V_{sub}) were fixed to V_d = 0.1 V and V_s = V_{sub} = 0 V during the measurements. The I_d–V_g showed hysteresis loops drawn in counter-clockwise directions because the FeFET was an *n*-channel-type one. In an I_d–V_g curve, threshold voltage (V_{th}) was defined as a V_g value at I_d/W = 1 × 10^{-7} A/cm. Two V_{th} values were extracted from the left- and right-side curves in an I_d–V_g hysteresis loop. A memory window was defined as the V_{th} difference. In this work, we call this a *static* memory window (V_w) because V_g sweep by 4156C is slow. The static V_w was, for instance, 1.0 V by sweeping V_g from −5 to 7 V then back to −5 V, or at $V_g = 1 \pm 6$ V as expressed in Figure 4. During the measurement of a wide-range I_d from 10^{-12} to 10^{-4} A as indicated in Figure 4, V_g sweep speed depends on the current range. Therefore, an I_d–V_g hysteresis curve only gives reference information that is not suitable for accurate discussion.

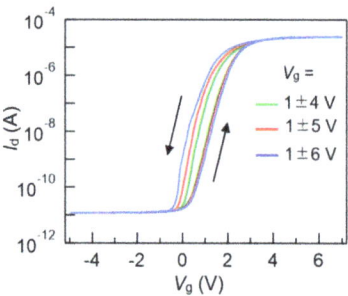

Figure 4. Static static drain current versus gate voltage (I_d–V_g) curves of a FeFET with L_{ch} = 85 nm. The channel width was W = 150 μm. V_g ranges were $V_g = 1 \pm 4$ V, 1 ± 5 V and 1 ± 6 V.

For an accurate understanding, the FeFET performance, a pulsed V_g with a controlled time width, was applied to the FeFETs for the erase (*Ers*) or program (*Prg*) operation. The V_g pulse heights with the time widths were (V_E, t_E) for *Ers*, and (V_P, t_P) for *Prg*, respectively. For the n-channel-type FeFET, the V_E was negative ($V_E < 0$ V) and V_P was positive ($V_P > 0$ V) [9]. The pulse time widths t_E and t_P were the same with each other in this work ($t_E = t_P = t_{EP}$). After, *Ers* and *Prg*, I_d–V_g curves were individually measured with a small common V_g range for *Read*. Two V_{th} values were defined in the I_d–V_g curves as the V_g at $I_d/W = 1 \times 10^{-7}$ A/cm. They were expressed as V_{thE} after *Ers* and V_{thP} after *Prg*. The V_{thE} was larger than the V_{thP} [9]. The V_{th} difference of $\Delta V_{th} = V_{thE} - V_{thP}$ was defined as a memory window obtained by read operation after erase-and-program pulse applications. The memory window ΔV_{th} is normally smaller than the above-mentioned static V_w, because slow switching components in a ferroelectric do not respond to short pulses [27,72,73]. The V_{thE} and V_{thP} were investigated by repeating a series of operations: *Ers*, *Read*, *Prg*, *Read*, in this order (Figure 5a). In *Ers*, a pulsed V_g of (V_E, t_{EP}) was applied with keeping $V_d = V_s = V_{sub} = 0$ V. In *Read* after *Ers*, a V_{thE} was extracted from an I_d–V_g curve drawn by narrow-range varying V_g from 0 to 1.1 V at $V_d = 0.1$ V and $V_s = V_{sub} = 0$ V. In *Prg*, a pulsed V_g of (V_P, t_{EP}) was applied, keeping $V_d = V_s = V_{sub} = 0$ V. In *Read* after *Prg*, a V_{thP} was extracted from an I_d–V_g curve drawn under exactly the same conditions as those in *Read* after *Ers*.

Figure 5b shows V_{thE} and V_{thP} by *Read* after *Ers* and *Prg* for three sets of (V_E, t_{EP}) and (V_P, t_{EP}) of $|V_E| = V_P = 6, 7$ and 8 V. Every marker corresponds to the measured V_{thE} and V_{thP}. Memory windows, $\Delta V_{th} = V_{thE}-V_{thP}$, as a function of pulse height $|V_E| = |V_P|$ (Figure 5c) and width t_{EP} (Figure 5d) can be seen in Figure 5b, where the V_{thE} and V_{thP} results (not shown in Figure 5b) of other V_P (=$|V_E|$) conditions were also used. Short V_g pulses of t_{EP} = 50 ns were available for *Ers* and *Prg* of the FeFET. Memory windows of $\Delta V_{th} > 0.7$ V were obtained using 8 and 8.5 V pulses.

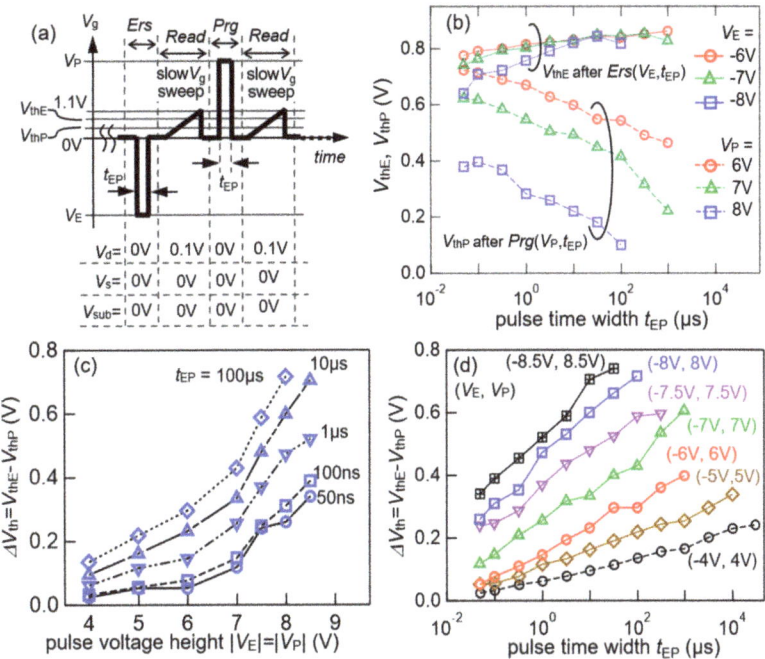

Figure 5. Investigation of V_{thE} and V_{thP} by applying V_g pulses to a FeFET with L_{ch} = 85 nm. The channel width was W = 100 μm. (**a**) The measurement procedure; (**b**) measured original V_{thE} and V_{thP}; (**c**) pulse-height dependence of $\Delta V_{th} = V_{thE} - V_{thP}$ and (**d**) pulse width dependence of ΔV_{th}.

Figure 5c,d show a clear monotonic ΔV_{th} increases when raising either the pulse height or width. Good analog V_{thE} and V_{thP} controllability was suggested by smooth and linear ΔV_{th} growths with raising $\log(t_{EP})$ as shown in Figure 5d. The similar tendencies of ΔV_{th} and t_{EP} have already been reported in our previous works [3,5,7,9,52]. In the prior FeFETs, poly-crystalized ferroelectrics were visualized by electron backscatter diffraction (EBSD) [44]. The EBSD indicated that the (C)SBT consisted of multi-grains with various crystal orientations in the FeFETs. The poly-crystalized ferroelectrics may bring the analog V_{thE} and V_{thP} controllability to the FeFETs. In the present FeFET, there must be numerous grains in channel-width direction with W = 100 μm whereas a single grain or a few were expected in channel-length with L_{ch} = 85 nm which was smaller than average diameters of SBT grains freely grown in-plane [44].

In a preferable geometry of the replacement-gate FeFET in the future, only the channel area $L_{ch} \times W$ will be intensively scaled down with remaining the height H. The H is decided by the gate-groove depth in *Step 7* in Section 2.1 and Figure 1. The ΔV_{th} in this report was not yet at its best ability considering the ferroelectric height H = 450 nm. In the vertical direction of FeFET, a gate stack by filling SBT should be essentially the same as a large L_{ch} conventional one by etching SBT. Therefore, potential ΔV_{th} will become the same as that of conventional FeFETs by improving the details in the fabrication process in Section 2.1. An immediate target for the present FeFET will be realizing ΔV_{th} = 0.7 V by *Ers* of (−6V, 10 μs) and *Prg* of (6V, 10 μs) for H = 190 nm as demonstrated before using Pt/CSBT/HfO$_2$/Si FeFETs [7].

3.2.2. Retention

Retention of a FeFET was measured by the procedures as shown in Figure 6a,b. After program (*Prg*), *Retain* and *Read* were repeated during the scheduled time. In *Prg*, a V_g pulse of (V_P, t_{EP}) was applied with $V_d = V_s = V_{sub} = 0$ V. In *Retain*, all the terminals were kept at zero as $V_g = V_d = V_s = V_{sub} = 0$ V. In *Read* at a certain time t, an I_d–V_g curve was drawn by varying V_g in a narrow range from 0 to 1.0 V at $V_d = 0.1$ V and $V_s = V_{sub} = 0$ V. A V_{thP} was extracted from the I_d–V_g and plotted with a marker at t as shown in Figure 6c. After completing the V_{thP}-t, V_{thE}-t started to be measured. In erase (*Ers*), a V_g pulse of (V_E, t_{EP}) was applied with $V_d = V_s = V_{sub} = 0$ V. After *Ers*, *Retain* and *Read* were repeated during the scheduled time. The *Retain* and *Read* conditions for V_{thE}-t were the same as those for V_{thP}-t. In the *Read* at a certain time t, an extracted V_{thE} was plotted with a marker at t as shown in Figure 6c. In this work, $V_P = 8$ V, $V_E = -8$ V and $t_{EP} = 10$ µs. The retention was measured for 10^5 s in each of V_{thP}-t and V_{thE}-t. At $t = 10^5$ s, they were still distinguishable with a difference $\Delta V_{th} = 0.26$ V. When $t > 10^3$ s, as shown in Figure 6c, the gradient of the V_{thP}-$\log(t)$ and V_{thE}-$\log(t)$ curves appeared to be nearly zero. A possible ten-year retention was suggested by extrapolation lines drawn on the last three markers in each branch. The present $L_{ch} = 85$ nm FeFET showed a good retention to the same extent as those of the conventional (C)SBT FeFETs [1–9,11,12,37–40,42,45,46,52].

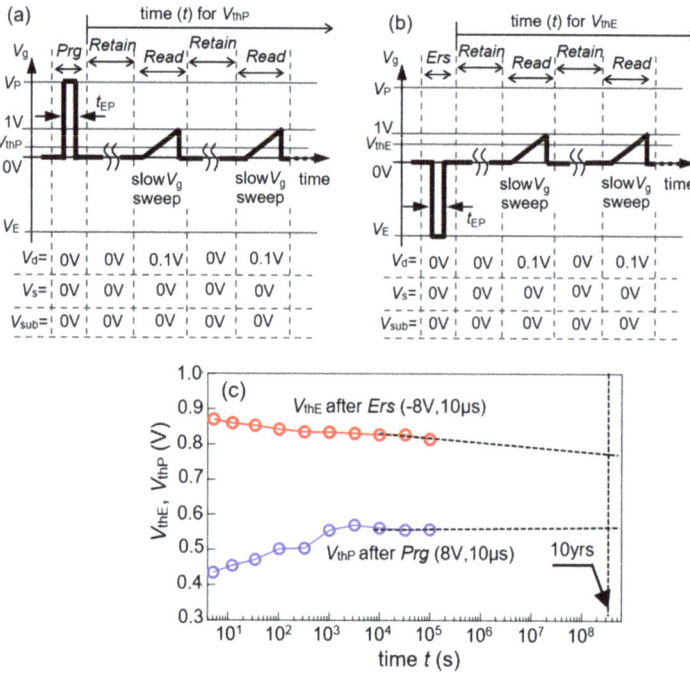

Figure 6. Retention investigation after applying V_g pulses to a FeFET with $L_{ch} = 85$ nm. The channel width was $W = 100$ µm. The measurement procedures for the retentions of (a) V_{thP} after *Prg* of (V_P, t_{EP}) and (b) V_{thE} after *Ers* of (V_E, t_{EP}). (c) The measured retentions for 10^5 s each. Dashed lines are extrapolations of V_{thP}–$\log(t)$ and V_{thE}-$\log(t)$ for estimating V_{thP} and V_{thE} after ten years.

3.2.3. Endurance

Endurance of a FeFET was measured by the procedure shown in Figure 7a. After imposing endurance cycles on FeFETs, pairs of V_{thE} and V_{thP} were obtained. The endurance cycles consisted of periodic bipolar V_g pulses for an alternate *Ers* of (V_E, t_{EP}) and *Prg* of (V_P, t_{EP}) with $V_d = V_s = V_{sub} = 0$ V. The endurance-cycle application was interrupted at certain scheduled cycle numbers (N). After the N cycle application, V_{thE} and V_{thP} were read as follows: a series operation of *Ers*, *Read*, *Prg*, and *Read*, in this order was performed. In *Ers*, a single V_g pulse of (V_E, t_{EP}) was applied with $V_d = V_s = V_{sub} = 0$ V. In *Read* after *Ers*, an I_d-V_g was measured by varying V_g in a narrow range from 0 to 1.5 V at $V_d = 0.1$ V and $V_s = V_{sub} = 0$ V. A V_{thE} was extracted from the $I_d–V_g$ and plotted with a marker at N as shown in Figure 7b. In *Prg*, a single V_g pulse of (V_P, t_{EP}) was applied with $V_d = V_s = V_{sub} = 0$ V. In *Read* after *Prg*, an $I_d–V_g$ was measured under the same conditions with *Read* after *Ers*. The obtained V_{thP} was plotted with a marker at N as shown in Figure 7b.

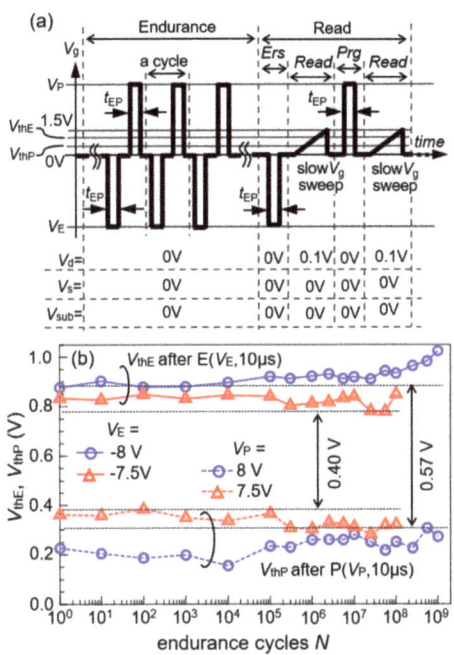

Figure 7. Endurance of a FeFET with L_{ch} = 85 nm. The channel width was W = 80 μm. (**a**) The measurement procedures of applying endurance cycles and reading V_{thE} and V_{thP}. (**b**) Endurances were measured up to $N = 10^8$ cycles for 7.5 V V_g pulse heights and $N = 10^9$ cycles for 8 V.

As shown in Figure 7b, the *Ers* of (−7.5 V, 10 μs) and *Prg* of (7.5 V, 10 μs) were first applied for an endurance up to $N = 10^8$ cycles. Next, a stronger input of (−8 V, 10 μs) and (8 V, 10 μs) was applied to the same FeFET up to $N = 10^9$ cycles. No significant sifts of V_{thE} and V_{thP} were observed throughout the measurements. By taking the minimum of the V_{thE} and the maximum of the V_{thP} in the endurance test, $\Delta V_{th} = 0.40$ V for $|V_E| = V_P = 7.5$ V and $\Delta V_{th} = 0.57$ V for $|V_E| = V_P = 8$ V were obtained. These were margins for distinguishing V_{thE} from V_{thP} as indicated in Figure 7b. In spite of using the rather complicated dummy-gate process, the L_{ch} = 85 nm FeFET fabricated showed high endurance up to $10^8 \sim 10^9$ cycles. This is the same as the endurance level that (C)SBT-FeFETs inherently have [1–12].

4. Summary

A new fabrication process of a FeFET was proposed and demonstrated. Dummy-gate patterns with self-aligned sources and drains were prepared on a Si substrate. HfO_2 with a thickness of 5 nm was inserted in advance between the dummy-gate substance and the Si substrate. The dummy substance was selectively removed to form a self-aligned groove on the gate. A thin SBT precursor film was deposited to fill up the groove. After forming the Ir gate electrode on the SBT, the whole gate stack was annealed for the SBT crystallization. The finished FeFET of Ir/SBT/HfO_2/Si had a channel length L_{ch} = 85 nm. The FeFET exhibited a 10^9 cycle-high endurance and long stable retentions measured for 10^5 s. By adopting the replacement-gate process, area-scalable SBT-FeFETs with the high endurance and long retention were successfully produced.

Author Contributions: Conceptualization followed by numerous improvements with respect to the device structure and processing, M.T.; the anneal and MOCVD processes, S.S.; SEM observation, M.T.; creation of PC-controlled measurement programs, S.S.; electrical measurement of the devices, S.S.; data analysis and discussion, S.S. and M.T.; writing—original draft preparation, M.T.; writing—review and editing, M.T. and S.S. All authors have read and agreed to the published version of the manuscript.

Funding: This research received no external funding.

Institutional Review Board Statement: Not applicable.

Informed Consent Statement: Not applicable.

Data Availability Statement: Not applicable.

Acknowledgments: This work was partially supported by WACOM R&D Corporation. We used the EB lithography system in the NPF of AIST, supported by MEXT, Japan.

Conflicts of Interest: The authors declare no conflict of interest.

References

1. Sakai, S.; Ilangovan, R. Metal-ferroelectric-insulator-semiconductor memory FET with long retention and high endurance. *IEEE Electron Device Lett.* **2004**, *25*, 369–371. [CrossRef]
2. Yan, K.; Takahashi, M.; Sakai, S. Electrical properties of ferroelectric-gate FETs with $SrBi_2Ta_2O_9$ formed using MOCVD technique. *Appl. Phys. A Mater. Sci. Process.* **2012**, *108*, 835–842. [CrossRef]
3. Sakai, S.; Zhang, W.; Takahashi, M. Dynamic analog characteristics of 10^9 cycle-endurance low-voltage nonvolatile ferroelectric-gate memory transistors. In Proceedings of the 2017 IEEE 9th International Memory Workshop, Monterey, CA, USA, 14–17 May 2017; pp. 95–98. [CrossRef]
4. Hai, L.V.; Takahashi, M.; Sakai, S. Fabrication and characterization of sub-0.6-μm ferroelectric-gate field-effect transistors. *Semicond. Sci. Technol.* **2010**, *25*, 115013. [CrossRef]
5. Zhang, W.; Takahashi, M.; Sakai, S. Electrical properties of $Ca_xSr_{1-x}Bi_2Ta_2O_9$ ferroelectric-gate field-effect transistors. *Semicond. Sci. Technol.* **2013**, *28*, 085003. [CrossRef]
6. Hai, L.V.; Takahashi, M.; Zhang, W.; Sakai, S. Novel process for widening memory window of sub-200nm ferroelectric-gate field-effect transistor by ferroelectric coating the gate-stack sidewall. *Semicond. Sci. Technol.* **2015**, *30*, 015024. [CrossRef]
7. Hai, L.V.; Takahashi, M.; Zhang, W.; Sakai, S. 100-nm-size ferroelectric-gate field-effect transistor with 10^8-cycle endurance. *Jpn. J. Appl. Phys.* **2015**, *54*, 088004. [CrossRef]
8. Zhang, W.; Takahashi, M.; Sasaki, Y.; Kusuhara, M.; Sakai, S. 3.3 V write-voltage $Ir/Ca_{0.2}Sr_{0.8}Bi_2Ta_2O_9/HfO_2/Si$ ferroelectric-gate field-effect transistors with 10^9 endurance and good retention. *Jpn. J. Appl. Phys.* **2017**, *56*, 04CE04. [CrossRef]
9. Sakai, S.; Takahashi, M.; Takeuchi, K.; Li, Q.-H.; Horiuchi, T.; Wang, S.; Yun, K.-Y.; Takamiya, M.; Sakurai, T. Highly scalable Fe(ferroelectric)-NAND cell with MFIS(metal-ferroelectric-insulator-semiconductor) structure for sub-10nm tera-bit capacity NAND flash memories. In Proceedings of the 2008 Joint Non-Volatile Semiconductor Memory Workshop and International Conference on Memory Technology and Design, Opio, France, 18–22 May 2008; pp. 103–105. [CrossRef]
10. Zhang, X.; Miyaji, K.; Takahashi, M.; Takeuchi, K.; Sakai, S. 0.5V bit-line-voltage self-boost-programming in ferroelectric-NAND flash memory. In Proceedings of the 2011 3rd IEEE International Memory Workshop, Monterey, CA, USA, 22–25 May 2011; pp. 155–158. [CrossRef]
11. Zhang, X.; Takahashi, M.; Takeuchi, K.; Sakai, S. 64 kbit ferroelectric-gate-transistor-integrated NAND flash memory with 7.5 V program and long data retention. *Jpn. J. Appl. Phys.* **2012**, *51*, 04DD01. [CrossRef]
12. Takahashi, M.; Zhang, W.; Sakai, S. High-endurance ferroelectric NOR flash memory using $(Ca,Sr)Bi_2Ta_2O_9$ FeFETs. In Proceedings of the 2018 IEEE 10th International Memory Workshop, Kyoto, Japan, 13–16 May 2018; pp. 58–61. [CrossRef]
13. De Araujo, C.A.P.; Cuchiaro, J.D.; McMillan, L.D.; Scott, M.C.; Scott, J.F. Fatigue-free ferroelectric capacitors with platinum electrodes. *Nature* **1995**, *374*, 627–629. [CrossRef]
14. Noguchi, T.; Hase, T.; Miyasaka, Y. Analysis of the dependence of ferroelectric properties of strontium bismuth tantalate (SBT) thin film on the composition and process temperature. *Jpn. J. Appl. Phys.* **1996**, *35*, 4900–4904. [CrossRef]
15. Lettieri, J.; Jia, Y.; Urbanik, M.; Weber, C.I.; Maria, J.-P.; Schlom, D.G.; Li, H.; Ramesh, R.; Uecker, R.; Reiche, P. Epitaxial growth of (001)-oriented and (110)-oriented $SrBi_2Ta_2O_9$ thin films. *Appl. Phys. Lett.* **1995**, *66*, 221–223. [CrossRef]
16. Ishikawa, K.; Funakubo, H. Electrical properties of (001)- and (116)-oriented epitaxial $SrBi_2Ta_2O_9$ thin films prepared by metalorganic chemical vapor deposition. *Appl. Phys. Lett.* **1999**, *75*, 1970–1972. [CrossRef]
17. Ishikawa, K.; Funakubo, H.; Saito, K.; Suzuki, T.; Nishi, Y.; Fujimoto, M. Crystal structure and electrical properties of epitaxial $SrBi_2Ta_2O_9$ films. *J. Appl. Phys.* **2000**, *87*, 8018–8023. [CrossRef]
18. Lee, H.N.; Visinoiu, A.; Senz, S.; Harnagea, C.; Pignolet, A.; Hesse, D.; Gösele, U. Structural and electrical anisotropy of (001)-, (116)-, and (103)-oriented epitaxial $SrBi_2Ta_2O_9$ thin films on $SrTiO_3$ substrates grown by pulsed laser deposition. *J. Appl. Phys.* **2000**, *88*, 6658–6664. [CrossRef]

19. Amanuma, K.; Hase, T.; Miyasaka, Y. Preparation and ferroelectric properties of SrBi$_2$Ta$_2$O$_9$ thin films. *Appl. Phys. Lett.* **1995**, *66*, 221–223. [CrossRef]
20. Atsuki, T.; Soyama, N.; Yonezawa, T.; Ogi, K. Preparation of Bi-based ferroelectric thin films by Sol-Gel method. *Jpn. J. Appl. Phys.* **1995**, *34*, 5096–5099. [CrossRef]
21. Robertson, J.; Chen, C.W.; Warren, W.L.; Gutleben, C.D. Electronic structure of the ferroelectric layered perovskite SrBi$_2$Ta$_2$O$_9$. *Appl. Phys. Lett.* **1996**, *69*, 1704–1706. [CrossRef]
22. Harnagea, C.; Pignolet, A.; Alexe, M.; Hesse, D.; Gösele, U. Quantitative ferroelectric characterization of single submicron grains in Bi-layered perovskite thin films. *Appl. Phys. A* **2000**, *70*, 261–267. [CrossRef]
23. Kalinin, S.V.; Gruverman, A.; Bonnell, D.A. Quantitative analysis of nanoscale switching in SrBi$_2$Ta$_2$O$_9$ thin films by piezoresponse force microscopy. *Appl. Phys. Lett.* **2004**, *85*, 795. [CrossRef]
24. Amorín, H.; Shvartsman, V.V.; Kholkin, A.L.; Costa, M.E.V. Ferroelectric and dielectric anisotropy in high-quality SrBi$_2$Ta$_2$O$_9$ single crystals. *Appl. Phys. Lett.* **2004**, *85*, 5667. [CrossRef]
25. Yu, T.; Shen, Z.X.; Toh, W.S.; Xue, J.M.; Wang, J. Size effect on the ferroelectric phase transition in SrBi$_2$Ta$_2$O$_9$ nanoparticles. *J. Appl. Phys.* **2003**, *94*, 618–620. [CrossRef]
26. Gruverman, A. Scaling effect on statistical behavior of switching parameters of ferroelectric capacitors. *Appl. Phys. Lett.* **1999**, *75*, 1452–1454. [CrossRef]
27. Tamura, T.; Arimoto, Y.; Ishiwara, H. A New Circuit Simulation Model of Ferroelectric Capacitors. *Jpn. J. Appl. Phys.* **2002**, *41*, 2654–2657. [CrossRef]
28. Pan, B.; Yu, H.; Wu, D.; Zhou, X.H.; Liu, J.-M. Dynamic response and hysteresis dispersion scaling of ferroelectric SrBi$_2$Ta$_2$O$_9$ thin films. *Appl. Phys. Lett.* **2003**, *83*, 1406–1408. [CrossRef]
29. Lee, W.-J.; Cho, C.-R.; Kim, S.-H.; You, I.-K.; Kim, B.W.; Yu, B.-G.; Shin, C.H.; Lee, H.C. Etching Behavior and Damage Recovery of SrBi$_2$Ta$_2$O$_9$ Thin Films. *Jpn. J. Appl. Phys.* **1999**, *38*, L1428–L1431. [CrossRef]
30. Asami, K.; Koiwa, I.; Yamanobe, T. Effects of Ion Etching and Annealing in O$_2$ Atmosphere Following Ion Etching on Properties and Chemistry of Sr$_{0.9}$Bi$_{2.1}$Ta$_2$O$_{9+\alpha}$ Thin Films. *Jpn. J. Appl. Phys.* **1999**, *38*, 5423–5427. [CrossRef]
31. Stafford, L.; Margot, J.; Delprat, S.; Chaker, M.; Pearton, S.J. Influence of redeposition on the plasma etching dynamics. *J. Appl. Phys.* **2007**, *101*, 083303. [CrossRef]
32. Efremov, A.M.; Kim, D.-P.; Kim, C.-I. Investigation of thin films etching mechanisms in plasma. *J. Vsc. Sci. Technol. A* **2003**, *21*, 1017–1023. [CrossRef]
33. Shimakawa, Y.; Kubo, Y.; Nakagawa, Y.; Goto, S.; Kamiyama, T.; Asano, H.; Izumi, F. Crystal structure and ferroelectric properties of ABi$_2$Ta$_2$O$_9$ (A = Ca, Sr, and Ba). *Phys. Rev. B* **2000**, *61*, 6559–6564. [CrossRef]
34. Noguchi, Y.; Shimizu, H.; Miyayama, M.; Oikawa, K.; Kamiyama, T. Ferroelectric properties and structure distortion in A-site-modified SrBi$_2$Ta$_2$O$_9$. *Jpn. J. Appl. Phys.* **2001**, *40*, 5812–5815. [CrossRef]
35. Das, R.R.; Bhattacharya, P.; Pe´rez, W.; Katiyar, R.S. Ferroelectric properties of laser-ablated Sr$_{1-x}$A$_x$Bi$_2$Ta$_2$O$_9$ thin films (where A = Ba, Ca). *Appl. Phys. Lett.* **2002**, *80*, 637–639. [CrossRef]
36. Das, R.R.; Bhattacharya, P.; Pe´rez, W.; Katiyar, R.S. Influence of Ca on structural and ferroelectric properties of laser ablated SrBi$_2$Ta$_2$O$_9$ thin films. *Jpn. J. Appl. Phys.* **2003**, *42*, 162–165. [CrossRef]
37. Development of the 1T FeRAM: Towards the Realization of the Ultra-Gbit Next-Generation Semiconductor Memory. AIST Research Results Archive, 24 October 2002. Available online: https://www.aist.go.jp/aist_e/list/latest_research/2002/20021024/20021024.html (accessed on 14 December 2020).
38. Sakai, S.; Takahashi, M.; Ilangovan, R. Long-retention ferroelectric-gate FET with a (HfO$_2$)$_x$(Al$_2$O$_3$)$_{1-x}$ buffer-insulating layer for 1T FeRAM. In Proceedings of the 2004 IEDM Technical Digest. IEEE International Electron Devices Meeting, San Francisco, CA, USA, 13–15 December 2004; pp. 915–918. [CrossRef]
39. Sakai, S.; Ilangovan, R.; Takahashi, M. Pt/SrBi$_2$Ta$_2$O$_9$/Hf-Al-O/Si field-effect-transistor with long retention using unsaturated ferroelectric polarization switching. *Jpn. J. Appl. Phys.* **2004**, *43*, 7876–7878. [CrossRef]
40. Li, Q.H.; Sakai, S. Characterization of Pt/SrBi$_2$Ta$_2$O$_9$/Hf-Al-O/Si field-effect transistors at elevated temperatures. *Appl. Phys. Lett.* **2006**, *89*, 222910. [CrossRef]
41. Li, Q.H.; Takahashi, M.; Horiuchi, T.; Wang, S.Y.; Sakai, S. Threshold-voltage distribution of Pt/SrBi$_2$Ta$_2$O$_9$/Hf-Al-O/Si MFIS FETs. *Semicond. Sci. Technol.* **2008**, *23*, 045011. [CrossRef]
42. Li, Q.H.; Horiuchi, T.; Wang, S.Y.; Takahashi, M.; Sakai, S. Threshold voltage adjustment of ferroelectric-gate field effect transistors by ion implantation. *Semicond. Sci. Technol.* **2009**, *24*, 025012. [CrossRef]
43. Sakai, S.; Zhang, W.; Takahashi, M. Method for disclosing invisible physical properties in metal-ferroelectric-insulator-semiconductor gate stacks. *J. Phys. D Appl. Phys.* **2017**, *50*, 165107. [CrossRef]
44. Zhang, W.; Takahashi, M.; Sakai, S. Investigation of ferroelectric grain sizes and orientations in Pt/Ca$_x$Sr$_{1-x}$Bi$_2$Ta$_2$O$_9$/Hf–Al–O/Si high performance ferroelectric-gate field-effect-transistors. *Materials* **2019**, *12*, 399. [CrossRef]
45. Takahashi, M.; Sakai, S. Self-aligned-gate metal/ferroelectric/insulator/semiconductor field-effect transistors with long memory retention. *Jpn. J. Appl. Phys.* **2005**, *44*, L800–L802. [CrossRef]
46. Horiuchi, T.; Takahashi, M.; Li, Q.H.; Wang, S.Y.; Sakai, S. Lowered operation voltage in Pt/SBi$_2$Ta$_2$O$_9$/HfO$_2$/Si ferroelectric-gate field-effect transistors by oxynitriding Si. *Semicond. Sci. Technol.* **2010**, *25*, 055005. [CrossRef]

47. Takahashi, M.; Horiuchi, T.; Li, Q.H.; Wang, S.Y.; Sakai, S. Basic operation of novel ferroelectric CMOS circuits. *Electron. Lett.* **2008**, *44*, 467–468. [CrossRef]
48. Takahashi, M.; Wang, S.Y.; Horiuchi, T.; Sakai, S. FeCMOS logic inverter circuits with nonvolatile-memory function. *IEICE Electron. Express* **2009**, *6*, 831–836. [CrossRef]
49. Wang, S.Y.; Takahashi, M.; Li, Q.H.; Takeuchi, K.; Sakai, S. Operational method of a ferroelectric (Fe)-NAND flash memory array. *Semicond. Sci. Technol.* **2009**, *24*, 105029. [CrossRef]
50. Miyaji, K.; Noda, S.; Hatanaka, T.; Takahashi, M.; Sakai, S.; Takeuchi, K. A 1.0 V power supply, 9.5 GByte/sec write speed, Single-Cell Self-Boost program scheme for Ferroelectric NAND Flash SSD. In Proceedings of the 2010 IEEE International Memory Workshop, Seoul, South Korea, 16–19 May 2010; pp. 1–4. [CrossRef]
51. Zhang, X.; Takahashi, M.; Sakai, S. FeFET logic circuits for operating a 64 kb FeNAND flash memory array. *Integr. Ferroelectr.* **2012**, *132*, 114–121. [CrossRef]
52. Sakai, S.; Zhang, X.Z.; Hai, L.V.; Zhang, W.; Takahashi, M. Downsizing and memory array integration of Pt/SrBi$_2$Ta$_2$O$_9$/Hf-Al-O/Si ferroelectric-gate field-effect transistors. In Proceedings of the 2012 12th Annual Non-Volatile Memory Technology Symposium, Singapore, 31 October–2 November 2012; pp. 55–59. [CrossRef]
53. Sakai, S.; Takahashi, M.; Motohashi, K.; Yamaguchi, Y.; Yui, N.; Kobayashi, T. Large-area pulsed-laser deposition of dielectric and ferroelectric thin films. *J. Vac. Sci. Technol. A* **2007**, *25*, 903–907. [CrossRef]
54. Sakai, S. Semiconductor-Ferroelectric Storage Devices and Processes for Producing The Same. U.S. Patent 7,226,795, 2007.
55. Böscke, T.S.; Müller, J.; Bräuhaus, D.; Schröder, U.; Böttger, U. Ferroelectricity in hafnium oxide: CMOS compatible ferroelectric field effect transistors. In Proceedings of the 2011 IEDM Technical Digest. IEEE International Electron Devices Meeting, Washington, DC, USA, 5–7 December 2011; pp. 24.5.1–24.5.4. [CrossRef]
56. Müller, J.; Yurchuk, E.; Schlösser, T.; Paul, J.; Hoffmann, R.; Müller, S.; Martin, D.; Slesazeck, S.; Polakowski, P.; Sundqvist, J.; et al. Ferroelectricity in HfO$_2$ enables nonvolatile data storage in 28 nm HKMG. In Proceedings of the 2012 Symposium on VLSI Technology, Honolulu, HI, USA, 12–14 June 2012; pp. 25–26. [CrossRef]
57. Ali, T.; Polakowski, P.; Riedel, S.; Büttner, T.; Kämpfe, T.; Rudolph, M.; Pätzold, B.; Seidel, K.; Löhr, D.; Hoffmann, R.; et al. Silicon doped hafnium oxide (HSO) and hafnium zirconium oxide (HZO) based FeFET: A material relation to device physics. *Appl. Phys. Lett.* **2018**, *112*, 222903. [CrossRef]
58. Fukuda, M.; Mizubayashi, W.; Kohno, A.; Miyazaki, S.; Hirose, M. Analysis of Tunnel Current through Ultrathin Gate Oxides. *Jpn. J. Appl. Phys.* **1998**, *37*, L1534–L1536. [CrossRef]
59. Shrenk, A.; Heiser, G. Modeling and simulation of tunneling through ultra-thin gate dielectrics. *J. Appl. Phys.* **1997**, *81*, 7900–7908. [CrossRef]
60. Takahashi, M.; Sakai, S. 2.3.3 Requirements to the F Layer, Chap.2 Development of high-endurance and long-retention FeFETs of Pt/Ca$_y$Sr$_{1-y}$Bi$_2$Ta$_2$O$_9$/(HfO$_2$)$_x$(Al$_2$O$_3$)$_{1-x}$/Si gate stacks. In *Ferroelectric-Gate Field Effect Transistor Memories*, 2nd ed.; Park, B.-E., Ishiwara, H., Okuyama, M., Sakai, S., Yoon, S.-M., Eds.; Springer: Singapore, Singapore, 2020; pp. 35–37. [CrossRef]
61. Kingston, R.; Neustadter, S.F. Calculation of the Space Charge, Electric Field, and Free Carrier Concentration at the Surface of a Semiconductor. *J. Appl. Phys.* **1955**, *26*, 718–720. [CrossRef]
62. Sze, S.M. Chap.7, MIS Diode and Charge-Coupled Device. In *Physics of Semiconductor Devices*, 2nd ed.; John Wiley & Sons: New York, NY, USA, 1981; pp. 366–369.
63. Zhang, F.; Hsu, S.T.; Ono, Y.; Ulrich, B.; Zhuang, W.; Ying, H.; Stecker, L.; Evans, D.R.; Maa, J. Fabrication and characterization of sub-micron metal-ferroelectric-insulator-semiconductor field effect transistors with Pt/Pb$_5$Ge$_3$O$_{11}$/ZrO$_2$/Si structure. *Jpn. J. Appl. Phys.* **2001**, *40*, L635–L637. [CrossRef]
64. Li, T.; Hsu, S.T.; Ulrich, B.; Ying, H.; Stecker, L.; Evans, D.R.; Ono, Y.; Maa, J.; Lee, J.J. Fabrication and characterization of a Pb$_5$Ge$_3$O$_{11}$ one-transistor-memory device. *Appl. Phys. Lett.* **2001**, *79*, 1661–1663. [CrossRef]
65. Müller, J.; Böscke, T.S.; Schröder, U.; Mueller, S.; Bräuhaus, D.; Böttger, U.; Frey, L.; Mikolajick, T. Ferroelectricity in simple binary ZrO$_2$ and HfO$_2$. *Nano Lett.* **2012**, *12*, 4318–4323. [CrossRef]
66. Shimizu, T.; Katayama, K.; Kiguchi, T.; Akama, A.; Konno, T.J.; Sakata, O.; Funakubo, H. The demonstration of significant ferroelectricity in epitaxial Y-doped HfO$_2$ film. *Sci. Rep.* **2016**, *6*, 32931. [CrossRef] [PubMed]
67. Yurchuk, E.; Müller, J.; Hoffmann, R.; Paul, J.; Martin, D.; Boschke, R.; Schlösser, T.; Müller, S.; Slesazeck, S.; Bentum, R.; et al. HfO$_2$-Based Ferroelectric Field-Effect Transistors with 260 nm Channel Length and Long Data Retention. In Proceedings of the 2012 IEEE International Memory Workshop, Milan, Italy, 20–23 May 2012; pp. 1–4. [CrossRef]
68. Trentzsch, M.; Flachowsky, S.; Richter, R.; Paul, J.; Reimer, B.; Utess, D.; Jansen, S.; Mulaosmanovic, H.; Müller, S.; Slesazeck, S.; et al. A 28nm HKMG super low power embedded NVM technology based on ferroelectric FETs. In Proceedings of the 2016 IEEE International Electron Devices Meeting, San Francisco, CA, USA, 3–7 December 2016; pp. 11.5.1–11.5.4. [CrossRef]
69. Mulaosmanovic, H.; Breyer, E.T.; Mikolajick, T.; Slesazeck, S. Ferroelectric FETs with 20-nm-Thick HfO$_2$ Layer for Large Memory Window and High Performance. *IEEE Trans. Electron. Devices* **2019**, *66*, 3828–3833. [CrossRef]
70. Zhou, H.; Ocker, J.; Mennenga, M.; Noack, M.; Müller, S.; Trentzsch, M.; Dünkel, S.; Beyer, S.; Mikolajick, T. Endurance and targeted programming behavior of HfO$_2$-FeFETs. In Proceedings of the 2020 IEEE International Memory Workshop, Dresden, Germany, 17–20 May 2020; pp. 1–4. [CrossRef]
71. Wong, H.; Iwai, H. On the scaling issues and high-κ replacement of ultrathin gate dielectrics for nanoscale MOS transistors. *Microelectron. Eng.* **2006**, *83*, 1867–1904. [CrossRef]

72. Tagantsev, A.K.; Stolichnov, I.; Setter, N.; Cross, J.S.; Tsukada, M. Non-Kolmogorov-Avrami switching kinetics in ferroelectric thin films. *Phys. Rev. B* **2002**, *66*, 214109. [CrossRef]
73. Jo, J.Y.; Yang, S.M.; Kim, T.H.; Lee, H.N.; Yoon, J.-G.; Park, S.; Jo, Y.; Jung, M.H.; Noh, T.W. Nonlinear dynamics of domain-wall propagation in epitaxial ferroelectric thin films. *Phys. Rev. Lett.* **2009**, *102*, 045701. [CrossRef]

Review

On the Thermal Models for Resistive Random Access Memory Circuit Simulation

Juan B. Roldán [1,*], Gerardo González-Cordero [1], Rodrigo Picos [2], Enrique Miranda [3], Félix Palumbo [4], Francisco Jiménez-Molinos [1], Enrique Moreno [5], David Maldonado [1], Santiago B. Baldomá [6], Mohamad Moner Al Chawa [7], Carol de Benito [2], Stavros G. Stavrinides [8], Jordi Suñé [3] and Leon O. Chua [9]

[1] Departamento de Electrónica y Tecnología de Computadores, Facultad de Ciencias, Universidad de Granada, Avd. Fuentenueva s/n, 18071 Granada, Spain; g2cordr@gmail.com (G.G.-C.); jmolinos@ugr.es (F.J.-M.); dmaldonado@ugr.es (D.M.)

[2] Industrial Engineering and Construction Department, University of Balearic Islands, 07122 Palma, Spain; rodrigo.picos@uib.es (R.P.); carol.debenito@uib.es (C.d.B.)

[3] Department Enginyeria Electrònica, Universitat Autònoma de Barcelona, Edifici Q., 08193 Bellaterra, Spain; enrique.miranda@uab.cat (E.M.); jordi.sune@uab.cat (J.S.)

[4] Consejo Nacional de Investigaciones Científicas y Técnicas (CONICET), Godoy Cruz 2290, Buenos Aires C1425FQB, Argentina; felix.palumbo@conicet.gov.ar

[5] UJM-St-Etienne, CNRS, Laboratoire Hubert Curien UMR 5516, Institute of Optics Graduate School, University Lyon, F-42023 St-Etienne, France; enrique.manuel.moreno.perez@univ-st-etienne.fr

[6] Unidad de Investigación y Desarrollo de las Ingenierías (UIDI), Facultad Regional Buenos Aires, Universidad Tecnológica Nacional, Medrano 951, Buenos Aires C1179AAQ, Argentina; sanboyeras@gmail.com

[7] Institute of Circuits and Systems, Technische Universität Dresden, 01062 Dresden, Germany; mohamad_moner.al_chawa@tu-dresden.de

[8] School of Science and Technology, Thermi University Campus, International Hellenic University, 57001 Thessaloniki, Greece; s.stavrinides@ihu.edu.gr

[9] Electrical Engineering and Computer Science Department, University of California, Berkeley, CA 94720-1770, USA; chua@berkeley.edu

* Correspondence: jroldan@ugr.es

Citation: Roldán, J.B.; González-Cordero, G.; Picos, R.; Miranda, E.; Palumbo, F.; Jiménez-Molinos, F.; Moreno, E.; Maldonado, D.; Baldomá, S.B.; Moner Al Chawa, M.; et al. On the Thermal Models for Resistive Random Access Memory Circuit Simulation. *Nanomaterials* **2021**, *11*, 1261. https://doi.org/10.3390/nano11051261

Academic Editor: Antonio Di Bartolomeo

Received: 11 April 2021
Accepted: 1 May 2021
Published: 11 May 2021

Publisher's Note: MDPI stays neutral with regard to jurisdictional claims in published maps and institutional affiliations.

Copyright: © 2021 by the authors. Licensee MDPI, Basel, Switzerland. This article is an open access article distributed under the terms and conditions of the Creative Commons Attribution (CC BY) license (https://creativecommons.org/licenses/by/4.0/).

Abstract: Resistive Random Access Memories (RRAMs) are based on resistive switching (RS) operation and exhibit a set of technological features that make them ideal candidates for applications related to non-volatile memories, neuromorphic computing and hardware cryptography. For the full industrial development of these devices different simulation tools and compact models are needed in order to allow computer-aided design, both at the device and circuit levels. Most of the different RRAM models presented so far in the literature deal with temperature effects since the physical mechanisms behind RS are thermally activated; therefore, an exhaustive description of these effects is essential. As far as we know, no revision papers on thermal models have been published yet; and that is why we deal with this issue here. Using the heat equation as the starting point, we describe the details of its numerical solution for a conventional RRAM structure and, later on, present models of different complexity to integrate thermal effects in complete compact models that account for the kinetics of the chemical reactions behind resistive switching and the current calculation. In particular, we have accounted for different conductive filament geometries, operation regimes, filament lateral heat losses, the use of several temperatures to characterize each conductive filament, among other issues. A 3D numerical solution of the heat equation within a complete RRAM simulator was also taken into account. A general memristor model is also formulated accounting for temperature as one of the state variables to describe electron device operation. In addition, to widen the view from different perspectives, we deal with a thermal model contextualized within the quantum point contact formalism. In this manner, the temperature can be accounted for the description of quantum effects in the RRAM charge transport mechanisms. Finally, the thermometry of conducting filaments and the corresponding models considering different dielectric materials are tackled in depth.

Keywords: resistive memories; thermal model; heat equation; thermal conductivity; circuit simulation; compact modeling; resistive switching; nanodevices

1. Introduction

Resistive memories (also known as resistive random access memories or RRAMs) base their operation on resistive switching mechanisms to modulate their conductance in a non-volatile manner [1–3]. Their promising potential is subject to scrutiny both in academia and in industry. These devices could be alternatives to flash devices in applications related to their non-volatility, such as storage class memories [4]. RRAMs show short read/write times, good enough endurance and retention behavior, low power operation, CMOS technology compatibility and the possibility to be built on 3D stacks [1,2]. Apart from non-volatile memory circuits, where certain applications are currently on the market, RRAMs show great potential for cryptographic circuits due to their inherent stochasticity, which can be employed for the design of random number generators and physical unclonable functions [5–9]. Nevertheless, currently, the hottest application for these devices is linked to neuromorphic circuits [10–15]. RRAMs can mimic biological synapses within a fully compatible CMOS technology context to facilitate the fabrication of hardware neural networks. This approach allows the use of a lower number of electronic components (by means of RS device crossbars) and low power consumption [1,10,11,14,16] than the purely CMOS alternative to neuromorphic circuits firstly introduced by Mead in the late eighties [17]. The number of papers on this subject including resistive switching devices is growing by leaps and bounds. Nevertheless, different issues should be improved for these devices in order to overcome the difficulties connected to massive industrial use; among them, the following should be counted: great temperature sensitivity, manufacturing processes, variability and the lack of well-established electronic design automation (EDA) tools, including in the latter issue strategies for parameter extraction. In relation to these essential aspects, we will deal here with the device thermal description and its modeling from a circuit simulation perspective.

The development of RRAM simulation and modeling infrastructure is key to step forward into industrial mature applications. In this respect, in the memory realm, it is important to highlight that DRAM and NAND Flash technologies will continue to hold their ground and even advance despite the slowing of Moore's Law in the short-medium term. Although a great number of papers have been published so far on modeling and simulation issues [18–41], there are many open questions that need to be addressed to improve RRAM position in the EDA context. One of the pressing modeling questions is connected with the device inherent stochasticity that produces cycle-to-cycle variability [19,42–51]. This type of variability has to be managed to achieve RRAM technological maturity; however, even if a variability reduction is achieved, taking into consideration its nature in the modeling is a must [52]. Another modeling battlefield lies in what is linked to thermal effects. It is known that most RS mechanisms are thermally activated [19,23,32,53–57]. The temperature evolution produced by Joule heating in device-relevant regions, where charge conduction is concentrated, determines the operation in many different types of RRAMs [18,19,38,53,58–60]. Consequently, an accurate thermal description is essential to implement both good RRAM physical simulators and compact models. It is also important to highlight that in cross-bar architectures, an optimum topology for hardware neural network implementation among other applications, the thermal evolution of one device might be influenced by neighbor cells. This effect, known as thermal crosstalk [60–63], has to be considered at the integration stage of chips based on RS devices.

Modeling of RRAM, as well as its physical simulation in general, shows notorious differences with respect to other electron devices. In this respect, in devices such as MOSFETs [64,65] (even multigate FETs [66]) or diodes [67,68], once a reasonable grid is established, the main differential equations are discretized and, in general, but for very scarce cases, convergence is searched for to obtain a solution. This is the main scheme to follow in drift-diffusion, hydrodynamic and Monte Carlo simulation approaches [69]. By contrast, in RRAMs the modeling paradigm is different due to the particularities of their operation. For the initial forming process (a pristine dielectric is assumed) and further set processes within RS cycles (in the common filamentary conduction regime, the case we will deal with henceforth), a conductive filament (CF) through the dielectric is formed which shorts the device electrodes and greatly reduce the device resistance [2,70]. Non-linear physical mechanisms (mostly thermally activated, following an Arrhenius' equation relationship) come into play in a positive feedback loop that leads certain magnitudes, such as the temperature, to shoot up. This process has an obvious reflection at the experimental level, the current has to be limited to avoid the device hard breakdown and its consequent destruction. All this leads to the caveat that we have to deal with numerical divergence from the simulation viewpoint. The current is limited in the context of forming or set processes to avoid the device rupture; in this manner, an uncontrolled temperature rise and the corresponding CF quick growth is avoided because after a hard breakdown process RS operation does not hold. At the simulation level, a current limit is also needed. The reset process is also linked to RRAM simulation divergence. As the reset goes on, the CF shrinks and the same current is strangled in a CF narrow section. Hence, Joule heating produces a temperature increase at this CF narrowing. The thermally activated mechanisms in the CF narrowing surroundings rise exponentially and the CF rupture takes place. If the rupture is thermally controlled, as in many unipolar devices, it is based upon a thermal run-away process that leads to the CF destruction. In summary, for a correct RRAM simulation description (both at the device and circuit levels, in the latter case it would be a compact modeling approach), we have to face numerical divergence in addition to nonlinearity in some of the physical magnitudes at hand in one way or other. This means, in general, as the reader can imagine, a numerical nightmare. For instance, when you set up a limit for the compliance current, there might be an important difference between the iteration prior to achieving the current limit and the following step (once the compliance current has been exceeded) in terms of the CF size and temperature in the hottest spot. If you miss to stop the iterations just when the compliance current is reached, and for some reason you iterate once more within the positive feedback loop the device is going through, you can end up wondering what is the dielectric melting temperature.

There are different RRAM models in the literature, and most of them consider thermal effects in one way or another. Some assume a simplified version of the steady-state heat equation (HE); others account for a non-steady-state model where the heat capacitance is included. In general, the main differences are found in the boundary conditions formulation to describe the device physics in the context of the HE or an equivalent energy balance equation. In any case, all these models can be formulated using the standard description proposed by [71], where they fit naturally. By using this formulation, it is clear that all these devices can be considered as extended memristors, this being the most general class of memristor devices according to usual classification [72]. Notice that, from this point of view, RRAM devices can be used inside the memristor framework as circuital elements for purposes further than memory applications [73–75].

Different flavors of these thermal models have been reported; however, as far as we know, they have not been brought together under one roof yet as has been done, for example, with electrical models [41]. We do so here. In Section 2, we comment on the HE in the RRAM operation context, in particular, we explain 3D physical simulation and compact modeling focusing on thermal effects. Section 3 is devoted to the RRAM thermal description through a general memristor model; the RRAM quantum point contact modeling including thermal effects is unfolded in Section 4, and finally, the thermometry of conducting filaments and corresponding modeling is developed in Section 5.

2. Mathematical Description of RRAM Thermal Effects
2.1. Heat Equation

We start by taking the 3D heat equation in the device into consideration, Equation (1):

$$\nabla \cdot (k_{th}(r)\nabla T(r,t)) + \dot{e}_{generated}(r) = \rho(r)c(r)\frac{\partial T(r,t)}{\partial t} \qquad (1)$$

where k_{th}—stands for the thermal conductivity (W/(m K)). This parameter depends on the temperature and geometry (assuming different material layers, which is the case for the usual RRAM architecture), c—stands for the specific heat or specific heat capacity (J/(kg K)). It is assumed that we are considering the specific heat capacity at constant pressure, which is why it is also denoted as c_p, ρ—stands for the material density (kg/m^3) and $\dot{e}_{generated}$—stands for the power density generated (rate of heat generation by means of Joule heating, per unit volume inside the system we are considering). It can be calculated as $\sigma(r)E^2(r)$, where $\sigma(r)$ is the local electrical conductivity and $E(r)$ is the local electric field [18,38]; i.e., the product of the field and the current density.

The RRAM thermal description requires the solution of this equation in the whole device active region. Nevertheless, in the compact modeling approach (CMA) some simplifying assumptions are made. Among others, we consider this equation in the region close to the conductive filament, where charge conduction takes place after a successful set or forming process (when the CF is created the device is said to be in the low resistance state, LRS, while if the CF is ruptured, after a successful reset process, the device resistance is much higher, the device enters in the high resistance state, HRS). If all the different device material layers are included (dielectric, possibly a multilayer stack, electrodes, etc.), the thermal conductivity, the density and specific heat of the different materials have to be considered [29,76,77].

A step forward consists in using the 1D HE version (a simplifying assumption that works well in many cases). If the x coordinate is assumed to be parallel to the CF longitudinal axis, from one of the dielectric-electrode interfaces to the other, and the CF is considered to be narrow enough to consider the same temperature in the transverse sections perpendicular to the x-axis; then, the HE could be written as follows:

$$\frac{\partial}{\partial x}\left(k_{th}(x)\frac{\partial T(x,t)}{\partial x}\right) + \dot{e}_{generated}(x) = \rho(x)c(x)\frac{\partial T(x,t)}{\partial t} \qquad (2)$$

This equation is most of the times solved within the device conductive filament, whose geometry is assumed to be a cylinder or a truncated-cone. For the HE particularization in the RRAM CMA some further assumptions are employed for the sake of simplicity:

(a) Constant thermal conductivity, i.e., $k_{th}(x,T) = k_{th}$. Neither geometric nor temperature dependencies are considered. In most cases, the CF thermal conductivity is the one considered.

(b) A single temperature in the whole conductive filament [38,78] is taken into account (this means a strong simplifying approach). Some models for circuit simulation can account for two different temperatures [79], this is a good strategy since the key (higher) temperature at the CF narrowing, where the CF is ruptured, is decoupled from the main CF bulk temperature; this latter temperature does not increase in the same manner. See Figure 4c in [80], where the CF temperature along the dielectric is plotted for different voltages. It is clear that the temperature is much higher in the CF narrowing while it shows a different behavior for the main CF body. The model with two different CF temperatures is more complex, hence, this issue has to be taken into account when dealing with circuits including hundreds or thousands of components.

Different RRAM cell schematics are shown in Figure 1. Assuming filamentary conduction, the CF evolution has to be calculated to describe RS operation and determine the device current. Several CF types (shapes) from the CMA employed in the literature are represented in Figure 1.

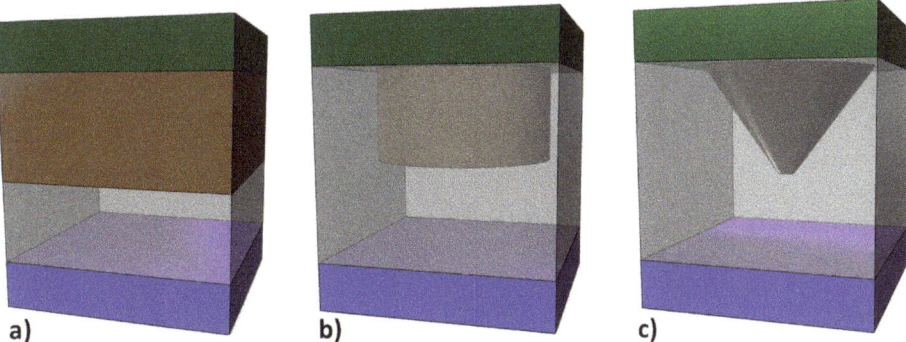

Figure 1. Different conductive filament shapes employed in RRAM compact models for circuit simulation. We will use this CF shapes in the thermal models described below. (**a**) CF that occupies all the modeling domain, (**b**) cylindrical CF, (**c**) truncated-cone shaped CF.

2.2. A Numerical Approach for the Heat Equation

Equation (1) is essential to all types of RRAM physical simulators. It is usually auto-consistently solved with other differential equations (Poisson equation, kinetic equations for the chemical reactions that control the CF evolution, etc.) [21,23,34,53,70,77,81]. Since the most common device structure is not based on curved surfaces or volumes, even in the more scaled cases, a finite difference approach could be a reasonable choice that simplifies the grid and the differential equations discretization. Boundary conditions are key to describe correctly the physics of the device operation. In many simplified models, the electrodes are supposed to be perfect heat sinks and, therefore, Dirichlet's boundary conditions are established at the electrode-dielectric interface (in most cases room temperature is assumed at this interface). However, to correctly describe heat transfer between the conductive filament, the dielectric layer and the electrodes, some parts of the latter should be included in the simulation domain (SD). The SD lateral interfaces (perpendicular to the dielectric-electrode interface) are usually described by Neumann boundary conditions. Sometimes the temperature derivative in the normal direction of these interfaces is assumed to be null. This means adiabatic conditions accordingly with Fourier's law for heat conduction.

We have included here some results to illustrate the HE role in a RRAM simulator. Our simulator calculates the RRAM current in the LRS. The internal resistance calculation is performed assuming fully formed metallic-like conductive filaments of different shapes. In addition to the current calculation, we solve the 3D HE [29]. In the SD we have included the dielectric stack and part of the electrodes; precisely, 10 nm of the Si-n$^+$ (bottom electrode) and Ni (top electrode). Consequently, the SD thermal boundary is shifted from the dielectric/electrode interfaces to the electrodes, as commented above. A 40 nm (X axis) $\times$ 40 nm (Y axis) $\times$ 30 nm (Z axis, vertical axis running from the Si layer to the Ni layer) SD is considered, see Figure 2.

Dirichlet's boundary conditions were supposed at the outer electrode layer surfaces. The constant temperature located outside the device was room temperature (a reasonable assumption accounting for the high electrode thermal conductivity). For the SD lateral faces we employed perfectly matched layers (PML) [82], an improved implementation of Neumann boundary conditions since PML are particularly appropriate for differential equation solution to deal with open boundary problems, our case here [83]. Joule heating takes place in the CFs. Some devices (schematics shown in Figure 2) were simulated. In our simulations we included two CFs to account for a different device configuration with respect to conventional studies with just one CF.

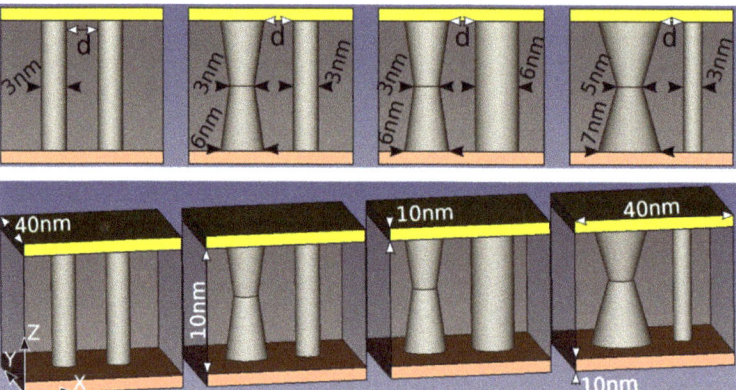

Figure 2. Simulated RRAMs. Four different LRS situations are considered, in all cases a double conductive filament was employed assuming a distance, d, between them (the bottom and top figures are the same in each case from different perspectives). The bottom electrode is assumed to be Si-n+ and the top electrode is made of Ni, the dielectric consists of HfO$_2$. The conductive filament shapes employed are shown for the different cases under study, they are assumed to be metallic-like, formed by Ni atom clusters [24,55,80]. The physical parameters are the same employed in the simulation in [29].

In Figure 3, symmetric temperature distributions are observed in (a) and (b), corresponding to similar CFs, and therefore, to alike Joule heating effects. See the effects of the low thermal conductivity in the dielectric. According to Fourier's law for heat conduction, the heat flux, q, is equal to the product of thermal conductivity, k$_{th}$, and the negative local temperature gradient ($q = -k_{th}\nabla T$). Since the HfO$_2$ thermal conductivity is around 1 W/(K m), the temperature drops off rapidly around the CF. See also the effects of the dielectric-electrode boundary at z = 10 nm and z = 30 nm, the temperature reduction is different from what is seen in the CF perpendicular direction along the x-axis. The maximum temperature is obtained in the narrowest section for the symmetrical truncated-cone shaped CF, as seen in (c) and (d). At this point, the physical mechanisms behind RS are more active and, consequently, they trigger the CF rupture at this location. See the thermal connection between the CFs for the different shapes and distances in between; in this respect, in tree-branch shaped filaments, the destruction of the branches and the thermal and current redistribution in the remaining intertwined branches makes the reset a complicated process.

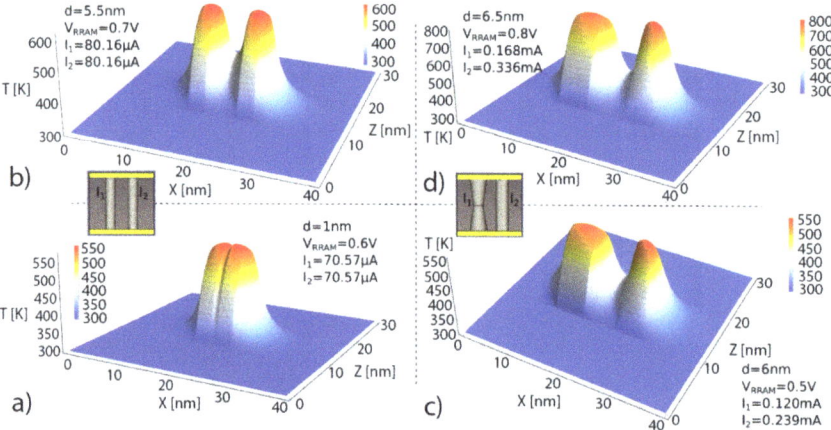

Figure 3. Temperature plots for some of the devices simulated as explained above (see the insets), the cross-section cuts corresponds to y = 20 nm in our SD. (**a**) RRAM with two cylindrical CFs (diameter = 3 nm) separated 1 nm apart for a bias of 0.6 V.

(**b**) RRAM with two cylindrical CFs (diameter = 3 nm) separated 5.5 nm apart for a bias of 0.7 V. (**c**) RRAM with one cylindrical CF (diameter = 6 nm) and a symmetrical truncated-cone shaped CF (low diameter = 3 nm, high diameter = 6 nm) separated 6 nm apart for a bias of 0.5 V. (**d**) RRAM with one cylindrical CF (diameter = 6 nm) and a symmetrical truncated-cone shaped CF (low diameter = 3 nm, high diameter = 6 nm) separated 6.5 nm apart for a bias of 0.8 V. For the sake of visibility, some of the 3D plots are rotated with respect to the 2D CF scheme.

In Figure 4 simulations of other RRAM configurations are shown. See that small changes in the device voltage can lead to important temperature variations in the CF bottleneck where RS mechanisms are thermally enhanced. In (c) and (d), the thermal crosstalk between CFs is observed when the distance between CFs is around 1 nm. For much higher inter CF distances, a lower thermal connection results even for higher currents.

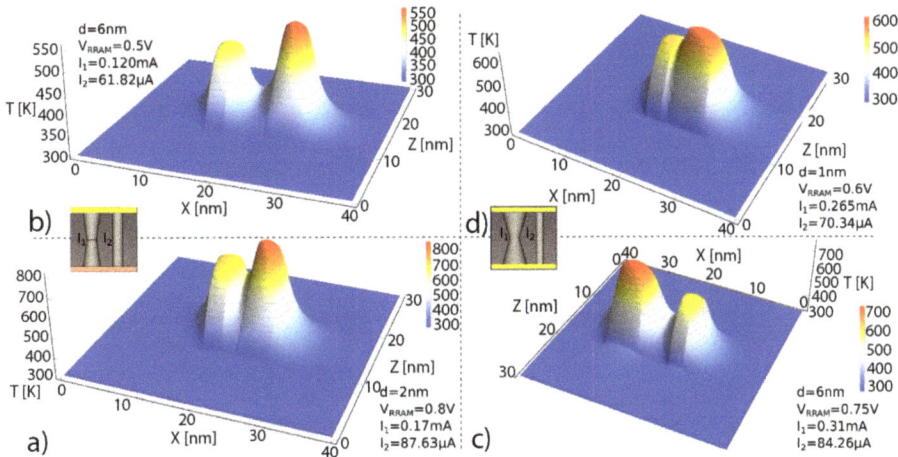

Figure 4. Temperature plots for some of the devices simulated as explained above (see the insets), the cross-section cuts corresponds to y = 20 nm in our SD. (**a**) RRAM with one cylindrical CF (diameter = 3 nm) and a symmetrical truncated-cone shaped CF (low diameter = 3 nm, high diameter = 6 nm) separated 2 nm apart for a bias of 0.8 V. (**b**) RRAM with one cylindrical CF (diameter = 3 nm) and a symmetrical truncated-cone shaped CF (low diameter = 3 nm, high diameter = 6 nm) separated 6 nm apart for a bias of 0.5 V. (**c**) RRAM with one cylindrical CF (diameter = 3 nm) and a symmetrical truncated-cone shaped CF (low diameter = 5 nm, high diameter = 7 nm) separated 6 nm apart for a bias of 0.75 V. (**d**) RRAM with one cylindrical CF (diameter = 3 nm) and a symmetrical truncated-cone shaped CF (low diameter = 5 nm, high diameter = 7 nm) separated 1 nm apart for a bias of 0.6 V. For the sake of visibility, some of the 3D plots are rotated with respect to the 2D CF scheme.

2.3. Explicit Heat Equation Solutions

2.3.1. RRAM with a Cylindrical Filament (Steady-State Operation, No Heat Transfer Term)

In the case under consideration, we assume a cylindrical CF with constant electrical and thermal conductivities. The boundary conditions are established at the extremes of the filament ($x = 0$ and $x = t_{ox}$, respectively, with temperatures $T(x = 0) = T(x = t_{ox}) = T_0$, where t_{ox} stands for the dielectric thickness), see Figure 5.

From Equation (2), we obtain [38]:

$$\sigma E^2 = -k_{th} \frac{\partial^2 T(x)}{\partial x^2} \qquad (3)$$

where E is the constant electric field in the CF ($E = V_{RRAM}/t_{ox}$). Figure 5 shows the different elements taken into account to solve the HE. The solution for the maximum temperature in the middle of the CF, with the boundary conditions sketched in Figure 5, is:

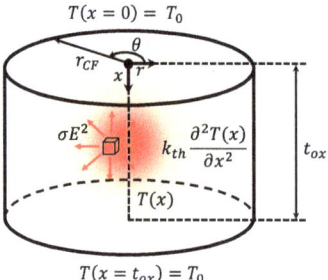

Figure 5. Schematic showing the different elements considered to solve the simplified HE in a cylindrical and homogenous conductive filament.

$$T_{max} = T_0 + \frac{\sigma\, t_{ox}^2\, E^2}{8\, k_{th}} \quad (4)$$

The single temperature that will represent the whole CF thermal state is chosen to be T_{max}, as shown below (see Appendix D.3 in [84]),

$$T_{max} = T_0 + \frac{\sigma\, V_{RRAM}^2}{8\, k_{th}} \quad (5)$$

Henceforth, this will be our thermal model 1, TM1. This assumption is justified by the fact that this maximum value controls the physical mechanisms that lead to the CF narrowing in a reset process and finally to the CF rupture. Nevertheless, among other issues in this model, the calculation of the ohmic resistance as the CF heats up is not correctly solved since the main CF body remains at a temperature much lower than the hottest spot where the maximum temperature is achieved. The Verilog-A implementation is shown in Table 1 (TM1).

2.3.2. RRAM with a Cylindrical Filament Including a Heat Transfer Term (Steady-State Operation)

We have added a term to account for the heat transfer from the CF to the surrounding insulator to Equation (3), see Figure 6. The heat losses are included by means of the heat transfer coefficient (h) [31,38,79,85], see Equation (6):

$$\sigma\, E^2 = -k_{th}\frac{\partial^2 T(x)}{\partial x^2} + 2\, h\frac{T(x) - T_0}{r_{CF}} \quad (6)$$

where r_{CF} stands for the conductive filament radius.

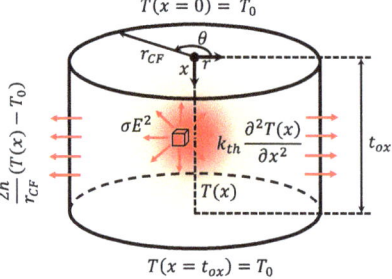

Figure 6. Sketch of a cylindrical filament with the different terms in the HE shown in Equation (6), including the heat transfer term.

Table 1. Verilog-A implementation of some of the thermal models described.

Thermal Model	Verilog-A Code for the Temperatures Calculation
TM1	T = T_0 + sigma*V**2/(8.0*kth);
TM2	E = V/tox; alpha = tox/2.0*sqrt(2*h/(kth*rcf)); T = T_0 + (sigma*E**2*rcf*(exp(alpha)−1)**2)/(2*h*(exp(2*alpha)+1));

TM3	LCF = tox−g;
	rg = sqrt(rt*rb);
	eta = rt/rb;
	E = V/LCF;
	alpha = LCF*sqrt(2*h/(kth*rg));
	T = T_0 + rg*sigma*E**2/(eta*h)*(0.5 − (exp(alpha/2.0)/(exp(alpha) + 1));

TM4	analog function real fdt$_0$;
	real sigmat,rcf,E,alpha;
	input sigmat,rcf,E,alpha;
	begin
	fdt$_0$ = sigmat*rcf*E**2*tanh(alpha*tox/2.0)/(sqrt(2*kth*h*rcf));
	end
	endfunction
	analog function real fT;
	real sigmat,rcf,eta,alpha,dt$_0$;
	input sigmat,rcf,eta,alpha,dt$_0$;
	begin
	fT = T_0 + sigmat*rcf*E**2/(2*h)*(1-cosh(alpha*tox/2.0)) + dt$_0$/alpha*sinh(alpha*tox/2.0);
	end
	endfunction
	analog function real falpha;
	real rcf;
	input rcf;
	begin
	falpha = sqrt(2*h/(kth*rcf));
	end
	endfunction
	analog function real fsigmat;
	real T;
	input T;
	begin
	fsigmat = sigma/(1 + alphat * (T − T_0));
	end
	endfunction

Equation (6) can be solved and the result is given below [27],

$$T_{max} = T_0 + \frac{\sigma\, E^2\, r_{CF}\, (e^\alpha - 1)^2}{2\, h\, (e^{2\alpha} + 1)} \quad (7)$$

where:

$$\alpha = \frac{t_{ox}}{2}\sqrt{\frac{2\,h}{k_{th}\, r_{CF}}} \quad (8)$$

In this case, as before, the electric field is assumed constant, and the CF temperature is considered to be T_{max}, as calculated in Equation (7). We will consider this the thermal model 2, TM2 (see the Verilog-A code in Table 1).

2.3.3. RRAM with a Truncated-Cone Shaped Filament Including Heat Transfer Coefficient (Steady-State Operation)

The boundary conditions and the CF geometry for this model are shown in Figure 7. Notice that the CF radius $r_{CF}(x)$ of the truncated cone depends on the x position. Consequently, the heat equation can be expressed now as follows:

$$\sigma(x)\, E(x)^2 - \frac{2h}{r_{CF}(x)}(T(x) - T_0) = -k_{th}\frac{\partial^2 T(x)}{\partial x^2} \quad (9)$$

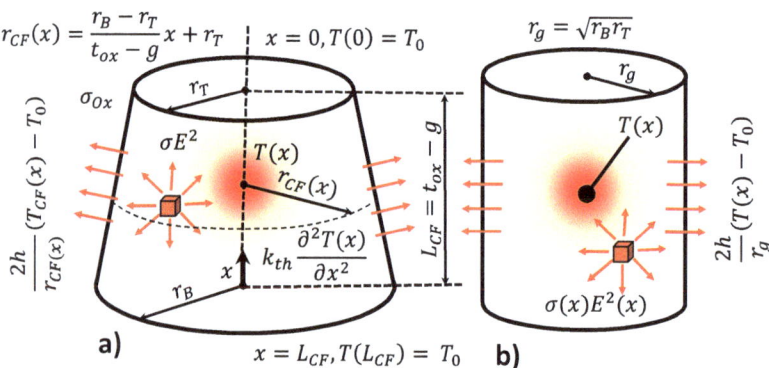

Figure 7. (a) Energy dissipation terms included in the heat equation and geometrical domain for the CF thermal description, (b) cylindrical CF equivalent employed to simplify the HE solution and obtain a compact analytical expression for the CF temperature. Note that the conductive filament length (L_{CF}) can be lower than the oxide layer (t_{ox}), due to the gap (g) between the top electrode and the conductive filament tip (see [27,78,86–88]).

This equation cannot be solved analytically because of the variable CF radius, $r_{CF}(x)$. In order to obtain an approximated analytical solution, we considered a transformation to simplify. A truncated-cone shaped CF with constant conductivity was found to be approximately equivalent in terms of this calculation to a cylinder with radius ($r_g = \sqrt{r_T r_B}$) and variable conductivity $\sigma_{CF}(x)$ [27], see Figure 7. For a fixed applied voltage, we include the maximum electric field. This value is affected by the ratio between the two truncated-cone radii ($\eta = r_T/r_B$). Under this assumption, the following simplified HE was obtained:

$$\frac{\sigma V_{RRAM}^2}{L_{CF}^2 \eta} - \frac{2h}{r_g}(T(x) - T_0) = -k_{th}\frac{\partial^2 T(x)}{\partial x^2} \quad (10)$$

Using this parameter:

$$\alpha = L_{CF}\sqrt{\frac{2h}{k_{th}\, r_g}} \quad (11)$$

The value of T_{max} can be obtained as follows (the one we assume for the whole CF, this will be the thermal model 3, TM3, see the Verilog-A code in Table 1),

$$T_{max} = T_0 + \frac{r_g\, \sigma\, E^2}{\eta\, h}\left[\frac{1}{2} - \frac{e^{\frac{\alpha}{2}}}{e^{\alpha} + 1}\right] \quad (12)$$

2.3.4. RRAM with a Truncated-Cone Shaped Filament Including Heat Transfer Coefficient (Steady-State Operation) and Two Temperature Values to Represent the CF Thermal Behavior

The use of two different CF temperatures allows a more accurate thermal description of the CF narrowing, where the temperature rises due to the thermal run-away process that leads to the RS operation, and a CF bulk temperature that accounts for the temperature in the CF wider part. This CF region could be left almost untouched in the sequence of set and reset processes. We will consider this version the thermal model 4, TM4 (see in Table 1 a Verilog-A implementation of the first thermal models proposed here). In the approach we followed, the electric field is calculated by means of two components associated with the CF top and bottom parts [79]. In this respect, the electric field can be calculated as: $E_{(T,B)} = \frac{V_{(T,B)}}{L/2}$, where $V_{(T,B)}$ is obtained considering the voltage divider formed by the resistances associated with the CF top and bottom portions (see the Appendix in [79]).

In the approximation strategy developed here, the maximum temperature (see the previous thermal models) is obtained for two cylinders of different radii (associated to the top and bottom CF temperatures), see Figure 8. These values are assumed to be the temperatures at the main CF volumes linked to the cylinders: for the thicker CF section (Figure 8b), T_T, and for the narrow CF (Figure 8c), T_B. The analytical expression for the temperature calculation is given below:

$$T_{(T,B)} = T_0 + \frac{\sigma_{(T,B)} r_{CF_{(T,B)}} E^2_{(T,B)}}{2h}\left(1 - \cosh\left(\frac{\alpha_{(T,B)} t_{ox}}{2}\right)\right) + \frac{dT_{0_{(T,B)}}}{\alpha_{(T,B)}} \sinh\left(\frac{\alpha_{(T,B)} t_{ox}}{2}\right) \quad (13)$$

where, parameters $\alpha_{(T,B)}$ and $dT_{0_{(T,B)}}$ are given in the equations below [79]:

$$\alpha_{(T,B)} = \sqrt{\frac{2h}{k_{th} r_{CF_{(T,B)}}}} \quad (14)$$

$$dT_{0_{(T,B)}} = \frac{\sigma_{(T,B)} r_{CF_{(T,B)}} E^2_{(T,B)} \tanh\left(\frac{\alpha_{(T,B)} t_{ox}}{2}\right)}{\sqrt{2 k_{th} h \, r_{CF_{(T,B)}}}} \quad (15)$$

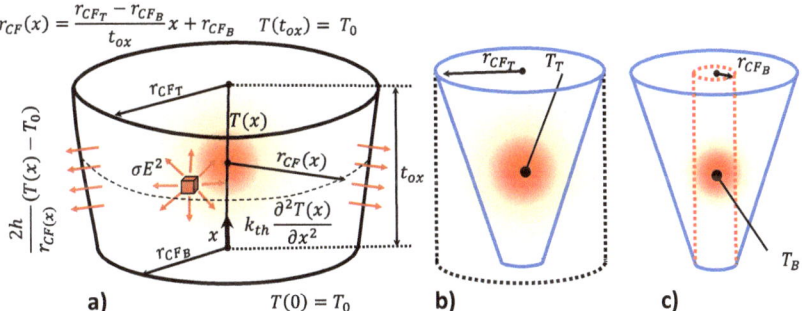

Figure 8. RRAM cell CF scheme for the thermal model based on two different CF temperatures. (**a**) Original filament with the corresponding boundary conditions. Cylindrical CFs (shown in dashed lines) employed to compute the (**b**) top temperature T_T and (**c**) the bottom T_B.

Equation (16) includes the CF conductance temperature dependence, assuming a metallic behavior:

$$\sigma_{(T,B)} = \frac{\sigma_0}{1 + \alpha_T\left(T_{(T,B)} - T_0\right)} \quad (16)$$

where σ_0 stands for the CF conductivity at room temperature (T_0) and α_T is the conductivity temperature coefficient. The Verilog-A code is shown in Table 1 (TM4).

2.4. Energy Balance in the Device

If we apply the first law of thermodynamics in terms of an energy balance in the device active region, we would obtain Equation (17) [78]:

$$\dot{e}_{generated} - \kappa(T(t) - T_0) = C_{th}\frac{\partial T(t)}{\partial t} \quad (17)$$

where T_0 stands for the temperature of the dielectric that surrounds the CF (usually assumed at room temperature) and κ is the inverse of the thermal resistance. In this case we do not account for a temperature distribution along the CF as in Equation (2). Our perspective here accounts for the whole CF, and even its surroundings, which is represented by a single temperature. In addition, we do not follow, as above, a scheme based on the HE solution and the association of the maximum temperature with the CF. The power generated can be calculated as $V_{RRAM}(t)I_{RRAM}(t)$, although we will employ $V(t)I(t)$ for short. We can study this differential equation accounting for different operation regimes.

2.4.1. Steady-State

This regime works well under the conventional ramped voltage stress, RVS. With long ramps to switch the device, Equation (17) can be written as follows:

$$\dot{e}_{generated} = \kappa(T(t) - T_0) \quad (18)$$

The power generated in the conductive filament (CF) (Joule heating effects calculated as current × voltage) equals the power dissipated toward the electrodes and the dielectric. Under the consideration of a single temperature to characterize the device active region, assuming that the electrodes and the dielectric are perfect heat sinks at a fixed temperature, T_0, Equation (18) can be written as follows:

$$R_{th} = \frac{T - T_0}{V I} \quad (19)$$

where R_{th} stands for the effective thermal resistance (it depends on the device physical features and is associated with heat conduction [89]). Using this simple model (thermal model 5, TM5), the device temperature can be estimated from Equation (19) [88,90–94].

At circuit simulation level, Equation (19) can be implemented with the equivalent electrical sub-circuit shown in Figure 9. The heat dissipated power is represented by a dependent current source whose value is described as $G_1 = VI$, where the voltage is determined by the two input sub-circuit terminals V^+ and V^-, and the current is sensed by a null voltage source V_{sense} connected in series between the input terminals I^+ and I^-. The thermal resistance is represented by an electrical resistance, R_{th}, and the room temperature by a constant voltage source, T_0, with a value that equals the room temperature (T_0), in K. The output sub-circuit terminal (T) provides a voltage that represents the device temperature T (in K).

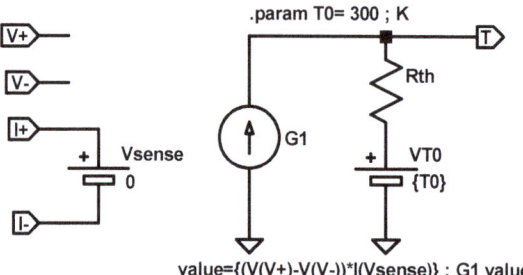

Figure 9. Equivalent electric circuit for the RS device thermal model based on a thermal resistance R_{th}.

2.4.2. Non-Steady-State Approach

Models based only on thermal resistances do not provide capacitive effects in terms of transient operation (mostly related to pulsed voltage stress, PVS, that can be employed to tune the device resistance in a multilevel operation regime, as needed in neuromorphic circuits). In order to include thermal inertia in the model, a capacitor (in the electrically equivalent thermal circuit) is added, C_{th}, the thermal or heat capacitance. This approach is used in different RRAMs compact models (thermal model 6, TM6), [78,95,96]. We can reformulate Equation (17) to the following expression:

$$V I = \frac{T - T_0}{R_{th}} + C_{th} \frac{dT}{dt} \quad (20)$$

From Equation (20), the temperature can be obtained as:

$$T = T_0 + V I R_{th} - \tau_{th} \frac{dT}{dt} \quad (21)$$

where τ_{th} (thermal time constant) is defined as follows:

$$\tau_{th} = C_{th} R_{th} \quad (22)$$

Equation (20) can be solved analytically if we assume a constant voltage (see Equation (23)).

$$T(t) = T_0 + V I R_{th} \left(1 - e^{-\frac{t}{\tau_{th}}}\right) \quad (23)$$

If we apply a time-dependent voltage, $V(t)$, Equation (23) does not work. In this case, we have to solve numerically Equation (20). Assuming a new function, $X(t) = T(t) - T_0$, we obtain,

$$V(t) I(t) = \frac{X(t)}{R_{th}} + C_{th} \frac{dX(t)}{dt} \quad (24)$$

Discretizing under equally distant temporal points $t_{i+1} = t_i + \Delta t$:

$$V_i I_i = \frac{X_i}{R_{th}} + C_{th} \frac{X_{i+1} - X_i}{\Delta t} \quad (25)$$

which gives us:

$$R_{th} V_i I_i = X_i + \tau_{th} \frac{X_{i+1} - X_i}{\Delta t} \quad (26)$$

and consequently,

$$X_{i+1} = \frac{\Delta t}{\tau_{th}} (R_{th} V_i I_i - X_i) + X_i \quad (27)$$

Finally, the device temperature could be calculated as $T_{i+1} = X_{i+1} + T_0$. From a circuit simulation point of view, Equation (20) can be implemented with the equivalent electrical sub-circuit shown in Figure 10. The values of the different electric elements and the role of the pins is the same as in Figure 9. However, a capacitor has been added to account for the thermal capacitance.

The values κ = 2.8–25 µJ/K s (R_{th} = 4 × 10^4–3.5 × 10^5 K/W) and C_{th} = 0.04–1.1 pJ/K were employed in [78]. In [95], the following values were given: C_{th} = 0.318 fJ/K and τ_{th} = 0.23 ns, from them the thermal resistance can be extracted $R_{th} = \tau_{th}/C_{th}$ = 7.23 × 10^5 K/W. The thermal resistance in [91] was taken R_{th} = 5 × 10^5 K/W. An estimation of 33 ps for the thermal time constant is reported in [18], which has to be compared to the electric pulse-width to assess the importance of thermal transient effects in conventional RRAM operation. The heat capacitance can be calculated as $C_{th} = C_p\, t_{ox}\, A$ [18], where A is the CF effective area, the effective CF length that approximately corresponds to the dielectric thickness (t_{ox}) and

C_p is the volumetric heat capacity (calculated as $\rho \times c$, Equation (2)) [89]. As detailed in [18], the thermal resistance can be calculated as follows:

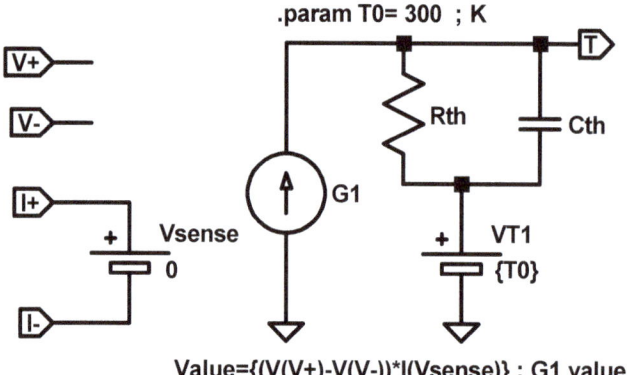

Figure 10. Equivalent electric circuit of a RRAM thermal model based on a thermal resistance and capacitance to implement Equation (20).

$$R_{th} \approx \frac{t_{ox}}{k_{th} A} \quad (28)$$

Assuming as the reference material Hf, we have the following values $k_{th} = 23$ Wm^{-1}K^{-1}, and $C_p = 1.92$ JK^{-1}cm^{-3}. Therefore, the thermal time constant can be estimated as:

$$R_{th} C_{th} = \frac{C_p\, t_{ox}^2}{k_{th}} \quad (29)$$

which is 33 ps for the case considered ($t_{ox} = 20$ nm).

A quick estimation to assess the role of the thermal resistance ($R_{th} = 4 \times 10^4$ K/W) can be performed if we assume an ideal device in the LRS under a steady-state regime with $I_{RRAM} = 1$ mA and $V_{RRAM} = 1$ V; using Equation (19), we would have $T = T_0 + R_{th} \times I \times V = T_0 + 40$ K, or $T = T_0 + 500$ K, if $R_{th} = 5 \times 10^5$ K/W.

The role of the heat capacitance can be easily seen in Figure 11. For a pulsed voltage signal of amplitude (peak to peak)= 0.025 V, offset = 0.0125 V and f = 0.5 GHz applied in an ideal device whose resistance is assumed to be $R_{RRAM} = 1\ \Omega$, the temperature can be obtained from Equation (27) for $R_{th} = 2 \times 10^5$ K/W and $C_{th} = 0.1$ fJ/K ($\tau_{th} = 20$ ps), $C_{th} = 0.25$ fJ/K ($\tau_{th} = 50$ ps), $C_{th} = 0.5$ fJ/K ($\tau_{th} = 100$ ps).

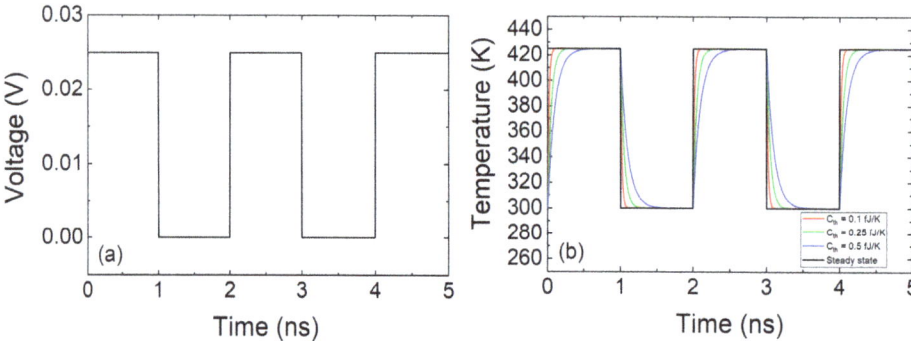

Figure 11. (a) Voltage applied to the device versus time, (b) Temperature versus time obtained for different values of C_{th} (assuming $R_{th} = 2 \times 10^5$ K/W).

As can be seen in the previous figure, the device thermal response should be faster than the electric pulses employed for an operation free of delays ("inertia") due to thermal effects. In fact, experimental techniques have been developed to estimate the device temperature with the application of ultra-short electrical pulses to RRAMs [97,98].

We have made use of some of the thermal models reported above. They cannot exist on their own since the conductive filament kinetics need to be considered to describe the device RS operation and, in doing so, calculate the current. The use of the thermal models TM1-TM4 has been presented previously in [27,56,79]. We show here some results of the Stanford model [78,88,93,95] along with the thermal models TM5 and TM6. For the device description, taking into consideration that no experimental data fitting is considered (since it was performed in the references where the models were introduced), we assumed a set of model parameters close to the one suggested in [88], see Table 2.

Table 2. Model parameters employed for the simulations performed with the Stanford model, in particular for Figures 12 and 13.

	Stanford-PKU Model Parameters		
Device Parameters	Unit	Resistive Switching	
		SET	RESET
V_0	V		0.4
I_0	mA		0.2
g_0	nm		0.35
v_0	m/s		10^6
α	-		1
β	-		3
γ_0	-		10

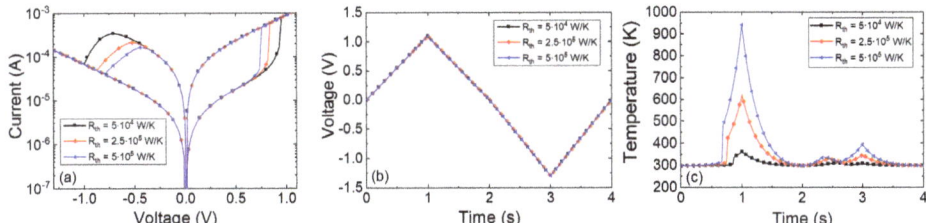

Figure 12. Simulations performed making use of the Stanford model including the TM5 with different thermal resistances. (a) Current versus voltage applied to the device, (b) voltage signal applied to the device, (c) temperature versus time.

Several I-V curves were plotted in Figure 12 considering different thermal resistances. As can be seen, the main dissimilarities are found in the set and reset regions. For the Stanford model, the highest temperatures are found in the set process, see that the Joule heating is higher in the set process and in the interval of positive voltages above V_{SET}. This is coherent with experimental findings that show that the Joule heating role is essential to describe the SET kinetics [81,99]. On average, these maximum temperatures achieved are in line with the estimations performed above for the thermal resistances considered. It is important to highlight the importance of the thermal resistance in the device design. See that higher R_{th} values lead to lower set and reset voltages to produce RS, and hence, lower power consumption. From this viewpoint, higher thermal resistances (i.e., devices showing a character thermodynamically more adiabatic with respect to the surroundings) might be more interesting. Since the heat flux from the CF to the metallic electrodes (operating these as heat sinks, a reasonable assumption, allows to calculate the heat flux with the material 3D thermal conductivity) could be in the same order of magnitude for different RRAMs, the dielectric could be the key (save the role of the contact thermal resistance). In this respect, we have to call the reader's attention to the fact that the usual RRAM dielectrics are grown in nanometric layers; consequently, the real thermal conductivity due to phonon quantization is far from the values corresponding to the corresponding 3D dielectric materials, as it was shown in [100–102].

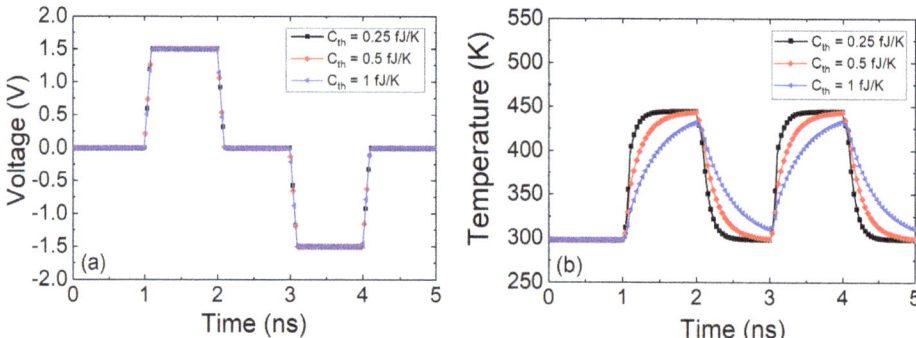

Figure 13. Simulations performed with the Stanford model (including TM6) making use of different thermal capacitances, C_{th}, assuming a common value of the thermal resistance, $R_{th} = 4 \times 10^5$ K/W. (**a**) Voltage applied to the device versus time, (**b**) Temperature versus time.

In the case of TM6 along with the Stanford model (using Table 2), we have plotted the results of a simulation using a pulsed voltage signal in Figure 13. A voltage signal such as the one in Figure 12b is close to DC, therefore the use of TM6 instead of TM5 is irrelevant. However, if a fast voltage signal is employed (Figure 13a), a high enough thermal capacitance makes a difference in terms of the device temperature transient (see Figure 13b).

The thermal time constants (Equation (22)) produced obvious delays for a voltage signal such as the one in Figure 13. These delays could seriously affect the device operation under pulsed input signals since RS is most of the times linked to thermal effects [1,24,53,81,99]. The thermal time constants corresponding to Figure 13b are the following: 0.4, 0.2 and 0.1 ns. These values are large compared to the value (33 ps) given by Ielmini [18] (we do not go into details of device materials at this point). An estimation of the C_{th} associated to a CF in a conventional RRAM, as described in [18], could help to shed light on this issue. Let us assume a cylindrical CF radius of 5 nm in a dielectric layer of 20 nm thick, if the heat capacity of Hf is considered ($C_p = 1.92$ JK^{-1}cm^{-3}) the CF thermal capacitance would be ($C_{th} = C_p\, t_{ox}\, A$) 0.003 fJ/K. Therefore, a value $\tau_{th} = 1.2$ ps is expected for the same thermal resistance employed in Figure 13. Although this thermal time constant is short, different authors [78,95] have used thermal capacitances values that lead to devices with higher thermal constants. A thermal device model described by Equation (20) and the thermal capacitance of an average CF produces so low thermal time constants that no transient term in Equation (20) would be worth being taken into account. From the experimental viewpoint, no delays linked to thermal inertia would be seen for conventional memory pulsed signals. Nevertheless, current transients on longer time scales than the previously calculated τ_{th}, linked to some extent to thermal effects have been reported previously [78]. In this respect, the thermal model, i.e., Equation (20), might not be enough to accurately describe RRAM thermal response.

The coupling of the CF temperature to a heat sink at room temperature with just two parameters (thermal resistance and capacitance) could not be described by the thermal features of a nanometric CF. We could use an intermediate temperature corresponding to an average region surrounding the CF that could help to build two different thermal circuits, one accounting for the coupling between the CF and this intermediate surrounding region (it could include the dielectric and electrode zones closer to the CF), and a second one coupling between this intermediate region and the outside world. This is in line with previous thermal descriptions (although introduced in another context) employed for magnetic current sensors [103] and AlGaAs/GaAs HBTs [104]. For this purpose, we present the following model. We will show below that the model based on Equation (20) can be used if a thermal capacitance that accounts for the whole device is taken into consideration. This means using a parameter much higher than the exclusively associated to the CF. In doing so, as always in compact modeling, the simplicity and accuracy trade-off has to be considered.

2.4.3. Non-Steady-State Approach with Two Different Temperatures Associated to the Device (Second-Order Memristor)

This thermal model, as suggested above, employs two different temperatures to describe the device from an energy balance perspective: the internal device temperature (approximately the CF temperature, T) that affects the RS mechanisms linked to the CF creation and destruction and a second temperature, associated to the CF surrounding regions (an effective temperature, T_S). The latter influences the internal device temperature T but it shows a different time evolution. The device intermediate surrounding region (at temperature T_S) is characterized by an outer boundary assumed to be at room temperature (T_0 = 300 K). This outer boundary is considered to be far away from the RS active region. The intermediate surrounding region can include different material layers; therefore, effective thermal constants are employed to account for the heat flux between this region and the exterior zone. Besides, the coupling between the inner (CF volume) and the intermediate CF surrounding region could be modeled by an effective thermal resistance and thermal capacitance: R_{th1} and C_{th1}. Under this approach, the device can be described by the following two equations (we assume this procedure to be the thermal model 7, TM7; see the circuital implementation in Figure 14).

$$C_{th1}\frac{d(T-T_S)}{dt} = V(t)I(t) - \frac{1}{R_{th1}}(T-T_s) \qquad (30)$$

$$C_{th2}\frac{dT_s}{dt} = V(t)I(t) - \frac{1}{R_{th2}}(T_s - T_0) \qquad (31)$$

where $V(t)I(t)$ allows the determination of $\dot{e}_{generated}$. The power dissipated by Joule heating affects the intermediate surrounding region temperature (modeled with parameters R_{th2} and C_{th2}) that accounts for the coupling between this region and the thermalized device exterior region. The approach described here is in line with the description of a second order memristor [100].

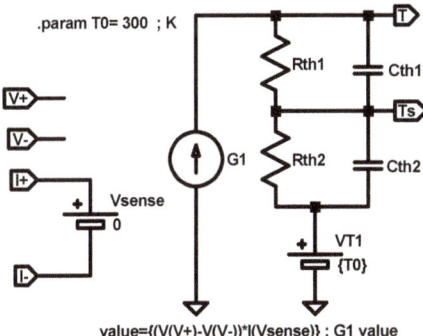

Figure 14. Equivalent electric circuit of a RRAM thermal model based on a double thermal circuit described by Equations (30) and (31).

The simulation was performed with this thermal model integrated in the Stanford compact model that was employed previously, see Figure 15.

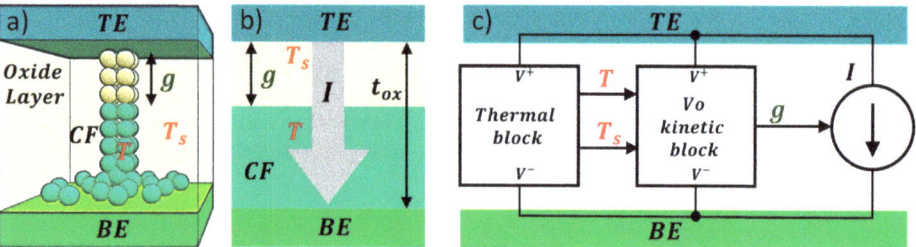

Figure 15. (**a**) Three-dimensional view of the Stanford scheme to model the different device areas (TE: top electrode, Oxide Layer, CF: conductive filament and BE: bottom electrode), (**b**) model parameters, g: gap between the TE and the filament tip and t_{ox}: dielectric thickness, (**c**) subcircuit representation for the implemented model. The connection between blocks represents the states variables used: g, which depends on kinetic block and it is linked to the two temperatures (T, T_S).

The results obtained for the set of parameters of the standard Stanford parameters [88] and the thermal model shown in Figure 14; Figure 15 are given in Figure 16.

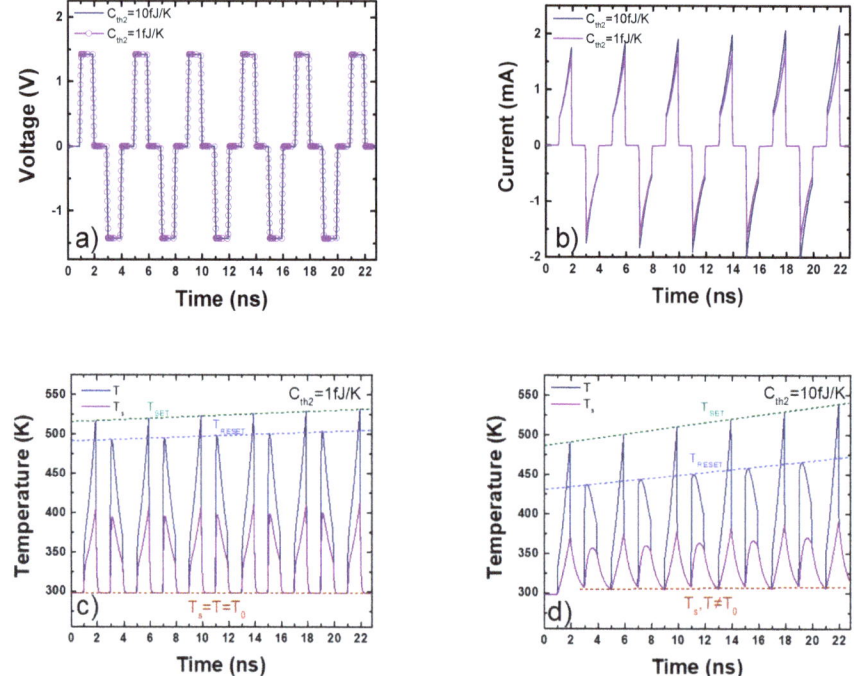

Figure 16. RRAM simulation making use of the Stanford model including a double RC thermal model R_{th1} = 40 kK/W, R_{th2} = 40 kK/W, C_{th1} = 0.003 fJ/K and C_{th2} with values 1 fJ/K and 10 fJ/K. (**a**) Applied voltage pulses for consecutive set and reset, (**b**) temporal current evolution, (**c**) temporal evolution of device filament temperature (T) and the intermediate surrounding region (T_S) with C_{th2} = 1 fJ/K and (**d**) C_{th2} = 10 fJ/K.

Depending on C_{th2}, different CF and intermediate surrounding region temperatures transient responses are obtained, producing the corresponding effects on the device current. This is noticeable when a consecutive series of set and reset pulses are applied, as shown in Figure 16a, in which a sequence of set pulses (1.5 V with 1 ns on time and 0.1 ns rise and fall times) and reset pulses (−1.5 V with 1 ns on time and 0.1 ns rise and fall times). In the first configuration, with the thermal capacities C_{th1} = 0.003 fJ/K, C_{th2} = 1 fJ/K and thermal resistances R_{th1} = R_{th2} = 40 kK/W, the current evolution is shown in Figure 16b. Figure 16c shows the CF (T) and intermediate surrounding region (T_S) evolution. In this first configuration, the corresponding transient shows low thermal inertia; after the pulse application, both temperatures reach room temperature ($T = T_S = T_0$). The devices show a slight increase in the maximum temperatures obtained in the set (T_{SET}) and reset (T_{RESET}) processes (Figure 16c).

In the second configuration, thermal capacities C_{th1} = 0.003 fJ/K, C_{th2} = 10 fJ/K and thermal resistances R_{th1} = R_{th2} = 40 kK/W, the current evolution is plotted in Figure 16b. Figure 16d shows the CF (T) and intermediate surrounding region (T_S) evolution. In this second configuration, the thermal inertia is higher in the second thermal circuit, after each set/reset pulse, the temperatures cannot go back to room temperature ($T, T_S \neq T_0$). As a result, each new cycle starts from a higher temperature than in the previous cycle; therefore, the maximum set (T_{SET}) and reset (T_{RESET}) temperatures show a growing trend (see Figure 16d). This temperature increase over the cycles implies that the device CF gap decreases in each new cycle, then the current increases (Figure 16b). This effect suggests the consideration of the temperature, in addition to the CF gap, as a state variable in line with the approach presented in [100] for second-order memristor. The temperature increase reported above could be employed with a series of pulses to tune the device conductivity in set cycles within a neuromorphic circuit context [100,105,106]. It is noteworthy that a third-order approach has been introduced in modeling devices for neuromorphic engineering [107].

2.4.4. SPICE-Based Circuital Models with Two or More CF Temperatures

In Section 2.3.4, a compact model based on two different CF representative temperatures was reviewed. In that model, some simplifications were performed in order to obtain analytical expressions for calculating these two temperatures although the flexibility linked to the consideration of different temperatures for the CF narrowing and CF main body added high value to the modeling process. In this section, an approach based on the electrical equivalent representation of this thermal framework is proposed in order to calculate numerically the temperature. It is noteworthy that most of the thermal models based on an electrical equivalent circuit (Sections 2.4.2 and 2.4.3) assume constant thermal resistances and capacitances, which can be used as fitting parameters. However, heat conduction through the CF and lateral heat dissipation depends on the filament size. This effect is included in physically-based simulators, such as those based on a kMC approach or on finite differences/elements, as far as the heat equation is solved using thermal parameters which are updated at simulation time according to the current filament size. Thermal models based on the heat equation analytical solutions in simplified CF geometries (Section 2.3) incorporate also this effect because the temperature analytical expression depends on the actual geometry, and it is evaluated at each simulation time step.

In this section, we present two thermal models based on an equivalent electrical representation (SPICE based), but including the effects of the CF evolution on the thermal properties, which also evolve as the simulation proceeds. The first one is a steady-state model, while the latter includes thermal capacitances. Furthermore, both models account for longitudinal heat conduction and lateral heat dissipation by means of several thermal resistances (or RC networks in the non-steady approach).

Figure 17 shows a general schema of the overall model. As explained before, the temperature of the CF main body is, in general, lower than that of the small portion of the filament where the filament evolves faster. Therefore, the CF is modeled by two different subcircuits (Figure 17), each of them characterized by different state variables (CF radius and temperature).

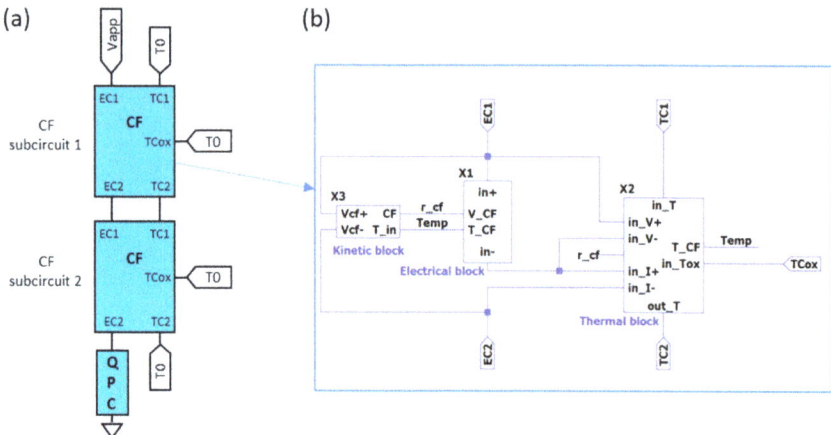

Figure 17. Schema of the circuital compact model. A truncated-cone shaped conductive filament is represented by connected cylinders for modeling purposes (**a**). The behaviour of each portion of the filament (cylinder) is modeled by the subcircuit inside the blue rectangle (**b**), which has electrical connections (EC) and thermal connections (TC). Each cylinder (subcircuit) is characterized by different state variables (radius, r_cf, and temperature, Temp). The cylinder subcircuit consists of several more subcircuits: a kinetic block for calculating the transient CF evolution; an electrical block for current calculation; and, finally, the thermal subcircuit, which includes the equivalent circuit for the thermal model. As can be seen, the subcircuits (thermal, kinetic and electrical blocks) are connected all together because they are interdependent. If necessary, a last subcircuit is added in series (**a**) in order to account for the conduction through a constriction by means of the quantum point contact model (see Section 4) [108].

Now, we focus on the description of the thermal subcircuit (Figure 18). The longitudinal heat conduction is modeled by R_{Thl1} and R_{Thl2}. For the sake of generality, it has been split off into two contributions in order to make easier the connection with other thermal sub-circuits and to build more complex thermal models. Their values are given by [89]:

$$R_{Thl1i} = R_{Thl2i} = \frac{1}{2} \frac{L_i}{k_{th} \pi r_i^2} \tag{32}$$

where k_{th} is the CF thermal conductivity, L_i is the length of the portion of the filament modeled by the sub-circuit and r_i, its radius (index i refers to the cylinder or sub-circuit number 1 or 2 in Figure 17a). On the other hand, R_{Thn} accounts for the lateral heat dissipation and it is calculated following this expression [89]:

$$R_{Thni} = \frac{1}{2 h L_i \pi r_i} \tag{33}$$

Note that in this model (TM8), the thermal resistances are not directly the fitting parameters since they are calculated according to the actual filament size. Therefore, as far as the complete device model is able to reproduce the geometrical evolution of the filament (kinetic block in Figure 17), the thermal resistances are not fixed, but their values evolve as the simulation runs. The implementation of such dependent resistances can be made by means of behavioural sources.

Although the model shown in Figure 17 uses two cylinders (and the corresponding two sub-circuits), the CF could be represented by more cylinders in order to get a more detailed CF description [31]. Indeed, in the limit with an infinite number of differential length cylinders, the circuit simulation would be equivalent to the resolution of the differential Equation (9). In fact, with a reduced number of filaments, the results are very similar to those obtained with a finite differences simulator [31,109]. Furthermore, complex filaments such as those with several branches forming a tree structure or interlaced between them could be simulated using more blocks and interconnecting them following a given structure (Figures 5 and 6 in [31]).

On the contrary, if only one block is used, this thermal model (TM8) would be equivalent to TM5, although the thermal resistance evolution is allowed in TM8.

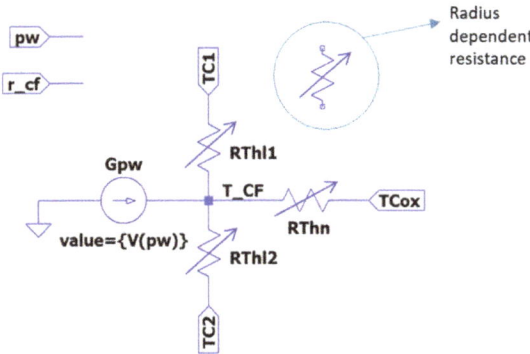

Figure 18. Circuital equivalent for thermal model TM8. The circuit inputs are the dissipated power (pw) and the CF radius (r_cf), while the output is the temperature (T_CF). The actual values of the thermal resistances depend on the filament radius (it is assumed to be a cylinder) and, therefore, they are updated as the CF evolves. The subcircuit has been prepared for being connected to other thermal subcircuits (through TC1, TC2 and TCox) in order to obtain a more complex thermal model of the whole device (with several temperatures along the filament or different temperatures for the surrounding insulator or bulk insulator, Figure 17). If only one block is used, all the resistances are in parallel and the model is equivalent to TM5, although the thermal resistance value keeps the dependency on the filament size in TM8 and it changes during the simulation.

Figure 19 shows the results provided by TM8 when is coupled to kinetic and conductive blocks fitted to simulate reset transitions in unipolar Ni/HfO$_2$/Si-n$^+$ resistive switching devices [80,109,110]. The QPC block has also been added. The two cylinders-TM8 model results have been compared with those provided by a finite differences simulator that was used to fit the experimental data [80]. The lateral heat dissipation parameter, h, has been changed in order to check its influence on the i-v curve. As can be seen, more heat dissipation requires a higher voltage to reach the thermally triggered reset transition, a well-known effect in RRAMs.

Thermal inertia can also be considered following this approach if thermal capacitances are added (Figure 20, thermal model TM9) [37]. In this new model, thermal capacitances could also be made dependent on the filament size instead of being fixed fitting parameters [37,111]. As previously mentioned, several blocks can be connected for modeling the CF. On the contrary, if only one segment is used, the model is equivalent to model TM6 (although TM9 lets the thermal components evolve at simulation time).

Figure 21 shows the simulation of the transient response of a Ni/20 nm-HfO$_2$/Si-n$^+$ resistive switching device [110] when a 3 V reset pulse is applied (for 100 ns) [37]. Several values of the thermal capacities have been considered. The simulation context here is different from the one shown in Section 2.4.3 since all the modeling components are linked to the device conductive filaments. Note also that only values higher than 0.2 fJ/K influence the device response. Fixed and variable thermal capacities have been used in order to analyze the role of size-dependent thermal capacities, which evolve at simulation time. As expected, variable thermal capacitors, whose value is reduced during a reset process, produce lower thermal inertia.

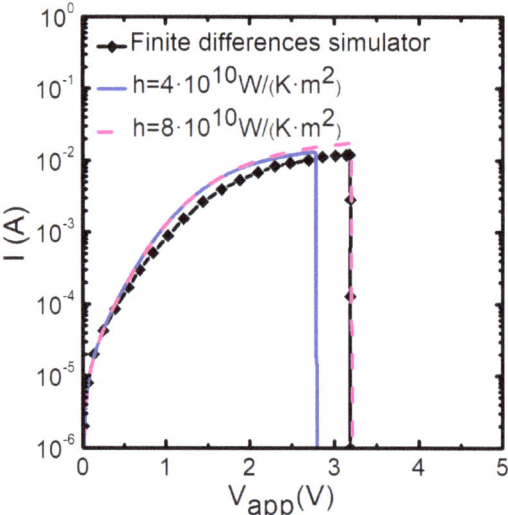

Figure 19. Simulation of a reset transition in unipolar Ni/20 nm-HfO$_2$/Si-n$^+$ resistive switching devices [109]. The *i-v* curve provided by a finite differences simulator used to fit the experimental data [80] is compared with the *i-v* curve calculated by means of the two cylinders model with TM8. Note that with only two subcircuits (Figure 17a) and taking variable electrical and thermal resistances into account, both types of simulators provide very close results, as far as the circuital model includes variable electric and thermal resistances. Two values of the lateral heat dissipation parameter, h, have been used for the sake of comparison.

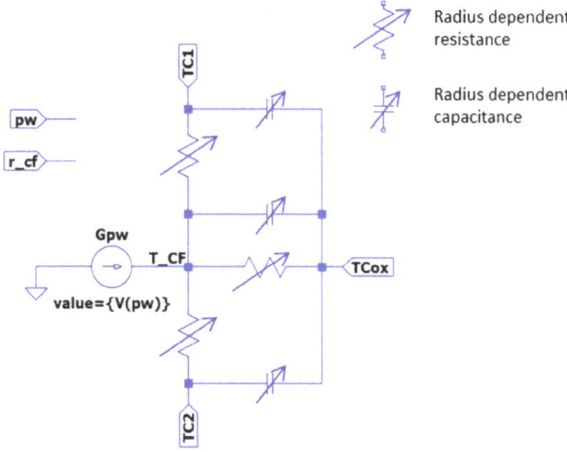

Figure 20. Circuital equivalent for thermal model TM9. It is similar to TM8 (Figure 18), but thermal inertia has been added by means of capacitances. As in TM8, the actual values of the thermal resistances and capacitances depend on the filament radius (it is assumed to be a cylinder) and, therefore, they are updated as the CF evolves [37].

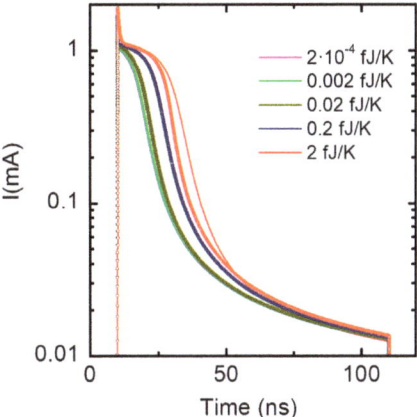

Figure 21. Simulated current in a Ni/20 nm-HfO$_2$/Si-n$^+$ resistive switching device [37,110] when a 3 V reset pulse is applied (for 100 ns). Different values of the thermal capacities have been assumed. Fixed thermal capacitances (solid lines) and size-dependent thermal capacitances (symbols) have been used [37,111].

Finally, it was previously seen that TM7 deals with two temperatures (at the filament and at the surrounding insulator). Note that although TM9 (following the two cylinders schema shown in Figure 17) also consider two temperatures, they are both linked to the conductive filament. TM7 can be obtained as a particular case of TM9 considering only one cylinder, but connecting another RC network between the node TCox and a voltage source for representing the bulk insulator temperature. It is important to note that in the TM9 case, variable (at simulation time) thermal components are allowed.

3. General Memristor Modeling Framework with Thermal Effects Emphasis

In this section, a different approach to model RRAM thermal features is proposed. For this purpose, we make use of the general memristor modeling workspace that was introduced by Corinto and Chua in [71]. This alternative perspective complements the developments presented in the previous section. In particular, the authors [71] developed a unified theoretical framework and also discussed the advantages of using the flux-charge (φ-Q) domain to study memristor elements. Within this framework, memristors, in the taxonomy proposed in [72] (the ideal, the generic, and the extended memristor), are described as the result of different approximations in the equations. This extended categorization emerged as a necessity in order to include theoretically the description of pinched, hysteretic behaviours demonstrated by various elements, not only in circuit theory and electronics but also in nature.

Among the different categories presented above, the most general class is linked to extended memristors, which refers to memristors that have extra state variables (in addition to φ and Q). For the specific case of charge-controlled memristors, they are described by the following equations:

$$v = M(Q, i, \mathbf{X})\, i \tag{34}$$

$$\frac{d\mathbf{X}}{dt} = g_Q(Q, i, \mathbf{X}) \tag{35}$$

$$\frac{dQ}{dt} = i \tag{36}$$

The memristance M of an extended memristor is implied in Equation (34), apparently bearing the feature of nonlinearity; v is the voltage across the memristor, i is the current flowing through it, and Q is the charge, i.e., the current first momentum. The vector $\mathbf{X}$ stands for a set of extra state variables, including all the necessary physical magnitudes according to the implemented memristive system; indicatively, they could be the device internal temperature, the conducting filament radius, or any other non-electrical variable influencing the memristor state that ultimately affects the device charge conduction. Apparently, the dynamics of the state variables X are governed by $g_Q(Q,i,X)$ and Equation (35). It is noted that the importance of the class of extended memristors comes from the fact that all real-world memristor devices known until now are indeed extended memristors. Notice that from Equation (34), we can define the memristance as follows:

$$M(Q, i, X) = \frac{v}{i} = \frac{d\varphi/dt}{dQ/dt} = \frac{d\varphi}{dQ} \quad (37)$$

where φ is the voltage first momentum, usually called flux in analogy with the charge. See, however, that a more useful way to obtain this relation is through derivation by assuming that the charge and the flux are related by a function f:

$$\varphi = f(Q, i, X) \quad (38)$$

Then, by deriving with respect to time, and using the chain rule, we obtain:

$$\frac{d\varphi}{dt} = v = \frac{\partial f(Q,i,X)}{\partial Q}\frac{dQ}{dt} + \frac{\partial f(Q,i,X)}{\partial i}\frac{di}{dt} + \frac{\partial f(Q,i,X)}{\partial X}\frac{dX}{dt} = \frac{\partial f(Q,i,X)}{\partial Q} i = \frac{\partial \varphi}{\partial Q} i \quad (39)$$

The latter part of Equation (39) is obtained under the assumption [71] described below,

$$\frac{\partial f(Q,i,X)}{\partial i}\frac{di}{dt} + \frac{\partial f(Q,i,X)}{\partial X}\frac{dX}{dt} = 0 \quad (40)$$

The system memory capability under no excitation is determined by a special case of Equation (35), often referred to as the power-off plot (POP) equation; in this case we have $i = 0$ or equivalently Q = constant. If a single state variable is considered, it is clear that if the POP equation is nil under these conditions, the system presents then a long-term memory since the state variable will not change with time; while if it is different to zero, the system is capable of exhibiting only short-term memory.

The consideration of the temperature, T, as the state variable is a peculiar case since there is an influence from external sources (i.e., the ambient –room– temperature, T_0); this implying a possible energy input in some cases if T_0 is not constant. In addition, as it has been discussed in Section 2, it is difficult to determine a single value for the device internal temperature (some models, as shown above, include two different temperatures to better describe the device operation). We can write the equations by separating the temperature as follows:

$$v = M(Q, i, X, T, T_0) \, i \quad (41)$$

$$\frac{dX}{dt} = g_Q(Q, i, X, T, T_0) \quad (42)$$

$$\frac{dT}{dt} = g_T(Q, i, X, T, T_0) \quad (43)$$

These equations include both temperatures: the internal device temperature, T, and the external T_0. Obviously, there is no equation governing T_0 dynamics since it can be considered as an external signal. Temperature, T, may be a position-dependent temperature $T(x,y,z)$, as already presented in Section 2.1. In this case, Equation (43) would correspond to the heat equation. As an additional note, it is important to highlight that a device will not present long-term memory characteristics associated solely with temperature, since the device will tend to reach thermal equilibrium with the external medium. In absence of any external electrical input, this would mean that the POP equation related to the evolution of the internal temperature is not zero in the general case. This does not preclude, however, that the system may have other internal variables that do present a long-term memory capability. As an example, we can think if the case of a phase change memory (PCM), where a phase change is activated by temperature, and it remains even after the device has cooled back to room temperature. A similar situation occurs when a RRAM conductive filament is ruptured because of an enhanced diffusion process favored by a temperature rise [24,80].

Example of Application

As an easy example, we can consider the case of the thermistor, which is one of the first elements identified as an extended memristor, i.e., a device whose resistance is dependent on some internal state variable that presents memory effects [112,113]. In this respect, and for the modeling developments henceforth, they display parallelism with RRAMs.

The model has been known since Steinhart and Hart published a function which fitted the variation of thermistor-resistance according to temperature [114] as a Taylor's expansion of the device conductance in terms of the temperature logarithm. This function, along with the equivalent Ohm's law in Equation (44), has proved to be suitable in a wide variety of thermistors, for ranges from a few degrees to a few hundred degrees, and it has been widely used to model this kind of devices when used as temperature sensors. The most usual way to describe it is by means of a simplification shown in Equation (45). In addition, a key thermistor characteristic is linked to self-heating, which can be described by Equation (46), by neglecting radiative heat dissipation:

$$v = M(T, T_0)\, i \tag{44}$$

$$M(T, T_0) = R_0\, exp\left(B \left(\frac{1}{T} - \frac{1}{T_0} \right) \right) \tag{45}$$

$$\frac{dT}{dt} = \frac{R_0}{C} i^2 - \frac{\delta}{C}(T - T_0) \tag{46}$$

In the above equations, T_0 is the room temperature, and T the device internal temperature. The rest of the symbols are parameters of the thermistor model and can be considered as constants for all practical purposes. At this point, it is noteworthy to point out that these equations bear exactly the same form as Equations (41) and (43) and, thus, identify the thermistor as a memristor. That is, the thermistor is a device whose resistance depends on its electrical history, and it has an internal state variable that governs the overall behaviour (the device internal temperature). Thus, the device can be classified as an extended memristor.

In addition, if we look at the POP equation (Equation (46) with $i = 0$), we see that the temperature derivative is different from zero for any situation other than the device thermal equilibrium with the surrounding environment. Thus, the device does not possess a feature linked to long-term memory. In this respect, it is also illustrative to point out that there are other memristive systems [115] that are also extended memristors due to self-heating, even if the thermal specific mechanisms are different from those of thermistors.

As an example to illustrate the memristive behavior of this device, we have simulated it when driven by a triangular current waveform, using specific values extracted from a datasheet for the thermistor constants: $\delta = 4 \times 10^{-3}$ W K^{-1}, $C = 60 \times 10^{-3}$ J K^{-1}, $B = 3950$ K, $T_0 = 298$ K, $R_0 = 10$ kΩ. Additionally, and in accordance with a typical thermistor datasheet, we have set a maximum current of 4.5 mA, and we have also used 5 different ramp slopes, as plotted in Figure 22.

Figure 23 plots the evolution of the memresistance as well as the current input versus time. The input signal shown in Figure 22 has been employed as well as the Equations (44)–(46).

In addition, we have also plotted these two magnitudes used in the Y axis previously against each other in Figure 24, showing the effects of the different slopes in the device memristance.

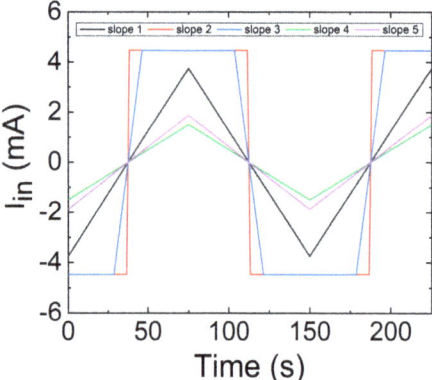

Figure 22. Input current waveform versus time for five different ramps. Colours are coherently employed in the following plots.

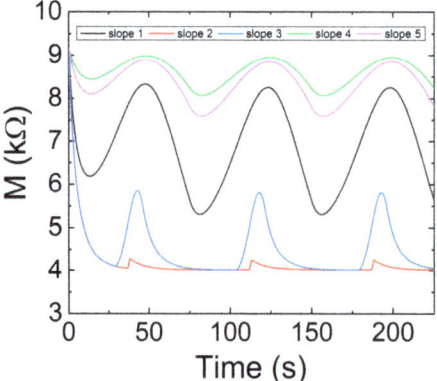

Figure 23. Memristance versus time for five different input voltage signals under ramped voltage stress.

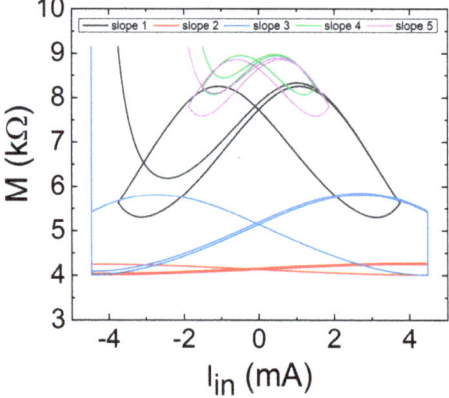

Figure 24. Memristance versus input current, for five different slopes. Colours are coherent with the results shown in the previous figures.

Then, the typical *i-v* memristor characteristics showing the famous loop are drawn in Figure 25. See that the shapes are in line with what is expected for memristors [71].

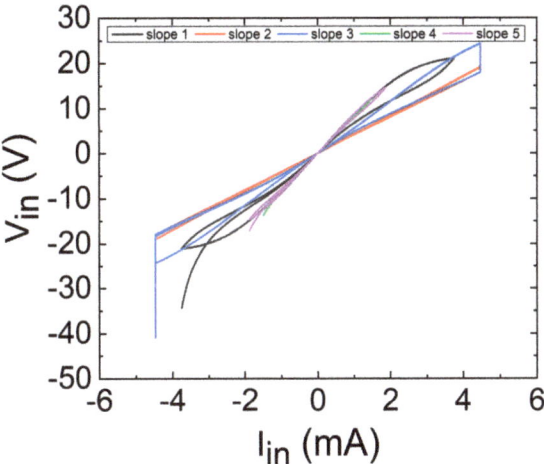

Figure 25. *i-v* thermistor characteristics for five different input voltages.

Figure 25 shows the two fingerprints of a memristor [116]: (1) a pinched loop; and (2) an area that varies with frequency, tending to a line at high frequencies. In fact, the behaviour at the highest frequency (cyan line) is nearly that of an ohmic resistor, with no loop area, while at lower frequencies the behaviour is different. It has to be noted that (see [115]) the situation is more interesting than simply an area increase at lower frequencies. As highlighted in [115], the thermistor control variable is the internal temperature and it tends to be in thermal equilibrium with the surroundings, which causes the loop area to reduce at a very low frequency. As we use it in the corresponding equations, we can see that for very low input signal slopes, the device always reaches thermal equilibrium, since the dT/dt is nearly zero, and its behaviour tends to be close to a nonlinear resistor, as shown in Figure 24; Figure 25 (red lines), with a null area enclosed in the loop.

At this point, the concept of dynamic route map (DRM) [36] comes up since it is quite useful to represent the device time evolution (again, in this facet, a full parallelism with RRAM is observed [36]). In fact, the DRM is a concept arising from non-linear dynamical systems, and represents the trajectories a system follows in the phase space of the state variable versus its derivative for different control parameter values. If we plot it as a 3D diagram, we find that all the trajectories, for a given constant T_0, are bound to fall on the same surface, as seen in Figure 26. Using this representation may provide very interesting insights into the device dynamics. Considering our thermistor, if a trajectory goes from a state with positive derivative to another characterized by a negative derivative with increasing temperature, then it will reach a stable equilibrium point at the temperature where the derivative nullifies. An equilibrium point is a state where the device tends to remain at even if it drifts from it in its operation; this idea resembles a similar concept related to the DC quiescent point in circuit theory, or memory in memristors. In the opposite case, when the trajectory goes from negative to positive, an equilibrium point might seem to come up at the zero-crossing temperature, but it is unstable, which means that the slightest change will force the system to come out of it.

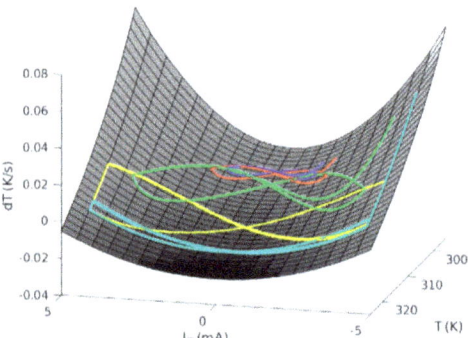

Figure 26. Memristor Dynamic Route Map (surface), showing as lines the five trajectories corresponding to the previous figures, using the same colour code. It can be seen that all these trajectories fall on the surface, which defines univocally the device behaviour. Notice that this surface is, in fact, a family of surfaces that depend on the room temperature T_0.

4. RRAM Quantum Point Contact Modeling, Thermal Effects

So far, we have studied thermal effects from a classical physics viewpoint. This is the approach commonly used in most compact models. However, the scale of the material layers that form part of a RRAM makes feasible for certain devices and for particular operation conditions the observation of quantum effects. In particular, when the conducting filament (CF) cross-sectional area in a RRAM device becomes very narrow, only a few atoms wide, the continuum description is expected to break down, so that the direct application of the heat equation becomes questionable [117,118]. We enter into the regime of heat transport and dissipation at the nanoscale [119]. Before starting with a discussion about these topics, it is important to discriminate between the role that temperature plays on the ion/vacancy movement across the insulating films (essentially governed by Kramers' theory [120]), and the temperature dependence of the mechanism adopted for the electronic transport in the CF itself (Schottky, Poole-Frenkel, tunneling, variable range hopping, space charge limited conduction, quantum point contact, etc.) [121]. Although both descriptions are intrinsically connected and they are at the heart of the complexity of the RRAM behavior, they are often treated separately for simplicity, or one of them completely dropped. To deepen into these intertwined approaches, a detailed RRAM dynamic simulation at the microscopic level is imperative. Ion/vacancy diffusion process, which defines the filamentary structure, depends on temperature, and the size of the structure determines the magnitude of the electron current that governs the power dissipation (Joule heating effects), which in turn affects the local temperature that drives the diffusion process. In this section we will exclusively focus the attention on the modeling of the electron transport at the nanoscale and the influence of temperature and power dissipation on it. The role of ions/vacancies will be indirectly addressed (more on this issue is explained in Section 5). Temperature evolution in the structures under study (e.g., Figure 1; Figure 2) is extensively covered in Section 2. First, a fixed ion/vacancy arrangement will be considered for simplicity, so that two particular extreme cases, LRS and HRS, will be examined. Second, a phenomenological model for the transition from HRS to LRS which takes into account the power dissipated at the CF bottleneck will be presented. As already discussed previously, while in LRS, the CF is completely formed establishing a metallic-like connection in between the electrodes; in HRS, the filament presents a gap along its structure as a consequence of the absence of conduction states [122]. Thereby, a common theory for both cases able to demonstrate consistency with the experimental observations is required.

Mesoscopic physics, a subdiscipline of condensed-matter physics, has resulted in a suitable framework for semi-empirically describing the temperature dependence of the electron flow in narrow constrictions and, in particular, in RRAMs. Mesoscopic physics describes the conducting properties of systems whose size lays in between the macroscopic (bulk material) and the microscopic (atoms and molecules) worlds. Since we are talking about atomic dimensions, quantum mechanics is at the foundations of mesoscopic physics [123]. Within this framework, the quantum confinement associated with filamentary conduction is described in terms of the electrochemical potential, potential wells, potential barriers, and bands (valence, conduction, gap). We also talk about a semi-empirical approach because the local temperature is frequently unknown and the external temperature is considered as a control parameter. This objection can be partly overcome if models including two different temperatures (for the cold and hot part of the CF, and for the CF and its surrounding region, see Sections 2.3.4 and 2.4.3) are employed. The idea of using a mesoscopic approach is the consequence of the observation of experimental RRAM conductance values around integer and non-integer multiples of the quantum conductance unit $G_0 = 2\,e^2/h$, where e is the electron charge and h the Planck's constant [124]. In terms of resistance, this unit is $R_0 = 1/G_0 = 12.9$ KΩ. The experimental conductance values for many cycles measured at a fixed bias, or the conductance measured at consecutive steps in one cycle at different or constant biases are often displayed using histogram plots with the x-axes normalized to G_0. In many cases, these histograms reveal a peak structure which is interpreted as an indicator of the number of channels available for conduction or as the occurrence of preferred atomic configurations for the CF [125]. Although the detection of peaks in the device histograms is recognized as the signature of quantum point-contact conduction, it should be taken into account that measurements can be seriously affected by a number of factors such as the existence of multiple conduction paths, series resistance, roughness and scattering caused by the granularity of matter, in general, non-adiabatic (non-smooth) potential profiles. Caution should also be exercised with the use of the term *conductance quantization*: only for simple s-electron metals, the transmission probability for the conductance channels is expected to open close to integer values [126]. For this reason, observations in the field of RRAM should be more appropriately considered to be in the quantum (rather than in the quantized) regime of conductance [125].

Many experimental results on resistive switching materials have been interpreted in terms of conduction through atom-sized filamentary structures [127]. This is the case of a wide variety of binary and ternary oxides such as SiO_x [128–131], HfO_2 [132–139], Ta_2O_5 [140–142], NiO [143,144], ZnO [145,146], a-Si:H [147], TiO_2 [148], V_2O_5 [149], YO_x [150], and $BiVO_4$ [151]. Nonlinear effects in HfO_2 were also reported by Degraeve et al. [152] and in CeO_x/SiO_2-based structures by Miranda et al. [153]. From the point of view of theory, it is worth mentioning that the CF formation in monoclinic- and amorphous-HfO_2 was investigated from first principles by Cartoixa et al. [154] and by Zhong et al. [155]. The filamentary paths are built from oxygen vacancies and using a Green's function formalism coupled to a density functional theory code, the conductance of filaments of different lengths was calculated. According to the obtained results, even the thinnest CFs can sustain conductive channels exhibiting signs of quantum conduction.

Very often, LRS is associated with conductance values $G \geq G_0$ and with a linear I-V curve (not to be confused with Ohmic behavior). In this case, the device conductance can reach values from 10 to 100 times G_0 which indicates the large number of atoms participating in the filament formation. On the other hand, HRS is associated with conductance values $G < G_0$ and with a non-linear I-V curve (mainly with exponential behavior). This state is characterized by a gap or potential barrier which acts as a blocking element for the electron flow. As the starting point for the inclusion of the thermal effects in RRAMs, the Buttiker-Landauer approach for quantum point contacts is considered [156]. Importantly, the analysis does not discriminate between CBRAMs and OxRAMs, so they are treated on equal grounds.

According to the finite-bias Landauer's formula [157], the I-V characteristic of a mesoscopic conductor can be expressed as:

$$I = \frac{2e}{h} \int D(E)[f(E - \beta eV) - f(E + (1-\beta)eV)]dE \quad (47)$$

where E is the energy, D the tunneling probability, f the Fermi-Dirac (FD) distribution function, and $0 \leq \beta \leq 1$ the fraction of the applied voltage that drops at the source side of the constriction. For a symmetrical structure $\beta = \frac{1}{2}$. Assuming an inverse parabolic potential barrier for the constriction bottleneck, D is given by [158]:

$$D(E) = \{1 + exp[-\nu(E - \varphi)]\}^{-1} \quad (48)$$

where ν is a coefficient related to the curvature of the potential barrier and φ the height of the potential barrier that represents the confinement effect (see Figure 27). For $T = 0$ K, (47) and (48) yield [159] (see Figure 27):

$$I(V) = G_0 \left\{ V + \frac{1}{e\nu} ln\left[\frac{1 + exp[\nu(\varphi - \beta eV)]}{1 + exp[\nu(\varphi + (1-\beta)eV)]}\right]\right\} \quad (49)$$

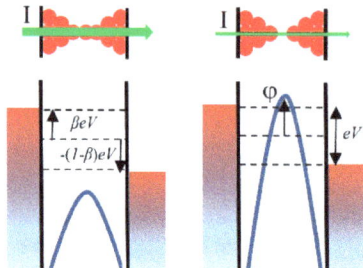

Figure 27. Schematic of the energy structure of the conducting filament. In LRS (high current), the CF is completely formed and the confinement potential barrier is low. In HRS (low current), the filament is broken and the confinement potential barrier is high. The green arrows width indicates the electron current magnitude.

Figure 28 shows some typical modeling results using Equation (49). Any additional potential drop along the confinement structure can be accounted for using the transformation $V \to V\text{-}I\, R_S$ in (49), where R_S is a series resistance. Equation (49) can be modified so as to include many parallel conducting channels [138]. For LRS, we can consider that there is no blocking element along the CF so that assuming $\varphi \to -\infty$ ($D \to 1$) in (49), we obtain:

$$I(V) = G_0 V \quad (50)$$

which is the celebrated Landauer formula for a monomode ballistic conductor [160]. Following [134], the temperature dependence can be introduced into (50), assuming $R_S(T) = R_{S0} \cdot [1 + \alpha_T(T - T_0)]$, where $R_{S0} = R_S(T_0)$, α_T is a temperature coefficient, and T_0 the room temperature. In this case, the I-V characteristic still follows a linear relationship but with a lower slope given by:

$$I(V) = \frac{G_0}{1 + G_0 R_S(T)} V \quad (51)$$

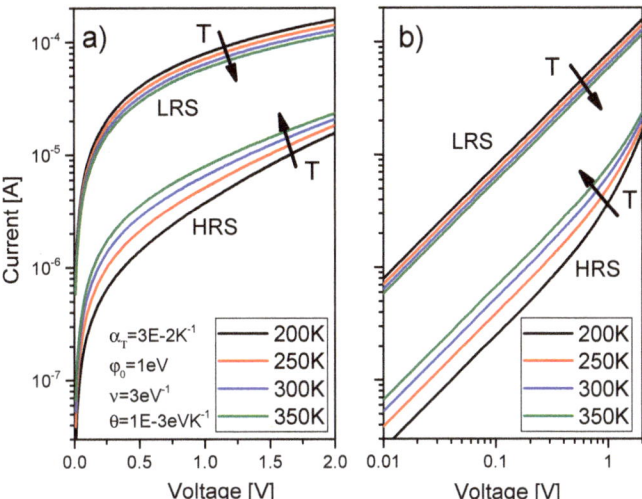

Figure 28. Effects of the temperature on the HRS and LRS I-V characteristics. (**a**) log-linear axis and (**b**) log-log axis.

If α_T is a positive coefficient, as expected for a metallic-like conductor, the current decreases as the temperature increases (see Figure 28). This behavior is in agreement with the experimental observations [134]. Notice that here the emphasis is put on the connection of the ballistic region with the rest of the device (internal or external) and in particular with the contacts. Nevertheless, R_S can also be viewed as the momentum relaxation factor along the filamentary structure. If we move to the opposite limit, for HRS, and we consider specifically the case $E \ll \varphi$, (48) reads:

$$D(E) \approx exp[\nu(E - \varphi)] \tag{52}$$

so that (47) can be integrated taking into account the temperature-dependent smearing of the FD distributions at the contacts. The result is [161]:

$$I(V) \approx \frac{2e}{h\nu} \frac{exp(-\nu\varphi)}{sinc(\pi\nu kT)} \{exp[\nu\beta eV] - exp[-\nu(1-\beta)eV]\} \tag{53}$$

which provides the exponential behavior observed for HRS. Now, notice that the temperature appears explicitly in (53) through the *sinc* function. In this case, the current increases with the temperature as expected from the availability of more energetic electrons at the injecting electrode. However, it can be shown that for a set of typical fitting parameters, the smearing of the FD functions is not enough to account for the observed temperature effects in HRS. In order to circumvent this problem, a new parameter is introduced into the model Equation (53) so that a larger variation of the current can be achieved. Following experimental observations for the soft breakdown conduction mode in SiO$_2$ [161], the confinement potential barrier height φ can be parameterized as $\varphi(T) = \varphi_0 - \theta(T - T_0)$, where $\varphi_0 = \varphi(T_0)$ and $\theta > 0$ is a linear temperature coefficient. This correction term arises from the thermal movement of ions/vacancies in the CF around their equilibrium positions. In this case, as the temperature increases, the tunneling current increases because of the reduction of the effective barrier height (see Figure 28). The temperature effect on the barrier profile was recently investigated in detail in [139] using inverse modeling in combination with the WKB approximation for the tunneling probability.

To conclude this section, it is worth mentioning that according to the standard theory of mesoscopic devices, heat largely dissipates at the electrodes (reservoirs) and thermal and electrical conductances are proportional through the Wiedemann-Franz law [119]. This idea is to heuristically explain why a CF of atomic dimensions is able to reach a stationary current state with conductance values of the order of G_0. Notice that the current density flowing through a nanoscale CF can be extraordinarily high. The question can be summarized as, where is power dissipated in a RRAM system exhibiting quantum properties? This is a fundamental question in mesoscopic physics [123]. Let us consider here the progressive increase of the current flow as a function of time when the device is subjected to a constant voltage stress after electroforming. This process corresponds to the transition HRS→LRS which arises because of the CF widening. Following [162], we can write first the following phenomenological equation for the current evolution:

$$\frac{dI}{dt} = \eta P_C \tag{54}$$

where η is a temperature- and material-dependent coupling coefficient and P_C is the power dissipated at the constriction bottleneck. For the simplest case of a constant applied bias V, Equation (54) expresses that the current levels off in the long run because power dissipation first increases and then progressively transfers from the constriction to the electrodes. Second, according to Landauer's formula, the transmission probability D (average) can be expressed as a function of the current flowing through the structure as:

$$\tilde{D} = G_0^{-1} G = (G_0 V)^{-1} I \tag{55}$$

and the power dissipated at the constriction can be calculated from the voltage drop V_C occurring at the constriction using:

$$P_C = V_C I = V\left(1 - \tilde{D}\right)I = VI\left(1 - \frac{I}{G_0 V}\right) \tag{56}$$

Then, from expression (54), an explicit differential equation for the current evolution is obtained:

$$\frac{dI}{dt} = \eta VI\left(1 - \frac{I}{G_0 V}\right) \tag{57}$$

Equation (57) is nothing but the logistic equation with effective transition rate ηV and carrying capacity $G_0 V$. The solution to Equation (57) for a constant bias reads:

$$I(t) = \frac{G_0 I_0 V exp(\eta V t)}{I_0 [exp(\eta V t) - 1] + G_0 V} \tag{58}$$

which complies with $I(t = 0) = I_0$ and $I(t = \infty) = G_0 V$, the initial and stationary conditions, respectively. Equation (58) expresses that, when a mesoscopic channel with conductance G_0 is formed, the power fundamentally dissipates at the electrodes and not at the constriction's bottleneck (see Figure 29). Power is indeed dissipated at the constriction during the CF formation as discussed in the next section. Of course, this is a simplistic view of a much more complex process.

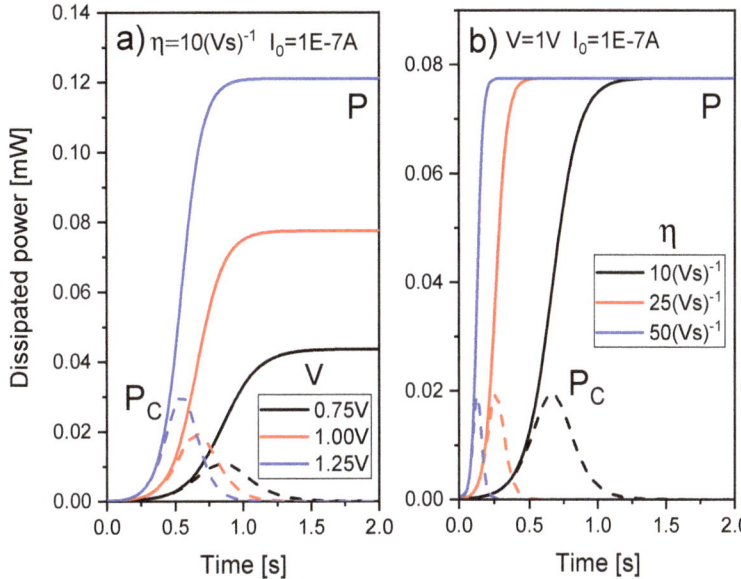

Figure 29. Evolution of the power dissipated in the structure P (solid lines), and at the constriction P_C (dashed lines). (**a**) Corresponds to different applied voltages V, and (**b**) corresponds to different transition rates η.

Although most of the models addressed in this manuscript are devoted to devices that show single filamentary conduction, some of them could also be applied to area-dependent devices and even to devices that do not require electroforming [1,2,70]. In particular, the Landauer's approach can be extended to area-dependent devices by assuming multifilamentary conduction. This is the case when the Landauer formula (49) includes a prefactor N dealing with the number of identical filaments assumed [138,159]. In addition, a modeling procedure in line with the general memristor framework presented in Section 3 could also be possible [71,72].

5. Thermometry of Conducting Filaments

In addition to the developments described above in relation to the HE solutions in different modeling approaches and levels of complexity, it is interesting to understand the dielectric breakdown (BD) phenomenon in the context of RRAM operation. In this respect, we shed light in this section on the structural damage that occurs during the BD current transient. In ultra-thin dielectric layers (<5 nm), there is a wide consensus around considering that the intrinsic BD is related to the generation of defects in the dielectric film [163–166]. When the density of bulk defects is high enough, the BD event is triggered by the local connection of the electrodes through a defect related conduction path. Once a defect percolation path is formed, the main feature is a progressive increase of the current across the dielectric. This phenomenon, often referred to as progressive breakdown (PBD), is an universal process that lies under a wide variety of dielectric materials, ranging from traditional oxides, such as SiO_2, SiO_XN_Y [167] to innovative 2D dielectrics, such as h-BN [168], passing through high-k materials such as Al_2O_3 and HfO_2 [169].

The physical structure of the filament formed during the PBD regime has been deeply studied. In the case of poly-Si/SiON/Si MOS devices during PBD, it was demonstrated that the filament is, at least in part, made of Si atoms, through the mechanism of dielectric breakdown induced epitaxy (DBIE) [170,171]. The filament sizes were directly observed by scanning transmission electron microscopy (STEM) after the BD of MIM structures with either $Ti/HfO_2/TiN$ or with $Hf/HfO_2/TiN$ devices, in which the top electrode (Ti or Hf) acted as cathode. Clear evidence of the formation of a metallic filament made of, respectively, Ti or Hf was reported by using electron energy loss spectroscopy (EELS) imaging [172,173]. In the case of 2D h-BN (CVD) dielectric layers, there is strong evidence that the CFs are formed by metal ions that penetrate from the electrodes into the h-BN stack under the action of the electric field [174,175].

Different experiments have probed that the SET event in RRAM devices [176,177] and the dielectric BD of gate oxides [169,178] have some common aspects. In addition to the clear dependence of the CF characteristics on the maximum current flowing through the device [18,179], TEM imaging of Si-based MOS capacitors prior to and post dielectric BD [163,170,180] and HfO$_2$-based RRAM cells after forming and cycling [172,181] show comparable microstructural changes in the oxide, suggesting the diffusion of the anodic atomic species into the oxide layer in both cases. Thus, these two phenomena share not only similar electrical characteristics, but also generate comparable microstructural changes, suggesting a common underlying physical mechanism. In such scenario, we propose to model the results for the SET event in RRAM devices similarly to the gate-oxide BD in MOSFETs.

The PBD effect has been captured by the model proposed by Palumbo et al. in [169,182], and later expanded by Lombardo in [183], clarifying the primary role played by the carrier energy loss through the PBD spot. Such model accounts for the physics behind the progressive evolution of the current, where the BD process is closely linked to the energy transfer from the CF itself to its surrounding atomic lattice. According to this idea, the high temperature associated with the localized current flow (being the BD spot area of 1–50 nm^2, the current density can reach a few MA/cm^2 [184–186]) would contribute to the generation and enlargement of the BD filament connecting the electrodes of the stack, enabling the promotion of the electro-migration of the fastest available atomic species. Since this technique unambiguously relate the transition rate (dI_{Tr}/dt) to the heat dissipation properties during the atomic diffusion of the cathode or anode atoms into the gate dielectric in the region of the percolation path, it is possible estimate the CF temperature. Considering the model reported in [169], we can express the current transition rate (marked as TR) as:

$$TR = \frac{dI_{Tr}}{dt} = \frac{q\,V\,f_1}{k_B\,T\,t_{ox}^2} D I_{SET} \tag{59}$$

where T is the temperature of the CF, t_{ox} is the dielectric thickness, k_B is the Boltzmann constant, D is the diffusion constant of the atomic species responsible for the generation of CF, I_{SET} is the current level at the onset of the transition, and $f_1 = n_e \lambda_e \sigma_e$, with n_e being the electron density, λ_e the electron mean free path and σ_e the cross-section for the electron-atom collision (responsible for the momentum transfer). V is the applied voltage across the BD spot which has been assumed to be equal to the overall externally applied bias between the metal contacts of the stack. f_1 value is around the unity since the defect concentration in the CF is most likely very high [172]. According to Equation (59), dI_{Tr}/dt is proportional to $D \times I_{SET}$. This means that the BD growth rate rises either by increasing the dominant diffusivity D of the fastest atomic species or by increasing the charge carrier flux.

The I-V characteristics under the PBD regime can be explained by some well-known physical models, for example invoking trap-assisted tunneling (TAT) current [187], co-tunneling [188,189], and the quantum point contact model [159]. Although the transport properties of stacks with different materials are fitted by considering different transport models, the underlying concept is similar in all cases, the electrons passing through the PBD spots experience a very large energy loss. To simplify the approach, the BD spot I_{SET}-V curve is usually modeled by assuming a simple analytical dependence as described in [190].

It is important to mention that independent experiments have probed that power dissipation taking place inside the dielectric layer is a reasonable assumption. According to Takagi [191], electrons tunneling through defects responsible for stress induced leakage current (SILC) in thin oxynitrides loose a fraction of energy, and as shown by Blochl and Stathis [192], this is caused by defect relaxation. It is reasonable to assume that a similar effect takes place for electron transport through the BD spot, since there is a clear dependence of the CF characteristic on the maximum current flowing through the device, both for the BD of gate oxides [179] and the SET event in RRAM devices [18,163,193], as well as for layered dielectrics, such as h-BN [168,190].

A simplification of spherical symmetry around the CF can be assumed to model the temperature in the BD spot. Within this approach, the temperature can be described by Equation (60), where the dissipated power at the CF is proportional to $I_{SET} \times V$, k_{th} is the thermal conductivity of the dielectric, T_0 is the room temperature and f_2 is the fraction of the energy lost at the constriction:

$$T = \frac{f_2 \, V \, I_{BD}}{2 \, \pi \, t_{ox} \, k_{th}} + T_0 \qquad (60)$$

The fitting parameters are f_1, f_2, D_0, and E_{act}; (taking into consideration that $D = D_0 * exp(-E_{act}/k_B T)$) and they describe the main features of the progressive BD effect on different stacks [190].

In this section we considered a RRAM device based on a MIM stack with a 10 nm thick atomic layer deposited HfO$_2$ film sandwiched between Ti and TiN electrodes [193]. During the HRS to LRS transition the current (I_{Tr}) increases gradually with time evidencing the progressive nature of the SET event (see Figure 30a,b). It is a noisy and progressive process well in agreement with the literature [176–178,194] whose duration shows a strong voltage dependence and dispersion. The time evolution of the HRS to LRS transition is quantified by the slope dI_{Tr}/dt, as defined in [169,185,195]. TR values were experimentally evaluated through measurements such as those shown in Figure 30a,b (approximately 100 measurements for each voltage value).

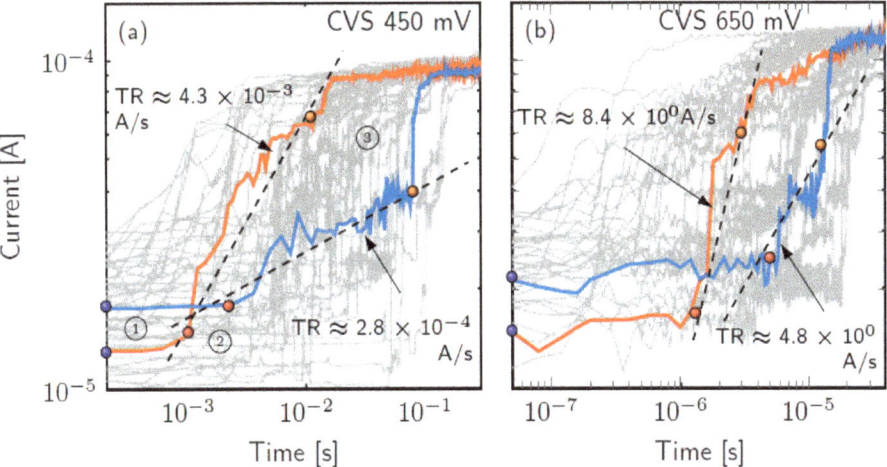

Figure 30. Current transient of the DUTs under constant voltage stress (CVS). (**a**) represents the lowest –450 mV– voltage whereas (**b**) the highest –650 mV–. Ball marker 1 points out the initial current (I$_{Init}$), whereas 2 the onset of the progressive increase of current (I$_{On}$) and 3 the final jump to the compliance level (I$_{End}$).

The fitting results for TR as a function of the applied voltage, obtained with the proposed model in Equations (59) and (60), are illustrated in Figure 31. The proposed fit accounts for both the t_{ox} reduction (t_{ox} considered is equal to t_{gap}~2 nm due to the forming step) and the increase in diffusivity (D_0 is in the order of ~10^{-6} cm^2/sec as other species are considered to complete the CF, i.e., oxygen vacancies). The rest of the parameters involved remain as previously mentioned in the literature (E_{act}~0.3–0.7 eV, f_2~0.1 and f_1~1) [193].

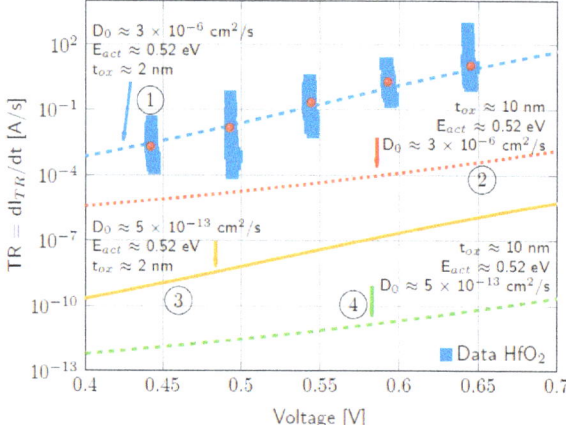

Figure 31. TR data (square markers –ball markers represent the mean value–) fitted assuming oxygen vacancies and $t_{gap} = t_{ox}$ (cyan dashed line – curve N° 1). Additionally, TR assuming literature values for t_{ox} and D is plotted –curves N° 2, 3 and 4–. TR presents a strong dependence with applied voltage, increasing almost one order of magnitude for every 50 mV step.

To implement this model for the SET event, the effect of the t_{ox} reduction after the forming step was considered. First, a forming operation (a controlled dielectric BD) creates the CF through the fresh oxide layer. Then, the switching mechanism is driven by the creation of a gap (RESET) and the restoration of the CF (SET). In the case under study, it has been demonstrated using the statistics of the SET switching time (t_{Set}) (i.e., the time to complete the HRS to LRS transition) that $t_{gap} \approx 2$ nm is a reasonable value [193].

Figure 32 presents the temperature calculations as a function of voltage provided Equation (60). f_2 represents the fraction of energy lost by the carriers, which ranges from 0 to 1. This parameter also depends on the temperature, mainly because of phonon-electron scattering [183]. Therefore, f_2 is a function of voltage and temperature whose behavior is found by a best fitting procedure. The influence of f_2 on the temperature is shown in Figure 32 for different f_2 values.

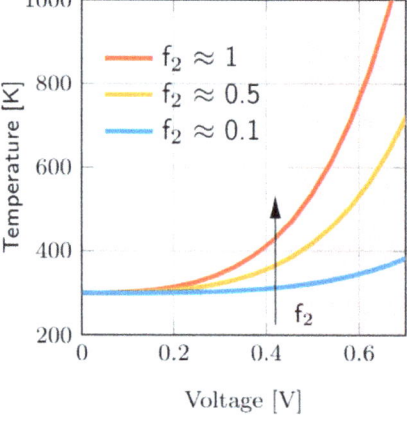

Figure 32. Temperature estimation according to Equation (60) as function of voltage and the energy loss in the CF. The red shaded zone indicates the voltages employed for the CVS (0.45 to 0.65 V).

The best fitting diffusivity required to reproduce the TR vs. voltage is observed in Figure 33. The data have been calculated assuming that D_0 is in the order of 3×10^{-6} cm^2/s and E_{act} = 0.52 eV as indicated in [193]. In HfO$_2$-based RRAM devices, the SET event is explained as the completion of the gap due to the migration of O$_2$-ions through a field-assisted and thermally activated effect, which creates the oxygen vacancies that fill the gap along the CF [38,44,53,195,196]. This is quite a relevant point to notice, as the diffusivity of oxygen vacancies (OVs), in a HfO$_2$ layer of thickness like t_{gap} spread over a range similar to the fitted diffusivity for the TR [197] (see Figure 33).

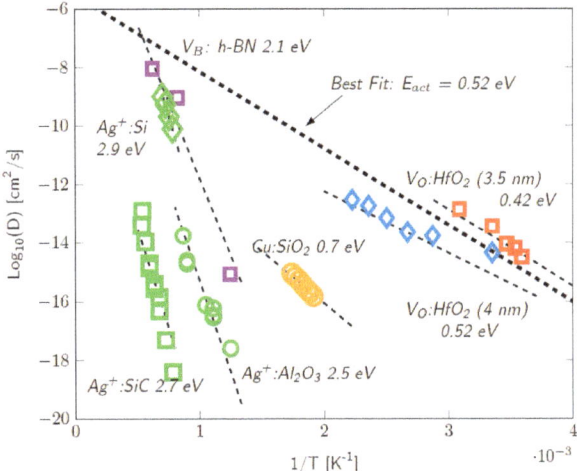

Figure 33. Reported values of diffusivity for different atomic species vs. reciprocal of temperature. The diffusivity D required for TR fitting is shown to be in the same range as the OVs diffusivity. OVs diffusivity [197] is ~10^4 times higher than for the metallic species as Cu:SiO$_2$ [198], Ag:SiC, Ag:Si and Ag:Al$_2$O$_3$ [199,200]. VB diffusivity in h-BN data corresponds to [201].

The diffusivity required to fit the experimental data of catastrophic BD in both SiO$_2$ and high-k (Al$_2$O$_3$ or HfO$_2$) stacks with metal electrodes are of the order of 10^{-13} cm^2/s at 1000 K, with activation energies ranging from 0.3 to 0.7 eV [169], where such values are in a range compatible with the diffusivity of metals in dielectrics (see in Figure 33. the case of Cu diffusion into SiO$_2$ layers [198]).

It should be mentioned that the state transition for a non-volatile regime in metal/h-BN/metal stacks (i.e., non-reversible event) has been studied with a similar approach where the best fitting value E_{act} is also much larger (E_{act} = 1.3 eV) [184,189]. Such discrepancies may lay on the fact that the particular species involved in the electromigration and/or diffusion process may change, depending on the severity of the SET event (volatile and non-volatile), as it occurs between the BD and SET events in HfO$_2$ stacks. While in the BD event in HfO$_2$ the diffusing ion species are considered to be the metallic ions from the electrodes ($D_0 = 1 \times 10^{-13}$ cm^2/sec, E_{act} = 0.3–0.7 eV [159,169,189]), the migration of oxygen vacancies from the TMO layer are responsible of the SET transition event ($D_0 = 1 \times 10^{-6}$ cm^2/s, E_{act} = 0.52 eV) [188].

To make clear the impact of both the t_{ox} reduction and the diffusivity increase (D_0), alternative fitting values were used to plot curves N° 2, N° 3 and N° 4 in Figure 31. Curve N°4 coincides with the TR for gate-oxide BD, as it considers diffusivity of metals in oxide layers and no t_{ox} reduction. The comparison of curves N° 1 and N° 4 evidence that TR is significantly higher than the TR expected for the voltage range considered. It is important to point out that TR calculated considering only a t_{ox} reduction or an increase in diffusivity (D_0) cannot meet the experimental data. This can be interpreted as that the two factors determine the dependence with the TR voltage, since none of them can separately adjust the results independently.

6. Conclusions

A comprehensive and exhaustive revision of RRAM thermal models is presented. Different approaches have been considered and described, including different conductive filament geometries, operation regimes, filament lateral heat losses, several temperatures to characterize each conductive filament, etc. A 3D numerical solution of the heat equation within a RRAM simulator was used. In addition, analytical models have been developed using equations describing the relevant physics behind the heat equation accounting for steady-state and non-steady-state device operation. A general memristor modeling framework was formulated considering the temperature as a state variable. Moreover, the quantum perspective was included in a mesoscopic context; this is a must due to the nanometric dimensions of the devices under study. In this respect, thermal effects were considered in the formulation of the quantum point contact model. Finally, conductive filament thermometry in usual RRAM technology was studied in detail. Since the physics underlying resistive switching is mainly based on thermally activated physical mechanisms, an accurate description of thermal effects is essential. As far as we know, there are not similar manuscripts that put together these types of effects under one roof.

Author Contributions: J.B.R., E.M., R.P., F.P., F.J.-M., S.G.S., J.S., G.G.-C., D.M., E.M. (Enrique Moreno) performed software development and simulations. D.M., G.G.-C., E.M. (Enrique Moreno), E.M. (Enrique Miranda), R.P., M.M.A.C., S.B.B., F.J.-M., J.B.R. wrote the original draft. J.B.R., E.M. (Enrique Miranda), R.P., F.P., F.J.-M., S.G.S., C.d.B., J.S., L.O.C. reviewed and edited the text. All the authors contributed to the English and reference checking. All authors have read and agreed to the published version of the manuscript.

Funding: This research was funded by Spanish Ministry of Science, Innovation and Universities, grant number TEC2017-84321-C4-3-R, TEC2017-84321-C4-4-R and by the Consejería de Economía y Conocimiento de la Junta de Andalucía and European Regional Development Fund (ERDF) under projects A-TIC-117-UGR18. It was also funded by MINCyT of Argentina (Contracts PICT2013/1210, PICT2016/0579 and PME2015-0196), CONICET (Project PIP- 11220130100077CO) and UTN.BA (Projects PIDUTN EIUTIBA4395TC3, CCUTIBA4764TC, MATUNBA4936 and CCUTNBA5182).

Data Availability Statement: The datasets generated during and/or analysed during the current study are available from the corresponding author on reasonable request.

Acknowledgments: We would like to thank F. Campabadal and M. B. González from the IMB-CNM (CSIC) in Barcelona for fabricating and measuring the devices which were employed to fit some of the compact models whose thermal blocks are presented here.

Conflicts of Interest: The authors declare no conflict of interest. The funders had no role in the design of the study; in the collection, analyses, or interpretation of data; in the writing of the manuscript, or in the decision to publish the results.

References

1. Lanza, M.; Wong, H.-S.P.; Pop, E.; Ielmini, D.; Strukov, D.; Regan, B.C.; Larcher, L.; Villena, M.A.; Yang, J.J.; Goux, L.; et al. Recommended Methods to Study Resistive Switching Devices. *Adv. Electron. Mater.* **2019**, *5*, 1800143. [CrossRef]
2. Pan, F.; Gao, S.; Chen, C.; Song, C.; Zeng, F. Recent progress in resistive random access memories: Materials, switching mechanisms, and performance. *Mater. Sci. Eng. R Rep.* **2014**, *83*, 1–59. [CrossRef]
3. Villena, M.A.; Roldán, J.B.; Jiménez-Molinos, F.; Miranda, E.; Suñé, J.; Lanza, M. SIM^2RRAM: A physical model for RRAM devices simulation. *J. Comput. Electron.* **2017**, *16*, 1095–1120. [CrossRef]
4. IRDS. *The International Roadmap for Devices and Systems: More Moore IEEE*; IRDS: New York, NY, USA, 2020.
5. Carboni, R.; Ielmini, D. Stochastic memory devices for security and computing. *Adv. Electron. Mater.* **2019**, *5*, 1900198. [CrossRef]
6. Puglisi, F.M.; Larcher, L.; Padovani, A.; Pavan, P. A Complete Statistical Investigation of RTN in HfO_2-Based RRAM in High Resistive State. *IEEE Trans. Electron Devices* **2015**, *62*, 2606–2613. [CrossRef]
7. Wei, Z.; Katoh, Y.; Ogasahara, S.; Yoshimoto, Y.; Kawai, K.; Ikeda, Y.; Eriguchi, K.; Ohmori, K.; Yoneda, S. True random number generator using current difference based on a fractional stochastic model in 40-nm embedded ReRAM. In Proceedings of the 2016 IEEE International Electron Devices Meeting (IEDM), IEEE, San Francisco, CA, USA, 3–7 December 2016; pp. 4.8.1–4.8.4.

8. Puglisi, F.M.; Zagni, N.; Larcher, L.; Pavan, P. random telegraph noise in resistive random access memories: Compact modeling and advanced circuit design. *IEEE Trans. Electron Devices* **2018**, *65*, 2964–2972. [CrossRef]
9. Lanza, M.; Wen, C.; Li, X.; Zanotti, T.; Puglisi, F.M.; Shi, Y.; Saiz, F.; Antidormi, A.; Roche, S.; Zheng, W.X.; et al. Advanced data encryption using two-dimensional materials. *Adv. Mater.* **2021**, in press.
10. Yao, P.; Wu, H.; Gao, B.; Tang, J.; Zhang, Q.; Zhang, W.; Yang, J.J.; Qian, H. Fully hardware-implemented memristor convolutional neural network. *Nat. Cell Biol.* **2020**, *577*, 641–646. [CrossRef] [PubMed]
11. Merolla, P.A.; Arthur, J.V.; Alvarez-Icaza, R.; Cassidy, A.S.; Sawada, J.; Akopyan, F.; Jackson, B.L.; Imam, N.; Guo, C.; Nakamura, Y.; et al. A million spiking-neuron integrated circuit with a scalable communication network and interface. *Science* **2014**, *345*, 668–673. [CrossRef]
12. Yu, S.; Gao, B.; Fang, Z.; Yu, H.; Kang, J.; Wong, H.-S.P. A neuromorphic visual system using RRAM synaptic devices with Sub-pJ energy and tolerance to variability: Experimental characterization and large-scale modeling. In Proceedings of the 2012 International Electron Devices Meeting, San Francisco, CA, USA, 10–13 December 2012; pp. 10.4.1–10.4.4.
13. Zidan, M.A.; Strachan, J.P.; Lu, W.D. The future of electronics based on memristive systems. *Nat. Electron.* **2018**, *1*, 22–29. [CrossRef]
14. Prezioso, M.; Merrikh-Bayat, F.; Hoskins, B.D.; Adam, G.C.; Likharev, K.K.; Strukov, D.B. Training and operation of an integrated neuromorphic network based on metal-oxide memristors. *Nature* **2015**, *521*, 61–64. [CrossRef] [PubMed]
15. Romero-Zaliz, R.; Pérez, E.; Jiménez-Molinos, F.; Wenger, C.; Roldán, J. Study of Quantized Hardware Deep Neural Networks Based on Resistive Switching Devices, Conventional versus Convolutional Approaches. *Electronics* **2021**, *10*, 346. [CrossRef]
16. Quesada, E.P.-B.; Romero-Zaliz, R.; Pérez, E.; Mahadevaiah, M.K.; Reuben, J.; Schubert, M.; Jiménez-Molinos, F.; Roldán, J.; Wenger, C. Toward Reliable Compact Modeling of Multilevel 1T-1R RRAM Devices for Neuromorphic Systems. *Electronics* **2021**, *10*, 645. [CrossRef]
17. Mead, C.; Ismail, M. *Analog VLSI Implementation of Neural Systems*; Springer: Berlin/Heidelberg, Germany, 1989.
18. Ielmini, D. Resistive switching memories based on metal oxides: Mechanisms, reliability and scaling. *Semicond. Sci. Technol.* **2016**, *31*, 063002. [CrossRef]
19. Ielmini, D.; Milo, V. Physics-based modeling approaches of resistive switching devices for memory and in-memory computing applications. *J. Comput. Electron.* **2017**, *16*, 1121–1143. [CrossRef]
20. Huang, P.; Gao, B.; Chen, B.; Zhang, F.; Liu, L.; Du, G. Stochastic simulation of forming, SET and RESET process for transition metal oxide-based resistive switching memory. *Proc. SISPAD* **2011**, *2012*, 312–315.
21. Aldana, S.; Roldán, J.B.; García-Fernández, P.; Suñé, J.; Romero-Zaliz, R.; Jiménez-Molinos, F.; Long, S.; Gómez-Campos, F.; Liu, M. An in-depth description of bipolar resistive switching in Cu/HfO$_x$/Pt devices, a 3D Kinetic Monte Carlo simulation approach. *J. Appl. Phys.* **2018**, *123*, 154501. [CrossRef]
22. Garcia-Redondo, F.; Gowers, R.P.; Crespo-Yepes, A.; Lopez-Vallejo, M.; Jiang, L. SPICE Compact modeling of bipolar/unipolar memristor switching governed by electrical thresholds. *IEEE Trans. Circuits Syst. I Regul. Pap.* **2016**, *63*, 1255–1264. [CrossRef]
23. Dirkmann, S.; Kaiser, J.; Wenger, C.; Mussenbrock, T. Filament growth and resistive switching in hafnium oxide memristive devices. *ACS Appl. Mater. Interfaces* **2018**, *10*, 14857–14868. [CrossRef]
24. Aldana, S.; García-Fernández, P.; Rodríguez-Fernández, A.; Romero-Zaliz, R.; González, M.B.; Jiménez-Molinos, F.; Campabadal, F.; Gómez-Campos, F.; Roldán, J.B. A 3D kinetic monte carlo simulationstudy of resistive switching processes in Ni/HfO$_2$/Si-n+-based RRAMs. *J. Phys. D* **2017**, *50*, 335103. [CrossRef]
25. Jagath, A.L.; Nandha Kumar, T.; Almurib, H.A.F. Modeling of Current Conduction during RESET Phase of Pt/Ta$_2$O$_5$/TaO$_x$/Pt Bipolar Resistive RAM Devices. In Proceedings of the 2018 IEEE 7th Non-Volatile Memory Systems and Applications Symposium (NVMSA), Hakodate, Japan, 28–31 August 2018; pp. 55–60.
26. Fang, X.; Yang, X.; Wu, J.; Yi, X. A Compact SPICE model of unipolar memristive devices. *IEEE Trans. Nanotechnol.* **2013**, *12*, 843–850. [CrossRef]
27. González-Cordero, G.; González, M.B.; García, H.; Campabadal, F.; Dueñas, S.; Castán, H.; Jiménez-Molinos, F.; Roldán, J.B. A physically based model for resistive memories including a detailed temperature and variability description. *Microelectron. Eng.* **2017**, *178*, 26–29. [CrossRef]
28. Karpov, V.; Niraula, D.; Karpov, I. Thermodynamic analysis of conductive filaments. *Appl. Phys. Lett.* **2016**, *109*, 093501. [CrossRef]
29. Maestro-Izquierdo, M.; Gonzalez, M.B.; JimenezMolinos, F.; Moreno, E.; Roldan, J.B.; Campabadal, F. Unipolar resistive switching behavior in Al$_2$O$_3$/HfO$_2$ multilayer dielectric stacks: Fabrication, characterization and simulation. *Nanotechnology* **2020**, *31*, 135202. [CrossRef] [PubMed]
30. Larentis, S.; Nardi, F.; Balatti, S.; Gilmer, D.C.; Ielmini, D. Resistive Switching by Voltage-Driven Ion Migration in Bipolar RRAM—Part II: Modeling. *IEEE Trans. Electron Devices* **2012**, *59*, 2468–2475. [CrossRef]
31. Jimenez-Molinos, F.; Villena, M.A.; Roldan, J.B.; Roldan, A.M. A SPICE compact model for unipolar RRAM reset process analysis. *IEEE Trans. Electron Devices* **2015**, *62*, 955–962. [CrossRef]
32. Menzel, S.; Kaupmann, P.; Waser, R. Understanding filamentary growth in electrochemical metallization memory cells using kinetic Monte Carlo simulations. *Nanoscale* **2015**, *7*, 12673–12681. [CrossRef] [PubMed]
33. Picos, R.; Roldán, J.B.; al Chawa, M.M.; García-Fernández, P.; García-Moreno, F.J.Y.E. Semiempirical modeling of reset transitions in unipolar resistive-switching based memristors. *Radioeng. J.* **2015**, *24*, 420–424. [CrossRef]

34. Vandelli, L.; Padovani, A.; Larcher, L.; Bersuker, G. Microscopic modeling of electrical stress-induced breakdown in polycrystalline hafnium oxide dielectrics. *IEEE Trans. Electron Devices* **2013**, *60*, 1754–1762. [CrossRef]
35. Blasco, J.; Ghenzi, N.; Suñé, J.; Levy, P.; Miranda, E. Equivalent circuit modeling of the bistable conduction characteristics in electroformed thin dielectric films. *Microelectron. Reliab.* **2015**, *55*, 1–14. [CrossRef]
36. Maldonado, D.; Gonzalez, M.B.; Campabadal, F.; JimenezMolinos, F.; Al Chawa, M.M.; Stavrinides, S.G.; Roldan, J.B.; Tetzlaff, R.; Picos, R.; Chua, L.O. Experimental evaluation of the dynamic route map in the reset transition of memristive ReRAMs. *Chaos Solitons Fractals* **2020**, *139*, 110288. [CrossRef]
37. Jiménez-Molinos, F.; González-Cordero, G.; Cartujo-Cassinello, P.; Roldán, J.B. SPICE modeling of RRAM thermal reset transition for circuit simulation purposes. In Proceedings of the Spanish Conference on Electron Devices, Barcelona, Spain, 8–10 February 2017.
38. Bocquet, M.; Deleruyelle, D.; Aziza, H.; Muller, C.; Portal, J.-M.; Cabout, T.; Jalaguier, E. Robust compact model for bipolar oxide-based resistive switching memories. *IEEE Trans. Electron. Devices* **2014**, *61*, 674–681. [CrossRef]
39. al Chawa, M.M.; Picos, R.; Tetzlaff, R. A Simple Memristor Model for Neuromorphic ReRAM Devices. In Proceedings of the 2020 IEEE International Symposium on Circuits and Systems (ISCAS), Seville, Spain, 10–21 October 2020.
40. al Chawa, M.M.; Picos, R. A simple quasi-static compact model of bipolar ReRAM memristive devices. *IEEE Trans. Circuits Syst. II* **2020**, *67*, 390–394. [CrossRef]
41. Panda, D.; Sahu, P.P.; Tseng, T.Y. A collective study on modeling and simulation of resistive random access memory. *Nanoscale Res. Lett.* **2018**, *13*, 1–48. [CrossRef] [PubMed]
42. Reuben, J.; Biglari, M.; Fey, D. Incorporating Variability of Resistive RAM in Circuit Simulations Using the Stanford–PKU Model. *IEEE Trans. Nanotechnol.* **2020**, *19*, 508–518. [CrossRef]
43. Mikhaylov, A.; Guseinov, D.; Belov, A.; Korolev, D.; Shishmakova, V.; Koryazhkina, M.; Filatov, D.; Gorshkov, O.; Maldonado, D.; Alonso, F.; et al. Stochastic resonance in a metal-oxide memristive device. *Chaos Solitons Fractals* **2021**, *144*, 110723. [CrossRef]
44. Aldana, S.; Pérez, E.; JimenezMolinos, F.; Wenger, C.; Roldán, J.B. Kinetic Monte Carlo analysis of data retention in Al:HfO$_2$-based resistive random access memories. *Semicond. Sci. Technol.* **2020**, *35*, 115012. [CrossRef]
45. Roldán, J.B.; Alonso, F.J.; Aguilera, A.M.; Maldonado, D.; Lanza, M. Time series statistical analysis: A powerful tool to evaluate the variability of resistive switching memories. *J. Appl. Phys.* **2019**, *125*, 174504. [CrossRef]
46. Miranda, E.; Mehonic, A.; Ng, W.H.; Kenyon, A.J. Simulation of cycle-to-cycle instabilities in SiO$_x$-based ReRAM devices using a self-correlated process with long-term variation. *IEEE EDL* **2019**, *40*, 28–31. [CrossRef]
47. Kvatinsky, S.; Ramadan, M.; Friedman, E.G.; Kolodny, A. VTEAM: A general model for voltage-controlled memristors. *IEEE Trans. Circuits Syst. II* **2015**, *62*, 786–790. [CrossRef]
48. Picos, R.; Roldan, J.B.; Al Chawa, M.M.; JimenezMolinos, F.; Garcia-Moreno, E. A physically based circuit model to account for variability in memristors with resistive switching operation. In Proceedings of the 2016 Conference on Design of Circuits and Integrated Systems (DCIS), Granada, Spain, 23–25 November 2016; pp. 1–6.
49. al Chawa, M.M.; de Benito, C.; Picos, R. A simple piecewise model of reset/set transitions in bipolar ReRAM memristive devices. *IEEE Trans. Circuits Syst. I* **2018**, *65*, 3469–3480. [CrossRef]
50. al Chawa, M.M.; Tetzlaff, R.; Picos, R. A Simple Monte Carlo Model for the Cycle-to-Cycle Reset Transition Variation of ReRAM Memristive Devices. In Proceedings of the 9th International Conference on Modern Circuits and Systems Technologies (MOCAST), Bremen, Germany, 7–9 September 2020.
51. Alonso, F.J.; Maldonado, D.; Aguilera, A.M.; Roldan, J.B. Memristor variability and stochastic physical properties modeling from a multivariate time series approach. *Chaos Solitons Fractals* **2021**, *143*, 110461. [CrossRef]
52. Pérez, E.; Maldonado, D.; Acal, C.; Ruiz-Castro, J.E.; Alonso, F.J.; Aguilera, A.M.; Jiménez-Molinos, F.; Wenger, C.; Roldán, J.B. Analysis of the statistics of device-to-device and cycle-to-cycle variability in TiN/Ti/Al:HfO$_2$/TiN RRAMs. *Microelectron. Eng.* **2019**, *214*, 104–109. [CrossRef]
53. Aldana, S.; García-Fernández, P.; Romero-Zaliz, R.; González, M.B.; Jiménez-Molinos, F.; Gómez-Campos, F.; Campabadal, F.; Roldán, J.B. Resistive switching in HfO$_2$ based valence change memories, a comprehensive 3D kinetic Monte Carlo approach. *J. Phys. D* **2020**, *53*, 225106. [CrossRef]
54. Guy, J.; Molas, G.; Blaise, P.; Bernard, M.; Roule, A.; Le Carval, G.; Delaye, V.; Toffoli, A.; Ghibaudo, G.; Clermidy, F.; et al. Investigation of forming, SET, and data retention of conductive-bridge random-access memory for stack optimization. *IEEE Trans. Electron Devices* **2015**, *62*, 3482–3489. [CrossRef]
55. Villena, M.A.; Roldán, J.B.; González, M.B.; González-Rodelas, P.; Jiménez-Molinos, F.; Campabadal, F.; Barrera, D. A new parameter to characterize the charge transport regime in Ni/HfO$_2$/Si-n$^+$-based RRAMs. *Solid State Electron.* **2016**, *118*, 56–60. [CrossRef]
56. González-Cordero, G.; Roldán, J.B.; Jiménez-Molinos, F. SPICE simulation of RRAM circuits. A compact modeling perspective. In Proceedings of the 2017 Spanish Conference on Electron Devices, Barcelona, Spain, 8–10 February 2017; pp. 26–29.
57. Huang, P.; Zhu, D.; Chen, S.; Zhou, Z.; Chen, Z.; Gao, B.; Liu, L.; Liu, X.; Kang, J. Compact model of HfO$_X$-based electronic synaptic devices for neuromorphic computing. *IEEE Trans. Electron. Devices* **2017**, *64*, 614–621. [CrossRef]
58. Kwon, S.; Jang, S.; Choi, J.-W.; Choi, S.; Jang, S.-J.; Kim, T.-W.; Wang, G. Controllable switching filaments prepared via tunable and well-defined single truncated conical nanopore structures for fast and scalable SiO$_x$ memory. *Nanoletters* **2017**, *17*, 7462–7470. [CrossRef]

59. Villena, M.; Gonzalez, M.B.; Roldán, J.; Campabadal, F.; Jiménez-Molinos, F.; Gómez-Campos, F.; Suñé, J. An in-depth study of thermal effects in reset transitions in HfO$_2$ based RRAMs. *Solid-State Electron.* **2015**, *111*, 47–51. [CrossRef]
60. Lohn, A.J.; Mickel, P.R.; Marinella, M.J. Analytical estimations for thermal crosstalk, retention, and scaling limits in filamentary resistive memory. *J. Appl. Phys.* **2014**, *115*, 234507. [CrossRef]
61. Sun, P.; Lu, N.; Li, L.; Li, Y.; Wang, H.; Lv, H.; Liu, Q.; Long, S.; Liu, S.; Liu, M. Thermal crosstalk in 3-dimensional RRAM crossbar array. *Sci. Rep.* **2015**, *5*, 13504. [CrossRef] [PubMed]
62. Deshmukh, S.; Islam, R.; Chen, C.; Yalon, E.; Saraswat, K.C.; Pop, E. Thermal modeling of metal oxides for highly scaled nanoscale RRAM. In Proceedings of the 2015 International Conference on Simulation of Semiconductor Processes and Devices (SISPAD), Washington, DC, USA, 9–11 September 2015; Volume 2015, pp. 281–284.
63. Wang, D.-W.; Chen, W.; Zhao, W.-S.; Zhu, G.-D.; Kang, K.; Gao, P.; Schutt-Aine, J.E.; Yin, W.-Y. Fully Coupled Electrothermal Simulation of Large RRAM Arrays in the "Thermal-House". *IEEE Access* **2018**, *7*, 3897–3908. [CrossRef]
64. Rodríguez, N.; Roldán, F.G.y.J.B. Modeling of inversion layer centroid and polysilicon depletion effects on ultrathin-gate-oxide MOSFET behaviour: The influence of crystallographic orientation. *IEEE Trans. Electron. Devices* **2007**, *54*, 723–732. [CrossRef]
65. González, B.; Roldán, J.; Iniguez, B.; Lazaro, A.; Cerdeira, A. DC self-heating effects modelling in SOI and bulk FinFETs. *Microelectron. J.* **2015**, *46*, 320–326. [CrossRef]
66. Roldán, J.B.; Gámiz, F.; JimenezMolinos, F.; Sampedro, C.; Godoy, A.; Rodríguez, N. An analytic I-V model for surrounding-gate MOSFET including quantum and velocity overshoot effects. *IEEE Trans. Electron. Devices* **2010**, *57*, 2925–2933. [CrossRef]
67. Blanco-Filgueira, B.; Roldán, P.L.Y.J.B. Analytical modeling of size effects on the lateral photoresponse of CMOS photodiodes. *Solid State Electron.* **2012**, *73*, 15–20. [CrossRef]
68. Blanco-Filgueira, B.; Roldán, P.L.y.J.B. A closed-form and explicit analytical model for crosstalk in CMOS photodiodes. *IEEE Trans. Electron Devices* **2013**, *60*, 3459–3464. [CrossRef]
69. Gámiz, F.; Godoy, A.; Donetti, L.; Sampedro, C.; Roldán, J.B.; Ruiz, F.; Tienda, I.; Jiménez-Molinos, N.R.Y.F. Monte Carlo simulation of nanoelectronic devices. *J. Comput. Electron.* **2009**, *8*, 174–191. [CrossRef]
70. Ielmini, D.; Waser, R. *Resistive Switching: From Fundamentals of Nanoionic Redox Processes to Memristive Device Applications*; Wiley-VCH: Hoboken, NJ, USA, 2015.
71. Corinto, F.; Civalleri, P.P.; Chua, L.O. A theoretical approach to memristor devices. *IEEE J. Emerg. Sel. Top. Circuits Syst.* **2015**, *5*, 123–132. [CrossRef]
72. Chua, L.O. Everything you wish to know about memristors but are afraid to ask. *Radioengineering* **2015**, *24*, 319–368. [CrossRef]
73. James, A.P. A hybrid memristor–CMOS chip for AI. *Nat. Electron.* **2019**, *2*, 268–269. [CrossRef]
74. Volos, C.K.; Kyprianidis, I.M.; Stavrinides, S.G.; Stouboulos, I.N.; Anagnostopoulos, A.N. Memristors: A new approach in nonlinear circuits design. In Proceedings of the 14th WSEAS International Conference on Communication, Cape Town, South Africa, 23–27 May 2010; pp. 25–30.
75. Li, Y.; Wang, Z.; Midya, R.; Xia, Q.; Yang, J.J. Review of memristor devices in neuromorphic computing: Materials sciences and device challenges. *J. Phys. D Appl. Phys.* **2018**, *51*, 503002. [CrossRef]
76. Padovani, A.; Larcher, L.; Pirrotta, O.; Vandelli, L.; Bersuker, G. Microscopic Modeling of HfO$_x$ RRAM operations: From forming to switching. *IEEE Trans. Electron. Devices* **2015**, *62*, 1998–2006. [CrossRef]
77. Cazorla, M.; Aldana, S.; Maestro, M.; González, M.B.; Campabadal, F.; Moreno, E.; Jiménez-Molinos, F.; Roldán, J.B. A thermal study of multilayer RRAMs based on HfO$_2$ and Al$_2$O$_3$ oxides. *J. Vac. Sci. Technol. B* **2019**, *37*, 012204. [CrossRef]
78. Guan, X.; Yu, S.; Wong, H.-S.P. A SPICE compact model of metal oxide resistive switching memory with variations. *IEEE Electron Device Lett.* **2012**, *33*, 1405–1407. [CrossRef]
79. González-Cordero, G.; Roldan, J.B.; Jiménez-Molinos, F.; Suñé, J.; Liu, S.L.y.M. A new model for bipolar RRAMs based on truncated cone conductive filaments, a Verilog-A approach. *Semicond. Sci. Technol.* **2016**, *31*, 115013. [CrossRef]
80. Villena, M.A.; González, M.B.; Jiménez-Molinos, F.; Campabadal, F.; Roldán, J.B.; Suñé, J.; Romera, E.; Miranda, E. Simulation of thermal reset transitions in resistive switching memories including quantum effects. *J. Appl. Phys.* **2014**, *115*, 214504. [CrossRef]
81. Von Witzleben, M.; Fleck, K.; Funck, C.; Baumkötter, B.; Zuric, M.; Idt, A.; Breuer, T.; Waser, R.; Böttger, U.; Menzel, S. Investigation of the impact of high temperatures on the switching kinetics of redox-based resistive switching cells using a high-speed nanoheater. *Adv. Electron. Mater.* **2017**, *3*, 1700294. [CrossRef]
82. Lantos, N.; Nataf, F. Perfectly matched layers for the heat and advection–diffusion equations. *J. Comput. Phys.* **2010**, *229*, 9042–9052. [CrossRef]
83. Moreno, E.; Hemmat, Z.; Roldan, J.B.; Pantoja, M.F.; Bretones, A.R.; Garcia, S.G.; Faez, R. Implementation of open boundary problems in photo-conductive antennas by using convolutional perfectly matched layers. *IEEE Trans. Antennas Propag.* **2016**, *64*, 4919–4922. [CrossRef]
84. González-Cordero, G. Compact Modeling of Memristors Based on Resistive Switching Devices. Ph.D. Thesis, Universidad de Granada, Granada, Spain, 2020.
85. Villena, M.A.; Jiménez-Molinos, F.; Roldan, J.B.; Suñe, J.; Long, S.; Lian, X.; Gamiz, F.; Liu, M. An in-depth simulation study of thermal reset transitions in resistive switching memories. *J. Appl. Phys.* **2013**, *114*, 144505. [CrossRef]
86. Guan, X.; Yu, S.; Wong, H.S.P. On the Variability of HfO$_x$ RRAM: From Numerical Simulation to Compact Modeling Technical. In Proceedings of the 2012 NSTI Nanotechnology Conference and Expo, NSTI-Nanotech, Santa Clara, CA, USA, 18–21 June 2012; Volume 2, pp. 815–820.

87. Jiang, Z.; Yu, S.; Wu, Y.; Engel, J.H.; Guan, X.; Wong, H.-S.P. Verilog-A compact model for oxide-based resistive random access memory (RRAM). In Proceedings of the 2014 International Conference on Simulation of Semiconductor Processes and Devices (SISPAD), Yokohama, Japan, 9–11 September 2014; pp. 41–44.
88. Jiang, Z.; Wu, Y.; Yu, S.; Yang, L.; Song, K.; Karim, Z.; Wong, H.-S.P. A compact model for metal–oxide resistive random access memory with experiment verification. *IEEE Trans. Electron Devices* **2016**, *63*, 1884–1892. [CrossRef]
89. Moran, M.J.; Shapiro, H.N.; Munson, B.R.; Dewitt, D.P.; Wiley, J.; Hepburn, K.; Fleming, L. *Introduction to Thermal Systems Engineering: And Heat Transfer*; John Wiley & Sons Inc.: New York, NY, USA, 2003; Volume 169, ISBN 0471204900.
90. Sheridan, P.; Kim, K.-H.; Gaba, S.; Chang, T.; Chen, L.; Lu, W. Device and SPICE modeling of RRAM devices. *Nanoscale* **2011**, *3*, 3833–3840. [CrossRef] [PubMed]
91. Huang, P.; Liu, X.Y.; Chen, B.; Li, H.T.; Wang, Y.J.; Deng, Y.X.; Wei, K.L.; Zeng, L.; Gao, B.; Du, G.; et al. A physics-based compact model of metal-oxide-based RRAM DC and AC operations. *IEEE Trans. Electron Devices* **2013**, *60*, 4090–4097. [CrossRef]
92. Li, H.; Huang, P.; Gao, B.; Chen, B.; Liu, X.; Kang, J. A SPICE Model of Resistive Random Access Memory for Large-Scale Memory Array Simulation. *IEEE Electron Device Lett.* **2013**, *35*, 211–213. [CrossRef]
93. Li, H.; Jiang, Z.; Huang, P.; Wu, Y.; Chen, H.Y.; Gao, B.; Liu, X.Y.; Kang, J.F.; Wong, H.S. Variation-Aware, Reliability-Emphasized Design and Optimization of RRAM using SPICE Model. In Proceedings of the Design, Automation & Test in Europe Conference & Exhibition, Grenoble, France, 9–13 March 2015; pp. 1425–1430.
94. Chen, A. A review of emerging non-volatile memory (NVM) technologies and applications. *Solid State Electron.* **2016**, *125*, 25–38. [CrossRef]
95. Chen, P.-Y.; Yu, S. Compact modeling of RRAM devices and its applications in 1T1R and 1S1R array design. *IEEE Trans. Electron. Devices* **2015**, *62*, 4022–4028. [CrossRef]
96. Chiang, M.-H.; Hsu, K.-H.; Ding, W.-W.; Yang, B.-R. A predictive compact model of bipolar RRAM cells for circuit simulations. *IEEE Trans. Electron. Devices* **2015**, *62*, 2176–2183. [CrossRef]
97. Kwon, J.; Sharma, A.A.; Chen, C.M.; Fantini, A.; Jurczak, M.; Herzing, A.A.; Bain, J.A.; Picard, Y.N.; Skowronski, M. Transient thermometry and high-resolution transmission electron microscopy analysis of filamentary resistive switches. *ACS Appl. Mater. Interfaces* **2016**, *8*, 20176. [CrossRef]
98. Sharma, A.A.; Noman, M.; Skowronski, M.; Bain, J.A. Technology, Systems and Applications (VLSI-TSA). In Proceedings of the 2014 International Symposium on VLSI Technology, Systems and Applications, Hsinchu, Taiwan, 28–30 April 2014; p. 1.
99. Nishi, Y.; Menzel, S.; Fleck, K.; Boettger, U.; Waser, R. Origin of the SET kinetics of the resistive switching in tantalum oxide thin films. *IEEE Electron. Device Lett.* **2014**, *35*, 259–261. [CrossRef]
100. Kim, S.; Du, C.; Sheridan, P.; Ma, W.; Choi, S.; Lu, W.D. Experimental demonstration of a second-order memristor and its ability to biorealistically implement synaptic plasticity. *Nano Lett.* **2015**, *15*, 2203–2211. [CrossRef]
101. Panzer, M.A.; Shandalov, M.; Rowlette, J.A.; Oshima, Y.; Chen, Y.W.; McIntyre, P.C.; Goodson, K.E. Thermal Properties of Ultrathin Hafnium Oxide Gate Dielectric Films. *IEEE Electron Device Lett.* **2009**, *30*, 1269–1271. [CrossRef]
102. Scott, E.A.; Gaskins, J.T.; King, S.W.; Hopkins, P.E. Thermal conductivity and thermal boundary resistance of atomic layer deposited high-k dielectric aluminum oxide, hafnium oxide, and titanium oxide thin films on silicon. *APL Mater.* **2018**, *6*, 058302. [CrossRef]
103. Roldán, A.M.; Roldán, J.B.; Reig, C.; Cubells-Beltrán, M.-D.; Ramírez, D.; Cardoso, S.; Freitas, P.P. A DC behavioral electrical model for quasi-linear spin-valve devices including thermal effects for circuit simulation. *Microelectron. J.* **2011**, *42*, 365–370. [CrossRef]
104. Busani, M.; Menozzi, R.; Borgarino, M.; Fantini, F. Dynamic thermal characterization and modeling of packaged AlGaAs/GaAs HBTs. *IEEE Trans. Compon. Packag. Technol.* **2000**, *23*, 352–359. [CrossRef]
105. Pedro, M.; Martin-Martinez, J.; Gonzalez, M.; Rodriguez, R.; Campabadal, F.; Nafria, M.; Aymerich, X. Tuning the conductivity of resistive switching devices for electronic synapses. *Microelectron. Eng.* **2017**, *178*, 89–92. [CrossRef]
106. González-Cordero, G.; Pedro, M.; Martin-Martinez, J.; González, M.; Jiménez-Molinos, F.; Campabadal, F.; Nafría, N.; Roldán, J. Analysis of resistive switching processes in TiN/Ti/HfO$_2$/W devices to mimic electronic synapses in neuromorphic circuits. *Solid-State Electron.* **2019**, *157*, 25–33. [CrossRef]
107. Kumar, S.; Williams, R.S.; Wang, Z. Third-order nanocircuit elements for neuromorphic engineering. *Nat. Cell Biol.* **2020**, *585*, 518–523. [CrossRef]
108. González-Cordero, G.; Jiménez-Molinos, F.; Roldán, J.B.; González, M.B.; Campabadal, F. Transient SPICE Simulation of Ni/HfO$_2$/Si-n$^+$ Resistive Memories. In Proceedings of the Design of Circuits and Integrated Systems Conference, DCIS, Granada, Spain, 23–25 November 2016.
109. González-Cordero, G.; Jiménez-Molinos, F.; Villena, M.A.; Roldán, J.B. SPICE Simulation of Thermal Reset Transitions in Ni/HfO$_2$/Si-n$^+$ RRAMs Including Quantum Effects. In Proceedings of the 19th Workshop on Dielectrics in Microelectronics, WoDiM, Catania, Italy, 27–30 June 2016.
110. González, M.B.; Rafí, J.M.; Beldarrain, O.; Zabala, M.; Campabadal, F. Analysis of the switching variability in Ni/HfO$_2$-based RRAM devices. *IEEE Trans. Device Mater. Reliab.* **2014**, *14*, 769–771.
111. Wang, W.; Laudato, M.; Ambrosi, E.; Bricalli, A.; Covi, E.; Lin, Y.-H.; Ielmini, D. Volatile Resistive Switching Memory Based on Ag Ion Drift/Diffusion—Part II: Compact Modeling. *IEEE Trans. Electron Devices* **2019**, *66*, 3802–3808. [CrossRef]
112. Chua Leon, O.; Kang, S.M. Memristive devices and systems. *Proc. IEEE* **1976**, *64*, 209–223. [CrossRef]

113. Ginoux, J.M.; Muthuswamy, B.; Meucci, R.; Euzzor, S.; Di Garbo, A.; Ganesan, K. A physical memristor based Muthuswamy-Chua-Ginoux system. *Sci. Rep.* **2020**, *10*, 1–10. [CrossRef]
114. Steinhart, J.S.; Hart, S.R. Calibration curves for thermistors. *Deep Sea Res. Oceanogr. Abstr.* **1968**, *15*, 497–503. [CrossRef]
115. Theodorakakos, A.; Stavrinides, S.G.; Hatzikraniotis, E.; Picos, R. A non-ideal memristor device. In Proceedings of the 2015 International Conference on Memristive Systems (MEMRISYS), Paphos, Cyprus, 8–10 November 2015; pp. 1–2.
116. Biolek, D.; Biolek, Z.; Biolkova, V.; Kolka, Z. Some fingerprints of ideal memristors. In Proceedings of the 2013 IEEE International Symposium on Circuits and Systems (ISCAS), Beijing, China, 19–23 May 2013; pp. 201–204.
117. Wagner, G.; Jones, R.; Templeton, J.; Parks, M. An atomistic-to-continuum coupling method for heat transfer in solids. *Comput. Methods Appl. Mech. Eng.* **2008**, *197*, 3351–3365. [CrossRef]
118. Xu, Z. Heat transport in low-dimensional materials: A review and perspective. *Theor. Appl. Mech. Lett.* **2016**, *6*, 113–121. [CrossRef]
119. Mosso, N.; Drechsler, U.; Menges, F.; Nirmalraj, P.; Karg, S.; Riel, H.; Gotsmann, B. Heat transport through atomic contacts. *Nat. Nanotech.* **2017**, *12*, 430–433. [CrossRef] [PubMed]
120. Hanggi, P.; Talkner, P.; Borkovec, H. Reaction-rate theory: Fifty years after Kramers. *Rev. Mod. Phys.* **1990**, *62*, 251. [CrossRef]
121. Chiu, F. A review on conduction mechsnisms in dielectric films. *Adv. Mater. Sci. Eng.* **2014**, *2014*, 578168. [CrossRef]
122. Waser, R.; Dittmann, R.; Saikov, G.; Szot, K. Redox-based resistive switching memories nanoionic mechanisms, prospects, and challenges. *Adv. Mater.* **2009**, *21*, 2632–2663. [CrossRef]
123. Datta, S. *Electronic Transport in Mesoscopic Systems*; Cambridge University Press: Cambridge, UK, 1995.
124. Kouwenhoven, L.P.; Van Wees, B.J.; Harmans, C.J.P.M.; Williamson, J.G.; Van Houten, H.; Beenakker, C.W.J.; Foxon, C.T.; Harris, J.J. Nonlinear conductance of quantum point contacts. *Phys. Rev. B* **1989**, *39*, 8040–8043. [CrossRef] [PubMed]
125. van Ruitenbeek, J.; Masis, M.M.; Miranda, E. Quantum point contact conduction. In *Resistice Switching: From Fundamentals of Nanoinic Redox Processes to Memristive Device Applications*; Ielmini, D., Waser, R., Eds.; John Wiley & Sons Inc.: New York, NY, USA, 2016; pp. 197–224.
126. Agrait, N.; Yeyati, A.L.; van Ruitenbeek, J.M. Quantum properties of atomic-sized conductors. *Phys. Rep.* **2003**, *377*, 81. [CrossRef]
127. Li, Y.; Long, S.; Liu, Y.; Hu, C.; Teng, J.; Liu, Q.; Lv, H.; Suñé, J.; Liu, M. Conductance quantization in resistive random access memory. *Nanoscale Res. Lett.* **2015**, *10*, 420. [CrossRef] [PubMed]
128. Suñé, J.; Miranda, E.; Nafría, M.; Aymerich, X. Point contact conduction at the oxide breakdown of MOS devices. In Proceedings of the IEEE International Electron Device Meeting (IEDM), San Francisco, CA, USA, 6–9 December 1998; p. 191.
129. Suñé, J.; Miranda, E.; Nafría, M.; Aymerich, X. Modeling the breakdown spots in silicon dioxide films as point contacts. *Appl. Phys. Lett.* **1999**, *75*, 959–961. [CrossRef]
130. Mehonic, A.; Vrajitoarea, A.; Cueff, S.; Hudziak, S.; Howe, H.; Labbe, C.; Rizk, R.; Pepper, M.; Kenyon, A.J. Quantum conductance in silicon oxide resistive memory devices. *Sci. Rep.* **2013**, *3*, 2708. [CrossRef] [PubMed]
131. Nandakumar, S.R.; Minvielle, M.; Nagar, S.; Dubourdieu, C.; Rajendran, B. A 250 mV Cu/SiO$_2$/W Memristor with Half-Integer Quantum Conductance States. *Nano Lett.* **2016**, *16*, 1602–1608. [CrossRef] [PubMed]
132. Miranda, E.; Walczyk, C.; Wenger, C.; Schroeder, T. Model for the resistive switching effect in HfO$_2$ MIM structures based on the transmission properties of narrow constrictions. *IEEE Electron. Device Lett.* **2010**, *31*, 609–611. [CrossRef]
133. Degraeve, R.; Roussel, P.; Goux, L.; Wouters, D.; Kittl, J.; Altimime, L.; Jurczak, M.; Groeseneken, G. Generic learning of TDDB applied to RRAM for improved understanding of conduction and switching mechanism through multiple filaments. In Proceedings of the 2010 International Electron Devices Meeting, San Francisco, CA, USA, 6–8 December 2010.
134. Walczyk, C.; Walczyk, D.; Schroeder, T.; Bertaud, T.; Sowinska, M.; Lukosius, M.; Fraschke, M.; Wolansky, D.; Tillack, B.; Miranda, E.; et al. Impact of temperature on the resistive switching behavior of embedded HfO$_2$-Based RRAM devices. *IEEE Trans. Electron. Dev.* **2011**, *58*, 3124–3131. [CrossRef]
135. Long, S.; Lian, X.; Cagli, C.; Cartoixà, X.; Rurali, R.; Miranda, E.; Jiménez, D.; Perniola, L.; Liu, M.; Suñé, J. Quantum-size effects in hafnium-oxide resistive switching. *Appl. Phys. Lett.* **2013**, *102*, 183505. [CrossRef]
136. Prócel, L.M.; Trojman, L.; Moreno, J.; Crupi, F.; Maccaronio, V.; Degraeve, R.; Goux, L.; Simoen, E. Experimental evidence of the quantum point contact theory in the conduction mechanism of bipolar HfO$_2$-based resistive random access memories. *J. Appl. Phys.* **2013**, *114*, 074509. [CrossRef]
137. Rahavan, N. Performance and reliability trade-offs for high-K RRAM. *Microelectron. Reliab.* **2014**, *54*, 2253–2257. [CrossRef]
138. Roldán, J.B.; Miranda, E.; González-Cordero, G.; García-Fernández, P.; Romero-Zaliz, R.; González-Rodelas, P.; Aguilera, A.M.; González, M.B.; Jiménez-Molinos, F. Multivariate analysis and extraction of parameters in resistive RAMs using the Quantum Point Contact model. *J. Appl. Phys.* **2018**, *123*, 014501. [CrossRef]
139. Calixto, D.; Maldonado, E.; Miranda, J.B.; Roldán, M. Modeling of the temperature effects in filamentary-type resistive switching memories using quantum point-contact theory. *J. Phys. D Appl. Phys.* **2020**, *53*, 295106. [CrossRef]
140. Tsuruoka, T.; Hasegawa, T.; Terabe, K.; Aono, M. Conductance quantization and synaptic behavior in a Ta$_2$O$_5$-based atomic switch. *Nanotechnology* **2012**, *23*, 435705. [CrossRef] [PubMed]
141. Chen, C.; Gao, S.; Zeng, F.; Wang, G.; Li, S.; Song, C.; Pan, F. Conductance quantization in oxygen-anion-migration-based resistive switching memory devices. *Appl. Phys. Lett.* **2013**, *103*, 043510. [CrossRef]
142. Yi, W.; Savelev, S.; Medeiros-Ribeiro, G.; Miao, F.; Zhang, M.; Yang, J.; Bratkovsky, A.; Williams, R.S. Quantized conductance coincides with state instability and excess noise in tantalum oxide memristors. *Nat. Commun.* **2016**, *7*, 11498. [CrossRef]

143. Ye, J.Y.; Li, Y.Q.; Gao, J.; Peng, H.Y.; Wu, S.X.; Wu, T. Nanoscale resistive switching and filamentary conduction in NiO thin films. *Appl. Phys. Lett.* **2010**, *97*, 132108. [CrossRef]
144. Nishi, Y.; Sasakura, H.; Kimoto, T. Appearance of quantum point contact in Pt/NiO/Pt resistive switching cells. *J. Mater. Res.* **2017**, *32*, 2631–2637. [CrossRef]
145. Zhu, X.-J.; Shang, J.; Li, R.-W. Resistive switching effects in oxide sandwiched structures. *Front. Mater. Sci.* **2012**, *6*, 183–206. [CrossRef]
146. Zhu, X.; Su, W.; Liu, Y.; Hu, B.; Pan, L.; Lu, W.; Zhang, J.; Li, R. Observation of conductance quantization in oxide-based resistive switching memory. *Adv. Mater.* **2012**, *24*, 3941–3946. [CrossRef]
147. Hajto, J.; Rose, M.J.; Snell, A.J.; Osborne, I.S.; Owen, A.E.; Lecomber, P.G. Quantised electron effects in metal/a-Si:H/metal thin film structures. *J. Non-Cryst. Solids* **1991**, *137*, 499–502. [CrossRef]
148. Samardzic, N.; Mionic, M.; Dakic, B.M.; Hofmann, H.; Dautovic, S.; Stojanovic, G. Analysis of Quantized Electrical Characteristics of Microscale TiO_2 Ink-Jet Printed Memristor. *IEEE Trans. Electron Devices* **2015**, *62*, 1898–1904. [CrossRef]
149. Yun, E.-J.; Becker, M.F.; Walser, R.M. Room temperature conductance quantization in V$\|$amorphous-$V_2O_5$$\|$V thin film structures. *Appl. Phys. Lett.* **1993**, *63*, 2493–2495. [CrossRef]
150. Petzold, S.; Piros, E.; Eilhardt, R.; Zintler, A.; Vogel, T.; Kaiser, N.; Radetinac, A.; Komissinskiy, P.; Jalaguier, E.; Nolot, E.; et al. Tailoring the Switching Dynamics in Yttrium Oxide-Based RRAM Devices by Oxygen Engineering: From Digital to Multi-Level Quantization toward Analog Switching. *Adv. Electron. Mater.* **2020**, *6*, 2000439. [CrossRef]
151. Zhao, M.; Yan, X.; Ren, L.; Zhao, M.; Guo, F.; Zhuang, J.; Du, Y.; Hao, W. The role of oxygen vacancies in the high cycling endurance and quantum conductance in $BiVO_4$-based resistive switching memory. *InfoMat* **2020**, *2*, 960–967. [CrossRef]
152. Degraeve, R.; Fantini, A.; Clima, S.; Govoreanu, B.; Goux, L.; Chen, Y.Y.; Wouters, D.; Roussel, P.; Kar, G.; Pourtois, G.; et al. Dynamic 'hour glass' model for SET and RESET in HfO_2 RRAM. In Proceedings of the Symposium on VLSI Technology, Honolulu, HI, USA, 12–14 June 2012.
153. Miranda, E.; Kano, S.; Dou, C.; Kakushima, K.; Suñé, J.; Iwai, H. Nonlinear conductance quantization effects in CeO_x/SiO_2-based resistive switching devices. *App. Phys. Lett.* **2012**, *101*, 012910. [CrossRef]
154. Cartoixa, X.; Rurali, R.; Suñé, J. Transport properties of oxygen vacancy filaments in metal/crystalline or amorphous HfO_2/metal structures. *Phys. Rev. B* **2012**, *86*, 165445. [CrossRef]
155. Zhong, X.; Rungger, I.; Zapol, P.; Heinonen, O. Oxygen modulated quantum conductance for ultra-thin HfO_2-based memristive switching devices. *Phys. Rev. B* **2016**, *94*, 165160. [CrossRef]
156. Büttiker, M. Quantized transmission of a saddle-point constriction. *Phys. Rev. B* **1990**, *41*, 7906. [CrossRef]
157. Hu, P. One-dimensional quantum electron system under a finite voltage. *Phys. Rev. B* **1987**, *35*, 4078. [CrossRef]
158. Senz, V.; Heinzel, T.; Ihn, T.; Lindermann, S.; Held, R.; Ensslin, K.; Wegscheider, W.; Bichler, M. Analysis of the temperature-dependent quantum point contact conductance in view of the metal-insulator transition in two dimensions. *J. Phys. Cond. Mat.* **2001**, *13*, 3831. [CrossRef]
159. Miranda, E.; Suñé, J. Electron transport through broken down ultra-thin SiO_2 layers in MOS devices. *Microelectron. Reliab.* **2004**, *44*, 1–23. [CrossRef]
160. Landauer, R. Spatial variation of currents and fields due to localized scatterers in metallic conduction. *IBM J. Res. Dev.* **1957**, *1*, 223–231. [CrossRef]
161. Avellán, A.; Miranda, E.; Schroeder, D.; Krautschneider, W. Model for the voltage and temperature dependence of the soft-breakdown current in ultrathin gate oxides. *J. Appl. Phys.* **2005**, *97*, 14104. [CrossRef]
162. Miranda, E. The role of power dissipation on the progressive breakdwon dynamics of ultra-thin gate oxides. In Proceedings of the IEEE Proc International Reliability Physics Simposium, Phoenix, AZ, USA, 15–19 April 2007; p. 572.
163. Lombardo, S.; Stathis, J.H.; Linder, B.P.; Pey, K.L.; Palumbo, F.; Tung, C.H. Dielectric breakdown mechanisms in gate oxides. *J. Appl. Phys.* **2005**, *98*, 121301. [CrossRef]
164. Stathis, J.H. Percolation models for gate oxide breakdown. *J. Appl. Phys.* **1999**, *86*, 5757–5766. [CrossRef]
165. Stathis, J.H. Reliability limits for the gate insulator in CMOS technology. *IBM J. Res. Dev.* **2002**, *46*, 265–286. [CrossRef]
166. Dumin, D.J. *Oxide Reliability: A Summary of Silicon Oxide Wearout, Breakdown, and Reliability*; World Scientific: Singapore, 2002.
167. Linder, B.; Lombardo, S.; Stathis, J.; Vayshenker, A.; Frank, D. Voltage dependence of hard breakdown growth and the reliability implication in thin dielectrics. *IEEE Electron Device Lett.* **2002**, *23*, 661–663. [CrossRef]
168. Palumbo, F.; Liang, X.; Yuan, B.; Shi, Y.; Hui, F.; Villena, M.A.; Lanza, M. Bimodal Dielectric Breakdown in Electronic Devices Using Chemical Vapor Deposited Hexagonal Boron Nitride as Dielectric. *Adv. Electron. Mater.* **2018**, *4*, 1700506. [CrossRef]
169. Palumbo, F.; Lombardo, S.; Eizenberg, M. Physical mechanism of progressive breakdown in gate oxides. *J. Appl. Phys.* **2014**, *115*, 224101. [CrossRef]
170. Tung, C.H.; Pey, K.L.; Tang, L.J.; Radhakrishnan, M.K.; Lin, W.H.; Palumbo, F.; Lombardo, S. Percolation path and dielectric-breakdown-induced-epitaxy evolution during ultrathin gate dielectric breakdown transient. *Appl. Phys. Lett.* **2003**, *83*, 2223–2225. [CrossRef]
171. Pey, K.L.; Ranjan, R.; Tung, C.H.; Tang, L.J.; Lin, W.H.; Radhakrishnan, M.K. Gate dielectric degradation mechanism associated with DBIE evolution. In Proceedings of the IEEE International Reliability Physics Symposium, Phoenix, AZ, USA, 25–29 April 2004; Volume 2004, pp. 117–121.

172. Privitera, S.; Bersuker, G.; Butcher, B.; Kalantarian, A.; Lombardo, S.; Bongiorno, C.; Geer, R.; Gilmer, D.; Kirsch, P. Microscopy study of the conductive filament in HfO₂ resistive switching memory devices. *Microelectron. Eng.* **2013**, *109*, 75–78. [CrossRef]
173. Privitera, S.; Bersuker, G.; Lombardo, S.; Bongiorno, C.; Gilmer, D. Conductive filament structure in HfO₂ resistive switching memory devices. *Solid-State Electron.* **2015**, *111*, 161–165. [CrossRef]
174. Yang, Y.; Gao, P.; Li, L.; Pan, X.; Tappertzhofen, S.; Choi, S.; Waser, R.; Valov, I.; Lu, W.D. Electrochemical dynamics of nanoscale metallic inclusions in dielectrics. *Nat. Commun.* **2014**, *5*, 4232. [CrossRef] [PubMed]
175. Pan, C.; Ji, Y.; Xiao, N.; Hui, F.; Tang, K.; Guo, Y.; Xie, X.; Puglisi, F.M.; Larcher, L.; Miranda, E.; et al. Coexistence of Grain-Boundaries-Assisted Bipolar and Threshold Resistive Switching in Multilayer Hexagonal Boron Nitride. *Adv. Funct. Mater.* **2017**, *27*. [CrossRef]
176. Rodriguez-Fernandez, A.; Cagli, C.; Perniola, L.; Suñé, J.; Miranda, E. Identification of the generation/rupture mechanism of filamentary conductive paths in ReRAM devices using oxide failure analysis. *Microelectron. Reliab.* **2017**, *76–77*, 178–183. [CrossRef]
177. Nishi, Y.; Fleck, K.; Böttger, U.; Waser, R.; Menzel, S. Effect of RESET Voltage on Distribution of SET Switching Time of Bipolar Resistive Switching in a Tantalum Oxide Thin Film. *IEEE Trans. Electron Devices* **2015**, *62*, 1561–1567. [CrossRef]
178. Palumbo, F.; Shekhter, P.; Weinfeld, K.C.; Eizenberg, M. Characteristics of the dynamics of breakdown filaments in Al₂O₃/InGaAs stacks. *Appl. Phys. Lett.* **2015**, *107*, 122901. [CrossRef]
179. Palumbo, F.; Miranda, E.; Ghibaudo, G.; Jousseaume, V. Formation and Characterization of Filamentary Current Paths in HfO₂-Based Resistive Switching Structures. *IEEE Electron Device Lett.* **2012**, *33*, 1057–1059. [CrossRef]
180. Palumbo, F.; Condorelli, G.; Lombardo, S.; Pey, K.; Tung, C.; Tang, L. Structure of the oxide damage under progressive breakdown. *Microelectron. Reliab.* **2005**, *45*, 845–848. [CrossRef]
181. Du, H.; Jia, C.-L.; Koehl, A.; Barthel, J.; Dittmann, R.; Waser, R.; Mayer, J. Nanosized conducting filaments formed by atomic-scale defects in redox-based resistive switching memories. *Chem. Mater.* **2017**, *29*, 3164–3173. [CrossRef]
182. Palumbo, F.; Eizenberg, M.; Lombardo, S. General features of progressive breakdown in gate oxides: A compact model. In Proceedings of the IEEE International Reliability Physics Symposium, Monterey, CA, USA, 19–23 April 2015; Volume 2015, pp. 5A11–5A16.
183. Lombardo, S.; Wu, E.Y.; Stathis, J.H. Electron energy dissipation model of gate dielectric progressive breakdown in n- and p-channel field effect transistors. *J. Appl. Phys.* **2017**, *122*, 085701. [CrossRef]
184. Lombardo, S.; Stathis, J.H.; Linder, B.P. breakdown transients in ultrathin gate oxides: Transition in the degradation rate. *Phys. Rev. Lett.* **2003**, *90*, 167601. [CrossRef] [PubMed]
185. Pagano, R.; Lombardo, S.; Palumbo, F.; Kirsch, P.; Krishnan, S.; Young, C.; Choi, R.; Bersuker, G.; Stathis, J. A novel approach to characterization of progressive breakdown in high-k/metal gate stacks. *Microelectron. Reliab.* **2008**, *48*, 1759–1764. [CrossRef]
186. Palumbo, F.; Lombardo, S.; Stathis, J.; Narayanan, V.; Mcfeely, F.; Yurkas, J. Degradation of ultra-thin oxides with tungsten gates under high voltage: Wear-out and breakdown transient. In Proceedings of the 2004 IEEE International Reliability Physics Symposium, Phoenix, AZ, USA, 25–29 April 2004; pp. 122–125. [CrossRef]
187. Larcher, L. Statistical simulation of leakage currents in mos and flash memory devices with a new multiphonon trap-assisted tunneling model. *IEEE Trans. Electron Devices* **2003**, *50*, 1246–1253. [CrossRef]
188. Nigam, T.; Martin, S.; Abusch-Magder, D. Temperature Dependence and Conduction Mechanism after Analog Soft Breakdown. In Proceedings of the 41st Annual Symposium 2003 IEEE International Reliability Physics, Dallas, TX, USA, 30 March–4 April 2003; pp. 417–423.
189. Condorelli, G.; Lombardo, S.A.; Palumbo, F.; Pey, K.-L.; Tung, C.H.; Tang, L.-J. Structure and conductance of the breakdown spot during the early stages of progressive breakdown. *IEEE Trans. Device Mater. Reliab.* **2006**, *6*, 534–541. [CrossRef]
190. Palumbo, F.; Wen, C.; Lombardo, S.; Pazos, S.; Aguirre, F.; Eizenberg, M.; Hui, F.; Lanza, M. A Review on Dielectric Breakdown in Thin Dielectrics: Silicon Dioxide, High-k, and Layered Dielectrics. *Adv. Funct. Mater.* **2020**, *30*, 1900657. [CrossRef]
191. Takagi, S.; Yasuda, N.; Toriumi, A. Experimental evidence of inelastic tunneling in stress-induced leakage current. *IEEE Trans. Electron Devices* **1999**, *46*, 335–341. [CrossRef]
192. Blöchl, P.E.; Stathis, J.H. Hydrogen electrochemistry and stress-induced leakage current in Silica. *Phys. Rev. Lett.* **1999**, *83*, 372–375. [CrossRef]
193. Aguirre, F.L.; RodriguezFernandez, A.; Pazos, S.M.; Sune, J.; Miranda, E.; Palumbo, F. Study on the connection between the set transient in RRAMs and the progressive breakdown of thin oxides. *IEEE Trans. Electron. Devices* **2019**, *66*, 1–7. [CrossRef]
194. Ielmini, D. Modeling the universal set/reset characteristics of bipolar RRAM by field-and temperature-driven filament growth. *IEEE Trans. Electron Devices* **2011**, *58*, 4309–4317. [CrossRef]
195. Pazos, S.; Aguirre, F.L.; Miranda, E.; Lombardo, S.; Palumbo, F. Comparative study of the breakdown transients of thin Al₂O₃ and HfO₂ films in MIM structures and their connection with the thermal properties of materials. *J. Appl. Phys.* **2017**, *121*, 094102. [CrossRef]
196. Rodríguez-Fernández, A.; Cagli, C.; Sune, J.; Miranda, E. Switching Voltage and Time Statistics of Filamentary Conductive Paths in HfO₂-Based ReRAM Devices. *IEEE Electron Device Lett.* **2018**, *39*, 656–659. [CrossRef]
197. Zafar, S.; Jagannathan, H.; Edge, L.F.; Gupta, D. Measurement of oxygen diffusion in nanometer scale HfO₂ gate dielectric films. *Appl. Phys. Lett.* **2011**, *98*, 152903. [CrossRef]

198. Shacham-Diamand, Y.; Dedhia, A.; Hoffstetter, D.; Oldham, W.G. Copper Transport in Thermal SiO_2. *J. Electrochem. Soc.* **1993**, *140*, 2427–2432. [CrossRef]
199. Nason, T.C.; Yang, G.; Park, K.; Lu, T. Study of silver diffusion into Si(111) and SiO_2 at moderate temperatures. *J. Appl. Phys.* **1991**, *70*, 1392–1396. [CrossRef]
200. Kim, B.G.; Yeo, S.; Lee, Y.W.; Cho, M.S. Comparison of diffusion coefficients and activation energies for Ag diffusion in silicon carbide. *Nucl. Eng. Technol.* **2015**, *47*, 608–616. [CrossRef]
201. Zobelli, A.; Ewels, C.P.; Gloter, A.; Seifert, G. Vacancy migration in hexagonal boron nitride. *Phys. Rev. B* **2007**, *75*, 094104. [CrossRef]

Article

Characterization and Design of Photovoltaic Solar Cells That Absorb Ultraviolet, Visible and Infrared Light

Sara Bernardes [1], Ricardo A. Marques Lameirinhas [1,2,*], João Paulo N. Torres [1,2,3] and Carlos A. F. Fernandes [1,2]

[1] Department of Electrical and Computer Engineering, Instituto Superior Técnico, 1049-001 Lisbon, Portugal; sarabernardes@tecnico.ulisboa.pt (S.B.); joaotorres@tecnico.ulisboa.pt (J.P.N.T.); ffernandes@tecnico.ulisboa.pt (C.A.F.F.)
[2] Instituto de Telecomunicações, 1049-001 Lisbon, Portugal
[3] Academia Militar, Av. Conde Castro Guimarães, 2720-113 Amadora, Portugal
* Correspondence: ricardo.lameirinhas@tecnico.ulisboa.pt

Abstract: The world is witnessing a tide of change in the photovoltaic industry like never before; we are far from the solar cells of ten years ago that only had 15–18% efficiency. More and more, multi-junction technologies seem to be the future for photovoltaics, with these technologies already hitting the mark of 30% under 1-sun. This work focuses especially on a state-of-the-art triple-junction solar cell, the GaInP/GaInAs/Ge lattice-matched, that is currently being used in most satellites and concentrator photovoltaic systems. The three subcells are first analyzed individually and then the whole cell is put together and simulated. The typical figures-of-merit are extracted; all the $I - V$ curves obtained are presented, along with the external quantum efficiencies. A study on how temperature affects the cell was done, given its relevance when talking about space applications. An overall optimization of the cell is also elaborated; the cell's thickness and doping are changed so that maximum efficiency can be reached. For a better understanding of how varying both these properties affect efficiency, graphic 3D plots were computed based on the obtained results. Considering this optimization, an improvement of 0.2343% on the cell's efficiency is obtained.

Keywords: concentrator systems; GaInP/GaInAs/Ge; multi-junction; photovoltaics; solar cells; space; triple-junction

Citation: Bernardes, S.; Lameirinhas, R.A.M.; Torres, J.P.N.; Fernandes, C.A.F. Characterization and Design of Photovoltaic Solar Cells That Absorb Ultraviolet, Visible and Infrared Light. *Nanomaterials* **2021**, *11*, 78. https://doi.org/10.3390/nano11010078

Received: 15 November 2020
Accepted: 26 December 2020
Published: 1 January 2021

Publisher's Note: MDPI stays neutral with regard to jurisdictional claims in published maps and institutional affiliations.

Copyright: © 2021 by the authors. Licensee MDPI, Basel, Switzerland. This article is an open access article distributed under the terms and conditions of the Creative Commons Attribution (CC BY) license (https://creativecommons.org/licenses/by/4.0/).

1. Introduction

The constant search for new energetic solutions to face the ever-demanding world's energy consumption has been one of the main focus amongst researchers in the twenty-first century. At the time this article is being written, a good and affordable alternative seems to be found in the use of renewable energies [1–19]. Even though the world is not yet prepared to switch completely to renewable sources, the installed capacity of these sources is increasing day by day, with the global renewable generation power already surpassing 2300 gigawatts. In 2018, 20% of this total generation capacity came from solar power, that continued to dominate in terms of new power installed, representing an increase of 24% [1].

This global solar expansion mainly derives from the capability of the photovoltaic (PV) industry to face the challenges that have been proposed until now.

In the years to come, PV has the capacity of becoming one of the major energy sources in the world—as the price of fossil fuels continuously rises [6–19], the cost of solar PV has been substantially decreasing over the last two decades, with its LCOE (Levelized Cost Of Energy) being estimated to be within the range of 0.03 to 0.10 $/kWh by 2020–2022 [2,3,20]. This prophetizes a solid future for the PV industry, especially if it is supported by the decrease in battery prices.

All of this motivates the industry to come up with new and improved solutions; one of those improvements in recent decades is the use of III-V multi-junction solar cells. These photovoltaic devices employ III-V semiconductors (made of elements in groups III and V of the Periodic Table), typically in a stacked distribution [4,5,21,22]. These cells have been demonstrating solid results in terms of efficiency, since the first III-V GaInP/GaAs tandem cell was demonstrated by Olson and Kurtz at NREL in 1996, with a record efficiency of more than 30% [21]. Today, III-V cells already hit the mark of 45.7% in concentrator photovoltaics (NREL, 4-junction GaInP/GaAs/GaInAs/GaInAs, 234 suns) [22], demonstrating extraordinary advances in choosing optimal bandgap distributions.

This work will focus on a specific III-V cell, the GaInP/GaInAs/Ge lattice-matched cell, the state-of-the-art cell for both concentrator photovoltaics and space applications. The main objective is then to build a simulation model that allows for a characterization of the subcells that form the whole cell, extracting $I-V$ curves and external quantum efficiencies, along with the most relevant figures-of-merit, such as fill-factors and efficiencies. A general optimization of the cell will also be attempted; this will be done by altering the thickness and doping of some layers.

It is used a Finite Element Tool, for being capable of simulating a 2D and 3D solar devices by providing a large set of physical models (drift-diffusion, general optoelectronic interactions with ray tracing, Fermi-Dirac statistics, etc.) for semiconductor device simulation.

2. Fields of Application of III-V Solar Cells

The III-V MJ (multi-junction) solar cells are utilized in the most varied fields of application, the most important two being space applications and concentrator photovoltaic (CPV) systems, as illustrated respectively in Figure 1a,b. These two fields represent very different operating conditions for solar cells, and thus different design approaches for each field must be considered. Record efficiencies of 35.8% (AM0 spectrum) [23] and 46% (AM1.5d spectrum, 508 suns) [22] were already demonstrated for space and CPV applications, respectively.

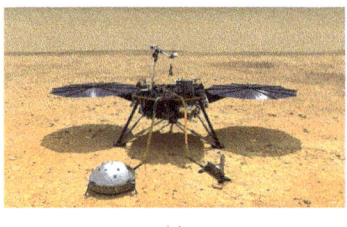

(a) (b)

Figure 1. Some examples of solar cells use in space and terrestrial applications: (**a**) NASA's InSight Lander robot, powered by solar energy, and already owns the off-world record of power generation. (**b**) A HCPV parabolic system that uses high-efficiency multi-junction modules by Solartron Energy Systems.

2.1. Space Applications

Regarding space applications, III-V cells have become the go-to technology, not only because of their high-efficiency results but also because of their high tolerance to radiation exposure. After being irradiated with high radiation doses, these cells showed an EOL (end-of-life) efficiency that was higher than a BOL (beginning-of-life) efficiency of a standard Si solar cell. Of course, this represented a major change for the spacecraft industry, since a good EOL efficiency is intrinsically connected to the weight and cost of the overall system, paramount factors when discussing the launch of a spacecraft, in which the cost is determined by €/kg, as opposed to €/W_p in terrestrial applications.

Therefore, these cells, given their high EOL efficiencies, good radiation tolerance, and high power-to-mass ratios (W/kg), meet the requirements of the majority of the NASA OSS (National Aeronautics and Space Administration Operational Support Services) missions, that call for high specific power values, making them the state-of-the-art cells for the majority of satellites and space vehicles.

Another important aspect concerning missions in space is the temperature at which PV modules must operate in certain harsher environments. Space PV arrays must be prepared to endure both high and low temperatures, depending on the mission's orbit. This leads to the necessity of studying the cell's temperature coefficient (dη/dT) to have a measure on how the performance of the cell will vary with temperature. When under the AM0 spectrum, the normalized temperature coefficient of a Si solar cell is in the range of -3×10^{-3} /°C to -5×10^{-3} /°C, while for tandem GaAs/Ge cells the temperature coefficient is approximately -2×10^{-3} /°C [24].

This notorious difference in temperature coefficients is explained by the variance of bandgap in both cells; solar cells that have in their composition materials with higher bandgap values show lower efficiency losses with temperature [25]. This means that there will be an ideal bandgap for each operating temperature.

2.2. Terrestrial Concentrator Systems

On Earth, the task of implementing III-V plate modules would represent a heavy cost of production, with the cost of a typical III-V high-efficiency cell being around 10 \$/cm^2 [26]. To counter this problem, solar PV companies developed concentrator photovoltaic systems (CPV), in which sunlight is concentrated with the use of mirror lenses. Usual concentration ratios for III-V cells may go from 500× to 2000×, the latter being commonly called high concentration PV (HCPV).

The increase in irradiance will directly affect the short-circuit current of the cell, increasing it. Resorting to Equation (1), it is easy to see that incrementing I_{SC} affects the open-circuit voltage of the cell, which increases logarithmically by several KT/q factors. This boost in the V_{OC} will be more evident for a multi-junction cell, in which every subcell will contribute for the increase of V_{OC} with concentration, and thus rising the fill-factor of the overall cell [6–19].

$$V_{OC} = nV_T \ln \frac{I_{SC}}{I_0} + 1 \tag{1}$$

For this reason, it would be fair to think the higher the concentration ratio, the higher the efficiency of the cell. Alas, in reality, no device is ideal, including solar cells; there are always losses that need to be considered, such as series and shunt resistances that must be taken into consideration. The concentration increase will have a dominant impact on the overall efficiency, diminishing the FF (Fill Factor), and changing the $I - V$ characteristic. The greater the concentration ratio, the higher the impact will be on the cell; e.g., for the TJ (triple-junction) GaInP/GaInAs/Ge, when incrementing the series resistance from $R_s = 0$ to $R_s = 0.1$ Ω, the FF is reduced from 90% (1 sun) to 87% at 83 suns, and to 71% at 500 suns [27].

Analyzing this data, it was then evident that some changes in series and shunt resistances had to be made in such a way that cells could operate under high concentration levels so that losses could be, to an extent, negligible. Every concentrator cell has a concentration limit for which the efficiency will start to drop, and several studies are being conducted in this matter. In the work of Steiner et al. [28], three tests were made using the single junction GaAs solar cell to prove the reduction in the FF and efficiency: three optimized grids for concentrations of $C = 100$, $C = 450$, and $C = 1000$ were tested, and the cell showed a maximum efficiency of 29.09% for a concentration of 450 suns.

3. III-V Solar Cell Design

For a better understanding of the fundamentals behind a III-V solar cell it is necessary to perceive where they differ from the simple junction cell. It has already been stated that III-V multi-junction cells are top performers in their fields of application, when compared with their single-junction counterparts, given that the latter have their efficiency limited a priori.

3.1. Bandgap versus Efficiency

In order to grasp why single-junction cells are limited efficiency-wise, one has to fathom how the bandgap is of paramount importance when discussing solar cells.

Taking into consideration a single-junction solar cell with bandgap W_G, only photons with their energy higher or equal to W_G are absorbed. Photons for which the energy is higher than the bandgap W_G, there is a certain amount of energy that is in excess and will be lost, an phenomenon also known as thermalization losses. This means that the energy that will be effectively converted into electric current will be just a portion of the photon's total energy. With this, it is evident that the device will only operate at maximum efficiency when the photon's energy, W_{ph}, is equal to the bandgap W_G. Alas, when considering the wide spectrum of sunlight, absorbing just the photons of a specific wavelength imposes quite a limitation on the overall efficiency of the cell.

In trying to solve this problem, a few solutions were developed. One of them is broadly used today in the PV industry: the concept of multi-junction solar cells. Instead of trying to make the cell operate only at a specific wavelength, one could try to divide the light spectrum into several spectral sections and associate a subcell with an appropriate bandgap to each one of them. This way, every subcell would have the unique function of absorbing photons of a specific wavelength range.

Now, there are different approaches to solve the problem and split the sunlight's spectrum. The first is a quite intuitive one, called the spatial distribution method, illustrated on Figure 2a, and consists in using a prism to separate a beam of white light into several different wavelengths and spatially arranging subcells with different bandgap values accordingly.

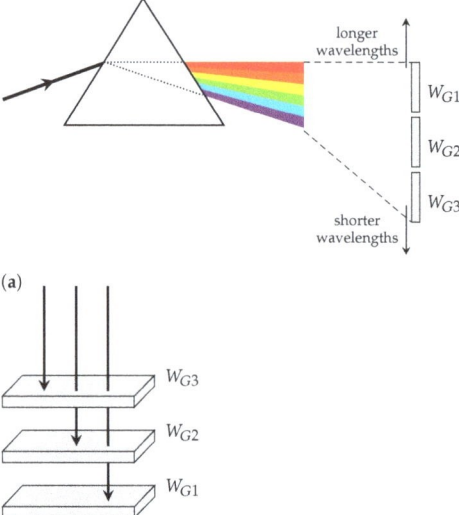

Figure 2. Spectral splitting approaches: (**a**) Spatial distribution, with the use of a prism, and (**b**) Stacked distribution of a 3-junction cell.

Even though the spatial distribution is employed in some CPV (concentrator photovoltaic) systems, there are some difficulties associated when using this method. The approach that is broadly used nowadays when designing MJ solar cells is the stacked distribution, as presented in Figure 2b. This method consists in stacking the subcells on top of each other by order of bandgap, so the subcell with a lower bandgap is placed on the bottom of the cell and the one with a higher bandgap is placed on the top. This way, the high energy photons can be absorbed right on top of the cell by subcells with high bandgap values, forcing the low energy photons to penetrate further into the lower layers, where the low bandgap subcells are placed. As a result, the photons will be efficiently distributed and absorbed throughout the stack, increasing overall performance.

For this reason, the choice of bandgap combinations is a decisive step in multi-junction design. Given that III-V semiconductors show high versatility in possible bandgap combinations, they are one of the best choices for designing state-of-the-art solar cells. Bearing this in mind, Fraunhofer ISE developed the etaOpt software, capable of predicting cell efficiencies based on how many p–n junctions they are made of and what are their respective bandgaps. According to the results obtained from etaOpt, the efficiency can increase substantially with the number of p–n junctions, however, this gain is dampened for higher counts, i.e., a jump from 2 to 3 junctions provides a much larger increase than one from 5 to 6 junctions [29]. Knowing this data *a priori* is quite important for manufacturers, since the amount of efficiency gained may not justify higher production costs that derive from augmenting the number of p–n junctions.

3.2. Bandgap versus Lattice Constant

The choice of an appropriate bandgap does not take into account only the spectral regions, but also the choice of the lattice constant, since one depends on the other. This selection determines the structure of a MJ solar cell—if the materials all have, approximately, the same lattice constant, the cell is said to be lattice-matched; on the contrary, when the materials have different lattice constants, one says that the cell is lattice-mismatched or metamorphic (MM).

This distinction is significant when discussing solar cell design, given that stacked materials with different lattice constants may create dislocations, which can ruin the quality of the material and thus its performance. The production of metamorphic cells has to consider appropriate strategies, such as step-graded buffers that make the transition between two materials with different lattice-constants less abrupt.

4. The GaInP/GaInAs/Ge Solar Cell

Regarding this work, it seems only relevant to discuss approaches in which the GaInP/GaInAs/Ge solar cells are utilized. The two most relevant examples are the lattice-matched triple-junction and the upright metamorphic structures [4,5].

4.1. III-V Solar Cell Designs

At the time this article is being written, the lattice-matched triple-junction $Ga_{0.5}In_{0.5}P/Ga_{0.99}In_{0.01}As/Ge$, on Figure 3a, is the state-of-the-art cell for both space and terrestrial concentrator applications. The subcells are all lattice-matched to Ge, assuring that no dislocations are created. The cell itself consists of three main p–n junctions composed of GaInP, GaInAs, and Ge, stacked on top of each other, connected in series. The light falls on the GaInP subcell, which has the higher bandgap, as it was already explained previously. Each one of these subcells is connected through tunnel junctions with low resistance and high optical transmissivity coefficients. However, one of the problems of this approach is that the spectrum splitting is not optimal, resulting in an excessive current in the bottom Ge cell.

One possible way to counter this problem is to increase the absorption of photons in the upper cells, resulting in less current discrepancy. This can be achieved by lowering the bandgaps of the top and middle subcells by increasing the In composition in both $Ga_xIn_{1-x}P$ and $Ga_xIn_{1-x}As$ materials. By doing this, the lattice constant also alters, and thus the materials no longer have the same lattice constant, making the cell lattice-mismatched or metamorphic (MM). This type of approach in monolithic structures may derive in dislocations that can harm material quality if no special measures are taken. In the case of the upright metamorphic TJ GaInP/GaInAs/Ge cell, presented in Figure 3b, one of those measures is to implement a GaInAs graded buffer between the middle and bottom cells, so that the lattice constant increases gradually and not abruptly.

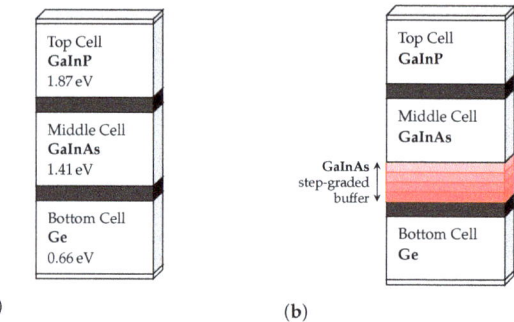

Figure 3. Simplified schematic of the triple-junction $Ga_{0.5}In_{0.5}P/Ga_{0.99}In_{0.01}As/Ge$ cell: (**a**) lattice-matched, and (**b**) upright metamorphic approaches.

4.2. Simulating the LM State-Of-The-Art Cell

In order to simulate this cell, one has to take into account that several companies are currently researching various approaches to its development, the two most important being Fraunhofer ISE and Spectrolab, Inc.

In this work, the approach that was utilized is identical to the one used at Spectrolab, where this cell already demonstrated an efficiency of 32% under 1-sun (AM1.5G spectrum) [30]. Moreover, it is assumed a 1 cm² active area. While there is published research of this cell concerning some of its specific structural information, there are not many details available about doping and thickness values and the material compositions of each layer, given that all of these specifics are treated as proprietary information of Spectrolab.

Having as basis the detailed Ph.D. dissertation of Sharma [31], it was possible to put together an accurate model to simulate the cell. Some modifications were made to best adapt the cell to the one demonstrated by Spectrolab in the research paper of King et al. [30]. The simulated cell structure with all its layers is illustrated in Figure 4.

Firstly, to comprehend how the stacked cell works, it is necessary to perceive the role that each subcell plays in the monolithic cell by analyzing the materials that constitute each layer.

4.2.1. The GaInP Top Subcell

Beginning from top to bottom, the first step was to simulate the GaInP top cell. This cell, as stated previously, has to absorb high energy photons, since it is on top of this cell that the light beams will fall onto. The $Ga_xIn_{1-x}P$ material is then chosen for its bandgap, which is $W_G = 1.89$ eV for a composition of $x = 0.5$. This is a pretty high value that allows for the first high energy photons to be absorbed.

Besides the main p–n junction being composed of GaInP, the top subcell also contains two extra layers: the back-surface (BSF) and the window or front-surface (FSF) layers.

The window layer acts as an absorber layer, and thus it will have to have a high bandgap, small thickness, and a low series resistance. The material chosen can be the AlInP since it has a pretty high bandgap value and it is capable of being lattice-matched to the rest of the cell.

In contrast, the BSF layer exists to boost the short-circuit current of the cell, given that sharing the applied voltage across the n–p–p+ junctions minimizes the reflection of minority carriers and therefore leads to the decrease of the dark current. The material that is chosen for this is the quaternary AlGaInP.

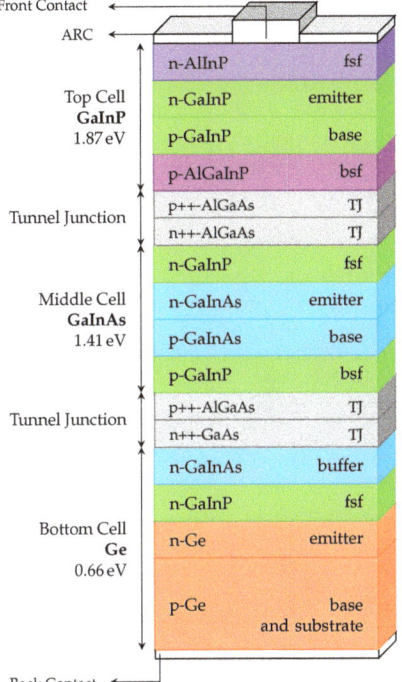

Figure 4. Detailed schematic of the simulated LM $Ga_{0.5}In_{0.5}P/Ga_{0.99}In_{0.01}As/Ge$ solar cell.

4.2.2. The GaInAs Middle Subcell

The second subcell to be simulated is the middle GaInAs cell, which is based in the more simple GaAs solar cell. It is lattice-matched to all the components that form the whole monolithic cell, with the main ternary compound, $Ga_xIn_{1-x}As$, having the composition $x = 0.99$ since its lattice constant corresponds to an exact-match to Ge's.

The subcell also has window and back-surface layers that are composed of highly-doped GaInP (composition of $x = 0.5$) given the high optical output of this material.

4.2.3. The Ge Bottom Subcell

Finally, the bottom subcell is made of a Ge substrate, instead of the typically used GaAs. This has two major advantages; firstly, Ge is cheaper than GaAs, and secondly, since Ge has a very low bandgap ($W_G = 0.66$ eV) the thickness of the subcell can be reduced from around 300 μm for the GaAs substrate to 170 μm for the Ge substrate.

Apart from a GaInP window layer similar to the middle cell one, the subcell also has a buffer layer made of highly-doped n-GaInAs (composition of $x = 0.99$) in order to reduce the ohmic contact between the bottom cell and the tunnel junction.

4.2.4. I–V Characteristic of the Stacked Cell

With the subcells already demonstrated, the next step was to try and assemble all of them in a monolithic cell.

Besides stacking the subcells on top of each other and separating them with appropriate tunnel junctions (AlGaAs–GaAs and AlGaAs–AlGaAs), it was also necessary to emulate the resistivity between subcell–tunnel diode and tunnel diode p–n junctions. This is made by establishing ohmic contacts with extremely high resistances that act as boundary conditions.

Two simulation models were tested: the first one, the cell was simulated in a Finite Element Tool without the metal grid (MG) on top, and the front contact had the same horizontal extension of the rest of the cell layers. This approach is a 1-D model since the structure only varies in one direction (vertical). The results were, then, artificially high since the contact effects were not being considered; the second method was employed so that the model would consider contact effects of the metal grid. Ergo, the cathode (top electrode) became smaller and a cap layer made of n+-GaAs was put below it with good ohmic contact formation in mind. Since there is this variation in the horizontal axis now, the model is a 2-D model.

Having as a reference the structure of the cell used at Spectrolab, the model developed in the Finite Element Tool was identical to the one depicted in Figure 4. In Figure 5, the obtained $I-V$ characteristics are presented for both simulation models: 1-D model (without the MG) and 2-D model (with the MG). The most important figures of merit obtained from the simulated results are shown in Table 1; for comparison purposes, the experimental results from Spectrolab, Inc. [30] are also presented.

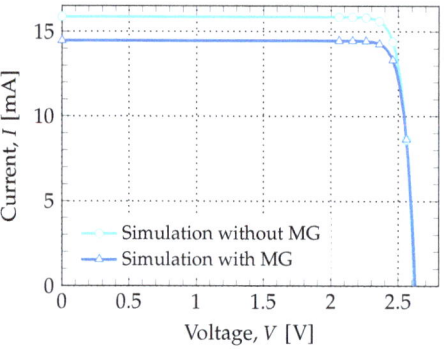

Figure 5. Simulated $I-V$ characteristics of the stacked cell. All curves were obtained using the AM0 spectrum. Figures of merit are presented in Table 1.

Table 1. Comparison of experimental and simulation values for the stacked cell.

	Experimental	Simulation	
	(Spectrolab)	without MG *	with MG *
I_{SC} [mA]	14.37	15.8771	14.4693
V_{OC} [V]	2.622	2.6296	2.6248
V_{MP} [V]	2.301	2.39	2.38
FF	0.85	0.89	0.88
Eff. [%]	32.0	36.9	33.65

* metal grid.

Analyzing the results, one can see that the best model to emulate the original cell's behavior is the 2-D model, in which some of the device's losses are being considered. The cell was emulated successfully to some extent: both the open-circuit voltage and short-circuit current were fairly replicated, which means that the overall structure (region materials, thickness, doping, etc.) was correctly modeled. Alas, both the fill-factor and efficiency were not consistent with the experimental results from Spectrolab. One explanation for this may be that losses were not properly accounted for in the final model, even taking the metal grid under consideration.

4.2.5. External Quantum Efficiencies

The final test was to obtain the External Quantum Efficiency (EQE) from each subcell when stacked. This analysis provides a frequency response of the cell, which can be precious information to understand and further optimize solar cells.

Resorting to the optical bias method, it was possible to extract the individual EQE of each subcell. This method consists of saturating all the subcells simultaneously, except the one under test, so that the saturated junctions will not limit the current, while that the cell that is not saturated (the one under study) will determine the current value, and thus its EQE can be computed.

When computing the EQE, it is necessary to have in mind that each cell will only absorb in a very specific wavelength range, that strongly depends on the bandgap of the other subcells. This dependence is due to the fact that the light spectrum is being split by the stacked distribution. In the lattice-matched approach, the GaInP top cell absorbs photons with energy $W_{ph} > 1.89\,\text{eV}$, the GaInAs middle cell will absorb between the range of $1.89 > W_{ph} > 1.41\,\text{eV}$ and, finally, the Ge bottom cell will absorb photons with energy $1.41 > W_{ph} > 0.661\,\text{eV}$. All of this is well illustrated in Figure 6, in which the simulated results in the Finite Element Tool are presented.

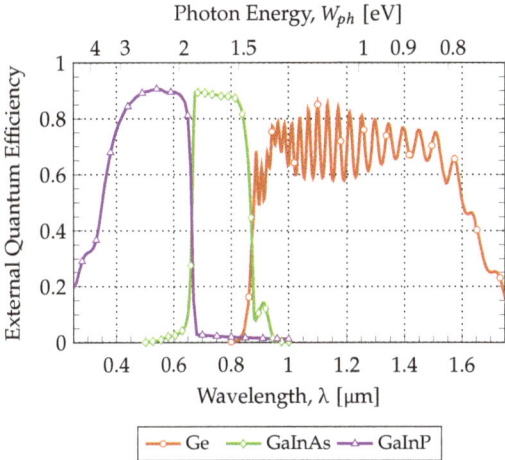

Figure 6. Simulated External Quantum Efficiencies of each subcell.

4.3. Temperature Effects

Temperature, naturally, is one of the most important factors when studying the behavior of semiconductors. This way, solar cells are usually tested for a nominal operating cell temperature (NOCT) of 25 °C, which is generally approximated to $T = 300\,\text{K}$ in absolute temperature values.

However, the photovoltaic cells under study have to be designed to withstand the extreme temperatures that only space can bestow. These temperatures can go from very high temperatures (HIHT (high intensity high temperature) missions) and deep-space temperatures like −170 °C, which is the cell temperature for Saturn-orbit missions. Therefore, it makes sense to try and emulate the cell under these conditions.

High and Low Temperatures

To try and perceive how high temperatures affect solar cell performance, a simulation was run first for $T = 300\,\text{K}$ and then for higher temperatures, in intervals of 50 K, to the final temperature of $T = 500\,\text{K}$. Besides studying the cell's behavior at high temperatures, it is also important to understand how they perform at temperatures below 0 °C. Even if some parameters variances can be expected, namely the increase in the open-circuit voltage and overall efficiency, there is some interest in how they vary for low temperatures.

The extracted $I - V$ curves for both ranges of temperature are illustrated in Figure 7, with the most relevant figures-of-merit from both plots (Figure 7a,b) being registered in Table 2.

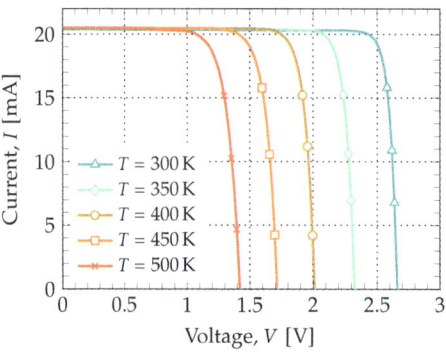

(a)

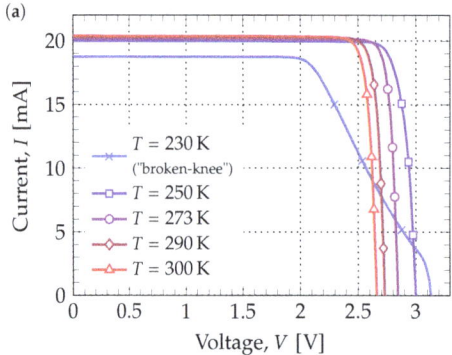

(b)

Figure 7. Tandem cell's $I - V$ characteristics obtained for two different intervals of temperature: (**a**) high temperature range, from $T = 300$ K to $T = 500$ K, and (**b**) low temperature range, from $T = 250$ K to $T = 300$ K. All curves were obtained using the AM0 spectrum.

Table 2. Measured values for both temperature ranges: high and low temperatures, from the respective plots (a) and (b), displayed in Figure 7.

	Figure 7a					Figure 7b			
	230 K	250 K	273 K	290 K	300 K	350 K	400 K	450 K	500 K
I_{SC} [mA]	18.7692	19.9959	20.2036	20.3397	20.4106	20.5206	20.5199	20.5445	20.5342
V_{OC} [V]	3.1344	3.0021	2.8466	2.7307	2.6627	2.3263	2.0162	1.7189	1.4237
FF	0.64	0.88	0.91	0.90	0.89	0.87	0.85	0.81	0.77
Eff. [%]	27.77	38.79	38.25	36.72	35.73	30.59	25.74	21.05	16.46

Both the open-circuit voltage and short-circuit current behave as expected: I_{SC} has an insignificant variance whereas the V_{OC} decreases substantially as temperature increases.

As for the efficiency and fill-factor, they both decrease as temperature rises, however, this is only valid to a certain point. As the array temperature gets colder, the variance in certain parameters begins to be non-linear. This is because, as temperature decreases, carriers start to enter the state of "freeze-out", in which there is not enough thermal energy for the dopants to be fully ionized, and thus there will be a shortage of charge carriers. Another issue is the phenomenon called "broken-knee" or "double-slope", in which the $I-V$ characteristic becomes degraded, generating a great reduction in the fill-factor and efficiency—this can be seen in the obtained curve for $T = 230$ K.

Notwithstanding, colder environments, to a certain extent, are good for solar cells since there is a boost in the overall performance; the obtained results confirm the need for some PV panels to have cooling systems installed so that the power conversion efficiency is maximized.

5. Cell Optimization

With the lattice-matched GaInP/GaInAs/Ge solar cell properly reproduced and simulated, an overall optimization of the cell is attempted. In order to do this, two studies on how thickness and doping affect the overall performance of the cell were made. The first study takes into account the top and middle subcells and their respective thicknesses. The second study will take into account the doping of the GaInP top subcell. The properties of the whole cell were maintained constant with the default, previously simulated parameter values.

Considering that the cell that was being simulated up to this point was optimized for CPV (concentrator photovoltaic) applications, this work will attempt to perform an optimization for space applications in LEO (low-Earth orbit, <1000 km) missions. The spectrum utilized was the AM0 and the cell temperature was $T = 300$ K.

5.1. Thickness Variation

When varying the cell thickness, it is necessary to select which layers are going to be altered. Since the photocurrent of the entire cell is determined by the top cell, the first layers to be chosen were the GaInP- base and emitter layers. The BSF and FSF layers were not altered, since their values were already at the minimum possible. The main goal of this study is to choose thickness values that establish a compromise between efficiency and size of the cell, given that the less cell bulkiness the better.

The first test consisted in varying both base and emitter thicknesses of the top cell and evaluate the efficiency, η, improvement. Other parameters like short-circuit current, I_{SC}, open-circuit voltage, V_{OC}, fill-factor, FF, and the variation in efficiency, $\Delta_{Eff.}$, were also registered. Both default (gray) and best (green) obtained results for the first test are displayed in Table 3. The best efficiency achieved was 31.80% which in comparison to the initial value of 31.76% corresponds to an improvement of +0.1107%.

Table 3. First study, first test: Top GaInP subcell thickness variation of the p-base and n-emitter layers.

Base [µm]	Emit. [µm]	I_{SC} [mA]	V_{OC} [V]	FF	η [%]	$\Delta_{Eff.}$ [%]
0.75	0.10	18.6750	2.6251	0.8847	31.7687	0.0000
0.70	0.11	18.5956	2.6254	0.8893	31.8039	+0.1107

Default values ; Best obtained values .

The second test was analogous to the first, except it was made considering only the middle subcell thickness. Once again, the BSF and FSF layers were not altered, varying only the thickness of both GaInAs- base and emitter layers. The top GaInP layers' thicknesses were the initial ones, without employing the optimization of the first test. The default values along with the best-obtained results are presented in Table 4. Alas, in this case, the best-obtained results (in green) correspond to a thickness increase of 0.5 µm in the base thickness. Since a bulkier cell is not the desired outcome, the second-best results (red) that achieved an efficiency of 31.8036% were chosen. This efficiency value corresponds to an improvement of +0.1098%.

Table 4. First study, second test: Middle GaInAs subcell thickness variation of the p-base and n-emitter layers.

Base [μm]	Emit. [μm]	I_{SC} [mA]	V_{OC} [V]	FF	η [%]	$\Delta_{Eff.}$ [%]
3.50	0.08	18.6750	2.6251	0.8847	31.7687	0.0000
4.00	0.08	18.6744	2.6272	0.8851	31.8074	+0.1220
3.75	0.09	18.6861	2.6262	0.8847	31.8036	+0.1098

Default values ; Best obtained values ; Second best values .

All of the obtained results for both tests are illustrated in two 3D plots, in which one can observe how cell the layers' thicknesses affect the overall performance of the cell. The 3D surface plots are presented in Figure 8 and were made resorting to the Curve Fitting Tool of MATLAB$^©$.

With this visual aid, it fairly clear that for the first test (Figure 8a), the efficiency depends on both GaInP- base and emitter thicknesses, being apparent that higher efficiencies concentrate in a range of values that are roughly in the center of the plot.

Similarly, analyzing the 3D plot for the second test (Figure 8b) it is evident that the higher the middle subcell's base thickness, the higher the efficiency. Unlike the first test, the GaInAs-base thickness is predominant in how the efficiency varies.

Finally, the best results from both tests were simulated, so that both subcell optimizations could be taken into account. The obtained parameters were: I_{SC} = 18.5943 mA, V_{OC} = 2.6276 V, FF = 88.98% and an efficiency of η = 31.8431%, which translates in an improvement of 0.2343%, in comparison with the initial value.

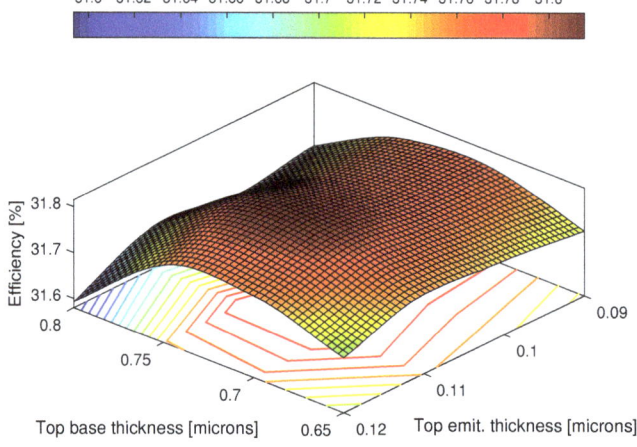

(**a**)

Figure 8. *Cont.*

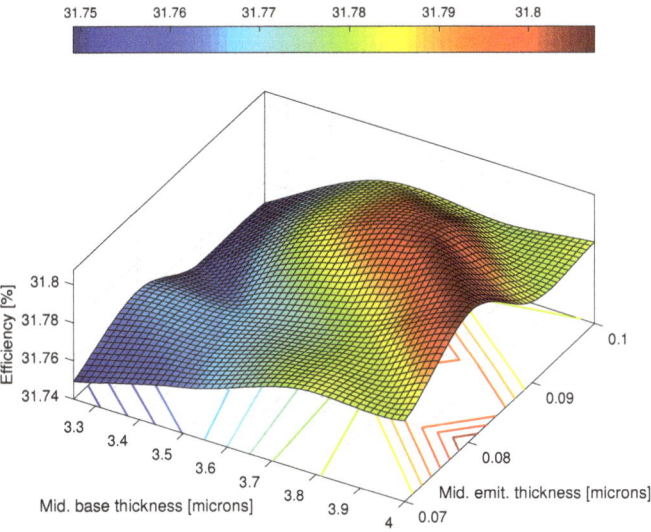

(b)

Figure 8. Graphic display of the obtained results for the: (**a**) first test: top GaInP subcell, and (**b**) middle GaInAs subcell. Both 3D plots were obtained using the 3D fitted surface with the cubic method of MATLAB Curve Fitting Toolbox.

5.2. Doping Variation

The second and final study was designed to evaluate how doping alters the performance of the cell. This last simulation is run with the best thickness values obtained in the first study.

Only the top cell's base and emitter layers are going to be contemplated in this study. Once more, Table 5 shows the best-obtained results of doping variation for the GaInP- base and emitter layers. The best obtained efficiency was 33.0194%, which corresponds to a total improvement of +3.9368% of the very first efficiency value that was η = 31.7687% (refer to Tables 3 and 4).

Table 5. Second study: doping variation of the p-base and n-emitter layers in the top subcell.

Base [cm^{-3}]	Emit. [cm^{-3}]	I_{SC} [mA]	V_{OC} [V]	FF	η [%]	$\Delta_{Eff.}$ [%]
1×10^{18}	1×10^{18}	18.6371	2.6805	0.90	33.02	+3.9368
1×10^{17}	5×10^{18}	18.5943	2.6276	0.89	31.84	+0.2343

Default values ; Best obtained values .

The doping values that were simulated were carefully chosen, given that the higher the doping, the lower the potential barrier to be overcome, making higher efficiencies possible to achieve. However, this efficiency increase can not be indefinite, since the minority carrier lifetime and diffusion length decrease with doping increase [32]. Hence, searching for the optimal doping value that increases efficiency without degrading the electronic properties of the semiconductor is of paramount importance. Values past 2.00×10^{18} cm^{-3} for the base and 1×10^{19} cm^{-3} were not chosen, given that simulations run with doping values higher than these resulted in deterioration of the $I - V$ curve.

Analogously to the first study, a 3D fitted cubic surface of the results was plotted and it is illustrated in Figure 9. It is clear that the base doping is predominant in efficiency variation; as it increases, efficiency values increase, reaching a peak region in which the efficiency is the highest possible. Beyond those values, there is an abrupt drop in the short-circuit current and open-circuit voltage, resulting in an efficiency reduction.

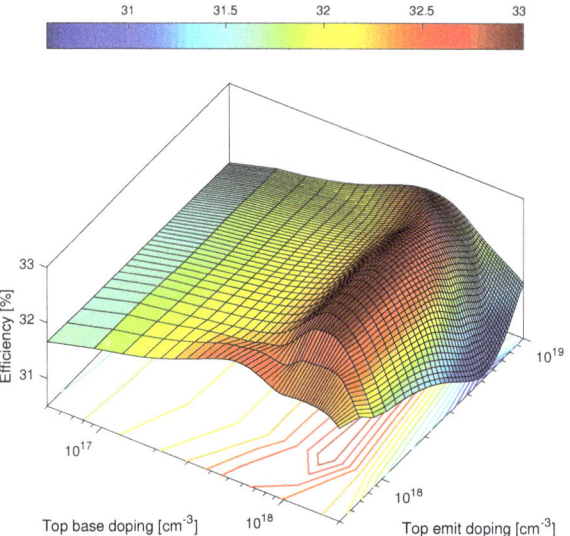

Figure 9. Graphic display of the obtained results of the second study. The 3D fitted surface with cubic method (MATLAB©).

This concludes the optimization of the cell for operation under the AM0 spectrum, at the nominal temperature of $T = 300$ K. As it has already been mentioned, temperatures in space can oscillate from extremely low to very high temperatures (sometimes in the same mission), and so each PV array must be optimized in accordance with the conditions it is planned to operate at.

6. Conclusions

The main aim of this work was to create a model so that a triple-junction state-of-the-art solar cell could be emulated and then analyzed with accuracy, without the need to resort to more advanced, and expensive, simulation technologies.

Comparing the simulated results with the actual experimental results by Spectrolab, Inc. one could say that the main goal was achieved, and the cell was emulated successfully. Both the open-circuit voltage and short-circuit current were fairly replicated, which means that the region materials, thickness, and doping were correctly modeled.

However, both the fill-factor and efficiency were not consistent with their experimental counterparts; this may have to do with the fact that losses were not properly accounted in the modeled cell since the only loss mechanisms present were the metal grid and the back/front contacts, and the fact that complex refractive indices were used in simulation (the imaginary part accounts for losses). Experimental values are calculated by appropriate measuring devices, such as multimeters, connecting them in series/parallel to a resistor, which in turn is connected to both terminals of the cell. This results in part of the losses not being accounted for in the simulation.

Other relevant differences are the external quantum efficiencies that were obtained for each subcell, in contrast with the experimental curves from Spectrolab, Inc. [33]. This is due mainly to the use of refractive indexes that do not correspond to the exact composition of a certain material. For instance, the most obvious difference is between the simulated and experimental frequency responses in the middle cell; this discrepancy may reside in the fact that the only refractive index available (from the databases) is not a rigorous match for the composition of $x = 0.99$ in $Ga_{0.99}In_{0.01}As$. This explanation is valid for other ternaries used as well.

Furthermore, bearing in mind that temperature plays a significant part in semiconductor performance, a test to evaluate how temperature influences the cell was also conducted. Most of the published research on how the GaInP/GaInAs/Ge solar cell behaves under different temperatures only has into consideration the higher range of temperature, given its paramount use in concentrator photovoltaic systems. With spacecraft implementation in sight, it was thought to be relevant to verify how the cell behaviors at low temperatures. Even though some plausible results were obtained, simulations in temperatures below 230 K did not obtain convergence, considering that the cell's design was not prepared for such low-temperature environments.

Finally, an optimization of the GaInP/GaInAs/Ge LM cell was also conducted. In this optimization, certain cell parameters were tweaked so it could reach its maximum potential for a 1-AM0 incidence. This could prove of some value for the photovoltaic industry that is dedicated to the manufacturing of solar cells for space applications, given that the doping can significantly boost the cell's efficiency.

Regarding the simulation times, depending on the mesh fineness and the voltage step that are being employed, the whole model takes roughly six minutes to simulate with Newton's method. This may be an advantage over more complex and detailed ways of simulation that are more time-consuming if the main objective is simply to obtain the major figures-of-merit of the cell.

Author Contributions: S.B. was responsible to write the original draft, J.P.N.T. and C.A.F.F. are her supervisors, J.P.N.T. and R.A.M.L. analysed the results and they were responsible to review and editing the final manuscript. All authors have read and agreed to the published version of the manuscript.

Funding: This research received no external funding.

Institutional Review Board Statement: Not applicable.

Informed Consent Statement: Not applicable.

Data Availability Statement: Not applicable.

Acknowledgments: This work was supported in part by FCT/MCTES through national funds and in part by cofounded EU funds under Project UIDB50008/2020.

Conflicts of Interest: The authors declare no conflict of interest.

References

1. IRENA. *Renewable Capacity Highlights 2019*; IRENA: Abu Dhabi, UAE, 2019.
2. Durão, B.; Torres, J.P.N.; Fernandes, C.A.F.; Lameirinhas, R.A.M. Socio-economic Study to Improve the Electrical Sustainability of the North Tower of Instituto Superior Técnico. *Sustainability* **2020**, *12*, 1923. [CrossRef]
3. Melo, I.; Torres, J.P.N.; Fernandes, C.A.F.; Lameirinhas, R.A.M. Sustainability economic study of the islands of the Azores archipelago using photovoltaic panels, wind energy and storage system. *Renewables* **2020**, *7*, 1–21. [CrossRef]
4. Bhattacharya, I.; Foo, S.Y. Indium phosphide, indium-gallium-arsenide and indium-gallium-antimonide based high efficiency multijunction photovoltaics for solar energy harvesting. In Proceedings of the 2009 1st Asia Symposium on Quality Electronic Design, Kuala Lumpur, Malaysia, 15–16 July 2009; pp. 237–241.
5. Bhattacharya, I.; Foo, S.Y. Effects of Gallium-Phosphide and Indium-Gallium-Antimonide semiconductor materials on photon absorption of multijunction solar cells. In Proceedings of the IEEE SoutheastCon 2010 (SoutheastCon), Concord, NC, USA, 18–21 March 2010; pp. 316–319.
6. Alves, P.; Fernandes, J.; Torres, J.; Branco, P.; Fernandes, C.; Gomes, J. Energy Efficiency of a PV/T Collector for Domestic Water Heating Installed in Sweden or in Portugal: Impact of Heat Pipe Cross-Section Geometry and Water Flowing Speed. In Proceedings of the Sdewes 2017, Dubrovnik, Croatia, 4–8 October 2017.
7. Gomes, J.; Luc, B.; Carine, G.; Fernandes, C.A.; Torres, J.P.N.; Olsson, O.; Nashih, S.K. Analysis of different C-PVT reflector geometries. In Proceedings of the 2016 IEEE International Power Electronics and Motion Control Conference (PEMC), Varna, Bulgaria, 25–30 September 2016.
8. Mota, F.; Torres, J.P.N.; Fernandes, C.A.F.; Lameirinhas, R.A.M. Influence of an aluminium concentrator corrosion on the output characteristic of a photovoltaic system. *Sci. Rep.* **2020**, *10*, 1–16. [CrossRef] [PubMed]

9. Marques, L.; Torres, J.; Branco, P. Triangular shape geometry in a Solarus AB concentrating photovoltaic-thermal collector. *Int. J. Interact. Des. Manuf. (IJIDeM)* **2018**, *12*, 1455–1468. [CrossRef]
10. Torres, J.P.N.; Fernandes, C.A.; Gomes, J.; Luc, B.; Carine, G.; Olsson, O.; Branco, P.J. Effect of reflector geometry in the annual received radiation of low concentration photovoltaic systems. *Energies* **2018**, *11*, 1878. [CrossRef]
11. Fernandes, C.A.; Torres, J.P.N.; Morgado, M.; Morgado, J.A. Aging of solar PV plants and mitigation of their consequences. In Proceedings of the 2016 IEEE International Power Electronics and Motion Control Conference (PEMC), Varna, Bulgaria, 25–30 September 2016.
12. Torres, J.P.N.; Nashih, S.K.; Fernandes, C.A.; Leite, J.C. The effect of shading on photovoltaic solar panels. *Energy Syst.* **2018**, *9*, 195–208. [CrossRef]
13. Fernandes, C.A.F.; Torres, J.P.N.; Branco, P.C.; Fernandes, J.; Gomes, J.R. Cell string layout in solar photovoltaic collectors. *Energy Convers. Manag.* **2017**, *149*, 997–1009. [CrossRef]
14. Fernandes, C.A.; Torres, J.P.N.; Gomes, J.; Branco, P.C.; Nashih, S.K. Stationary solar concentrating photovoltaic-thermal collector—Cell string layout. In Proceedings of the 2016 IEEE International Power Electronics and Motion Control Conference (PEMC), Varna, Bulgaria, 25–30 September 2016.
15. Campos, C.; Torres, J.; Fernandes, J. Effects of the heat transfer fluid selection on the efficiency of a hybrid concentrated photovoltaic and thermal collector. *Energies* **2019**, *12*, 1814. [CrossRef]
16. Torres, J.P.N.; Fernandes, J.F.; Fernandes, C.; Costa, B.P.J.; Barata, C.; Gomes, J. Effect of the collector geometry in the concentrating photovoltaic thermal solar cell performance. *Therm. Sci.* **2018**, *22*, 2243–2256. [CrossRef]
17. Torres, J.; Seram, V.; Fernandes, C. Influence of the Solarus AB reflector geometry and position of receiver on the output of the concentrating photovoltaic thermal collector. *Int. J. Interact. Des. Manuf. (IJIDeM)* **2019**, *14*, 153–172. [CrossRef]
18. Alves, P.; Fernandes, J.F.; Torres, J.P.N.; Branco, P.C.; Fernandes, C.; Gomes, J. From Sweden to Portugal: The effect of very distinct climate zones on energy efficiency of a concentrating photovoltaic/thermal system (CPV/T). *Sol. Energy* **2019**, *188*, 96–110. [CrossRef]
19. Nashih, S.K.; Fernandes, C.A.F.; Torres, J.P.N.; Gomes, J.; Costa, Branco, P.J. Validation of a simulation model for analysis of shading effects on photovoltaic panels. *ASME. J. Sol. Energy Eng* **2016**, *138*, 044503. [CrossRef]
20. IRENA. *Renewable Power Generation Costs in 2017*; IRENA: Abu Dhabi, UAE, 2018.
21. NREL. *NREL Scientists Spurred the Success of Multijunction Solar Cells*; NREL: Golden, CO, USA, 2012.
22. Green, M.A.; Hishikawa, Y.; Dunlop, E.D.; Levi, D.H.; Hohl-Ebinger, J.; Yoshita, M.; Ho-Baillie, A.W. Solar cell efficiency tables (Version 52). *Prog. Photovoltaics Res. Appl.* **2019**, *27*, 3–12. [CrossRef]
23. Chiu, P.T.; Law, D.; Woo, R.; Singer, S.; Bhusari, D.; Hong, W.; Zakaria, A.; Boisvert, J.; Mesropian, S.; King, R.; et al. 35.8% space and 38.8% terrestrial 5J direct bonded cells. In Proceedings of the 2014 IEEE 40th Photovoltaic Specialist Conference (PVSC), Denver, CO, USA, 8–13 June 2014; pp. 35–37.
24. Landis, G.A. Review of solar cell temperature coefficients for space. In Proceedings of the 13th Space Photovoltaic Research and Technology Conference, Cleveland, OH, USA, 14–16 June 1994; pp. 385–399.
25. Landis, G.A.; Merritt, D.; Raffaelle, R.P.; Scheiman, D. *High-Temperature Solar Cell Development*; NASA John Glenn Research Center: Cleveland, OH, USA, 2005; pp. 241–247.
26. King, R.R.; Bhusari, D.; Larrabee, D.; Liu, X.; Rehder, E.; Edmondson, K.; Cotal, H.; Jones, R.K.; Ermer, J.H.; Fetzer, C.M.; et al. Solar cell generations over 40% efficiency. *Prog. Photovolt. Res. Appl.* **2012**, *20*, 801–815. [CrossRef]
27. Cotal, H.; Fetzer, C.; Boisvert, J.; Kinsey, G.; King, R.; Hebert, P.; Yoon, H. III-V multijunction solar cells for concentrating photovoltaics. *Energy Environ. Sci.* **2009**, *2*, 174–192. [CrossRef]
28. Steiner, M.; Philipps, S.P.; Hermle, M.; Bett, A.W.; Dimroth, F. Validated front contact grid simulation for GaAs solar cells under concentrated sunlight. *Prog. Photovolt. Res. Appl.* **2011**, *19*, 73–83. [CrossRef]
29. Philipps, S.P.; Dimroth, F.; Bett, A.W. High-Efficiency III-V Multijunction Solar Cells. In *McEvoy's Handbook of Photovoltaics: Fundamentals and Applications*, 3rd ed.; Kalogirou, S.A., Ed.; Academic Press: Cambridge, MA, USA, 2018; pp. 439–463.
30. King, R.R.; Fetzer, C.M.; Law, D.C.; Edmondson, K.M.; Yoon, H.; Kinsey, G.S.; Krut, D.D.; Ermer, J.H.; Hebert, P.; Cavicchi, B.T.; et al. Advanced III-V multijunction cells for space. In Proceedings of the 2006 IEEE 4th World Conference on Photovoltaic Energy Conversion, Waikoloa, HI, USA, 7–12 May 2006; Volume 2, pp. 1757–1762.
31. Sharma, P. Modeling, Optimization, and Characterization of High Concentration Photovoltaic Systems Using Multijunction Solar Cells. Ph.D. Thesis, School of Electrical Engineering and Computer Science, University of Ottawa, Ottawa, ON, USA, 2017.
32. Dugas, J.; Oualid, J. Modelling of base doping concentration influence in polycrystalline silicon solar cells. *Sol. Cells* **1987**, *20*, 145–154. [CrossRef]
33. King, R.; Law, D.; Edmondson, K.; Fetzer, C.; Kinsey, G.; Hojun, Y.; Krut, D.; Ermer, J.; Sherif, R.; Karam, N. Advances in High-Efficiency III-V Multijunction Solar Cells. *Adv. Optoelectron.* **2007**. [CrossRef]

Article

Optical Nanoantennas for Photovoltaic Applications

Francisco Duarte [1], João Paulo N. Torres [1,2,3], António Baptista [1,4] and Ricardo A. Marques Lameirinhas [1,2,*]

- [1] Department of Electrical and Computer Engineering, Instituto Superior Técnico, 1049-001 Lisbon, Portugal; joaoptorres@hotmail.com (F.D.); joaptorres@tecnico.ulisboa.pt (J.P.N.T.); baptista@tecnico.ulisboa.pt (A.B.)
- [2] Instituto de Telecomunicações, 1049-001 Lisbon, Portugal
- [3] Academia Militar, Av. Conde Castro Guimarães, 2720-113 Amadora, Portugal
- [4] Centro de Investigação, Desenvolvimento e Inovação da Academia Militar, Av. Conde Castro Guimarães, 2720-113 Amadora, Portugal
- * Correspondence: ricardo.lameirinhas@tecnico.ulisboa.pt

Abstract: In the last decade, the development and progress of nanotechnology has enabled a better understanding of the light–matter interaction at the nanoscale. Its unique capability to fabricate new structures at atomic scale has already produced novel materials and devices with great potential applications in a wide range of fields. In this context, nanotechnology allows the development of models, such as nanometric optical antennas, with dimensions smaller than the wavelength of the incident electromagnetic wave. In this article, the behavior of optical aperture nanoantennas, a metal sheet with apertures of dimensions smaller than the wavelength, combined with photovoltaic solar panels is studied. This technique emerged as a potential renewable energy solution, by increasing the efficiency of solar cells, while reducing their manufacturing and electricity production costs. The objective of this article is to perform a performance analysis, using COMSOL Multiphysics software, with different materials and designs of nanoantennas and choosing the most suitable one for use on a solar photovoltaic panel.

Keywords: nanoantennas; optics; optoelectronic devices; photovoltaic technology; rectennas

Citation: Duarte, F.; Torres, J.P.N.; Baptista, A.; Marques Lameirinhas, R.A. Optical Nanoantennas for Photovoltaic Applications. *Nanomaterials* **2021**, *11*, 422. https://doi.org/10.3390/nano11020422

Academic Editor: Antonio Di Bartolomeo

Received: 5 January 2021
Accepted: 3 February 2021
Published: 7 February 2021

Publisher's Note: MDPI stays neutral with regard to jurisdictional claims in published maps and institutional affiliations.

Copyright: © 2021 by the authors. Licensee MDPI, Basel, Switzerland. This article is an open access article distributed under the terms and conditions of the Creative Commons Attribution (CC BY) license (https://creativecommons.org/licenses/by/4.0/).

1. Introduction

In the last decade, the advances in the nanoscale dimension enabled the development of new devices, such as nanoantennas or optical antennas, due to the emergence of a new branch of science known as nanooptics, which studies the transmission and reception of optical signals at the nanoscale. These devices have been the object of intense research and development activity, with the goal to reach the captivating possibility of confining the electromagnetic radiation in spatial dimensions smaller than the wavelength of light.

The transmission through a metal plane with subwavelength-sized holes can be drastically increased if a periodic arrangement of holes is used. This phenomenon is widely known as Extraordinary Optical Transmission [1]. The usage of nanoantennas with apertures smaller than the light wavelength can locally enhance light–matter interaction. Thus, nanoantennas are devices that have the ability to manipulate and control optical radiation at subwavelength scales.

Nanoantennas are a nanoscale version of radio-frequency (RF) or microwave antennas. However, throughout this article it will be proven that in the process of sizing the nanoantennas, it will not be enough to reduce the size of the RF antennas to the optical domain, mainly because of the unique material properties of metals that influence the behavior of antennas at the nanoscale: the existence at the interface between metals and dielectrics of surface plasmon-polariton electromagnetic waves, which gives rise to resonant effects not available at RF [1,2].

The use of optical antennas for solar energy harvesting has received significant interest as they represent a viable alternative to the traditional energy harvesting technologies.

Economical large-scale fabrication of nanoantenna devices would support applications such as building integrated photovoltaics and supplementing the power grid [3].

2. Rectenna System for Solar Energy Harvesting

The nanoantenna itself does not convert the collected AC current into DC current, and so it needs to be complemented with a rectifying element. The whole structure is commonly referred to as a rectenna [4].

A rectenna is a circuit containing an optical antenna, filter circuits, and a rectifying diode or bridge rectifier for the conversion of electromagnetic energy propagating through space (solar energy) into DC electric power (through the photovoltaic effect).

A schematic representation of a nano-rectenna system is depicted in Figure 1.

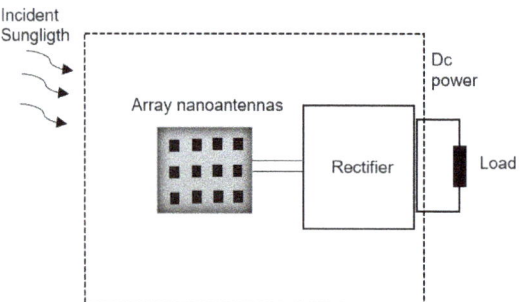

Figure 1. Representation of the nano-rectenna system (adapted from the work in [5]).

First, electromagnetic radiation is collected by the nanoantenna device. However, the output obtained from a single nanoantenna element is not enough to drive the rectifier and to provide DC power to an external load. The efficiency of a single optical antenna is generally low and its functionality is limited. Therefore, nanoantennas are arranged into arrays to increase their signal. The total field captured by the array is the addition of the fields captured by each nanoantenna [6].

The AC current generated in the nanoantenna arrays is collected and rectified into DC current by the rectifier system. This system has different rectifiers whose outputs can be DC coupled together, allowing arrays of nanoantennas to be networked to further increase output power [3].

As optical radiation requires high-speed rectification, high frequency metal–insulator–metal (MIM) diodes—also known as tunneling diodes—are commonly used for this purpose.

According to Moddel and Grover, the MIM diodes must have three key characteristics in order to have an efficient rectifier system [6]: high responsivity, that is, a measure of the rectified DC voltage or current as a function of the input radiant power; low resistance, in order to have a good impedance matching between the antenna and the diode; and asymmetry in the I–V curve, so the diode must have asymmetric characteristics for the rectenna be operated without applying an external DC bias.

Examples of material combinations used for diode rectifiers include Ni/NiO/Ni, Nb/Nb2O5/Pt, Nb/TiO2/Pt, Cu/TiO2/Pt, Nb/MgO/Pt, and Nb/Al2O3/Nb [6].

3. Experimentally Studied Nanoantenna Materials and Designs

A large variety of nanoantenna geometries has been researched for multiple potential applications. Currently, nanoantennas structures are mainly made of plasmonic materials, i.e., specially designed metal (usually gold or silver) nanoparticles with unique optical properties. Plasmonic materials exhibit strong light absorption in the visible region of the spectrum [4].

The advances in the manufacturing techniques allowed the construction of different formats of nanoantennas. The main types of plasmonic nanoantennas that have been proposed and investigated experimentally are represented in Figure 2.

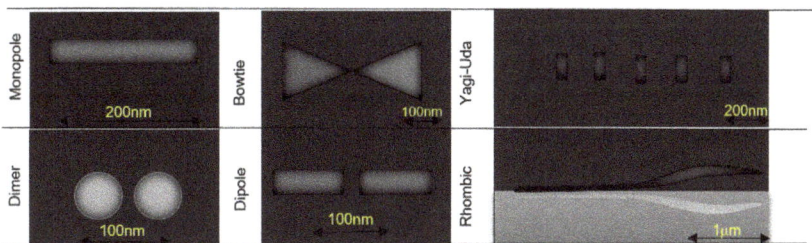

Figure 2. Main types of plasmonic nanoantennas (adapted from the work in [7]).

3.1. Plasmonic Monopole Nanoantenna

The most basic type of plasmonic nanoantenna, a monopole, is a single metallic nanoparticle that can enhance the electromagnetic field strength in its surrounding area upon excitation of plasmon resonances. Monopole nanoantennas have advantages over other geometries, because they are easier to engineer and are well isolated from interference due to the ground plane. Their characteristics are dependent on the shape, size, material, and dielectric environment of the nanoparticle [7].

Another great utility of the monopole optical antenna is when it is integrated in a Near-field Scanning Optical Microscopy (NSOM), to be used as a near-field probe for measurements [8]. An effective nanoantenna can be used in spectroscopy: it needs to interact strongly with incident electromagnetic radiation in order to measure its intensity.

3.2. Plasmonic Dipole Nanoantenna

Dipole configurations are widely used in radio frequency and microwave ranges. Therefore, it is not a surprise that analogs of such antennas also appeared in the optical range. This type of optical antenna is widely used in near-field optical probes, just like the monopole. The dipole optical antenna is constituted either by dimers or two monopoles separated by a small space (gap). Usually, there is a high field confinement in the gap between the two metallic nanoparticles [7].

The design of plasmonic nanoantennas may rely on the same principles used in RF antennas. For example, the length of the dipole RF antenna is approximately half the wavelength of the incident radio waves, whereas the length of the dipole plasmonic nanoantenna is smaller than the wavelength, λ, of incident light in free space [9].

3.3. Plasmonic Bowtie Nanoantenna

Another typical structure is the bowtie nanoantenna, consisting of two triangular shape nanoparticles aligned along their axes and forming the feed gap with their tips. These optical antennas are a variant of the dipole nanoantennas. Such geometry ensures a wider bandwidth together with large field localizations in the feed gap compared to the straight dipole.

The bowtie topology is considered to be one of the most efficient nanoantenna geometries for solar energy harvesting. According to Sen Yan [5], in their study it is shown that the bowtie topology can increase the total radiation efficiency and rectenna efficiency compared to the straight dipole by a considerable 10%.

3.4. Plasmonic Yagi-Uda Nanoantenna

RF Yagi–Uda type antennas are usually used to receive TV signals from remote stations, due to their high directivity. Their plasmonic counterparts consist of a reflector and one or several directors.

Yagi–Uda optical antennas can be useful in many applications: in wireless communications, in the fields of biology and medicine, in nanophotonic circuits, in quantum information technology, in data storage (as an optical chip), in photodetectors, and in photovoltaic (PV) systems.

3.5. Plasmonic Spiral-Square Nanoantenna

This design of nanoantenna allows the electromagnetic radiation to be harvested in one specific point in its structure—the gap (feed point) between two metallic arms, as presented on Figure 3. Thus, this topology has a wider angle of incidence exposure in comparison to other formats, which makes it an ideal geometry for solar energy harvesting.

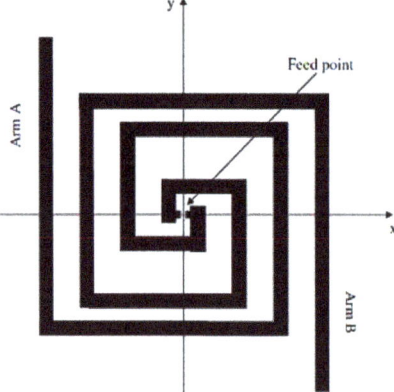

Figure 3. Geometry of a square-spiral nanoantenna (sourced from the work in [10]).

They also demonstrate a high directivity that can be further improved by increasing the number of arms.

3.6. Dielectric Nanoantennas

A new research direction of optical antennas has recently been suggested with the introduction of dielectric nanoantennas. Optical antennas constructed with dielectric materials have several advantages over their metallic counterparts due to unique features not found in plasmonic nanoantennas [4].

Dielectric nanoantennas are fabricated from optically transparent materials that have low dissipative losses at optical frequencies. Unlike gold or silver, dielectric nanoantennas are usually made from silicon nanoparticles which are widely used in nanoelectronics to fabricate transistors and diodes. Furthermore, silicon has a high permittivity and exhibits very strong electric and magnetic resonances at the nanoscale, and thus improves radiation efficiency and antenna directivity, expanding the range of applications for nanoantenna structures [4,11].

The authors of [11] used silicon nanoparticles to demonstrate the performance of all-dielectric nanoantennas. They have analyzed an all-dielectric analog of the plasmonic Yagi–Uda nanoantenna consisting of an array of nanoelements: four directors and one reflector particle made of silicon. In this type of structure, the optimal performance is obtained when the director nanoparticles sustain a magnetic resonance and the reflector nanoparticle sustains an electric resonance [4]. schematic representation of this antenna is shown in Figure 4.

Figure 4. 3D view of an all-dielectric optical Yagi–Uda nanoantenna, consisting of the reflector 1 of the radius Rr = 75 nm, and smaller director 2–5 of the radii Rd = 70 nm (adapted from the work in [7]).

The dipole source is placed equally from the reflector and the first director surfaces at the distance D. The separation between surfaces of the neighboring directors is also equal to D.

The operational regime of a dielectric Yagi–Uda nanoantenna strongly depends on the distance between its elements. According to Krasnok [11], in their study it was verified that the radiation efficiency of the dielectric Yagi–Uda nanoantenna slowly decreased with decreasing distance between its elements, while the radiation efficiency of a plasmonic antenna of similar design and dimensions was greatly affected by the decrease in distance between particles. This is due to increased metal losses caused by proximity of adjacent metallic nanoparticles.

However, for larger separation distances, D, the radiation efficiencies of both types of nanoantennas were very identical. Although dissipation losses of silicon are much smaller than those of silver, the dielectric particle absorbs the EM energy by the whole spherical volume, while absorption only occurs at the surface of metallic particles. As a result, there is no substantial difference in the performance of these two types of nanoantennas for relatively large distances between its elements.

To sum up, based on the results of this study, a conclusion could be made that all-dielectric nanoantennas demonstrate major advantages over their metallic counterparts: much lower Joule losses and strong optically induced magnetization [11].

3.7. Aperture Nanoantennas

There is another type of optical antenna that is interesting for the topic of this article: aperture optical antennas. Light passing in a small aperture is the subject of intense scientific interest since the very first introduction of the concept of diffraction by Grimaldi in 1665 [12].

The first theory of diffraction due to a slit, that is much less than the light wavelength, in a thin metal layer was developed by Bethe. This theory predicted that the power transmitted by the slit would decrease as the slit diameter decreased relative to the wavelength of the EM radiation. This theory proved to be incorrect when Ebbesen, in 1998, observed the extraordinary optical transmission phenomenon (EOT) [1]. The EOT is an optical phenomenon, in which a structure containing subwavelength apertures transmits more light than might naively be expected. Ebbesen et al. observed that when focusing a light beam in a thick metallic film where there was a subwavelength hole array, a large increase of incident electromagnetic wave transmission occurs, i.e., a periodic array of subwavelength holes, as presented in Figure 5, transmits more light than a large macroscopic hole with the same area as the sum of all the small holes [1,2,13–19].

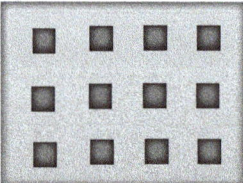

Figure 5. Schematic view of 200 nm diameter aperture arrays with 1 um period (adapted from the work in [12]).

This discovery would be fundamental, as it not only allowed great technological developments during the last decade, but also allowed a better understanding of the diffraction by small slits in relation to the light wavelength [20,21].

According to Wenger, there are three main types of aperture antennas [12]: single subwavelength aperture, single aperture surrounded by shallow surface corrugations, and subwavelength aperture arrays.

4. Surface Plasmon Resonance

As referred in the introduction, incident light on the optical antenna causes the excitation of free electrons in metallic particles. More precisely, EM waves induce time-varying electric fields in the nanoantenna that apply a force on the gas of electrons inside the device, causing them to move back and forth at the same frequency range as the incoming light. This phenomenon is known as surface plasmon. At specific optical frequencies the nanoantenna resonates at the same frequency as the incoming light which enables the absorption of the incoming radiation [4,15–19].

It should be taken into account that, at optical frequencies, metals do not act as perfect conductors: their conductivity changes dramatically, and so they are unable to respond to the time-varying electric field immediately. The wave propagation within the material is affected, which means that the penetration of EM radiation into metals can no longer be neglected.

Thus, at optical frequencies an antenna no longer responds to external wavelength but to a shorter effective wavelength that depends on the material properties [20].

EM radiation penetrates the metal of the nanoantenna and gives rise to oscillations of the free-electron gas. These electron oscillations can give rise to plasmon resonances, depending on the size, shape, and index of refraction of the particle as well as the optical constants of its surrounding [21].

When these oscillations are optimized, i.e., when the metal structure is sized to achieve the resonance condition, it is called Surface Plasmon Resonance (SPR). It is also important to mention that there are two types of surface plasmons [15–19,22]: Surface Plasmon Polariton (SPP), when the EM waves strike a metallic film and are confined to the surface of this film, and Localized Surface Plasmon (LSP), when the coupling is made with a metal nanoparticle with a diameter much smaller than the incident wavelength.

Surface plasmons are highly confined energy fields made by the oscillation of electrons on the surface of nanoantennas. When a metallic nanoparticle is illuminated by light, surface plasmons will be coupled with the photons of incident light in the form of a propagating surface wave [23].

SPPs are infrared or visible frequency EM waves trapped at or guided along metal–dielectric interfaces [24]. This coupling of plasmons—either SPPs or LSPs—and photons results in charge oscillation in the visible and infrared regimes depending on the metal used. SPPs are shorter in wavelength than the incident light (photons). Therefore, SPPs provide a significant reduction in effective wavelength and have tighter spatial confinement and higher local field intensity [24].

Recent development of nanofabrication techniques enabled construction of a variety of metal structures at the subwavelength scale and opened the research area called plasmonics, a subfield of nanophotonics studying the manipulation of light coupled to electrons at the nanoscale.

The properties of optical antennas are still under the intensive study and so research efforts to relate plasmonics with subwavelength optical antenna are in a developing stage [23].

5. Efficiency

The radiation efficiency of nanoantennas is a key parameter for solar energy harvesting. It is the first factor in the total efficiency product by which nanoantennas can convert incident light to useful energy. This efficiency depends directly on the type of metal used as conductor and the dimensions of the nanoantenna [6].

The main advantage of this type of technology in comparison to the conventional solar photovoltaic cells is its far greater efficiency by which the transformation of electromagnetic energy into DC electric power is performed. Typical efficiencies for traditional silicon cells are in the order of 20%, whereas nanoantennas go from a stunning 70% for silver nanodipoles [25] to a more realistic 50% for aluminum dipoles [26]. Most solar radiation is in the visible and infrared (IR) wavelength region, and so nanoantennas need to be designed for this part of the spectrum, with the aim of being an alternative to conventional solar photovoltaic cells.

The total efficiency of a rectenna consists of two parts: (1) the efficiency by which the light is captured by the nanoantenna and brought to its terminals, also known as radiation efficiency, η_{total}^{rad}, and (2) the efficiency by which the captured light is transformed into low frequency electrical power by the rectifier, η_{total}^{mat}.

According to Kotter, the total radiation efficiency could be given by expression 1 [25], where λ is the wavelength of the incident light and the upper and lower integration limits λ_{start} and λ_{stop} should cover the optical bandwidth for the solar energy harvesting.

$$\eta_{total}^{rad} = \frac{\int_{\lambda_{start}}^{\lambda_{stop}} P_{inc}(\lambda) \eta^{rad}(\lambda) d\lambda}{\int_{\lambda_{start}}^{\lambda_{stop}} P_{inc}(\lambda) d\lambda} \quad (1)$$

Furthermore, $P_{inc}(\lambda)$ is a function of the wavelength that follows Planck's law for black body radiation according to expression 2, with T being the absolute temperature of the black body that in this case is the temperature of the surface of the sun, h the Planck's constant, c the speed of light in vacuum, and k the Boltzmann constant.

$$P_{inc}(\lambda) = \frac{2\pi h c^2}{\lambda^5} \frac{1}{e^{\frac{hc}{\lambda kT}} - 1} \quad (2)$$

η^{rad} is the radiation efficiency of the antenna as a function of the wavelength that is given by expression 3, where P^{rad}, P^{inj}, and P^{loss} are the radiated power, the power injected at the terminals, and the power dissipated in the metal of the nanoantenna, respectively.

$$\eta^{rad} = \frac{P^{rad}}{P^{inj}} = \frac{P^{rad}}{P^{rad} + P^{loss}} \quad (3)$$

In order to generate DC power in the load, a rectifier is connected to the input port to rectify the current flowing in the antenna's structure that oscillates around hundreds of THz. Like the total radiation efficiency, it is also possible to define the total matching efficiency as described on expression 4, where η^{mat} is the matching efficiency of the nanoantenna rectifier system given by expression 5, with Z_{rec} being the impedance of the rectifier and Z_{ant} the input impedance of the nanoantenna. Moreover, R_{rec} is the real part of the impedance of the rectifier and R_{ant} the real part of the nanoantenna input impedance.

$$\eta_{total}^{mat} = \frac{\int_{\lambda_{start}}^{\lambda_{stop}} P_{inc}(\lambda)\eta^{rad}(\lambda)\eta^{mat}(\lambda)d\lambda}{\int_{\lambda_{start}}^{\lambda_{stop}} P_{inc}(\lambda)\eta^{rad}(\lambda)d\lambda} \quad (4)$$

$$\eta^{rad} = \frac{4R_{rec}R_{ant}}{|Z_{rec} + Z_{ant}|^2} \quad (5)$$

All these quantities are marked in Figure 6, an equivalent circuit of the total rectenna system, where both the transmitting and receiving processes can be easily described.

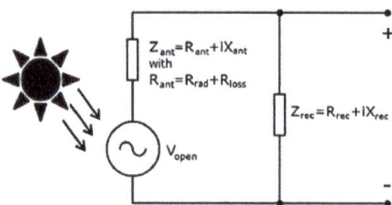

Figure 6. Equivalent circuit for the rectenna system (adapted from the work in [5]).

V_{open} is the voltage generated by the receiving antenna at its open terminals, while V_{rec} is the voltage seen at the terminals when a current is flowing to the rectifier. The useful power is the power going to the impedance of the rectifier Z_{rec} and it is given by expression 6.

$$P_{rec} = \frac{R_{rec}}{2}\frac{V_{open}^2}{|Z_{rec} + Z_{ant}|^2} \quad (6)$$

This power is maximal under optical matching conditions, i.e., $Z_{rec} = Z_{ant}*$, leading to expression 7.

$$P_{rec} = \frac{V_{open}^2}{8R_{ant}} \quad (7)$$

Finally, to define the total rectenna efficiency, η_{total}^{rec}, presented on expression 8, is just needed to sum expressions 1 and 4.

$$\eta_{total}^{rec} = \eta_{total}^{rad}\eta_{total}^{mat} \quad (8)$$

6. Model: Solar Cell

A solar cell, shown in Figure 7, is a PIN structure device with no voltage directly applied across the junction. The solar cell converts light into electrical power and delivers this power to a load. This process requires a material that can absorb the light photons. The interaction of an electron with a photon leads to the promotion of an electron from the valence band into the conduction band leaving behind a hole, i.e., the absorption of a photon by a semiconductor material results in the generation of an electron–hole pair. After an electron–hole pair is created, the electron and the hole move from the solar cell into an external circuit, producing a photocurrent I. The electron then dissipates its energy in the external circuit and returns to the solar cell [26–42].

Some processes illustrated in Figure 7 are (1) absorption of a photon leads to the generation of an electron–hole pair; (2) recombination of electrons and holes; (3) electrons and holes can be separated with semipermeable membranes; (4) the separated electrons can be used to drive an electric circuit; and (5) after all electrons passed through the circuit, they will recombine with holes.

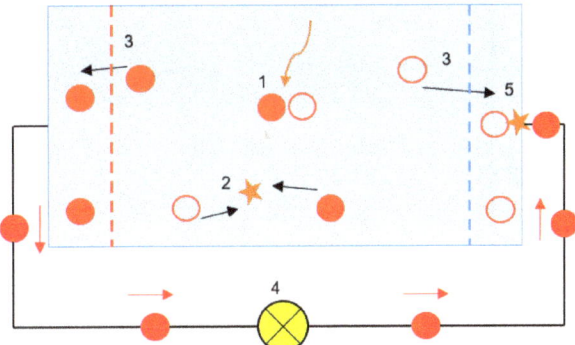

Figure 7. Simple model a solar cell connected to a load (sourced from the work in [43]).

That solar cell is a PIN junction, also illustrated in Figure 8. The PIN structure consists of a p region and a n region separated by an intrinsic layer. The p region and n region have different electrons concentration: the n-type has an excess of electrons while the p-type has an excess of holes, i.e., positive charges. The intrinsic layer width W is much larger than the space charge width of a normal PN junction [28–42].

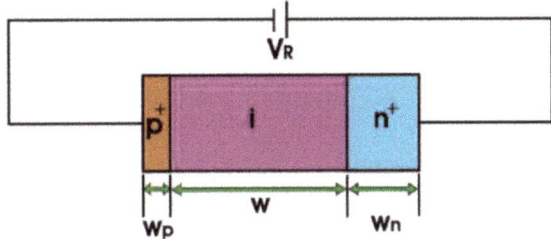

Figure 8. Circuit of a PIN junction, where W is the intrinsic layer width.

Absorption of light occurs in the intrinsic zone. A voltage V_R is applied so that there is an electric field in the intrinsic zone large enough so when the photons are absorbed, an electron–hole pair is created, i.e., a negative charge, electron, goes to the conduction band of the semiconductor and in the valence band a positive charge is going to move on the action of the electric field [28–42]. Therefore, there is an electric field that immediately separates the positive from the negative charge (the negative goes to one of the terminals and the positive one goes to the other).

The output of the PV cell is often represented with the relation between the current and voltage. This is known as the current–voltage curve (I–V curve). The I–V curve, represented in Figure 9, is a snapshot of all the potential combinations of current and voltage possible from a cell under standard test conditions (STC) [28–44]: (i) cell temperature: 25 °C (298.16 K); (ii) incident irradiance on the cell: $G = 1000 \text{ W m}^{-2}$; and (iii) spectral distribution of solar radiation: AM 1.5 spectrum.

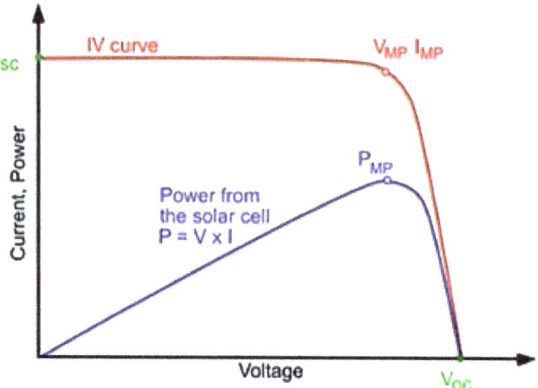

Figure 9. I–V curve (red) and power curve (blue) of a solar cell (sourced from the work in [45]).

The point in the I–V curve at which the maximum power is attainable is called Maximum Power Point (MPP), being that power calculated by expression 9 [28–42].

$$P_{MP} = V_{MP} \times I_{MP} \tag{9}$$

The representation of equipment through equivalent electrical circuits is a technique used in the field of electrical engineering. In order to study the PV equipment, a simplified electrical model is presented in Figure 10 [28–42].

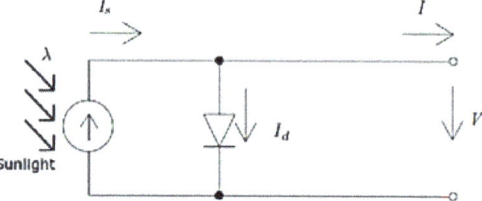

Figure 10. Equivalent circuit of a PV cell (1 diode and 3 parameters model-1M3P).

This model has three parameters: I_s, I_0, and n.

I_s, also known as I_{pv}, represents the electric current generated by the beam of light radiation, consisting of photons, upon reaching the active surface of the cell. The level of this current depends on the irradiance [28–42].

The PIN junction functions as a diode that is traversed by an internal unidirectional current I_d which depends on the voltage V at the terminals of the cell and on the parameters I_0 and n, as it is possible to verify from expression 10 [28–42].

$$I_d = I_0 \left(e^{\frac{V}{n v_T}} - 1 \right) \tag{10}$$

Then, I_0 is the he reverse saturation current of the diode, n is the diode ideality factor and v_T is the thermal voltage for a given temperature, determined using expression 11, from the Boltzmann's constant, k, and electron charge value, q [28–42].

$$v_T = \frac{kT}{q} \tag{11}$$

Using the Kirchhoff's Current Law (KCL) on that internal node, expression 12 is revealed [28–42].

$$I = I_s - I_d = I_s - I_0 \left(e^{\frac{V}{n v_T}} - 1 \right) \quad (12)$$

However, the simplified model of 1 diode and 3 parameters is not a strict representation of the PV cell. It is necessary to take into account the voltage drop in the circuit up to the external contacts, which can be represented by a series resistance R_s and also the leakage currents, which can be represented by a parallel resistance, R_p. The influence of these parameters on the I–V characteristic of the solar cell can be studied using the equivalent circuit presented on Figure 11 [28–42].

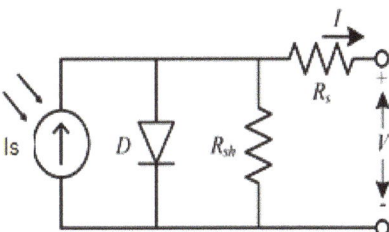

Figure 11. Equivalent circuit of a PV cell (1 diode and 5 parameters model-1M5P).

The model parameters are I_s, I_0, n, R_s, and R_p, and thus the output current can be related to the output voltage based on expression 13 [28–42].

$$I = I_s - I_d - I_{R_p} = I_s - I_d = I_s - I_0 \left(e^{\frac{V}{n v_T}} - 1 \right) - \frac{V + R_s I}{R_p} \quad (13)$$

7. Simulation Results

In this section, a set of simulations are going to be presented. The main software used for this study was COMSOL Multiphysics®. It is generally used for modeling and simulation of real-world multiphysics systems.

First, we begin to module a PIN junction (solar cell). The purpose of the simulation is to study the propagation of light inside the semiconductor device. The incident light, an EM wave with a wavelength of 530 nm in the visible band, hits a silicon PIN junction with dimensions 150 nm, length of the p-junction; 2 um, length of the intrinsic layer; and 80 nm, length of the n-junction. The width is 0.5 um, while the PIN junction depth is 640 nm. These values are representative for a 0.35 um CMOS process.

The geometry consists of two parts: the first part is air (in gray), whose edge on top is used as the source for the EM wave that arrives to the solar cell, and the second part, in blue, is the PIN junction (from top to bottom, n-junction, intrinsic zone, and the p-junction).

The results are obtained through the simulations performed on COMSOL Multiphysics®, which uses the finite element method (FEM). This is a numerical method for solving problems of engineering and mathematical physics. To solve a problem, it subdivides a large system into smaller, simpler parts called finite elements.

In this case, FEM is used to calculate the electric field, so that the program needs to define a mesh to solve the system of equations.

A customized mesh with triangular elements and a maximum element size of 10 nm was defined, as presented on Figure 12. The basic condition is that the mesh size should be lower than wavelength, in order not to have numerical errors in the calculation of the solution.

The parameters used for the mesh on the different simulations are represented on Table 1.

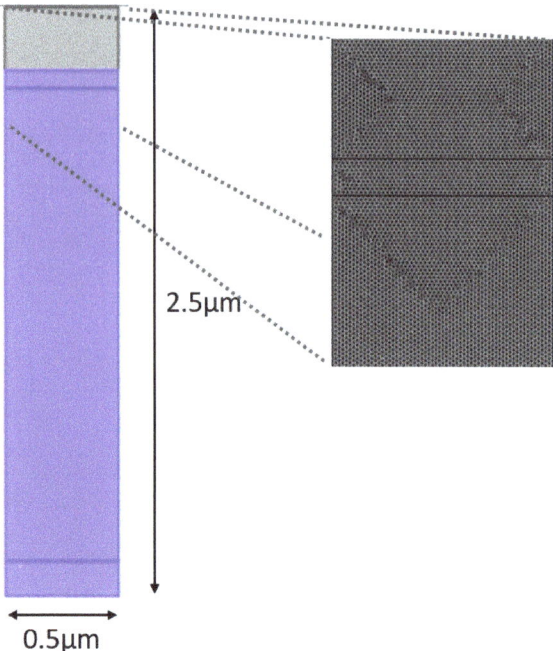

Figure 12. Schematic representation of a PIN junction on COMSOL Multiphysics®, as well as its mesh.

Table 1. Mesh parameters COMSOL Multiphysics®.

Parameter	Value
Maximum element size	1×10^{-8} [m]
Minimum element size	5×10^{-11} [m]
Maximum element growth rate	1.1
Curvature factor	0.2
Resolution of narrow regions	1

The mesh settings determine the resolution of the finite element mesh used to discretize the model. A higher value results in a finer mesh in narrow regions. In this example, because the geometry contains small edges and faces, an extremely fine mesh was designed. This will better resolve the variations of the stress field and give a more accurate result. Refining the mesh size to improve computational accuracy always involves some sacrifice in speed and typically requires increased memory usage [46].

This study is focus on the Transverse Electric (TE) polarization. TE polarized light is characterized by its electric field being perpendicular to the plane of incidence. For TE light, the magnetic field lies in the plane of incidence, thus its always perpendicular to the electric field in isotropic materials. On the other hand, Transverse Magnetic (TM) polarized light is characterized by its magnetic field being perpendicular to the plane of incidence [47].

In this case, the electric field has only one component along the z-direction (horizontal axis).

The PIN junction was tested for different values of λ (light wavelength): 400 nm (blue), 530 nm (green), and 800 nm (IR), as observed on Figure 13.

For a light wavelength of 400 nm, in the blue region, the photons are absorbed mainly in the top of the intrinsic region. The electric field is zero in the bottom part of the intrinsic region.

For a light wavelength of 530 nm, the electric field is stronger in the n-junction and decreases along the intrinsic zone, due to the fact that the photons are absorbed mainly in this area.

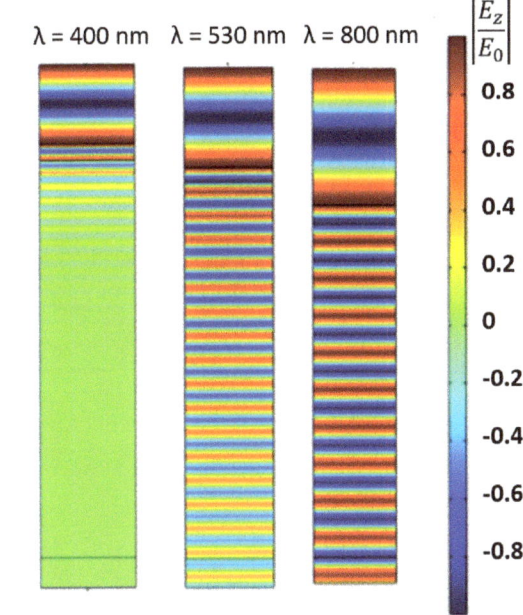

Figure 13. Normalized Electric field, z-component of the cross section of a PIN junction.

For a light wavelength of 800 nm, it is observed that the electric field practically does not decrease along the intrinsic zone. Thus, it is concluded that there is almost no absorption of photons for this wavelength.

When a nanoantenna with an array of air slits or apertures is introduced on top of the silicon PIN junction, the behavior of the electric field changes.

The main purpose of the simulations with a nanoantenna is to observe the difference between a PIN junction without nanoantenna and with a nanoantenna. Furthermore, it is our interest to analyze the evolution of the diffraction pattern as the number of air slits increases, namely, a three-slit, a seven-slit, and a fifteen-slit array, and to compare the simulation results with the results expected by the classical theory [48].

The simulation environment used is similar to that of Figure 12, where an incident light wave hits the PIN junction by propagating through the air slit arrays and absorbed along the intrinsic region.

Various experiments were performed, where the electric field was normalized to E(0), that is, the incident electric field. The incident light wave has an electric field whose amplitude is registered. This amplitude is constant for all the simulated cases and thus it will serve for normalization. It is necessary to have a normalization constant in order to better compare the electric field values for the cases when there is a nanoantenna on top of the PIN junction and when there is no nanoantenna (the structure will be different).

When light hits the surface, the electric field is no longer the incident field. It is the incident field plus the reflected field, and the reflected field varies whether or not there is a nanoantenna.

In these experiments, it was considered that the dimensions of the air slits and their spacing had subwavelength dimensions as well as the metal thickness. Furthermore, for four different values of the light wavelength, four particular cases were considered: (i) nanoantenna metal thickness, $\lambda/10$ and air slit width, $\lambda/10$; (ii) nanoantenna metal thickness, $\lambda/100$ and air slit width, $\lambda/2$; (iii) nanoantenna metal thickness, $\lambda/100$ and air slit width, $\lambda/5$; and (iv) nanoantenna metal thickness, $\lambda/100$ and air slit width, $\lambda/10$.

For each case, on top of the PIN junction a three-slit, a seven-slit, and a fifteen-slit array were tested. The procedures required to study and simulate a fifteen-slit array are identical to those used to simulate a three-slit or a seven-slit array. The parameters are the same, differing only in the number of slits. The maximum absolute values of the normalized electric field along the intrinsic region for an aluminum nanoantenna were registered on Table 2.

Table 2. Maximum absolute values of the normalized electric field along the intrinsic region.

Light Wavelength [nm]	Metal Thickness	Air Slit Width	3 Slits	7 Slits	15 Slits
400	$\lambda/10$	$\lambda/10$	0.087	0.069	0.860
400	$\lambda/100$	$\lambda/5$	0.536	0.369	0.577
400	$\lambda/100$	$\lambda/10$	0.335	0.356	0.517
530	$\lambda/10$	$\lambda/10$	0.190	0.181	0.122
530	$\lambda/100$	$\lambda/5$	1.019	1.018	1.040
530	$\lambda/100$	$\lambda/10$	0.956	0.893	0.908
800	$\lambda/10$	$\lambda/10$	0.188	0.098	0.140
800	$\lambda/10$	$\lambda/2$	1.787	2.575	2.633
800	$\lambda/100$	$\lambda/5$	1.704	2.547	1.612
800	$\lambda/100$	$\lambda/10$	1.605	1.010	1.027
1550	$\lambda/10$	$\lambda/10$	0.177	0.063	0.272
1550	$\lambda/10$	$\lambda/2$	10.053	8.071	5.806
1550	$\lambda/100$	$\lambda/5$	11.467	4.508	4.724
1550	$\lambda/100$	$\lambda/10$	2.304	1.369	1.083

When the total electric field is normalized by the incident field, it is possible to immediately check whether the radiation through the intrinsic region is higher or lower than the incident radiation. In other words, if any numerical value obtained by the different simulations is greater than 1, it means that the structure itself has the capacity to transmit more light than its incidence, which indicates the occurrence of the Extraordinary Optical Transmission phenomenon. The results highlighted in green indicate the occurrence of the EOT phenomenon.

The metal thickness $\lambda/100$ proved to be more efficient and thus more simulations were performed with this size. This metal thickness was the most efficient as it can be in part attributed to the fact that aluminum, for very small film thicknesses, has a very large transmission coefficient and a low reflection coefficient. Meanwhile, for a metal thickness of $\lambda/10$ there was no occurrence of the EOT phenomenon. Contrary to what happens in the previous case, in this case practically everything is reflected and little transmitted.

The results obtained from the simulations indicate that (i) if the nanoantenna metal thickness is much smaller in relation to the wavelength, the stronger will be the electric field intensity in the intrinsic region, and (ii) the smaller the air slit width in relation to the wavelength, the smaller the intensity of the electric field in the intrinsic region, as expected given the classical theories of diffraction.

These results are confirmed by the classical theory as EOT is observed mainly due to the constructive interference of SPPs propagating between the slits of the nanoantenna, where they can be coupled from/into radiation.

The shape, dimensions, and the spacing between apertures are fundamental parameters that must be carefully sized to allow the propagation of SPPs and the occurrence of the EOT phenomenon. With the aid of MATLAB software, a 1D plot was made to compare the values of the normalized electric field along the intrinsic zone for the light wavelength of 400 nm with an aluminum nanoantenna and without nanoantennas.

It is observed in all cases that the electric field is stronger in the n-junction and then rapidly reaches the zero value in the middle of the intrinsic zone.

By analyzing Figure 14, it is observable that the normalized electric field is stronger without nanoantennas. For this light wavelength, the results for other parameters of metal thickness and air slit width in Table 2 are quite identical, and thus for a light wavelength of 400 nm, the introduction of nanoantennas for solar harvesting does not contribute for a bigger efficiency of the solar cell.

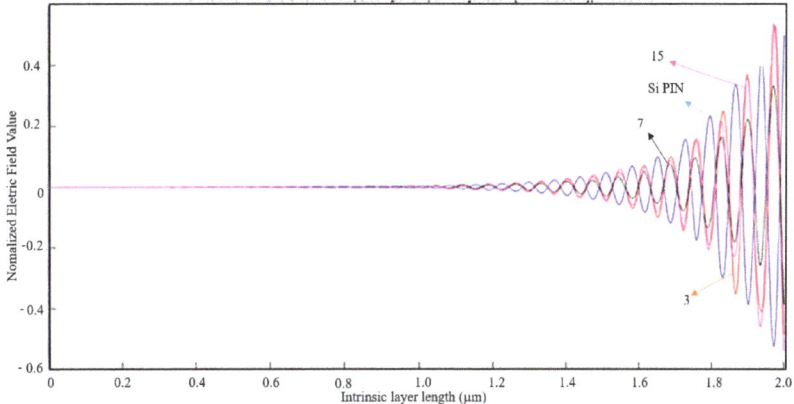

Figure 14. 1D Plot of the normalized electric field, z-component, along the intrinsic zone for a light wavelength of 400 nm: Si PIN junction (blue); 3-slit array Al nanoantenna (red); 7-slit array Al nanoantenna (black); and 15-slit array Al nanoantenna (magenta).

Given a light wavelength of 530 nm, according to Table 2 for a metal thickness of $\lambda/100$ and an air slit width of $\lambda/5$ the EOT phenomenon barely occurs. Like in the previous case, a 1D plot was made on MATLAB and it is presented on Figure 15.

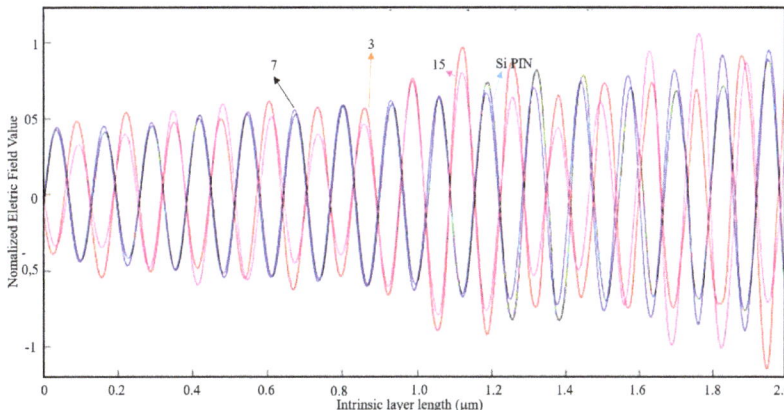

Figure 15. 1D Plot of the normalized electric field, z-component, along the intrinsic zone for a light wavelength of 530 nm: Si PIN junction (blue); 3-slit array Al nanoantenna (red); 7-slit array Al nanoantenna (black); and 15-slit array Al nanoantenna (magenta).

It is observable on Figure 15 that the results obtained for the normalized electric field with and without an aluminum nanoantenna are very similar. Therefore, one can conclude that for 530 nm of light wavelength the introduction of nanoantennas for solar harvesting barely contributes for a bigger efficiency of the solar cell.

For a light wavelength of 800 nm, the EOT phenomenon does not occur if the metal thickness is $\lambda/10$. For a metal thickness of $\lambda/100$, the EOT phenomenon occurs for every case and thus it is concluded that the nanoantennas are indeed efficient for this wavelength where $\lambda/100$ is the optimum thickness (see Table 2).

Below in Figures 16–18, the cases where the EOT phenomenon occurs are represented.

By analyzing Figure 16, although the 15-slit array nanoantenna has recorded the maximum absolute value of the normalized electric field, the seven-slit array is the most efficient nanoantenna type, as the normalized electric field is higher along the entire intrinsic zone.

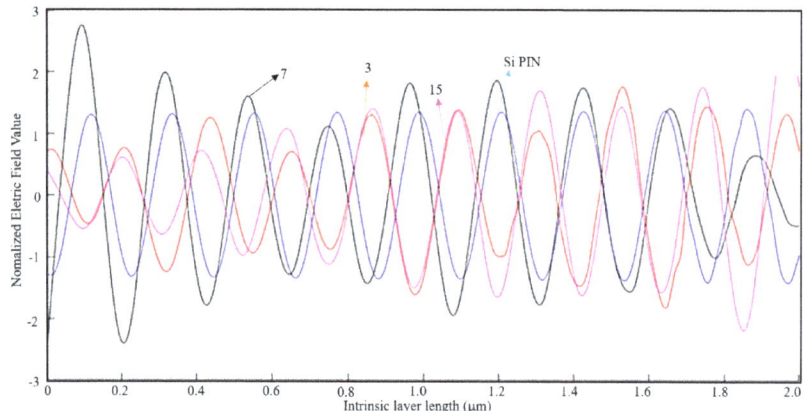

Figure 16. 1D Plot of the normalized electric field, z-component, along the intrinsic zone for a light wavelength of 800 nm (metal thickness: $\lambda/100$; air slit width: $\lambda/2$).

By analyzing Figure 17, one can conclude that a seven-slit array is the most efficient along the intrinsic zone, and from Figure 18, it is concluded that it is the three-slit array.

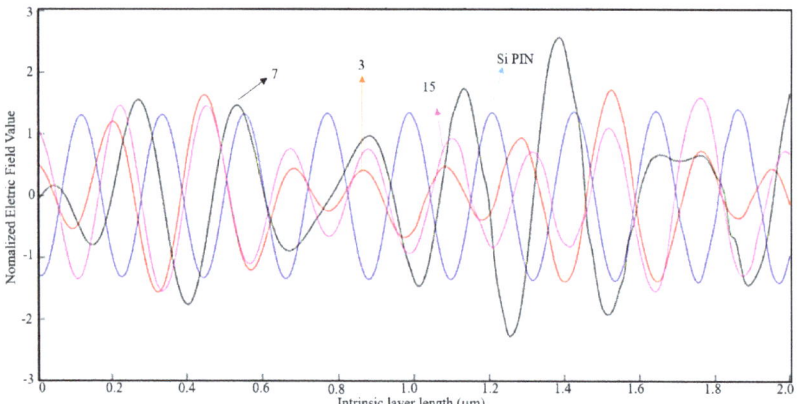

Figure 17. 1D Plot of the normalized electric field, z-component, along the intrinsic zone for a light wavelength of 800 nm (metal thickness: $\lambda/100$; air slit width: $\lambda/5$).

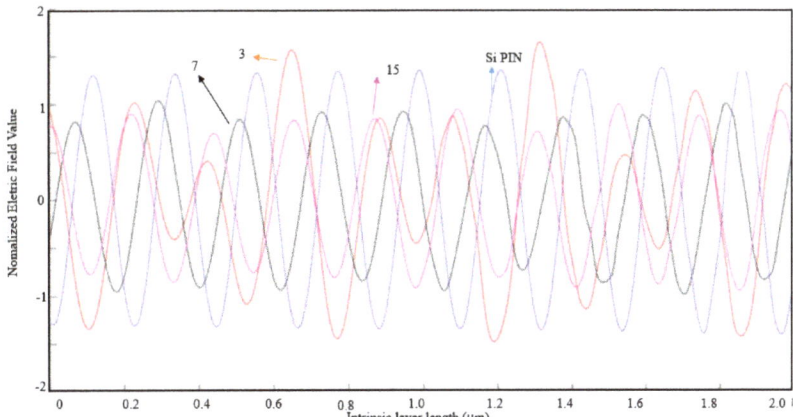

Figure 18. 1D Plot of the normalized electric field, z-component, along the intrinsic zone for a light wavelength of 800 nm (metal thickness: $\lambda/100$; air slit width: $\lambda/10$).

Even though there is the occurrence of EOT, the nanoantennas are less efficient for this air slit width and thus there is no visible advantage on their implementation.

The procedures that are necessary to carry out the study and simulation of an array of slits with different material types are identical to those used previously. The metals that will be considered in the following simulations using the COMSOL Multiphysics® software are Gold (Au) and Platinum (Pt).

In Tables 3 and 4 are registered the maximum absolute values of the normalized electric field along the intrinsic region for a nanoantenna of gold and for another of platinum, respectively, on top of a silicon PIN junction.

Table 3. Maximum absolute values of the normalized electric field along the intrinsic region for a gold nanoantenna.

Light Wavelength [nm]	Metal Thickness	Air Slit Width	3 Slits	7 Slits	15 Slits
400	$\lambda/10$	$\lambda/10$	0.228	0.340	0.171
400	$\lambda/100$	$\lambda/5$	0.539	0.541	0.483
400	$\lambda/100$	$\lambda/10$	0.571	0.570	0.522
530	$\lambda/10$	$\lambda/10$	0.657	0.913	0.302
530	$\lambda/100$	$\lambda/5$	1.078	0.955	0.902
530	$\lambda/100$	$\lambda/10$	0.932	0.928	0.900
800	$\lambda/10$	$\lambda/10$	0.755	0.235	0.318
800	$\lambda/100$	$\lambda/5$	1.392	1.413	1.612
800	$\lambda/100$	$\lambda/10$	1.083	1.058	1.280
1550	$\lambda/10$	$\lambda/10$	0.045	0.076	0.207
1550	$\lambda/100$	$\lambda/5$	3.441	4.489	2.810
1550	$\lambda/100$	$\lambda/10$	1.503	1.407	2.525

Table 4. Maximum absolute values of the normalized electric field along the intrinsic region for a platinum nanoantenna.

Light Wavelength [nm]	Metal Thickness	Air Slit Width	3 Slits	7 Slits	15 Slits
400	$\lambda/10$	$\lambda/10$	0.130	0.223	0.152
400	$\lambda/100$	$\lambda/5$	0.584	0.578	0.569
400	$\lambda/100$	$\lambda/10$	0.572	0.578	0.969
530	$\lambda/10$	$\lambda/10$	0.210	0.411	0.197
530	$\lambda/100$	$\lambda/5$	1.013	1.002	0.994
530	$\lambda/100$	$\lambda/10$	1.215	0.957	0.968
800	$\lambda/10$	$\lambda/10$	0.191	0.139	0.145
800	$\lambda/100$	$\lambda/5$	1.588	1.591	1.243
800	$\lambda/100$	$\lambda/10$	1.261	1.048	1.105
1550	$\lambda/10$	$\lambda/10$	0.053	0.011	0.031
1550	$\lambda/100$	$\lambda/5$	1.633	1.726	2.333
1550	$\lambda/100$	$\lambda/10$	1.317	1.253	1.234

From the observation of both tables above, and comparing the results with an aluminum nanoantenna in Table 2, one can verify that the EOT phenomenon is present in all material types. In addition, it is possible to observe that the EOT phenomenon is stronger with an aluminum nanoantenna, as maximum absolute values of the normalized electric field along the intrinsic region of 10 × the incident field were registered for a three-slit array.

For a gold or a platinum nanoantenna, the results obtained show that the EOT phenomenon is mostly present for the light wavelengths of 800 nm and 1550 nm. These results show clear evidence of the EOT phenomenon and constitute an interesting result for the implementation of an aperture nanoantenna, as the electric field in the near-field region is strongly enhanced.

In Figure 19, the case where the maximum absolute value of the normalized electric field along the intrinsic region for an aluminum nanoantenna on top of a Si PIN junction had the highest value, as compared with the other nanoantenna material types. From the observation of Figure 19, it is clearly visible the difference of the normalized electric field along the intrinsic zone for the aluminum nanoantenna and the other material types.

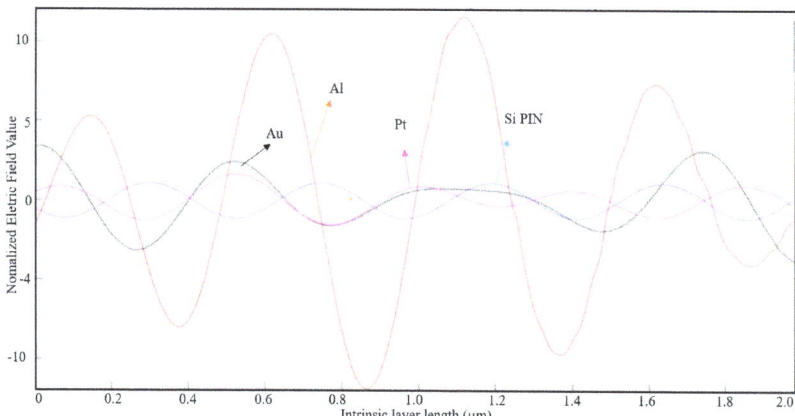

Figure 19. 1D Plot of the normalized electric field, z-component, along the intrinsic zone for different nanoantenna material types: Si PIN junction (blue), Al nanoantenna (red), Au nanoantenna (black), and Pt nanoantenna (magenta) (3-slit array; light wavelength: 1550 nm; metal thickness: $\lambda/100$; and air slit width: $\lambda/5$).

For the same parameters, in Figures 20 and 21 are represented the simulation results for a seven-slit array and a fifteen-slit array nanoantenna, respectively, for the three materials types and the Si PIN junction.

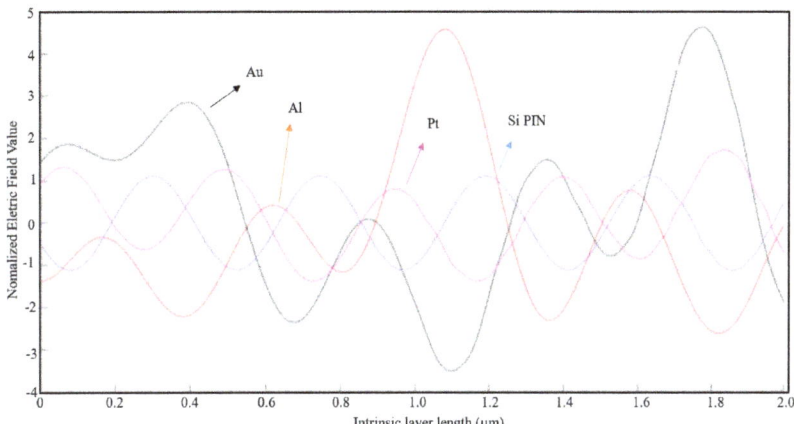

Figure 20. 1D Plot of the normalized electric field, z-component, along the intrinsic zone for different nanoantenna material types: Si PIN junction (blue), Al nanoantenna (red), Au nanoantenna (black), and Pt nanoantenna (magenta) (7-slit array; light wavelength: 1550 nm; metal thickness: $\lambda/100$; air slit width: $\lambda/5$).

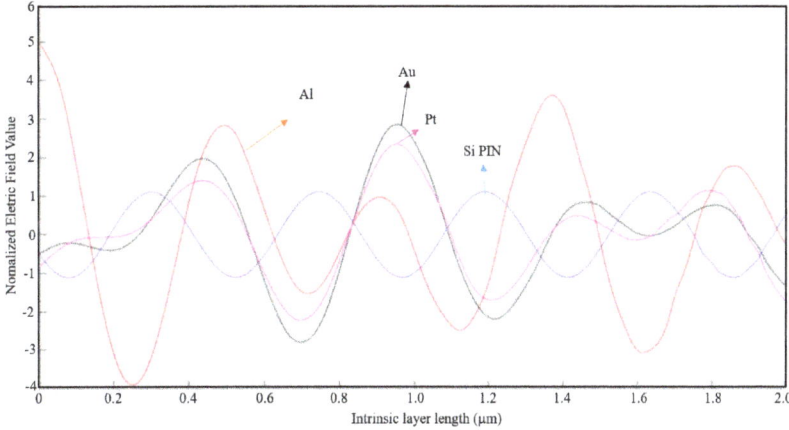

Figure 21. 1D Plot of the normalized electric field, z-component, along the intrinsic zone for different nanoantenna material types: Si PIN junction (blue), Al nanoantenna (red), Au nanoantenna (black), and Pt nanoantenna (magenta) (15-slit array; light wavelength: 1550 nm; metal thickness: $\lambda/100$; air slit width: $\lambda/5$).

By analyzing these figures, it is verified that the aluminum and the gold nanoantenna have by far a stronger normalized electric field along the entire intrinsic region compared to the platinum nanoantenna and the case without any nanoantennas. Comparing the three cases above, one can conclude that aluminum is the most appropriate material for the application of an optical antenna.

8. Study of the Short-Circuit Current and the Open-Circuit Voltage on the Solar Cell

As previously referred, a solar cell can be modeled using the single diode and 3 parameters model, that includes the I–V and the P–V characteristics of a typical module.

The problem of modeling a PV system is further compounded by the fact that the I–V curve of a PV module is dependent on the irradiance and temperature, which are continuously changing. Consequently, the parameters required to model a PV module must be adjusted according to the ambient temperature and irradiance [43]. Two main parameters that are used to characterize the performance of a solar cell are the short-circuit current, I_{sc}, and the open-circuit voltage, V_{oc}.

In order to prove that the model used during the simulations on COMSOL Multiphysics® is indeed a solar cell, the short-circuit current and the open-circuit voltage were measured upon variation of the irradiance and temperature. As the software does not simulate directly the short-circuit current in the cell, a simulation of the current density norm, J_{sc}, was made. In this simulation, the solar cell was short-circuited as depicted in Figure 22.

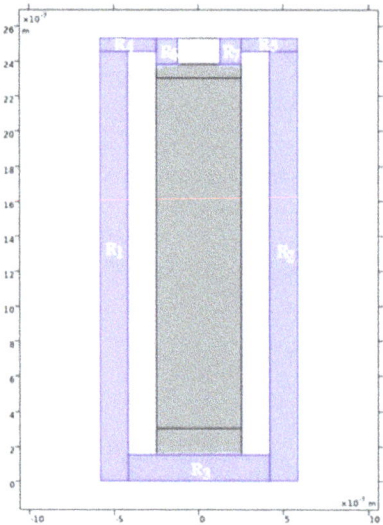

Figure 22. Short-circuited solar cell model (gray: Si PIN junction; dark blue: aluminum; light blue: Air).

According to Ibrahim, the complete equation for the short-circuit current, taking into account that it varies with the irradiance and the temperature on the solar cell, is described by expression 14, where α_{STC} is the thermal coefficient of the short-circuit current, measuring the variation of I_{sc} with an increase of 1 °C of temperature T [49].

$$I_{sc}(G,T) = \frac{G}{G_{STC}}[I_{sc_{STC}} + \alpha_{sc}(T - T_{STC})] \tag{14}$$

Although COMSOL can simulate the variation in the temperature, during the simulations the temperature T on the PV cell is considered to be constant and equal to STC. Considering that the software does not simulate directly the short-circuit current in the cell, but the current density norm, given by expression 15.

$$J_{sc} = \frac{G}{G_{STC}} J_{sc_{STC}} \tag{15}$$

Table 5 contains the average values of the current density norm with the input irradiance.

Table 5. Values of the current density norm with the input irradiance.

Irradiance [W m^{-2}]	$J_{sc_{min}}$ [×10^6 A m^{-1}]	$J_{sc_{max}}$ [×10^6 A m^{-1}]	$J_{sc_{avg}}$ [×10^6 A m^{-1}]
400	0.88	10.05	5.47
500	0.92	11.25	6.09
600	1.00	12.33	6.67
700	1.10	13.30	7.20
800	1.20	14.20	7.70
900	1.25	15.10	8.18
1000	1.29	15.97	8.63
1100	1.35	16.78	9.07
1200	1.40	17.60	9.50
1300	1.48	18.33	9.91
1400	1.60	18.96	10.28

From Figure 23, the current density norm varies almost linearly with the input irradiance for this range of values on the PV cell. The slight nonlinearity can be attributed to the resistance of the material (in this case, aluminum). The resistance of any material is a function of the material's resistivity, ρ, and the material's dimensions, and it is given by expression 16, where L, t, and W are the length, the thickness, and the width of the material, respectively [43].

$$R = \frac{\rho L}{t W} \quad (16)$$

As presented on Figure 22, there are 7 blocks or sections of aluminum surrounding the solar cell (in order to perform a short-circuit of the PV cell). Based on expression 16, it is possible to determine the value of that blocks resistance, which is presented on Table 6, for a $\rho(T = 25\,°C) = 2.70 \times 10^{-8}\,\Omega\,m$ and $t = 640$ nm.

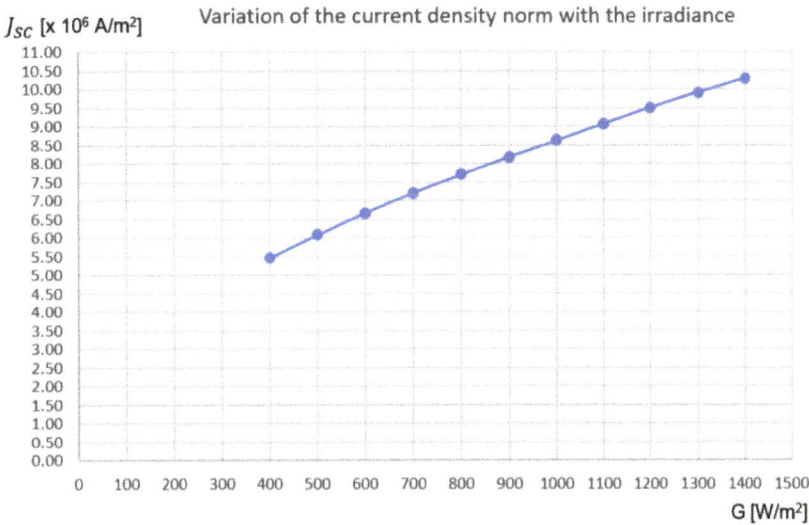

Figure 23. 1D Plot of the variation of J_{sc} with the irradiance (x-axis: Irradiance [W/m2]; y-axis: Average value of the current density norm, $J_{sc_{avg}}$ [×10^6 A m^{-1}].

Table 6. Aluminum sections dimensions and resistance value.

Section	Length, L [m]	Width, W [m]	Resistance, R [mΩ]
R_1	2.455×10^{-6}	1.666×10^{-7}	621.447
R_2	2.455×10^{-6}	1.666×10^{-7}	621.447
R_3	150×10^{-9}	8.335×10^{-7}	7.692
R_4	0.075×10^{-6}	3.336×10^{-7}	9.485
R_5	0.075×10^{-6}	3.336×10^{-7}	9.485
R_6	150×10^{-9}	1.250×10^{-7}	50.625
R_6	150×10^{-9}	1.250×10^{-7}	50.625

By analyzing the values of the resistance for each block of aluminum, one can conclude that the resistance is an important factor to consider. All the values obtained for the resistance of each block are in agreement with the 0.35 um CMOS process. Therefore, the nonlinearity of the current density norm with the input irradiance is explained.

Similar to the procedure to the I_{sc}, it is possible to verify how V_{oc} varies with the irradiance, as verified on Table 7.

Table 7. Values of the open-circuit voltage with the input irradiance.

Irradiance [W m^{-2}]	V_{bot} [V]	V_{bot} [V]	V_{oc} [V]
100	−4.5189	−5.3311	0.8121
200	−4.5189	−5.3311	0.8121
400	−4.5189	−5.3311	0.8121
800	−4.5189	−5.3311	0.8121
1000	−4.5189	−5.3311	0.8121
1200	−4.5189	−5.3311	0.8121

The open-circuit voltage has a steady value equal to 0.8121 V, for different values of the irradiance, G, leading to the conclusion that it is not dependent on the irradiance. This value is the maximum voltage the solar cell on this model can deliver.

The open-circuit voltage varies with the irradiance by expression 17, leading to the conclusion that this variations is not very significant, because it follows a logarithmic function, where N_s is the number of series-connected cells in a PV module (if it is a single PV cell, this value is equal to 1) and α_{oc} is the thermal coefficient of the open-circuit voltage.

$$V_{oc}(G, T) = V_{oc_{STC}} + \frac{N_s k T}{q} ln(G) + \alpha_{oc}(T - T_{STC}) \qquad (17)$$

To conclude, the short-circuit current, I_{sc}, varies nonlinearly with irradiance and its variation with temperature is fairly small depending on its temperature coefficient. When determining the dependence of the open-circuit voltage, V_{oc}, on temperature and irradiance, it is found that it is strongly dependent only on the temperature. It has been observed that the results obtained in this study are is accordance with what is expected by the classical theory of a photovoltaic cell and so the model that was tested on COMSOL software is valid.

9. Conclusions

The main objective of this article is the study and simulation of the behavior of an optical antenna with subwavelength dimensions for solar harvesting on PV panels. To perform such study, the COMSOL Multiphysics® software was used, to obtain the simulation numerical results of the studied structures.

It has been demonstrated with several simulations in different conditions that the EOT phenomenon was always confirmed on nanoantennas with three materials: aluminum (Al), gold (Au), and platinum (Pt). Thus, it means that these structures have the capacity to transmit more light than its incidence, in orders of magnitude greater than predicted by standard aperture theory. These experiments provide evidence that these unusual optical properties are due to the coupling of light with SPPs on the surface of the metallic nanoantennas.

Additionally, it has been verified with the simulation results that optimum results were obtained for light wavelengths of 800 nm and 1550 nm. These results constitute an interesting result for the implementation of an aperture nanoantenna, as they cover a wide range of the spectrum: the EOT phenomenon was verified on almost the entire visible region as well as the IR region. Typical silicon solar cells have proven to be inefficient at these wavelengths.

Although most of the researchers use gold or silver to fabricate the optical antennas, the results obtained in this article show that aluminum can have even better results than the other material types, mainly due to its transmission and reflection coefficients. Furthermore, among all metals analyzed, aluminum has the smallest skin depth in the visible spectrum, as well as being cheaper than gold or platinum. However, aluminum is unstable. It oxidizes quickly, and the optical properties are lost. Therefore, aluminum has to be coated with an antioxidant compound.

Author Contributions: F.D. was responsible to write the original draft, J.P.N.T. and A.B. are his supervisors, J.P.N.T. and R.A.M.L. analyzed the results and they were responsible to review and editing the final manuscript. All authors have read and agreed to the published version of the manuscript.

Funding: This research received no external funding.

Institutional Review Board Statement: Not applicable.

Informed Consent Statement: Not applicable.

Data Availability Statement: Not applicable.

Acknowledgments: This work was supported in part by FCT/MCTES through national funds and in part by cofounded EU funds under Project UIDB50008/2020.

Conflicts of Interest: The authors declare no conflicts of interest.

References

1. Ebbesen, T.W.; Lezec, H.J.; Ghaemi, H.F.; Thio, T.; Wolff, P.A. Extraordinary optical transmission through sub–wavelength hole arrays. *Nature* **1998**, *86*, 1114–1117. [CrossRef]
2. Agio, M. *Optical Antennas*; Cambridge University Press: Cambridge, UK, 2013.
3. Kotter, D.K.; Novack, S.D.; Slafer, W.D.; Pinhero, P.J. Theory and Manufacturing Processes of Solar Nanoantenna Electromagnetic Collectors. *J. Solar Energy Eng.* **2010**, *132*, 1. [CrossRef]
4. Ameziane, M. *Solar Nanoantenna Electromagnetic Collectors for Energy Production*; Tampere University of Applied Sciences: Tampere, The Netherland, 2015.
5. Yan, S.; Tumendemberel, B.; Zheng, X.; Volskiy, V.; Vandenbosch, G.A.; Moshchalkov, V.V. Optimizing the bowtie nano–rectenna topology for solar energy harvesting applications. *Solar Energy* **2017**, *157*, 259–262. [CrossRef]
6. Moddel, G.; Sachit, G. Metal Single–Insulator and MultiInsulator Diodes for Rectenna Solar Cells. In *Rectenna Solar Cells*; Springer: New York, NY, USA, 2013; pp. 89–109.
7. Krasnok, A.E.; Maksymov, I.S.; Denisyuk, A.I.; Belov, P.A.; Miroshnichenko, A.E.; Simovski, C.R.; Kivshar, Y.S. Optical Nanoantennas. *Phys. Uspekhi* **2013**, *56*, 539. [CrossRef]
8. Taminiau, T.H.; Segerink, F.B.; Van Hulst, N.F. A Monopole Antenna at Optical Frequencies: Single–Molecule Near–Field Measurements. *IEEE Trans. Antennas Propag.* **2007**, *55*, 11. [CrossRef]
9. Maksymov, I.S. Magneto–plasmonic nanoantennas: Basics and applications. *Rev. Phys.* **2016**, *1*, 36–51. [CrossRef]
10. Gallo, M.; Mescia, L.; Losito, O.; Bozzetti, M.; Prudenzano, F. Design of optical antenna for solar energy collection. *Energy* **2012**, *39*, 27–32. [CrossRef]
11. Krasnok, A.E.; Miroshnichenko, A.E.; Belov, P.A.; Kivshar, Y.S. All–dielectric optical nanoantennas. *Opt. Express* **2012**, *20*, 18. [CrossRef] [PubMed]
12. Wenger, J. *Aperture Optical Antennas*; École Centrale de Marseille: Marseille, France, 2013.
13. Rivera, V.; Ferri, F.; Silva, O.; Sobreira, F.; Marega, E., Jr. *Light Transmission via Subwavelength Apertures in Metallic Thin Films*; Intech: London, UK, 2012; pp. 157–182.
14. Kim, K.Y. *Plasmonics–Principles and Applications*; BoD–Books on Demand: Norderstedt, Germany, 2012.
15. Torres, J.P.N.; Machado, V.; Baptista, A. A New Hybrid Finite Element Method: Electromagnetic Propagation in Bent Waveguides. *IEEE Photonics J.* **2020**, *12*, 2966256. [CrossRef]

16. Torres, J.; Baptista, A.; Maló Machado, V. Coupling analysis in concentric ring waveguides. *J. Lightwave Technol.* **2013**, *31*, 2140–2145. [CrossRef]
17. Lameirinhas, R.A.M.; Torres, J.P.N.; Baptista, A. The Influence of Structure Parameters on Nanoantennas' Optical Response. *Chemosensors* **2020**, *8*, 42. [CrossRef]
18. Lameirinhas, R.A.M.; Torres, J.P.N.; Baptista, A. Sensors Based on Nanoantennas: Fundamentals. *Eur. J. Appl. Phys.* **2020**, *2*, 3. [CrossRef]
19. Lameirinhas, R.A.M.; Torres, J.P.N.; Baptista, A. A Sensor Based on Nanoantennas. *Appl. Sci.* **2020**, *10*, 6837. [CrossRef]
20. Novotny, L.; Van Hulst, N. Antennas for light. *Nat. Photonics* **2011**, *5*, 83–90. [CrossRef]
21. Kalkbrenner, T.; Håkanson, U.; Schädle, A.; Burger, S.; Henkel, C.; Sandoghdar, V. Optical microscopy via spectral modifications of a nanoantenna. *Phys. Rev. Lett.* **2005**, *95*, 200801. [CrossRef] [PubMed]
22. Gomes, R.D.F.R.; Martins, M.J.; Baptista, A.; Torres, J.P.N. Study of a nano optical antenna for intersatellite communications. *Opt. Quantum Electron.* **2017**, *49*, 135. [CrossRef]
23. Park, Q.H. Optical antennas and plasmonics. *Dep. Phys.* Korea University, Seoul, **2009**, *50*, 407–423. [CrossRef]
24. Opto–Mechanical Devices for Measuring Nanoplasmonic Metamaterials. Available online: https://www.nist.gov/pml/microsystems--and--nanotechnology--division/photonics--and--plasmonics--group/opto--mechanical--devices (accessed on 4 February 2019).
25. Novack, S.; Kotter, D.K.; Slafer, W.D.; Pinhero, P. Solar nanoantenna electromagnetic collectors. In Proceedings of the 2nd International Conference on Energy Sustainability, Jacksonville, FL, USA, 10–14 August 2008.
26. Sarehraz, M.; Buckle, K.; Weller, T.; Stefanakos, E.; Bhansali, S.; Goswami, Y.; Krishnan, S. Rectenna developments for solar energy collection. In Proceedings of the Conference Record of the Thirty-first IEEE Photovoltaic Specialists Conference, Lake Buena Vista, FL, USA, 3–7 January 2005.
27. Solar Cell Structure. Available online: https://www.pveducation.org/pvcdrom/solar--cell--operation/solar--cell--structure (accessed on 20 May 2019).
28. Durão, B.; Torres, J.P.N.; Fernandes, C.A.F.; Lameirinhas, R.A.M. Socio-economic Study to Improve the Electrical Sustainability of the North Tower of Instituto Superior Técnico. *Sustainability* **2020**, *12*, 1923. [CrossRef]
29. Melo, I.; Torres, J.P.N.; Fernandes, C.A.F.; Lameirinhas, R.A.M. Sustainability economic study of the islands of the Azores archipelago using photovoltaic panels, wind energy and storage system. *Renewables* **2020**, *7*, 4. [CrossRef]
30. Alves, P.; Fernandes, J.; Torres, J.; Branco, P.; Fernandes, C.; Gomes, J. Energy Efficiency of a PV/T Collector for Domestic Water Heating Installed in Sweden or in Portugal. The Impact of Heat Pipe Cross–Section Geometry and Water Flowing Speed. In Proceedings of the Sdewes 2017 (Sustainable Development of Energy, Water And Environment System), Dubrovnik, Croatia, 4–8 October 2017.
31. Gomes, J.; Luc, B.; Carine, G.; Fernandes, C.A.; Torres, J.P.N.; Olsson, O.; Branco, P.C.; Nashih, S.K. Analysis of different C–PVT reflector geometries. In Proceedings of the 2016 IEEE International Power Electronics and Motion Control Conference (PEMC), Varna, Bulgaria, 25–28 September 2019.
32. Mota, F.; Torres, J.P.N.; Fernandes, C.A.F.; Lameirinhas, R.A.M. Influence of an aluminium concentrator corrosion on the output characteristic of a photovoltaic system. *Sci. Rep.* **2020**, *10*, 21865. [CrossRef]
33. Marques, L.; Torres, J.; Branco, P. Triangular shape geometry in a Solarus AB concentrating photovoltaic–thermal collector. *Int. J. Interact. Des. Manuf. (IJIDeM)* **2018**, *12*, 1455–1468. [CrossRef]
34. Torres, J.P.N.; Fernandes, C.A.; Gomes, J.; Luc, B.; Carine, G.; Olsson, O.; Branco, P.J. Effect of reflector geometry in the annual received radiation of low concentration photovoltaic systems. *Energies* **2018**, *11*, 1878. [CrossRef]
35. Fernandes, C.A.; Torres, J.P.N.; Morgado, M.; Morgado, J.A. Aging of solar PV plants and mitigation of their consequences. In Proceedings of the 2016 IEEE International Power Electronics and Motion Control Conference (PEMC), Varna, Bulgaria, 25–28 September 2016.
36. Torres, J.P.N.; Nashih, S.K.; Fernandes, C.A.; Leite, J.C. The effect of shading on photovoltaic solar panels. *Energy Syst.* **2018**, *9*, 195–208. [CrossRef]
37. Fernandes, C.A.; Torres, J.P.N.; Branco, P.C.; Fernandes, J.; Gomes, J. Cell string layout in solar photovoltaic collectors. *Energy Convers. Manag.* **2017**, *149*, 997–1009. [CrossRef]
38. Fernandes, C.A.; Torres, J.P.N.; Gomes, J.; Branco, P.C.; Nashih, S.K. Stationary solar concentrating photovoltaic–thermal collector—Cell string layout. In Proceedings of the 2016 IEEE International Power Electronics and Motion Control Conference (PEMC), Varna, Bulgaria, 25–28 September 2016.
39. Campos, C.; Torres, J.; Fernandes, J. Effects of the heat transfer fluid selection on the efficiency of a hybrid concentrated photovoltaic and thermal collector. *Energies* **2019**, *12*, 1814. [CrossRef]
40. Torres, J.P.N.; Fernandes, J.F.; Fernandes, C.; Costa, B.P.J.; Barata, C.; Gomes, J. Effect of the collector geometry in the concentrating photovoltaic thermal solar cell performance. *Therm. Sci.* **2018**, *22*, 2243–2256. [CrossRef]
41. Torres, J.; Seram, V.; Fernandes, C. Influence of the Solarus AB reflector geometry and position of receiver on the output of the concentrating photovoltaic thermal collector. *Int. J. Interact. Des. Manuf. (IJIDeM)* **2019**, *14*, 153–172. [CrossRef]
42. Alves, P.; Fernandes, J.F.; Torres, J.P.N.; Branco, P.C.; Fernandes, C.; Gomes, J. From Sweden to Portugal: The effect of very distinct climate zones on energy efficiency of a concentrating photovoltaic/thermal system (CPV/T). *Solar Energy* **2019**, *188*, 96–110. [CrossRef]

43. The Working Principle of a Solar Cell. Available online: https://ocw.tudelft.nl/wpcontent/uploads/solar_energy_section_3.pdf (accessed on 20 May 2019).
44. Shakya, S.R. *Training Manual for Engineers on Solar PV System*; Technical Report of Alternative Energy Promotion Centre (Aepc) & Energy Sector Assistance Programme (Esap); Alternative Energy Promotion Centre/Energy Sector Assistance Programme: Kathmandu, Nepal, 2011.
45. IV Curve. Available online: https://www.pveducation.org/pvcdrom/solar-cell-operation/iv-curve (accessed on 22 May 2019).
46. Comsol, A.B. *Multiphysics, COMSOL, Comsol Multiphysics Reference Manual*; COMSOL: Grenoble, France, 2013; p. 1084.
47. Polarization Definitions. Available online: https://ibsen.com/technology-2/polarization-definitions (accessed on 17 June 2019).
48. Brown, W.C. The history of power transmission by radio waves. *IEEE Trans. Microw. Theory Tech.* **1984**, *32*, 1230–1242. [CrossRef]
49. Ibrahim, H.; Anani, N. Variations of PV module parameters with irradiance and temperature. *Energy Procedia* **2017**, *134*, 276–285. [CrossRef]

Review

A Brief Review of the Role of 2D Mxene Nanosheets toward Solar Cells Efficiency Improvement

T. F. Alhamada [1,2], M. A. Azmah Hanim [2,3,*], D. W. Jung [4,*], A. A. Nuraini [2] and W. Z. Wan Hasan [5]

[1] Northern Technical University, Mosul 41001, Iraq; thaerfaez@ntu.edu.iq
[2] Department of Mechanical and Manufacturing Engineering, Faculty of Engineering, Universiti Putra Malaysia, Serdang 43400, Selangor, Malaysia; nuraini@upm.edu.my
[3] Advanced Engineering Materials and Composites Research Center (AEMC), Faculty of Engineering, Universiti Putra Malaysia, Serdang 43400, Selangor, Malaysia
[4] Department of Mechanical Engineering, Jeju National University, 1 Ara 1-dong, Jeju 690-756, Korea
[5] Department of Electrical and Electronic Engineering, Faculty of Engineering, Universiti Putra Malaysia, Serdang 43400, Selangor, Malaysia; wanzuha@upm.edu.my
* Correspondence: azmah@upm.edu.my (M.A.A.H.); jungdw77@naver.com (D.W.J.)

Abstract: This article discusses the application of two-dimensional metal MXenes in solar cells (SCs), which has attracted a lot of interest due to their outstanding transparency, metallic electrical conductivity, and mechanical characteristics. In addition, some application examples of MXenes as an electrode, additive, and electron/hole transport layer in perovskite solar cells are described individually, with essential research issues highlighted. Firstly, it is imperative to comprehend the conversion efficiency of solar cells and the difficulties of effectively incorporating metal MXenes into the building blocks of solar cells to improve stability and operational performance. Based on the analysis of new articles, several ideas have been generated to advance the exploration of the potential of MXene in SCs. In addition, research into other relevant MXene suitable in perovskite solar cells (PSCs) is required to enhance the relevant work. Therefore, we identify new perspectives to achieve solar cell power conversion efficiency with an excellent quality–cost ratio.

Keywords: power conversion efficiency; solar cells; MXenes; electrodes; additives; HTL/ETL

1. Introduction

The development of innovative materials for efficient solar cells has garnered a lot of attention [1–10] because of the ever-increasing need for renewable and clean energy supplies [11–15]. Sunlight has been identified as the most prevalent, cheapest, and cleanest source of energy for meeting society's long-term energy requirements. Solar cells convert sunlight directly into electricity—the most efficient and practical method to utilise solar energy. Earth-rich silicon (Si)-based solar cells dominate the industry, with power conversion efficiencies (PCEs) of over 26 percent and a 25-year average module living standard [16–18]. However, since Si solar cells have high initial production costs, researchers are turning their attention to less expensive alternatives, such as perovskite solar cells (PSCs), organic solar cells (OSCs), quantum dot solar cells (QDSCs), and dye-sensitised solar cells (DSSCs) [19].

PSCs are the most feasible option among these new PV technologies for providing a PCE equivalent to maturing silicon solar cells. Furthermore, compared to traditional Si-based technologies, their lower costs, adjustable band gap, processability at low temperatures, long charge carrier diffusion lengths, high light absorption coefficients, lower exciton binding energy, numerous options for much simpler mass production processes lacking additional advantages, and increasing performance make it a more lucrative option [20–26]. Additionally, in contrast to traditional Si solar cells, PSCs operate well even in diffuse or weak light, making them suitable for specialised purposes [27]. Due to the development of various architectures, chemical compositions, manufacturing protocols, advances in materials, and phase stabilisation techniques, efficiencies have increased dramatically since the first report on all-solid-state PSCs in 2012, from 9.7% in 2012 to 25.5% percent in 2021 [28–31]. Between the highest observed efficiency and its theoretical maximum, PSCs may be split into two categories: the normal (n-i-p) structure and the inverted (p-i-n) structure [32,33].

Furthermore, concerns regarding PSC stability have been highlighted because a thin-film solar device must pass the IEC 61,646 environment stability test before it can be sold commercially [34]. A lot of research is now underway to improve the stability and performance of PSCs [19]. Scientists have been attempting to integrate perovskite into solar cells since the material's initial breakthrough in 2009. The solar cells in this material are more efficient than those in current solar modules [35]. On average, existing solar modules capture 15 to 18 percent of the sun's energy, while perovskite solar cells have an efficiency of up to 28 percent [36]. Dou's research team developed a sandwich-like material that mixes organic and inorganic components to form a composite structure that does not need lead and improves stability considerably. According to Yao Gao, the new organic–inorganic hybrid perovskite materials are cheaper and perform better than traditional inorganic semiconductors. Solar cells can be highly efficient using this new method; the authors made hybrid perovskite materials that are intrinsically more stable. These novel materials are better for the environment and safer for bioelectronic sensors on humans because the researchers removed hazardous lead [37].

Transition-metal nitrides, or carbides (MXenes), were first found in 2011 by Gogotsi and his coworkers as star materials from MAX phases, which are layered compounds resembling graphite with monoatomic A element layers sandwiched between electrically conductive and stiff MX-blocks [38–40]. It was proposed that the generated material be labelled MXenes to highlight the removal of the A element from the MAX phase and its two-dimensional (2D) shape, related to graphene. The material has recently shown promising applications in solar cells [41–44], biomedical fields [45–47], light-emitting diodes [48–50], sensors [51–55], energy storage [56–62], catalysis [63–66], water purification [67–72], and electromagnetic applications [41–44,73]. The nanoengineering of these 2D materials is a hot topic right now. Due to its adjustable work function, high electrical conductivity, good transparency, and charge-carrier mobility, $Ti_3C_2T_x$ (T stands for certain surface-terminating functional groups such as O, OH, and F) leads the current research on MXene in solar cells [74–76]. MXenes are currently divided into transition metals in either an out-of-plane or in-plane ordered form. Furthermore, most 2D transition-metal MXenes exist in the form of random solid solutions, which are characterised by two randomly distributed transition metals across the 2D structure. This review paper detailed the basic principles for the creation of each 2D transition-metal MXene structure, as well as their tunable characteristics depending on the transition-metal composition. 2D transition-metal MXenes vary from their counterparts mono-transition-metal MXenes, where two transition metals can occupy the metal sites.

Guo and his group included $Ti_3C_2T_x$ as an additive in the photoactive layer of methylammonium lead iodide ($MAPbI_3$) in the first research on MXene materials in perovskite solar cells, which was published in 2018 [77]. Since then, its application has been extended to the electrode, electron transport layer (ETL)/hole transport layer (HTL). The $Ti_3C_2T_x$ functions on MXenes in solar cell applications may be classified into three categories: electrode [78], additive [77], and ETL/HTL [79,80]. Figure 1 below summarises the synthesis, properties, and application of MXene. The solar cells (SCs) in Figure 1 have been widely investigated [73].

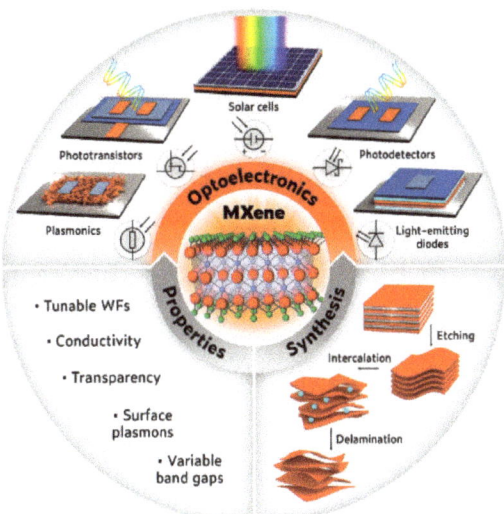

Figure 1. MXene synthesis, properties, and their applications. Reprinted with permission from ref. [73]. Copyright 2021 John Wiley & Sons, Inc.

This article summarises all previously reported work on incorporating MXene into solar cells to improve solar power generation and operational stability. The next section defines the efficiency improvement of SC and how it is classified. Section 3 lists the types of roles that MXene mainly plays in solar cells. A conclusion and prospect are given in Section 4.

2. The Efficiency Improvement of Solar Cells

The conversion efficiency of a solar cell is a measurement of incident light that can be converted to electrical energy. The incident light's power is the denominator, while the solar cell's electrical power is the numerator; thus, this conversion efficiency may be expressed as a fraction [77].

The power conversion efficiency (PCE) of solar cells is one of the most significant parameters [81]. The PCE has improved rapidly since the PSC's introduction in 2009 [82]. The PCE of Kojima et al. initial's PSC was just 3.8 percent [83]. Im et al. [84] claimed a PCE of 6.5 percent in 2011, while Kim et al. [28] recorded a PCE of nearly 9 percent in 2012. In 2016, approximately 22% of PCEs were verified, to the best of our knowledge [85]. All of these remarkable outcomes and conclusions in such a short period of time demonstrated PSC's tremendous potential [86]. Below is the equation used to calculate the conversion efficiency:

$$\text{Conversion efficiency (\%)} = \text{Generated electrical power (W)}/\text{Incident light power (W)} \times 100 \quad (1)$$

Fu et al. published a paper in 2019 that can be applied to various MXene compositions as possible electrodes for the creation of high-performance solar cells. Solar cells with a maximum power conversion efficiency (PCE) of 11.5 percent were delaminated from a few stacked $Ti_3C_2T_x$ MXene-contacted Si layers [87]. The authors recently suggested integrating an inorganic 2D Cl-terminated Ti_3C_2 ($Ti_3C_2Cl_x$) MXene into the volume and surface area of $CsPbBr_3$ lm to substantially decrease the superficial lattice tension. The faulty surface is healed, and a champion efficiency of 11.08 percent is obtained with an ultra-high open-circuit voltage of up to 1.702 V on the fully inorganic $CsPbBr_3$-PSC, which is the greatest efficiency record for this kind of PSC to date. In addition, at 80 percent relative humidity for 100 days and 85 degrees Celsius for 1 month, the unencapsulated device performs nearly as well as the enclosed device [86]. Y. Zhang et al. used density functional theory calculations to thoroughly assess 64 2D transition-metal carbide (MXene) to determine that they were acceptable semiconductors for solar cells via material screening. Ti_2CO_2/Zr_2CO_2 and Ti_2CO_2/Hf_2CO_2 heterostructure solar cells, in particular, have really high power conversion efficiency of 22.74 and 19.56 percent, respectively (Most PCEs inside this paper were evaluated at AM-1.5G-illumination). This research opens the path for MXenes to be used as solar materials in the future [88]. According to Saeed et al., many new opportunities for creating effective indoor organic photovoltaics (OPVs) for practical applications can be explored. With the introduction of different optoelectronic methods to improve device performance under low indoor lighting with varied spectra, the indoor efficiency of OPVs (for PCE > 30%) has taken a quantum leap [89]. Saeed et al. demonstrated additional enhancements to dye-sensitised photovoltaic cells (DSPVs) in indoor solar applications for light energy recycling due to its outstanding light-harvesting performance under ambient lighting conditions. DSPVs' suitability for ambient energy harvesting is proven by their record high power conversion efficiency (PCE) of over 30% under indoor lighting circumstances, consistent device operation, cost-effectiveness, colorful aesthetics, and PCE retention of up to 99% [90].

3. Applications of MXene in Solar Cells

3.1. MXene as Conducting Additives in Solar Cells' Photoactive Active Layer

MXene as a photoactive layer additive in SCs is discussed in this section. Despite significant advances in PCE, charge-carrier recombination inside of the photoactive layer and at perovskite/ETL and perovskite/HTL interfaces still limits PSC performance. Improvements in charge-carrier management are essential to closing the gap between the existing PCEs and the theoretic efficiency frontier of CSs. Prior to mass manufacturing, the intrinsic instability of perovskite in humidity and at high temperatures, as well as the device's limited scalability, must be addressed. Two-dimensional nanomaterials with distinct characteristics have been investigated as additions in photoactive perovskite layers of the HTL/ETL of PSC in recent years. The use of additive engineering to enhance the surface coverage and crystallisation of perovskite films has proven to be successful.

Guo et al. investigated the inclusion of $Ti_3C_2T_x$ in the $MAPbI_3$-based perovskite absorber for the first time in 2018 [77], kicking off research on MXenes in solar cells. Their findings indicate that adding $Ti_3C_2T_x$ to $MAPbI_3$ may prolong the nucleation process, resulting in larger crystals. Furthermore, the $Ti_3C_2T_x$ additive is extremely helpful in speeding electron transport across the grain boundary, similar to a carrier bridge [91–94]. This is measured by the reduced charge-transfer resistance for the Ti_3C_2Tx additive, as revealed by the electrochemical impedance spectra. The median power conversion efficiency (PCE) rises from 15.2 percent to 16.8 percent because of these factors. In addition to adding $Ti_3C_2T_x$ to the photoactive $MAPbI_3$ layer, similarly, Agresti et al. added $Ti_3C_2T_x$ to the TiO_2/ETL to fine-tune its work function (WF). This lowered it from 3.91 to 3.85 eV, which is beneficial for tuning the interfacial energy levels between the perovskite absorber and the TiO_2/ETL, improving charge transfer and lowering the barrier height. The device achieves a PCE of 20.14 percent, which is 26.5 percent greater than the control device without the $Ti_3C_2T_x$ addition, thanks to the double addition and optimisation of both the photoactive $MAPbI_3$ and the TiO_2 electron transport layer. Furthermore, the inclusion of $Ti_3C_2T_x$ to the current density-voltage (JV) curves was shown to decrease hysteresis while enhancing the PSCs' long-term exposure stability. Recently, this group used density functional calculations to further investigate the $MAPbI_3$ perovskite/$Ti_3C_2T_x$-based MXene interface. When the relative concentrations of the OH, O, and F termination groups were changed, the findings indicate that the work function interface displays highly nonlinear behaviour, and they offer a profound insight into the alignment of the energy level for the manufacture of high-performance materials [15].

Agresti et al. used $Ti_3C_2T_x$ MXene in $MAPbI_3$ PSCs to modify the work function of perovskite films and ETLs, resulting in a power conversion efficiency improvement of 26%, as compared to $Ti_3C_2T_x$-free control devices [95]. Di Vito and his colleagues used DFT to conduct first-principles calculations on a $Ti_3C_2/MAPbI_3$ perovskite-coupled system, linking WF tuning to changes in the various concentrations of OH-, O-, and F-MXene-Terminations, and found that OH collections had the greatest impact in reducing work function [94].

Zhang and his colleagues used an in situ solution growth technique to synthesise $MAPbBr_3$ nanocrystals (NCs) on the surface of multilayer MXene ($Ti_3C_2T_x$) nanosheets that form heterostructures in 2020 [96]. PSCs were manufactured utilising the $C-TiO_2/m-TiO_2$-TQD/TQD-Perovskite/Spiro-OMeTAD-$Cu_{1.8}S$ design to enhance PCE and device stability while retaining a champion hysteresis-free power conversion efficiency of 21.64% compared to 18.31% for control devices, with substantially better long-term air and light stability. The entire potential of MXene materials in SCs must be explored as a new area. Various groups, on the other hand, revealed different methods for making use of 2D MXene materials' higher electrical conductivity. 2D $Ti_3C_2T_x$ MXene nanosheets were used as nanoscale additives in 2D Ruddles-den-Popper PSCs by Jin et al. The PCE of 2D PSCs rose from 13.69 percent (control device without MXene additive) to 15.71 percent [97] due to passivated trap states, optimal orientation, reduced charge transfer resistance, and enhanced crystallinity. Yang et al. utilised SnO_2-Ti_3C_2 MXene nanocomposites as electron transport layers (ETLs) in planar PSCs [98].

Zhao et al. utilised $Ti_3C_2T_x$ MXene nanosheets as a multifunctional additive in a two-step method to create extremely efficient planar PSCs in 2021. The findings indicate that single-layer $Ti_3C_2T_x$ nanosheets improve the reactivity of the PbI_2-layer by inducing the formation of a porous PbI_2-layer, which increases the perovskite grain size and lowers the amount of residual PbI_2 in the perovskite film. Random stacking of large PbI_2 grains readily leads to the formation of pores, according to previous research [99]. The mechanism diagram to produce high-quality perovskite films is shown in Figure 2. $Ti_3C_2T_x$ can also improve the WF of $MAPbI_3$, allowing for better energy-level alignment between the perovskite layer and the ETL. Finally, by interacting with the under-coordinated Pb_{2+}, the terminal collections on the surface of $Ti_3C_2T_x$ play a critical role in the passivation of perovskite films. The maximum PCE of 16.45 percent and a PCE rate of 15.94 percent were obtained at the optimum $Ti_3C_2T_x$ dose of 0.03 percent by weight. These values are about 18 percent better than those of pure PSCs, which had the greatest power conversion efficiency of 16.45 percent and a PCE rate of 15.94 percent. As a result, this research established $Ti_3C_2T_x$ as an effective and feasible addition for the manufacture of greatly efficient two-stage produced PSCs, paving the path for their application to other 2D materials [100].

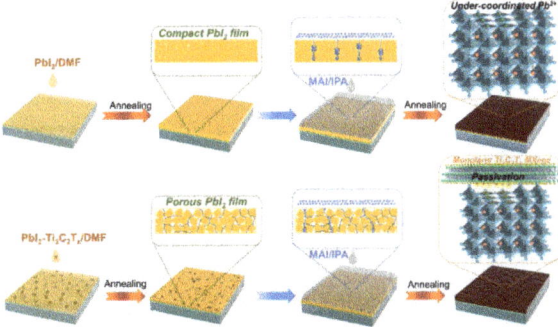

Figure 2. Mechanism diagram for the production of high-quality perovskite films processed in two steps, supported by the additive $Ti_3C_2T_x$. Reprinted with permission from ref. [100]. Copyright 2020 Elsevier B.V.

Larciprete et al. investigated pure environmental aging and the thermally driven breakdown of the mixed halide perovskite Csx (FA$_{0.83}$MA$_{0.17}$) (1x) Pb$_3$ using X-ray photo-electron spectroscopy (I$_{0.83}$Br$_{0.17}$) and high-resolution ultraviolet. The scientists also looked at the impacts of the Ti$_3$C$_2$T$_x$ MXene additive on photovoltaic stability as part of their research. Furthermore, the absence of any negative impact on PV stability, as well as a significant stabilising effect of the additional MXene, contribute to long-term aging. In the fresh samples, we observed a modest decrease in the initial halide migration rate, but this needs more investigation. In conclusion, we believe that our findings on Csx (FA$_{0.83}$MA$_{0.17}$) (1x) Pb$_3$ (I$_{0.83}$Br$_{0.17}$) show severe criticality in the stability of certain mixed perovskites that are comparable to single-halide materials. As a result, it appears that the effectiveness of agents based on electronic and chemical stabilisation of their functional properties, as well as the creative development of device architectures capable of interacting with disruptive agents, are critical for the long-term use of mixed perovskite [101].

For the first time, Hou & Yu showed further improved IPSCs using Ti$_3$C$_2$T$_x$ nanosheets as an additive in ZnO. The creation of the Zn–O–Ti bond enhances the PCE when ZnO is modified with Ti$_3$C$_2$T$_x$, because of the recently created charge transfer routes between both the passivated surface of ZnO films and the ZnO nanocrystals. Figures 3 and 4 illustrate energy level diagrams of the materials utilised in IPSCs. When compared to the control device that utilises pure ZnO as ETL, ITIC-based IPSCs with ZnO/Ti$_3$C$_2$T$_x$/ETL achieve an average power conversion efficiency of 12.20 percent, which is a 15.53 percent improvement (10.56 percent). PM6: Y6 IPSCs reach a champion power conversion efficiency of 16.51 percent based on the ZnO/Ti$_3$C$_2$T$_x$ interface layer, compared to 14.99 percent for the reference device [102].

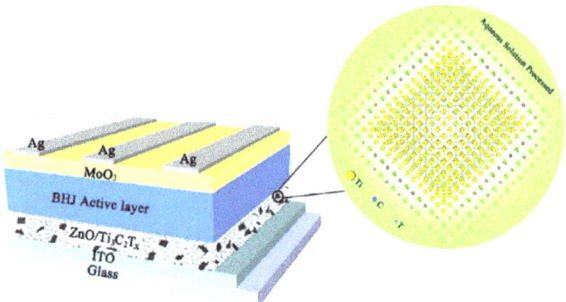

Figure 3. Schematic representation of the IPSCs configuration. Reprinted with permission from ref. [102]. Copyright 2020 Elsevier B.V.

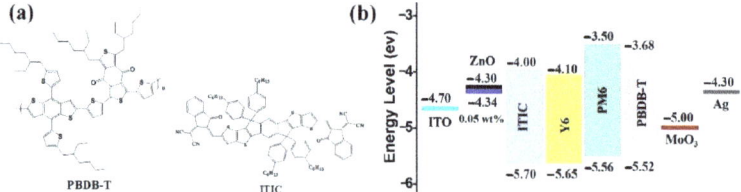

Figure 4. (**a**) Chemical structures of PBDB-T and ITIC. (**b**) Band diagram of the materials used in IPSCs. Reprinted with permission from ref. [102]. Copyright 2020 Elsevier B.V.

According to Jin et al., a modest doping level of Ti$_3$C$_2$Tx nanosheets significantly enhanced the quality of 2D perovskite (BA) 2 (MA) 4Pb$_5$I$_{16}$ films and the photovoltaic performance of the associated device, with a PCE increase from 13.7 to 15.7 percent due to the increase in current. Figure 5a depicts the architecture of the current PSCs, as well as an example of Ti$_3$C$_2$T$_x$ incorporation into a 2D perovskite film. Figure 5b shows the

JV curves of the devices constructed using the control, $Ti_3C_2T_x$ 0.1 mM, $Ti_3C_2T_x$ 0.3 mM, $Ti_3C_2T_x$ 0.5 mM, and $Ti_3C_2T_x$ 0.7 mM samples. The external quantum efficiency (EQE) spectrum displayed in Figure 5c supports this growth in short-circuit current density (Jsc). Furthermore, a steady power output compatible with the JV curves is shown by the photocurrent evaluated for much more than 5 min at a point of maximum power (0.80 V) (Figure 5d). The enhanced vertically directed growth, uniform phase distribution in the thin film, and the crystallinity, which eventually improves charge transfer, are primarily responsible for the $Ti_3C_2T_x$-doped components' superiority. Furthermore, owing to the superior crystallinity and passivation effect of the perovskite film, the components doped with $Ti_3C_2T_x$ nanosheets had a greater moisture stability than the shell components [99]. We can conclude that MXene has many functions in solar cells. As an additive, it accelerates electron transport by acting as an "electron" bridge. Hence, by its addition, it influences the carrier transport materials' work function and other characteristics like conductivity. This research offers a viable approach for enhancing the efficiency of 2D perovskite film and expands the scope of $Ti_3C_2T_x$'s photovoltaic applications [99].

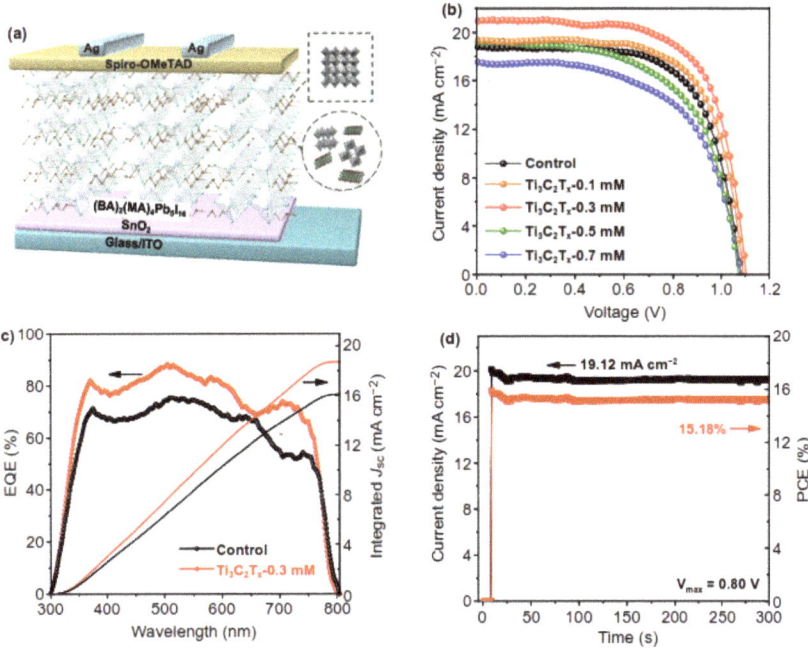

Figure 5. (a) Schematic representation of devices with the structure glass/ITO/SnO$_2$/2D perovskite/SpiroOMeTAD/Ag. (b) JV curves from devices with different amounts of Ti3C2Tx doping. (c) EQE spectra and integrated Jsc of the control and optimised $Ti_3C_2T_x$ doping devices. (d) Stabilised power output and current density at a constant bias 0.80 V for the $Ti_3C_2T_x$ dopant devices. Reprinted with permission from ref. [99]. Copyright 2021 Springer Nature Switzerland AG. Part of Springer Nature.

3.2. Novel Metal Transparent Conductive Electrode

In PSCs, MXene is used as an electrode. An electrode is one of the most essential components of a PSC for controlling the charge collecting process; it is important for long-term stability and affects the device's overall cost. Metal thin-film electrodes, nanostructured metal electrodes [103], carbon electrodes [104], and graphene electrodes [105], Ref. [106] are some of the newly described electrode materials for PSC.

The $Ti_3C_2T_x$ MXene recently reported an electrical conductivity of up to 15,100 S cm^{-1} [107], as well as great transparency, good flexibility, and tunable WF [108–110]. Because of these characteristics, $Ti_3C_2T_x$ may be used as an electrode in optoelectronic devices such as solar cells. The next sections elaborate on Si-wafer-based, organic, perovskite-based, and dye-sensitised solar cells, in that sequence. In quantum-dot-sensitised solar cells, the $Ti_3C_2T_x$ MXene was also utilised to make the counter electrode (CE) (QDSCs). Chen et al. described a hybrid CE made up of hydrothermally produced CuSe nanoparticles on $Ti_3C_2T_x$-MXen nanosheets screen printed on graphite foil [111]. This composite CE offers higher electrical conductivity for electron transport and a greater specific surface area than CuSe and $Ti_3C_2T_x$-based CEs, allowing for more active centers for polysulfide electrolyte reduction. The device can obtain a PCE of 5.12 percent by employing a CuSe- $Ti_3C_2T_x$ hybrid CE with an optimum mass ratio. Devices that utilise CuSe and $Ti_3C_2T_x$-based CEs, on the other hand, have a PCE of 3.47 percent and 2.04 percent, respectively. Similarly, Tian et al. used a simple ion-exchange technique at ambient temperature to produce CuS/Ti_3C_2 composite CEs, which exhibited a substantially higher electrocatalytic rate for polysulfide reduction than pure CuS [112]. The overall PCE of the QDSC based on this composite CE is 5.11 percent, which is 1.5 times higher than that of a device with pure CuS CE. The combined benefits of the Ti_3C_2 framework's high conductivity and the numerous catalytically active centers of the CuS nanoparticles are mostly responsible for the improved performance [15].

Cao et al. utilised 2D MXene material (Ti_3C_2) as a back electrode in non-precious metal PSCs and hole-transport materials in 2019 [78]. This increase in PCE was ascribed to the Ti_3C_2 electrode's superior charge extraction capacity and reduced square resistance when compared to carbon electrodes. Jiang and his colleagues recently reported that, by using a combination of one-dimensional carbon nanotubes (CNTs), two-dimensional Ti_3C_2-MXene nanosheets, and commercial carbon paste as the electrode material in CsP-bBr$_3$-PSC, they were able to obtain a power conversion efficiency of 7.1% [19,113].

In dye-sensitised solar cells, the 2D-layered Ti_3C_2 counter electrode substantially surpassed V2C in 2021 when compared to the iodide redox couple. According to Xu et al., the catalytic activity of Ti_3C_2 may be enhanced by increasing the etching time suitably. A PCE of 6.2 percent was found in DSCs with a Ti_3C_2 counter electrode etched for 24 h. Furthermore, K + intercalation has the potential to substantially boost Ti_3C_2's catalytic activity, which is affected by the increased number of catalytic activity centers and the increased interlayer spacing for smooth iodide electrolyte transport. The PCE of the DSCs with the K + -Ti_3C_2 counter electrode was 7.11 percent, which was notably similar to the PCE of the conventional DSCs using Pt counter electrodes (7.2%) [114]. Chen et al. made the first effort to utilise MXene/CoS as an electrocatalytic CE for QDSSCs in their research. When compared to QDSSCs with bare MXene (4.25%) and bare CoS (5.77%) CEs, the QDSSCs with an Mxene/CoS/CE exhibit a substantial improvement in cell performance and provide a promising PCE of 8.1% [115].

Additionally, a fan was installed to aid in the construction of flexible OSCs. This study emphasises the significance of developing FTEs and demonstrates their essential importance in flexible OSCs. With a sheet resistance of 110 sq^{-1}, the transparent $Ti_3C_2T_x$ Mxene electrodes have the lowest sheet resistance to date. As a result, scientists and engineers should collaborate to develop FTEs with the high electrical and optical compromise needed for highly efficient flexible OSCs. Tang et al. [116] demonstrated a flexible non-fullerene OSC with Ag NW/Mxene component electrodes and PBDB-T: ITIC: PC71BM active layers utilising the Ag NW/Mxene component electrodes (Figure 6) [117].

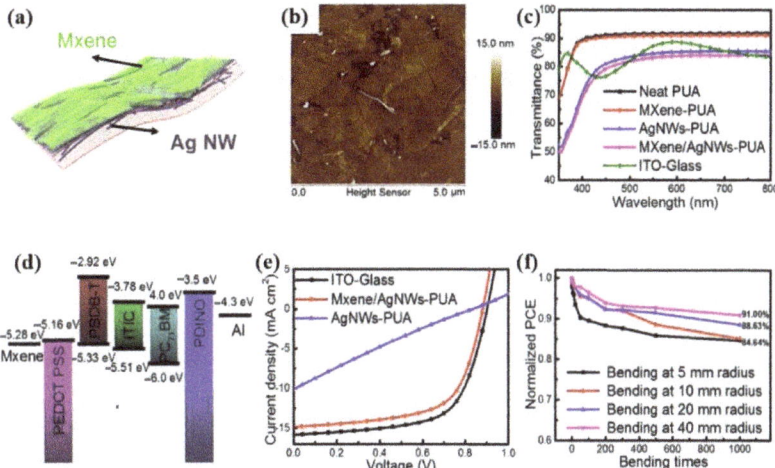

Figure 6. (a) Schematic representation of the MXene/AgNW hybrid electrodes on PUA substrates. (b) AFM images of the MXene/AgNW PUA films. (c) Transmission spectra of pure PUA, MXene-PUA, Ag NW-PUA, optimised MXene/Ag NW-PUA, and ITO glass. (d) Energy level diagrams of the flexible OSCs. (e) JV curves of the flexible OSCs with PBDB-T: ITIC: PC71BM active layers. (f) Normalised PCE of the flexible OSCs with MXene/Ag NW electrodes as a function of the number of bending cycles. Reproduced with permission. Reprinted with permission from ref. [116,117]. Copyright 2019 American Chemical Society.

Ahmed et al. studied the application of single-layer delaminated 2-D-MXene (Ti_3C_2) created by the leaching method to replace both TCO and Pt as a conductive layer and a catalyst. Each test required at least five samples. To prevent human error and obtain the greatest possible conversion efficiency for reliable comparisons, a pre-built TCO Pt meter was utilised as the reference counter electrode (CE). Figure 7 depicts the whole procedure. Furthermore, Ti3C2 was adjusted in thickness for optimum conversion efficiency. At optimum thickness, the TCO/Pt/free MXen-based CE had a PCE of 8.68%, which was 4.03% higher than the conventional TCO/Pt-based counter electrode. The high efficiency is attributable to the high conductivity, the large number of accessible catalytic centers owing to the delaminated structure, and Ti_3C_2's excellent catalytic activity towards iodide and triiodide electrolytes [118].

Hence, we can conclude that MXene serves a variety of roles in solar cells. As an electrode, it improves the form of hybrid electrodes with other conducting nanomaterials, such as metallic nanowires or carbon nanotubes. In addition, it enhances transparency, increases flexibility, metallic conductivity, and influences the work functions.

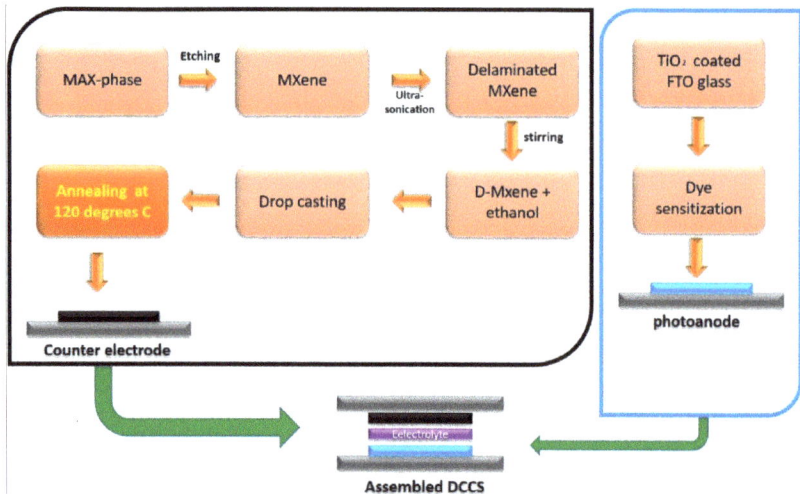

Figure 7. Schematic representation of an experimental procedure. Reprinted with permission from ref. [118]. Copyright 2021 Elsevier Ltd. and Techna Group S.r.l.

3.3. Mxene as Transfer Layer HTL/ETL in Solar Cells

The Electron Transport Layer (ETL) and Hole Transport Layer (HTL) in perovskite solar cells play an essential role in increasing stability (PSCs) and photovoltaic performance. The ETL's primary function is to collect and transmit electrons from the perovskite layer while also preventing hole backflow, efficiently segregating charges, and reducing charge recombination [119]. The HTL's primary function is to collect and transport holes from the photoactive perovskite layer to the electrode while also acting as an energy barrier to inhibit electron transmission to the anode. Furthermore, the HTL efficiently divides the photoactive perovskite layer from the anode and isolates air moisture, which enhances the stability of PSCs by reducing deterioration and corrosion [120]. The HTL PSC performance of component prototypes with various Mo_2C @ CNT nanocomposite loading (1, 1.5, and 2 wt.-percent) was also investigated. Then, the Mo_2C-CNT @ PEDOT: PSS HTL-based device was utilised as an X-ray photodetector, with a maximum sensitivity of 3.56 mA/Gycm2. Figure 8a depicts the schematic structure of the ITO/HTL/$CH_3NH_3PbI_3$/ETL/LiF/Al-PSC using Mo_2C-CNT @ PEDOT: PSS as HTL in the ITO/HTL/$CH_3NH_3PbI_3$/ETL/LiF/Al-PSC using Mo_2C-CNT @ PEDOT: PSS as HTL. The architecture of this composite perovskite solar cell was studied using cross-sectional FESEM (Figure 8b), and the associated energy level diagram is presented in Figure 8c. The findings show that Mxene/CNT nanocomposites with a perovskite layer have the potential to improve the efficiency of SCs and photodetectors. A high PCE of 11.98 percent was obtained for the HTL containing 1.5 percent by weight Mo_2C-CNTs mixed with PEDOT: PSS in a component architecture of ITO/HTL/$CH_3NH_3PbI_3$/PCBM/LiF/Al, which is greater than the HTLs with Mo_2C (9.82%) and CNT (10.61%) mix [121].

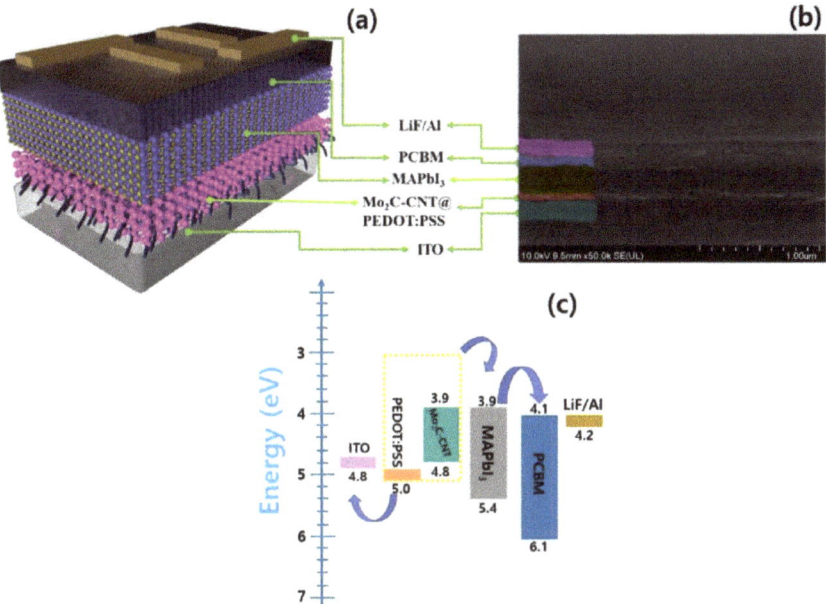

Figure 8. (a) Device architecture of the prepared ITO/HTL/CH$_3$NH$_3$PbI$_3$/PCBM/LiF/Al prototype using Mo$_2$C-CNTs @ PEDOT: PSS HTL and (b) FESEM cross-sectional image; (c) Energy level diagram for ITO/Mo$_2$C-CNTs @ PEDOT: PSS/CH$_3$NH$_3$PbI$_3$/PCBM/LiF/Al structure. Reprinted with permission from ref. [121]. Copyright 2021 Elsevier B.V.

According to Bati et al., the incorporation of 2D MXenes into the ETL of PSCs produces extremely effective photovoltaic (PV) components. A power conversion efficiency of over 21% is obtained with the optimum composition [122]. In a planar PSC with a regular structure, Zheng et al. examined a hybrid film of SnO$_2$ nanoparticles and Ti$_3$C$_2$T$_x$ MXene nanoflakes as an electron transport layer (ETL). The ETL and perovskite layer production procedures are shown in Figure 9. The results show that the film qualities of the upper perovskite layers can be controlled by changing the Ti$_3$C$_2$T$_x$/SnO$_2$ ratios (2.02 wt percent in ETLs), such as crystallinity, crystal size, compactness, defect density, optical absorption, surface roughness, and so on, by changing the Ti$_3$C$_2$T$_x$/SnO$_2$ ratios (2.02 wt percent in ETLs) [123].

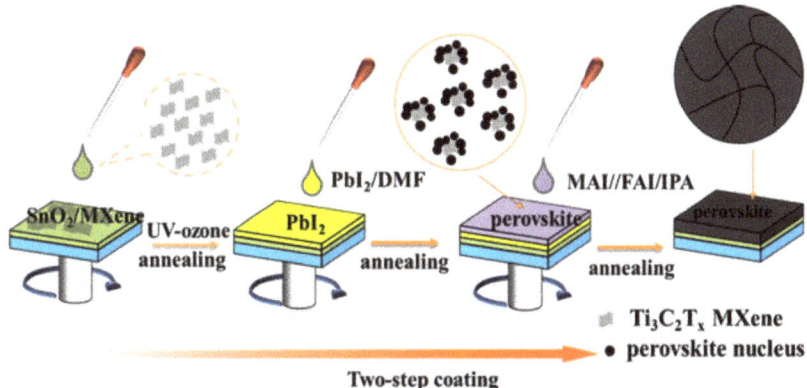

Figure 9. Schematic representation of the manufacturing processes of the perovskite film and the ETL. Reprinted with permission from ref. [123]. Copyright 2021 American Chemical Society.

J. Zhang et al. developed the Nb$_2$CTx-MXene, which has outstanding photoelectric characteristics and can be utilised as the HTL in fabricating the inverted PVSCs. Enhancing the O-terminated functional groups on the Nb$_2$CT$_x$ surface, oxygen plasma treatment altered the work function (WF) of Nb$_2$CT$_x$ HTL. PVSCs with oxygen-plasma-treated Nb$_2$CT$_x$ HTL have the greatest PCE of 20.74 percent and excellent stability. Figure 10 shows a schematic representation of the device construction as well as the structure of Nb$_2$CT$_x$ MXene, as seen in Figure 10a. The PVSCs' current density–voltage curves (JV) are presented in Figure 10b for various scan directions. As demonstrated in Figure 10, the enhanced Jsc is attributed to the greater external quantum efficiency values (EQE) owing to more effective charge separation and collecting efficiency (Figure 10c). The Nb$_2$CT$_x$-HTL treated with oxygen plasma similarly produces flexible and large-area (0.99 cm^2) PVSCs with PCE of 17.26 percent and 17.94 percent (Figure 10d,e). Furthermore, employing Nb$_2$CT$_x$ treated with oxygen plasma as HTL, the flexible and large-area (0.99 cm^2) PVSCs obtain the greatest PCE of 17.26 percent and 17.94 percent, respectively [124].

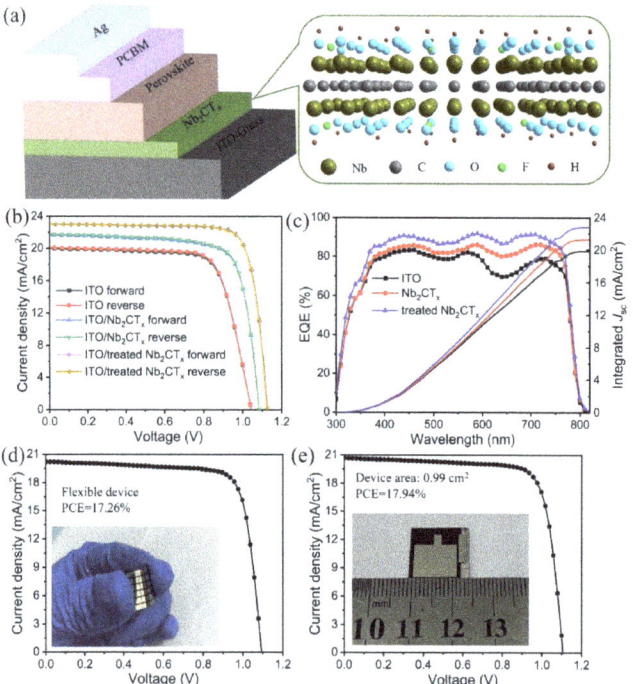

Figure 10. (a) The schematic diagram of the device structure and the structure of Nb$_2$CT$_x$ MXene. (b) JV curves of PVSCs measured under different scan directions. (c) External quantum efficiency (EQE) and integrated Jsc curves of various PVSCs. JV curves of the flexible (d) and large-area (e) PVSCs using Nb$_2$CT$_x$-HTL treated with oxygen plasma. Reprinted with permission from ref. [124]. Copyright 2021 AIP Publishing LLC.

Wang et al. used a solution procedure at room temperature to show the potential of Ti$_3$C$_2$T$_x$ Mxene as an ETL for efficient PSCs with traditional design. The authors modified the MXene surface using an oxygen plasma treatment and attempted to establish a link between the surface characteristics and MXene termination groups. The contact angle and topography measurements were used to study the surface tension of MXene and the morphology of the associated perovskite. The PbO interactions between perovskite and MXene were shown by high-resolution XPS spectra, which improved device stability [125].

Yang et al. found a superior match in energy levels between the ETL layer and the perovskite in the case of a hybrid of oxidised and pure $Ti_3C_2T_x$, with a champion PCE of 18.29 percent, compared to PSCs with pure $Ti_3C_2T_x$ as ETL, with a PCE of 16.50 percent. The intersection of the baseline with the tangent line of the spectra determined the highest occupied molecular orbital (HOMO) and the highest energy levels, while the results of the UV-Vis absorption spectra calculated the lowest unoccupied molecular orbital (LUMO). The enhanced electron mobility in the ETL, which increases electron transport and decreases hole–electron recombination, is responsible for the improvement in PCE. This research shows that these materials have a lot of promise for use in low-temperature-produced PSC and other solar technologies [126].

To develop a new $ZnO/Ti_3C_2T_x$ nanohybrid composite film, Hou & Yu utilised $Ti_3C_2T_x$, a representative of MXene, as an additive in zinc oxide (ZnO). By establishing the Zn–O–Ti bond on the ZnO surface, $Ti_3C_2T_x$ nanosheets generate new electron transport routes between ZnO nanocrystals and passivates the ZnO surface. As a consequence, the PBDB-T: ITIC based photovoltaic devices with $ZnO/Ti_3C_2T_x$ ETLs have a power conversion efficiency of 12.20 percent, compared to 10.6 percent for the comparable device utilising pure ZnO as the ETL, which is a 15.53 percent improvement. Furthermore, PM6: Y6-based IPSCs obtain a champion power conversion efficiency of 16.5 percent, compared to 15 percent for the reference device, demonstrating the $ZnO/Ti_3C_2T_x$—ETL's applicability [102]. Saranin et al. showed that by utilising MXenes as doping for the forming layers, it is possible to adjust the optoelectronic characteristics of inverted p-i-n-perovskite components. When compared to reference cells, the MXene-based devices had a maximum PCE of over 19% and an average growth of +8%, which is a surprising result, given that the $MAPbI_3$-based p-i-n cell used spin-coated NiO [127].

4. Conclusions and Prospect

From the discovery of MXene in 2011 up to now, MXene has achieved tremendous technological developments. In 2018, MXene entered into the development of solar cell production by enhancing the effectiveness of energy produced and the stability of solar cells. This review attempts to compile all previously published research on adding MXene into PSCs to enhance operational stability and solar energy collection. According to MXene's function, the most essential device parameters are given in Tables S1–S3 (Supplementary Materials).

The main conclusions of this work are:

1. Adoption of perovskite solar cells for effective use in solar energy technology due to their good stability against moisture, heat, and light as well as good crystallisation and low density of defects in perovskite films.
2. The use of titanium carbide ($Ti_3C_2T_x$) in perovskite solar cells resulted in a steady-state energy conversion efficiency of 23.3% and outstanding stability.
3. MXenes combine with other materials to create hybrids and nanocomposites with improved or additional functions. These innovative materials could be used in applications such as renewable energy, energy storage, and conversion.
4. It has become clear to us that the use of a hybrid MXene with carbon nanotubes (m-SWCNTs) can effectively improve the photovoltaic performance of perovskite solar cells due to the presence of hybrid interfacial layers that can reduce defect density and thus improve charge extraction and transfer.
5. From the above tables, it is clear to us that in the last year, the use of MXene as an electron transport layer (ETL) for solar cells has dominated scientific research due to efficient PSCs with conventional design through a solution method at room temperature.
6. All kinds of 2D transition-metal MXenes demonstrated behavior not previously seen in mono-M MXenes, indicating the potential for the use of 2D transition-metal MXenes in a variety of novel applications. Researchers can tune the performance of MXenes for a variety of applications, including nanomagnets, transparent electronics,

semiconductors, supercapacitors, and structural materials, by controlling the composition of the 2D transition-metal MXenes phase. This level of control over their composition and structure is unique in the area of 2D materials, and it opens up new avenues for nanomaterial design. The addition of 2D transition-metal MXenes to the category of 2D materials has increased the design options for nanomaterials to satisfy the needs of growing technology.

Supplementary Materials: The following are available online at https://www.mdpi.com/article/10.3390/nano11102732/s1, Tables S1–S3: Summary of the key parameters for the solar cells employing MXenes.

Funding: This research was fully funded by the Universiti Putra Malaysia (UPM) Research Grant (UPM-GRANT Putra, UPM/GP-IPB/2020/9688700), the Ministry of Higher Education Malaysia (KPT) Research Grant (FRGS/2012/5524194), and Department of Mechanical Engineering, Jeju National University, Korea.

Acknowledgments: The authors would like to acknowledge the Ministry of Higher Education Malaysia (KPT), Universiti Putra Malaysia (UPM), and Jeju National University for providing necessary resources in completing this study.

Conflicts of Interest: The authors declare no conflict of interest.

References

1. Ma, X.; Mi, Y.; Zhang, F.; An, Q.; Zhang, M.; Hu, Z.; Liu, X.; Zhang, J.; Tang, W. Efficient Ternary Polymer Solar Cells with Two Well-Compatible Donors and One Ultranarrow Bandgap Nonfullerene Acceptor. *Adv. Energy Mater.* **2018**, *8*, 1702854. [CrossRef]
2. Zhao, D.; Zhang, C.; Kim, H.; Guo, L.J. High-Performance Ta_2O_5/Al-Doped Ag Electrode for Resonant Light Harvesting in Efficient Organic Solar Cells. *Adv. Energy Mater.* **2015**, *5*, 1500768. [CrossRef]
3. Li, Y.; Yu, H.; Li, J.; Wong, S.-M.; Sun, X.; Li, X.; Cheng, C.; Fan, H.J.; Wang, J.; Singh, N.; et al. Novel Silicon Nanohemisphere-Array Solar Cells with Enhanced Performance. *Small* **2011**, *7*, 3138–3143. [CrossRef] [PubMed]
4. Zhang, S.; Qin, Y.; Zhu, J.; Hou, J. Over 14% Efficiency in Polymer Solar Cells Enabled by a Chlorinated Polymer Donor. *Adv. Mater.* **2018**, *30*, e1800868. [CrossRef]
5. Wan, Z.; Lai, H.; Ren, S.; He, R.; Jiang, Y.; Luo, J.; Chen, Q.; Hao, X.; Wang, Y.; Zhang, J.; et al. Interfacial engineering in lead-free tin-based perovskite solar cells. *J. Energy Chem.* **2021**, *57*, 147–168. [CrossRef]
6. Zhao, Y.; Han, X.; Chang, L.; Dong, C.; Li, J.; Yan, X. Effects of selenization conditions on microstructure evolution in solution processed $Cu_2ZnSn(S,Se)_4$ solar cells. *Sol. Energy Mater. Sol. Cells* **2019**, *195*, 274–279. [CrossRef]
7. Ren, A.; Zou, J.; Lai, H.; Huang, Y.; Yuan, L.; Xu, H.; Shen, K.; Wang, H.; Wei, S.; Wang, Y.; et al. Direct laser-patterned MXene–perovskite image sensor arrays for visible-near infrared photodetection. *Mater. Horiz.* **2020**, *7*, 1901–1911. [CrossRef]
8. Li, J.; Yu, H.; Li, Y.; Wang, F.; Yang, M.; Wong, S.M. Low aspect-ratio hemispherical nanopit surface texturing for enhancing light absorption in crystalline Si thin film-based solar cells. *Appl. Phys. Lett.* **2011**, *98*, 021905. [CrossRef]
9. Zhao, D.; Ding, L. All-perovskite tandem structures shed light on thin-film photovoltaics. *Sci. Bull.* **2020**, *65*, 1144–1146. [CrossRef]
10. Li, J.; Yu, H.; Li, Y. Aligned Si nanowire-based solar cells. *Nanoscale* **2011**, *3*, 4888–4900. [CrossRef]
11. Ren, A.; Lai, H.; Hao, X.; Tang, Z.; Xu, H.; Jeco, B.M.F.Y.; Watanabe, K.; Wu, L.; Zhang, J.; Sugiyama, M.; et al. Efficient Perovskite Solar Modules with Minimized Nonradiative Recombination and Local Carrier Transport Losses. *Joule* **2020**, *4*, 1263–1277. [CrossRef]
12. Wang, Y.; Shao, P.; Chen, Q.; Li, Y.; Li, J.; He, D. Nanostructural optimization of silicon/PEDOT:PSS hybrid solar cells for performance improvement. *J. Phys. D Appl. Phys.* **2017**, *50*, 175105. [CrossRef]
13. Shi, B.; Duan, L.; Zhao, Y.; Luo, J.; Zhang, X. Semitransparent Perovskite Solar Cells: From Materials and Devices to Applications. *Adv. Mater.* **2020**, *32*, e1806474. [CrossRef]
14. Li, J.; Yu, H.; Wong, S.M.; Li, X.; Zhang, G.; Lo, P.G.-Q.; Kwong, D.-L. Design guidelines of periodic Si nanowire arrays for solar cell application. *Appl. Phys. Lett.* **2009**, *95*, 243113. [CrossRef]
15. Yin, L.; Li, Y.; Yao, X.; Wang, Y.; Jia, L.; Liu, Q.; Li, J.; Li, Y.; He, D. MXenes for Solar Cells. *Nano-Micro Lett.* **2021**, *13*, 78. [CrossRef] [PubMed]
16. Green, M.A.; Dunlop, E.D.; Hohl-Ebinger, J.; Yoshita, M.; Kopidakis, N.; Hao, X. Solar cell efficiency tables (Version 58). *Prog. Photovolt. Res. Appl.* **2021**, *29*, 657–667. [CrossRef]
17. Punathil, L.; Mohanasundaram, K.; Tamilselavan, K.S.; Sathyamurthy, R.; Chamkha, A.J. Recovery of Pure Silicon and Other Materials from Disposed Solar Cells. *Int. J. Photoenergy* **2021**, *2021*, 5530213. [CrossRef]
18. Chowdhury, S.; Rahman, K.S.; Chowdhury, T.; Nuthammachot, N.; Techato, K.; Akhtaruzzaman, M.; Tiong, S.K.; Sopian, K.; Amin, N. An overview of solar photovoltaic panels' end-of-life material recycling. *Energy Strat. Rev.* **2020**, *27*, 100431. [CrossRef]
19. Shah, S.A.A.; Sayyad, M.H.; Khan, K.; Sun, J.; Guo, Z. Application of MXenes in Perovskite Solar Cells: A Short Review. *Nanomaterials* **2021**, *11*, 2151. [CrossRef]

20. Shah, S.A.A.; Sayyad, M.H.; Sun, J.; Guo, Z. Hysteresis Analysis of Hole-Transport-Material-Free Monolithic Perovskite Solar Cells with Carbon Counter Electrode by Current Density–Voltage and Impedance Spectra Measurements. *Nanomaterials* **2020**, *11*, 48. [CrossRef]
21. Shah, S.A.A.; Sayyad, M.H.; Khan, K.; Guo, K.; Shen, F.; Sun, J.; Tareen, A.K.; Gong, Y.; Guo, Z. Progress towards High-Efficiency and Stable Tin-Based Perovskite Solar Cells. *Energies* **2020**, *13*, 5092. [CrossRef]
22. Li, Y.; Ji, L.; Liu, R.; Zhang, C.; Mak, C.H.; Zou, X.; Shen, H.-H.; Leu, S.-Y.; Hsu, H.-Y. A review on morphology engineering for highly efficient and stable hybrid perovskite solar cells. *J. Mater. Chem. A* **2018**, *6*, 12842–12875. [CrossRef]
23. Wu, Y.; Wang, D.; Liu, J.; Cai, H. Review of Interface Passivation of Perovskite Layer. *Nanomaterials* **2021**, *11*, 775. [CrossRef] [PubMed]
24. Li, B.; Zhang, Y.; Fu, L.; Zhang, L.; Liu, Z.; Yin, L. Two-dimensional black phosphorous induced exciton dissociation efficiency enhancement for high-performance all-inorganic $CsPbI_3$ perovskite photovoltaics. *J. Mater. Chem. A* **2019**, *7*, 22539–22549. [CrossRef]
25. Wang, H.; Chan, C.C.S.; Chu, M.; Xie, J.; Zhao, S.; Guo, X.; Miao, Q.; Wong, K.S.; Yan, K.; Xu, J. Interlayer Cross-Linked 2D Perovskite Solar Cell with Uniform Phase Distribution and Increased Exciton Coupling. *Sol. RRL* **2020**, *4*, 1900578. [CrossRef]
26. Wu, T.; Liu, X.; Luo, X.; Lin, X.; Cui, D.; Wang, Y.; Segawa, H.; Zhang, Y.; Han, L. Lead-free tin perovskite solar cells. *Joule* **2021**, *5*, 863–886. [CrossRef]
27. Juang, S.S.-Y.; Lin, P.-Y.; Lin, Y.-C.; Chen, Y.-S.; Shen, P.-S.; Guo, Y.-L.; Wu, Y.-C.; Chen, P. Energy Harvesting Under Dim-Light Condition with Dye-Sensitized and Perovskite Solar Cells. *Front. Chem.* **2019**, *7*, 209. [CrossRef] [PubMed]
28. Kim, H.-S.; Lee, C.-R.; Im, J.-H.; Lee, K.-B.; Moehl, T.; Marchioro, A.; Moon, S.-J.; Humphry-Baker, R.; Yum, J.-H.; Moser, J.E.; et al. Lead Iodide Perovskite Sensitized All-Solid-State Submicron Thin Film Mesoscopic Solar Cell with Efficiency Exceeding 9%. *Sci. Rep.* **2012**, *2*, 591. [CrossRef]
29. Yoo, J.J.; Seo, G.; Chua, M.R.; Park, T.G.; Lu, Y.; Rotermund, F.; Kim, Y.-K.; Moon, C.S.; Jeon, N.J.; Correa-Baena, J.-P.; et al. Efficient perovskite solar cells via improved carrier management. *Nat. Cell Biol.* **2021**, *590*, 587–593. [CrossRef]
30. Zhang, F.; Zhu, K. Additive Engineering for Efficient and Stable Perovskite Solar Cells. *Adv. Energy Mater.* **2020**, *10*, 1902579. [CrossRef]
31. Park, N. Research Direction toward Scalable, Stable, and High Efficiency Perovskite Solar Cells. *Adv. Energy Mater.* **2020**, *10*, 1903106. [CrossRef]
32. Pazos-Outón, L.M.; Xiao, T.P.; Yablonovitch, E. Fundamental Efficiency Limit of Lead Iodide Perovskite Solar Cells. *J. Phys. Chem. Lett.* **2018**, *9*, 1703–1711. [CrossRef]
33. Brenes, R.; Laitz, M.; Jean, J.; Dequilettes, D.W.; Bulović, V. Benefit from Photon Recycling at the Maximum-Power Point of State-of-the-Art Perovskite Solar Cells. *Phys. Rev. Appl.* **2019**, *12*, 014017. [CrossRef]
34. Wang, D.; Wright, M.; Elumalai, N.K.; Uddin, A. Stability of perovskite solar cells. *Sol. Energy Mater. Sol. Cells* **2016**, *147*, 255–275. [CrossRef]
35. Zuo, C.; Bolink, H.; Han, H.; Huang, J.; Cahen, D.; Ding, L. Advances in Perovskite Solar Cells. *Adv. Sci.* **2016**, *3*, 1500324. [CrossRef]
36. Chen, B.; Baek, S.-W.; Hou, Y.; Aydin, E.; De Bastiani, M.; Scheffel, B.; Proppe, A.; Huang, Z.; Wei, M.; Wang, Y.-K.; et al. Enhanced optical path and electron diffusion length enable high-efficiency perovskite tandems. *Nat. Commun.* **2020**, *11*, 1257. [CrossRef]
37. Gao, Y.; Shi, E.; Deng, S.; Shiring, S.B.; Snaider, J.M.; Liang, C.; Yuan, B.; Song, R.; Janke, S.M.; Liebman-Peláez, A.; et al. Molecular engineering of organic–inorganic hybrid perovskites quantum wells. *Nat. Chem.* **2019**, *11*, 1151–1157. [CrossRef] [PubMed]
38. Anasori, B.; Gogotsi, Y. *2D Metal Carbides and Nitrides (MXenes)*; Springer: Cham, Switzerland, 2019.
39. Numan, A. *Contemporary Nanomaterials in Material Engineering Applications*; Springer: Cham, Switzerland, 2021; Volume 1.
40. Gogotsi, Y.; Huang, Q. MXenes: Two-Dimensional Building Blocks for Future Materials and Devices. *ACS Nano* **2021**, *15*, 5775–5780. [CrossRef] [PubMed]
41. Zhao, S.; Zhang, H.-B.; Luo, J.-Q.; Wang, Q.-W.; Xu, B.; Hong, S.; Yu, Z.-Z. Highly Electrically Conductive Three-Dimensional $Ti_3C_2T_x$ MXene/Reduced Graphene Oxide Hybrid Aerogels with Excellent Electromagnetic Interference Shielding Performances. *ACS Nano* **2018**, *12*, 11193–11202. [CrossRef] [PubMed]
42. Iqbal, A.; Sambyal, P.; Koo, C.M. 2D MXenes for Electromagnetic Shielding: A Review. *Adv. Funct. Mater.* **2020**, *30*, 2000883. [CrossRef]
43. Deng, B.; Xiang, Z.; Xiong, J.; Liu, Z.; Yu, L.; Lu, W. Sandwich-Like Fe&TiO_2@C Nanocomposites Derived from MXene/Fe-MOFs Hybrids for Electromagnetic Absorption. *Nano-Micro Lett.* **2020**, *12*, 55. [CrossRef]
44. Cao, W.; Ma, C.; Tan, S.; Ma, M.; Wan, P.; Chen, F. Ultrathin and Flexible CNTs/MXene/Cellulose Nanofibrils Composite Paper for Electromagnetic Interference Shielding. *Nano-Micro Lett.* **2019**, *11*, 72. [CrossRef]
45. Ma, Y.; Yue, Y.; Zhang, H.; Cheng, F.; Zhao, W.; Rao, J.; Luo, S.; Wang, J.; Jiang, X.; Liu, Z.; et al. 3D Synergistical MXene/Reduced Graphene Oxide Aerogel for a Piezoresistive Sensor. *ACS Nano* **2018**, *12*, 3209–3216. [CrossRef]
46. Kalambate, P.K.; Gadhari, N.S.; Li, X.; Rao, Z.; Navale, S.; Shen, Y.; Patil, V.R.; Huang, Y. Recent advances in MXene–based electrochemical sensors and biosensors. *TrAC Trends Anal. Chem.* **2019**, *120*, 115643. [CrossRef]
47. Lei, Y.; Zhao, W.; Zhang, Y.; Jiang, Q.; He, J.; Baeumner, A.J.; Wolfbeis, O.S.; Wang, Z.L.; Salama, K.N.; Alshareef, H.N. A MXene-Based Wearable Biosensor System for High-Performance In Vitro Perspiration Analysis. *Small* **2019**, *15*, e1901190. [CrossRef] [PubMed]

48. Xu, Q.; Yang, W.; Wen, Y.; Liu, S.; Liu, Z.; Ong, W.-J.; Li, N. Hydrochromic full-color MXene quantum dots through hydrogen bonding toward ultrahigh-efficiency white light-emitting diodes. *Appl. Mater. Today* **2019**, *16*, 90–101. [CrossRef]
49. Ahn, S.; Han, T.-H.; Maleski, K.; Song, J.; Kim, Y.-H.; Park, M.-H.; Zhou, H.; Yoo, S.; Gogotsi, Y.; Lee, T.-W. A 2D Titanium Carbide MXene Flexible Electrode for High-Efficiency Light-Emitting Diodes. *Adv. Mater.* **2020**, *32*, e2000919. [CrossRef]
50. Lee, S.; Kim, E.H.; Yu, S.; Kim, H.; Park, C.; Park, T.H.; Han, H.; Lee, S.W.; Baek, S.; Jin, W.; et al. Alternating-Current MXene Polymer Light-Emitting Diodes. *Adv. Funct. Mater.* **2020**, *30*, 2001224. [CrossRef]
51. Cai, Y.; Shen, J.; Ge, G.; Zhang, Y.; Jin, W.; Huang, W.; Shao, J.; Yang, J.; Dong, X. Stretchable $Ti_3C_2T_x$ MXene/Carbon Nanotube Composite Based Strain Sensor with Ultrahigh Sensitivity and Tunable Sensing Range. *ACS Nano* **2018**, *12*, 56–62. [CrossRef] [PubMed]
52. Kim, S.J.; Koh, H.-J.; Ren, C.E.; Kwon, O.; Maleski, K.; Cho, S.; Anasori, B.; Kim, C.-K.; Choi, Y.-K.; Kim, J.; et al. Metallic $Ti_3C_2T_x$ MXene Gas Sensors with Ultrahigh Signal-to-Noise Ratio. *ACS Nano* **2018**, *12*, 986–993. [CrossRef]
53. Li, S.; Zhang, Y.; Yang, W.; Liu, H.; Fang, X. 2D Perovskite $Sr_2Nb_3O_{10}$ for High-Performance UV Photodetectors. *Adv. Mater.* **2020**, *32*, 1905443. [CrossRef]
54. Chen, J.; Li, Z.; Ni, F.; Ouyang, W.; Fang, X. Bio-inspired transparent MXene electrodes for flexible UV photodetectors. *Mater. Horiz.* **2020**, *7*, 1828–1833. [CrossRef]
55. Ouyang, W.; Chen, J.; He, J.; Fang, X. Improved Photoelectric Performance of UV Photodetector Based on ZnO Nanoparticle-Decorated BiOCl Nanosheet Arrays onto PDMS Substrate: The Heterojunction and $Ti_3C_2T_x$ MXene Conduction Layer. *Adv. Electron. Mater.* **2020**, *6*, 2000168. [CrossRef]
56. Zhao, M.-Q.; Ren, C.E.; Ling, Z.; Lukatskaya, M.R.; Zhang, C.; Van Aken, K.L.; Barsoum, M.W.; Gogotsi, Y. Flexible MXene/Carbon Nanotube Composite Paper with High Volumetric Capacitance. *Adv. Mater.* **2015**, *27*, 339–345. [CrossRef] [PubMed]
57. Pang, J.; Mendes, R.G.; Bachmatiuk, A.; Zhao, L.; Ta, H.Q.; Gemming, T.; Liu, H.; Liu, Z.; Rummeli, M.H. Applications of 2D MXenes in energy conversion and storage systems. *Chem. Soc. Rev.* **2019**, *48*, 72–133. [CrossRef] [PubMed]
58. Jia, L.; Li, Y.; Su, L.; Liu, D.; Fu, Y.; Li, J.; Yan, X.; He, D. TiO_2 Nanoparticles In Situ Formed on Ti_3C_2 Nanosheets by a One-Step Ethanol-Thermal Method for Enhanced Reversible Lithium-Ion Storage. *ChemistrySelect* **2020**, *5*, 3124–3129. [CrossRef]
59. Zang, X.; Wang, J.; Qin, Y.; Wang, T.; He, C.; Shao, Q.; Zhu, H.; Cao, N. Enhancing Capacitance Performance of $Ti_3C_2T_x$ MXene as Electrode Materials of Supercapacitor: From Controlled Preparation to Composite Structure Construction. *Nano-Micro Lett.* **2020**, *12*, 77. [CrossRef]
60. Jiang, H.; Wang, Z.; Yang, Q.; Tan, L.; Dong, L.; Dong, M. Ultrathin $Ti_3C_2T_x$ (MXene) Nanosheet-Wrapped $NiSe_2$ Octahedral Crystal for Enhanced Supercapacitor Performance and Synergetic Electrocatalytic Water Splitting. *Nano-Micro Lett.* **2019**, *11*, 31. [CrossRef] [PubMed]
61. Liu, H.; Zhang, X.; Zhu, Y.; Cao, B.; Zhu, Q.; Zhang, P.; Xu, B.; Wu, F.; Chen, R. Electrostatic Self-assembly of 0D–2D SnO_2 Quantum Dots/$Ti_3C_2T_x$ MXene Hybrids as Anode for Lithium-Ion Batteries. *Nano-Micro Lett.* **2019**, *11*, 65. [CrossRef]
62. Zhang, S.; Ying, H.; Yuan, B.; Hu, R.; Han, W.-Q. Partial Atomic Tin Nanocomplex Pillared Few-Layered $Ti_3C_2T_x$ MXenes for Superior Lithium-Ion Storage. *Nano-Micro Lett.* **2020**, *12*, 78. [CrossRef]
63. Li, Z.; Zhuang, Z.; Lv, F.; Zhu, H.; Zhou, L.; Luo, M.; Zhu, J.; Lang, Z.; Feng, S.; Chen, W.; et al. The Marriage of the FeN_4 Moiety and MXene Boosts Oxygen Reduction Catalysis: Fe 3d Electron Delocalization Matters. *Adv. Mater.* **2018**, *30*, e1803220. [CrossRef]
64. Ahmed, B.; EL Ghazaly, A.; Rosen, J. i-MXenes for Energy Storage and Catalysis. *Adv. Funct. Mater.* **2020**, *30*, 2000894. [CrossRef]
65. Wang, J.; Zhang, Z.; Yan, X.; Zhang, S.; Wu, Z.; Zhuang, Z.; Han, W.-Q. Rational Design of Porous $N-Ti_3C_2$ MXene@CNT Microspheres for High Cycling Stability in Li–S Battery. *Nano-Micro Lett.* **2020**, *12*, 4. [CrossRef] [PubMed]
66. Sun, Y.; Meng, X.; Dall'Agnese, Y.; Dall'Agnese, C.; Duan, S.; Gao, Y.; Chen, G.; Wang, X.-F. 2D MXenes as Co-catalysts in Photocatalysis: Synthetic Methods. *Nano-Micro Lett.* **2019**, *11*, 79. [CrossRef] [PubMed]
67. Ihsanullah, I. Potential of MXenes in Water Desalination: Current Status and Perspectives. *Nano-Micro Lett.* **2020**, *12*, 72. [CrossRef]
68. Zhang, Q.; Teng, J.; Zou, G.; Peng, Q.; Du, Q.; Jiao, T.; Xiang, J. Efficient phosphate sequestration for water purification by unique sandwich-like MXene/magnetic iron oxide nanocomposites. *Nanoscale* **2016**, *8*, 7085–7093. [CrossRef] [PubMed]
69. Xie, X.; Chen, C.; Zhang, N.; Tang, Z.-R.; Jiang, J.; Xu, Y.-J. Microstructure and surface control of MXene films for water purification. *Nat. Sustain.* **2019**, *2*, 856–862. [CrossRef]
70. Lu, Y.; Fan, D.; Xu, H.; Min, H.; Lu, C.; Lin, Z.; Yang, X. Implementing Hybrid Energy Harvesting in 3D Spherical Evaporator for Solar Steam Generation and Synergic Water Purification. *Sol. RRL* **2020**, *4*, 2000232. [CrossRef]
71. Wu, X.; Ding, M.; Xu, H.; Yang, W.; Zhang, K.; Tian, H.; Wang, H.; Xie, Z. Scalable $Ti_3C_2T_x$ MXene Interlayered Forward Osmosis Membranes for Enhanced Water Purification and Organic Solvent Recovery. *ACS Nano* **2020**, *14*, 9125–9135. [CrossRef]
72. Ming, X.; Guo, A.; Zhang, Q.; Guo, Z.; Yu, F.; Hou, B.; Wang, Y.; Homewood, K.P.; Wang, X. 3D macroscopic graphene oxide/MXene architectures for multifunctional water purification. *Carbon* **2020**, *167*, 285–295. [CrossRef]
73. Liu, Z.; Alshareef, H.N. MXenes for Optoelectronic Devices. *Adv. Electron. Mater.* **2021**, *7*, 2100295. [CrossRef]
74. Xu, M.; Lei, S.; Qi, J.; Dou, Q.; Liu, L.; Lu, Y.; Huang, Q.; Shi, S.; Yan, X. Opening Magnesium Storage Capability of Two-Dimensional MXene by Intercalation of Cationic Surfactant. *ACS Nano* **2018**, *12*, 3733–3740. [CrossRef] [PubMed]
75. Khazaei, M.; Ranjbar, A.; Arai, M.; Sasaki, T.; Yunoki, S. Electronic properties and applications of MXenes: A theoretical review. *J. Mater. Chem. C* **2017**, *5*, 2488–2503. [CrossRef]
76. Shi, M.; Xiao, P.; Lang, J.; Yan, C.; Yan, X. Porous $g-C_3N_4$ and MXene Dual-Confined FeOOH Quantum Dots for Superior Energy Storage in an Ionic Liquid. *Adv. Sci.* **2020**, *7*, 1901975. [CrossRef] [PubMed]

77. Guo, Z.; Gao, L.; Xu, Z.; Teo, S.; Zhang, C.; Kamata, Y.; Hayase, S.; Ma, T. High Electrical Conductivity 2D MXene Serves as Additive of Perovskite for Efficient Solar Cells. *Small* **2018**, *14*, e1802738. [CrossRef] [PubMed]
78. Cao, J.; Meng, F.; Gao, L.; Yang, S.; Yan, Y.; Wang, N.; Liu, A.; Li, Y.; Ma, T. Alternative electrodes for HTMs and noble-metal-free perovskite solar cells: 2D MXenes electrodes. *RSC Adv.* **2019**, *9*, 34152–34157. [CrossRef]
79. Yu, Z.; Feng, W.; Lu, W.; Li, B.; Yao, H.; Zeng, K.; Ouyang, J. MXenes with tunable work functions and their application as electron- and hole-transport materials in non-fullerene organic solar cells. *J. Mater. Chem. A* **2019**, *7*, 11160–11169. [CrossRef]
80. Cheng, M.; Zuo, C.; Wu, Y.; Li, Z.; Xu, B.; Hua, Y.; Ding, L. Charge-transport layer engineering in perovskite solar cells. *Sci. Bull.* **2020**, *65*, 1237–1241. [CrossRef]
81. Wolverton, M. Perovskite solar cells reveal excitonic optical transitions. *Scilight* **2018**, *2018*, 080003. [CrossRef]
82. Green, M.A.; Hishikawa, Y.; Dunlop, E.D.; Levi, D.H.; Hohl-Ebinger, J.; Yoshita, M.; Ho-Baillie, A.W. Solar cell efficiency tables (Version 53). *Prog. Photovolt. Res. Appl.* **2019**, *27*, 3–12. [CrossRef]
83. Kojima, A.; Teshima, K.; Shirai, Y.; Miyasaka, T. Organometal Halide Perovskites as Visible-Light Sensitizers for Photovoltaic Cells. *J. Am. Chem. Soc.* **2009**, *131*, 6050–6051. [CrossRef]
84. Im, J.-H.; Lee, C.-R.; Lee, J.-W.; Park, S.-W.; Park, N.-G. 6.5% efficient perovskite quantum-dot-sensitized solar cell. *Nanoscale* **2011**, *3*, 4088–4093. [CrossRef]
85. Green, M.A.; Ho-Baillie, A. Perovskite Solar Cells: The Birth of a New Era in Photovoltaics. *ACS Energy Lett.* **2017**, *2*, 822–830. [CrossRef]
86. Zhou, Q.; Duan, J.; Du, J.; Guo, Q.; Zhang, Q.; Yang, X.; Duan, Y.; Tang, Q. Tailored Lattice "Tape" to Confine Tensile Interface for 11.08%-Efficiency All-Inorganic $CsPbBr_3$ Perovskite Solar Cell with an Ultrahigh Voltage of 1.702 V. *Adv. Sci.* **2021**, *2101418*, 2101418. [CrossRef]
87. Fu, W.; Ramalingam, V.; Kim, H.; Lin, C.-H.; Fang, X.; Alshareef, H.N.; He, J. MXene-Contacted Silicon Solar Cells with 11.5% Efficiency. *Adv. Energy Mater.* **2019**, *9*, 1–9. [CrossRef]
88. Zhang, Y.; Xiong, R.; Sa, B.; Zhou, J.; Sun, Z. MXenes: Promising donor and acceptor materials for high-efficiency heterostructure solar cells. *Sustain. Energy Fuels* **2021**, *5*, 135–143. [CrossRef]
89. Saeed, M.A.; Kim, S.H.; Kim, H.; Liang, J.; Woo, H.Y.; Kim, T.G.; Yan, H.; Shim, J.W. Indoor Organic Photovoltaics: Optimal Cell Design Principles with Synergistic Parasitic Resistance and Optical Modulation Effect. *Adv. Energy Mater.* **2021**, *11*, 2003103. [CrossRef]
90. Saeed, M.A.; Yoo, K.; Kang, H.C.; Shim, J.W.; Lee, J.-J. Recent developments in dye-sensitized photovoltaic cells under ambient illumination. *Dye. Pigment.* **2021**, *194*, 109626. [CrossRef]
91. Wang, Y.; Zhang, Y.; Zhang, L.; Wu, Z.; Su, Q.; Liu, Q.; Fu, Y.; Li, J.; Li, Y.; He, D. Enhanced performance and the related mechanisms of organic solar cells using Li-doped SnO_2 as the electron transport layer. *Mater. Chem. Phys.* **2020**, *254*, 123536. [CrossRef]
92. Wu, Z.; Zhang, W.; Xie, C.; Zhang, L.; Wang, Y.; Zhang, Y.; Liu, Q.; Fu, Y.; Li, Y.; Li, J.; et al. Bridging for Carriers by Embedding Metal Oxide Nanoparticles in the Photoactive Layer to Enhance Performance of Polymer Solar Cells. *IEEE J. Photovolt.* **2020**, *10*, 1353–1358. [CrossRef]
93. Di Vito, A.; Pecchia, A.; Der Maur, M.A.; Di Carlo, A. Nonlinear Work Function Tuning of Lead-Halide Perovskites by MXenes with Mixed Terminations. *Adv. Funct. Mater.* **2020**, *30*, 1909028. [CrossRef]
94. Shao, P.; Chen, X.; Guo, X.; Zhang, W.; Chang, F.; Liu, Q.; Chen, Q.; Li, J.; Li, Y.; He, D. Facile embedding of SiO_2 nanoparticles in organic solar cells for performance improvement. *Org. Electron.* **2017**, *50*, 77–81. [CrossRef]
95. Agresti, A.; Pazniak, A.; Pescetelli, S.; Di Vito, A.; Rossi, D.; Pecchia, A.; Der Maur, M.A.; Liedl, A.; Larciprete, R.; Kuznetsov, D.V.; et al. Titanium-carbide MXenes for work function and interface engineering in perovskite solar cells. *Nat. Mater.* **2019**, *18*, 1228–1234. [CrossRef] [PubMed]
96. Zhang, Z.; Li, Y.; Liang, C.; Yu, G.; Zhao, J.; Luo, S.; Huang, Y.; Su, C.; Xing, G. In Situ Growth of $MAPbBr_3$ Nanocrystals on Few-Layer MXene Nanosheets with Efficient Energy Transfer. *Small* **2020**, *16*, e1905896. [CrossRef] [PubMed]
97. Jin, X.; Yang, L.; Wang, X.-F. Efficient Two-Dimensional Perovskite Solar Cells Realized by Incorporation of $Ti_3C_2T_x$ MXene as Nano-Dopants. *Nano-Micro Lett.* **2021**, *13*, 68. [CrossRef]
98. Yang, L.; Dall'Agnese, Y.; Hantanasirisakul, K.; Shuck, C.E.; Maleski, K.; Alhabeb, M.; Chen, G.; Gao, Y.; Sanehira, Y.; Jena, A.K.; et al. SnO_2–Ti_3C_2 MXene electron transport layers for perovskite solar cells. *J. Mater. Chem. A* **2019**, *7*, 5635–5642. [CrossRef]
99. Cao, X.; Zhi, L.; Jia, Y.; Li, Y.; Zhao, K.; Cui, X.; Ci, L.; Zhuang, D.; Wei, J. A Review of the Role of Solvents in Formation of High-Quality Solution-Processed Perovskite Films. *ACS Appl. Mater. Interfaces* **2019**, *11*, 7639–7654. [CrossRef]
100. Zhao, Y.; Zhang, X.; Han, X.; Hou, C.; Wang, H.; Qi, J.; Li, Y.; Zhang, Q. Tuning the reactivity of PbI_2 film via monolayer $Ti_3C_2T_x$ MXene for two-step-processed $CH_3NH_3PbI_3$ solar cells. *Chem. Eng. J.* **2021**, *417*, 127912. [CrossRef]
101. Larciprete, R.; Agresti, A.; Pescetelli, S.; Pazniak, H.; Liedl, A.; Lacovig, P.; Lizzit, D.; Tosi, E.; Lizzit, S.; Di Carlo, A. Mixed Cation Halide Perovskite under Environmental and Physical Stress. *Materials* **2021**, *14*, 3954. [CrossRef]
102. Hou, C.; Yu, H. $ZnO/Ti_3C_2T_x$ monolayer electron transport layers with enhanced conductivity for highly efficient inverted polymer solar cells. *Chem. Eng. J.* **2021**, *407*, 127192. [CrossRef]
103. Wei, J.; Xu, R.; Li, Y.-Q.; Li, C.; Chen, J.-D.; Zhao, X.-D.; Xie, Z.-Z.; Lee, C.-S.; Zhang, W.; Tang, J.-X. Enhanced Light Harvesting in Perovskite Solar Cells by a Bioinspired Nanostructured Back Electrode. *Adv. Energy Mater.* **2017**, *7*, 1700492. [CrossRef]

104. Tran, V.-D.; Pammi, S.; Park, B.-J.; Han, Y.; Jeon, C.; Yoon, S.-G. Transfer-free graphene electrodes for super-flexible and semi-transparent perovskite solar cells fabricated under ambient air. *Nano Energy* **2019**, *65*, 104018. [CrossRef]
105. Bogachuk, D.; Zouhair, S.; Wojciechowski, K.; Yang, B.; Babu, V.; Wagner, L.; Xu, B.; Lim, J.; Mastroianni, S.; Pettersson, H.; et al. Low-temperature carbon-based electrodes in perovskite solar cells. *Energy Environ. Sci.* **2020**, *13*, 3880–3916. [CrossRef]
106. Liu, Z.; He, H. Counter Electrode Materials for Organic-Inorganic Perovskite Solar Cells. In *Nanostructured Materials for Next-Generation Energy Storage and Conversion*; Springer: Berlin/Heidelberg, Germany, 2019; pp. 165–225. [CrossRef]
107. Zhang, J.; Kong, N.; Uzun, S.; Levitt, A.; Seyedin, S.; Lynch, P.A.; Qin, S.; Han, M.; Yang, W.; Liu, J.; et al. Scalable Manufacturing of Free-Standing, Strong $Ti_3C_2T_x$ MXene Films with Outstanding Conductivity. *Adv. Mater.* **2020**, *32*, e2001093. [CrossRef]
108. Hantanasirisakul, K.; Gogotsi, Y. Electronic and Optical Properties of 2D Transition Metal Carbides and Nitrides (MXenes). *Adv. Mater.* **2018**, *30*, e1804779. [CrossRef] [PubMed]
109. Xiong, D.; Li, X.; Bai, Z.; Lu, S. Recent Advances in Layered $Ti_3C_2T_x$ MXene for Electrochemical Energy Storage. *Small* **2018**, *14*, e1703419. [CrossRef]
110. Li, K.; Liang, M.; Wang, H.; Wang, X.; Huang, Y.; Coelho, J.; Pinilla, S.; Zhang, Y.; Qi, F.; Nicolosi, V.; et al. 3D MXene Architectures for Efficient Energy Storage and Conversion. *Adv. Funct. Mater.* **2020**, *30*, 2000842. [CrossRef]
111. Chen, Y.; Wang, D.; Lin, Y.; Zou, X.; Xie, T. In suit growth of CuSe nanoparticles on MXene (Ti_3C_2) nanosheets as an efficient counter electrode for quantum dot-sensitized solar cells. *Electrochim. Acta* **2019**, *316*, 248–256. [CrossRef]
112. Tian, Z.; Qi, Z.; Yang, Y.; Yan, H.; Chen, Q.; Zhong, Q. Anchoring CuS nanoparticles on accordion-like Ti_3C_2 as high electrocatalytic activity counter electrodes for QDSSCs. *Inorg. Chem. Front.* **2020**, *7*, 3727–3734. [CrossRef]
113. Mi, L.; Zhang, Y.; Chen, T.; Xu, E.; Jiang, Y. Carbon electrode engineering for high efficiency all-inorganic perovskite solar cells. *RSC Adv.* **2020**, *10*, 12298–12303. [CrossRef]
114. Xu, C.; Zhao, X.; Sun, M.; Ma, J.; Wu, M. Highly effective 2D layered carbides counter electrode for iodide redox couple regeneration in dye-sensitized solar cells. *Electrochim. Acta* **2021**, *392*, 138983. [CrossRef]
115. Chen, X.; Zhuang, Y.; Shen, Q.; Cao, X.; Yang, W.; Yang, P. In situ synthesis of $Ti_3C_2T_x$ MXene/CoS nanocomposite as high performance counter electrode materials for quantum dot-sensitized solar cells. *Sol. Energy* **2021**, *226*, 236–244. [CrossRef]
116. Tang, H.; Feng, H.; Wang, H.; Wan, X.; Liang, J.; Chen, Y. Highly Conducting MXene–Silver Nanowire Transparent Electrodes for Flexible Organic Solar Cells. *ACS Appl. Mater. Interfaces* **2019**, *11*, 25330–25337. [CrossRef] [PubMed]
117. Fan, X. Doping and Design of Flexible Transparent Electrodes for High-Performance Flexible Organic Solar Cells: Recent Advances and Perspectives. *Adv. Funct. Mater.* **2021**, *31*, 1–30. [CrossRef]
118. Ahmad, M.S.; Pandey, A.; Rahim, N.A.; Aslfattahi, N.; Mishra, Y.K.; Rashid, B.; Saidur, R. 2-D Mxene flakes as potential replacement for both TCO and Pt layers for Dye-Sensitized Solar cell. *Ceram. Int.* **2021**, *47*, 27942–27947. [CrossRef]
119. Pan, H.; Zhao, X.; Gong, X.; Li, H.; Ladi, N.H.; Zhang, X.L.; Huang, W.; Ahmad, S.; Ding, L.; Shen, Y.; et al. Advances in design engineering and merits of electron transporting layers in perovskite solar cells. *Mater. Horiz.* **2020**, *7*, 2276–2291. [CrossRef]
120. Li, S.; Cao, Y.-L.; Li, W.-H.; Bo, Z.-S. A brief review of hole transporting materials commonly used in perovskite solar cells. *Rare Met.* **2021**, *40*, 2712–2729. [CrossRef]
121. Hussain, S.; Liu, H.; Vikraman, D.; Hussain, M.; Jaffery, S.H.A.; Ali, A.; Kim, H.-S.; Kang, J.; Jung, J. Characteristics of Mo2C-CNTs hybrid blended hole transport layer in the perovskite solar cells and X-ray detectors. *J. Alloys Compd.* **2021**, *885*, 161039. [CrossRef]
122. Bati, A.S.R.; Hao, M.; Macdonald, T.J.; Batmunkh, M.; Yamauchi, Y.; Wang, L.; Shapter, J.G. 1D–2D Synergistic MXene-Nanotubes Hybrids for Efficient Perovskite Solar Cells. *Small* **2021**, *17*, 2101925. [CrossRef]
123. Zheng, H.; Wang, Y.; Niu, B.; Ge, R.; Lei, Y.; Yan, L.; Si, J.; Zhong, P.; Ma, X. Controlling the Defect Density of Perovskite Films by MXene/SnO_2 Hybrid Electron Transport Layers for Efficient and Stable Photovoltaics. *J. Phys. Chem. C* **2021**, *125*, 15210–15222. [CrossRef]
124. Zhang, J.; Huang, C.; Yu, H. Modulate the work function of Nb_2CT_x MXene as the hole transport layer for perovskite solar cells. *Appl. Phys. Lett.* **2021**, *119*, 033506. [CrossRef]
125. Wang, J.; Cai, Z.; Lin, D.; Chen, K.; Zhao, L.; Xie, F.; Su, R.; Xie, W.; Liu, P.; Zhu, R. Plasma Oxidized $Ti_3C_2T_x$ MXene as Electron Transport Layer for Efficient Perovskite Solar Cells. *ACS Appl. Mater. Interfaces* **2021**, *13*, 32495–32502. [CrossRef] [PubMed]
126. Yang, L.; Kan, D.; Dall'Agnese, C.; Dall'Agnese, Y.; Wang, B.; Jena, A.K.; Wei, Y.; Chen, G.; Wang, X.-F.; Gogotsi, Y.; et al. Performance improvement of MXene-based perovskite solar cells upon property transition from metallic to semiconductive by oxidation of $Ti_3C_2T_x$ in air. *J. Mater. Chem. A* **2021**, *9*, 5016–5025. [CrossRef]
127. Saranin, D.; Pescetelli, S.; Pazniak, A.; Rossi, D.; Liedl, A.; Yakusheva, A.; Luchnikov, L.; Podgorny, D.; Gostischev, P.; Didenko, S.; et al. Transition metal carbides (MXenes) for efficient NiO-based inverted perovskite solar cells. *Nano Energy* **2021**, *82*, 105771. [CrossRef]

Article

Nanostructured Molybdenum-Oxide Anodes for Lithium-Ion Batteries: An Outstanding Increase in Capacity

Hua Wang [1], Tianyi Li [1], Ahmed M. Hashem [2,*], Ashraf E. Abdel-Ghany [2], Rasha S. El-Tawil [2], Hanaa M. Abuzeid [2], Amanda Coughlin [3], Kai Chang [1], Shixiong Zhang [3], Hazim El-Mounayri [1], Andres Tovar [1], Likun Zhu [1,*] and Christian M. Julien [4,*]

1. Department of Mechanical and Energy Engineering, Indiana University-Purdue University Indianapolis, Indianapolis, IN 46202, USA; wanghua@iu.edu (H.W.); tl41@iupui.edu (T.L.); kc59@iupui.edu (K.C.); helmouna@iupui.edu (H.E.-M.); tovara@iupui.edu (A.T.)
2. National Research Centre, Inorganic Chemistry Department, Behoes Street, Dokki, Giza 12622, Egypt; achraf_28@yahoo.com (A.E.A.-G.); r2samir@yahoo.com (R.S.E.-T.); hanaa20619@hotmail.com (H.M.A.)
3. Department of Physics, Indiana University, Bloomington, IN 47405, USA; amacough@iu.edu (A.C.); sxzhang@indiana.edu (S.Z.)
4. Institut de Minéralogie, de Physique des Matériaux et Cosmologie (IMPMC), Sorbonne Université, UMR-CNRS 7590, 4 Place Jussieu, 75752 Paris, France
* Correspondence: ahmedh242@yahoo.com (A.M.H.); likzhu@iupui.edu (L.Z.); christian.julien@sorbonne-universite.fr (C.M.J.)

Abstract: This work aimed at synthesizing MoO_3 and MoO_2 by a facile and cost-effective method using extract of orange peel as a biological chelating and reducing agent for ammonium molybdate. Calcination of the precursor in air at 450 °C yielded the stochiometric MoO_3 phase, while calcination in vacuum produced the reduced form MoO_2 as evidenced by X-ray powder diffraction, Raman scattering spectroscopy, and X-ray photoelectron spectroscopy results. Scanning and transmission electron microscopy images showed different morphologies and sizes of MoO_x particles. MoO_3 formed platelet particles that were larger than those observed for MoO_2. MoO_3 showed stable thermal behavior until approximately 800 °C, whereas MoO_2 showed weight gain at approximately 400 °C due to the fact of re-oxidation and oxygen uptake and, hence, conversion to stoichiometric MoO_3. Electrochemically, traditional performance was observed for MoO_3, which exhibited a high initial capacity with steady and continuous capacity fading upon cycling. On the contrary, MoO_2 showed completely different electrochemical behavior with less initial capacity but an outstanding increase in capacity upon cycling, which reached 1600 mAh g^{-1} after 800 cycles. This outstanding electrochemical performance of MoO_2 may be attributed to its higher surface area and better electrical conductivity as observed in surface area and impedance investigations.

Keywords: molybdenum oxides; green synthesis; biological chelator; additional capacity; anodes; lithium-ion batteries

1. Introduction

Understanding and realization of the benefit of efficient energy storage is one of the most important strategies for achieving sustainable development [1,2]. Nowadays, lithium-ion batteries (LIBs) have become one of the most important energy storage technologies due to the fact of their higher storage capacity and power density compared to other rechargeable batteries [3–5]. The development and rapid increase in portable electronic devices and electric vehicles have accelerated the pursuit of developing LIBs with high energy and power densities [6,7]. Therefore, it is essential to develop high-capacity electrode materials for LIBs [8–13]. Graphite has become the standard anode material for LIBs since their commercialization by Sony Corporation [14]. However, graphite has relatively low theoretical capacity (372 mAh g^{-1} and 850 mAh cm^{-3}), which cannot meet the demand of current large-scale energy applications [15]. To address this issue, there is a continuous effort to explore alternative anode materials. For instance, transition metal oxides (TMOs), such as NiO, MnO$_2$, TiO$_2$, Fe$_3$O$_4$, MoO$_3$, and MoO$_2$, have been studied as anode materials for LIBs. These oxides are abundant, low cost, and have a high theoretical specific capacity of approximately 500–1200 mAh g^{-1} due to the fact of their conversion reaction upon lithiation [16–21].

Molybdenum oxides with different oxidation states (e.g., MoO$_3$, MoO$_{3-\delta}$, Mo$_n$O$_{3n-1}$, and MoO$_2$) and a broad spectrum of electrical properties ranging from wide band gap semiconducting (MoO$_3$) to metallic (MoO$_2$) character are considered as promising anode materials for LIBs [22]. Their specific capacities are significantly higher than that of graphite [23–29]. In particular, MoO$_3$ with an orthorhombic crystal structure is a thermal stable, abundant, cost effective, and a rather safe oxide with a theoretical capacity of 1117 mAh g^{-1} and a typical discharge potential plateau around 0.45 V [30–34]. It has a unique layered structure that is convenient for fast lithium diffusion transport [15,35–38]. The overall first lithiation reaction for MoO$_3$ is described by two reactions: the lithium insertion (addition) at a potential >1.5 V up to $x \approx 1.2$ (Equation (1)) and the conversion (transformation) reaction at a potential <0.5 V up to $x \approx 6.0$ (Equation (2)) as follows [22]:

$$MoO_3 + xLi^+ + xe^- \rightarrow Li_xMoO_3, \quad (1)$$

$$Li_xMoO_3 + (6-x)Li^+ + (6-x)e^- \rightarrow Mo + 3Li_2O. \quad (2)$$

Some drawbacks have been reported for MoO$_3$, such as phase transformation accompanied by volume expansion with repeating cycling, which leads to a rapid capacity fading [39,40].

On the other hand, MoO$_2$ crystallizes in the monoclinic structure with space group $P2_1/c$, which can be viewed as a distorted rutile phase. This structure is composed of MoO$_6$ octahedra joined by edge-sharing, which form a (1 × 1)-tunneling network [41,42]. In addition, MoO$_2$ has outstanding properties for energy storage applications, e.g., metal-like conductivity (~6 × 10^3 S cm^{-1}), very low toxicity, cost-effectiveness, high chemical and thermal stability, high volumetric capacity due to the fact of its high density (6.5 g cm^{-3}), and high theoretical capacity (838 mAh g^{-1}) [43–45]. The first lithiation mechanism is an insertion-type reaction that takes place in the bulk and amorphous MoO$_2$ electrodes with only one-electron reduction as described by Equation (3) [46]:

$$MoO_2 + xLi^+ + xe^- \leftrightarrow Li_xMoO_2, \quad (3)$$

with $0 \leq x \leq 0.98$. The second mechanism is a conversion reaction that gradually resolves Li$_x$MoO$_2$ as described by Equation (4) [47]:

$$Li_xMoO_2 + (4-x)Li \leftrightarrow 2Li_2O + Mo. \quad (4)$$

that shows the formation of metallic Mo and Li$_2$O.

MoO$_3$ and MoO$_2$ have been prepared in different morphologies, e.g., nanoparticles [48], nanowires [49,50], nanorods [51,52], nanotubes [53], nanosheets [54], and nanobelts [55]. These nanosized fabrications were expected to improve the electrochemical performance [56]. However, these fabrication methods are complicated, expensive, energy- and time-consuming, and non-scalable [57]. To alleviate these limitations, to some extent, an attempt was made to use a rather benign approach via simple, green, and eco-friendly reducing agents for nanoparticles formation [58]. Green synthesized particles have low toxicity and are more stable than those prepared by traditional methods, as biological sources provide a stabilizing and capping effect for the synthesized particles, especially extracts of plants [58].

Extracts of waste products have been used as cost-effective, eco-friendly, and efficient raw materials for various energy storage applications [59,60]. In our previous work, we used extracts of lemon and orange peels to synthesize manganese dioxides, which has been used as cathode materials in LIBs and supercapacitors [60,61]. Further processing and using large quantities of orange peels as a byproduct will reduce hazardous impacts and serious environmental pollution [60]. Orange peels contain polyphenolic and flavonoid compounds which have hesperidin, narirutin, naringin, and eriocitrin [62]. It is well known that the phenolic compounds have at least one aromatic ring. The latter is attached to one or more hydroxyl groups. The number and position of the carboxylic group has a direct impact on reducing the antioxidant ability of flavonoids and phenolic acids. As the number of hydroxyl group increases, the antioxidant activity increases [63]. Orange is considered as one of the most important fruits with a global production of 48.8 (2016/17) million tons. Industrial extraction of citrus juice consumed a large portion of this production. As a result of this industry, there are large amounts of residues, e.g., peel and segment membranes. A high percent of these residues is related to peel byproduct that represents between 50% and 65% of the total weight of the fruit; reported chemical analysis for orange peel showed 7.1% protein and 12.79% crude fiber. In addition, limonoids and flavonoids with antioxidant activity were also found in orange peel. This antioxidant activity of citrus peel extracts comes from glycosides hesperidin and naringin present in this extract. Orange peel also contains coniferin and phlorin as additional phenols that help in radical scavenging when administered in the form of orange peel molasses, and this will promote sustainable disposal of orange peels [64].

In this study, orange peel extract was used as an effective chelating agent to synthesize molybdenum oxides. MoO_3 and MoO_2 were prepared by altering the calcination conditions: in air for MoO_3 and in vacuum for MoO_2 at a low temperature of 450 °C. The as-prepared oxides were subjected to various characterizations, including X-ray diffraction (XRD), thermogravimetric analysis (TGA), scanning electron microscopy (SEM), transmission electron microscopy (TEM), Raman scattering (RS) spectroscopy, and X-ray photoelectron spectroscopy (XPS), to elucidate their morphological and structural properties. Further electrical and electrochemical characterizations, including cyclic voltammetry (CV), galvanostatic charge–discharge (GCD), electrochemical impedance spectroscopy (EIS), and area-specific impedance (ASI), were carried out for the as-prepared molybdenum oxides as anode materials for LIBs.

2. Materials and Methods

Ammonium molybdate, conductive carbon black super C65 (Timcal Co., Bodio, Switzerland), binder polyvinylidene fluoride (PVDF, 12 wt.%, Kureha Battery Materials Japan Co., Tokyo, Japan), solvent 1-methyl-2-pyrrolidinone (NMP, anhydrous 99.5%, Sigma–Aldrich, Burlington, MA, USA), electrolyte 1 mol L^{-1} $LiPF_6$ in ethylene and dimethyl carbonate solution mixed as a 1:1 volume ratio (BASF Corporation, Ludwigshafen-am-Rhein, Germany), and lithium ribbon (thickness 0.38 mm, 99.9% trace metals basis, Sigma–Aldrich, Burlington, MA, USA) were employed as received.

Molybdenum oxides were prepared by the sol-gel method using ammonium molybdate tetrahydrate, $(NH_4)_6Mo_7O_{24} \cdot 4H_2O$ as the source of molybdenum, and extract of orange peel as the chelating agent. Pure filtrated extract of orange peel was obtained through boiling small pieces of cleaned waste peels in distilled water at 100 °C for 10 min. A schematic representation of the MoO_3 and MoO_2 growth process is shown in Figure 1. Pure orange peel extract drops were added with vigorous stirring to a 100 mL solution of 4 g of $(NH_4)_6Mo_7O_{24} \cdot 4H_2O$. During this operation, the solution changed in color from yellow to blue until conversion to a dark gel. The dry xerogel (precursor) was divided into two parts: one part was calcined in air at 450 °C for 5 h (MOA, yellow color) and the second was calcined under vacuum at 450 °C for 5 h (MOV, black color).

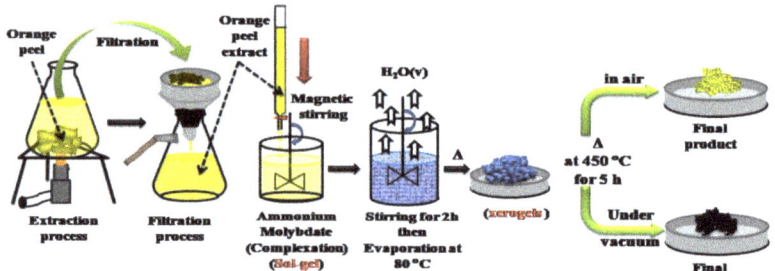

Figure 1. Schematic diagram for the synthesis of MoO₃ (yellow color) and MoO₂ (black).

XRD analyses of as-prepared samples were processed using a Bruker D8 Discover XRD Instrument equipped with CuK$_\alpha$ radiation (λ = 1.5406 Å). The scanning rate was 1.2° min^{-1}, for 2θ between 10° and 80°. Raman spectra were recorded at room temperature with a micro-Raman spectrometer (Renishaw, Wotton-under-Edge, UK) with a confocal Raman microscope inVia™ system at a 532 nm laser-line excitation. The spectra were calibrated with the reference Si phonon peak at 520 cm^{-1}. The morphology of the materials was studied by field emission scanning electron microscopy (FESEM, JEOL JSM-7800F) and by transmission electron microscopy (TEM, JEOL, JEM-2100 microscope, Japan). BET surface area and pore size distribution of synthesized samples were determined from an N$_2$-physisorption analyzer (ASAP 2020 system, Micromeritics Corporate, Norcross, GA, USA). The BET surface area was calculated from the isotherms in the range from 0.02 to 0.4 of relative pressures (P/P_0). TGA measurements were carried out for the prepared samples using a thermal gravimetric analyzer (Perkin Elmer, TGA 7 series) in a temperature range of 50–1000 °C at a heating rate of 10 °C min^{-1} in air. X-ray photoelectron spectra were recorded using a PHI VersaProbe II Scanning X-Ray Microprobe system equipped with a Mg Kα source (λ = 1253.6 eV).

LIB electrodes were fabricated as a mixture of active materials (Mo oxide powders), carbon black (CB), and polyvinylidene fluoride binder (PVDF) in a 5:3:2 mass ratio. We used a high percentage of carbon black and PVDF binder in the electrode to maintain the mechanical integrity and good electrical connection in the electrode during long-term cycling experiment. The mixture was added to N-methyl-2-pyrrolidone (NMP) solvent. The mixed slurry was magnetically stirred for 24 h to form a homogeneous blend. The well-blended slurry was cast on a copper foil by a doctor blade and was dried under vacuum at 100 °C for 24 h. Finally, electrodes were punched out as ~0.97 cm^2 discs (Φ = 11 mm). CR2032 coin cells processed in an argon-filled glovebox using 30 µL electrolyte dripped on the electrode, then on a Celgard 2400 separator. Electrochemical tests were carried out using an Arbin BT2000 battery cycler at room temperature. Before cycling, cells were initially maintained at rest for 30 min. Cells were cycled galvanostatically at C/10 and 1C-rate (1C = 838 mA g^{-1} for MoO$_2$ and 1C = 1117 mA g^{-1} for MoO$_3$) in a voltage range between 0.01 and 3.0 V. Cyclic voltammetry was conducted at room temperature on a BioLogic VSP workstation in which the potential was set to sweep from open-circuit voltage to 0.01 V and then to sweep back to 3.0 V at a 0.02 mV s^{-1} scanning rate. Electrochemical impedance spectroscopy was also conducted by the VSP workstation in the frequency range from 5 × 10^5 to 0.1 Hz with an amplitude of 5 mV.

3. Results

3.1. Structure and Morphology

The X-ray diffractograms of MOA and MOV materials are shown in Figure 2a. Patterns display well-resolved reflections with a very smooth background indicating the high crystallinity of Mo oxides prepared by the sol-gel method with biological chelating agent and final calcination at 450 °C. The XRD spectrum of MOA exhibited the typical pattern of the α-MoO$_3$ phase and can be indexed in the orthorhombic structure with *Pbnm* space group (JPCDS card 76-1003) [65]. The presence of a preferred orientation of (0k0) planes was evidenced by the (020), (040), and (060) Bragg lines with large intensities. The XRD spectrum of the MOV material displayed sharp diffraction peaks indicating the formation of highly crystallized MoO_2, which can be indexed using the monoclinic structure with the $P2_1/c$ space group (JPCDS card 68-0135). In order to characterize the phase purity as well as the phase composition, the full structural identification of the MoO_3 and the MoO_2 powders were analyzed using Rietveld refinements. The results are listed in Table 1, and the refined XRD spectra are displayed in Figure 2b,c. The small values of the residual and reliability parameters (R_p, R_w, and χ^2) of the Rietveld refinement indicate the successful identification of the orthorhombic and monoclinic phases of MoO_3 and MoO_2 powders, respectively, even in the presence of some impurity phases as in the case of MOV. The lattice parameters obtained from Rietveld refinement are in good agreement with values of our previous work as well as other literature [22,66–68]. A careful examination of the MoO_2 sample calcinated in vacuum reveals the presence of a small amount of Mo-suboxides such as Mo_4O_{11}, Mo_8O_{23}, and Mo_9O_{26} (Table 1). These compositions belong to Mo_nO_{3n-1} suboxides (Magnéli phases, $n = 4$–9), which crystallize into the ReO_3-type structure characterized by the presence of empty channels due to the loss of oxygen [23,68,69]. These compositions (Mo_4O_{11}, Mo_8O_{23}, and Mo_9O_{26}) deduced form Rietveld refinement imply the presence of a mixture of Mo with oxidation states between +6 and +4. This electronic configuration implies a concentration of free carriers and, thus, a large electrical conductivity, which is beneficial to electrochemical properties [68].

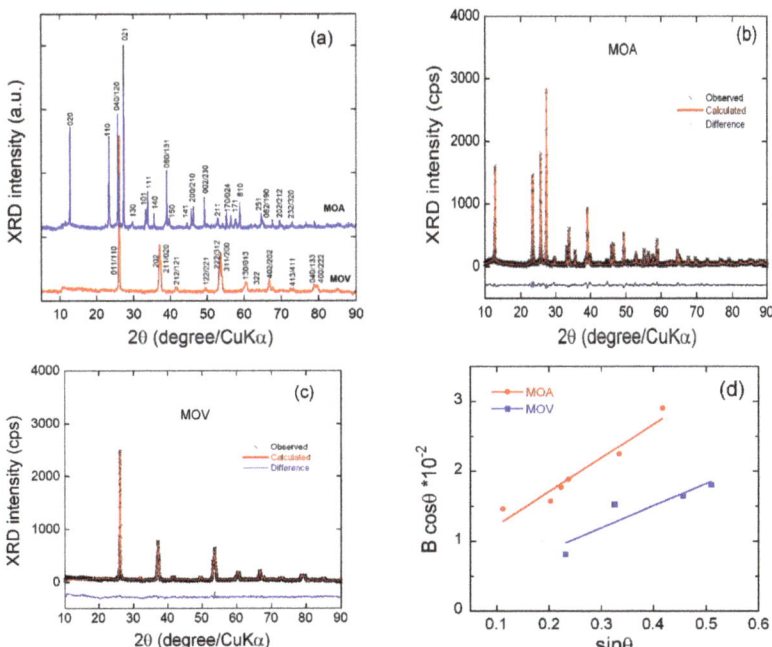

Figure 2. (a) XRD patterns of the as-prepared MOA and MOV samples. (b) Rietveld refinement of the MOA sample. (c) Rietveld refinement of the MOV sample. Cross marks are experimental data and solid lines (in red) are calculated diagrams. The curve at the bottom is the difference between the calculated and observed intensities. (d) Analysis of micro-strain from the full-width B at half-maximum of the XRD peaks according to Equation (1).

Table 1. Results of the Rietveld refinements for the MOA and MOV samples.

Crystal data	MOA	MOV
Lattice parameters		
a (Å)	3.69(5)	5.61(3)
b (Å)	13.84(8)	4.85(3)
c (Å)	3.95(9)	5.62(1)
V (Å^3)	202.6	131.3
L_c (nm)	29.5	45.6
$\varepsilon \times 10^{-2}$ (rd)	11.9	7.9
Reliability factors		
R_p (%)	10.9	8.1
R_{wp} (%)	16	11.2
R_{exp}	9.1	7.7
χ^2	3.1	2.1
Materials fraction (mol%)		
MoO_3	100	0
MoO_2	0	90.2
Mo_4O_{11}	0	2.2
Mo_8O_{23}	0	4.5
Mo_9O_{26}	0	3.1

The formation of Mo_4O_{11}, Mo_8O_{23}, and Mo_9O_{26} suboxides under vacuum is due to the presence of not only the ammonia in ammonium molybdate but also the CO and CO_2 gases generated by the combustion reaction of carbon found in the organic components of orange peel (i.e., ascorbic and citric acid) which reduce the Mo^{6+} ions in absence of O_2. The average crystalline sizes of the prepared samples were calculated using the Debye–Scherrer's formula from the full-width of diffraction peaks. They were found to be ≈29 and 45 nm for MOA and MOV, respectively. Further information on the structural properties can be obtained from the broadening of diffraction peaks that is considered an indicator, not only of the crystallinity of the MOA and MOV powder, but also of the homogeneous distribution of cations over the structure. The micro-strain (ε) of the MOA and MOV particles was determined using the Williamson–Hall equation [70]:

$$B_{hkl} \cos \theta_{hkl} = (K\lambda/L_c) + 4\varepsilon \sin \theta_{hkl} \quad (5)$$

where B_{hkl} is the line broadening of a Bragg reflection (*hkl*), K is the shape factor, L_c is the effective crystallite size, and λ is the X-ray wavelength. The micro-strain is estimated from the slope of the plot ($B_{hkl} \cos \theta_{hkl}$) vs. ($\sin \theta_{hkl}$) and the intersection with the vertical axis provides the crystallite size. The B_{hkl} value used here was the instrumentally corrected one. From Figure 2d, the micro-strain was determined to be 11.9×10^{-2} and 7.9×10^{-2} rd for MOA and MOV, respectively, showing a slight difference in the crystallinity of the samples, as the micro-strain was strongly affected by the heat-treatment conditions.

Figure 3 displays the thermogravimetry (TG) curves of MOA and MOV samples recorded at a heating rate of 10 °C min^{-1}. The MOA sample showed a stable, flat, and straight-line TG profile without weight change until the start of decomposition above 730 °C. These features indicate a stochiometric MoO_3 material without any oxygen vacancies or carbon coating due to the burning of the extract of organic peel. On the contrary, the thermal behavior of reduced MOV looked different. The TG curve was stable and flat until approximately 400 °C. Above 400 °C, a gradual and pronounced weight gain occurred until reaching the highest value of 10.4% weight gain, which was due to the re-oxidation and filling of oxygen vacancies in the suboxide (Mo_4O_{11}, Mo_8O_{23}, and Mo_9O_{26}) lattices, and the transformation of MoO_2 to the stoichiometric MoO_3 phase at T = 600 °C. Theoretically, the weight gain for the conversion of MoO_2 to MoO_3 was approximately 12.5%. From the TG analysis, it was observed that the weight of the sample increased by ≈10.4% from room temperature to 600 °C in the air. Thus, the calculated value for conversion of MoO_2 and the suboxides (i.e., Mo_4O_{11}, Mo_8O_{23}< and Mo_9O_{26}) to the stoichiometric MoO_3 is close to the theoretical value. It is worth noting that the color of MoO_2 was black before the TG measurements and converted to the color yellow after the TG runaway to 600 °C. In addition, this TG of MOV confirmed that there was no carbon coating around their particles. This was because there was no weight loss above 500 °C related to the emission of CO_2 as a result of the reaction between oxygen in the air and carbon, if present. However, some mass loss might occur, which was masked by oxygen gain during the oxidation process.

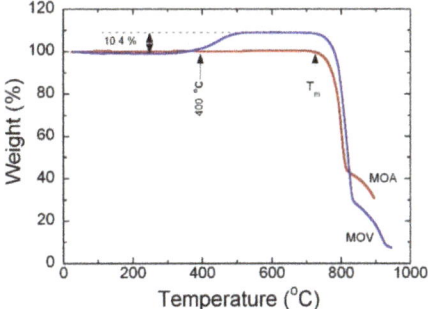

Figure 3. Thermogravimetry (TG) curves of the MOA and MOV samples recorded at a heating rate of 10 °C min^{-1}. MOA displays the typical behavior of the stoichiometric MoO_3 orthorhombic phase, while MOV shows the oxidation of the suboxide at 400 °C and the conversion to MoO_3 at 600 °C.

The SEM images (a–c) and TEM image (d) of the MOA and MOV samples depicted in Figure 4 illustrate the influence of the synthesis conditions on the particle size and morphology. There is a significant difference between the morphology of molybdenum oxide prepared in air and that prepared in vacuum from the same ammonium molybdate tetrahydrate precursor. Air calcination gives heterogeneous MOA particles with well-crystallized crystals a platelet-like shape (Figure 4a,c). The sizes of the MOA particles were in a wide range from the sub-micrometer to ~10 μm [71]. On the contrary, calcination in vacuum provided homogeneous MOV powders with an ash-like morphology at the nanometer size (Figure 4b). SEM (Figure 4c) and TEM images (Figure 4d) show that the MOA platelets had sizes larger than 1 μm, while the MOV powders had smaller sizes, in the 40–100 nm range. The size and morphology differences of the MOA and MOV particles were mainly due to the heat treatment conditions.

Figure 4. (**a**,**b**) SEM images of the MOA and MOV samples synthesized using a sol-gel method assisted by a biological chelator (scale bar of 10 μm). (**c**) Magnified SEM image of the MOA (scale bar of 1 μm) and a (**d**) TEM image of the MOV sample (scale bar of 100 nm).

Raman spectroscopy is a sensitive tool for investigating the coordination, structure, lattice vibrations, and symmetry of molybdenum and oxygen atoms in the presence of different phases. Further structural analyses of as-prepared molybdenum oxides were carried out by Raman scattering spectroscopy using the excitation line at λ_{exc} = 532 nm (Figure 5a–d). The Raman spectrum of the MOA sample (Figure 5a) displays the typical vibrational features of the orthorhombic α-MoO$_3$ phase. Twelve vibrational modes were evidenced by the peaks located at 197, 216, 245, 283, 290, 336, 364, 378, 471, 665, 818, and 995 cm^{-1}. The wavenumbers and relative intensities matched closely with the single crystal Raman spectrum given in the literature [72–76]. Most of the Raman active modes were dominated by either interlayer or intralayer contributions. More specifically, the peak at 665 cm^{-1} was related to the ν(O-Mo$_3$) stretching mode of the triply-coordinated oxygen atoms, which are shared by three MoO$_6$ octahedra. The intense peak at 818 cm^{-1} was linked to the doubly-coordinated oxygen ν(O-Mo$_2$) stretching mode. The high-wavenumber peak at 995 cm^{-1} was associated with the ν(Mo^{6+} = O) asymmetric stretching mode of terminal singly-coordinated (unshared) oxygen atoms, which had bonds that were responsible for the layered structure of the α-MoO$_3$ orthorhombic phase [75]. Figure 5b–d presents the micro-Raman spectra of the MOV sample recorded on different areas of the sample using 1% laser power (0.5 mW) at a 532 nm laser-line excitation. The micro-Raman results were in good agreement with the XRD findings. The mixture of vibrational features of the MoO$_2$ and Mo$_n$O$_{3n-1}$ suboxide phases (i.e., o-Mo$_4$O$_{11}$, m-Mo$_8$O$_{23}$, o-Mo$_9$O$_{26}$ Magnéli) can be identified [77–83]. The Raman bands of the MOV sample located at 126, 203, 228, 346, 362, 458, 470, 495, 570, 585, and 741 cm^{-1} (Figure 5b) correspond to a rutile-type (monoclinic) structure and agreed well with the vibrational features of the m-MoO$_2$ reported in the literature [77–80]. Two weaker peaks, located at 425 and 820 cm^{-1}, were attributed to the orthorhombic o-Mo$_4$O$_{11}$ suboxide [81,83].

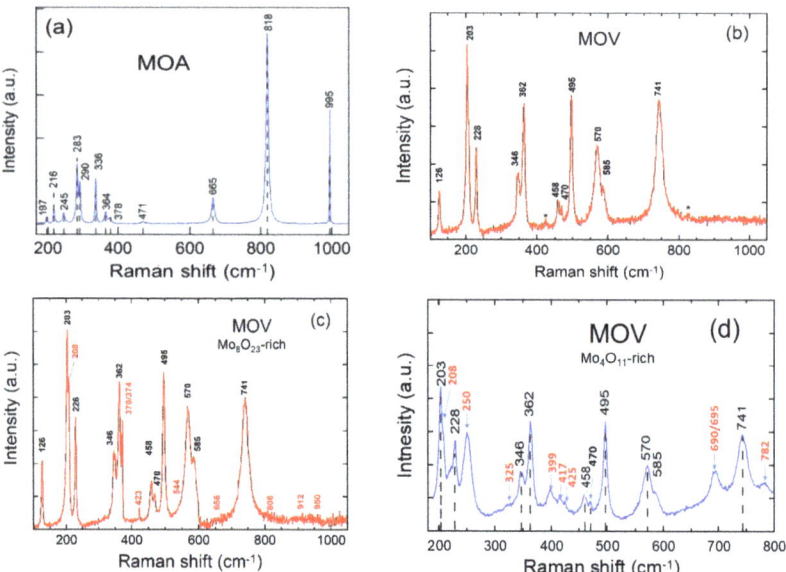

Figure 5. Raman spectra of the (**a**) MOA powders, (**b**) MOV (MoO$_2$-rich sample where the stars correspond to Raman peaks of suboxides), (**c**) MOV with m-Mo$_8$O$_{23}$-rich particles, and (**d**) MOV with o-Mo$_4$O$_{11}$-rich particles. Spectra were recorded at a spectral resolution of 1 cm^{-1}.

Vibrational analysis of the MoO$_2$ spectrum reveals that the bands in the 500–800 and 200–400 cm^{-1} regions were due to Mo–O stretching and bending modes, respectively. The low-frequency region (<200 cm^{-1}) corresponded to the lattice modes. The Raman spectra of suboxide-rich areas are displayed in Figure 5c,d for the MOV with m-Mo$_8$O$_{23}$-rich and o-Mo$_4$O$_{11}$-rich particles, respectively (Raman peaks of suboxides are marked in red). The monoclinic m-Mo$_8$O$_{23}$ phase is identified through the Raman peaks at 208, 370/374, 656, 912, and 950 cm^{-1}, whereas peaks located at 208, 250, 325, 399, 417, 425, 695, 782, 806, and 912 cm^{-1} are assigned to the o-Mo$_4$O$_{11}$ phase. Moreover, the MOV sample contained a small amount of the o-Mo$_9$O$_{26}$ suboxide identified by the peaks at 208, 544, 782, 912, and 950 cm^{-1}. The spectroscopic results are listed in Table 2 and compared with the literature data [81,82].

Table 2. Reported Raman peak frequencies (cm^{-1}) of M–O oxides.

α-MoO$_3$		m-MoO$_2$		o-Mo$_4$O$_{11}$		m-Mo$_8$O$_{23}$		o-Mo$_9$O$_{26}$	
Exp.	[81]	Exp.	[82]	Exp.	[82]	Exp.	[82]	Exp.	[82]
197	-	126	-	208	208	-	-	208	208
216	217	203	208	250	253	208	208	-	465
245	245	228	232	-	281	-	222	544	575
283	284	346	353	325	339	374	373	-	622
290	291	362	370	399	380	-	384	-	637
336	338	458	448	417	413	-	592	-	679
364	365	470	473	425	435	656	654	782	761
378	379	495	501	695	714	-	875	912	906
471	472	570	572	782	787	912	918	-	931
665	666	585	590	806	837	950	951	950	951
818	820	741	748	912	916			-	989
995	996			-	963				

XPS measurements were carried out to evaluate the chemical composition and investigate the surface valance states of Mo in MOA and MOV samples. The results are shown in Figure 6. The survey spectra (Figure 6a) display the fingerprints of the Mo 3d, Mo3p$_{3/2}$, Mo3p$_{1/2}$, and O1s core levels (their binding energies are listed in Table 3). The Mo 3d and O1s peaks were analyzed by evaluating the peak area of elements using Gaussian profiles after removing the secondary electron background. All XPS spectra can be deconvoluted using two Mo 3d doublets with 3d$_{5/2}$ and 3d$_{3/2}$ species. For the MOA sample (Figure 6b), the Mo 3d$_{5/2}$ and Mo3d$_{3/2}$ characteristic peaks were located at 232.6 and 235.7 eV, respectively (with a spin–orbit separation of ~3.1 eV), suggesting the sole existence of Mo^{6+} species on the MOA surface [23,84,85]. The binding energy of the Mo 3d$_{5/2}$ line for polycrystalline MoO$_3$ has been reported to be 231.6–s232.7 eV [86–88]. For the MOV sample, the deconvoluted peaks in Figure 6c unambiguously reveal the co-existence of mixed Mo valence states (Table 3).

Table 3. XPS analysis of the MOA and MOV samples.

Sample	Binding Energy (eV)									Average Mo Valence State
	Mo3p$_{3/2}$	Mo3p$_{1/2}$	O1s	Mo3d$_{5/2}$			Mo3d$_{3/2}$			
				Mo^{4+}	Mo^{5+}	Mo^{6+}	Mo^{4+}	Mo^{5+}	Mo^{6+}	
MOA	398.9	415.5	530.5	-	-	232.6	-	-	235.7	6.00
MOV	398.9	415.5	530.6	233.1	230.0	231.6	236.3	233.3	234.7	4.39

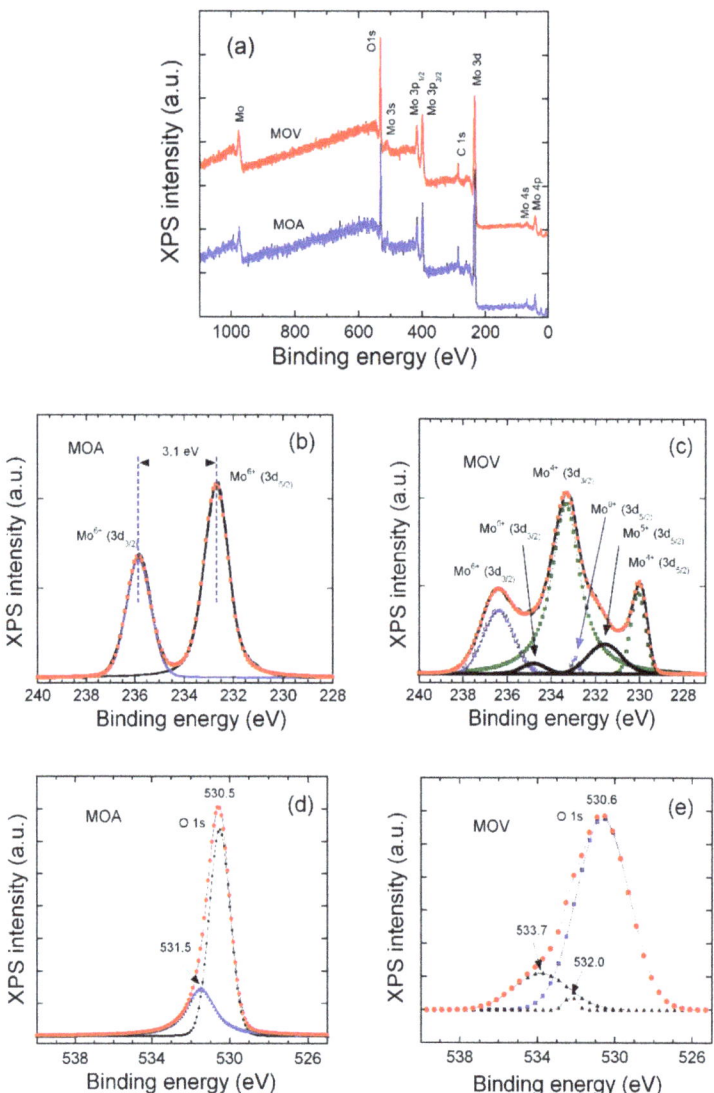

Figure 6. (a) XPS survey spectra of the MOA and MOV samples. High-resolution XPS spectra of (b) Mo 3d in MOA, (c) Mo 3d in MOV, (d) O1s in MOA, (e) O1s in MOV.

The first doublet centered at 230 and 233.3 eV was typically the Mo $3d_{5/2}$ and Mo $3d_{3/2}$ of Mo^{4+}, respectively, whereas the second one located at 231.6 and 234.7 eV was due to the Mo^{5+}, and, finally, the last one located at 233.1 and 236.3 eV was due to the Mo^{6+} [88,89]. The XPS spectra of O1s are presented in Figure 6d,e for the MOA and MOV samples, respectively. The intense peak located at ∼530.5 ± 0.1 eV was attributed to the binding energy of Mo–O bonds, whereas the peak at a higher binding energy was assigned to surface states. Therefore, the surface states of the MOV observed in the XPS patterns ascribed the presence of MoO_2, Mo_4O_{11}, Mo_8O_{23}, and Mo_9O_{26} (Figure 6c). From XPS peak deconvolution, the average Mo valence state of the MOA and MOV sample was determined to be 6.00 and 4.39, respectively.

The porous texture of the MOA and MOV samples was investigated by the N_2 adsorption–desorption isotherm measurement. The isotherm profiles of samples can be categorized as a type IV curve with a H3 hysteresis loop at the relative pressure of 0.8–1.0, thus implying the existence of a large number of mesopores. The average pore size was below 2 nm in the MOV material, while the MOA sample exhibits an average pore size of 10 nm. Moreover, the Brunauer–Emmett–Teller (BET) specific surface area of the MOV was 4.0 m^2 g^{-1}, which was higher than that of the MOA (0.23 m^2 g^{-1}). The mesoporous structure of the Mo–O samples may be beneficial for the electrolyte to penetrate completely into the pores and diffuse efficiently to active sites with less resistance, and can also buffer large volume change during the Li$^+$-ion insertion/extraction processes. The equivalent particle size of the MOA and MOV samples can be calculated from the BET data and compared using SEM images. The average particle size (nm) is expressed by Equation (6) below [90]:

$$L_{BET} = \frac{6000}{S_{BET} d}, \qquad (6)$$

where S_{BET} is the specific surface area (in m^2 g^{-1}) measured by BET experiments, and d is the gravimetric density (4.70 and 6.47 g cm^{-3} for MoO$_3$ and MoO$_2$, respectively). Results of the sample texture are summarized in Table 4. Note that the L_{BET} values corresponded to the average size of the secondary particles (agglomerates observed in SEM images).

Table 4. BET specific surface area (S_{BET}) and average pore size and pore volume of the MOA and MOV samples.

Sample	S_{BET} (m^2 g^{-1})	Pore Size (nm)	Pore Volume (cm^3 g^{-1})	L_{BET} (nm)
MOA	0.23	10	0.0012	3500
MOV	4.00	~2	0.0002	231

3.2. Electrochemical Properties

The electrochemical properties of as-prepared MOA and MOV as anode materials of LIBs were investigated in a potential range of 0.01–3.0 V vs. Li$^+$/Li. Figure 7a shows the cyclic voltammetry (CV) curves of MoO$_3$ performed at a scanning rate of 0.01 mV s^{-1}. MoO$_3$ demonstrates four prominent peaks in the first discharge process located at 2.7, 2.28, 0.7, and 0.3 V. The peaks at 2.7, 2.28, and 0.7 V appear only in the first discharge cycle and disappear in the subsequent cycles. This feature has been attributed to the intercalation of Li ions into the interlayer space between MoO$_6$ slabs, which occurs as the Li$_x$MoO$_3$ phase (see Equation (1)) and causes irreversible structural change to MoO$_3$ in a lithiated amorphous phase [91]. The peak at 0.3 V originates from a conversion reaction (see Equation (2)) of Li$_x$MoO$_3$ to Mo^0 and Li$_2$O [92]. The shift to a rather low voltage for the peak at 0.3 V with subsequent cycles may be attributed to a structure evolution. Two broad anodic peaks observed at approximately 1.18 and 1.73 V correspond to the de-lithiation process and are maintained in the forthcoming cycles. Note that the strong cathodic peak slightly shifts by 0.25 V after the first cycle. Figure 7b displays the galvanostatic charge–discharge profiles of the MOA sample. The upper voltage discharge plateau, observed in the first discharge, disappear in the subsequent cycles and the plateau at approximately 0.3 V shifts to lower voltage as noticed in CV results. These electrochemical features are those of the MoO$_3$ phase reported so far [93]. At 1C-rate (current density of ~1.1 A g^{-1}), the discharge capacity of the MoO$_3$ electrode decreased abruptly from the initial value of 1613 to 330 mAh g^{-1} over the first 50 cycles and then slightly increased in subsequent discharge-charge cycles at a rate of 0.35 mAh g^{-1} per cycle, reaching the specific capacity of 435 mAh g^{-1} after 725 cycles (Figure 7c). The Coulombic efficiency remained almost at 100% during long-term cycling. The initial large capacity decay revealed the poor electrochemical stability of MoO$_3$ electrode, which was due to the huge volume expansion and/or the structural change during the conversion reaction [91]. The rate capability displayed in Figure 7d for MOA showed significant capacity fading upon increasing the loading current. Moreover, after returning to the initial low C-rate (0.1C), the capacity did not return to its initial value and lost more than half of its value.

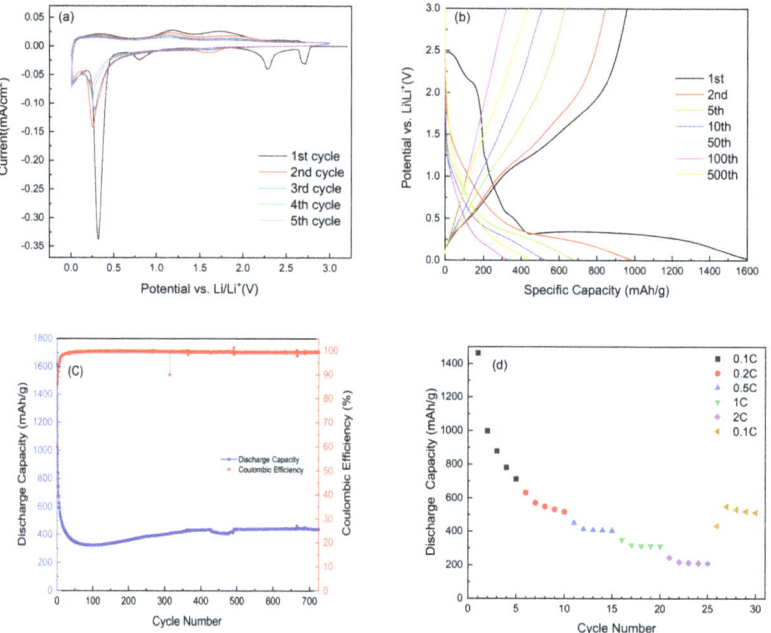

Figure 7. Electrochemical performance of MOA as anode material: (**a**) five first cyclic voltammograms recorded 0.01 mV s^{-1} scanning rate, (**b**) galvanostatic charge/discharge curves carried out at 1C-rate (~1.1 A g^{-1}) in the potential window 0.01–3.0 V vs. Li$^+$/Li, (**c**) specific discharge capacity and Coulombic efficiency as a function of cycle numbers performed at a 1C-rate, and (**d**) rate capability.

Figure 8a shows the first five cyclic voltammograms of the MOV electrode material, which exhibited five cathodic peaks located at 2.03, 1.53, 1.25, 0.78, and 0.42 V vs. Li$^+$/Li. Note that the cathodic peaks located at 2.03 and 0.78 V disappeared starting from the 2nd cycle, and it may be related to the reduction in solution species and formation of a solid electrolyte interphase (SEI) on the anode surface, while the one at 0.42 V shifted to lower potential. The two strong cathodic peaks at 1.25 and 1.53 V were maintained in the subsequent cycles with a slight shift toward higher potentials (1.27 and 1.56 V, respectively). This high potential shift makes them close to the two strong anodic peaks at 1.43 and 1.7 V. A decrease in the potential difference ΔE between the redox peaks started from the 2nd cycle to 0.16 and 0.14 V instead of 0.18 and 0.17 observed in the 1st cycle. In the subsequent cycles, these voltage sets 1.27/1.43 and 1.56/1.7 V were assigned to the reversible phase transitions (monoclinic–orthorhombic–monoclinic) of partially lithiated Li$_x$MoO$_2$ during Li intercalation (discharge) and de-intercalation (charge) processes, which are in a good agreement with previous reports [92–95].

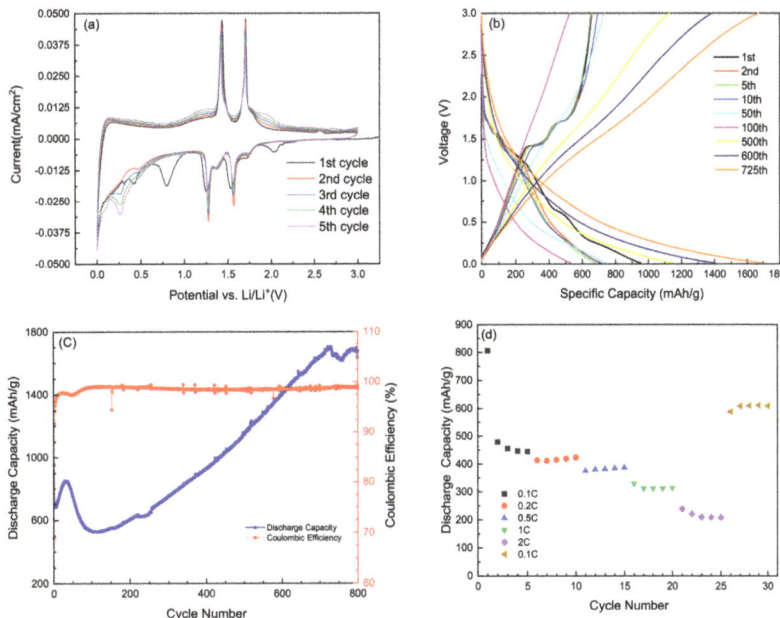

Figure 8. Electrochemical performance of MOV as anode material. (**a**) First five cyclic voltammograms recorded at scanning rate of 0.01 mV s^{-1}. (**b**) Galvanostatic charge/discharge curves of MoO$_2$ performed at 1C-rate (~0.86 A g^{-1}). (**c**) Specific discharge capacity and Coulombic efficiency as a function of cycle number performed at 1C-rate. (**d**) Rate capability.

It is worth noting also that the CV curves starting from the 2nd cycle to the 5th cycle almost overlapped. This demonstrates that the as-prepared material (i.e., the mixture of MoO$_2$ and Mo$_n$O$_{3n-1}$ suboxides) had good stability and reversibility for lithium-ion insertion and extraction during the first several cycles. Figure 8b illustrates the galvanostatic discharge–charge profiles of the MOV anode material tested at 1C-rate (~0.86 A g^{-1}) in a potential window 0.01–3.0 V vs. Li$^+$/Li. Two prominent plateaus at 1.25 and 1.53 V were observed during discharge process besides other small plateaus. The first lithiation mechanism was an insertion-type reaction that took place in the bulk and amorphous MoO$_2$ electrodes with only one-electron reduction as described (see Equation (3)) [46]. The second step was a conversion reaction that gradually resolved Li$_x$MoO$_2$ as described by Equation (4) [47], showing the formation of metallic Mo and Li$_2$O. In the charge curve, two plateaus were evidenced at 1.43 and 1.70 V and assigned to the deintercalation of Li$^+$ from Li$_x$MoO$_2$ framework. The disappearance of small plateaus starting from the 2nd cycle is related to an irreversible structural change suggesting that part of Li$^+$ cannot be extracted during the charge process [69]. Starting from the 2nd cycle, discharge and charge redox plateaus were clearly observed as noticed in the cyclic voltammograms. A voltage upgrading was detected upon cycling the MoO$_2$ phase, which did not exist for MoO$_3$. Figure 8c exhibits the electrochemical performance of the MOV anode material cycled at 1C-rate. An initial discharge capacity around 900 mAh g^{-1} was delivered in the 1st cycle, which decreased to ~500 mAh g^{-1} after 100 cycles and then increased on subsequent cycles reaching a value of 1625 mAh g^{-1} after 700 cycles. The Coulombic efficiency increased also from 93% to almost 99.4% after 100 cycles This better electrochemical behavior of the MOV electrode in comparison with that of MOA is attributed to several factors: (i) the smaller size of the nanoparticles, (ii) the presence of highly conductive suboxide phases, (iii) the higher BET specific surface area, (iv) the high intrinsic electrical conductivity of the MoO$_2$ phase, and (v) the meso-porosity. The importance of cycling at a high C-rate was also evidenced in Figure 8d, showing the rate capability of the MOV electrode. The rate capability of the MOV electrode is shown in Figure 8d. When the C-rate increased from 0.1C to 2C, the discharge capacity decreased from approximately 450 mAh g^{-1} to approximately 200 mAh g^{-1}. However, when the rate returned back to 0.1C after 2C testing, the capacity also returned back to approximately 600 mAh g^{-1}, which is slightly higher than the capacity during the initial 0.1C test. This slight increase was consistent with the capacity change pattern shown in Figure 8c. The capacity slightly increased from the 5th cycle to about the 50th cycle.

The gradual increase in the discharge capacity and additional capacities beyond the correlating theoretical value upon long-term cycling is worthy to be discussed. This characteristic is common in a large number of conversion reaction metal-oxide anode materials [96–106]. Keppeler and Srinivasan stated that the mechanism leading an experimental capacity larger than the theoretical value remains speculative [98]. The literature reveals a lithium storage capacity higher by 10–100% at high current densities of 30–2000 mA g^{-1} after being tested beyond 50 cycles [96,97]. Different capacity shapes have been reported that exhibit additional capacity occurrences. Cobalt oxides frequently show a type I (mount-shape) capacity profile [99], type II (upward-shape) is observed for additional capacity occurrence for Fe- or Mn-oxide-based electrodes [100], type III (U-shape) is a typical capacity profile found for several cases when the anode material contains Mn or Fe [101], and iron-oxide-based electrodes tend to form a type IV (horizontal-shape) capacity profile [96]. Here, the MOV negative electrode material exhibited a capacity profile type III with a pronounced U-shape. The specific discharge capacity was almost twice the theoretical value after 800 cycles monitored at a high 1C-rate with a Coulombic efficiency, which remained constant at 99.4%. This is in contrast with the type IV profile reported by Shi et al. [102] for the mesoporous MoO_2 electrode synthesized at 500 °C via a nanocasting strategy. However, the self-assembled porous MoO_2/graphene microspheres, fabricated by Palanisamy et al. [103], exhibited a weak U-profile when cycled at a low current rate (C/10). A different capacity profile (upward-shape) was reported by Tang et al. [104] for an MoO_2–graphene nanocomposite electrode cycled at 100 mA g^{-1}. Thus, not only the morphology plays an important role in the excess capacity but also the operating mode is modifying the electrochemical performance upon long-term cycling of nanostructured oxides.

After the 100th test, the MOV anode displayed a gradual increase in specific capacity during cycling (Figure 8c). This anomalous behavior can be attributed to: (i) the activation of the porous structure with nano-cavities; the presence of numerous mesopores might be beneficial for the gradual access of the electrolytes in the porous structure of the electrode, and (ii) an additional Li-ion accommodation through reactions with the grain boundary phase in nanostructures; other scenarios associated with additional capacities, such as electrode/electrolyte interphases and electrocatalytic effect of metallic particles, have been identified [98]. The existence of numerous mesopores might be beneficial for more electrolytes accessing in the porous framework of the electrode, which favors the Li$^+$ insertion/extraction process. Such a characteristic was evidenced in cobalt-based anodes [105], MnO/graphene composite [100], and graphene-wrapped Fe_3O_4 [106]. In MnO_x anodes, it might be based on mixed effects such as transition-metal cluster aggregation and formation of defects and deformation [101].

Table 5 summarizes the electrochemical performance of various MoO_2 anode materials prepared by various synthetic processes [107–125]. The different strategies demonstrate the ability to mitigate the particle pulverization as a consequence of Li insertion/extraction and improve the MoO_2 electrochemical performance via the fabrication of nanocomposites including carbonaceous materials. The particle size reduction results in the transport path shortening for both ions and electrons, while the carbonaceous matrix maintains high conductivity, large surface area, and chemical stability. The MoO_2-based composites studied as lithium battery anodes involve various forms including mesoporous and monolith MoO_2; nanostructured powders such as nanowires (NWs), nanospheres (NSs), hollow spheres (HSs), and nanobelts (NBs); MoO_2/carbon materials; various binary composites. Thermoelectrochemical activation of MoO_2 is also an attractive synthetic approach. A comparison of the electrochemical properties of these anode materials shows that the MoO_2/Mo_nO_{3n-1} composite prepared by a simple sol-gel technique assisted by a green chelator exhibits the best performance.

Table 5. Electrochemical performance of various MoO_2 composites as anode materials for LIBs. The cycle number at which the specific capacity is reported is given in parenthesis.

Material	Synthesis	Reversible Capacity (mAh g^{-1})	Current Rate (mA g^{-1})	Reference
Nano MoO_2	rheology	402	100 (40)	[118]
MoO_2/Mo_2N	reduction of MoO_3	815	100 (150)	[119]
MoO_2/graphene	chemical vapor deposition	986	50 (150)	[120]
MoO_2/C	ion exchange	574	100 (100)	[121]
MoO_2/C	carbothermal reduction	500	100 (50)	[108]
MoO_2/C hollow spheres	solvothermal	580	200 (200)	[122]
Mesoporous MoO_2	template casting	750	42 (30)	[103]
Activated MoO_2	thermoelectrochemical activation	850	100 (30)	[123]
MoO_2 HCSMSs	hydrolysis	420	50 (30)	[124]
W-doped MoO_2	nanocasting	670	75 (20)	[111]
C/WO_x/MoO_2	hydrothermal	670	90 (50)	[125]
MoO_2/C NWs	solvothermal	500	200 (20)	[109]
C/MoO_2 NSs	hydrothermal+annealing	675	838 (30)	[113]
MoS_2/MoO_2	sulfur assisted	654	500 (80)	[115]
C/MoO_2 NBs	hydrothermal+annealing	617	100 (30)	[110]
MoO_2 monolith	morphosynthesis	719	200 (20)	[112]
α-MoO_3@β-MnO_2	two-step hydrothermal	286	6C (50)	[107]
MoO_2/N-doped C NWs	calcination	700	2000 (400)	[114]
C-coated MoO_2	hydrothermal	312	10000 (268)	[116]
MoO_2/flexible C	electrospinning	451	2000 (500)	[117]
MoO_2/Mo_nO_{3n-1}	sol-gel with green chelator	1600	800 (800)	this work

To further investigate the electrochemical kinetics as well as characterize the improved electrochemical properties of MOA and MOV negative electrode materials, EIS measurements were carried out using a fresh cell. Figure 9a shows the Nyquist plots for the MOA and MOV electrodes. The equivalent circuit model (Figure 9b) used to analyze the EIS results is composed of a series of four elements: the cell resistance R_s, a resistance in parallel with a constant phase element corresponding to the solid electrolyte interphase (SEI) layer, a second R-CPE parallel component, which figures out the charge transfer process, and finally the diffusion Warburg component (Z_W). All Nyquist plots can be decomposed as follows: (i) the intercept at high frequency with the Z'-axis is related to the uncompensated ohmic resistance of the cell (R_s); (ii) in the high-frequency region, the first depressed semicircle is associated with the SEI (R_{SEI}, CPE_{SEI}); (iii) a second depressed semicircle in the medium-frequency region is ascribed to the charge transfer impedance and the interfacial capacitance at the electrode/electrolyte interface (R_{ct}, CPE_{dl}); finally, (iv) in the low-frequency range, the inclined line is ascribed to the Li$^+$-ion diffusion-controlled process characterized by the Warburg impedance. The values of R_s for the two samples are quite small (~7 Ω) implying a negligible ohmic polarization of the MOA and MOV electrodes. The R_{ct} value is lower in the MOV material (211 Ω) compared to the MOA (272 Ω) electrode. This matches well with the electrochemical performance of MOV mentioned above. This is attributed to the presence of Mo suboxides in MOV electrode (mixture of MoO_2, o-Mo_4O_{11}, m-Mo_8O_{23}, and o-Mo_9O_{26}), which leads to a significant increase in the electronic conductivity as compared to MOA.

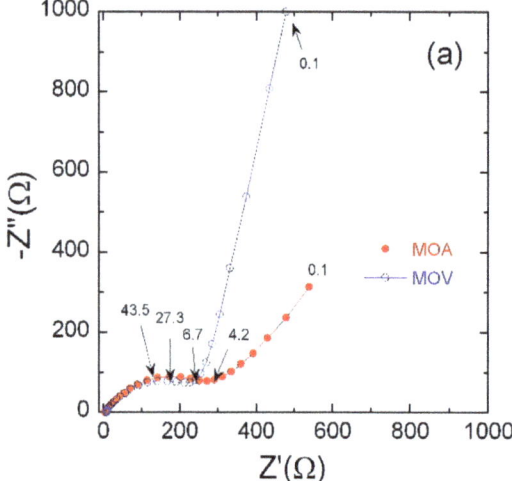
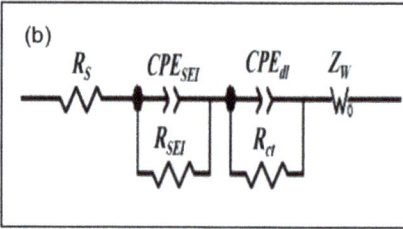

Figure 9. (**a**) Nyquist plots of fresh cells including the MOA and MOV electrodes. (**b**) The equivalent circuit model used for EIS data fitting.

More information on the change in the overall cell potential as a function of the depth-of-charge (DOD) can be obtained by evaluating the area-specific impedance (ASI expressed in Ω cm^2) given by the relation [126,127]:

$$ASI = A \frac{OCV - V_{cell}}{I}, \qquad (7)$$

where A is the cross-sectional area of the electrode, $\Delta V = OCV - V_{cell}$ is the potential change during current interruption for 60 s at each DOD step, and I is the current passing throughout the cell. ASI is affected also by ohmic drop, Li-ion diffusion through the electrolyte and solid-state diffusion within the electrode. This is like EIS measurements without the need to reach the equilibrium. Moreover, ASI could be more representative than data from EIS in terms of evaluation of the total cell resistance. However, ASI results confirmed the features observed by EIS. Figure 10a displays the variation of ASI for the MOA and MOV electrodes for the 1st discharge at 1C-rate. ASI values at 90% DOD are 22 and 16 Ω cm^2 for the MOA and MOV samples, respectively. The curves in Figure 10a indicate that, during battery discharging, the charge–transfer resistance is dependent on DOD. To further verify the effect of ASI on the electrochemical properties of MOA and MOV electrodes, ASI was calculated at various discharge cycles at 20% and 90% DOD as shown in Figure 10b. These results show that there were two different behaviors represented by an increase in the ASI values during the first five cycles, followed by a continuous decrease until the 725th cycle. The degree of decay in ASI values was much larger for MOV than for MOA at 20% DOD. By going to a deep discharge of 90% DOD, the situation looks rather different. ASI values increased after the 1st cycle then almost stabilizes until the 725th cycle for the MOA electrode. On the contrary, MOV showed smaller ASI values than MOA with a continuous reduction upon cycling upon shallow discharge (20% DOD). These results show that the lower ASI value was obtained for the MOV sample, and it is beneficial for the long-life cycling behavior.

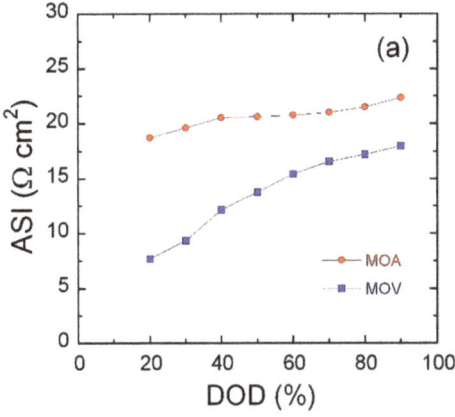
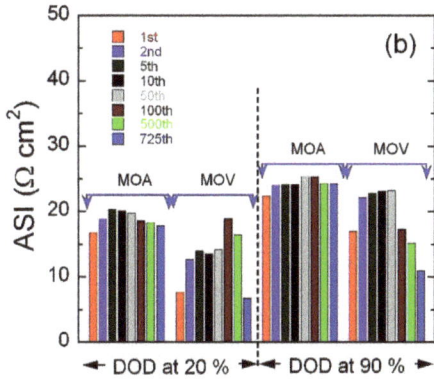

Figure 10. Area specific impedance (ASI) of the MOA and MOV as a function of depth of discharge (DOD) for the 1st discharge (**a**) and as a function of cycling for the MOA and MOV electrodes at 20% and 90% DOD (**b**).

4. Conclusions

This research article sheds light on the promising design strategies of molybdenum oxides for high kinetic energy storage. The green and facile preparation of nanosized molybdenum oxides (i.e., MoO_3 and MoO_2) by thermal decomposition of ammonium molybdate tetra hydrate (i.e., $(NH_4)_6Mo_7O_{24} \cdot 4H_2O$) in air and in an inert atmosphere, respectively, has been demonstrated. The efficiency of the synthetic method is attributed to the use of orange peel extract as a chelator. The as-prepared MOA and MOV materials have the structure of MoO_3 and $MoO_2 + Mo_nO_{3n-1}$ suboxides as estimated from XRD, XPS, and Raman spectroscopy. Thermal analysis emphasized the thermal stable phase of MoO_3 up to approximately 800 °C and the presence of oxygen vacancies in the MOV sample. BET measurements show the mesoporous texture of molybdenum oxides; MOA had a lower specific surface area than MOV due to the easy crystal growth in the MoO_3 phase. Electrochemical characterizations showed the outstanding properties in terms of capacity upgrading upon cycling for the MOV negative electrode material, which shows a pronounced U-shape capacity profile when cycled 800 times at 1C-rate. Finally, EIS and ASI experiments confirmed the superiority of the MOV (mixture of MoO_2, Mo_4O_{11}, Mo_8O_{23}, and Mo_9O_{26} phases) over the MOA (stoichiometric MoO_3 insulator) sample as an anode material for Li-ion batteries.

Author Contributions: Conceptualization, L.Z. and A.M.H.; Formal analysis, T.L.; A.E.A.-G., R.S.E.-T., H.M.A., H.W., K.C. and A.C.; Investigation: T.L.; A.E.A.-G, R.S.E.-T, H.M.A., H.W., K.C. and A.C.; Writing—original draft preparation, A.M.H., A.E.A.-G., R.S.E.-T., H.W. and A.C.; Writing—review and editing, C.M.J., A.M.H., L.Z., S.Z., H.E.-M. and A.T.; Supervision, L.Z. and A.M.H.; Project administration, L.Z. and A.M.H.; Funding acquisition: L.Z. and A.M.H. All authors have read and agreed to the published version of the manuscript.

Funding: This article was derived from the subject data funded in part by the United States Agency for International Development (USAID) and the National Academy of Sciences (NAS) through Subaward 2000010562. Any opinions, findings, conclusions, or recommendations expressed in this article are those of the authors alone and do not necessarily reflect the views of USAID or NAS.

Institutional Review Board Statement: Not applicable.

Informed Consent Statement: Not applicable.

Data Availability Statement: Data are contained within the article.

Acknowledgments: The Egyptian authors are grateful for the financial support from the Science, Technology, and Innovation Funding Authority (STIFA, STDF previously) through project number 42691 entitled "Microstructure-Based, Multi-Physics Simulation and Optimization to Improve Battery Performance". Access to XPS at the Nanoscale Characterization Facility at Indiana University was provided by the NSF Award DMR MRI-1126394. S.X.Z. and A.L.C. acknowledge support from the US National Science Foundation through grant number ECCS-1936406 (Raman Studies at Indiana University).

Conflicts of Interest: The authors declare no conflict of interest.

References

1. Zhao, X.; Jia, W.; Wu, X.; Lv, Y.; Qiu, J.; Guo, J.; Wang, X.; Jia, D.; Yan, J.; Wu, D. Ultrafine MoO_3 anchored in coal-based carbon nanofibers as anode for advanced lithium-ion batteries. *Carbon* **2020**, *156*, 445–452. [CrossRef]
2. Jiang, J.; Li, Y.; Liu, J.; Huang, X.; Yuan, C.; Lou, X.W.D. Recent advances in metal oxide-based electrode architecture design for electrochemical energy storage. *Adv. Mater.* **2012**, *24*, 5166–5180. [CrossRef] [PubMed]
3. Cheng, X.; Li, Y.; Sang, L.; Ma, J.; Shi, H.; Liu, X.; Lu, J.; Zhang, Y. Boosting the electrochemical performance of MoO_3 anode for long-life lithium ion batteries: Dominated by an ultrathin TiO_2 passivation layer. *Electrochim. Acta* **2018**, *269*, 241–249. [CrossRef]
4. Manthiram, A.; Chemelewski, K.; Lee, E.S. A perspective on the high-voltage $LiMn_{1.5}Ni_{0.5}O_4$ spinel cathode for lithium-ion batteries. *Energy Environ. Sci.* **2014**, *7*, 1339–1350. [CrossRef]
5. Sun, Y.; Liu, N.; Cui, Y. Promises and challenges of nanomaterials for lithium based rechargeable batteries. *Nat. Energy* **2016**, *1*, 16071. [CrossRef]
6. Li, H.; Liu, P.; Zhou, N.; Huang, X.; Wang, H. Electrochemical presodiation promoting lithium storage performance of Mo-based anode materials. *Ceram. Int.* **2017**, *43*, 11967–11972. [CrossRef]
7. Goodenough, J.B.; Kim, Y. Challenges for rechargeable batteries. *J. Power Sources* **2011**, *196*, 6688–6694. [CrossRef]
8. Hua, R.; Liu, T.; Chen, B.; Cai, R.; Zhou, J. Computational atomic mechanical properties of structure and diffusion in the MoO_3 anode materials during lithiation. *Mater. Sci.* **2018**, *145*, 8–13.
9. Baldoni, M.; Craco, L.; Seifert, G.; Leoni, S. A two-electron mechanism of lithium insertion into layered α-MoO_3: A DFT and DFT+U study. *J. Mater. Chem. A* **2013**, *1*, 1778–1784. [CrossRef]
10. Zhao, K.; Pharr, M.; Wan, Q.; Wang, W.L.; Kaxiras, E.; Vlassak, J.J.; Suo, Z. Concurrent reaction and plasticity during initial lithiation of crystalline silicon in lithium-ion batteries. *J. Electrochem. Soc.* **2012**, *159*, A238–A243. [CrossRef]
11. Shang, H.; Zuo, Z.; Li, L.; Wang, F.; Liu, H.; Li, Y. Ultrathin graphdiyne nanosheets grown in situ on copper nanowires and their performance as lithium-ion battery anodes. *Angew. Chem. Int. Ed.* **2018**, *57*, 774–778. [CrossRef]
12. Tabassum, H.; Zou, R.; Mahmood, A.; Liang, Z.; Wang, Q.; Zhang, H.; Gao, S.; Qu, C.; Guo, W.; Guo, S. A universal strategy for hollow metal oxide nanoparticles encapsulated into B/N co-doped graphitic nanotubes as high-performance lithium-ion battery anodes. *Adv. Mater.* **2018**, *30*, 1705441. [CrossRef]
13. Feng, K.; Li, M.; Liu, W.; Kashkooli, A.G.; Xiao, X.; Cai, M.; Chen, Z. Silicon-based anodes for lithium-ion batteries: From fundamentals to practical applications. *Small* **2018**, *14*, 1702737. [CrossRef]
14. Nagaura, T.; Tozawa, K. Lithium ion rechargeable battery. *Prog. Batteries Solar Cells* **1990**, *9*, 209–212.
15. Zhang, W.; Wang, B.; Luo, H.; Jin, F.; Ruan, T.; Wang, D. MoO_2 nanobelts modified with an MOF-derived carbon layer for high performance lithium-ion battery anodes. *J. Alloys Compd.* **2019**, *803*, 664–670. [CrossRef]
16. Chen, S.; Zhu, J.; Wu, X.; Han, Q.; Wang, X. Graphene oxide-MnO_2 nanocomposites for supercapacitors. *ACS Nano* **2010**, *4*, 2822–2830. [CrossRef]
17. Liu, D.; Wang, X.; Tian, W.; Liu, J.; Zhi, C.; He, D.; Bando, Y.; Golberg, D. Ultrathin nanoporous Fe_3O_4 carbon nanosheets with enhanced supercapacitor performance. *J. Mater. Chem. A* **2013**, *1*, 1952–1955. [CrossRef]
18. Mondal, A.K.; Su, D.; Chen, S.; Xie, X.; Wang, G. Highly porous $NiCo_2O_4$ nanoflakes and nanobelts as anode materials for lithium-ion batteries with excellent rate capability. *ACS Appl. Mater. Interfaces* **2014**, *6*, 14827–14835. [CrossRef]
19. Huo, J.; Xue, Y.; Liu, Y.; Ren, Y.; Yue, G. Polyvinyl alcohol-assisted synthesis of porous MoO_2/C microrods as anodes for lithium-ion batteries. *J. Electroanal. Chem.* **2020**, *857*, 113751. [CrossRef]
20. El-Deen, S.S.; Hashem, A.M.; Abdel-Ghany, A.E.; Indris, S.; Ehrenberg, H.; Mauger, A.; Julien, C.M. Anatase TiO_2 nanoparticles for lithium-ion batteries. *Ionics* **2018**, *24*, 2925–2934. [CrossRef]
21. Su, Y.; Tong, R.-A.; Zhang, H.; Liang, P.; Wang, C.-A.; Zhong, M. Defocused laser ablation process. A high-efficiency way to fabricate MoO_3-Mo integrative anode with excellent electrochemical performance for lithium ion batteries. *J. Alloys Compd.* **2019**, *787*, 295–300. [CrossRef]
22. Ramana, C.V.; Mauger, A.; Julien, C.M. Growth, characterization and performance of bulk and nanoengineered molybdenum oxides for electrochemical energy storage and conversion. *Prog. Cryst. Growth Charact. Mater.* **2021**, *67*, 100533. [CrossRef]
23. Lakshmi-Narayana, A.; Hussain, O.M.; Ramana, C.V.; Camacho-Lopez, M.; Abdel-Ghany, A.; Hashem, A.; Mauger, A.; Julien, C.M. Molybdenum-suboxide thin films as anode layers in planar lithium microbatteries. *Electrochem* **2020**, *1*, 160–187. [CrossRef]
24. Julien, C.M.; Mauger, A.; Vijh, A.; Zaghib, K. *Lithium Batteries: Science and Technology*; Springer: Cham, Switzerland, 2016; pp. 120–124.

25. Chen, X.; Huang, Y.; Zhang, K. α-MoO$_3$ nanorods coated with SnS$_2$ nano sheets core-shell composite as high-performance anode materials of lithium ion batteries. *Electrochim. Acta* **2016**, *222*, 956–964. [CrossRef]
26. Tang, W.; Peng, C.X.; Nai, C.T.; Su, J.; Liu, Y.P.; Reddy, M.; Lin, M.; Loh, K.P. Ultrahigh capacity due to multi-electron conversion reaction in reduced graphene oxide-wrapped MoO$_2$ porous nanobelts. *Small* **2015**, *11*, 2446–2453. [CrossRef]
27. Petnikota, S.; Teo, K.W.; Chen, L.; Sim, A.; Marka, S.K.; Reddy, M.V.; Srikanth, V.V.; Adams, S.; Chowdari, B.V. Exfoliated graphene oxide/MoO$_2$ composites as anode materials in lithium-ion batteries: An insight into intercalation of Li and conversion mechanism of MoO$_2$. *ACS Appl. Mater. Interfaces* **2016**, *8*, 10884–10896. [CrossRef]
28. Zhang, W.; Xing, L.; Chen, J.; Zhou, H.; Liang, S.; Huang, W.; Li, W. Improving the cyclic stability of MoO$_2$ anode for sodium ion batteries via film-forming electrolyte additive. *J. Alloys Compd.* **2020**, *822*, 153530. [CrossRef]
29. Ramana, C.V.; Atuchin, V.V. Electrochemical properties of sputter-deposited MoO$_3$ films in lithium microbatteries. *J. Vacuum Sci. Technol. A* **2012**, *30*, 04D105. [CrossRef]
30. Li, Y.; Sun, H.; Cheng, X.; Zhang, Y.; Zhao, K. In-situ TEM experiments and first principles studies on the electrochemical and mechanical behaviors of α-MoO$_3$ in Li-ion batteries. *Nano Energy* **2016**, *27*, 95–102. [CrossRef]
31. Ma, F.; Yuan, A.; Xu, J.; Hu, P. Porous α-MoO$_3$/MWCNT nanocomposite synthesized via a surfactant-assisted solvothermal route as a lithium-ion-battery high-capacity anode material with excellent rate capability and cyclability. *ACS Appl. Mater. Interfaces* **2015**, *7*, 15531–15541. [CrossRef]
32. Xia, W.; Xu, F.; Zhu, C.; Xin, H.L.; Xu, Q.; Sun, P.; Sun, L. Probing microstructure and phase evolution of α-MoO$_3$ nanobelts for sodium-ion batteries by in situ transmission electron microscopy. *Nano Energy* **2016**, *27*, 447–456. [CrossRef]
33. Zheng, C.; Chen, C.R.; Chen, L.; Wei, M.D. A CMK-5-encapsulated MoSe$_2$ composite for rechargeable lithium-ion batteries with improved electrochemical performance. *J. Mater. Chem.* **2017**, *5*, 19632. [CrossRef]
34. Zeng, L.X.; Huang, X.X.; Chen, X.; Zheng, C.; Liu, R.P.; Chen, G.; Qian, Q.R.; Chen, Q.H.; Wei, M.D. Ethanol thermal reduction synthesis of hierarchical MoO$_2$-C hollow spheres with high rate performance for lithium ion batteries. *RSC Adv.* **2016**, *6*, 105558. [CrossRef]
35. Zhao, K.; Tritsaris, G.A.; Pharr, M.; Wang, W.L.; Okeke, O.; Suo, Z.; Vlassak, J.J.; Kaxiras, E. Reactive flow in silicon electrodes assisted by the insertion of lithium. *Nano Lett.* **2012**, *12*, 4397–4403. [CrossRef]
36. Yang, T.; Yu, X.; Liu, C.; Liang, L.; Wang, W. High-performance lithium storage properties based on molybdenum trioxide nanobelts. *Solid State Ion.* **2018**, *326*, 1–4. [CrossRef]
37. Atuchin, V.V.; Gavrilova, T.A.; Grigorieva, T.I.; Kuratieva, N.V.; Okotrub, K.A.; Pervukhina, N.V.; Surovtsev, N.V. Sublimation growth and vibrational microspectrometry of α-MoO$_3$ single crystals. *J. Cryst. Growth* **2011**, *318*, 987–990. [CrossRef]
38. Mai, L.Q.; Hu, B.; Chen, W. Lithiated MoO$_3$ nanobelts with greatly improved performance for lithium batteries. *Adv. Mater.* **2017**, *19*, 3712–3716. [CrossRef]
39. Xia, W.; Zhang, Q.; Xu, F.; Sun, L. New insights into electrochemical lithiation/delithiation mechanism of α-MoO$_3$ nanobelt by in situ transmission electron microscopy. *ACS Appl. Mater. Interfaces* **2016**, *8*, 9170–9177. [CrossRef]
40. Huang, J.; Yan, J.; Li, J.; Cao, L.; Xu, Z.; Wu, J.; Zhou, L.; Luo, Y. Assembled-sheets-like MoO$_3$ anodes with excellent electrochemical performance in Li-ion battery. *J. Alloys Compd.* **2016**, *688*, 588–595. [CrossRef]
41. Zhang, P.; Guo, S.; Liu, J.; Zhou, C.; Li, S.; Yang, Y.; Wu, J.; Yu, D.; Chen, L. Highly uniform nitrogen-doped carbon decorated MoO$_2$ nano popcorns as anode for high-performance lithium/sodium-ion storage. *J. Colloid Interface Sci.* **2020**, *563*, 318–327. [CrossRef]
42. Wang, W.; Shi, G.; Cai, H.; Zhao, C.; Wu, J.; Yu, Y.; Hu, J.; Fang, Z.; Yan, J.; Liu, B. Yolk-shell structured Mo/MoO$_2$ composite microspheres function as high-performance anode materials for lithium-ion batteries. *J. Alloys Compd.* **2019**, *792*, 191–202. [CrossRef]
43. Zhang, L.; Shen, K.; Jiang, Y.; Song, Y.; Liu, Y.; Yuan, X.; Guo, S. Facile construction of flower-like MoO$_2$@N, P co-doped carbon on carbon cloth as self-standing anode for high-performance sodium ion battery. *J. Electroanal. Chem.* **2019**, *852*, 113510. [CrossRef]
44. Ma, J.; Fu, J.; Niu, M.; Quhe, R. MoO$_2$ and graphene heterostructure as promising flexible anodes for lithium-ion batteries. *Carbon* **2019**, *147*, 357–363. [CrossRef]
45. Tang, S.; Shen, C.; Ji, W.; Liu, J.; Fichou, D. Template-free synthesis of hierarchical MoO$_2$ multi-shell architectures with improved lithium storage capability. *Mater. Res. Bull.* **2017**, *91*, 85–90. [CrossRef]
46. Dahn, J.R.; McKinnon, W. Structure and electrochemistry of Li$_x$MoO$_2$. *Solid State Ion.* **1987**, *23*, 1–7. [CrossRef]
47. Zhou, L.; Wu, H.B.; Wang, Z.; Lou, X.W. Interconnected MoO$_2$ nanocrystals with carbon nanocoating as high-capacity anode materials for lithium-ion batteries. *ACS Appl. Mater. Interfaces* **2011**, *3*, 4853–4857. [CrossRef]
48. Xia, Q.; Zhao, H.L.; Du, Z.H. Facile synthesis of MoO$_3$/carbon nanobelts as high-performance anode material for lithium ion batteries. *Electrochim. Acta* **2015**, *180*, 947–956. [CrossRef]
49. Chen, L.; Jiang, H.; Jiang, H.; Zhang, H.; Guo, S.; Hu, Y.; Li, C. Mo-Based ultra-small nanoparticles on hierarchical carbon nanosheets for superior lithium ion storage and hydrogen generation catalysis. *Adv. Energy Mater.* **2017**, *7*, 1602782. [CrossRef]
50. Meduri, P.; Clark, E.; Kim, J.H.; Dayalan, E.; Sumanasekera, G.U.; Sunkara, M.K. MoO$_3$-x nanowire arrays as stable and high capacity anodes for lithium-ion batteries. *Nano Lett.* **2012**, *12*, 1784–1788. [CrossRef]
51. Yang, L.; Li, X.; Ouyang, Y.; Gao, Q.; Ouyang, L.; Hu, R.; Liu, J.; Zhu, M. Hierarchical MoO$_2$/Mo$_2$C/C hybrid nanowires as high-rate and long-life anodes for lithium-ion batteries. *ACS Appl. Mater. Interfaces* **2016**, *8*, 19987–19993. [CrossRef]

52. Zhou, J.; Lin, N.; Wang, L.; Zhang, K.; Zhu, Y.; Qian, Y. Synthesis of hexagonal MoO_3 nanorods and a study of their electrochemical performance as anode materials for lithium-ion batteries. *J. Mater. Chem. A* **2015**, *3*, 7463–7468. [CrossRef]
53. Xiu, Z.; Kim, D.; Alfaruqi, M.H.; Song, J.; Kim, S.; Duong, P.T.; Mathew, V.; Baboo, J.P.; Kim, J. Ultrafine molybdenum oxycarbide nanoparticles embedded in N-doped carbon as a superior anode material for lithium-ion batteries. *J. Alloys Compd.* **2017**, *696*, 143–149. [CrossRef]
54. Zhang, H.-J.; Shu, J.; Wang, K.-X.; Chen, X.-T.; Jiang, Y.-M.; Wei, X.; Chen, J.-S. Lithiation mechanism of hierarchical porous MoO_2 nanotubes fabricated through one-step carbothermal reduction. *J. Mater. Chem.* **2014**, *2*, 80–86. [CrossRef]
55. Yang, L.C.; Gao, Q.S.; Zhang, Y.H.; Tang, Y.; Wu, Y.P. Tremella-like molybdenum dioxide consisting of nanosheets as an anode material for lithium-ion batteries. *Electrochem. Commun.* **2008**, *10*, 118–122. [CrossRef]
56. Xiao, X.; Peng, Z.; Chen, C.; Zhang, C.; Beidaghi, M.; Yang, Z.; Wu, N.; Huang, Y.; Miao, L.; Gogotsi, Y.; et al. Freestanding MoO_{3-x} nanobelt/carbon nanotube films for Li-ion intercalation pseudocapacitors. *J. Nano Energy* **2014**, *9*, 355–363. [CrossRef]
57. Zhang, P.; Zou, L.; Hu, H.; Wang, M.; Fang, J.; Lai, Y.; Li, J. 3D Hierarchical carbon microflowers decorated with MoO_2 nanoparticles for lithium ion batteries. *Electrochim. Acta* **2017**, *250*, 219–227. [CrossRef]
58. Nadimicherla, R.; Zha, R.; Wei, L.; Guo, X. Single crystalline flowerlike α-MoO_3 nanorods and their application as anode material for lithium-ion batteries. *J. Alloys Compd.* **2016**, *687*, 79–86. [CrossRef]
59. Hashem, A.M.; Abuzeid, H.; Kaus, M.; Indris, S.; Ehrenberg, H.; Mauger, A.; Julien, C.M. Green synthesis of nanosized manganese dioxide as positive electrode for lithium-ion batteries using lemon juice and citrus peel. *Electrochim. Acta* **2018**, *262*, 74–81. [CrossRef]
60. Abuzeid, H.M.; Hashem, A.M.; Kaus, M.; Knapp, M.; Indris, S.; Ehrenberg, H.; Mauger, A.; Julien, C.M. Electrochemical performance of nanosized MnO_2 synthesized by redox route using biological reducing agents. *J. Alloys Compd.* **2018**, *746*, 227–237. [CrossRef]
61. Abuzeid, H.M.; Elsherif, S.A.; Abdel-Ghany, N.A.; Hashem, A.M. Facile, cost-effective and eco-friendly green synthesis method of MnO_2 as storage electrode materials for supercapacitors. *J. Energy Storage* **2019**, *21*, 156–162. [CrossRef]
62. Bampidis, V.A.; Robinson, P.H. Citrus byproducts as ruminant feeds: A review. *Anim. Feed Sci. Technol.* **2006**, *128*, 175–217. [CrossRef]
63. Hashem, A.M.; Abuzeid, H.M.; Winter, M.; Li, J.; Julien, C.M. Synthesis of high surface area α-K_yMnO_2 nanoneedles using extract of broccoli as bioactive reducing agent and application in lithium battery. *Materials* **2020**, *13*, 1269. [CrossRef] [PubMed]
64. Olabinjo, O.O.; Ogunlowo, A.S.; Ajayi, O.O.; Olalusi, A.P. Analysis of physical and chemical composition of sweet orange (citrus sinensis) peels. *Int. J. Environ. Agric. Biotechnol.* **2017**, *2*, 2201–2206. [CrossRef]
65. Kihlborg, L. Least squares refinement of crystal structure of molybdenum trioxide. *Ark. Kemi.* **1963**, *21*, 357–364.
66. Hashem, A.M.; Abbas, S.M.; Abdel-Ghany, A.E.; Eid, A.E.; Abdel-Khalek, A.A.; Indris, S.; Ehrenberg, H.; Mauger, A.; Julien, C.M. Blend formed by oxygen deficient $MoO_{3-δ}$ oxides as lithium-insertion compounds. *J. Alloys Compd.* **2016**, *686*, 744–752. [CrossRef]
67. Anderson, S.; Magnelli, A. Structure of MoO_3. *Acta Chem. Scand.* **1950**, *4*, 793–799.
68. Kihlborg, L. Studies on molybdenum oxides. *Acta Chem. Scand.* **1959**, *13*, 954–962. [CrossRef]
69. Magnéli, A. The crystal structures of Mo_9O_{26} (beta'-molybdenum oxide) and Mo_8O_{23} (beta-molybdenum oxide). *Acta Chem. Scand.* **1948**, *2*, 501–517. [CrossRef]
70. Hashem, A.M.; Abdel-Ghany, A.E.; El-Tawil, R.S.; Indris, S.; Ehrenberg, H.; Mauger, A.; Julien, C.M. Amorphous Mo_5O_{14}-type/carbon nano composite with enhanced electrochemical capability for lithium-ion batteries. *Nanomaterials* **2020**, *10*, 8. [CrossRef]
71. Troitskaia, I.B.; Gavrilova, T.A.; Gromilov, S.A.; Sheglov, D.V.; Atuchin, V.V.; Vemuri, R.S.; Ramana, C.V. Growth and structural properties of α-MoO_3 (010) microplates with atomically flat surface. *Mater. Sci. Eng. B* **2010**, *174*, 159–163. [CrossRef]
72. Williamson, G.K.; Hall, W.H. X-ray line broadening from filed aluminium and wolfram. *Acta Metall.* **1953**, *1*, 22–31. [CrossRef]
73. Py, M.; Maschke, K. Intra-and interlayer contributions to the lattice vibrations in MoO_3. *Physica B + C* **1981**, *105*, 370–374. [CrossRef]
74. Dieterle, M.; Weinberg, G.; Mestl, G. Raman spectroscopy of molybdenum oxides. Part I. Structural characterization of oxygen defects in MoO_{3-x} by DR UV/Vis, Raman spectroscopy and X-ray diffraction. *Phys. Chem. Chem. Phys.* **2002**, *4*, 812–821. [CrossRef]
75. Py, M.; Schmid, P.E.; Vallin, J. Raman scattering and structural properties of MoO_3. *Il Nuovo Cimento B* **1977**, *38*, 271–279. [CrossRef]
76. Nazri, G.-A.; Julien, C. Far-infrared and Raman Studies of orthorhombic MoO_3 single crystal. *Solid State Ion.* **1992**, *53*, 376–382. [CrossRef]
77. Srivastava, R.; Chase, L.L. Raman spectra of CrO_2 and MoO_2 single crystals. *Solid State Commun.* **1972**, *11*, 349–353. [CrossRef]
78. Spevack, P.A.; Mcintyre, N.S. Thermal reduction of MoO_3. *J. Phys. Chem. C* **1992**, *96*, 9029–9035. [CrossRef]
79. Dierle, M.; Mestl, G. Raman spectroscopy of molybdenum oxides. *Phys. Chem. Chem. Phys.* **2002**, *4*, 822–826. [CrossRef]
80. Navas, I.; Vinodkumar, R.; Lethy, K.J.; Detty, A.P.; Ganesan, V.; Sathe, V.; Mahadevan Pillai, V.P. Growth and characterization of molybdenum oxide nanorods by RF magnetron sputtering and subsequent annealing. *J. Phys. D Appl. Phys.* **2009**, *42*, 175305. [CrossRef]
81. Camacho-López, M.A.; Escobar-Alarcón, L.; Picquart, M.; Arroyo, R.; Córdoba, G.; Haro-Poniatowski, E. Micro-Raman study of the m-MoO_2 to α-MoO_3 transformation induced by cw-laser irradiation. *Opt. Mater.* **2011**, *33*, 480–484. [CrossRef]

82. Blume, A. Synthese und Strukturelle Untersuchungen von Molybdän-, Vanadium- und Wolframoxiden als Referenzverbindungen für die Heterogene Katalyse. Ph.D. Thesis, Universität Berlin, Berlin, Germany, 2004.
83. Zhao, Y.; Liu, X.; Lei, D.Y.; Chai, Y. Effects of surface roughness of Ag thin films on surface-enhanced Raman spectroscopy of graphene: Spatial nonlocality and physisorption strain. *Nanoscale* **2014**, *6*, 1311–1317. [CrossRef]
84. Choi, J.-G.; Thompson, L.T. XPS study of as-prepared and reduced molybdenum oxides. *Appl. Surf. Sci.* **1996**, *93*, 143–149. [CrossRef]
85. Novotny, P.; Lamb, H.H. Nanostructured MoO_x films deposited on c-plane sapphire. *J. Vac. Sci. Technol. A* **2019**, *37*, 051504. [CrossRef]
86. Colton, R.J.; Guzman, A.M.; Rabalais, J.W. Electrochromism in some thin-film transition-metal oxides characterized by x-ray electron spectroscopy. *J. Appl. Phys.* **1978**, *49*, 409. [CrossRef]
87. Fleisch, T.H.; Mains, G.J. An XPS study of the UV reduction and photochromism of MoO_3 and WO_3. *J. Chem. Phys.* **1982**, *76*, 780. [CrossRef]
88. Ramana, C.V.; Atuchin, V.V.; Kesler, V.G.; Kochubey, V.A.; Pokrovsky, L.D.; Shutthanandan, V.; Becker, U.; Ewing, R.C. Growth and surface characterization of sputter-deposited molybdenum oxide thin films. *Appl. Surf. Sci.* **2007**, *253*, 5368–5374. [CrossRef]
89. Cimino, A.; DeAngelis, B.A. the application ox X-ray photoelectron spectroscopy to the study of molybdenum oxides and supported molybdenum oxide catalysts. *J. Catal.* **1975**, *36*, 11–22. [CrossRef]
90. Thiele, G.; Poston, M.; Brown, R. A Case Study in Sizing Nanoparticles. Micromeritics Instrument Corporation. Available online: http://www.particletesting.com/library (accessed on 1 January 2019).
91. Jung, Y.S.; Lee, S.; Ahn, D.; Dillon, A.C.; Lee, S.-H. Electrochemical reactivity of ball-milled MoO_{3-y} as anode materials for lithium-ion batteries. *J. Power Sour.* **2009**, *188*, 286–291. [CrossRef]
92. Wu, D.; Shen, R.; Yang, R.; Ji, W.; Jiang, M.; Ding, W.; Peng, L. Mixed molybdenum oxides with superior performances as an advanced anode material for lithium-ion batteries. *Sci. Rep.* **2017**, *7*, 44697. [CrossRef]
93. Cho, J.S. Large scale process for low crystalline MoO_3-carbon composite microspheres prepared by one-step spray pyrolysis for anodes in lithium-ion batteries. *Nanomaterials* **2019**, *9*, 539. [CrossRef]
94. Yang, L.C.; Gao, Q.S.; Tang, Y.; Wu, Y.P.; Holze, R. MoO_2 synthesized by reduction of MoO_3 with ethanol vapor as an anode material with good rate capability for the lithium-ion battery. *J. Power Sour.* **2008**, *179*, 357–360. [CrossRef]
95. Sen, U.K.; Mitra, S. Synthesis of molybdenum oxides and their electrochemical properties against Li. *Energy Proc.* **2014**, *54*, 740–747. [CrossRef]
96. Su, L.; Zhong, Y.; Zhou, Z. Role of transition metal nanoparticles in the extra lithium storage capacity of transition metal oxides: A case study of hierarchical core–shell $Fe_3O_4@C$ and Fe@C microspheres. *J. Mater. Chem. A* **2013**, *1*, 15158–15166. [CrossRef]
97. Zheng, F.; Zhu, D.; Chen, Q. Facile fabrication of porous $Ni_xCo_{3-x}O_4$ nanosheets with enhanced electrochemical performance as anode materials for Li-ion batteries. *ACS Appl. Mater. Interfaces* **2014**, *6*, 9256–9264. [CrossRef]
98. Keppeler, M.; Srinivasan, M. Interfacial phenomena/capacities beyond conversion reaction occurring in nano-sized transition-metal-oxide-based negative electrodes in lithium-ion batteries: A review. *ChemElectroChem* **2017**, *4*, 2727–2754. [CrossRef]
99. Grugeon, S.; Laruelle, S.; Dupont, L.; Tarascon, J.M. An uptake on the reactivity of nanoparticles Co-based compounds towards Li. *Solid State Sci.* **2003**, *5*, 895–904. [CrossRef]
100. Sun, Y.; Hu, X.; Luo, W.; Xia, F.; Huang, Y. Reconstruction of conformal nanoscale MnO on graphene as a high-capacity and long-life anode material for lithium ion batteries. *Adv. Funct. Mater.* **2013**, *23*, 2436–2444. [CrossRef]
101. Guo, J.; Liu, Q.; Wang, C.; Zachariah, M.R. Interdispersed amorphous MnO_x-carbon nanocomposites with superior electrochemical performance as lithium-storage material. *Adv. Funct. Mater.* **2012**, *22*, 803–811. [CrossRef]
102. Shi, Y.F.; Guo, B.K.; Corr, S.A.; Shi, Q.H.; Hu, Y.S.; Heier, K.R.; Chen, L.Q.; Seshadri, R.; Stucky, G.D. Ordered mesoporous metallic MoO_2 materials with highly reversible lithium storage capacity. *Nano Lett.* **2009**, *9*, 4215–4220. [CrossRef]
103. Palanisamy, K.; Kim, Y.; Kim, H.; Kim, J.M.; Yoon, W.-S. Self-assembled porous MoO_2/graphene microspheres towards high performance anodes for lithium ion batteries. *J. Power Sour.* **2015**, *275*, 351–361. [CrossRef]
104. Tang, Q.; Shan, Z.; Wang, L.; Qin, X. MoO_2-graphene nanocomposite as anode material for lithium-ion batteries. *Electrochim. Acta* **2012**, *79*, 148–153. [CrossRef]
105. Mei, W.; Huang, J.; Zhu, L.; Ye, Z.; Mai, Y.; Tu, J. Synthesis of porous rhombus-shaped Co_3O_4 nanorod arrays grown directly on a nickel substrate with high electrochemical performance. *J. Mater. Chem.* **2012**, *22*, 9315–9321. [CrossRef]
106. Zhou, G.; Wang, D.-W.; Li, F.; Zhang, L.; Li, N.; Wu, Z.-S.; Wen, L.; Lu, G.Q.; Cheng, H.-M. Graphene-wrapped Fe_3O_4 anode material with improved reversible capacity and cyclic stability for lithium ion batteries. *Chem. Mater.* **2010**, *22*, 5306–5313. [CrossRef]
107. Wang, Q.; Zhang, D.-A.; Wang, Q.; Sun, J.; Xing, L.-L.; Xue, X.-Y. High electrochemical performances of α-MoO_3@MnO_2 core-shell nanorods as lithium-ion battery anodes. *Electrochim. Acta* **2014**, *146*, 411–418. [CrossRef]
108. Zeng, L.; Zheng, C.; Deng, C.; Ding, X.; Wei, M. MoO_2-ordered mesoporous carbon nanocomposite as an anode material for lithium-ion batteries. *ACS Appl. Mater. Interfaces* **2013**, *5*, 2182–2187. [CrossRef]
109. Gao, Q.; Yang, L.; Lu, X.; Mao, J.; Zhang, Y.; Wu, Y.; Tang, Y. Synthesis, characterization and lithium-storage performance of MoO_2/carbon hybrid nanowires. *J. Mater. Chem.* **2010**, *20*, 2807–2812. [CrossRef]
110. Yang, L.; Liu, L.; Zhu, Y.; Wang, X.; Wu, Y. Preparation of carbon coated MoO_2 nanobelts and their high performance as anode materials for lithium ion batteries. *J. Mater. Chem.* **2012**, *22*, 13148–13152. [CrossRef]

111. Fang, X.P.; Guo, B.L.; Shi, Y.F.; Li, B.; Hua, C.X.; Yao, C.H.; Chang, Y.C.; Hu, Y.S.; Wang, Z.X.; Stucky, G.D.; et al. Enhanced Li storage performance of ordered mesoporous MoO_2 via tungsten doping. *Nanoscale* **2012**, *4*, 1541–1544. [CrossRef]
112. Sun, Y.; Hu, X.; Yu, J.C.; Li, Q.; Luo, W.; Yuan, L.; Zhang, W.; Huang, Y. Morphosynthesis of a hierarchical MoO_2 nanoarchitecture as a binder-free anode for lithium-ion batteries. *Energy Environ. Sci.* **2011**, *4*, 2870–2877. [CrossRef]
113. Wang, Z.; Chen, J.S.; Zhu, T.; Madhavi, S.; Lou, X.W. One-pot synthesis of uniform carbon-coated MoO_2 nanospheres for high-rate reversible lithium storage. *Chem. Commun.* **2010**, *46*, 6906–6908. [CrossRef]
114. Yang, L.C.; Sun, W.; Zhong, Z.W.; Liu, J.W.; Gao, Q.S.; Hu, R.Z.; Zhu, M. Hierarchical MoO_2/N-doped carbon heteronanowires with high rate and improved long-term performance for lithium-ion batteries. *J. Power Sour.* **2016**, *306*, 78–84. [CrossRef]
115. Xu, Z.; Wang, H.; Li, Z.; Kohandehghan, A.; Ding, J.; Chen, J.; Cui, K.; Mitlin, D. Sulfur refines MoO_2 distribution enabling improved lithium ion battery performance. *J. Phys. Chem. C* **2014**, *118*, 18387–18396. [CrossRef]
116. Wang, Y.; Huang, Z.; Wang, Y. A new approach to synthesize MoO_2@C for lithium ion batteries. *J. Mater. Chem. A* **2015**, *3*, 21314–21320. [CrossRef]
117. Zhang, X.; Gao, M.; Wang, W.; Liu, B.; Li, X. Encapsulating MoO_2 nanocrystals into flexible carbon nanofibers via electrospinning for high-performance lithium storage. *Polymers* **2021**, *13*, 22. [CrossRef]
118. Liang, Y.; Yang, S.; Yi, Z.; Lei, X.; Sun, J.; Zhou, Y. Low temperature synthesis of a stable MoO_2 as suitable anode materials for lithium batteries. *Mater. Sci. Eng. B* **2005**, *121*, 152–155. [CrossRef]
119. Liu, J.; Tang, S.; Lu, Y.; Cai, G.; Liang, S.; Wang, W.; Chen, X. Synthesis of Mo_2N nanolayer coated MoO_2 hollow nanostructures as high-performance anode materials for lithium-ion batteries. *Energy Environ. Sci.* **2013**, *6*, 2691–2697. [CrossRef]
120. Huang, Z.X.; Wang, Y.; Zhu, Y.G.; Shi, Y.; Wong, J.I.; Yang, H.Y. 3D graphene supported MoO_2 for high performance binder-free lithium ion battery. *Nanoscale* **2014**, *6*, 9839–9845. [CrossRef]
121. Che, Y.; Zhu, X.Y.; Li, J.J.; Sun, J.; Liu, Y.Y.; Jin, C.; Dong, C.H. Simple synthesis of MoO_2/carbon aerogel anodes for high performance lithium ion batteries from seaweed biomass. *RSC Adv.* **2016**, *6*, 106230–106236. [CrossRef]
122. Wang, Y.W.; Yu, L.; Lou, X.W. Formation of triple-shelled molybdenum–polydopamine hollow spheres and their conversion into MoO_2/carbon composite hollow spheres for lithium-ion batteries. *Angew. Chem. Int. Ed.* **2016**, *55*, 14668–14672. [CrossRef]
123. Ku, J.H.; Jung, Y.S.; Lee, K.T.; Kim, C.H.; Oh, S.M. Thermoelectrochemically activated MoO_2 powder electrode for lithium secondary batteries. *J. Electrochem. Soc.* **2009**, *156*, A688–A693. [CrossRef]
124. Lei, Y.Z.; Hu, J.C.; Liu, H.W.; Li, J.L. Template-free synthesis of hollow core-shell MoO_2 microspheres with high lithium-ion storage capacity. *Mater. Lett.* **2012**, *68*, 82–85. [CrossRef]
125. Yoon, S.; Manthiram, A. Microwave-hydrothermal synthesis of $W_{0.4}Mo_{0.6}O_3$ and carbon-decorated WO_x-MoO_2 nanorod anodes for lithium ion batteries. *J. Mater. Chem.* **2011**, *21*, 4082–4085. [CrossRef]
126. Sun, Y.-K.; Myung, S.-T.; Park, B.-C.; Yashiro, H. Improvement of the electrochemical properties of $Li[Ni_{0.5}Mn_{0.5}]O_2$ by AlF_3 coating. *J. Electrochem. Soc.* **2008**, *155*, A705–A710. [CrossRef]
127. Amine, K.; Liu, J.; Kang, S.; Belharouak, I.; Hyung, Y.; Vissers, D.; Henriksen, G. Improved lithium manganese oxide spinel/graphite Li-ion cells for high-power applications. *J. Power Sour.* **2004**, *129*, 14–19. [CrossRef]

MDPI
St. Alban-Anlage 66
4052 Basel
Switzerland
Tel. +41 61 683 77 34
Fax +41 61 302 89 18
www.mdpi.com

Nanomaterials Editorial Office
E-mail: nanomaterials@mdpi.com
www.mdpi.com/journal/nanomaterials

www.ingramcontent.com/pod-product-compliance
Lightning Source LLC
LaVergne TN
LVHW070430100526
838202LV00014B/1562